DATE DUE		
DEC 09 '92 DEC 0 2 2013		

Food Policy

Integrating Supply, Distribution, and Consumption

EDI SERIES IN ECONOMIC DEVELOPMENT

Food Policy

Integrating Supply, Distribution, and Consumption

Edited by

J. Price Gittinger
Joanne Leslie
Caroline Hoisington

PUBLISHED FOR THE WORLD BANK
The Johns Hopkins University Press
BALTIMORE AND LONDON

© 1987 The International Bank
for Reconstruction and Development / THE WORLD BANK
1818 H Street, N.W., Washington, D.C. 20433, U.S.A.
Manufactured in the United States of America
First printing March 1987
Second printing May 1988

The Johns Hopkins University Press
Baltimore, Maryland 21211, U.S.A.

Manuscript editor: Alice S. Dowsett
Research assistant: Anne Stokes

Library of Congress Cataloging-in-Publication Data
Food policy.
  (EDI series in economic development)
  Bibliography: p.
  Includes index.
  1. Food supply—Developing countries. 2. Nutrition policy—Developing
countries. 3. Agriculture and state—Developing countries. I. Gittinger,
J. Price (James Price), 1928—   . II. Leslie, Joanne. III. Hoisington,
Caroline. IV. Economic Development Institute (Washington, D.C.).
V. Series.
HD9018.D44F665   1987   363.8'56'091724   86-27613
ISBN 0-8018-3500-3

Contents

Preface   ix

Contributors   x

Abbreviations and Data Notes   xiii

Introduction: Changing Concepts of Food Policy   1
J. Price Gittinger, Joanne Leslie, and Caroline Hoisington

PART I. THE FRAMEWORK OF WORLD FOOD POLICY   11

1. The World Food and Hunger Problem: Changing
   Perspectives and Possibilities, 1974–84   15
   *Walter P. Falcon, C. T. Kurien, Fernando Monckeberg, Achola P.
   Okeyo, S. O. Olayide, Ferenç Rabar, and Wouter Tims*

2. The World Food Equation: Interrelations among
   Development, Employment, and Food Consumption   39
   John W. Mellor and Bruce F. Johnston

3. The Changing Context of Food and Agricultural
   Development Policy   72
   G. Edward Schuh

4. Food Growth Slowdown: Danger Signal for the Future   89
   Lester R. Brown

PART II. THE IMPLICATIONS OF PROGRAMS TO
   INCREASE PRODUCTION   103

5. The Impact of the Green Revolution and Prospects
   for the Future   106
   Per Pinstrup-Andersen and Peter B. R. Hazell

6. Broadening Production Increase Programs to Reach
   Low-Income Farmers   119
   Graeme Donovan

7. Women in African Food Production and Food Security   133
   Food and Agriculture Organization

8. Food Policy Options for Secondary Regions:
   A Framework for Applied Research   141
   Bruce M. Koppel

9. The Nutritional Impact of Agricultural Projects   153
    Shlomo Reutlinger
10. An Overview of Farming Systems Research
        and Development: Origins, Applications, and Issues   165
    John S. Caldwell
11. Cash Crops versus Subsistence Crops: Income
        and Nutritional Effects in Developing Countries   179
    Joachim von Braun and Eileen Kennedy

PART III. FOOD SECURITY, TRADE, AND AID   195

12. Poverty and Entitlements   198
    Amartya Sen
13. Food Security and Poverty in Developing Countries   205
    Shlomo Reutlinger
14. Food Security and the Role of the Grain Trade   215
    Graham Donaldson
15. Trends in Trade and Food Aid   224
    Barbara Huddleston
16. The Nutritional Impact of Food Aid: Criteria
        for the Selection of Cost-Effective Foods   234
    Shlomo Reutlinger and Judit Katona-Apte
17. The Evolution of Food Aid: Toward a Development-First
        Regime   246
    Raymond F. Hopkins

**PART IV. DOMESTIC MARKETING, PRICE POLICIES,
    AND SUBSIDIES**   261

18. Price Policy and the Political Economy of Markets   264
    C. Peter Timmer
19. Transitional Measures and Political Support for Food Price
        Policy Reform   277
    Paul Streeten
20. Food Prices and the Poor in Developing Countries   282
    Per Pinstrup-Andersen
21. The Relationship between Price Policy and Food
        Marketing   293
    C. Peter Timmer
22. Food Marketing Activities of Low-Income Households   304
    Benson Ateng
23. Post-Harvest Food Losses in Developing Countries   309
    E. R. Pariser

PART V. MALNUTRITION AND NUTRITION INTERVENTIONS 327

24. Strategies for the Control of Malnutrition and the Influence of the Nutritional Sciences 330
    Michael C. Latham

25. Energy in Human Nutrition: A Reconsideration of the Relationship between Intake and Functional Consequences 346
    George H. Beaton

26. Interactions of Malnutrition and Diarrhea: A Review of Research 355
    Joanne Leslie

27. Women's Activities and Impacts on Child Nutrition 371
    Sandra L. Huffman

28. Variable Access to Food 385
    Michael Lipton

29. Nutritional Risk: Concepts and Implications 393
    Wendy P. McLean

30. Nutritional Surveillance 402
    John B. Mason and Janice T. Mitchell

31. Supplementary Feeding Programs for Young Children in Developing Countries: A Summary of Lessons Learned 413
    George H. Beaton and Hossein Ghassemi

32. Nutrition Education: An Overview 429
    Robert C. Hornik

33. Nutrition Education: Lessons Learned 436
    Richard K. Manoff

PART VI. FOOD AND NUTRITION PLANNING 443

34. Nutrition Policies and Programs: A Decade of Redirection 446
    Alan Berg and James Austin

35. National Nutrition Policy: Lessons of Experience 457
    James M. Pines

36. China's Food and Nutrition Planning 467
    Dean T. Jamison and Alan Piazza

37. Dilemmas and Options in the Formulation of Agricultural Policies in Africa 485
    Alain de Janvry

38. Experience with Food Strategies
   in Four African Countries   497
   Kees Tuinenburg

Bibliography   509

Index   556

Preface

Food is the basic human need. Providing sufficient food of adequate nutritional quality for everyone is the first development objective for all World Bank member governments, and the Bank has placed great emphasis on helping governments realize this objective. Yet in many developing countries hunger remains a persistent problem. Usually the basic difficulty is not lack of food but lack of purchasing power on the part of households, individuals, and, in some cases, nations. World Bank research on food security during the past decade has contributed significantly to our understanding of the relation between poverty and hunger.

Economic growth—the primary objective of the World Bank—will ultimately provide most households with the purchasing power needed to secure an adequate diet. Until that time, explicit policies to make food available to low-income households and to encourage appropriate use of food within households will be necessary. Even where national income is relatively high, special health and nutrition measures are needed for vulnerable groups.

As our understanding of the complexities and interactions of food and nutrition issues has deepened, developing country leaders and the development community have recognized that a broadly based, integrated policy approach to supply, distribution, and consumption is essential if everyone is to be assured of access to food. This volume brings together some of the best current thinking about food policy, in selections that were chosen to emphasize the broader view of this subject. Originally assembled in the Economic Development Institute of the World Bank as background readings for a policy seminar, the collection is now made available for a wider audience of developing country officials, scholars, and others interested in realistic approaches to eliminating hunger.

The editors wish to express their appreciation for the assistance and counsel of Per Pinstrup-Andersen of the International Food Policy Research Institute in selecting the materials for this volume and reviewing the commentaries.

Contributors

The affiliations shown are those at the time of writing.

Benson Ateng
: West Africa Projects Department, World Bank, Washington, D.C.

James Austin
: Graduate School of Business Administration, Harvard University, Cambridge, Massachusetts

George H. Beaton
: Department of Nutritional Sciences, University of Toronto, Toronto, Canada

Alan Berg
: Population, Health, and Nutrition Department, World Bank, Washington, D.C.

Lester R. Brown
: President, Worldwatch Institute, Washington, D.C.

John S. Caldwell
: Department of Horticulture, Virginia Polytechnic Institute and State University, Blacksburg, Virginia.

Alain de Janvry
: Department of Agricultural and Resource Economics, University of California, Berkeley, California

Graham Donaldson
: Operations Evaluation Department, World Bank, Washington, D.C.

Graeme Donovan
: Agriculture and Rural Development Department, World Bank, Washington, D.C.

Walter P. Falcon
: Food Research Institute, Stanford University, Stanford, California

Hossein Ghassemi
: Health and Nutrition Section, United Nations Children's Fund, New York

Peter B. R. Hazell
: Agricultural Growth Linkages and Development Policy Program, International Food Policy Research Institute, Washington, D.C.

Raymond F. Hopkins
: Department of Political Science, Swarthmore College, Swarthmore, Pennsylvania

Robert C. Hornik — Annenberg School of Communications, University of Pennsylvania, Philadelphia, Pennsylvania

Barbara Huddleston — Food Security and Information Service, Food and Agriculture Organization of the United Nations, Rome, Italy

Sandra Huffman — School of Hygiene and Public Health, Johns Hopkins University, Baltimore, Maryland

Dean T. Jamison — Education and Training Department, World Bank, Washington, D.C.

Bruce F. Johnston — Food Research Institute, Stanford University, Stanford, California

Judit Katona-Apte — Consultant, Durham, North Carolina

Eileen Kennedy — Consumption and Nutrition Program, International Food Policy Research Institute, Washington, D.C.

Bruce M. Koppel — East-West Center Resource Systems Institute, Honolulu, Hawaii

C. T. Kurien — Madras Institute of Development Studies, Madras, India

Michael C. Latham — Division of Nutritional Sciences, Cornell University, Ithaca, New York

Joanne Leslie — International Center for Research on Women, and Manoff International, Inc., Washington, D.C.

Michael Lipton — Institute of Development Studies, University of Sussex, Brighton, England

Richard K. Manoff — President, Manoff International, Inc., Washington, D.C.

John B. Mason — Nutritional Surveillance Program and Division of Nutritional Sciences, Cornell University, Ithaca, New York

Wendy P. McLean — Department of Human Nutrition, London School of Hygiene and Tropical Medicine, London, England

John W. Mellor — Director, International Food Policy Research Institute, Washington, D.C.

Janice T. Mitchell — Nutritional Surveillance Program, Cornell University, Ithaca, New York

Fernando Monckeberg — Institute of Nutrition and Food Technology, University of Chile, Santiago, Chile

Achola P. Okeyo	Institute for Development Studies, University of Nairobi, Nairobi, Kenya
S. O. Olayide	Department of Agricultural Economics, University of Ibadan, Ibadan, Nigeria
E. R. Pariser	Sea Grant Program, Massachusetts Institute of Technology, Cambridge, Massachusetts
Alan Piazza	East Asia and Pacific Projects Department, World Bank, Washington, D.C.
James M. Pines	Consultant, Alexandria, Virginia
Per Pinstrup-Andersen	Consumption and Nutrition Program, International Food Policy Research Institute, Washington, D.C.
Ferenç Rabar	Institute of Planning Economy, Budapest, Hungary
Shlomo Reutlinger	Agriculture and Rural Development Department, World Bank, Washington, D.C.
G. Edward Schuh	Agriculture and Rural Development Department, World Bank, Washington, D.C.
Amartya Sen	All Souls College, Oxford University, Oxford, England
Paul Streeten	Economic Development Institute, World Bank, Washington, D.C.
C. Peter Timmer	Graduate School of Business Administration, Harvard University, Cambridge, Massachusetts
Wouter Tims	Centre for World Food Studies, Free University, Amsterdam, The Netherlands
Kees Tuinenburg	Rural Development Programme, Royal Tropical Institute, Amsterdam, The Netherlands
Joachim von Braun	Consumption and Nutrition Program, International Food Policy Research Institute, Washington, D.C.

Abbreviations and Data Notes

Abbreviations

ACC/SCN	Administrative Committee on Coordination/Subcommittee on Nutrition of the United Nations
AVRDC	Asian Vegetable Research and Development Center
CARE	Committee for American Relief Everywhere
CFA	Committee on Food Aid Policies and Programs of the WFP
CGIAR	Consultative Group on International Agricultural Research
CIAT	Centro Internacional de Agricultura Tropical
CIMMYT	Centro Internacional de Mejoramiento de Maíz y Trigo
EC	European Community
ECLA	See ECLAC
ECLAC	Economic Commission for Latin America and the Caribbean of the United Nations (formerly ECLA)
ESN	Food Policy and Nutrition Division (FAO)
FAO	Food and Agriculture Organization of the United Nations
FSIP	Farming systems infrastructure and policy support
FSR&D	Farming systems research and development
FSR/E	Farming systems research and extension
GAO	General Accounting Office
GDP	Gross domestic product
GNP	Gross national product
GOBI	Growth monitoring, oral rehydration, breastfeeding, and immunization
IBRD	International Bank for Reconstruction and Development
ICDDR	International Centre for Diarrhoeal Diseases Research
ICRISAT	International Crops Research Institute for the Semi-Arid Tropics
IDA	International Development Association
IDB	Inter-American Development Bank
IDRC	International Development Research Centre
IDS	Institute of Development Studies
IFAD	International Fund for Agricultural Development
IFARD	International Federation for Agricultural Research and Development
IFPRI	International Food Policy Research Institute
ILO	International Labour Organisation

IMF	International Monetary Fund
INACG	International Nutritional Anemia Consultative Group
INCAP	Institute of Nutrition of Central America and Panama
IRRI	International Rice Research Institute
IVACG	International Vitamin A Consultative Group
NAS	National Academy of Sciences
NCHS	National Center for Health Statistics
ODC	Overseas Development Council
OECD	Organisation for Economic Co-operation and Development
OPEC	Organization of Petroleum Exporting Countries
ORT	Oral rehydration therapy
OTA	Office of Technical Assessment
PEM	Protein-energy malnutrition
SEARCA	Southeast Asia Regional Center for Graduate Study and Research in Agriculture
UNCTAD	United Nations Conference on Trade and Development
UNDP	United Nations Development Programme
UNECA	United Nations Economic Commission for Africa
UNICEF	United Nations Children's Fund
UNRISD	United Nations Research Institute for Social Development
UNU	United Nations University
USAID	U.S. Agency for International Development
USDA	U.S. Department of Agriculture
WFC	World Food Council
WFP	World Food Programme
WHO	World Health Organization

Data Notes

Measures are metric system. Currency amounts are U.S. dollars unless otherwise indicated.

INTRODUCTION

Changing Concepts of Food Policy

J. Price Gittinger, Joanne Leslie, and Caroline Hoisington

Since the end of World War II, total world food production has increased substantially, and—despite significant population growth—per capita food production has also increased. However, averages mask variations, and in some areas, population growth has outstripped agricultural growth, so that per capita food production has fallen. Even within regions of increased per capita food production, the poor or unemployed often go hungry. In all, hundreds of millions of people still lack secure access to adequate food and many suffer from outright malnutrition. This persistence of widespread hunger and malnutrition in spite of increased food production has led to the view that a broader concept of food policy is needed.

Policymakers in developing countries increasingly recognize that an explicit food policy implemented through a strategy of coordinated programs is fundamental to their development goals, a view shared by the donor agencies that work with them. Both accept that a broadly conceived food policy, one that takes into consideration all aspects of the food system—supply, distribution, and consumption—has the best chance of meeting each individual's nutritional needs. Experience shows, however, that such a policy is not easy to implement.

Components of Food Policy

A food policy should be concerned with both short-term and long-term needs. It should include programs to alleviate current malnutrition, such as fortifying food, providing school lunches, setting up ration shops, and distributing vitamin A capsules. At the same time, it should include programs to increase supply and access in the long term, such as pursuing research to increase crop yields, building infrastructure for improved transportation, increasing incentives for farmers, expanding employment and income-generating oppor-

1

tunities, and using futures markets appropriately. Governments can ignore neither the current generation of malnourished nor the needs of future generations.

The scope of food policy issues ranges from the macro to the micro. On the macro level, many policies not normally considered as food policies can have a significant effect on food supply and consumption. An example is the disincentive effect of overvalued foreign exchange on domestic producers, which leads to cheap imported food and relatively high-priced, noncompetitive exports. Policies that favor an industrialized urban sector over the more agricultural rural sector have generally led to serious disincentives to agricultural production and to stagnating output. A common element of such policies is to keep food prices low so that wages may be kept low.

Although price policies that increase farmer incentives are essential, by themselves they may not be enough to bring about continued production increases. Infrastructure to give farmers access to more efficient technologies, such as high-yielding seed, and to reliable water supplies, pesticides, and credit to purchase production inputs, is necessary to ensure sustained increases in agricultural output. Otherwise, higher prices may only lead farmers to produce one crop instead of another, with little or no increase in total production. Research into locally adapted agricultural technologies is also vital to increase production and to reduce cost in the long run.

On the micro level, social and cultural contexts are important determinants of food supply and consumption. Small farmers may wish to avoid risk; extension work may be directed toward men and not reach women, who are often the major food producers, especially in Africa; and the dynamics of decision making, time allocation, and food distribution within households may vitally affect nutritional status, especially of weaning-age children and pregnant and lactating women.

An analogy may be drawn between the nutritional status of an individual and the food sector of a society. An individual with marginally inadequate food intake cannot build up reserves of energy and other nutrients to resist a crisis. Such an individual is thus vulnerable to infectious disease or variations in seasonal food availability, both of which can precipitate severe malnutrition. Similarly, a society in which a substantial proportion of the population receives only a marginal food intake is vulnerable to the food shortages and high prices resulting from a poor crop or an economic crisis. The result can be famine. Thus one of the goals of a broad-based food policy should be to prevent marginal inadequacies, both at the individual level and at the national level, so that if crises do occur they will not result either in individual cases of acute malnutrition or in famines.

Supply

The essential foundation of an efficient food system is a stable food supply, obtained through production, trade, or both. Although many decisionmakers have concentrated on increasing food production, from an economic point of view—but not necessarily from a political one—food security may best be served by a combination of production and imports. The variability of domestic production, and therefore of national supply and price levels, is generally greater than the variability of international supply and prices.

Distribution

Although adequate supplies of food on an aggregate level are absolutely necessary, experience has shown they are insufficient to guarantee adequate nutritional status for the population as a whole. Marketing bottlenecks, ranging from inefficient government marketing boards to the lack of such infrastructure as roads, bridges, and efficient telecommunications, may affect food availability. Distribution networks may be inadequate to cope with movement between regions in times of deficit.

Consumption

An unfettered market probably will not achieve some important food policy goals, and direct nutrition intervention will be necessary. A segment of the population may not earn enough to purchase food, foods may be of inferior quality nutritionally, or people may not know how to improve their family's diet. In most countries, targeted programs to help vulnerable groups—biologically vulnerable mothers and children and economically vulnerable low-income groups—will be a key component of national food policy, although governments must also be concerned about the cost of nutrition interventions. Targeted interventions are usually more cost effective and produce fewer market distortions than very broad-scale interventions such as general food subsidies. The drawback is that the complexity and cost of administering a targeted program may be high. Sometimes, however, subsidies and rations can be successfully targeted to low-income groups—for example, by subsidizing a staple that is consumed widely by the poor but less so by the better off. Interventions such as fortification of foods with micronutrients that are missing or low in local diets—such as iron, iodine, and vitamin A—can be cost-effective and much cheaper than treatment programs. Nutrition education programs, which are relatively inexpensive compared to other direct nutritional interventions, have in some instances caused significant improvements in nutritional status, even when not associated with feeding or food distribution programs.

The appropriate balance between supply issues, distribution issues, and consumption issues in food policy will vary from country to country and from region to region. In this decade in Africa, the overriding issue is producing enough food. Yet it is precisely at times of overall food shortfalls that a country must have a food strategy that pays explicit attention to distribution and consumption. Otherwise, the burden of shortage will fall inequitably on low-income or other vulnerable groups. In Asia and Latin America, in contrast, this decade has not seen overall food shortages but has seen a growing concern with issues of distribution and consumption. Nonetheless, because of the size of Asia's population, the bulk of the world's hungry people are still found there, while pockets of extreme deprivation persist in Latin America. Governments of all countries face a similar problem of ensuring that everyone receives adequate energy plus sufficient protein and other needed nutrients.

Analyzing the food situation, setting food policies, and then implementing them are extraordinarily complex tasks. To carry them through, policymakers must have access to good information and be able to analyze it to understand the situation in their countries and the effects of their policies. Monitoring and evaluation of policies and programs are essential. The food sector is complex and interacts dynamically with all other sectors of the economy. Incorporating a food policy into national planning is a good step, but political realities influence its implementation. Coordinating efforts of various agencies, ministries, and other institutions is a central task, as indeed is building a consensus among the technical and political leadership about the place of a broad-based food policy in national development.

Problems of Discipline Orientation

Despite growing recognition of the need for an integrated food policy, few governments, in either developed or developing countries, have as yet adopted more than the beginnings of such a policy. A major reason is the form of modern knowledge—expertise tends to be discipline based. Agriculturists tend to focus on production, those active in the commercial food sector on market improvement, and physicians and nutritionists on clinical aspects of malnutrition. Ministries have characteristically grown up around these disciplines, so that most governments have a ministry of agriculture, which focuses on production, a ministry of health, which is responsible for reducing severe malnutrition, and perhaps a parastatal marketing board with agricultural marketing responsibilities. Few governments have a ministry whose responsibility is to address all aspects of food policy.

International agencies face the same limitation. Since they work with governments and are staffed with specialists—often drawn from member governments—they too tend to be organized along disciplinary lines. Thus the Food and Agriculture Organization has been historically most concerned with food production issues and the World Health Organization with health and nutrition interventions, although recently both have begun to include broader elements in their programs. Even when an agency has a mandate that covers all aspects of food policy, its internal organization tends to be discipline oriented. Within the World Bank, for example, separate departments deal with food production and nutrition interventions. Even the World Food Council frequently finds itself supporting discipline-oriented programs of member governments despite a commitment to a broader food policy.

One obvious problem with this discipline orientation is that some aspects of food policy tend to "fall through the cracks" and policies may even develop inconsistencies. Agriculturists assume nutritionists will deal with consumption issues, and nutritionists assume someone else is responsible for monitoring economically vulnerable groups not yet suffering from overt malnutrition. Distribution issues and market improvement receive inadequate attention because they are not the core responsibility of any ministry. The ministry of agriculture may be working mostly on high-status foods or export crops while the ministry of health would prefer that those responsible for agriculture focus on increasing production of the main foods eaten by the poor.

The Purpose and Organization of This Volume

Since the World Food Conference in 1974, much work has gone into efforts to ensure adequate food for all, with some successes and some failures. One purpose of this collection of readings is to review some of the experience to date.

The collection focuses on food policy issues in developing countries. Its basic tenets are that effective food policy must be concerned with supply, distribution, and consumption—which includes explicit nutritional goals—and that malnutrition is unlikely to be eliminated in the foreseeable future through growth of national income alone.

The collection is intended for specialists or students concerned with food policy who are discipline oriented but who recognize that food policy must be broadly based. Thus the collection includes selections drawn from all aspects of food policy. In each area, the intent is to provide the nonspecialist with the best of current thinking, since none of us can lay claim to being a specialist in all aspects of food policy, however expert we may be in our own particular discipline. We hope readers will gain a perspective on a range of food policy issues and see where their responsibilities fit into the whole food policy continuum. We encourage readers whose interest is stimulated by a particular selection to return to the original article, as these excerpts may omit material of interest to specialists and citations important for the scholar.

The emphasis in the collection is on broad policy aspects, on distribution, and particularly on consumption. This is because a rich literature dealing with agricultural production is readily available, while many aspects of distribution and consumption are more poorly served by the available literature, and such summary articles as do exist tend to be found in less accessible publications.

We have also assembled this collection keeping in mind several excellent recent collections in the general field of food policy. (See the bibliography for full citations.) We expect readers will turn to those volumes in addition to this collection, so we have not included any excerpts from them. *Agricultural Development in the Third World*, edited by Carl K. Eicher and John M. Staatz (1984), has an excellent selection focused on agricultural development policy issues. *Nutrition and Development*, edited by Margaret Biswas and Per Pinstrup-Andersen (1985), is a collection focused more on the distribution and consumption aspects of food policy. *Food Policy: Frameworks for Analysis and Action*, edited by Charles K. Mann and Barbara Huddleston (1985), also emphasizes the need for a broad food policy; particularly interesting in their collection are descriptions of country experiences in Kenya, Thailand, and Tunisia. This collection could be viewed as a companion volume to *Food Policy Analysis*, written by C. Peter Timmer, Walter P. Falcon, and Scott R. Pearson (1983). Their prizewinning work emphasizes the economic aspects of food policy and the analytical, techniques necessary to formulate food policy.

Part I of this collection is an overview of current thinking about food policy and the world food situation. The opening chapter is an assessment by an international group of academic leaders who focus on changing perceptions about food policy since the World Food Conference of 1974. Then two leaders in the field, John W. Mellor of IFPRI and Bruce F. Johnston of the Food Research Institute at Stanford University, assess current thinking about agricultural development and its relationships to broader issues of food policy and overall economic development. G. Edward Schuh emphasizes a point that a number of other authors also comment on: the growing need to see food policy in the context of the national and, indeed, international economic scene. Schuh reflects a common view that it is issues of poverty and broader economic forces that must dominate food policy formulation in the next decade. A contrasting view is that of Lester R. Brown, who warns that a distinct possibility exists that past increases in food production will not be replicated in the future. If that is so, then chronic food shortages may again appear and supply concerns merit much more attention than they currently receive.

Part II deals with food production but emphasizes elements of agricultural production that are particularly relevant in the context of a broad food policy. It addresses the problems of low-income producers, small farmers, and producers struggling in marginal areas. The importance of women as food producers is noted, particularly the growing recognition that production increase programs have too often ignored women farmers, who are frequently the key actors in food production, especially in sub-Saharan Africa and among lower-income groups throughout the world. This section also notes that agricultural development efforts have too often failed to pay adequate attention to nutritional aspects and discusses ways to improve project design to avoid unfavorable nutritional consequences. The issues of cash crops versus food crops and the nutritional impact of cash crop development are analyzed.

Part III takes up food security, trade, and aid. "Entitlement," the concept introduced by Amartya Sen of Oxford University, is the first issue covered in this section. A point made by articles in this section is that at the household level, lack of a secure food supply is predominantly a result of poverty, and there is a danger that if the mechanisms that cause food insecurity are not understood, treating food security at the national level may actually reduce security at the household level. Food shortages can be either chronic or transitory, and this section discusses policies to address these different problems. The section also points out that governments may not attach sufficient importance to use of the world market as a way to increase food security. Trade and food aid are both examined, including recent trends in volume and direction of movement of primary grains. A controversial proposal as to how governments should select food aid commodities is presented. Finally, there is a review of the evolution of food aid to date, with recommendations for its future course.

Part IV addresses distribution issues. It proposes a price policy that can both act as an incentive for farmers and provide affordable food for everyone. However, it recognizes that the transition to a price system that can encourage greater production (by raising the prices farmers receive for their crops and thereby increasing food prices paid by consumers) is a difficult policy issue, even when decisionmakers agree that in the longer run, price incentives will increase the food supply and reduce food costs by increasing production efficiency. How food prices and food price policy affect particular groups within the society and influence income distribution is discussed, as are frequently ignored relationships between price policy and market structure. One way to increase effective food supply and to reduce food costs is to reduce post-harvest food losses, which experts estimate total some 10 percent of food grains and 20 percent of starchy staple crops, other perishables, and fish.

Part V develops the concept that disaggregation is the key to understanding nutrition problems and to developing policies to address them. The articles included in this section make it clear that malnutrition must be disaggregated in two ways: identification of nutritionally vulnerable groups and identification of specific nutrition deficiencies. Nutritional vulnerability may be related to economic causes (seasonal work or food production, landlessness, or urban unemployment, for example), to biological characteristics (the high prevalence of disease among weaning-age children and the increased food needs of pregnant and lactating women), or to sociocultural causes (inappropriate intrahousehold food distribution, multiple demands on women's time, or ignorance about how to maintain good nutritional status when circumstances change, as when a rural family migrates to an urban area and has to purchase food).

The four major nutrient deficiencies in the developing world—protein-energy malnutrition, iron deficiency anemia, vitamin A deficiency, which causes blindness and other problems, and goiter and cretinism caused by iodine deficiency—are susceptible to quite different interventions. The latter three, all of which are micronutrient deficiencies, may be alleviated or prevented by what might be termed "technical fixes," such as food fortification or mass distribution of the missing nutrient, although they will eventually disappear with the dietary diversity that comes with rising incomes and greater interregional trade. In contrast, protein-energy malnutrition is a more difficult problem to resolve, since it results from an inadequate intake of food. Supplementary feeding programs have generally been expensive for the small effects they have had. However, recent positive results from carefully designed, relatively inexpensive nutrition education interventions have been extremely encouraging.

Part VI takes a look at the experience in food and nutrition planning and concludes that generally it has not been broadly integrated. Food policy has often really consisted of programs to increase agricultural production, and food and nutrition plans have tended to be either price policy initiatives or designs for nutrition interventions. Even then, implementation has proved difficult. In light of this, the review of China's successful experience with improving food availability is particularly instructive. In contrast, the falling per capita production of food in Africa in the past decade, not to mention tragic famines in many countries, has been a source of worldwide concern and is partially responsible for the increased focus on food and nutrition issues in this decade. In the past few years, the World Food Council has focused on national food strategies, and many governments and agencies are working to develop integrated food policies. The last piece in the collection describes some recent experience in designing food strategies in four countries in Africa and suggests both the difficulties and the possibilities for success in trying to turn the concept of a broad-based food policy into a reality.

PART I

The Framework
of World Food Policy

The World Food Conference of 1974 convened in Rome amid an atmosphere of crisis. Delegates feared that the world was entering a period of chronic food shortage; most discussion focused on the simple core issue of how global food production could be increased. Today, as G. Edward Schuh comments in this part, "the situation could not be more different." Food supplies worldwide are more than adequate, and large surplus stocks are building up in the industrialized food exporting countries. As the crisis atmosphere has receded, the world community has had time to refine and deepen its understanding of the structure of food availability, the formulation of food policy, and the political context of policy implementation. Analysts have disaggregated the problem of hunger into elements more susceptible to resolution by perceptive food policies. As Walter P. Falcon and his colleagues note below: "Experts no longer perceive the 'hunger problem' as one of starvation or protein deficiency, but rather of chronic undernutrition, affecting a range of vulnerable groups whose common bond is their poverty."

Focusing on what Falcon and his group term the dichotomy between "the world *hunger* problem and the world *food* problem," most experts now agree that hunger issues center either on catastrophes—natural or man-made—or on chronic problems of food availability among vulnerable groups. This emphasis on the links between hunger and poverty is the most important change in thinking about world food policy since the World Food Conference.

While the links between hunger and poverty are the most significant deepening of the understanding about food policy, "one of the least anticipated developments . . . since the World Food Conference has been the growing complexity of the international economic environment and its effects on the food systems of the developing countries," as Falcon and his colleagues comment. "Few people recognized the extent to which such nonagricultural factors as trade, capital markets, exchange rates, and a host of other elements would exert tremendous pressure on the food systems of the developing countries . . . ," a theme later developed in more detail by Schuh.

The selections in this part review the changing perception of the world community about the structure of food availability and the food policy to which this leads. They summarize contemporary thinking and provide a background for the later parts that deal with more specialized aspects of food policy. The authors agree on the major outlines of the global food experience since the World Food Conference (although there are minor differences in the figures they use to review the experience, depending on the source and aggregation of their data), but they do not all agree on what the experience of the past decade or so implies for future food availability. All agree that careful food policy formulation will be needed if every person in the society is to be assured of adequate food, but they do not dwell on recent experience with food and nutrition planning. That topic is taken up in greater detail by the authors in part VI, who point out that attempts at comprehensive food and nutrition planning have generally not been politically realistic and have therefore been ineffective. Instead, incrementalist approaches closely linked to other policy initiatives appear to offer more promise.

The opening selection is a review by an international group of seven experts under the chairmanship of Falcon, prepared at the request of the World Food Council. The group examines the global food experience in the decade following the World Food Conference (at which the council was established). As noted above, they find an improvement in food supplies and an awareness that the world must change the focus of its food policy concerns "from numbers to vulnerable groups." As do most other specialists, the group notes that agricultural prices must be high enough to create incentives for farmers to expand output, but they go on to assert that as a result, "policies to promote agricultural production must go hand-in-hand with measures to provide a minimum of food to vulnerable groups."

At the time of the World Food Conference, delegates paid much attention to the idea of a system of international coordinated stocks. Such a system was never established, and the group identifies a growing consensus that an international agreement on food stocks probably would not increase significantly the reserves available to food-deficit countries and would probably prove to be very expensive for them. Increasing market instability caused by attempts to isolate national agricultural policies from the world market, especially in industrialized countries, has become a much more serious problem for food-deficit countries than the rising real prices of traded foods feared in 1974. The group feels only concerted international efforts can overcome this problem and calls on donor countries and multilateral agencies "to take the lead to improve the functioning of the global food economy and help ease the food burdens of the developing countries."

John W. Mellor and Bruce F. Johnston look at the changing understanding of agricultural development and food availability. Given the growing numbers of people seeking employment in developing countries, they conclude that only a food- and labor-intensive development strategy can balance the world food equation at levels high enough to eliminate malnutrition and poverty. They note that food production plays two vital roles in labor-intensive development. It leads to a demand structure appropriate to low capital-labor ratios and to capital accumulation, and at the same time it provides wage goods essential to labor mobilization. "Both needs," they comment, "were glossed over in the dominant thinking about development strategies in the 1950s and 1960s."

Schuh details the growing importance of the links between all aspects of food supply, distribution, and consumption and the broader national and international economy. He emphasizes the impact that the tremendous expansion of the international monetary system has had on the international economy. "Today," he comments, "the food and agricultural sector can be understood only in the context of the larger economy, both national and international." Policy considerations once far removed from food policy considerations are now very important. Indeed, "a decade ago the value of a nation's currency was largely ignored as an issue of domestic food and agricultural policy. Today, it is probably the most important price in the economy." In this context, he concludes, policymakers must take into account the poverty and income distribution implications of proposed food policies, not just the production implications. "The changing international economy, as well as altered concepts of what properly should be paramount in shaping food and agricultural policy, have changed significantly the context policymakers face as they address the complex challenges of improving the welfare of their people in the decades ahead."

While most specialists assessing current thinking about food policy feel that broader issues of poverty and of integrating national food policies into an international context must now be the paramount focus, Lester R. Brown sounds a note of warning about the underlying assumption of continued production increases. He points to a leveling off of productivity gains—partly due to rising fertilizer cost—and to growing constraints on water for expanded agricultural production, while population continues to grow. To re-establish an upward trend in per capita food production, he concludes, will require both more rapid production increases—which will be very difficult considering the resource constraints of land, water, and energy—and vigorous population control policies. Otherwise, rising food prices will "translate into political unrest and instability."

1

The World Food and Hunger Problem: Changing Perspectives and Possibilities, 1974–84

Walter P. Falcon, C. T. Kurien,
Fernando Monckeberg, Achola P. Okeyo,
S. O. Olayide, Ferenç Rabar, and Wouter Tims

The 1974 World Food Conference represented a benchmark in thinking about the global food system. The immediate threats of famine in the Indian subcontinent and the African Sahel, coupled with the reduction of world grain reserves to their lowest levels in 25 years and corresponding increases in food prices, shocked the international community into a mood of serious concern and reappraisal.

On the tenth anniversary of the conference, the World Food Council asked us to assess progress made in the last decade toward meeting food objectives. Instead of attempting comprehensiveness, we have sought to focus on a select number of issues, primarily those concerning food problems in the developing countries. Our analysis draws on the vast flow of contributions about food issues from scholars, policymakers, and practitioners. Without their efforts, our assessment would not have been possible.

Selected Food Issues of the Last Decade

Our analysis starts from a set of shared views about the world food situation. These are different from the views that prevailed at the time of the 1974 conference, putting the policy framework in a somewhat different light.

Excerpted from *The World Food and Hunger Problem: Changing Perspectives and Possibilities, 1974–84*, an independent assessment presented to the World Food Council, Rome, February 10, 1984 (WFC/1984/86).

Evolving Perceptions, 1974–84

The first, overriding assumption of delegates at the World Food Conference was that the world was entering a period of tight food supplies and that mass starvation was a distinct possibility. Demand was in danger of outpacing supplies, especially in Asia. Delegates feared that the major food-producing countries would not be able to grow enough grain to meet the demand, nor did they think that the large projected imports envisaged could be transported, even assuming that countries had the foreign exchange to pay for them. Since the balance of supply and demand would be close, they thought that recurrent food crises were likely, given climatic variability and man-made disruptions.

The answer proposed was essentially to increase agricultural production in the food-deficit developing regions. Delegates were reasonably confident about the availability of technical means to increase production if agriculture were given sufficient priority and if the necessary resources were allocated. Hence, delegates were optimistic that with increased production in food-deficit areas, the worst aspects of hunger could be eradicated in a decade and the threat of starvation could be eliminated.

Because the 1974 conference stressed the man-made and political dimensions of the world food problem, delegates emphasized mobilizing political will. To maintain political momentum, they created special follow-up and oversight bodies, including the World Food Council, the FAO Committee on World Food Security, and the Committee on Food Aid Policies and Programs. They also felt that international agreements were needed to establish a system of nationally held food reserves.

The emphasis on increased agricultural production and international agreements formed the basic tenets of food security thinking in 1974. Hence, food security was implicitly identified with commercial food prices and physical availability rather than with demand and consumption of poor people or nutritionally vulnerable groups.

By 1984, many of the assumptions made at the 1974 conference had proved to be ill-founded. After a slow start in 1975, cereal production and reserves recovered substantially. At the end of the 1970s, surpluses reached record levels and the real market prices for cereals were the lowest in 30 years. Despite the fluctuations, market adjustments were fairly smooth, even without an effective international wheat agreement.

The net addition to global population since the conference is approaching one billion people. Much of this increase has taken place in those countries or regions with acute food problems, but this has not led to any strain on the world food situation. Demand for grainfed livestock has grown rapidly in the U.S.S.R., Eastern Europe, and some middle-income developing countries, and trade in coarse grains has increased four-fold, yet supplies have proved more than ample.

While the threat of rising international food prices has not been borne out during the last decade, international agricultural trade has been marked by disruptive market instability. Often this has arisen as a result of insulating domestic production from international market conditions, which creates distortions and fluctuations both in price and in production levels. The effects are particularly adverse for low-income countries heavily dependent on commodity exports.

The decade since the conference has also witnessed a clearer understanding of the nature and extent of malnutrition. Experts no longer perceive the "hunger problem" as one of starvation or protein deficiency, but rather of chronic undernutrition, affecting a range of vulnerable groups whose common bond is their poverty. Chronic hunger is still a staggering problem for millions of people. Reaching them—as opposed to disaster or famine victims—has proved to be much more intractable than imagined in 1974. The hungry are no longer seen as existing in isolation from the surrounding economic and social environment. Instead, experts now realize that the hungry are closely linked to their particular food and labor market conditions and to the impact of changing technologies on their societies. Ironically, the undernourished are often engaged in food production.

International concern about food and hunger has slowly shifted from Asia to Africa. Asia, as a whole, has made rapid strides in agricultural production and reduced its dependence on imported cereals, although it is still the home of the largest absolute number of poor and chronically undernourished people. Africa, however, seems to be bearing out the 1974 fears. Population growth has outstripped food production and food imports are increasingly essential. The undernourished in Africa are now a much higher proportion of total population than they are in Asia.

Finally, experts now have a greater understanding of the role that food strategies and policies play in facilitating programs to address hunger. While production must be increased to resolve hunger problems, experts now better appreciate the connections between hunger, viable employment opportunities, and income generation.

Identifying the Undernourished: From Numbers to Vulnerable Groups

Experts still disagree about who the world's hungry are, where they are located, and the best way to help them. In part, this reflects the imprecise usage of terms such as hunger, starvation, malnutrition, and undernutrition. It also reflects gaps in our knowledge about malnutrition and how it affects various groups, in both the short and the long run.

Globally, experts now see the principal nutritional problem as inadequate food consumption in terms of quantity—energy—rather than quality—say, protein (see Latham in part V). The importance of protein, especially for children, is unquestionable; but the growing consensus is that most diets meet protein requirements as long as people consume them in quantities adequate to satisfy energy needs. Hence, hunger is primarily related to undernutrition rather than malnutrition. Basic energy requirements vary significantly between individuals of different ages, body weights, sexes, and activity levels and vary for an individual at different times. Thus, specifying a uniformly acceptable cutoff point for undernutrition is not easy. Also, experts are uncertain about the functional consequences of food deprivation in terms of productivity, human development, health, and well-being.

Measuring actual food consumption is just as difficult as specifying consumption norms. Consumption estimates are frequently derived from aggregate national accounts of food production, stock movements, external trade, food use, and availability of food for direct human consumption. Only a few studies have assessed actual household consumption, and fewer still have observed food distribution among family members.

Given all these problems, the variation in estimates of the total number of undernourished around the world is not surprising: 450 million according to the FAO, 840 million according to the World Bank, and 1.3 billion according to IFPRI. Even the least of these estimates is staggering, especially remembering the 1974 conference theme that hunger should be eliminated within a decade.

Some factors that lead to food deprivation are, of course, easily identifiable. Weather conditions are the commonest. Floods and droughts can both cause crop failure. The continuing latent hunger of millions, however, is not related to such occasional calamities. In many parts of the world people are hungry because they lack either enough land to produce food for themselves or jobs that pay enough to buy food.

The common bond of undernourished people is poverty. Their poverty results from the way in which landowners use their land, from low agricultural productivity, from agricultural technologies that do not provide enough employment to the rural labor force, and from lack of nonfarm employment opportunities. Consequently, policies designed to eradicate hunger must address this range of complex problems—problems made more complex by the international factors relating to food production and trade.

Not only have we made important advances in our understanding of the nature of malnutrition and the overall numbers involved since the World Food Conference, but we have also come to appreciate the need for different measures for different groups of people. Disaggregating the malnourished into identifiable groups by recognizing their particular but changing needs and designing appropriate programs remain urgent tasks.

The majority of the undernourished live in rural areas. Here it is the families of landless laborers and households headed by women (men are often away at distant jobs for most of the year) who are most threatened by undernutrition, followed by marginal farmers and poor coastal fishing families. Regional factors within countries, such as remoteness and access only to inferior land and marginal water resources, further aggravate the nutritional problems of many rural people.

In many instances, the undernourished are also squeezed by shifts in the food sector itself. In many countries, the increased income resulting from economic development leads to the production of more convenient, more easily digestible cereals, such as rice and wheat, to the neglect of the "inferior" cereals that constitute the staple diet of the poor. Simultaneously, shifts from the traditional payment in kind to cash payment may expose low wage earners in agriculture to the caprice of market forces in the context of a rapidly commercializing agriculture.

Although a smaller proportion of the world's hungry, the undernourished in urban areas also face severe difficulties in meeting their food needs. In several countries, the urban poor in cities do benefit from urban-biased food policies and ration schemes that keep consumer prices down and assure reasonably stable food supplies throughout the year. Yet the urban poor are often the hardest hit by economic downturns, inflation, fixed wage dependency, and unemployment. Their health, because of crowded living conditions, may be worse than that of the rural poor of equivalent or even lower incomes.

Women—whether in urban or rural areas—represent a disproportionately heavy share of the undernourished (see Huffman in part V). Their undernutrition stems from both physiological and sociocultural factors. In the first instance, pregnant and lactating women must nourish not only themselves but their babies as well. When the woman's food intake is inadequate, both mother and child suffer. Second, women in most rural areas account for a higher proportion of agricultural labor than men, requiring them to carry their family and childbearing responsibilities along with full-time field work. In addition, new technologies introduced into traditional farming systems and into traditional social structures have often actually increased women's work and reduced their material well-being.

Finally, young children face particular nutritional risks (see Leslie in part V). They require food with an especially high concentration of both energy and protein, as well as other nutrients. Failure to meet this spectrum of nutritional requirements results in various forms of growth-inhibiting malnutrition, the most significant of which is protein-energy malnutrition. In both cause and consequence, infant malnutrition is inextricably interlocked with illness and infection, which both sharpen and are sharpened by malnutrition. Perhaps one-half of all cases of severe child malnutrition are precipitated by such illnesses as diarrhea, measles, chicken pox, tuberculosis, or intestinal parasites that depress the child's appetite, sap energy, and drain away body weight. Customs that lead to withholding nutritious foods during some of these episodes further aggravate illness, malnutrition, and the risk of death.

National Food Security Concerns

A nation's food security is achieved when it can assure both physical and economic access to food for all its citizens over both the short and the long run. Behind this simplified definition, however, lie a number of complex and overlapping components involving agricultural production, international trade and economic interdependence, national stocking policies, development aid, and a range of direct measures designed to enhance household consumption levels.

CHANGING CONCEPTS OF FOOD SECURITY. For some time following the World Food Conference, experts discussed food security concerns largely in terms of increasing domestic food production and creating international reserve stocks. The goal of increasing local production was based on an implicit assumption, arising from the 1974 trade squeeze felt by many low-income countries, that food imports must be decreased to achieve food self-sufficiency. Great efforts and hopes were placed on establishing an international grain reserve and on meeting multilateral food aid targets. Although the food aid targets were substantially met, the 1979 International Wheat Agreement negotiations foundered because of irreconcilable North-South positions and divergent East-West and West-West negotiating stances.

This supply-oriented concept of food security had begun to change by the late 1970s. At the 1979 Ottawa session of the World Food Council, food security was discussed as "a function of all factors affecting the maintenance and improvement of per capita food consumption, particularly in the poorest countries, including food production, income generation, [and the] capacity to earn foreign exchange." This broader concept recognized the conclusion emerging from a number of analyses: the economic and food production growth policies prevailing in most countries would not solve the hunger problem unless they were reoriented to ensure increased income and improved consumption for the poor and malnourished. Thus, equal attention was given to the demand and consumption sides of the equation.

Mutual attention to the demand and supply sides of food security has, in turn, pointed to the need to identify various policy options at the national level. Supply-side policy options include national buffer stocks, imports, and even the use of futures markets, as well as increased domestic production. Consumption-side policy options include a host of direct measures designed to reach low-income consumers and, more recently, growing attention to the importance of food price policy. Implicitly, supply-side policies are concerned with macroeconomic efficiency—determining the set of aggregate food security policies that is the most efficient and therefore the least costly to the economy. Implicitly, consumption-side policies are concerned with maximizing benefits—obtaining consumer equity for the most disadvantaged. Food price policy is the link between the supply and consumption objectives.

However, we think that analysts have not paid enough attention to the inherent long-term and short-term trade-offs and policy conflicts that arise when attempting to meet both the supply and consumption sides of the food security equation simultaneously.

PRICE POLICIES TO ACHIEVE FOOD SECURITY. From a macroeconomic standpoint, aggregate food security is achieved through a policy goal of price stabilization, which implies adequate supply. Most discussions of food security thus examine the policy tools available to ensure domestic availability and to protect prices from extreme fluctuation—buffer stocks, trade, and possibly futures market purchases. The "best" combination of trade and reserve stock strategies will be different from different vantage points—producer or consumer, urban or rural, rich or poor—and involve directly conflicting interests. Each "best" combination will lead to a particular price. Needless to say, the analytically determined, supply-oriented policies that prescribe food prices rarely lead to the prices observed in reality. Though analytically sound, this type of analysis misses an important dimension of political economy. Major political forces may be at work when, say, a government holds inefficiently large buffer stocks beyond operational needs or resorts to trade to meet constant production shortfalls.

Nearly all governments separate domestic food prices from international prices. This recognizes that international prices may not always be the best to protect the special interests of producers and consumers as well as special categories of low-income combined producer-consumers, such as marginal farmers and landless laborers whose income and food output are directly affected by food price policy. In this sense, price policy has food security implications not only for income transfer consequences between producers and consumers but also for various producers. Short-run, consumption-oriented food security can be obtained in part by pricing policies that benefit the poor and the undernourished. The difficulty is that such price policies may be in direct conflict with longer-term food security objectives such as increased food production or a certain food trade policy. Equally important, the political economy of a country may make it extremely difficult to alter an existing price structure to further equity concerns.

THE FOOD SECURITY DILEMMA. A government confronting its food problems must choose a path that strikes a balance between short- and long-term considerations and the needs and claims of different groups. In the long run, the agricultural sector requires positive incentives to increase production and adopt new technologies, so food prices must be high enough to create incentives to expand output. Yet the same price incentives may be a poor prescription for meeting the needs of the poor and undernourished. In the short run, high food prices may increase suffering among those who do not immediately benefit from production incentives.

The food security dilemma occurs when a government must choose between long-run aggregate food security and short-run food security to improve consumption of specific groups. In actual policy making, the dilemma will be resolved. In fact, policymakers make these choices continuously, whether by way of conscious weighting of appropriate policy mixes or, in the extreme, by neglecting the existence of the dilemma altogether. The conclusion is that policies to promote agricultural production must go hand-in-hand with measures to provide a minimum of food to vulnerable groups. Governments faced with the dilemma—and donors supporting their efforts—should be clear about the need for a mix of the two policy elements and about the economic rationale governing both.

The Increasing Complexity of the External Economic Environment

One of the least anticipated developments during the decade since the World Food Conference has been the growing complexity of the international economic environment and its effects on the food systems of the developing countries. Experts anticipated expanded food shipments to feed developing countries. However, few people recognized the extent to which such nonagricultural factors as trade, capital markets, exchange rates, and a host of other elements would exert tremendous pressure on the food systems of the developing countries, directly influencing their capacity to confront their food problems.

INTERNATIONAL FOOD TRADE TRENDS. In 1982–83, world production of wheat, coarse grains, and milled rice reached a record of approximately 1.7 billion tons. Carryover stocks were a record 217 million tons, or 21 percent of world cereal consumption. International grain trade was 201 million tons, some 7 percent less than the record volume achieved the year before, a drop closely tied to the economic recession. Even this smaller grain trade, however, was still more than double the grain trade of a decade earlier. Twenty-one percent of world wheat production was exported, 11 percent of coarse grains, and 13 percent of rice.

The driving force behind this rapid increase in cereal trade during the past decade was not, however, the needs of the poor or expanding population, but rising incomes and changing dietary patterns. In 1982–83, almost 47 percent of the imports of wheat and coarse grains went to the U.S.S.R., Eastern Europe, Western Europe, and Japan. If China, the middle-income developing countries, and the oil exporting countries of the Middle East are included, the proportion of imports reaches more than 90 percent. In general, the rapid increases in cereal imports are due to agricultural trade policies in those countries that encourage increased consumption of wheat and grainfed livestock and that seek to supplement and stabilize domestic supplies through imports. The United States as the major cereal exporter and the U.S.S.R. as the largest importer have come to play a preponderant role in the international cereal trade.

As for the developing countries, grain imports have provided a buffer for internal shortfalls in domestic production. In 1982, developing countries as a whole imported 100 million tons of cereals valued at $25 billion. The major importing developing countries were the middle-income countries and the oil exporting countries. While low-income developing countries have also greatly increased their cereal imports, the amounts are a relatively small proportion of total cereal trade, reaching 12 million tons in 1982–83. This small proportion is contrary to expectations at the time of the World Food Conference that demand from low-income countries would place tremendous burdens on available supply.

This lower demand can be explained in part by the turnaround during the last decade in the food trade position of South Asia, which ceased being a major market for grain in the 1970s. Instead, Africa has become increasingly dependent on cereal imports. In the last five years, African commercial and food aid imports have doubled, and this dependence is likely to continue to grow. Currently, imported food feeds most of urban Africa.

While wheat continues to be the major grain imported by developing countries, their demand for feed grain and meat products has been growing at a rapid 7 percent annually. Present projections suggest they will double their consumption of grainfed livestock in the next ten years.

With the rapid expansion of food imports by developing countries, they are on the verge of becoming net importers of agricultural products. Consequently, their ability to continue to expand food imports depends on larger earnings from commodity exports; expansion of their nonagricultural exports, especially manufactured foods; or a contraction of nonagricultural imports.

NATIONAL AGRICULTURAL POLICIES AND FOOD TRADE INSTABILITY. One result of expanded international trade has been to bring national agricultural policies into direct conflict with each other, thereby increasing market instability as countries try to insulate their agricultural sectors from international fluctuations. For the food-deficit developing countries, international market instability has proven to be a much more serious problem than the rising real prices of traded foods feared by many observers in 1974.

When governments isolate domestic markets from trade, particularly in thin markets such as rice where trade includes only a small proportion of production, they contribute to a vicious cycle: instability motivates isolation from international markets, reduced supply and demand increase price fluctuations, and thus new incentives arise to protect domestic markets even further. In the case of the major food exporters, largely OECD countries, world market instability is exacerbated because of their preponderant role in determining food prices and because of their trade practices that limit imports from developing countries when they are in direct competition with domestically grown—hence, domestically protected—commodities. Paradoxically, world market instability is also the cause for, as well as the partial result of, the national agricultural policies of the major food producing countries, even as they attempt to assure their own domestic stability.

Protecting domestic agricultural markets occurs in the wake of national policies that attempt to encourage two sometimes conflicting public policy objectives: to promote greater productivity and efficiency in agricultural output and to maintain or improve the economic and social welfare of the farm sector. Generally speaking, these dual objectives are pursued through a range of policies to influence supply and, to a lesser extent, demand. On the supply side, most food-exporting countries have a whole inventory of pricing policies, supply management and production policies, and marketing assistance policies, as well as concomitant trade promotion policies. On the demand side, one finds measures designed to encourage use of food products by consumers or targeted groups of consumers through such policies as subsidized pricing and food distribution schemes.

The international sugar market is a clear-cut example of how national agricultural policies in OECD countries have led to restricted markets, instability, and lower foreign exchange earnings for developing country producers. As a result of their wartime experience, the United States and several EC countries embarked on a policy to become self-sufficient in sugar through sugar beet production. To encourage their industries, the United States and the EC countries heavily subsidized their internal markets for sugar and effectively excluded substantial imports of more efficiently produced cane sugar, largely from developing countries. The EC has even become a net sugar exporter. In the United States, high prices have led to development and widespread use of high fructose corn syrup, a maize-based sugar substitute, which in turn has led to even further subsidies for beet sugar. As the United States and the EC have subsidized beet sugar, the international price of sugar has fluctuated wildly, generally in a downward direction, dropping 16 percent, for example, in just one two-week period in October 1983. However valid the original decision for the United States and the EC to become major sugar producers, the result has been to maintain a costly program at the taxpayers' and consumers' expense, to create further price distortions to justify past policy decisions, and all the while to force down the international price of sugar to the detriment of developing country producers. The situation has been further compounded in recent years because the U.S.S.R. and the Eastern European countries have also limited their cane sugar imports to protect domestic beet sugar production.

INTERNATIONAL FINANCIAL AND MACROECONOMIC POLICIES. Apart from food trade instability, the general international macroeconomic setting and world financial markets are another major international influence on the developing countries' ability to overcome their food problems. The spectrum of macroeconomic issues adversely affecting the developing countries' economic maneuverability is disturbingly wide. Currently, the debt and debt-servicing issue receives a great deal of attention. Equally significant are issues such as volatility of exchange and interest rates and currency markets, the scarcity of capital for long-term investment, and finally, the looming and ominous potential for increased trade protectionism.

An improved international economic environment represents the bedrock on which governments can make the long-term commitment to reorient their national policy frameworks and to undertake the investment decisions necessary to meet the requirements not only of their food sectors, but of the other economic and social sectors as well. In the present international economic environment, governments of low-income countries will be able to initiate these changes only with great difficulty, if at all.

Priorities for Confronting Developing Country Food Problems

A small number of critical areas exist where appropriate policy and funding shifts could make a substantial difference in overcoming existing programming and implementation bottlenecks, thus creating a more efficient and equitable global food economy. We make no pretence of offering "quick fixes" or newly discovered policy pronouncements. Indeed, we will discuss public policy choices that involve considerable political and social cost, that entail clear trade-offs among short- and long-term objectives, and that require substantial financial commitment over the long haul.

Short-Term Requirements: Special Measures for the Poor and Hungry

As we noted earlier, experts now recognize that poverty is the basic cause of hunger today and that hunger is essentially a rural problem. Most of the world's undernourished have neither the land to grow their own food nor the income to purchase it. The key to the long-term reduction of hunger is meaningful agrarian reform in certain countries coupled with additional productive jobs to raise the effective demand of the rural poor. But helping the undernourished through the income-generating effects of agricultural and rural development is a complex, inevitably slow process. Moreover, some groups—the urban poor, the unemployed, landless laborers, and migrant workers—may not benefit appreciably from these development efforts. Special short-term programs are therefore needed for these groups and for the present generation of undernourished people who may not see the benefits of development activities in their lifetimes.

CONSUMER FOOD SUBSIDIES. Consumer food subsidies in various forms—general retail price subsidies for basic food, coupons, rationing, and free food distribution—are the most direct short-term measures, and many countries have used them. Subsidies have the potential to reduce hunger quickly, although they lack the direct income-generating effects of employment-oriented measures and can become a burden on the public exchequer.

Careful targeting can reduce cost. Experts now recognize that the foods consumed by poor families vary significantly from those bought by higher-income groups. Once national data are available on food consumption by income groups, governments can institute subsidies more narrowly focused on the specific food staples of the poor. Such subsidies are normally more efficient and less administratively cumbersome than wider subsidies and can also be applied seasonally or regionally, thereby having the intended nutritional impact in those months and areas in which the incidence of undernutrition is highest.

Another promising approach is food subsidy programs aimed at poor households with young children, combined with health, educational, and related services provided through primary health care networks. This approach could be used to establish selected household entitlements to food supplements with actual food distribution handled through regular commercial outlets.

Where food subsidies are accepted as a short-term measure, policymakers must bear in mind that frequently they become shortcuts to keep down the cost of urban living rather than to benefit the poor and the hungry. Once they are firmly established, strong political pressures to prevent dismantling them are likely.

DIRECT MEASURES FOR SMALL FARMERS. Paradoxically, about half of the world's hungry people—and the majority of those in Africa—could probably grow their own food. This underlines the importance of specific measures for small landholders and tenant farmers even though in many cases the land is marginal and its occupants are partially dependent on off-farm employment. Low cost, simple-technology packages emphasizing improved cultivation practices could increase smallholders' food production and consequently their consumption in a comparatively short time. However, if smallholder programs are to realize this potential, they will require a higher degree of political priority and administrative support than do programs for larger farms, which are more highly organized at the outset. Given the appropriate support, small producers can achieve high standards of husbandry and market orientation.

In the same fashion, improved credit arrangements can result in high returns to smallholders in the short term. Better credit facilities, emphasizing improvement of loan administration, will be a key element in any package of smallholder assistance. Landless families have also been penalized by the denial of credit on reasonable terms. Providing small loans to this group for productive purposes is a promising new approach to asset and income generation. Early experience from India and Bangladesh suggests high returns on capital, few defaults, and considerable economic multiplier effects at low cost. Although relatively high administrative demands tend to limit expansion of such schemes in the short run, they could make an important contribution to reducing hunger and poverty in the longer run.

Special measures must be undertaken within the policy framework of longer-term food sector objectives and investments. Policymakers must decide on the appropriate blend of direct measures, recognizing that the most immediate palliative measures, such as food subsidies, tend to be expensive and to make limited contributions to long-term solutions, while the more productive ones, such as employment creation and small farmer programs, are administratively more demanding and structurally more involved.

The Long-Term Requirements

The long-term actions for the food-deficit countries require a blend of human and capital investments, institutional arrangements, agricultural and macroeconomic policy reform, and, perhaps more important, political commitment—the lynchpin upon which success will ultimately depend.

INVESTMENTS IN TECHNOLOGY, RESEARCH, AND RESOURCE DEVELOPMENT. Most of the increase in future agricultural production must come from increased output per unit of land area rather than from bringing new land under production. Yield increases will be necessary not only to feed growing populations in proximity to where they live, but also to spur income-generating opportunities in non-farm activities. Yield-increasing agriculture is dependent on the scientific and technical capacity to invent and sustain appropriate new chemical, biological, and mechanical technologies. Agriculture will become increasingly tied to the capacity of a nation's agroindustrial sector and the institutions that disseminate more productive inputs— seeds, herbicides, insecticides, and farm management technology.

Relevant technology depends, in the first instance, on a long-term commitment to agricultural research and relevant research in the social and nutritional sciences. Despite the much-heralded green revolution in Asia and the laudable efforts of the international research centers, the technologies to increase yields in all the diverse environments where the poor and the undernourished live are still in their infancy, most notably in the harsh, resource-poor areas such as arid regions that require dry-farming technologies.

Equally as important as agronomic research is the need for research in the social and nutritional sciences. As is now well known, the application of new technologies is often not socially neutral, but causes significant shifts—if not upheavals—in local traditions, economic relationships, and labor market conditions. In practically all developing countries, rural women tend to be the last to benefit from new technological packages, even though they account for the majority of the farm labor force. Hence, research is needed on the societal ramifications of introducing new technology, particularly as it applies to small farmers and to their relationships with farm workers and the rural poor. Many food-deficit developing countries still do not have national research facilities capable of carrying research through to the practical implementation stage, nor the long-term commitments to funding and manpower development to enable them to overcome the weak link in the research chain to date—ensuring self-sustaining infrastructure and institutions.

The conversion to more yield-oriented agriculture will also require careful attention to the resource base upon which it depends. Unless special efforts are made to avoid the depletion of soil and water resources, the world could face the ecological disaster and paradox of making green fields into deserts rather than deserts into green fields.

Nowhere is the case more clear for large-scale capital investments in the decades ahead than in water resource management. Experts estimate that unused irrigation potential around the world is 1.1 billion hectares, and in sub-Saharan Africa less than 1 percent of total arable land is now irrigated. For most of the world's undernourished, the supply and physical control of water is perhaps the key factor in the food production–poverty–hunger equation. Water is a critical factor in the semiarid regions as well as in regions with monsoon flooding and runoff. Many of the world's undernourished live in large river basins in Asia where lack of irrigation, erosion, flooding, high salinity, and poor drainage represent major obstacles to improved productivity. In the semiarid regions of Africa and Asia, the inability to harness rainfall effectively severely limits the length of the growing seasons, and what rains occur often take a heavy toll in flooding and soil erosion.

Increasing irrigation efficiency through better control and allocation of water can often double crop yields with existing technologies. What is generally required is improved maintenance, better linkages to seasonal production requirements of individual crops, more responsiveness to farmers, and stepped-up management training and supervision. All this requires tremendous outlays of capital, not only for new projects but also to maintain existing ones. A 1977 study by the Trilateral Commission concluded that an annual irrigation investment of $4.5 billion (at 1975 prices)—about six times the current investment rate—would be needed to meet a 3 to 4 percent growth in the demand for food during this decade and the next.

ECONOMIC ENVIRONMENT AND INSTITUTIONAL ARRANGEMENTS. Scientific knowledge and financial resources are not the only preconditions for adopting improved practices in agriculture. A suitable economic environment is equally essential.

Institutions capable of timely delivery of the inputs on which a modernizing agriculture depends are one critical requirement. Arrangements for credit and marketing are further institutional supports that will become necessary, especially for small farmers. Credit to purchase inputs and to meet other operational costs and arrangements will be crucial for small and marginal farmers, many of whom are not in a position to cultivate even the small plots of land that they have because the initial investment is beyond their means. Small farmers are often at a great disadvantage in terms of marketing and trade. Dealers and large farmers exploit the vulnerability of small farmers by making inputs or credit available at unremunerative terms. Appropriate institutional arrangements for marketing at the local level where small farmers as a whole can safeguard their interests are vital, both for their survival and for their contribution to the national effort to increase food production and to make food available to those who need it.

In many traditional societies, land ownership is highly skewed and the actual cultivators are frequently tenants with no direct interest in land improvement. Rental arrangements may retard incentives to increase output. In other situations, land ownership is so traditionally communal that even enterprising farmers may face severe social and economic constraints. In such cases, appropriate land reform may be an essential prerequisite for agricultural change to become effective, even when the scientific knowledge and the technical requirements may be readily available.

In the long run, the solution of the food problem will also depend on an adequate expansion and diversification of nonfarm activities to provide employment and income-generating opportunities to those at present dependent on agriculture for their livelihood. This is particularly so where landless agricultural laborers now constitute a large segment of the rural population. In countries where pressure on land is already high, a well thought out and effectively implemented policy to bring down the growth rate of the population is also necessary.

MACROECONOMIC POLICIES AND THE FOOD SECTOR. Every government influences, directly or indirectly, the quantities and kinds of food produced, traded, and consumed. This is done in part through the kinds of agricultural and food sector policies we have discussed earlier. At the same time, broader macroeconomic policy decisions have a pervasive, albeit often unrecognized, effect on the food sector and the consumption level. Even if appropriate food sector policies are established, they are, by themselves, insufficient. In the long run, macroeconomic forces are too powerful for even the best food sector policies to overcome.

Overvalued currency may make the import of fertilizers appear to be a cheaper alternative than domestic production. Tax and credit policies favoring the industrial sector may use up available resources and result in the food sector being starved of funds. An export promotion policy may divert attention from rural employment programs. In short, the institutional structure of the economy, the rate of growth and the direction of that growth, the distribution of income, trade policy and exchange rates, the management of money supply and credit, and many more macroeconomic decisions will have an important bearing on the overall food situation in a country, however remote some of these factors may appear to be from agriculture and food as such.

This added dimension to a country's food sector has major implications for a government's attempts to confront its food problems. The necessary policies and programs cannot come solely from the ministries of agriculture and public works, for example. Important policy decisions being made by a government's central bank and finance ministry will likewise have important ramifications.

The political and administrative directive thus becomes quite clear. To deal with a country's food problem requires close and coordinated consultations among a whole range of government ministries. Attaining this kind of cooperation obviously requires solid and unwavering political support from the highest level. This kind of support may thus represent the ultimate test of a country's commitment to confront its food problems, for the kinds of decision making involved may run against the grain of long-standing economic and bureaucratic institutions.

POLITICAL WILL AND POLICY IMPLEMENTATION. Political will is usually the "given" in food sector analysis, after which discussion focuses on the technocratic and managerial means to increase production and assure consumption levels for the poor. However, perhaps to a greater extent than in the developed industrial countries, the process of implementing public policy—as opposed to formulating public policy—is the focal point of political participation and competition in the developing countries. At the same time, a government's policies have a great bearing on the daily lives of citizens. Many policies include distributive and redistributive measures or deal with agriculture, urban development, education, health, and employment, to name but a few areas that vitally affect the lives of individual citizens, particularly in areas with poor communications and scarce resources. Policies that propose significant changes to existing social and economic structures intensify the political activities engendered during the policy implementation phase and will generate opposition from those whose interests are threatened. Even intended beneficiaries may not fully support new policies if their long-term advantages are not immediately apparent.

The point is that simply formulating effective policies and programs and redirecting capital and human resources to the food sector, however difficult that may be, are still only initial steps. Overcoming the formidable hurdles to implementation requires policies that are widely accepted by the entire government, not just the food sector ministries. In addition, the policy formulation process must be open to as much participation as possible to ensure support from various political and economic groups throughout the implementation phase. At the same time, policymakers must make a considerable effort to protect the interests of the rural poor and undernourished, precisely because their economic and political power is so minimal. All of this means that governments must be willing to legitimize policy debate and dissent, to encourage feedback and policy readjustment, and to reward officials who seek to meet policy and program targets, whatever their political acceptability. In the long run, the political interests of a government are met when its social and economic policy interests are promoted and served.

External Actions by the International Community

The developing countries cannot unilaterally deal with the increasing complexity of the external economic environment, and most cannot realize efforts to alleviate undernutrition and to revitalize their agricultural and rural sectors solely with domestic capital and manpower. The donor countries and the multilateral agencies will have to take the lead to improve the functioning of the global food economy and help ease the food burdens of the developing countries.

AGRICULTURAL POLICIES IN THE INDUSTRIALIZED COUNTRIES. Virtually all industrialized countries have excluded their agricultural sectors from international negotiations and, consequently, from the general trend of trade liberalization. This has had profound effects on international relations regarding food and results in often overlooked burdens for developing countries.

Insulation of the agricultural and food sectors in the major industrialized countries has led to increased stability for the remaining countries participating in the world market. It has also encouraged greater self-sufficiency in the industrialized countries and even surplus production due to high support prices domestically and the restriction of competing imports. The consequence is that growing surpluses enter the world market and depress the prices of most agricultural commodities that are of interest to the developing countries. We contend the result is international prices that are too low to reflect either the marginal costs of efficient producers or, conversely, the real scarcities of these commodities. In this regard, our concern is quite the opposite of that expressed by the World Food Conference in 1974, which feared continuous shortages and high world market prices.

The long-term solution is a return of the industrial countries to a system that generates international prices more in line with underlying scarcities and production costs. Price policy mechanisms that currently set internal prices independent of world market prices should be modified. Needless to say, this can only be a gradual process, given the production and income distortions that have been created in the past. Nevertheless, the essence of this change should be toward internal prices set to take into account their impact on international prices. In the initial stages of the process, limitations on the quantities produced under support price systems will be needed to curtail excessive surplus production and further disruption of international price formation.

Higher international prices that in due course will result from these policy changes have the advantage of giving the appropriate signals to developing countries as they decide on their own price policies and resource allocations. In addition, closer ties between internal food prices in the industrial countries and international prices will enhance the stability of the international markets, as some of the present instability will be absorbed by industrial country markets reacting to internal price movements.

In the present international situation, most developing nations cannot shape their agricultural policies without reference to international market conditions and prices. Developed countries must begin to shape their agricultural policies with an understanding of their implications for international prices and their impact on the low-income countries. This is a central requirement for any meaningful long-term global strategy toward the eradication of hunger.

AID FLOWS. External financing can make a crucial difference in whether countries meet development goals in the near term, in the more distant future, or not at all. Recently, a significant shift in official financing toward promoting small-farm food crop production and rural infrastructure in marginal areas and strengthening the capacity of supportive public institutions has occurred. Appraisal criteria in official projects have been broadened beyond economic rates of return to newer and still emerging concepts of social benefit-cost analysis. Equally important has been a slow shift toward program assistance to support policy changes, a move we strongly endorse and believe should be encouraged even more.

Agriculture in the developing countries received a larger share of international financial flows after the food crisis of 1972–74. The multilateral organizations, in particular, increased the share of their aid to agriculture, which grew by 12 percent a year between 1973 and 1980. During the same period, bilateral commitments from OECD countries grew by 11 percent a year, and OPEC commitments grew by 4 percent a year. Aid to agriculture declined slightly in 1981 and 1982.

Notwithstanding these increases, analysis by IFPRI and the FAO shows that food objectives cannot be achieved without higher external capital flows. We would not disagree with the recent FAO projection that about $1.7 thousand billion in aggregate direct investment in agriculture will be needed by the developing countries between 1980 and 2000 to achieve increased agricultural production of 3.7 percent annually.

Even if increases in total aid continue to be inadequate, scope for increased sectoral emphasis on agriculture still remains. The share of OPEC development assistance directed to agriculture is only about 5 percent. Among the OECD countries, considerable disparity exists in the proportion of aid directed to agriculture. If the donors at the low end of the spectrum (those directing as little as 9 to 10 percent of their aid to agriculture) were to increase their emphasis to match that of donors at the high end of the spectrum (who direct 30 to 35 percent of their aid to agriculture), total real flows to agriculture from OECD sources would increase by 11 percent.

Bilateral aid efforts should be in addition to commitments to sustain multilateral flows. Beginning in 1979–80, changes in political support for multilateral aid have begun to affect total flows of aid to agriculture. Multilateral aid is important, since it provides the largest share of aid to agriculture and tends to provide the largest share to poor countries.

AID EFFECTIVENESS. In a climate of uncertainty about aid prospects, effectiveness takes on added importance. From the standpoint of food security, the most important criterion is the degree to which the poor and hungry benefit.

Judged only by the narrow criteria of project implementation and rates of return, aid projects for agriculture have done reasonably well, although donors and the public at large continue to raise questions about appropriate scale, missed opportunities, poor management, and inadequate consultations with beneficiaries. Aid donors should direct more attention toward assisting local institutions to serve development goals and helping them avoid overdependence on central government financing. The role of private voluntary organizations can be expanded. Their record of involving the beneficiaries in program design and responding to changed needs is well established. At the program level, examples can still be found of investment projects that perform below potential because of inappropriate policies or simply a lack of concern for the poor. Furthermore, problems of aid coordination abound. In some cases, donors compete for projects or influence. In others, projects are designed in ignorance of other projects, with the result that they prove counterproductive.

Countries should not underwrite projects without programs or programs without policies. Food sector strategies, which encourage long-term investment programming accompanied by regular policy review, serve not only to bring about better coordination among agencies involved in food policy but also to involve the donors in a well-coordinated and long-term endeavor to which they can commit themselves.

Finally, we stress that the donor countries need to exhibit greater awareness of the pressures facing developing country leaders and decisionmakers in the current difficult economic and political circumstances. To expect them to make policy and program changes overnight—as if the developed countries are any more able to make sudden reversals in their own policies—is to promote an attitude that is naively technocratic and possibly disruptive to the interests of both parties.

THE FOOD RESERVE DEBATE. In 1974, the world community was shocked into a recognition that it lacked the means to mitigate a tight market situation and that the burden of the shortfall fell disproportionately on the poor. One of the recommendations of the World Food Conference was to set up a system of international coordinated stocks as the centerpiece for dealing with shortages. Efforts to improve the operation of the unregulated international grain market have been frustrated by the divergent interests of producer and consumer nations, by different North-South perspectives, and by different East-West perspectives. The now defunct discussions at the International Wheat Council demonstrate the inherent difficulties of getting grain exporting and importing countries to negotiate the size, price bands, and organizational arrangements for an international grain reserve.

Recent analysis of food reserve options has called into question the importance to developing countries of either an international stock agreement or large nationally held buffer stocks. An international agreement would probably not increase significantly the net amount of reserves available to food-deficit countries and would probably substitute in part for national and commercial stocks that would have been held in any event. By the same token, large nationally held reserves would prove to be very expensive for food-deficit countries. In the Sahel, for example, one ton of buffer stock grain might cost as much as $500, as opposed to a world price of $200 a ton landed in the importing country. A 6 million ton stock held in developing countries has been estimated to cost as much as $82 million annually to operate. Moreover, because of the random occurrence of poor crop years, stocks might be held much longer than is economically feasible. In the capital-scarce mood of the 1980s, investing in the construction and maintenance of large, expensive storage facilities would divert scarce resources away from long-term food sector development and more immediate measures to help the poor and undernourished.

While we recognize the political pressure to establish large nationally held grain reserves in the absence of an international reserve, we would nonetheless argue that importing countries should only hold operational stocks and that exporting countries should hold the preponderance of reserves. To make these arrangements work effectively, however, two requirements must be met. These requirements would be particularly important if a tight international supply situation for food grain with rising prices were to occur in the latter half of the 1980s or early 1990s, as some observers predict.

The first requirement is a thorough reexamination by national policymakers of the role of existing reserves in meeting the food needs of all people in their country. Poor families benefit from national and international stocks and market stabilization policies only to the extent that such policies enhance their market access and that stocks cover the low-cost staples of the poor. (Wheat is generally not the food of the poor and undernourished.) Hence, establishing reserves of whatever sort requires an initial query: who benefits from such a reserve? If the undernourished are excluded, then the stocking policy may be overlooking the beneficiaries who should be helped the most by its very existence.

The second requirement is guaranteed access to food supply in high-price periods at some concessional rate. North America and the European Community have particular responsibility in this area, since they would undoubtedly hold the lion's share of aggregate reserves for the foreseeable future.

INSTITUTIONAL CONSIDERATIONS. We have concentrated on the general direction in which we feel policy and resources should be moving in the years ahead. However, we would like to focus attention on four specific institutions that in our view urgently require increased funding and support: the research centers of the Consultative Group on International Agricultural Research (CGIAR), the International Development Association (IDA) of the World Bank group, the International Fund for Agricultural Development (IFAD), and the Cereal Import Facility of the IMF.

Since 1979, IFAD and CGIAR, which devote all their activities to agriculture, have seen their funding reduced in real terms. The concessional IDA, which devotes 40 to 50 percent of its grants to agriculture, is also facing a cutback in commitments. A given proportion of reduction in funding to these institutions results in a greater proportionate reduction in their investment capacity, affecting not only new projects, but the stream of funds for ongoing projects as well. In agricultural research, even greater proportionate reductions in capacity and eventual on-site applicability are incurred.

We take exception to the argument that investment for development should correspond to the "real costs" of borrowing in the capital markets and that subsidized loans somehow represent a long-term disservice to recipient countries because they do not correspond to the actual value of capital. As an instrument of public policy, all governments, developed and developing, subsidize capital investments for programs that do not have an initial financial appeal but which further important social and economic objectives. In turn, these initial concessional investments lay the groundwork in areas where poverty, malnutrition, and low productivity previously made lending at market rates unlikely. Moreover, IDA and IFAD loans have an admirable record of returns on investment based on project appraisal criteria, despite their concessional nature.

The creation of the IMF Cereal Import Facility represents a conceptual departure from previous remedies put forward to ease the low-income countries' food problem. The principle behind the facility is simple: it enables low-income countries to maintain a minimally adequate food supply by providing financing to import cereals in times of domestic crop failure or high international grain prices. It is thus premised on the valid observation that in the short term, foreign exchange, not food itself, is the limiting factor for meeting many countries' food consumption needs. Despite its inherent usefulness, the facility has thus far not been used to its full potential, nor has it been tested in times of high international price conditions. Moreover, its future may be in jeopardy due to the IMF's present difficulties in the context of the larger international debt crisis. Be that as it may, the concept behind the facility remains valid, and its capacity to operate must be safeguarded in the years to come, whatever the broader economic circumstances. We also recommend that the facility be expanded to cover noncereal imports. If the purpose of the facility is to assure adequate food supplies to poor people, its coverage should include all food items, cereals and noncereals, consumed by the poor.

Conclusion: The Nexus of the World Food and Hunger Problem

In the decade since the 1974 World Food Conference, the realities of the world food and hunger problem have shifted appreciably. Most of the dire forecasts heard at the 1974 conference have not been borne out. Aggregate food and agricultural production is at record levels, with correspondingly low real prices for most internationally traded cereals and agricultural commodities. The threat of global food scarcity now seems remote, although the possibility of major production shortfalls still remains. Yet between 400 and 800 million people in different parts of the world, especially in the low-income countries of Asia, Africa, and Latin America, still go without adequate food. Growing output and starving millions—that is the paradox, the dilemma, of the world food situation.

Thus, there is a dichotomy between the world *hunger* problem and the world *food* problem, even though the two are closely intertwined. While the production of more food is important to deal with hunger, especially at the local level and to meet population growth, hunger will not be ultimately overcome until the undernourished have access to meaningful employment and income-generating opportunities. These opportunities can come about, at least for the rural sector where most of the poor and undernourished live, through greater output and productivity of the food and agricultural sectors. In the meantime, direct measures will be needed to provide the poor and undernourished with access to the food they require.

The problem of hunger must be tackled primarily at the national level. It is at this level that decisions are made about agricultural production and consumption, the institutional structure of the economy, employment opportunities and income distribution, management of money supply and credit, and trade policy and exchange rates—all of which have an important bearing on the overall food situation and the access of vulnerable groups to food. Decisions are required to provide for the short-term needs of the undernourished without hindering long-term solutions to the problem of hunger.

The global food problem we have identified is the inability to reconcile the increasing commercialization of domestic and international agricultural trade with divergent national agricultural policies and expanding food surpluses. Without some measure of adjustment, the low-income countries will continue to bear the greatest part of the burden caused by this incongruity, reducing not only their prospects for agricultural growth but the food available to the undernourished as well.

To deal with the global food problem, changes in agricultural trade policies in the industrially advanced countries are necessary. In the present international situation, most developing countries cannot shape their agricultural policies without reference to international market conditions and prices. Developed countries must begin to shape their own national agricultural policies with an understanding of the implications of their policies for international prices and their impact on low-income countries and on hungry people. This is the nexus where the world food and hunger problems come together.

2

The World Food Equation: Interrelations among Development, Employment, and Food Consumption

John W. Mellor and Bruce F. Johnston

Since Malthus published his *Essay on the Principle of Population* (1798), people have viewed the world food equation as a race between food supply and population growth. However, current concerns about world food scarcity focus almost entirely on the developing countries.

The unprecedented growth in population since World War II brought on a number of pessimistic predictions in the Malthusian tradition. Beginning with the *First World Food Survey,* published by the FAO in 1948, researchers have tried to quantify the global extent of malnutrition. (In current usage, malnutrition falls in the general category of undernutrition.) Food shortages and a sharp upsurge in food prices during 1973–74 focused attention on the views of neo-Malthusians. Concern receded because of the excellent food crops of the early 1980s and attention shifted to the worldwide recession, even though the underlying problems of massive poverty and inadequate, highly unreliable food intake remained.

The low-income countries especially subject to these problems have important structural and demographic characteristics in common. A large proportion of the population depends on agriculture for employment, and growth rates of the population and labor force are high. This means that the agricultural share of employment will decline slowly and that the absolute size of the farm work force will continue to increase for many years.

Although no precise definition of malnutrition exists, nutritionists agree that adequate nutrition depends primarily on overall food intake, and that the aggregate deprivation is massive. Unless a country's

Excerpted from "The World Food Equation: Interrelationships Among Development, Employment, and Food Consumption," *Journal of Economic Literature,* vol. 22 (June 1984), pp. 531–74.

agricultural development pattern permits the absorption of more workers into the rural labor force, even a large increase in food output will leave many households with inadequate access to food.

The food equation should be viewed as a dynamic balance between food supply and demand in individual countries rather than as a race between food and population. This balance depends on complex relationships between a number of variables. Equilibrium in this vital food equation can range from a low one of a small increase in food supplies and little purchasing power in the hands of the poor to high levels of each. Consensus is growing among economists and development experts that a high-level equilibrium of food production and employment is not only desirable on social welfare grounds but also represents a strategy that will achieve faster overall growth.

Failure to choose and pursue this growth strategy has led to a pessimistic view of prospects for reducing food deprivation through growth. Instead, it has turned attention, unproductively, to direct, welfare-oriented approaches. These seem likely to have adverse effects on rapid, broad-based development.

Because of the dominant position of agriculture as a source of income and employment in low-income countries, we emphasize the central importance of a broad-based, "unimodal" pattern of agricultural development. This pattern is characterized by gradual but widespread increases in productivity by small farmers who adopt innovations appropriate to their labor-abundant, capital-scarce situation. It contrasts with the dualistic or "bimodal" pattern of agricultural development based on rapid modernization of a subsector of large, capital-intensive farm units, along with capital-intensive industrialization, that many developing countries have pursued.

Reduction of malnutrition and related manifestations of poverty requires a set of interacting forces. These may be viewed as a ring that links nutrition needs, generation of effective demand for food by the poor, increased employment, a development strategy that structures demand toward labor-intensive goods and services, production of wage goods, and an emphasis on growth in agriculture. Moreover, the structure of rural demand generated by a unimodal pattern of agricultural development fosters more rapid growth of output and employment in manufacturing and other nonfarm sectors than do development strategies characterized by pronounced dualism in capital allocation.

Trends in Food Production, Trade, and Consumption

Three dynamic features mark the contemporary global food scene. First, countries and regions vary considerably in the extent to which their food production growth rates differ from their population growth rates. Second, increasing exports from the most developed to the developing countries are the major source of increased per capita consumption in developing countries as a group. Third, the growth in food crop production in developing countries is increasingly dependent on increased yields per unit area rather than on area expansion.

Production

During 1961–77, the growth rate of staple food production in developing countries as a group slightly exceeded their population growth rate—2.7 percent versus 2.6 percent (table 2-1). However, in Latin America and Asia, food production growth rates substantially exceeded those for population—by 18 percent and 12 percent respectively—while, in sharp contrast, in sub-Saharan Africa the food production growth rate was only 58 percent of the population growth rate. Moreover, developing countries with slow per capita GNP growth rates, which are concentrated largely in sub-Saharan Africa, have done least well in agricultural production.

Between 1961–70 and 1971–80, Asia and North Africa and the Middle East increased their staple food production growth rate by 22 and 16 percent, respectively, while that rate declined by 50 percent in sub-Saharan Africa and by 60 percent in Latin America (table 2-2). The regions accelerating their staple food growth rates were the ones with the highest growth rates in output per hectare. Africa, with the slowest food production growth rate by far, also had the slowest growth in output per hectare.

Trade

From 1961–65 to 1973–77, net imports of staple foods by developing countries (excluding China) increased nearly five-fold, from 5 to 23 million tons per year. Linear projections of consumption and production suggest an increase of net staple food imports to 80 million tons by the year 2000 (table 2-3). Net imports have risen from 1.5 percent of developing country production in the mid-1950s to 5 percent in the mid-1970s and are projected to reach 8.5 percent of production by the year 2000.

For each regional and GNP growth rate category in table 2-3, food imports grew more rapidly than food exports. Sub-Saharan Africa, with the slowest growth rate for agricultural production, changed from a net exporter to a significant importer and is projected to account for a substantial share of world food imports by the year 2000. Although production growth rates in Latin America have been relatively rapid, the growth rate of imports has been similar to that in sub-

Table 2-1. *Growth Rates of Population and of Production and Consumption of Staple Foods in Developing and Developed Countries, 1961–77*
(percent, except as specified)

Country group	Population, 1977 (millions)	Average annual growth rate, 1961–77			Production growth rate as percentage of population growth rate	Consumption growth rate as percentage of population growth rate	Production growth rate as percentage of consumption growth rate
		Population	Production	Consumption[a]			
Developing countries	2,092	2.6	2.7	2.9	103	111	93
By region							
Asia	1,207	2.5	2.8	2.5	112	103	109
North Africa and Middle East	240	2.6	2.6	3.5	97	132	74
Sub-Saharan Africa	311	2.7	1.6	2.4	58	86	67
Latin America	333	2.7	3.2	3.6	118	132	89
By GNP per capita growth rate, 1966–77							
Less than 1.0 percent	338	2.5	1.3	2.3	53	94	56
1.0–2.9 percent	1,019	2.5	2.9	2.6	117	105	111
3.0–4.9 percent	279	2.8	3.0	3.3	110	120	91
5.0 percent and over	456	2.7	2.8	3.3	101	123	83

Developed countries	1,139	1.0	2.6	2.3	274	237	115
EEC	269	0.6	1.8	1.1	290	178	163
Eastern Europe and U.S.S.R.	369	1.0	2.8	3.5	294	364	81
United States	217	1.0	3.0	0.9	291	91	321
Others	284	1.2	2.3	2.7	182	216	84
World	3,230	2.0	2.6	2.5	135	128	105

Notes: As used here, "basic staple foods" include cereals, roots and tubers, pulses, groundnuts, and bananas and plantains. According to FAO data these commodities accounted for about three-fourths of the average per capita intake in developing countries (about three-fifths for the world as a whole) during 1973–77. The data are analyzed only through 1977 because the consumption data were available only through that date as of writing. Because of interaction among supply and demand forces, it is desirable to keep the same time periods for all items. Trend growth rates are computed using the semilogarithmic trend equation fitted to the time-series data based on the least squares method.

China, with a population of approximately 1 billion, is excluded because the major disruptions occasioned by the "Great Leap Forward" in the early 1960s and the subsequent slow recovery make 1961–77 a particularly biased period for that country.

a. Because of the nature of available data sets, the consumption growth rate is calculated between the 1961–65 and 1973–77 averages.

Sources: Calculated by Leonardo Paulino and others, IFPRI, from FAO (1975c, 1980a, 1980b, 1981b); IFPRI (1977); Paulino (1984); United Nations (1979); World Bank (1979).

Table 2-2. *Growth Rates of Production, Area Harvested, and Output Per Hectare for Major Food Crops in Developing and Developed Countries, 1961–70 and 1971–80*
(percent)

Country group	Production[a]		Area harvested		Output per hectare		Growth rate for output per hectare as share of production growth rate	
	1961–70	1971–80	1961–70	1971–80	1961–70	1971–80	1961–70	1971–80
Developing countries	2.9	2.6	1.5	0.9	1.5	1.6	52	62
Asia	2.7	3.3	0.8	1.0	1.9	2.3	70	70
North Africa and Middle East	2.5	2.9	1.2	1.0	1.2	1.8	48	62
Sub-Saharan Africa	2.3	1.2	2.5	1.1	-0.2	0.1	-9	8
Latin America	4.3	1.7	2.7	0.6	1.5	1.0	35	59
Developed countries	3.0	1.7	-0.5	0.7	3.5	1.0	117	59
EEC	2.5	1.3	-0.5	-0.4	2.9	1.7	116	131
Eastern Europe and U.S.S.R.	3.6	0.8	-0.8	0.4	4.4	0.4	126	50
United States	2.6	2.8	-0.4	1.5	3.1	1.3	119	46
Others	2.7	1.7	0.3	1.0	2.5	0.7	92	41
World	3.0	2.0	0.5	0.8	2.4	1.2	80	60

Note: China is excluded (see note to table 2-1).
a. Major food crops here exclude bananas and plantains, for which estimates on area harvested are not available.
Sources: Same as for table 2-1.

Table 2-3. *Trade in Food Staples in Developing Countries, 1961–65 and 1973–77, and Projections of Net Imports to 2000*

	Net imports (millions of tons)			Annual growth rate, 1961–65 to 1969–73 (percent)	
Country group	1961–65	1973–77	2000[a]	Exports	Imports
Developing countries	5.3	23.0	80.3	2.1	5.4
By region					
Asia	6.3	10.9	−17.9	2.5	3.5
North Africa and					
Middle East	3.6	10.6	57.3	−2.0	7.3
Sub-Saharan Africa	−0.9	2.9	35.5	−4.6	7.1
Latin America	−3.7	−1.4	5.4	3.6	6.9
By GNP per capita growth rate					
Less than 1.0 percent	1.6	8.0	39.5	−5.1	7.7
1.0–2.9 percent	2.8	−1.1	−48.5	1.8	3.3
3.0–4.9 percent	1.7	4.0	24.1	4.8	5.5
5.0 percent and over	4.7	12.1	65.2	2.9	6.6

Note: China is excluded (see note to table 2-1).

a. The projections are based on differences between extrapolations of 1961–77 country trend production and the aggregate projections of demand for food, animal feed, and other uses. Projections of demand for animal feed were assumed to follow the country growth rates of meat consumption, that is, no change in feeding efficiency. A basis for such adaptation is being pursued at IFPRI, but the results are not yet available.

Sources: Same as for table 2-1.

Saharan Africa, so that net exports have dropped by nearly two-thirds.

Concurrently with dramatic growth in developing country imports of cereals, the U.S.S.R. changed from a major exporter prior to the 1960s to a large net importer in 1980.

Increased staple food exports have come principally from the United States, which increased its net cereal exports from an average of 37 million tons per year in 1961–65 to 115 million tons in 1981.

Consumption

Food consumption in developing countries grew at 111 percent of the population growth rate during 1961–77 (table 2-1). However, only a small part of this improvement came from growth in domestic production. The significant factor was rapid growth in net imports. Only Asia had a faster growth rate of production than consumption, and this was largely due to changes in India, where reduced imports were associated with stagnating per capita consumption.

Those countries with the slowest GNP growth, largely in sub-Saharan Africa, had such poor agricultural growth that per capita consumption fell despite high import growth. Without the rapid import growth, staple food consumption would have grown at only 53 percent of the population growth rate instead of at 93 percent.

Paradoxically, countries with high agricultural production growth also tend to have large and increasing food imports. The relationship is illustrated dramatically by reference to the 16 developing countries with the fastest growth rates in staple food production for 1961–76 (Bachman and Paulino 1979). Despite production growth at the extraordinary pace of 3.9 percent per year, they more than doubled their net imports of food staples in that period and the consumption met by domestic production declined from 96 to 94 percent.

Sources of Growth

During the 1960s and 1970s, increased yield per unit area of land has increased its weight, relative to expanded area, from 52 percent to 62 percent in explaining increased production of staple food crops in developing countries (table 2-2). Among the major developing country regions, yield growth exceeded 2 percent only for Asia, and then only in 1971–80. However, more than half of the 16 countries with fast growth rates of staple food production had yield growth rates exceeding 2 percent (Bachman and Paulino 1979).

Developing countries may experience faster growth rates while "catching up." The Punjab of India experienced a 13.9 percent annual growth rate of wheat output and a 10.2 percent growth rate in foodgrain production from 1967–68 to 1971–72 at the height of the green revolution. Even this unusually rapid rate was significantly dependent on an area expansion rate of 6.9 and 2.5 per year for wheat and foodgrains, respectively. Nonetheless, for the longer period 1967–68 to 1981–82, the growth rate of Punjab foodgrain production was still a rapid 6 percent.

Current high population growth rates demand much more of agriculture than was the case for the early developers. For example, in Japan the foodgrain production growth rate of 1.6 percent from 1880 to 1920 was equal to 160 percent of the population growth rate. India, in its recent period of fastest growth rate of foodgrain production, achieved a growth rate over 100 percent higher than Japan in its early phase, but this still was only 138 percent of the population growth rate.

Phases of Supply-Demand Balance

The extraordinary quantities of grain that now move in international trade, the growing imports and declining self-sufficiency of even those developing countries with high growth rates for staple food production, and the virtual monopoly of exports by high-income developed countries tell an important story about the transition in the food supply-demand balance during the course of development. This transition may be divided into three phases (Mellor 1966, 1983; Tsujii 1982).

The first phase is rough parity of domestic supply and demand with real food prices constant except for sharp year to year, weather-induced fluctuations. This phase typifies low-income countries prior to acceleration of their growth rates. Slow population growth is associated with slow growth in effective demand that is substantially met by applying a slowly growing labor force to an expanded land area or by raising yield per unit area. Equilibrium between supply and demand is maintained without significant trade or price changes except for weather-induced fluctuations. To the extent that accelerated population growth brings diminishing returns, per capita income tends to decline. In this phase, domestic agricultural production will tend to be inelastic with respect to price, due to nonprice constraints.

The second phase is rapid growth in demand that generally exceeds growth in domestic supply. The result is either an upward trend in the real price of food or a rapid growth in net imports. This phase typifies developing countries as they first accelerate their growth. When individual incomes initially accelerate, laborers typically spend 70 to 90 percent of their additional income on food. That is, their marginal propensity to expend on food is 0.7 to 0.9 (Mellor 1978). Thus, if the growth strategy results in sharply rising employment, demand for food will grow rapidly. Subsiding population growth rates are likely to accelerate further per capita income growth. Agricultural growth itself is likely to lead to a growth of demand and thus of employment in other sectors (Bell and others 1982; Rangarajan 1982; Mellor 1976; Mellor and Lele 1973). This fast growth in demand because of rising incomes makes it increasingly difficult for food supply to keep pace with demand. It is these relationships that provide the powerful links between food production, an employment-oriented strategy of economic growth, and improved nutrition, discussed later.

In phase two, growing demand for livestock products becomes the major factor in growth of per capita demand for cereals (Mellor 1966, 1983). For example, the income elasticity of demand for livestock products averages about 1.0 for Asia and the Far East while that for cereals for direct human consumption averages about 0.2 (FAO 1977a). Initially livestock are fed mainly waste and by-products, the supply of which is inelastic with respect to livestock production. As demand grows, cereals usable for direct human consumption are fed increasingly to livestock. These tendencies are reflected in the 63 percent increase in livestock feed use in the Middle East for the period

1966–70 to 1976–80 compared to a 49 percent increase in livestock production (Khaldi 1984). The data for Taiwan are dramatic. In 1961, feed use of cereals was less than 1 percent of total use; in 1981, it was 60 percent (Taiwan 1981). Since the initial proportion of imports in cereal consumption is normally low, net imports may undergo a period of explosive growth.

Given the diminishing returns to limited land area, plus the great difficulty and lack of experience with increasing the yield per unit of land by more than 2 percent per year, we can expect this phase to be one of rising real prices or rising imports of food. Even for countries with substantial areas of unexploited land, expansion of output in pace with demand is likely to be difficult because of deficiencies in their physical and institutional infrastructure.

The third phase is a virtual cessation of demand growth while production growth is maintained at a high level. The consequence is a downward trend in the real price of food or rapid growth in net exports. In this phase, the marginal propensity to spend on food (measured at the farm) eventually declines to near zero. The institutions that support a substantial rate of food production growth are likely to be in place so that food supply shifts more rapidly than demand. Stocks or exports constantly increase or food prices decline drastically. The relative size of the agricultural sector declines sharply, rural-urban income disparities are substantial, and income transfers to redress those disparities become likely. Developed countries have usually carried out such income transfers through higher prices that provide additional incentives to increase production.

This outline of the changing structural relationships of production and consumption helps explain the contrasting elements of the global food scene at a single point in time as well as how it will evolve over time. Clearly, within these broad tendencies factor endowments affect the food supply-demand balances in any given phase of development. For example, Thailand may export food throughout its development and Western Europe may generate smaller exports later in its development than North America. Similarly, agricultural price policy may change the levels of production and consumption within the context of changing structural relationships.

Economists generally agree that in developing countries, over the short- and medium-term, aggregate food supply tends to be highly inelastic with respect to price—on the order of 0.1 to 0.2 (Herdt 1970). Differences in interpretation arise as the adjustment period is extended. Those attempting to measure very long-run response to price argue that the whole set of policy differences between developed and developing countries is induced by relative price differences that are themselves a matter of policy (Petersen 1979; Hayami and Ruttan

1971). However, it is probably more useful to separate public policies and macrorelationships that may change independently of price, even though price changes may also induce changes in those policies and relationships. Thus, in a later section ("Lessons from Past Experience: Structure, Organization, and Human Resources"), we discuss acceleration of growth rates in staple food production as basically a function of complex institutional changes needed to accelerate the generation and adoption of appropriate technology. Within that slowly changing context, price policy has an important but subsidiary role.

Global Prospects

The preceding analysis defines long-term structural processes that result in the developing countries' generating a faster shift in food demand than in supply, while the converse is true for developed countries. In that context, three questions need particular attention.

First, will the pace of development in the developing countries be maintained at the same rapid rate as in the 1960s and 1970s? If that growth is closely linked to the growth rate in the developed countries, as argued in several World Bank reports (for example, 1983b), and if the growth of developed countries slows as they further mature, then one can expect slower growth in developing countries and hence in their imports of staple foods. However, if, as Lewis (1980) argues, trade among developing countries can expand quickly and technological and organizational improvements can proceed rapidly, further increase in the aggregate growth rate of developing countries can still occur and thereby further accelerate growth in food imports.

Second, will food exports from developed countries continue to grow rapidly? The rate of yield increase in developed countries slowed down in the 1970s and, except in the United States, so did production (table 2-2). However, the "new biology" of genetic engineering may result in future yield increases (Shemilt 1983). The United States has large areas of land that could come into production with, at most, modest increases in real prices (Paarlberg 1982). As for the European Community, Koester (1982) projects net cereal exports will rise from 3 million tons in 1980 to 25 million tons in 1990 if current policies are not changed.

Third, will Africa continue to have an extraordinarily low growth rate in food production and rapid growth in staple food imports financed largely by oil revenues or foreign aid? Given that accelerating African food production growth is bound to be a lengthy process (Lele 1979, 1984) and that real oil price increases have abated, a growth in imports in the next decade depends substantially on the political context of foreign assistance to Africa. In the past, rapid increases in foreign aid have accompanied African food difficulties.

The implicit, and yet inconclusive, judgment from the preceding analysis is that demand in developing countries will continue to grow more rapidly than supply and that exports from developed countries will meet this demand with at most modest increases in real food prices.

Our conclusion, that real food prices are likely to increase only modestly, is consistent with data for the past 125 years. These show no trend in real maize prices, although wheat prices have declined closer to parity with maize during that period (Martin and Brokken 1983).

While the longer-term trend may be expected to be one of stable or modestly increasing prices, the situation is very different if we consider short-term price variability. Except for the unusually stable conditions in the 1950s and 1960s, real cereal prices have fluctuated 50 percent and more at least once every six years throughout the last 125 years. In the 1950s and 1960s, the United States maintained large stocks of staple foods, holding world food prices unusually stable. The United States is no longer willing to do this. In the meantime, the very application of biological science that accelerates the growth rate in yield seems associated with increased variation in the level of production. Although the reasons for this are complex, narrowing the genetic base of crop varieties grown over large areas is probably an important factor (Hazell 1982; Mehra 1981).

The demand of low-income people for staple foods is quite elastic with respect to price due to their high budget share of food. Hence, food supply changes impose the bulk of adjustment on the poor, with consequent great privation (Mellor 1978). Programs of food subsidies and employment guarantees or flexible public works programs play an increasing role in protecting low-income consumers from these fluctuations. At the international level, the IMF Cereal Import Facility can finance expanded food imports to alleviate a short-term deficit (Adams 1983; Valdés 1981). Over the very long term, as livestock consumption continues to grow rapidly and rising incomes of the poor lower their demand elasticity for staple foods below those of higher-income consumers for livestock products, fluctuations in livestock numbers and production can become a major device for absorbing fluctuations in grain supplies.

In the meantime, fluctuations in welfare of the poor are immense. The proportion of the rural population in India that is below the poverty line, using Ahluwalia's poverty index, has fluctuated repeatedly from 40 to 60 percent, largely due to the effects of changing agricultural production and prices (Mellor and Desai 1985). Such fluctuations involve major changes in the nutritional status of the rural population.

Nutritional Implications of Supply-Demand Balances

Food ranks at the top of the hierarchy of human needs, while the concept of diminishing marginal utility of income affirms the view that redistribution of income in favor of the poor is just. Thus discussions of income distribution, poverty, food intake, and nutrition are inseparable until food needs are met. Concern about poverty in low-income countries has focused substantially on absolute poverty, often related to a nutritional base, even though defining nutritional requirements is difficult.

Extent of Malnutrition

FAO calculations of per capita food availability indicate that the nutritional situation in the developing countries has not changed significantly since 1961, when the average per capita availability of food provided 2,130 calories, or 93 percent of defined requirements (FAO 1976c, 1982b). Such estimates are, of course, only rough indicators. Nevertheless, the broad picture is consistent with the trends in food production and trade reviewed in the preceding section. Even in terms of national averages, food consumption has remained marginal in much of Asia and Africa.

According to FAO estimates in the *Fourth World Food Survey* (1977a), the number of people in developing countries consuming less than a "critical minimum energy intake" increased from 400 million in 1969–71 to over 450 million during 1972–74. Reutlinger and Selowsky (1976) estimate that 1.1 billion people had "calorie deficient" diets in the mid-1960s. A major reason for the difference between the two estimates is that the FAO approach was related to the "critical minimum energy intake" for survival, whereas Reutlinger and Selowsky used a requirement concept relevant to "moderately active" individuals.

Three fundamental difficulties arise when assessing nutritional status. First, nutritional status is a continuum, so that it is extremely difficult, if not impossible, to define minimum requirements; yet governments' desire to define absolute poverty for public policy purposes urges them to draw up specific requirements. Energy requirements for adults, for example, depend not only on sex, body size, and age, but also on the level of activity. Second, individuals of the same size and other measurable characteristics exhibit considerable biological variability that gives rise to different nutritional requirements. Infectious or parasitic diseases may also increase requirements. Third, an individual's energy and other nutritional requirements are often conditioned by past food intake that has restricted growth and ultimate body size. This means that the low levels of food intake characteristic of the poor in low-income countries correlate with lower requirement levels unless the effect of body size is offset by a higher level of activity because members of poor households have to work harder or longer.

Children have the greatest potential for adapting to restricted food intake because, in addition to changing their activity level, they adjust by growing more slowly and attaining a smaller body size. Martorell (1984) shows that differences between children of high economic status in developing countries are small. However, the differences between low and high socioeconomic groups are much larger. Martorell offers persuasive evidence that environmental factors are far more important than genetic factors in accounting for most of the observed differences in body size within and among countries.

Distinctive Nutritional Problems and Vulnerable Groups

Malnutrition among infants, small children, and pregnant and lactating women represents a distinctive set of problems. Those groups are exceptionally vulnerable because of the special nutritional requirements for growth, fetal development, and lactation.

Excessively high rates of mortality and morbidity among infants and small children are usually related to interactions between food deprivation and infection. Frequent episodes of illness reduce food intake, and inadequate and inappropriate food intake increases the duration, severity, and fatality levels of infection (Chandra 1982; Martorell 1980; also part V of this collection). A large-scale investigation of mortality in children carried out under the auspices of the Pan American Health Organization demonstrated that nutritional deficiency was the underlying or associated cause in 52 percent of deaths among children under five years of age (Puffer and Serano 1973).

Although increasing the availability of food at the household level facilitates efforts to improve the nutritional status of the most vulnerable groups, also needed are social service programs that include a judicious mix of hygiene and nutrition education, immunization programs, environmental sanitation, a safe and more adequate water supply, and selected promotional activities related to oral rehydration therapy and family planning. The effectiveness of such programs depends on achieving a broad coverage of the rural population. This means that difficult problems of organizational design and implementation must be overcome. The section on lessons from past experience suggests programs that may do so at a cost that even low-income countries can afford.

Energy-Protein Malnutrition and "High"-Level Food Supply Balance

In the 1960s and early 1970s, nutritionists believed that a "protein gap" was the major nutritional problem in developing countries. The current consensus is that the major problem is energy-protein malnutrition. Nutritional deficiencies, including protein malnutrition, "are the result of inadequate intake of food, being thus unavoidably associated with inadequate intake of energy" (FAO/WHO 1973, p. 23).

Once governments recognize that the fundamental nutrition problem is inadequate food intake, it should be obvious that no simple, low-cost solutions exist. To realize large increases in the food supply and in the purchasing power of the poor seems achievable only in the context of a broad-based development strategy.

Development Strategy, Employment, and Food

A strategy, widely adopted in developing countries, of highly capital-intensive growth in the "modern" sector, combined with rapid population growth in the dominant rural sector and a small initial capital stock, fosters a dualism that not only results in slower rates of capital formation and employment but also causes lower growth in effective demand for food and poorer performance in agriculture. This lessens the domestic food supply and causes a poorer export performance that reduces the capability to finance food imports. Thus the food equation balances at low levels of food production, employment, income of the poor, effective demand for food, food intake, and nutrition.

High rates of population growth add to a large stock of agricultural labor used at very low average and marginal productivities and make the labor absorption problem much more difficult for contemporary developing countries than for their predecessors. The problem is exacerbated by the fact that there is little land left suitable for agricultural settlement. In this context, agriculture can play a critical role in restraining the growth in capital intensity in the industrial sector. Agriculture provides wage goods essential to mobilization of labor and facilitates a level and structure of demand consistent with appropriately labor-intensive techniques of production. These, in turn, facilitate increased exports. The advantage of applying modern agricultural science can offset other disadvantages faced by contemporary developing countries. To reap this advantage, concentration of capital in a capital-intensive industrial sector must not deprive agriculture of the capital essential to use the technology potentially available. (For an extensive treatment of these relationships see Mellor and Desai 1985; Singh 1983; Mellor 1976, 1978.)

Given the global food prospects presented earlier, and in the context of an economy open in every respect except for massive migration of labor, the operative constraint on balancing the food equation at a high level is rapid growth in employment and in the purchasing power of the poor.

Structural and Demographic Characteristics of the Farm Labor Force

In the course of development, the occupational structure shifts from predominantly agricultural to predominantly nonagricultural. Eventually, the absolute size of the agricultural labor force declines. In early stages of development, the transformation proceeds slowly because of high population growth rates and the initially dominant weight of the agricultural sector (Dovring 1959). The supply of labor to nonagricultural occupations is highly elastic; the optimal choice of agricultural production techniques will be highly labor-intensive for a considerable period of time.

The population growth rate in Japan for 1872–1942 was 1.2 percent. In contrast, during the next few decades, labor force growth is expected to rise at a 2.7 percent rate in developing countries (World Bank 1982). In Africa, the rate of population growth is still steadily increasing, rising from 2.1 percent in 1950–55 to 2.8 percent in 1975–77 (Kirk 1978). In Asia, although population growth rates have been high, they are now slowing down. During 1980–2000, India's labor force is expected to grow at 2.0 percent a year and China's at 1.4 percent.

Projections for Kenya, extending to the year 2024, are particularly sobering because of an exceptionally rapid growth of the country's population and labor force and the extent to which the land area for expanded cultivation has already been reduced by past growth of the farm population. Shah and Willekens (1978) projected that Kenya's rural work force would increase four-fold between 1969 and 2024— this in spite of an assumed 16-fold increase in the working age population in urban areas that will reduce the share of the rural labor force from 87 percent of the total in 1969 to 65 percent in 2024.

Capital Availability

Extremely low initial capital-labor ratios in a dominant rural sector are at the heart of the development problem. This deficiency lies particularly with the human capital of skills and technical and organizational knowledge. The scarcity of the latter further limits capacity to coordinate the growth of various forms of capital so as to keep the respective rates of return roughly aligned (Johnson 1969).

Fortunately, it has become apparent that marginal savings rates rise quickly once development is under way and rates of return rise. Most Asian countries now have domestic savings rates well over 20 percent of GDP (World Bank 1982). The high marginal savings rates of farmers in the Punjab when returns to investments in wells and fertilizer soared with the new technology in the late 1960s are notable in this context. In much of sub-Saharan Africa, where net domestic savings rates are typically under 10 percent of GNP (World Bank 1982), the bar to domestic savings is the low rate of return to investment due to price distortions and gross misallocation of the existing capital stock (Lele 1979, 1984). Savings and investment by African farmers in the past have been very high when attractive investment opportunities existed—for instance, planting cocoa trees.

Capital-Intensive Development Strategies

Developing countries commonly follow strategies that foster dualism, concentrating capital in large-scale, capital-intensive industries. The intellectual base for India's Second Five-Year Plan provides a notable case of one approach (Mellor 1976; Bhagwati and Chakravarty 1969; Mahalanobis 1953). This approach is essentially the same as that of China (Tang and Stone 1980) and the U.S.S.R. (Feldman as stated in Domar 1957) and has close intellectual links to the family of Harrod-Domar—related growth models.

In this dualistic approach, growth is seen as a direct function of an increase in capital stock, which is to be accelerated by channeling resources into the capital goods industries and away from consumption. Then the output from capital goods production is reinvested to provide a high marginal savings rate and hence a rapidly rising average savings rate. Employment growth, consistent with a view of fixed factor proportions, is seen as a direct function of growth in the capital stock. Since labor is assumed not only to be in surplus, but also to be consuming its subsistence needs, no further supply of consumer (wage) goods is needed as employment increases (for example, Chakravarty 1969). In India, it was understood that improved welfare for the laboring classes was to be postponed in favor of large increases in the future. In the short run, agriculture and the cottage industries were to provide employment and consumer goods without drawing on the scarce capital of other sectors. Thus the approach was explicitly highly dualistic in capital intensity.

Many problems arose with this dualistic approach. The capital intensity of the modern sector was even greater than expected and increased over time (Mellor 1976). This was for reasons inherent in the investment pattern, including inability to operate large-scale capital-intensive industries at a high proportion of capacity and underinvestment in infrastructure. The consequence was slower growth and a lower savings reinvestment rate than expected. The strategy of relying on extremely low capital intensity in agriculture and the cottage industries was not as successful as hoped, either in producing goods or in mitigating poverty. Thus, the strategy neglected agriculture even though that was not the intent. Despite low growth rates in employment, an upward pressure on food prices took hold with deleterious social effects and a drain of foreign exchange (Tang and Stone 1980; Mellor 1976). The investment strategy put severe demands on forms of capital requiring foreign exchange at the same time that resources were diverted from traditional export industries (Mellor and Lele 1975). Thus foreign exchange became a limiting factor.

An import substitution strategy is another dualistic approach commonly adopted in developing countries. The intellectual base for this approach is the view most articulately advanced by Prebisch (for example, 1971) that terms of trade for primary commodities are deteriorating. The strategy is to start with displacement of imports produced by relatively labor-intensive industries and then to proceed to more capital-intensive ones. With neglect of agriculture, the structure of domestic demand growth tends to be narrow, urban biased, and oriented to high-income consumers, accelerating the increase in capital intensity (Furtado 1964). The result is innately highly dualistic with all the characteristics indicated above (Bhagwati 1978; Krueger 1978).

Economies characterized by either of these two dualistic approaches tend to have grossly overvalued exchange rates, a situation which discriminates further against the agricultural sector. Argentina is a prime example (Cavallo and Mundlak 1982), as are Colombia (García García 1981) and the bulk of African countries. Not only are direct price incentives to agriculture dulled but, far more important, critical government attention is diverted from the policy and institutional needs of agricultural development (Lele 1984).

Given the highly dualistic nature of the above strategies, which result in slow growth of both food production and employment, development of a strong interest in redistributive and structuralistic approaches to poverty reduction is not surprising. These growth strategies tend to be associated with the term "trickle down" in reference to the slow rate of amelioration of absolute poverty. In India, concern about redistributive measures and programs for fulfilling basic needs continued (India 1961), perhaps in recognition that the poor would not share the time preference of planners. These concerns were reinforced in India when growth proved slower than expected, and spread more widely in the late 1960s and early 1970s with the World Bank's strong association with a more direct attack on poverty (McNamara 1973; Haq 1971). These "basic needs" approaches became pervasive in the foreign assistance community in the 1970s and even into the 1980s.

Food and Labor-Intensive Development

Food production plays two vital roles in labor-intensive development. It contributes to a structure of demand appropriate to low capital-labor ratios and to capital accumulation, and it provides the wage goods essential to labor mobilization. Both needs were glossed over in the dominant thinking about development strategies in the 1950s and 1960s.

RURAL DEMAND, CAPITAL INTENSITY, AND CAPITAL ACCUMULATION. Modern high-yielding crop varieties distribute a large factor share of the incremental income they generate to land and therefore to landowners. Food sales, cash income, and demand for other goods and services are all elastic with respect to this increased income. In contrast, rural wage employment is inelastic with respect to the increased output (Mellor 1976; Mellor and Lele 1973).

In Asia, peasant farmers typically spend some 40 percent of incremental income on locally produced nonagricultural goods and services (Hazell and Röell 1983). The income multipliers are substantial—on the order of 0.7 (Bell and others 1982; Rangarajan 1982; Mellor and Lele 1973)—and the employment multipliers are probably larger, given the nature of the production processes. Thus, if agricultural development spearheaded by the introduction of high-yielding varieties spreads the factor income returned to land to large numbers of small peasant landowners, as would be the case in the peasant agriculture typical in much of Asia, then the base on which increments to rural consumption of locally manufactured consumer goods occurs will also be large.

If, however, agricultural development is highly concentrated in a large-scale subsector with consequent concentration of the added income in high-income families, the capital and import intensity of the demand generated for goods and services may be much higher (Johnston and Kilby 1975; Furtado 1964). Thus, the nature of consumption linkages and of production relationships argues for a broad, unimodal pattern of agricultural growth.

In Africa, growth linkages between agriculture and other sectors seem weaker than in Asia. Hazell and Röell (1983) note this in comparing the Gusau District of northern Nigeria and the Muda region of Malaysia. King and Byerlee (1978) find a marginal propensity to spend on rural nonfood products in Africa of 0.1, much lower than is usual in Asia. They also find much higher marginal propensities to spend on imported products than on products from all urban centers combined or even from large urban centers. The weak domestic linkages in Africa can be traced to the much lower average productivity of labor used in agriculture, the consequent lesser differentiation of the rural economy (Mellor and Desai 1985), a less well-developed infrastructure, and a particularly suboptimal pattern of non-agricultural investment.

Note an important interaction between the effects of agricultural growth on capital intensity and capital accumulation. Given the labor market conditions in developing countries, the more labor-intensive the goods and services demanded, the more elastic will be the supply. Because the cost of agricultural production has been reduced by technological progress, if a capital constraint exists, agriculture can contribute to breaking that constraint. This applies whether the capital constraint is in public sector infrastructure and education, which calls for higher local or national taxes on agriculture; in small-scale rural industries, for which direct investment by prosperous farmers may be appropriate; or in a more distant industry where a temporary change in terms of trade against agriculture may be in order. Farmers—or their children—will benefit if transferred resources are used productively. In many developing countries, especially in Africa, agriculture has been "taxed" heavily, but the resources transferred from agriculture have often financed inefficient investments and supported nonfarm income and wages far above the income levels of the farm population. Côte d'Ivoire represents a sharp contrast to many other African countries by "taxing" agriculture heavily but reinvesting substantially in agriculture (Gbetibouo and Delgado 1984).

Taiwan epitomizes these processes whereby rapid growth and rising productivity in agriculture stimulate growth in other sectors. Increases in factor productivity accounted for well over half of the 3.5 percent annual rate of agricultural production increase in the decades preceding and following World War II (Lee 1971). The widespread increase in the commercialization of the agricultural sector provided incentives for investment in roads, electrification, and telephones as well as for strictly agricultural infrastructure such as irrigation. The growth of nonfarm activities was also stimulated by increasing rural demand for consumer goods and services and for agricultural inputs as farm cash incomes rose. The growth pattern of rural demand in Taiwan had its greatest impact on the growth of output and employment in decentralized small- and medium-scale manufacturing firms that employed labor-intensive technologies and economized on the use of capital and foreign exchange. Expanded manufacture and unsophisticated farm equipment played an especially significant role in fostering growth and diffusion of the metalworking skills that are so important to industrial development (Johnston and Kilby 1975).

FOOD PRODUCTION TECHNOLOGY AND THE PRICE OF WAGE GOODS. Accelerated growth in productive nonfarm employment accelerates growth in the wage bill and demand for wage goods. Since the marginal propensity of laborers in developing countries to spend on food is on the order of 0.7 to 0.9 (Mellor 1973), the supply of wage goods may constrain employment growth. Thus labor supply is usefully described as a function of simultaneously determined labor and food markets (Lele and Mellor 1981). Given the inelasticity of the aggregate production of food in developing countries (Herdt 1970), the food market is a function of technological change in agriculture and the factor bias of that technology. The strong factor bias toward land of modern yield-increasing technology and the low marginal propensity of landowners to spend on food tend to favor rapid growth in food marketing and therefore act to restrain growth in capital-labor ratios at any given level of capital formation.

COMPARATIVE ADVANTAGE AND DOMESTIC FOOD PRODUCTION. Whether a developing country has a comparative advantage at the margin in food production depends on the underlying land resource and the pace and pattern of technological possibilities for agriculture. Intuitively, a country with the bulk of its rapidly growing population in food production, facing immense labor absorption problems in nonagriculture, and with limits on net capital inflows or labor outmigration faces a bleak prospect indeed if it does not have a comparative advantage for a very considerable expansion of food production. Given the balance of payments difficulties of most developing countries, relief from food import pressures must appear attractive, at least until export expansion has accelerated. Perhaps more important, the market-broadening feature of income expenditures generated by domestic agricultural development provides training for later entering the export market of manufactured products, a factor of considerable importance to Taiwan's early export success (Liang and Lee 1972). Finally, the bulky nature of food causes the difference between export and import prices to be large, further encouraging food production for domestic use.

There is a biological logic to the argument that the agroclimatic conditions that allowed the growth of large stocks of surplus agricultural labor are conducive to further large productivity gains from new agricultural technology. That is, where rural population densities are already high, a comparative advantage is likely to lie with large increases through modern technology because such areas have generally favorable conditions for agricultural production, and the modern high-yielding varieties respond best to favorable conditions, for example, plentiful water and fertilizer (Mellor and Desai 1985).

Why did such growth not occur earlier? Colonial regimes typically stifled modern industry while destroying major elements of traditional industry, with the consequent creation of a large underemployed rural landless class. For a striking case, note India's preeminent precolonial position in textiles (Gittinger 1982). Subsequently, the takeoff is delayed if these same conditions lead to very low rates of capital accumulation or, in recent development history, if a dualistic growth strategy concentrates capital on only a small portion of the labor force. Note the self-inflicted damage to India's textile industry in the 1950s (Mellor and Lele 1975).

Less certain are the prospects in regions such as the drier areas of West Africa where labor productivity in agriculture has been too low to have permitted "surplus" labor, and where the average and marginal product of agricultural labor are roughly comparable at close to the subsistence level (Mellor and Desai 1985). In such circumstances, labor transfer not only adds to food demand but detracts from food supply. The technology package must include both land-augmenting and labor-augmenting innovations.

Because accelerated agricultural growth is itself apt to be region specific, at least at a particular time, and because of the strong local linkages (in itself a generally desirable feature), such growth is likely to exacerbate regional disparities, although obviously not to the same extent as capital-intensive urban development (Mellor 1976). However, the problem of regional disparities tied closely to ethnic differences may be a particularly serious political barrier to such an approach to development in Africa.

Lessons from Past Experience: Structure, Organization, and Human Resources

Achieving accelerated growth in the agricultural sector—which is essential to balance the food equation at a high level—involves problems that are extremely complex and ill-structured. Useful policy analysis must include interactive learning from past experience (Johnston and Clark 1982). In this analysis, we emphasize Japan, the Republic of Korea, and Taiwan, where economic development has run its course to the point where analysts can draw relatively confident conclusions. More recent experience in India's Punjab, Indonesia, Malaysia, Thailand, and Kenya's high-potential farming regions provides additional evidence. At the same time, their experience directs attention to constraints on the transferability of the East Asian experience.

The common feature of the success achieved in Japan, Korea, and Taiwan is that each created an effective agricultural research system, a comprehensive rural infrastructure and input delivery system, and a broad educational system. These are the basic building blocks of rural development.

Sen has rightly emphasized that in today's developing countries a "shift in focus to technological and institutional details is long overdue" (quoted in Hunter 1978, p. 37). In Japan, Korea, and Taiwan, careful attention was given to those details, but in the context of a strategic perspective that took account of the complementarities among program interventions and of the long-term consequences of investment decisions and policy choices.

The Structure of Agricultural Production

The East Asian economies followed a unimodal pattern of development characterized by a widespread but gradual increase in productivity and expansion in the use of purchased inputs by small farmers. This pattern is consistent with the famous inverse relationship between farm size and productivity—small farmers, whether owner-cultivators or tenants, tend to use nonland inputs, especially labor, more intensively than larger farmers. This tendency may be offset, however, by differentiating factors, such as a policy environment in which small farmers do not have access to credit or large farmers have access to tractors at artificially low prices. In our view, the most significant implication of the induced innovation hypothesis of Hayami and Ruttan (1971) is that the indirect long-term effects of price distortion on the orientation of research and on the bias of technological change may well be even more important than its adverse effects on short-run allocational efficiency. (For a useful summary of the extensive empirical evidence about the relationship between farm size and productivity, see Berry and Cline 1979, p. 134. They note that "the special efficiency advantages of small farms tend to disappear" when the opportunity cost of labor is relatively high.)

The relevance of the experience of Japan, Korea, and Taiwan for places where there have not been "extensive redistributive reforms" has frequently been challenged (for example, de Janvry 1981). This is a serious charge because the land reforms in the three economies depended on special circumstances following World War II. Often overlooked, however, is that in the prewar period, although land ownership was highly skewed, farm operational units were small and the bias of technical change was in a labor-using, capital-saving direction. The explanation, in brief, is that the large landowners found it profitable to rent out their land to tenant households operating small units (Smith 1959). Even so, in the few areas of the world still dominated by feudal systems, particularly Latin America, land redistribution may well be a necessary condition for moving toward a unimodal pattern.

A widespread belief that economies of scale are important in agriculture has been a pervasive force contributing to bimodal patterns of agricultural development. Many economists, agricultural scientists, and other specialists assume that only a large and fairly capital-intensive farm unit can be "modern" and efficient. An emphasis on economies of scale has been a persistent tenet in Marxist views on agricultural development (Kozlowski 1975; Wittfogel 1971).

Several socialist regimes in tropical Africa have established state farms because of the presumed importance of economies of scale and to facilitate grain purchases for urban areas. Since the concentration of scarce capital, foreign exchange, and trained manpower in large mechanized state farms is achieved by depriving the great majority of the farm population of inputs and supporting services, the inevitable consequence is a bimodal pattern.

In other countries, especially in Latin America, land reform has often been linked with the objective of instituting group farming. The performance of group farming schemes has almost invariably been poor (Gurley 1983; Wong 1979; Dorner 1977). Even in China officials have questioned the effectiveness of the commune system as an organizational framework to guarantee a high rate of growth (Khan 1983).

Large operational units, whether for group farming or by private landowners, create strong pressures to make excessive investments in labor-displacing mechanization. A big operational unit that relies on a large work force, whether hired laborers or members of a group farm, encounters supervision problems when trying to avoid work shirking. The manager of a large operational unit, whether private or collective, finds the use of capital-intensive technologies to minimize the problems of supervising a large work force attractive; but the social opportunity cost of using scarce capital to displace labor for which alternative employment opportunities are not available is high.

Owing to the high degree of variability that characterizes farming activities, many on-the-spot supervisory decisions have to be made by individuals performing what are normally routine tasks (Brewster 1950). Efficient production based on labor-using, capital-saving technologies therefore depends on decentralized decision making and the incentive that owner-cultivators or tenants have to exercise judgment and initiative because of their direct interest in the outcome.

In many countries, the neglect and ineffectiveness of agricultural research has seriously limited possibilities for modernizing the agricultural sector. Profitable technological innovations suited to the needs of small farmers have simply not been available. In many Asian countries, that situation changed as the green revolution demonstrated that high returns are possible with improved varieties adapted to local environmental conditions. Expenditure on national research systems in developing countries has increased in real terms at an annual rate of 10 percent during the past decade (Oram and Bindlish forthcoming). Nevertheless, many of these systems are ineffective.

The great variation in farming systems associated with differences in the physical environment and in socioeconomic conditions limits the effectiveness of traditional approaches to research and extension, especially in sub-Saharan Africa and other rainfed farming areas. During the past decade, agriculturists have focused on increasing the relevance of research to the needs of small farmers. This approach emphasizes on-farm adaptive research in specific "recommendation domains" characterized by relatively homogeneous farming systems associated with similar agroclimatic conditions. A recent paper by Byerlee and others (1982) gives an exceptionally succinct statement of the importance of on-farm research based on a farming systems perspective (see Caldwell in part II). Although they share the current optimism about the potential contribution of farming systems research to the effectiveness of agricultural research, they are concerned that unfocused efforts and failure to apply cost-effective methods in collecting data, selecting technological alternatives for experimentation, and identifying important opportunities in light of farmer circumstances may lead to disappointment.

Organizational Requirements of Agricultural Development

Failure to meet the organizational requirements for agricultural development has been common in developing countries, but it has been especially conspicuous in sub-Saharan Africa. Moris (1983, p. 11) details a long and depressing litany of organizational shortcomings, including a severe revenue-expenditure squeeze, excessive politicization of technical functions traceable to acute scarcity of resources, and the emergence of distinctive managerial styles. These managerial styles are subject to a number of "routine operational difficulties," such as "a bad fit between objectives and organizational capacities," "high rates of staff transfer and turnover," "top staff over-worked while bottom staff loaf," a "large amount of energy [by the top staff] required to accomplish routine tasks," "inability to adhere to schedules," "unreliable technical and support services," "failure to repair or maintain equipment," and "low morale of field staff."

The common failure to meet the organizational requirements of rural development cannot be explained as simply a problem of weak management. It is the result of a "system of interactions" in which managers are "put again and again into impossible working situa-tions." The proximate difficulties that result in "persistent administra-tive malfunctioning" are compounded by failure of macroeconomic management that results in inflation, overvalued exchange rates, and import restrictions that raise the prices of imported and locally man-ufactured products and generally distort relative prices (Timmer and others 1983). Marketing board pricing policies further discourage export crop production. A common consequence, increasingly in evi-dence in some African countries, is a severe shortage of farm inputs and consumer goods in rural areas (Lele 1984). The agricultural sector's terms of trade may also be affected adversely by cheap food policies, a common manifestation of the urban bias of government policy in many developing countries (Lipton 1977).

Mellor (1976, p. 289) points to a fundamental factor underlying organizational problems when he states, "imbalance between public sector responsibilities and the availability of resources is particularly likely, yet receives little explicit attention in planning exercises." Re-cent discussions of Africa's food crisis have put particular emphasis on the imbalance between the heavy responsibility assigned to parastatals and the limited administrative capacity of those organizations. There is little doubt that administrative problems have been especially se-rious when quasi-governmental organizations have been given opera-tional responsibilities related to producing and marketing food crops. Bates (1981) has presented a particularly vigorous critique of the adverse effects of government interventions in Africa.

A useful view of organization in general terms is "as a framework for calculation and control through which collections of individuals determine what each should do and ensure that each does what is expected of him" (Johnston and Clark 1982, p. 156). The various tasks of calculation and control can be performed by at least three different types of organizations: local "participatory" organizations that link rural people with each other and with the larger social system, bu-reaucratic organizations staffed by government employees, and pri-vate firms or cooperatives.

Olayide and Idachaba (1986) suggest there should be a transition from "parastatals that engage directly in farm input supply and food marketing" to "facilitating institutions" that, for example, provide market information and coordinate price policies. They also stress the importance of improvements in a country's road and communications network, storage facilities, and the like. A recent paper by Jones (1984) also focuses on identifying the most useful roles that governmental marketing boards might perform in promoting more efficient marketing of food crops in tropical Africa. The World Bank (1981) places great emphasis on the need for "privatization" of operations now being performed ineffectually and at high cost by parastatals.

In recent years, interest in promoting participation in local organizations has increased. Unfortunately, there has been a tendency "to treat participation as a free good, desirable in unlimited quantities" (Johnston and Clark 1982, p. 171). Participation should, however, be viewed as a form of investment. Individuals will not invest their time and effort in local organizations unless they perceive that the benefits derived from collective action exceed the costs of that participation. Three design features determine whether efforts to induce participation will succeed: the attractiveness of benefits, the harmony of participants' objectives, and the simplicity of techniques that can be used to realize the organization's objectives (Johnston and Clark 1982).

Encouraging the formation of effective participatory organizations capable of problem solving, able to use local knowledge to mobilize local resources, and able to enforce accountability is a difficult, time-consuming process. Nevertheless, the effort may be highly rewarding. In Japan, Korea, and Taiwan, irrigation associations played a major role. The economies of scale in constructing irrigation and drainage systems are significant, and there are distinct advantages to local participation in their design and management, as well as in the mobilization of money and labor for projects in which local farmers have a direct interest (Alfonso 1983). Indeed, we think that government funds for investment in a pump or a tubewell to improve the quality and quantity of water available in a rural community should be given only as grants-in-aid to the local organization that provides most of the resources required and assumes responsibility for management and maintenance. As with irrigation, rural health programs are activities for which efforts to promote local participation may be particularly desirable and feasible.

Note also that price and market mechanisms and private firms and farmers' associations played a major role in the three East Asian economies in fulfilling many calculation and control tasks that are essential to agricultural development. Nor is it surprising that the ambitious attempts in many developing countries to determine prices administratively and to rely on parastatals for the performance of essentially commercial functions have caused many problems.

Galbraith (1979, p. 111), who can scarcely be accused of having an instinctive preference for a price and market system, has emphasized that market mechanisms "economize on scarce and honest administrative talent," whereas reliance on detailed planning and administratively determined prices is likely to jeopardize the prospects for rapid and efficient growth. "The consequence—reliance on a large, centrally planned and administered public sector—is that the greatest possible claim is placed on the scarcest possible resource. That is administrative talent, with its complementary requirements in expert knowledge, experience, and discipline." Moreover, the large literature on rent seeking emphasizes that quantitative restrictions on imports and other measures give rise to "contrived rents" that result in a deadweight loss to society because of resources that are wasted in competing for those rents (Tollison 1982; Krueger 1974).

The other side of the coin is equally important. Direct government action is indispensable in a wide range of activities because markets would otherwise perform poorly, if at all. Agricultural research and extension, roads and other rural infrastructure, and certain types of social service programs are important examples.

Determining Priorities for Social Service Programs

Japan, Korea, and Taiwan supplemented their production-oriented programs with strategic interventions to enhance the quality of human resources. The rural population had access to formal education that enhanced their ability to evaluate innovations, to participate effectively in local organizations, and to influence public institutions to be responsive to rural interests. Expansion of higher education institutions provided the large number of trained people required by modern agriculture. They were also in the vanguard in applying modern medical knowledge and public health technologies and in promoting improvements in health.

Recent demographic experience has demonstrated that the current unprecedented rapid reduction in mortality in developing countries can be followed by a similarly rapid reduction in birthrates (Kirk 1971). Interventions that reduce fertility and lead to better health of infants and small children do more than ease the task of labor absorption or increase the coverage of education programs. Children whose physical and cognitive development has not been impaired by frequent infections and malnutrition can be expected to perform better in school and to become more productive workers. Moreover, a broad-based, employment-oriented development strategy increases the likelihood that investments in education and health will have an economic payoff.

The determinants of levels of and changes in fertility are so complex that understanding of the importance of various causal factors is still limited (Cassen 1978). We find the eclectic view of Mauldin and Berelson (1978) most persuasive. They conclude that a family planning effort has a significant independent effect, but they stress that the best results are obtained when family planning programs are associated with a favorable social setting, particularly for health and education.

Considerable evidence now exists that well-designed programs that emphasize a limited range of preventive and promotional activities can reduce infant and child mortality substantially and fairly quickly. A review of ten demonstration projects by Gwatkin and others (1980) also indicates that the cost of such programs is low enough to be affordable even in low-income countries.

Between 1960 and 1981, ten economies achieved significant declines in fertility, defined arbitrarily as a reduction in the crude birthrate of 14 points or more (table 2-4). The ten are quite diverse. However, they all had family planning programs rated as strong or moderate. In contrast, of 94 economies classified according to their family planning effort, more than 70 percent had weak programs or no programs at all (Mauldin and Berelson 1978). Among the ten economies in table 2-4, per capita GNP in 1981 ranged from $300 in China to nearly $5,700 in Trinidad and Tobago. All ten ranked relatively high in education, but with considerable variation (World Bank 1983b).

In 1981, the share of agriculture in the labor force ranged from less than 10 percent in Trinidad and Tobago to more than three-quarters in Thailand. Six of the eight economies in table 2-4 in which agriculture's share was still in excess of 50 percent in 1960 have experienced fairly broad-based agricultural development. Colombia and Tunisia are the exceptions, but note that in Colombia, the share of agriculture in the labor force declined sharply, from 51 percent in 1960 to only 26 percent in 1980. Probably the most striking common feature that emerges from table 2-4 is that by 1981 the infant and child mortality rates in the ten economies were, with one exception, far below the average levels in low- and middle-income economies. Tunisia's estimated infant mortality rate in 1981 was slightly above the average for the middle-income group, but it is significant that the reduction in both infant and child mortality in Tunisia between 1960 and 1981 was exceptionally large. These characteristics of economies with significant declines in fertility are consistent with the child survival hypothesis that parents are more receptive to family planning when they are confident that their children will survive to maturity.

Table 2-4. Crude Birthrates, Infant Mortality Rates, and Child Death Rates and the Share of Agriculture in the Total Labor Force in Economies with Significant Declines in Fertility, 1960 and 1981

Economy	Crude birthrate (per 1,000 population)		Infant mortality rate (per 1,000 live births)		Child death rate, ages 1–4 (per 1,000 in age group)		Share of agriculture in labor force (percent)	
	1960	1981	1960	1981	1960	1981	1960	1981
China	39	21	165	71	26	7	n.a.	69
Colombia	46	29	103	55	14	4	51	26
Costa Rica	47	30	83	27	8	1	51	29
Cuba	32	18	66	19	5	1	39	23
Korea, Republic of	43	24	78	33	9	2	66	34
Malaysia	45	31	72	30	7	2	63	50
Taiwan	39	21[a]	56	25	8	1	56	37
Thailand	44	30	103	53	13	4	84	76
Trinidad and Tobago	38	23[b]	54	31	4	1	22	10
Tunisia	49	34	159	88	36	9	56	35
Average[c]	42	26	94	43	13	3	49	39
Thirty-two low-income economies	48	44	163	124	30	21	82	73
Fifty-nine middle-income economies[d]	43	35	127	81	22	11	62	45

n.a. Not available.

Note: A significant decline in fertility is defined as a decline in the crude birthrate of 14 per 1,000 population or more. Hong Kong and Singapore also experienced significant declines but, as city states, are special cases.

a. 1978 (World Bank 1980).

b. 1980 (World Bank 1982).

c. Unweighted average.

d. Population-weighted averages; these figures for 32 low-income economies exclude China and India (where the birthrate declined from 44 to 35 per 1,000 population).

Source: World Bank (1983b).

The availability of appropriate technology for health, nutrition, and family programs does not mean that it is easy to secure the necessary political, financial, and administrative support to adopt and implement them. Experience in Costa Rica is of special interest since it demonstrates the feasibility of introducing a rural health program without the social control that characterizes communist nations such as China or Cuba (Mata and Mohs 1978).

Ness (1979) and others have stressed the importance of involving local community organizations in the promotion of family planning. Community participation is important "when new norms and group processes are needed to support behavior change" (Korten 1983, p. 195). Community involvement is thus likely to facilitate the behavioral changes required for better hygiene, child feeding practices, and waste disposal as well as family planning. Group efforts can also reduce dependence on outside funds and personnel by mobilizing local resources, and they may lead to greater accountability and to emphasis on cost-effective preventive and promotional activities rather than on individual curative care.

Conclusion

Will the world food equation be balanced at a high or a low level? Clearly, no simple answer exists. In the future, as in the past, outcomes will vary from country to country. Achieving a balance between food supply and demand at levels high enough to eliminate malnutrition and other manifestations of poverty will require sustained and effective action to accelerate growth of food production, to expand employment opportunities, to improve human capital, to strengthen organizational capabilities, and to slow population growth. These are complex, dynamic processes.

Trade flows of agricultural commodities from developed to developing countries can be expected to continue to grow rapidly because of the long-term structural forces at work. Whether real prices will move upward or downward is less certain. The configuration of forces is such, however, that it is reasonable to expect that high growth rates in per capita income in the bulk of the developing world will cause at least some intermediate-term increase in the real price of staple foods at the global level.

Although estimating aggregate nutritional inadequacies is uncertain and fraught with questions, the needs are clearly massive. Further, nutritional inadequacies seem inseparable from broader issues of poverty. However, the high marginal propensity of the poor to spend on food means that a major reduction of poverty will bring massive increases in food consumption that will carry per capita consumption well beyond the minimum requirements now prescribed by international agencies. We have therefore emphasized that improvements in nutrition require a set of interacting forces: accelerated growth in agriculture, production and ready availability of goods that low-income people want to purchase, a strategy of agricultural development that structures demand toward high-employment-content goods and services, increased employment, and effective demand for food by the poor.

Diminishing returns to agriculture in the face of population growth and limited land area make land-augmenting technological change essential if agriculture is to play its productive role. Continuous technological change for an accelerated rate of growth in agriculture requires a complex organizational structure and massive investment in human capital—an investment fully consistent with the welfare objectives of improved food intake. Employment-oriented effective demand is most likely to arise from a smallholder agriculture, which is also fully consistent with high rates of technological change. Where labor productivity is unusually low, as in sub-Saharan Africa, or where seasonal bottlenecks occur, labor-augmenting technological change may also be necessary.

The policy implications of this analysis and of the lessons of past experience can now be succinctly distilled. The actions needed for unimodal rural development are clear from wide experience, and those actions can be successfully applied in a broad range of land ownership patterns. The most common barrier to the interrelated strategy indicated is pronounced dualism in capital allocation—too much to industry and the unproductive elements of the public sector, and to capital-intensive elements within those, rather than to agriculture and, within agriculture, to large-scale and therefore capital-intensive allocations.

Given the diseconomies of scale, it is essential not to promote large-scale agricultural units, with a consequent misallocation of capital, within a bimodal pattern of development. The organizational requirements for rural development are so complex that they require allocation of substantial responsibilities to the private sector and to local organizations with a clear setting of priorities among the activities to be carried out by the public sector. Developing the necessary organizational structure and allocation of responsibilities are difficult, time-consuming processes that are greatly facilitated and accelerated by use of market forces. Having stated the importance of market forces, we must also recognize that their role is limited and that the government must initiate activities and organization. Within this context, interacting health, nutrition, and family planning programs are important claimants of organizational resources. They not only directly increase human welfare, but they also enhance the effectiveness of the labor force and restrain its growth.

The outcome of this strategy will depend upon national-level decisions about macroeconomic policies, exchange rates, interest rates, and investment allocations among sectors and regions, not just within agriculture itself. Indeed, the whole strategy fails if it is viewed simply as the responsibility of agriculture ministries. Higher levels of foreign economic and technical assistance can, of course, improve the prospects of success, but only if aid programs focus on the same high-priority strategic objectives.

3

The Changing Context of Food and Agricultural Development Policy

G. Edward Schuh

Food and agricultural development policy today is carried out in a completely different world from that which prevailed even a decade or so ago. In the past, sectoral approaches were appropriate. Today, the food and agricultural sector can be understood only in the context of the larger economy, both national and international.

A decade ago, the emphasis was on food and food self-sufficiency. Today, the emphasis should be on generating income streams and remaining competitive. A decade ago, policymakers were only just beginning to talk about international capital markets. Today, they cannot understand agricultural commodity markets in isolation from international financial markets. A decade ago, the value of a nation's currency was largely ignored as an issue of domestic food and agricultural policy. Today, it is probably the most important price in the economy. A decade ago, a national perspective was appropriate. Today, food and agricultural policies must take account of changes in international comparative advantage. A decade ago, long-term changes in an economy were understood to arise from technological evolution and rising per capita income. Today a powerful new insight sees that rising per capita income has important collateral effects through the rising value of time.

The Evolution of an International Food and Agricultural System

One of the remarkable achievements since the end of World War II has been the evolution of an international food and agricultural system built on international trade and supported by a rapidly evolving

Written for this collection.

institutional infrastructure. The key to this evolving system is an international trade structure that enables consumers to tap supplies of food and agricultural products in almost any part of the world. This global trade structure has become possible because of technical and institutional innovations that have lowered transportation costs and made information available almost instantly around the world.

As with other forms of trade, trade in agricultural products grew rapidly in the 1970s. Virtually all countries now engage in trade of agricultural products of one kind or another, either as exporters or as importers, and thus are bound together in a common system. As a result, domestic and international policies are inseparable in today's world. Developments in the international economy, generally beyond the reach of domestic policies, often change the articulation and effect of domestic policies, making them different from those originally intended.

This system of trade has become an important means of national food security if and when national governments want to take advantage of it (see Reutlinger in part III). Associated with the international food and agricultural system has been the virtual elimination of major famines except in those cases where national governments do not let the outside world know about food shortages or make them known too late to overcome difficult transportation problems. Even in the recent African famine, the problem was not lack of available food in a global sense or of the means to get food to the distressed areas. People perished because the international community did not know about the problem in time or failed to act quickly enough once it did know.

Parallel to the evolving system of trade, an international infrastructure for the food and agricultural system has been evolving as well. At the end of World War II, this infrastructure consisted primarily of the FAO, with near universal membership, and the General Agreement on Tariffs and Trade among industrialized countries, its agricultural provisions honored primarily in the breach. Various attempts to develop international commodity agreements occurred during the post–World War II period but have not been notably successful. UNCTAD, although it provides a forum for discussion of international commodity problems, has otherwise been of limited effectiveness. In the late 1960s, CGIAR was formed to support a network of international centers. Following the World Food Conference in 1974, the WFC and IFAD were established. In the early 1980s, arrangements for financing food imports through the IMF Compensatory Financing Facility came into effect.

The system still has some important deficiencies. The social science research institutions to parallel the international agricultural research centers are lacking and consist primarily of IFPRI and the modest research capability of the FAO and the World Bank. These institutions are inadequate in the light of the rapid internationalization of the global food and agricultural economy and the changed conditions that development has created for both international trade and domestic policy making in national economies. It may be time to consolidate these institutions according to some well-conceived overall plan and to sort out what is needed and what is not functioning up to standard.

Food and Agricultural Self-Sufficiency

The emergence of a well-articulated international food and agricultural system and the potential for increasing productivity change the focus of food and agricultural policy. The motivating force of this policy today should not be food production per se, and above all it should not be food self-sufficiency. Lack of access to food by individual households is almost wholly associated with poverty and will have to be attacked with income- and employment-generating policies, together with income redistribution policies. The emphasis in agricultural development should be to improve the income of the rural population, which in most developing countries is still the main component of poverty, and to improve export performance so as to acquire the resources needed for development.

Rising Food Production and Long-Term Price Declines

Brown (1982, p. 14) echoed a theme commonly heard in discussions of the world food situation: "the period of global food security is over . . . the worldwide effort to expand food production is losing momentum . . . world food supplies are tightening and the slim margin between food production and population growth continues to narrow" (see also his chapter in part I).

Much of the recent debate exemplified by Brown's comments was engendered in the early 1970s when international commodity prices surged. Yet neither trends in world food production nor those in food prices imply that the world is running out of production potential or that the developing countries are unable to feed themselves, although the per capita food production data suggest a mixed and uneven performance. Indeed, by the end of the 1970s, the very decade which gave rise to so much Malthusian pessimism, food production in the developing countries as a whole had increased an impressive 58 percent over 1961–65, compared to 42 percent in the developed countries as a whole, as shown in table 3-1. Africa was the poorest performer. There, food production expanded only 32 percent during this

Table 3-1. *World Agricultural and Food Production Indexes, 1979*
(1961–65 = 100)

Region	Total agricultural production	Total food production	Per capita food production
Developed countries[a]	140	142	123
Developing countries	154	158	106
East Asia	176	175	120
South Asia	144	146	108
West Asia	167	168	108
Africa	131	132	88
Latin America	161	173	113
World	145	147	118

a. Including U.S.S.R.
Source: USDA (1980), summarized in Johnson (1982). Figures for 1979 are preliminary.

period. Elsewhere, food output expanded by 75 percent in East Asia, by 73 percent in Latin America, and by 68 percent in West Asia.

Even if one takes into account the rapid growth of population, table 3-1 shows that the performance of the developing countries as a whole was still substantial. Total per capita food production in the developing countries was 6 percent more than in 1961–65. The total masks a great deal, however. Per capita food production had declined by some 12 percent in Africa, and the increase for South and West Asia was only 8 percent. Bangladesh actually experienced a significant decline, and per capita production also declined in the Caribbean countries.

Now, a decade after the Malthusian wave of pessimism in the mid-1970s, the situation could not be more different. There is a chronic food problem in Africa, but food production in the rest of the world is relatively abundant. Farmers in the United States are in dire straits as their capacity to produce has outpaced the ability of the market to absorb their output, especially in the face of a strong dollar and the interference of commodity programs with the free play of market forces. India, which in the early 1970s was widely predicted to become an international basket case, has instead become a net exporter of cereals, with substantial potential for output expansion still remaining. China has emerged as an exporter of rice and feedgrains despite rapid short-term increases in per capita income. Brazil has steadily eroded the previously dominant position of the United States in the international soybean market.

The price of food is another measure of scarcity. If the demand for food were outpacing supply, the price of food would increase. Wheat and maize prices during a span of somewhat more than 100 years are plotted in figure 3-1. The United States has traditionally been a significant exporter of both wheat and maize, so in a very real sense, the U.S. price represents the international opportunity cost of these grains. The story told by this graph is a dramatic one. The real price of wheat has experienced a long-term decline. In constant value terms, its price in the 1980s is approximately half what it was 100 years earlier. This decline occurred despite the enormous increase in world population and significant increases in per capita income for many of the world's inhabitants. The story for maize is somewhat less dramatic in that its decline extends over a relatively shorter period, primarily the period since the end of World War II. The decline, however, is no less significant, since maize is both a food grain and an input into the livestock industry for which demand grows fairly rapidly as per capita incomes increase. Demand for maize has, in fact, grown tremendously.

Figure 3-1. *U.S. Wheat and Maize Prices, 1866–1981*
(constant 1967 U.S. dollars per bushel)

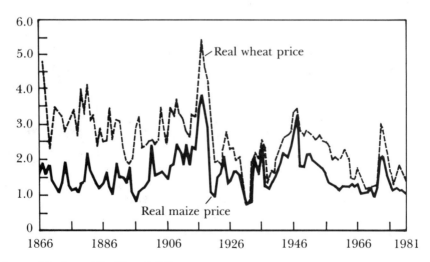

Source: Martin and Brokken (1982).

The rising food production of the last two decades and the long-term decline in the price of food grains hardly point to a Malthusian crisis. To the contrary, they point to a situation of growing abundance, interrupted by short-term problems associated with weather cycles, wars, and international monetary disturbances.

Using Productivity Increases to Generate New Income

The reason for rising food output and the decline in the real price of food is the use of new agricultural technology. The process started in Europe, Japan, and the United States and in recent years has been extended to the developing countries. The data on yield in table 3-2 tell a great deal of the story. In the mid-1930s, average yield of cereals was the same in the industrialized countries as in the developing countries. By the mid-1950s, average yield in the industrialized countries had spurted some 19 percent to 1.37 metric tons a hectare, while that in the developing countries stayed at its original level. By the end of the 1960s, yield in the developing countries was finally beginning to increase and had risen 23 percent compared to the mid-1950s, but the yield in industrialized countries had spurted another 56 percent. During the 1980s, grain yield has continued to increase around the world.

Table 3-2. *Average Grain Yield, Developing
and Industrialized Countries*
(metric tons per hectare)

Group	1934–38	1952–56	1967–70	1981–83
Developing countries	1.15	1.15	1.41	2.01
Industrialized countries	1.15	1.37	2.14	2.67

Source: FAO data.

The data on food production and productivity have far-reaching implications. First, they demonstrate that production of food and other agricultural products is not based solely on natural or physical resources. Instead, the capacity to produce food and agricultural products is man-made, based on science and technology, new knowledge, and people's skills.

Second, these data support optimism about the ability to feed the world's rapidly growing population. An expanded food supply is based on reproducible human capital, not on the natural endowment of the land. In the United States, food prices in the early part of this century were rising as all available agricultural land was brought under cultivation. Moreover, as noted, grain yield was basically no different from that in countries now referred to as developing. The experience of the United States, Europe, Japan, and now many parts of the developing world indicates what can be done with proper investments in research and extension, in education and training of the rural labor force, and in the development of industries to supply modern inputs.

Third, for countries that have not made such investments, the implications are both sobering and hopeful. They are sobering in that output produced in countries experiencing rapid productivity growth is stiff competition for producers in countries that have not yet experienced such productivity growth. They are hopeful in that late adopters of new production technology can catch up rather quickly if they are willing to make the proper investments. At the same time, consumers in lagging countries can benefit from the technological advances elsewhere if those countries play to their own prevailing comparative advantage and earn the wherewithal to have their food produced elsewhere. In any case, consumers worldwide can benefit and have benefited from the technological progress that has occurred to date.

Finally, this analysis points to the poverty or income dimension of the food problem, which has both a production and an income distribution dimension. Building agricultural research capability is no less important than in the past, but the perspective should be one of producing new income streams rather than producing food itself. That will give a very different commodity mix emphasis, with cash, export, and raw material crops emerging to be as important as food crops.

Changes in the International Monetary System

No part of the international system has experienced more change than the international monetary system, nor is there any part of the system for which the changes are more significant. The system is now huge. Recent estimates are that international financial flows are running at a level of approximately $40 trillion a year, while the flow of international trade amounts to approximately $2 trillion a year. Clearly, financial flows dominate the international system and swamp international trade as a factor influencing the value of national currencies in foreign exchange markets.

Parallel to this has been the shift beginning in 1973 from the Bretton Woods system of fixed exchange rates to a system of bloc-floating, with major currencies floated relative to each other, but with a large number of individual currencies pegged to the major floating currencies.

The emergence of a well-integrated international capital market and the shift to a system of bloc-flexible exchange rates significantly changed the way in which monetary and fiscal policies affect national economies. International capital flows influence the economies of countries with flexible exchange rates by inducing changes in the value of their currencies. These changes in exchange rates in turn shift resources among export- and import-competing sectors and nontraded sectors. For countries in which agricultural commodities are important tradables, agriculture has to bear a large share of the burden of adjustment to changing monetary conditions, with incentives to expand output as conditions in domestic money markets ease and to contract output as domestic monetary conditions tighten. The important change from the old fixed exchange rate system is that it is changes in foreign demand and foreign supply that force adjustments in the agricultural sector, not changes in the domestic cost structure of agriculture.

Another change in the international monetary system was the significant increase in monetary instability that started about 1968, the same time that agriculture in many countries became quite sensitive to changes in monetary conditions. The result has been a significant increase in instability in international commodity markets. Since this instability comes from shifts in foreign demand and supply rather than domestic conditions, it changes the instruments policymakers can use to deal with it. Stability in monetary and fiscal policy is now much more important than grain stocks or reserves as a means to create stable market conditions.

The emergence of a well-integrated international capital market and the shift to flexible exchange rates also established a strong link between financial markets and commodity markets. Somewhat of a link has always existed, since conditions in money markets influenced the cost of carrying stocks. In today's configuration, however, the link is through the exchange rate and its impact on the competitive position of domestic agriculture in international markets. Realignments in exchange rates are reflected immediately in the price of tradable commodities, independently of what is happening on the supply side. This creates very different policy choices and dilemmas than when the price is fluctuating because of changes in supply.

The emergence of a well-integrated international capital market with the shift to flexible exchange rates complicates agricultural policy in a number of additional senses. For instance, minimum price and price support policies become much more difficult to manage. If domestic prices are fixed, realignments in exchange rates that have little to do with the underlying conditions of agricultural supply and demand will influence how competitive tradable agricultural commodities are in foreign markets, with dramatic short-term implications for domestic markets. These disturbances are further complicated when countries that are large in a trade sense are subject to these same conditions. The role of the United States in the international grain and soybean markets is a perfect example. The significant decline in the value of the U.S. dollar in the 1970s caused the price of these commodities to decline in terms of other currencies, thus causing the quantity imported by other countries to increase and United States exports to increase as well. This had important dampening effects on the agricultural sectors of other countries, independently of whether they were export competitors or importers. By the same token, the rise in the value of the dollar in the early 1980s led to higher prices of these same commodities in terms of the currencies of other countries: The United States' share of these markets has declined significantly, and the price in other countries has risen. This effect has been exaggerated by the rigidity of the United States' support level, but that only further emphasizes the significance of international interdependence. The agriculture of other countries is affected not only by U.S. monetary and fiscal policies and the changes in the value of the U.S. dollar but also in important ways by the domestic commodity policies the United States implements.

To the extent that national governments isolate their domestic agricultural sectors from international markets, some of these external forces may be attenuated, but the extent to which domestic sectors can be isolated is deceptive. Realignments in exchange rates can bring about implicit changes in domestic relative prices even though domestic and border prices are fixed in relative terms. This can alter the domestic conditions of supply and demand. Consider a country that pegs its currency to the value of the U.S. dollar. If that country is either an exporter or an importer of agricultural commodities, its agriculture will benefit from a decline in the value of the dollar. It will not benefit relative to the United States, of course, but relative to the agriculture of countries whose currencies are rising against the dollar. This includes the agriculture of all those countries that have the value of their currencies pegged to the value of other major currencies. The reverse occurs when the value of the dollar rises, again with important resource allocation effects in these other countries.

Finally, there is the whole issue of international commodity agreements in the context of a flexible exchange rate system. In the new configuration of the international economy, with flexible exchange rates and well-integrated capital markets, such agreements now appear infeasible. Typically, such agreements involve some attempt to support prices in U.S. dollar terms at some agreed-to level, and some means of enforcing that price, by international marketing quotas, imposed production adjustments, or both. Under the fixed exchange rate system, such an agreement was at least feasible in principle. Under a flexible exchange rate system it may not be feasible at all, and with a system of bloc-floating it may be well nigh impossible. Exchange rate realignments induce changes in the domestic prices within member countries. This influences the quantity exported or the quantity imported. More generally, it makes it difficult for some countries to comply with the provisions of the agreement, while creating in other countries very strong pressures to cheat or break out of the cartel.

There are those, of course, who would like to abandon the present flexible exchange rate system because of its perceived instability and go back to the old fixed exchange rate system. That would not be possible even if it were desirable unless one were willing to give up all the advantages of a well-integrated capital and financial market and the benefits from trade. The shift to a system of flexible exchange rates in 1973 was nothing more than a tacit recognition that exchange rates could no longer be fixed. Recent attempts to influence the value of the dollar by coordinated and massive central bank interventions have illustrated the difficulties of influencing exchange rates and confirmed the decisions taken in 1973.

This is not to say the system cannot be improved. That will require either that the IMF become an international central bank, that the United States manage its monetary policy as if it were that international central bank, or that there be a great deal of policy coordination among national economies. Part of the present problem arises from the fact that the industrialized countries have never given the IMF resources commensurate with its originally assigned objectives, while the United States has managed its monetary policy primarily as if it were a closed economy when, in fact, since the world is on a dollar standard, the United States is in reality the central banker for the world.

The conditions now unfolding in the international monetary system are cause for serious concern. The rapid growth in barter and countertrade indicates that the international economy is facing a serious liquidity crisis. The emergence of the United States as a debtor country will have major exchange rate and monetary implications. Already it has led to a decline in the value of the dollar. Under circumstances that are quite feasible, the decline could be significant. The result could well be enormous shocks to international commodity markets, to world agriculture, and to the international economy as a whole.

Developments in the System of International Trade

Developments in the system of international trade are almost as farreaching as developments in the international monetary system, and almost as poorly perceived and understood. In part this is because of the tendency to consider international economic intercourse as a real trade phenomenon without fully appreciating the significance of the international capital market.

Much of the debate about the current United States trade deficit illustrates the failure to understand the new system. It is popular to predict that the value of the dollar should soon decline because the United States is running a large trade deficit. In point of fact, of course, the United States has a large trade deficit because the dollar is strong, and the dollar is strong because of what is happening in the international capital market. The emergence of the United States as a major debtor country is far more likely to have an effect on the value of the dollar than what happens on the trade account because financial flows are so much larger than trade flows.

The emergence of a well-integrated capital market and the shift to a system of bloc-floating exchange rates has significantly altered the constraints faced by individual nations as they attempt to develop their economies. At the same time, it provides them with new means and opens new development opportunities, but within significant new limitations on international trade policies.

Consider events in the international economy these last three to four years and the dilemmas they present to both developed and developing countries. To service and repay past debts, the developing countries have to provide a surplus on their trade account. That surplus implies a deficit in the trade accounts of the developed or previously capital-exporting countries, which for the most part the United States has been supplying. For these countries, however, the deficit on the trade account implies that they are capital importers, as illustrated by recent United States experience. This, in turn, pulls much-needed capital away from the developing countries.

The opportunities, constraints, and dilemmas are real. Developing countries now have a well-developed capital market they can access for development purposes. Yet if they are to repay that debt and remain good risks for further borrowing, they have to improve their export performance. This forces them to turn outward in the configuration of their economies, to implement policies that use their resources more efficiently, and to develop productive export sectors. It also implies expanded international trade.

Paradoxically, the present crisis in international financial markets may be the harbinger of a brighter future for agriculture in many of the countries most affected by the crisis. Policymakers will be forced to realign their exchange rates to bring their external accounts in line to service and eventually to pay off their debts. They will also have to reduce the import subsidies that have caused food imports to grow so rapidly in some developing countries. Overvalued currency has probably been the single most common policy distortion among developing countries, and the degree of overvaluation is substantial. The implicit export tax from overvaluation of the currency alone in Brazil, for example, ranged from 22 to 27 percent between 1954 and 1966 (Bergsman and Malan 1971; Bergsman 1970). The recent floating of the Mexican peso provides another example of how overvalued currencies often are. Little wonder that the agriculture of these countries has done so poorly. Little wonder also that countries imposing such distortions shift from being net exporters of food to being net importers. After all, the overvalued currency is an implicit import subsidy as well as an implicit export tax.

Trade and exchange rate policies, the main instruments by which governments have intervened to influence food and agricultural prices, have played a major role in shifting the domestic terms of trade against agriculture. The failure to address the effects of trade and exchange rate policy on the domestic terms of trade is ironic in light of the importance the developing countries have attached to the external terms of trade. At the very time many of these countries issued complaints about declining external terms of trade and lack of export opportunities, they have severely overvalued their currency in foreign exchange markets, levied export taxes, and imposed complicated licensing provisions to limit exports. The net effect of these policies has been to divert agricultural output away from viable export markets and to the domestic market. To put it succinctly, limitations on external markets have in important respects been self-imposed.

The developed countries that have been supplying loan capital to developing countries in the past are faced with no less serious policy dilemmas than the debtor countries. If the developed countries want their past credits to be repaid, they must be willing to accept imports from the debtor countries. This places great stress on the traditional sectors of the developed countries, forcing significant restructuring and greater efficiencies in their economies as well as those of the debtors. This is burden sharing at its best, but it is painful for all concerned.

The international economy has been passing through an enormously stressful period. It has accommodated two petroleum crises in the 1970s, suffered from misguided policies in developed and developing countries alike, and learned to live with the system of bloc-floating exchange rates and a burgeoning international capital market. As the international economy recovers from this difficult period, individual countries will have choices to make at the margin between increasing exports or importing capital, and between exporting capital and accepting more imports. In the process, pressures for expanded trade and further integration of the international economy will be great.

One of the major implications of this analysis is the importance of general trade liberalization if international adjustment burdens are to be truly shared. Another is the need for symmetry in conditionality and insistence on policy rationality among the developed countries. Developing countries will not benefit from their domestic policy reforms if the developed countries are unwilling to accept their exports and at the same time supply capital as the demand for it grows.

Changes in International Comparative Advantage

Probably at no time in modern history have such powerful forces been acting to change international comparative advantage. In the case of world agriculture, there is the growing capacity to produce a modern technology adapted to developing countries, particularly those in the tropics. An important part of this capacity is the CGIAR network of 13 research centers. Of even greater importance is the growing research capacity in many developing countries. India and Brazil are outstanding examples, but many others exist.

Another factor that has great potential to change international comparative advantage in agriculture is the new biotechnology. It is not clear whether this new potential source of technological breakthroughs will benefit developed or developing countries the most. It is likely, however, that this new technology will prove highly transferable, with potentially great effects in the developing countries. For example, a new hormone ready to be adopted in the United States promises to increase a dairy cow's milk production by 40 percent. This hormone ought to be highly transferable.

The rapid diffusion of modern poultry technology is also transforming international agriculture and altering international comparative advantage. Poultry production is a relatively easy way for a country to upgrade the quality of its diet as per capita income increases. An expansion of this sector gives rise to a strong derived demand for feedgrains. As economic development proceeds, therefore, there likely will be a relative shift away from foodgrains as a source of food, with feedgrain use making possible additional value added from local labor and pasture resources.

These examples suggest that a worldwide surge in agricultural technology is under way. That surge can bring enormous benefits, but it can also cause serious adjustment problems. The need to transfer labor out of agriculture will probably be quite great. When agriculture makes up a large part of the economy, managing this adjustment is not easy.

In the industrial sector, the big news is the newly industrialized countries that have already penetrated the developed countries with their exports and forced significant restructuring of their economies. Manufacturing is declining and the service sector is growing. Now, a new round of exporters is coming on the scene, including China, India, Pakistan, and the Philippines. The shocks to trade patterns as important industrial sectors shift from one country to another can be great.

The service sector is probably the least understood sector of the international economy. International trade in services is growing rapidly and can be expected to continue to grow in the future. The service sector probably will be the comparative advantage of the developed countries in the decades ahead.

In today's world, comparative advantage is increasingly influenced by human capital and less and less by the underlying endowment of physical resources. This is a problem for those countries that lag in developing their stock of human capital, but it holds out the promise that in the future countries can, within limits, make their comparative advantage whatever they want it to be. This is not to say that national governments should ignore the principles of comparative advantage when they design their development policy. To the contrary, it is the only viable principle as long as efficiency is important. It is to say that the traditional concept of comparative advantage has to be broadened to include the concept of human capital, and that countries do not have to accept their "original" resource endowment as a basis for their future comparative advantage. Moreover, it implies that investment policy designed to augment and shape a nation's stock of human capital is a more viable way to alter and improve its comparative advantage than protectionist measures, which distort resource use and reduce the ability to compete in the international economy without at the same time building a strong basis for longer-term economic development.

As new agricultural technology becomes increasingly important to agricultural change, individual cultivators must have greater knowledge about opportunities, management choices, and markets, with obvious implications about the education they must receive. Countries will need a whole stock of middle-level workers to provide such services as input and output marketing. Outside agriculture, countries will need an increasingly well-educated work force if they are to take advantage of international trade to energize economic growth. In the case of training the high-level cadres needed for modernization, and in the case of developing the capacity for agricultural research, the resources needed are modest, but the gestation period is long. Most countries need significantly improved human capital services if they are to compete effectively in international markets. These include an analytical capability to analyze trade opportunities, a market information system to give private decisionmakers an improved basis for decision making, and improved means by which participants in risky markets can transfer that risk to other members of the society through futures markets for commodities and foreign exchange and through marketing instruments, such as warehouse warrants.

Changes in International Competitive Advantage

Competitive advantage is what is left after policy interventions by governments have had their effect on national economies. Government policies can suppress underlying comparative advantage or they can distort it away from what underlying conditions of supply and demand would imply. The exchange rate can have the same effect. In the absence of large international capital and financial markets, exchange rates were important reflections of underlying comparative advantage. Today, they are more properly a part of competitive advantage, since changes in exchange rates induced by capital and financial flows can distort the extent to which underlying comparative advantage is expressed. Capital flows may reflect differences in savings rates as much as conditions of trade. Until institutional means are developed to create stable international monetary conditions, large shifts in competitive advantage may be expected in response to large swings in the relative values of national currencies.

The international debt crisis that is causing many countries to undertake significant reforms of domestic economic policies is bringing about major shifts in competitive advantage. Subsidies are being phased out, export taxes and other discriminations against exports are being reduced, and exchange rates are being realigned to more realistic levels. These reforms will have major impacts on trade flows in the future.

The manner in which protection is provided to domestic industries has changed significantly over the last 10 to 15 years. Tariff protection has declined as a consequence of multilateral trade negotiations, at least among Western industrialized countries, and nontariff barriers have become more significant. In addition, new forms of protectionism have arisen in the form of voluntary export agreements, semicartel arrangements, and various orderly marketing arrangements. These newer forms of protectionism distinguish themselves by being selective and focusing on one or a small group of countries, by tending to be self-limiting, and by rewarding countries that practice restraint in their exports with economic rents of various kinds. Their negative aspects are that they compensate foreign and domestic producers at the expense of domestic consumers. These selective forms of protectionism are likely to proliferate in the years ahead as the export imperative spreads worldwide. They are an aspect of trade policy that will increasingly have to be taken into account as pressures for exports grow.

Fortunately, the growth of international trade worldwide since the end of World War II has created valuable vested interests against protectionism and in favor of trade liberalization. Protectionist initiatives are tempered by the threat of retaliation as country after country finds it has as much to lose as to gain from the spread of protectionism. This, more than anything else, explains the relative success in staving off protectionism despite enormous realignments in real exchange rates and the emergence of strong new competitors. An important phenomenon that promises to strengthen further these forces against protectionism is the growth in subsector integration across national boundaries. As industries become more international in scope, they generate multicountry forces in favor of freer trade and against protectionism.

It is not well recognized that the new system of bloc-floating exchange rates means there are smaller national gains from protectionist measures of any kind. Both protectionist measures and export subsidies lead to changes in exchange rates. The exchange rate realignments may help spread the burden of adjustment in the domestic economy, but the nation as a whole still has to bear the adjustment. The ability to dump problems abroad, as under the old fixed exchange rate system, is no longer available.

These new dimensions to trade policy are important both in shaping food and agricultural development policy and in shaping economic policy more generally.

The Rising Value of Time

One of the most powerful forces a country experiences as it undergoes economic development is the rising value of human time. In the past, long-term changes in an economy have been understood in large part to be a function of increased per capita income and technological evolution. The newer perspective recognizes that increased per capita incomes raise the opportunity cost of human time, given that time is the one finite resource.

The rise in the value of time has important collateral economic effects in addition to the rise in per capita income. Consider the issue of population growth. Modern economic theories of population view children as consumer durables that families demand just as they demand other consumer goods. Children are labor-intensive consumables that are produced in the household. As increases in per capita income raise the opportunity cost of the labor to produce these children, the number of children declines even as the demand for the services of children rises. Furthermore, the demand is for a higher-quality child, so families increase their child services by investing more in them in the form of education, improved nutrition, and health as their incomes rise.

Another impact of the rising value of time is that it leads to changes in the agricultural commodity mix that consumers demand. For example, rice is quite time-intensive since it requires considerable time to prepare. Wheat, in contrast, is converted into bread in modern factories and the family has only to consume it directly. As the value of time rises, the commodity mix can be expected to change in favor of less time-intensive goods independently of the more familiar income effect. The implications extend to food, trade, and agricultural development policy.

Finally, the rising value of time has important implications for institutional development. This is a complex set of issues that goes beyond the scope of this paper, but some of the immediate interest focuses on the need to develop institutions that produce human capital for the society—institutions concerned with education, research, health, and nutrition. It also has to do with that great empty box, "the role of women in development." It is time to put some content into this slogan rather than to continue the empty rhetoric that has characterized it in the past. The content has to do with household technology and human capital investment in women to improve productivity both in the household and in economic activities outside the home, whether in agriculture, industry, or commerce.

Conclusion

Food and agricultural development policy in most countries has traditionally been shaped in the narrow confines of sectoral policy, neglecting other sectors of the economy, other aspects of economic policy, and often the international economy. In today's world, that is no longer a sound approach. Policymakers must pay attention to the poverty and income distribution implications of food policy, not just the production implications. The changing international economy, as well as altered concepts of what properly should be paramount in shaping food and agricultural policy, have changed significantly the context policymakers face as they address the complex challenges of improving the welfare of their people in the decades ahead.

4

Food Growth Slowdown: Danger Signal for the Future

Lester R. Brown

Two major developments dominate the current world food economy. One is the leveling off of per capita food production since 1973 following a quarter-century of steady gain. The other is the increasing differences in food production among continents and major countries. In some regions, per capita food production is surging ahead; in others it is falling steadily.

China and Africa illustrate these contrasts. China's impressive rise in per capita grain production has given it a substantial safety margin that will permit it to weather two successive poor harvests without any serious malnutrition. In contrast, Africa's food situation is deteriorating. The 1 percent annual decline in per capita grain output since 1967 has been aggravated by the 1983–84 drought. Even before the drought, nearly a fifth of Africa's population was being sustained by imported grain (USDA 1984c).

Stagnating Cropland Expansion

From the beginning of agriculture until roughly the 1950s, the yearly increases in food production were due largely to expansion of the area cultivated. Growth in world cropland slowed markedly during the 1950s, fell to below 0.3 percent per year in the 1970s, and is expected to drop to 0.2 percent in the 1980s and to 0.15 percent in the 1990s (Urban and Vollrath 1984).

Net growth in world cropland area in any given year reflects the difference between countries that are still adding cropland and a

Adapted from "Reducing Hunger," *State of the World, 1985,* by Lester R. Brown, William U. Chandler, Christopher Flavin, Cynthia Pollock, Sandra Postel, Linda Starke, and Edward C. Wolf, with the permission of Lester R. Brown and W. W. Norton & Company, Inc. Copyright © 1985 by the Worldwatch Institute.

much smaller, though growing, number whose cropland area is shrinking. Expansion results from pushing back the frontiers of settlement or else from irrigation projects, drainage projects, clearing forests, or plowing grassland. Examples of countries that have added to cropland by new settlement projects are Brazil, which is encouraging new farms and ranches in the Cerrado and the Amazon Basin, and Indonesia, which is resettling people from densely populated Java to the outer islands of Sumatra, Kalimantan, and Sulawesi.

New irrigation projects have played a central role in adding to the cultivated area of semiarid countries such as Mexico and Pakistan. Land reclamation by drainage figures prominently in the U.S.S.R., which planned to reclaim some 700,000 hectares a year during the early 1980s. In Central America, cropland area expansion comes at the expense of forests. In East Africa, Argentina, and the Great Plains states in the United States, grassland conversion accounts for the bulk of recent growth.

On the other side of the ledger, roughly a third of the world's people live in countries where cropland area is shrinking (table 4-1). Japan has lost nearly 20 percent of its cropland since the early 1960s, and China has lost 5 percent. Cropland is largely lost to urbanization and industrialization. The amount of cropland engulfed by cities is unknown, but individual countries provide an indication. The United States built on some 2.5 million hectares of prime cropland between 1967 and 1975 (Lee 1978). In Europe from 1960 to 1970, West Germany lost about 2.5 percent of its agricultural land to urbanization, and France and the United Kingdom each lost nearly 2 percent (OECD 1976).

Village expansion also accounts for cropland loss. Unfortunately, little research has been conducted on this topic. A study of Bangladesh pointed out that growth in the number of families is closely related to growth of the area occupied by the village. Homes made of locally available materials such as bamboo, thatch, and corrugated iron sheets are not strong enough to hold an upper story. Thus every new village homestead is built on cropland (Quazi 1978).

Chinese planners are becoming alarmed over the loss of cropland to village home construction. One consequence of the shift to a family-based, market-oriented farm system is that for the millions of peasants becoming wealthy, building a new home is a top priority. Planners in Beijing have concluded that one way to minimize cropland conversion is to encourage peasants to construct two-story homes (Hendry 1983).

Since the 1950s, one of the principal causes of cropland shrinkage in Western Europe and Japan has been factory construction. More recently, industrial development has begun to claim land in developing countries.

Table 4-1. *Decline in Cropland Area, Selected Countries*

Country	Postwar year of peak cropland area	Decline from peak year to 1980 (percent)
China	1963	5.1
France	1960	13.3
Germany, Federal Republic of	1955	13.9
Ireland	1960	29.4
Italy	1955	4.8
Japan	1960	19.6
Korea, Republic of	1968	5.3
Netherlands	1955	18.0
Poland	1955	9.7
Portugal	1963	18.1
Sweden	1955	21.0
Yugoslavia	1960	5.6

Source: Urban and Vollrath (1984).

In addition to growing nonfarm uses, excessive economic demands and mismanagement are destroying cropland through desertification, erosion, waterlogging, and salinization of irrigated land. In other cases, irrigation water is diverted to nonfarm uses. A U.N. report on cropland in Latin America notes severe erosion in the Andean countries, where gullys are advancing through the steeply sloping countryside like the tentacles of a gigantic malignancy (United Nations, ECLAC 1976). In Italy, some 2 million hectares have been abandoned in the last ten years because "the farming methods used on this marginal land have led to deterioration of the soil so that the land was consumed in the literal sense of the term" (*OECD Observer* 1976, p. 26).

Other sources of cropland loss have received little attention. For example, land for burial has claimed millions of hectares in the past 20 years. In most countries, this loss is minimized by using cemeteries, but in China the dead are buried under mounds often located on good farmland. The government has launched a campaign to encourage cremation. "Otherwise," an official in the Ministry of Civil Affairs observed, "the living and the dead will have to scramble for land" (*Mazingira* 1984, p. 15).

Another factor in the world cropland equation is the low productivity of the newly cultivated area. In Brazil and Nigeria, where expansion of cropland has been the greatest, cereal yields have increased little or none since 1950. Increasing use of fertilizer and other inputs is offset by the declining quality of cropland (USDA 1984c). In Canada, it takes an estimated 2.4 hectares of new land in the western provinces to replace every hectare of land lost to urban expansion in the wetter eastern provinces (Canada 1976). Elsewhere, there has been a "retreat from the margin" such as occurred in the U.S.S.R. in the early 1980s following overexpansion into marginal lands.

Although all projections of world food supply and demand incorporate projections for cropland area, none take into account the record amount of topsoil being lost from the world cropland base by erosion. The net loss of some 25 billion tons of topsoil annually from the world's cropland is reducing the inherent productivity of the land (Brown and Wolf 1984). An interdisciplinary team in southern Iowa has studied the link between soil erosion and production cost in detail. The team concluded that as cropland changes from slightly to severely eroded, fertilizer requirements per hectare increase by some 45 kilograms of nitrogen, 3 kilograms of phosphate, and 14 kilograms of potash (Rosenberry and others 1980).

The combination of slowing cropland expansion and continuing population growth has led to a sharp reduction in the area of cropland per person. In 1950, a quarter of a hectare of grain was harvested per person worldwide. By 1984 this had shrunk to 0.15 hectare per person (table 4-2).

For planning purposes, it is best to assume that by the end of the century virtually all growth in world food production will have to come from increasing land productivity.

Water Constraints on Increased Food Production

The lack of unexploited water resources may constrain future growth in world food output even more than the scarcity of unex-

Table 4-2. *World Per Capita Grain Area and Fertilizer Use, 1950–84*

| | Grain area per capita (hectares) | Fertilizer use | |
Year		Per capita (kilograms)	Total (million tons)
1950	0.24	5.4	13.5
1955	0.23	6.7	18.3
1960	0.21	8.9	27.0
1965	0.20	11.9	23.1
1970	0.18	17.1	63.0
1975	0.18	20.4	82.4
1980	0.16	25.6	113.1
1984	0.15	25.4	121.0

Source: FAO (1978); Andrilenas (personal communication, 1983); Worldwatch Institute estimates based on data from USDA and FAO.

ploited fertile land. In countries such as Mexico and Pakistan, fresh-water scarcity prevents the spread of high-yielding wheats. In the U.S.S.R., water shortages are frustrating efforts to expand feedgrain production for the country's increasing livestock herds.

Although irrigated agriculture started several thousand years ago, the bulk of its expansion has occurred since 1950. As of 1980, some 46 percent of the world's 261 million hectares of irrigated land was in Asia. The Middle East and North Africa, the U.S.S.R., the United States, and Latin America each accounted for somewhat less than 10 percent of the irrigated land. Sub Saharan Africa had only 2 percent.

Irrigation plays an important role in the four major food producers: the United States, the U.S.S.R., China, and India. The increase of irrigated land in China since 1950 has been impressive, rising from about 20 million hectares in 1950 to some 48 million by 1980 (Stone n.d.). In 1950, India's net irrigated area was 21 million hectares—almost exactly the same as China's—and by 1980 it totaled some 39 million hectares. The most rapid growth has occurred since the mid-1960s following the introduction of high-yielding wheat and rice varieties that were both more responsive to water and required more exacting cultivation techniques. As small farmers perceived an opportunity to make greater profit, they invested in wells of their own so that they could exploit the yield potential of the new varieties (Centre for Monitoring Indian Economy 1984).

The area of irrigated land in the United States expanded during 1950–78, but at a decelerating rate (USDA 1983a). Since 1978, the area of irrigated land has declined because of depletion of the Ogallala aquifer in the southern Great Plains and the diversion of water to nonfarm uses in the sunbelt states (U.S. Department of Commerce 1984). The U.S.S.R.'s irrigated area has grown steadily in recent decades, with some 18 million hectares now under irrigation. Plans call for an addition of roughly 700,000 hectares a year during the mid-1980s, an annual growth of nearly 4 percent. Such an increase reflects the urgency that the U.S.S.R. attaches to expansion because it both boosts food production and minimizes the wide swings in crop output resulting from highly variable rainfall (USDA 1984b).

Irrigation often holds the key to cropping intensity, especially in monsoon climates where the wet season is followed by warm, dry months with little or no rain. Irrigation permits production of two, three, or even more crops per year.

Given the projected growth in world food demand, the world's irrigated area is certain to expand. The question is, how rapidly. FAO projections show a possible addition of 53 million hectares between 1980 and 1990, but this depends on capital availability. Not only does it take a great deal of capital to irrigate this much land, but the cost of irrigation per hectare is rising as most of the least costly sites have been developed.

As the cost of bringing new land under irrigation and the cost of energy to pump underground water rise, attention will focus more on improving the efficiency of water use. Modification of irrigation practices to use water more economically will be the key to expanding irrigated food production.

The Fertilizer Link

As the areas suitable for new agricultural settlement disappeared after World War II and population growth accelerated, demand for fertilizer climbed rapidly. In 1950, the world used less than 14 million tons of chemical fertilizer. By 1984, world fertilizer consumption totaled 121 million tons, nearly a nine-fold increase in 34 years (table 4-2). The reduction in world cropland per person since 1950 has been offset by increased per capita fertilizer use. Eliminating its use today would probably cut world food production by at least a third. At least one and a half billion people are now fed with the additional food produced with chemical fertilizer.

The soil nutrients most likely to be limiting to plant growth are nitrogen, phosphorus, and potassium. Hence, chemical fertilizers usually supply these three elements. Of the three, nitrogen accounts for just over half of world fertilizer output and phosphate and potash account for roughly one-quarter each (USDA 1984a).

Historically, Western Europe, the United States, and Japan dominated world fertilizer output, but as nitrogen fertilizer is synthesized from atmospheric nitrogen, it can be produced wherever energy is available. Following the 1973 oil price increase, most new nitrogen plants have been built in oil exporting countries, particularly those that flare natural gas. This shift has markedly boosted the developing country share of nitrogen fertilizer production (USDA 1984a). Phosphate and potash, in contrast, are mined by only a handful of countries that have large indigenous reserves. In 1980, three-fifths of world phosphate rock exports came from Morocco and from Florida in the United States. The remainder came from a number of smaller exporters. The U.S.S.R. and Canada dominate potash production. Together they produce 55 percent of the world's potash. The Democratic Republic of Germany and the Federal Republic of Germany each produce 10 to 11 percent, and the United States and France produce most of the remainder (Lastigzon 1981).

As of 1981, the industrial countries were consuming 72 million tons of chemical fertilizer annually, 63 percent of the world total. Developing countries were using 43 million tons annually, but their consumption has been growing far more rapidly. Experts predict that by the year 2000, fertilizer use by the industrial and the developing countries may be about the same (Fertilizer Institute 1982).

In recent years, the growth in world fertilizer use has slowed markedly. After increasing 7.5 percent annually from 1950 through 1973, it dropped to 5.6 percent a year following the 1979 oil price increase (table 4-2). Where fertilizer use is high, diminishing returns are setting in. As applications increase, so do crop yields, but only up to a point. The ratio between the prices of grain and fertilizer has changed in recent decades, and the real cost of fertilizer now constrains use to some extent (USDA 1984c; Andrilenas, personal communication, 1983; FAO 1978). In many developing countries, mounting foreign debt has limited fertilizer use. The more foreign exchange is required to service debt, the less is available to import fertilizer. Brazil, for example, has severely restricted its fertilizer imports (USDA 1983b). Because of external debt and internal deficits, many governments are under pressure to reduce or eliminate subsidies, thus making fertilizer use less attractive to farmers. In some instances, the pressure has come from international agencies and creditors as a condition of continued funding or debt rescheduling (USDA 1984a).

Future fertilizer use will be influenced heavily by the energy-food price relationship and by the continuing spread of irrigation. Energy prices will almost inevitably rise in the long term. Offsetting this to some extent is the temporary shift toward the use of flared natural gas as a nitrogen fertilizer feedstock. As long as gas supplies last, this will check the rising cost of manufacturing nitrogen fertilizer.

Advances in Technology

The doubling of world food output over the past generation is due largely to advances in agricultural technology, especially the expanded use of irrigation and chemical fertilizers, and to improved crop varieties. As cereals dominate food output, the development of hybrid maize and dwarf varieties of rice and wheat has been critical.

The mid-1980s is a particularly active time for agricultural research, with advances in biotechnology—including recombinant DNA, tissue culture, and cloning—opening new frontiers in farm technology. Exciting though these technologies are, they "will be used to complement, but not replace, the well-established practices of plant and animal breeding" (Cowan 1981, p. 3).

The historical trends of three principal cereals grown in the United States—maize, wheat, and sorghum—suggest that the potential exists to raise crop yields in countries where agricultural modernization is only beginning and indicate the longer-term constraints in agriculturally advanced societies.

The yield trend for sorghum in the United States since 1950 illustrates clearly the S-shaped curve that scientists expect all biological growth functions to follow (figure 4-1). From the mid-1950s until the late 1960s, sorghum yield nearly tripled, climbing from 1.3 tons to 3.3 tons per hectare. This remarkable growth was achieved by the rapid spread of hybrid sorghum and irrigation, particularly in the southern plains, and by increased use of chemical fertilizer. Although yields have fluctuated since the late 1960s, average yield has not increased.

Maize yield has also increased dramatically, nearly tripling between 1950 and the early 1980s (figure 4-2). The increased yield is due to continuously improved hybrids and the increased application of chemical fertilizer. Yields are still rising, although not as rapidly since the early 1970s. Year to year fluctuations from 1950 through 1969 were quite modest. In 1970, however, when the maize blight struck, yield dropped sharply because the predominant maize varieties contained little resistant stock. Yields declined even further in 1974 because of bad weather, and in 1980 and 1983 because of drought. However, agriculturists will not be able to determine whether U.S. maize yield is leveling off in the same way as sorghum yield for some years.

The wheat yield increase in the United States has been less dramatic than the maize and sorghum yield increases, but after several years of static or declining levels during the 1970s, wheat yield is again increasing.

Although Japan's rice yield started increasing well before that of cereals in the United States, the steady rise that spanned several decades has been interrupted in recent years (figure 4-3). Japan's rice yield, which averaged roughly 4.5 tons a hectare of milled rice, has increased little in the last decade. As with sorghum and maize in the United States, increasing present fertilizer use has little effect on yield (USDA 1984c).

To assess fully the potential for boosting world food output, current yields in developing countries must be compared with those of the more agriculturally advanced countries. For example, in the mid-1980s, Argentine maize yield was scarcely half that of the United States, suggesting that over time, given that soils and climate are similar in Argentina and the United States, Argentine maize yield could double as agriculture modernizes.

Two of the most widely discussed potential breakthroughs in agricultural research are the development of nitrogen fixing cereals and of more photosynthetically efficient crops. However, evidence is

Figure 4-1. *U.S. Sorghum Yield Per Hectare, 1950–84*

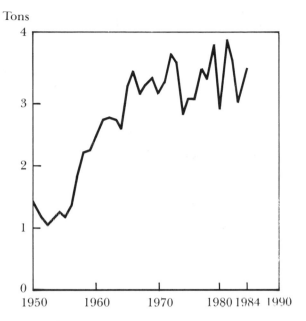

Source: USDA data.

Figure 4-2. *U.S. Maize Yield Per Hectare, 1900–84*

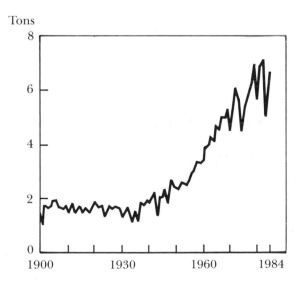

Source: USDA data.

Figure 4-3. *Japanese Rice Yield Per Hectare, 1900–84*

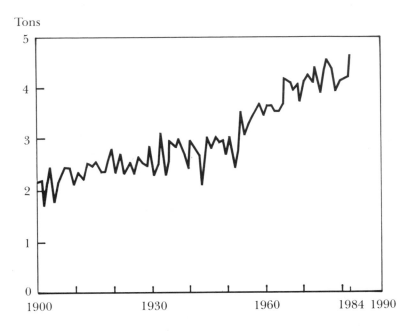

Source: USDA data.

mounting that if cereals are modified to behave like legumes, they will pay a yield penalty. In other words, a plant that supports nitrogen fixing bacteria living on its roots will have less energy to form grain.

In applied agricultural research, as in any other area of endeavor governed by economics, researchers tackle the easy tasks first. After several decades of sustained progress in increasing crop and livestock productivity, maintaining the rate of growth is becoming more difficult. Returns on agricultural research investment may be diminishing. Doubling or tripling U.S. research expenditure on sorghum, for example, is unlikely to have much effect on yield. Likewise, the ability of researchers in Japan to raise rice yield appears limited, regardless of how much is spent.

Food Security Trends

Since 1973, world grain production has barely kept pace with population growth (table 4-3). The difference between a 3 percent growth rate of grain production and one of 2 percent is the difference between a world where increased food output is improving diets across the board and one where food production is barely keeping pace with population growth. The lack of growth in per capita income for the world since 1979 has virtually eliminated food demand growth arising from increased income.

Discussions of food security at the global level commonly focus on food reserves, typically measured in terms of carryover stocks—those stores of grain on hand when harvest of the new crop begins (table 4-4). The cropland idled under U.S. farm programs is also a reserve, though one year removed. Except during 1972–75, these two reserves together have maintained a remarkable stability in the world grain market.

A poor harvest in the U.S.S.R. in the summer of 1972, followed by a decision in Moscow to offset crop shortfalls by imports rather than by belt-tightening, and also a United States election year decision to idle a large amount of cropland, caused the severe world wheat shortages beginning in the late summer of 1972. When poor harvests followed

Table 4-3. *Growth of Total and Per Capita World Grain Production, 1950–84*
(percent)

Period	Grain production	Population	Grain production per capita
1950–73	3.1	1.9	1.2
1973–79	1.9	1.8	0.1
1979–84	2.0	1.7	0.3

Sources: IMF (1950–84); USDA (1984c); U.N., various years.

Table 4-4. *Indicators of World Food Security, 1960–84*
(millions of tons, except as specified)

Year	World carryover stocks of grain	Grain equivalent of idled U.S. cropland	Total reserves	World consumption (days)
1960	200	36	236	104
1965	142	70	212	81
1970	164	71	235	75
1975	141	3	144	43
1980	187	0	187	47
1984[a]	205	38	243	56

a. Projection based on May 15 estimates of U.S. cropland idled.

Sources: Reserve stocks from USDA (1983d, 1984d); cropland idled from Weber (personal communication, 1983, 1984).

during the next two years in major food-producing regions such as China, the Indian subcontinent, the U.S.S.R., and the United States, the rebuilding of world grain stocks was unfortunately delayed.

The combination of carryover stocks and idled U.S. cropland amounted to the equivalent of 243 million tons of grain in 1984, equal to 56 days of world food consumption, and more than enough to maintain relatively stable prices in world grain markets.

With over 90 percent of the world grain harvest consumed in the country in which it is produced, food security, particularly in the poor countries, is dominated by the relationship between growth in food output and population growth (USDA 1983c, 1984c, 1984d). Since 1973, the race between food production and population has been a standoff. Although per capita grain production for the world as a whole has been static during this period, it has steadily increased in some regions of the world, declined in others, and showed no perceptible movement up or down in still others.

Among the trouble spots are Africa and the south Andean countries of Latin America. These regions with declining food production per person typically have fragile ecosystems, are most often semiarid or mountainous, and have rapid population growth.

Africa is losing the battle to feed itself. Malnutrition and hunger are on the increase. The postwar peak in African per capita grain production of 180 kilograms came in 1967. By 1982, it had fallen 20 percent. In 1983, it fell an additional 14 percent because of the continentwide drought. Although in 1970 Africa was nearly self-sufficient in food, by 1984 imports had reached 24 million tons (table 4-5). That so many Africans are starving today is a tragedy, but the even greater tragedy is

Table 4-5. *Changes in World Grain Trade, 1950–84*
(millions of tons)

Region	1950	1960	1970	1980	1984[a]
North America	+23	+39	+56	+131	+126
Australia and New Zealand	+3	+6	+12	+19	+20
Latin America	+1	0	+4	−10	−4
Eastern Europe and U.S.S.R.	0	0	0	−46	−51
Africa	0	−2	−5	−15	−24
Asia	−6	−17	−37	−63	−80
Western Europe	−22	−25	−30	−16	+13

Note: Plus sign indicates net exports, minus sign, net imports.
a. Preliminary.
Sources: FAO (1976b, 1980b, 1981b); USDA (1983c, 1984e); adjustments by Worldwatch Institute.

that African governments and the international community are doing so little about the causes. More often than not, food price policies are designed to pacify urban consumers rather than to stimulate development in the countryside. Except for a few countries such as Kenya, soil conservation programs are largely nonexistent. African leaders are only beginning to sense the urgency of slowing population growth. Family planning programs, where they exist, are still in an embryonic stage.

After Africa, food security is deteriorating most rapidly in mountainous developing countries, largely because their ecosystems are fragile and highly vulnerable to mismanagement. Land hunger in the Andean countries—Bolivia, Chile, Ecuador, and Peru—is evident in the push of unterraced farming up the mountainsides. It is obvious even to the casual observer that much of the soil on the steeply sloping, freshly plowed mountainsides will soon be washed away, leaving only bare rock and hungry people. One of the most fragile mountain ecosystems is that of Nepal. Grain production per person there peaked in 1961 and has declined some 27 percent since then (USDA 1984c). Nothing is pending in Nepal in either farming or family planning that promises to arrest this deterioration in the foreseeable future.

Food Prices: The Bottom Line

Assessing the food prospect is not simply a matter of determining in a technical sense how much food the world's farmers can produce. The real issue is the cost of food production and the relationship of this cost to the purchasing power of the billion and a half poorest people in the world, who already spend most of their income on food.

The cost of food production is determined by the resources available, such as land, water, fertilizer, and pesticides, and the skill with which they are combined. Historically, advancing technology has more than offset any restrictions imposed by resource availability, but this has been less true in the past decade. As a result, growth in food production has slowed.

As noted earlier, growth in the world cropland area is now slight. Although irrigation has recently played a major role in boosting land productivity, for much of humanity, water is becoming scarce. Perhaps the most important force driving up the cost of food production is the shrinking cropland per person. Given the difficulties of expanding cropland area and the momentum of world population growth, this pattern is certain to continue.

As the harvested area per person moves toward one-tenth of a hectare at the turn of the century, farmers will have to apply ever larger amounts of fertilizer to maintain per capita food output, contributing to higher production costs. As the amount of fertilizer required to satisfy food needs continues to increase, the world is faced with two rising cost curves. The first is the additional expenditure due to shrinking cropland per person. The second is the rising cost of energy, which will increase the cost per unit of chemical fertilizer.

For the world as a whole to reestablish the upward trend in per capita food production, either the growth of food production must accelerate or population growth must slow down. Given the resource constraints described earlier—land, water, and energy—reestablishing a 3 percent rate of growth in food production will be difficult. The hope of reducing hunger thus rests more heavily than ever on population policies and family planning programs.

Headlines describing food price protests and food riots are becoming commonplace: witness recent demonstrations in Brazil (Hoge 1983), the Dominican Republic (Hornblower 1984), Morocco (Randal 1984), Poland (*New York Times* 1983), and Tunisia (Rupert 1984). Rising demands on the earth's food-producing resources as some 81 million people are added each year are beginning to translate into political unrest and instability.

PART II

The Implications
of Programs
to Increase Production

Increasing agricultural production in the developing world has been a primary concern of national policymakers and international development agencies for many years. By now something of a consensus exists about how increased production can be achieved. Improved farming technologies, which are the results of scientific research, must be available to farmers, along with full information on how to use the new technologies. Essential inputs, such as fertilizer and improved seed, must be readily available, and sometimes capital investments must be made. Often farmers will need credit to finance inputs and other investments. Lastly, this new production package must make economic sense for farmers, which implies that a good market must exist with reliable demand for the farmers' products at remunerative prices.

The use of modern inputs, which must be paid for in cash, implies that even the farm family that farms primarily for subsistence must sell some produce to pay for the inputs. The additional production should, in theory, more than pay for the cost of the inputs; otherwise the family may finish up worse off. Clearly the level of risk is a central issue. When availability of inputs, reliability of output, or prices of inputs or outputs vary too much, the risk of adopting a new technology will override the possible gain. In sum, incentives to increase production must be clear and all of the means to respond to them must be reliably available.

A number of good texts and collections of readings on agricultural production and agricultural development, several of which are listed in the Introduction, discuss these major issues. The selections in this section focus instead on issues that have begun to emerge in recent years as a consequence of the experience gained by those working to increase agricultural production.

Several distinct areas are treated. The first is the impact of technological change, specifically the green revolution, and the direct and indirect effects of increasing overall production. Per Pinstrup-Andersen and Peter B. R. Hazell look at these impacts, particularly at the charges that negative effects have resulted—for example, that fluctuations in production have increased, that small farmers have been bypassed by the new technologies, causing uneven distribution of benefits, and that low-income producers and consumers have been made poorer. The authors conclude that while some of these things have happened, the causes are complex. Technological change may, depending on the environment in which it takes place, either exacerbate such problems or solve them, and the indirect effects of agricultural growth, including income and employment generation in rural economies, are substantial and measurable.

The rest of part II deals with other difficulties and opportunities inherent in introducing technological changes and the relationships between technological change and social and institutional issues. Some groups of producers have been particularly difficult to reach: low-income farmers with few resources and low ability to take risks are the ones on whom Graeme Donovan focuses, while producers living in poor and ecologically difficult areas are discussed by Bruce M. Koppel. A staff group from the FAO notes the importance of women as agricultural producers, especially in Africa, and the critical contribution they make to their families' nutritional well-being. The group points out, however, that new technology may impinge on women's time in ways that interfere with their ability to maintain this contribution. The group suggests that particular attention needs to be paid to developing technologies suitable to the tasks, both agricultural and domestic, for which women are responsible. Then, if women are to make good use of these technologies, information must be made available to them through programs adjusted to their work and time allocation patterns.

Shlomo Reutlinger addresses the circumstances under which agricultural projects can have nutritionally negative effects and suggests that once these situations are clearly understood, project designers may be better able to avoid them. John S. Caldwell describes farming systems research, an approach to introducing change that has been developed over the past several years in an attempt to deal with some of the problems noted by other authors in this part. Farming systems research recognizes that inducing technological change is a complex process that causes many effects throughout a farming system. Taking a systems approach leads to a better understanding of farms as complex organizations with many components and helps ensure that the changes promoted will make the whole system function better. Joachim von Braun and Eileen Kennedy look analytically at the currently very controversial topic of the relationship between food and cash crops. They find that cash crops occupy nearly half the cultivated area in developing countries and contribute substantially to higher incomes for farmers who grow them. Little evidence supports a contention that cash crops lead to nutritionally adverse effects, except in isolated local instances.

The issues treated in part II form a complementary set—or perhaps a secondary round—of issues relating to the primary issues of inputs, credit, and prices. They are, however, issues that in recent years experts have found to be crucial to achieving the central task of increasing agricultural production in developing countries.

5

The Impact of the Green Revolution and Prospects for the Future

Per Pinstrup-Andersen and Peter B. R. Hazell

The importance of the interaction between technological change and the institutional policy environment has been recognized in much of the debate about the impact of the green revolution, but a great deal of the literature has failed to distinguish between the impacts of the two. This has led to the argument that the green revolution was to blame for undesirable developments that occurred as a consequence of inappropriate institutions and policies. The nature of the technology plays a certain role, but where policies and institutions have been favorable, the distribution of the benefits from the green revolution has been widespread, and where they have been unfavorable and appropriate changes have not been made, the potential of the green revolution to promote economic growth, reduce poverty, and facilitate self-sustaining development has not been fully exploited.

The Impact of the Green Revolution on Food Production

The impact of the green revolution on wheat and rice production is a function of both the area sown with the new wheat and rice varieties and the increase in yields per unit of land. Because increasing yields have made rice and wheat more profitable for farmers than some other crops, more land has been brought into cultivation of these two crops.

The green revolution has also facilitated significant expansion of irrigation and multiple cropping because the new crop varieties have

Excerpted from "The Impact of the Green Revolution and Prospects for the Future," *Food Review International*, vol. 1, no. 1 (1985), pp. 1–25, by courtesy of Marcel Dekker, Inc.

shorter growing periods and reduced sensitivity to day length and can therefore be grown in different latitudes. Agriculturists estimate that between one-third and one-half of the rice areas in the developing world are planted with high-yielding varieties (HYVs) and that total annual production increases due to the use of rice HYVs are around 2.5 million tons per year in Latin America, worth approximately $500 million (CIAT 1981). Although these estimates are rough and subject to considerable error, they do indicate that the production impact is very large. Evidence from Asia supports a similar conclusion. Herdt and Capule (1983) estimate that in 1980, modern rice varieties added 27 million tons to the production of rice in eight Asian countries that produce 85 percent of Asia's rice (Bangladesh, Burma, China, India, Indonesia, Philippines, Sri Lanka, and Thailand). The use of fertilizers added another 29 million tons, and irrigation contributed 34 million tons. Note that as HYVs generally have a higher response to fertilizers and possibly to other inputs, a clear distinction between the contribution of each factor is difficult.

The wheat areas grown with modern varieties are of magnitudes similar to those for rice. Researchers estimate that these varieties were grown on about 30 million hectares during 1976–77 (Pinstrup-Andersen 1982b) and about 35 million today (James 1983). However, since much more land is used for rice than for wheat in developing countries, modern varieties occupy a larger percentage of the wheat area. Estimates of the contribution of new HYVs to increased wheat production in developing countries vary from 7 to 27 million tons per year, worth $1,200 to $2,500 million (James 1983; Pinstrup-Andersen 1982a; CIMMYT 1978). The large difference in the estimates is due primarily to the different assumptions about average yield increases. However, irrespective of whether the actual increase is closer to the lower or the higher estimates, it is still impressive.

While the term green revolution originally referred to wheat and rice, researchers have developed high-yielding varieties for a number of other food crops important to the developing countries. These include sorghum, maize, cassava, and beans. The area grown with improved maize varieties and hybrids derived from CIMMYT germ plasm in developing countries runs into millions of hectares (James 1983). Major efforts to develop high-yielding technologies for many other food crops grown under developing country conditions have begun more recently, and it is too soon to estimate the impact on global production. However, results for some crops in a few countries, such as beans and cassava in Cuba and beans in several Central American countries, show considerable promise. Similarly, results from farm trials of improved varieties and cultural practices for various food crops show great potential for yield increases.

The Impact of the Green Revolution
on Production Fluctuations

The green revolution has clearly enabled many developing countries to achieve impressive rates of growth in national foodgrain production since the mid-1960s. At the same time, however, the variability of national foodgrain production has also increased. Increased production variability can, in the absence of stabilization policies, lead to more volatile prices, creating problems for farmers and consumers alike. The degree of price instability induced can be quite large in countries where a high proportion of total production is consumed on the farm. This is because year to year fluctuations in production are then transmitted to relatively thin markets. In India, only one-third of foodgrain production is actually marketed, and farm price variability has more than doubled since the mid-1960s for wheat and rice.

Mehra (1981) and others argue that much of this increased instability is due to the widespread adoption of improved seed/fertilizer-intensive technologies since the mid-1960s (Barker and others 1981). The yields of crops grown with the new technologies may be more sensitive to year to year variations in input use arising from shortages or price changes.

Although it is an extreme example, the 1970 southern maize leaf blight epidemic, during which about 15 percent of the United States maize crop was lost, illustrates how maize yields have become increasingly correlated over time as varieties became more genotypically similar, with a common susceptibility to the same kinds of pest, disease, and weather conditions (Hargrove and others 1979). Similar problems exist in other crops and other areas of the world, such as Asia (Chang 1984). Plant breeders have recognized the risk associated with this loss in genetic variation and have in recent years attempted to reverse the trend.

Other causes of these increased yield correlations may be important. Kothare (1977) provides evidence that rainfall was more erratic in many parts of India during the more recent period of analysis. The use of fertilizers and irrigation on cereal crops has also increased at a time when the supplies of these inputs have become more variable. For example, an increase in use of electric irrigation pumps since the mid-1960s has coincided with increased irregularities in electricity supplies. Since power outages affect large areas of India simultaneously, they are likely to have a simultaneous effect on crop yields in many states. Other important sources of the increased variability in India's total cereal production were increases in the cropped area, in the year to year variability of the areas sown with individual crops, and in positive correlations between areas sown and yields.

Cereal yields in India are also responsive to price signals, increasingly so since the widespread adoption of input-intensive technologies. The standard deviation around the long-term growth trend of harvest prices for rice in West Bengal (the most important rice growing state) and for wheat in Uttar Pradesh (the most important wheat growing state) have both increased over ten-year periods (Hazell 1984). Since price variations affect all farmers, any adjustments they make in input use in response to price movements could lead to more highly correlated yields across states. In India, interstate yield correlations have increased for all crops except sorghum and minor millets.

Given the potential link between the new technologies and increased instability, should greater priority in agricultural research be given to reducing yield instability? In developing countries, continued growth in foodgrain production is of paramount importance, and any trade-off between breeding for growth and breeding for stability may prove costly. But a strengthening of ongoing efforts to develop genetic resistance or tolerance to pests may meet growth as well as stability goals. Also, some of the other important sources of increased variability in production are amenable to, or even the consequence of, government policy. For example, policies to provide more stable farm prices and electricity supplies could help stabilize cereal production in India.

Appropriate policy interventions can also alleviate some of the problems posed by increased instability. Storage schemes and international trade can stabilize food supplies for consumers, and credit and insurance schemes and futures markets can help farmers cope with yield risks. Governments could also give greater priority to increasing production in more stable areas and in areas where production is not strongly correlated with that in other regions.

The Direct Impact of the Green Revolution on Poverty and Nutrition

A number of early studies of the impact of the green revolution concluded that the rural poor did not receive their fair share of the benefits generated. Agriculturists argued that mostly large farmers adopted the new yield-increasing technology, leaving small farmers unaffected or even worse off because the green revolution resulted in (a) downward pressures on the prices of the commodities small farmers produced; (b) upward pressures on the prices of the inputs they purchased; (c) efforts by large farmers to either increase tenants' rents or force the tenants off the land; and, (d) attempts by large farmers to increase their landholdings by purchasing smaller farms, thus forcing small farmers into landlessness.

Furthermore, some agriculturists argued that the green revolution resulted in reduced rural employment. The net result, they said, was a rapid increase in the inequality of income and asset distribution and a worsening of rural poverty in areas affected by the green revolution (Griffin 1972, 1979; Harriss 1977; Fraenkel 1976; Hewitt de Alcantara 1976).

While others have always questioned the validity of these conclusions, recent studies have produced a sizable body of evidence that proves beyond reasonable doubt that as a general rule the green revolution has resulted in a significant improvement in the material well-being of the poor. First, the early studies failed to distinguish between early and subsequent adoption of new technology. While it was true that early adopters were primarily large farmers, these studies failed to recognize that small farmers would follow quickly once they saw the success of the new technologies under farm conditions. Second, the studies largely overlooked the benefits of lower prices to the poor as consumers of rice and wheat. Third, the studies gave little or no attention to the multiplier effects of the green revolution and the resulting impact on incomes of the rural poor. Fourth, the impact of the green revolution was frequently confused with the impact of institutional arrangements, agricultural policies, and labor-saving mechanization. Such confusion led to incorrect identification of the causes of rural poverty and thus incorrect recommendations for action to reduce poverty.

Five important factors determine the distribution of economic gains from technological change in agriculture, and therefore the direct impact on the poor. These are (a) the nature of the technology; (b) the general structure of the agricultural sector and the land tenure system in particular; (c) the structure of the markets for inputs, such as fertilizers and labor, and for credit; (d) the market for agricultural products; and (e) the prevailing agricultural policy.

The poor may be affected by the green revolution through changes in their assets, income, and/or the prices they pay for food. The impact on a particular household is influenced by the extent to which it depends on rice or wheat for its income and the importance of these commodities in the household budget. The impact will differ among poor producers, landless laborers, and poor consumers.

Impact on Poor Producers

Producers have widely adopted high-yielding wheat and rice varieties irrespective of farm size and tenurial status. In many regions suited for the high-yielding varieties, low-income farmers have adopted them to at least the same extent as larger farmers, and the most recent studies suggest that net gains per unit of land tend to be larger on smaller farms (Blyn 1983; Herdt and Capule 1983; Prahladachar 1983; Byerlee and Harrington 1982; Chaudhry 1982; Pinstrup-Andersen 1982a). However, many regions are not suited for high-yielding rice and wheat varieties. Thus the green revolution has contributed to a considerable change in regional income distribution in some countries, as illustrated in India. The green revolution has primarily benefited producers who control optimal production environments or who have access to such environments, irrespective of farm size, and in some countries, particularly in Latin America, the larger and better-off farmers tend to control the best production environments. In many other areas, including those where good soil has been distributed through land reforms, such environments are often controlled by low-income farmers.

The most important lesson from these findings is that soil quality, access to irrigation water, and other aspects of the physical production environment are much more important in determining adoption patterns than farm size. Therefore, as long as new technology is suited only or mainly for optimal production environments, farmers without access to such environments, irrespective of farm size, will not benefit. While a great deal of research is now under way to increase the productivity of less favored areas, available technology is still limited.

The impact of technological change on poor farmers depends very much on institutions and policies. Although in many developing countries small farmers generally use available land more efficiently than those with larger farms, policymakers often see large farms as more desirable. Therefore, attempts by early adopters of the green revolution technology to enlarge their farms by land purchase or termination of rental arrangements were supported by public policy. Such policies were fueled during early phases of the green revolution by the belief that smaller farmers would not adopt new technologies. Hindsight reveals that what was needed during those initial phases was policy measures and institutional changes to reduce the time lag between the adoption of the new technology on large and on small farms, such as the removal of input market constraints for small farmers.

Until a few years ago, indications suggested that a combination of early adoption, generation of large economic gains among large farmers, and policies adverse to small farmers led to increasing land concentration and increasing numbers of landless farm workers during the initial phases of the green revolution. However, solid empirical evidence that this is a widespread phenomenon does not exist. While changes in land tenure have occurred, the role of the green revolution is not clear. Demographic pressures, regional migration, and other factors may have been important.

Impact on Landless Labor

The green revolution is based on a combination of new production inputs: seed varieties with high yield potential, fertilizers, irrigation, and in some cases, chemical pesticides and mechanization. One result of this combined package has been higher labor productivity and increased labor demand. In areas with high unemployment and an abundant labor supply, this has resulted in a considerable expansion in employment. In regions with little unemployment and limited labor supply, considerable wage increases have occurred. However, migration of labor from other regions and availability of labor-saving mechanical technology have limited such wage increases. Also, in many regions where technological change has made a significant impact on production, real wages have increased little if at all in spite of increased labor demand. The primary reason is that these regions have also experienced high rates of population growth, and the growth in labor demand may merely have kept pace with the growth in the labor force. The important question is how the landless would have fared in the absence of the technological change. Clearly they would have been worse off without the growing demand for labor.

Mechanical technology has not always reduced employment. Much of the investment in irrigation equipment, and in some cases investments in machines for land preparation and harvesting, has resulted in large production increases, due partly to a shorter cropping season and expansion from single to double cropping. The result has been increased employment. However, in many cases mechanization has been introduced for the explicit purpose of reducing labor demands while the output effects have been minimal. For example, Binswanger (1978) concluded that existing studies of the effects of tractors in South Asia failed to provide evidence that they substantially contributed to increases in cropping intensity, yields, and timeliness, but they did substitute for labor. Investment in labor-saving technology has frequently been a reaction to labor shortages at the local level and to difficulties in labor management. Increasing labor mobility, whether within or among countries, would make such investments less attractive while increasing employment.

Impact on Poor Consumers

Empirical evidence of consumer gains from technological change in developing country agriculture is plentiful (for example, Pinstrup-Andersen 1979; Scobie 1979; Evenson and Flores 1978; Scobie and

Posada 1978; Akino and Hayami 1975; Mellor 1975). The consumer gains come about because food prices are lower than they would have been in the absence of the production increases induced by technological change. Import-substitution, export, and domestic price policies can dampen the price reduction. In fact, governments have used price and foreign trade policies extensively to strike a desired balance between the harmful effects of lower prices on farmers and future food production and the beneficial effects on consumers (see Timmer in part IV). Since the green revolution generates an economic surplus by more efficient use of resources and reduced unit costs, consumer gains need not imply producer losses. Both may gain.

The distribution of consumer gains between the poor and the rest depends primarily on the amount spent by each group on the commodities in question. In most cases, the poor spend less on wheat and rice than the better-off population; thus the latter obtain larger absolute gains. However, in many countries, the share of total incomes spent on wheat and rice is larger for the poor than for the better-off. Thus, real income gains relative to current incomes are larger for the poor (Pinstrup-Andersen 1977).

The Impact of the Green Revolution on Nutritional Status

Technological change in agriculture influences human nutrition through its impact on:

o The incomes acquired by households at risk of having malnourished or undernourished members

o The prices of food commodities

o The nature of the production systems among semisubsistence farmers

o The risks and fluctuations in food production, storage, prices, and incomes

o The nutrient composition of the foods available to malnourished households

o Household income composition, intrahousehold income and budget control, and women's time allocation

o Labor demand and energy expenditures

o Infectious diseases.

The degree to which expanded food production is translated into expanded food consumption by the malnourished varies greatly depending on the crop or livestock species for which production is expanded, the nature of the technology that brought about the expansion, and who produces the increase. Thus, using total production expansion as a proxy for nutritional impact is likely to be misleading.

Since nutritional problems are found among the urban as well as the rural poor, the most desirable technologies from a nutritional point of view are those developed for food commodities primarily produced by poor farmers or, if produced by better-off farmers, those which occupy a large share of the budget of poor consumers and which markedly increase the demand for farm labor. In many developing countries, particularly in Asia, wheat and rice are such commodities. In other countries, millet, sorghum, maize, cassava, or beans would better meet these criteria.

The higher productivity of rice and wheat relative to other crops for which no green revolution has yet occurred has led many farmers to substitute wheat or rice for other crops on their land. Nutritionists have expressed some concern that such substitution may have resulted in negative nutrition effects. Substitution of wheat for pulses in India is a case in point. However, the net impact of this substitution has been an increase in the production of energy and protein per unit of land (Ryan 1977). The impact on the poor and malnourished is not known.

Shifts from multiple cropping to monocropping present another risk of negative nutrition effects among semisubsistence farmers. Empirical evidence on this topic is very limited, and more research is needed to assess the nutrition effects of such shifts and how negative effects may be avoided and positive ones enhanced (Pinstrup-Andersen 1982b). In particular, further study of these and other on-farm linkages between agricultural production activities and the nutritional status of the semisubsistence farm family as part of farming systems research would be useful.

The Indirect Income and Employment Effects of the Green Revolution

The indirect effects of technological change and agricultural growth can substantially increase the demand for goods and services, thereby stimulating economic growth (Lele and Mellor 1981; Mellor and Lele 1973). An empirical study of agricultural and industrial performance in India (Rangarajan 1982) found that a 1 percent addition to the agricultural growth rate stimulated a 0.5 percent addition to the growth rate of industrial output and a 0.7 percent addition to the growth rate of national income. At a regional level, in a province in the Philippines Gibb (1974) found that each 1 percent increase in agricultural income generated a 1 to 2 percent increase in employment in most sectors of the local nonfarm economy. Similarly, a study of technological change in rice in Malaysia (Bell and others 1982) found that for each dollar of income created directly in agriculture by the project, an additional 80 cents of value added was created indirectly in the local nonfarm economy.

An important aspect of growth linkages to the nonfarm economy is that they are predominantly due to increases in household consumption expenditure. In the Malaysian study, about two-thirds of the 80 percent "income multiplier" was due to increased rural household demand for consumer goods and services. Only one-third was due to agriculture's increased demand for inputs and processing, transport, and marketing services. These findings strongly support Mellor's contention that because much of the accepted wisdom on development strategy ignores these consumption linkages, it has tended to seriously underestimate the potential importance of agriculture (Mellor 1976).

In addition to enhancing agriculture's contribution to national economic growth, the existence of strong consumer expenditure linkages between agricultural households and the nonfarm economy is important for two other reasons. First, the income and employment generated by these linkages is predominately concentrated in rural areas. Rurally focused growth is desirable in many countries where rural areas have been severely disadvantaged in the past through urban-biased policies (Lipton 1977). Such policies have encouraged excessive migration from rural to urban areas and have exacerbated problems of rural underemployment. Second, the kinds of goods and services demanded are typically produced by small labor-intensive enterprises. They are focused on such sectors as transportation, hotels and restaurants, entertainment, personal services, health, distributive trades, and housing and residential construction. Increased household demands for specialized agricultural products, particularly fresh fruits and vegetables and fish and livestock products, can also provide important increases in rural employment.

Strong household links to the rural nonfarm economy not only help alleviate problems of rural underemployment; because the major beneficiaries of the increased employment earnings are typically the poor, they also contribute to the reduction of rural poverty and malnutrition. Survey evidence from many countries confirms that small farmers and landless workers obtain substantial shares of their total income from nonagricultural sources. Consequently, the beneficiaries of the indirect employment gains generated by agricultural growth need not be limited to poor nonagricultural households residing in towns. Rather, the potential beneficiaries include a wide range of occupation groups within the poor segments of society.

The indirect benefits from agricultural growth are not restricted to the poor. They can increase the earnings of skilled workers as well as provide lucrative returns to capital and to managerial skills. In the Malaysian study, for example, the indirect benefits of the project were skewed in favor of the nonfarm households in the region, many of which were relatively well off. Even among agricultural households, the landed households fared better than the landless. The point is that although the indirect effects of agricultural growth do not necessarily improve the relative distribution of income within rural areas, they can still have wide-reaching effects in alleviating absolute poverty.

Lessons for the Future

What are some of the lessons learned from recent studies of the green revolution? First, it has become abundantly clear that the technological barriers to expanded food production among small and large farmers in developing countries can be alleviated.

Another lesson learned from the green revolution is that while technological change in agriculture provides a vehicle for development that reaches far beyond the more immediate goals of satisfying food and nutrition needs, its full potential for achieving growth as well as equity goals will be realized only if it is properly integrated into the overall development strategy and accompanied by appropriate public policy and institutional changes. The short-term impact on the poor is particularly sensitive to institutional arrangements and public policies. Where existing institutions favor very unequal asset and income distributions, technological change has tended to amplify the inequality. However, although the impact on the relative income distribution varies among regions, in most cases the green revolution has contributed to higher incomes of both poor and rich.

The principal message coming from recent studies of the role of women in technological change in agriculture is that gender specificity in labor activities, decision making in production and consumption, and the general level of well-being among the rural poor are important issues to be considered explicitly in technology design and diffusion as well as in related policies and institutional changes (Agarwal 1983; C. W. Jones 1983; Unnevehr and Standford 1983; White 1983; Lewis 1981; Tinker 1979a). Ignoring these gender specificities may lead to inappropriate technologies and policies from the point of view of both growth and equity.

To further reduce rural poverty and inequalities, policy measures and institutional changes should focus on the uneven distribution of the ownership of productive resources, inequitable power structures, poor training and education, differential access to factor and product markets, and lack of access to health facilities. Such measures might include land reform, development of infrastructure and irrigation facilities, improved marketing facilities, access to credit for the poor, expansion of health facilities for the poor, and a series of other government interventions to change the socioeconomic environment and strengthen human resources.

In addition to those interventions aimed at self-sustaining, long-term reductions in rural poverty, income transfers to the poor, such as food and credit subsidies, are needed to alleviate poverty and malnutrition in the short run. This does not mean that technological change should await such policies and institutional changes. Technological change is needed to generate an economic surplus that, together with appropriate policies and institutional changes, will facilitate growth and reduce poverty. However, technological change by itself cannot be expected to remove serious inequities. The interaction between technological change and government policies is complex, and additional research on this matter is urgently needed to facilitate effective policy design in pursuit of growth and equity goals.

Although the most obvious successes of recent technological change in agriculture pertain to wheat and rice grown under relatively good physical environments, ongoing agricultural research is likely to result in significant yield and production gains for other crops under less favorable production environments. Furthermore, if such gains are to materialize, investors in agricultural research must make a long-term commitment and should not expect quick results. Agricultural research must be viewed as an investment with a high but long-term payoff. However, unless new, highly visible successes in crops other than rice and wheat come about relatively soon, the incentive for continued support of agricultural research at current or increasing levels may begin to falter.

An extremely difficult food production situation has already arisen in sub-Saharan Africa. While the causes are complex, it is possible that this situation could have been avoided if massive investments in agricultural research, including manpower training for the food crops and production environments of sub-Saharan Africa, had been made during the past 20 to 25 years. The lesson to be learned is not that hindsight is better than foresight but that such massive long-term investments in agricultural research are long overdue.

A continuation of current efforts to find "quick fixes" through price policies and increased dependence on export crop production as a substitute rather than a complement to long-term investments in research, training, and technological change will not lead to self-sustaining improvements in food production and human nutrition in Africa. Neither will it provide the vehicle for the economic growth so badly needed in African agriculture. But technological change just might provide such a vehicle.

6

Broadening Production Increase Programs to Reach Low-Income Farmers

Graeme Donovan

The literature on agricultural production focuses on the generation and introduction of new technologies, availability of inputs and credit, incentives—especially price incentives—to the farmer, infrastructure building, and institutional support. These are widely agreed to be the main issues. This paper concentrates on certain specific aspects of these issues, an understanding of which is now essential for making sound agricultural policy. Some of these issues are particularly critical in programs designed to meet the needs of poorer farmers and those farming the more difficult lands of the world—very often the same people.

Demand-Led Growth in Agricultural Production and the Role of New Technologies

Families with very low incomes spend more than 75 percent of their income on food. Furthermore, if their incomes increase, they spend a high proportion of each additional amount of income on food. If their incomes continue to rise, however, the proportion of additional income spent on food begins to decline, and the pattern of spending on different food commodities changes. A low-income family may, for example, spend 60 percent of additional income on food grains, 9 percent on livestock products, 5 percent on vegetable oils, 4 percent on sweeteners, and 1 percent on other foods, with very little on other family needs such as clothing and education. By contrast, a higher-income family experiencing an income increase may spend only 6 percent of the addition on food grains, 4 percent on vegetable oils,

Excerpted from Production Increase Programs, background note for Economic Development Institute Food Policy Seminar, World Bank, 1984; processed.

and 2 percent on sweeteners, but 15 percent on livestock products, 12 percent on other foods, and five times as much as the low-income family on education.

From changes in preferences as incomes change springs the pattern of demand for agricultural products, which helps to determine the pattern of agricultural growth. Research has shown that families begin to substitute one starchy staple food, often wheat or rice, for another, often a coarse grain or starchy root, even at extremely low levels of income. This suggests that these consumers at least perceive their diets to be nutritionally adequate at that point, which suggests in turn that some estimates of the extent of undernutrition may be exaggerated. As incomes rise, families partially shift their demand to foods that are more valuable nutritionally, such as eggs, milk, meat, fish, vegetables, and fruits, and partially to foods that have less nutritional value, such as polished rice, instead of rough rice or legumes, which have greater food value but lower status.

Since these changing patterns of demand depend upon both income and relative commodity prices, policymakers have room to shape the demand pattern, to some extent, through measures relating to prices and incomes. What is most important, however, is for policymakers to understand the fundamental shifts in demand that occur as incomes rise, because these shifts are the basis for the major economic changes that occur with development. These changes include the shifting relative importance of food grains, legumes, sugar, oilseeds, livestock products, vegetables, fruits, beverages, cotton, other fiber crops, tobacco, and specialty crops; the eventual relative decline of the agricultural sector as a whole; and the changes in productivity in that sector that lead to an outflow of workers to other parts of the economy.

During 1960–82, a small but noticeable shift occurred in the global allocation of cereals as food for humans and feed for livestock. For all cereals taken together, the proportion fed to livestock rose from just over 32 percent in the early 1960s to just over 36 percent in the early 1980s. A shift away from the coarse grains has also occurred. Wheat, rice, and maize together now account for 78 percent of all cereals, compared with 71 percent in the early 1960s. Wheat and rice alone make up about 50 percent of current production versus 46 to 47 percent in the early 1960s.

An interesting example of a shift in demand at a fairly high level of aggregation is the case of tea in India. In the medium-term past, India's tea consumption was rising at 6 to 7 percent per year, while production rose at only 2.6 percent per year. In the past two years, with good monsoons and higher agricultural incomes, domestic tea

Table 6-1. *Wheat Prices, 1890–1982*
(1967 U.S. dollars per bushel, Kansas City #3 wheat)

Year	Price per bushel	Year	Price per bushel
1890	3.09	1950	2.72
1900	2.44	1960	2.10
1910	3.01	1970	1.34
1920	3.08	1980	1.40
1930	2.02	1984 (preliminary)	1.20
1940	2.15		

consumption rose exceptionally rapidly, cutting exports from 72 percent of production in 1951 to 35 percent in 1984. In spite of this diversion, strong domestic demand has pushed local prices to record levels. The government restricted exports to take the edge off these prices twice in a nine-month period.

The price signals to which farmers react arise from the marketplace in which the demand and the supply of a certain commodity interact. On the supply side, the important elements that govern amounts produced are the relative prices of inputs, the available production technologies, and the relative profitabilities of specific farm enterprises. The mix of these elements in the case of wheat, for example, has led to a long-term downward trend in price, in real terms, as illustrated in table 6-1.

In other words, the demand for wheat has spurred technological changes that have allowed substantially greater quantities of wheat to be supplied over the years. Farmers have found it profitable to keep growing wheat in spite of the falling prices because the productivity of wheat-growing land has increased rapidly. In the past 15 years, the global area of wheat harvested has increased 20 percent, from just over 200 million hectares to about 240 million hectares, while average yields have increased almost 40 percent, from around 1.5 tons to about 2.1 tons per hectare. During the same period, by contrast, world production of pulses, where new technology has not been available, has virtually stagnated. In one of the leading producing countries, India, production in the early 1980s has been only at levels achieved 30 years previously, and per capita availability fell more than 30 percent between 1957 and 1982. The price has risen substantially, but with a stagnant production technology even higher prices have not made the crop attractive to farmers. As legumes are the most important vegetable source of protein, it is likely that this has had undesirable nutritional effects. The rising prices have certainly made it more difficult for the poor to afford legumes.

A lowering of market prices of basic foods over time is extremely important for low-income groups, who are significant purchasers of food and include most landless families, the smallest farmers in rural areas, and the urban poor. For families in these groups, falling real food prices represent rising real incomes. For farmers, of course, falling prices are disincentives to production. This gives rise to one of the most fundamental policy dilemmas concerning food production in development. For the major foodgrains, what one writer has called "the technological treadmill" has played a key role in helping to resolve this dilemma and sustain growth in the face of falling real prices. Even with new technologies available, however, considerable skill in "getting prices right" for basic foodstuffs is needed to balance the interests of consumers and producers (see Timmer in part IV).

The Farm Family and Technological Change

Unlike other productive sectors of the economy, agriculture is organized into a huge number of small family production units. Policymakers concerned with raising farm production should appreciate the complexity of decision making this implies. For any kind of change in production to take place on a wide scale, millions of decisionmakers have to be convinced to adopt whatever innovations will make such production changes possible. Furthermore, in most cases the decisions emerge from families rather than from single managers, so that many competing and sometimes conflicting factors complicate the decision process. Work and home, employment and leisure are intertwined in agriculture much more closely than in other sectors. The appearance of a new production possibility may set in motion a series of negotiations and decisions within the family in which traditional roles, power, asset balances, and status all play their part in the decision making as well as being affected by it. These negotiations may include such things as the allocation of food among male and female adults and children; the balance between home-consumed and marketed production; the amount of off-farm wage labor sought by various family members and its timing throughout the year; the allocation of time (especially by women) among crop and livestock production, field crops and home gardens, fuelwood and water collection, household maintenance, childcare, food preparation, marketing activities, and participation in ceremonies and other social affairs; the balance of consumption expenditures among food, clothing, education, health, shelter, traditional ceremonies, and consumer durables and between consumption and saving; the investment profile; and so on.

A common mistake is to underestimate the role of women both in agricultural production itself and in the wider decision-making processes in the family (see FAO in part II). Another common error is not to take a wide enough view of the effects of a change in farming practice and to wonder why an apparently beneficial change is not adopted when a more careful analysis would show its net effect to be negative for family welfare. One example is the apparent paradox that adoption of high-yielding varieties of food grains may in some situations adversely affect family nutrition. The process may start with a new emphasis in the family on producing a marketable surplus of, say, rice, using a high-yielding modern variety that will bring the family into the cash economy on a scale never experienced before. The new rice variety needs a lot more labor for weeding and other tasks traditionally performed by women. Intensified participation by women in these field cropping activities may compete with another of their traditional tasks, care of a home vegetable garden, so that the garden is neglected in the drive for cash production that is perhaps forced through in the family by a husband who may also assume control over the cash from rice sales. The family's diet may suffer as a result of not having the quantity and variety of vegetables it had previously, even though its cash income is higher than before, if the income is used for nonfood purposes, including reinvestment in the farm.

There are other documented effects of changing the roles of men and women, and especially of changing the demands made on them for labor. Several studies estimate that women in farm families work longer hours than men, and that in most cases a demand for more of their labor in some farm activity leads to a decrease in effort elsewhere. Evidence from the Philippines suggests that food preparation may suffer, leading in turn to a lower-quality family diet. Another study documents premature weaning of children. In Cameroon, when families contracted to produce rice commercially on government-owned land (for which husbands received the cash proceeds), wives worked on the rice transplanting only when they were paid to compensate them for loss of sorghum in their own fields as a result of less weeding. (Sorghum weeding clashed with rice transplanting in the month of July.)

Other studies suggest that increasing the cash incomes of women has more certain positive effects on family nutrition than does increasing men's income. When women are thrown out of wage labor by modern harvesting technology, for example, the loss of income may affect their families' nutrition adversely. The women's activities in gathering fuel must be a central consideration for farm forestry projects. Rural water supply schemes that place their outlets inconveniently for women, their chief users, may have much less than the expected effects on reducing diseases spread by poor hygiene in food preparation. Much more attention is also needed to developing labor-saving improvements in food processing and cooking technologies.

Rainfed Farming and Its Constraints

As we have seen, it is vital for policymakers to understand how the farm family works if policies are to achieve their intended results. Equally important, scientists must understand how the farm works, what constrains farmers' agricultural decisions, and how various elements of biological systems interact with one another if they are to devise new, productive technologies that will succeed.

The total area in the world that is arable or under permanent crops is about 1.47 billion hectares, while the total area irrigated is estimated to be only 213 million hectares, approximately 14 percent as much as the arable area. Furthermore, at least some of the land nominally under irrigation does not enjoy water control sufficient to allow perennial cropping or even single cropping of maximum intensity. The majority of the world's crops are therefore grown under rainfed conditions, subject to the numerous risks which that implies. For a considerable proportion of this area, the rainfall is so low in quantity and so uncertain in timing as to make water the overriding constraint that determines the timing and scope of various husbandry practices as well as overall crop performance.

A farmer depending on erratic and uncertain rains pays very close attention to the weather—in monsoonal areas, for example, searching the skies daily in May or early June, looking with great anticipation for the small clouds that herald the approach of the rains. The initial plowing of the land is often done only after early rains have softened the soil. The choice of crop may depend on the degree of certainty with which rain is expected. In drier areas of Burma, for example, farmers plant sesame rather than the more profitable groundnut because if the early rains fail after planting, as they frequently do, it is not so great a loss to replow the land and plant sesame a second time. The seeds for groundnut are much more expensive and are not worth the risk to these farmers. In rainfed agriculture, the pattern of rainfall after planting will help to determine the degree of weediness, the scope of insect attacks, whether or not destructive flooding occurs, the timing of interrow cultivation and of the harvest, the size of the harvest, the magnitude of drying problems for both grain and straw, pest attacks during storage, and so on.

To deal with these uncertainties, farmers have devised various strategies to give themselves more control over the complex, unpredictable physical and biological environment with which they have to deal, usually by creating possibilities for making numerous decisions in sequence as the season progresses. In many rainfed areas, particularly in Africa, strategies involve repeated interplanting of crops among other crops, creating plots and subplots with different mixtures. This requires complicated decisions about times of planting, spacing of different crops, density of planting any particular crop, and, above all, the allocation of labor to various activities. The procurement and storage of inputs (especially seeds and fertilizers) also requires sometimes tricky scheduling in this setting.

The improved husbandry practice most strongly affected by expectations about rainfall is the use of fertilizer. Where rainfall is adequate, most crops will respond to fertilizer, and it becomes worthwhile to adopt better crop varieties bred specifically to respond to fertilizer. Where water supply is inadequate, however, crops may not respond at all, or fertilizer may actually harm the crop by burning it. In any case, traditional varieties adapted to local conditions may give at least some minimum yield under low rainfall, while new varieties with high potential may fail completely. The decision about application of fertilizer is often a complex and risky one, especially since for many farmers it represents their first use of an input for which they have to pay cash or take out credit. Research on soil, water, and plant management under risky conditions of low and erratic rainfall that improves the effectiveness of water supply use might pay off better than fertilizer subsidies, for example, in encouraging fertilizer use.

Another complicating factor in rainfed farming is the source of power used. The move from human-powered, hand-hoe husbandry (which may involve either shifting or sedentary cultivation) to one using livestock draft is not merely a substitution of one input for another, but a change in the entire farming system. Livestock draft implies sedentary cultivation, and farmers must learn how to manage and look after animals, which requires specialized husbandry practices. A livestock-powered agriculture is characterized by many links between humans, animals, and plants through use of crop wastes and by-products as feeds, recycling of animal wastes to the fields or for use as fuel, production of animal by-products such as milk, meat, and hides for sale or home use, stabling of animals (frequently within the family household), changes in the rhythm of daily work, and so on.

If at a later stage mechanical power is substituted for animal power, substantial adjustments are needed in the off-farm systems to support and sustain the mechanization. These include a good transport and communications infrastructure, a reliable supply of clean, uniform fuel, a flow of spare parts and access to repair and maintenance facilities, the emergence of a substantial cadre of persons trained in machine operation and repair, the growth of assembly and manufacturing industries, dealer networks, and provision of credit facilities to support all these activities with appropriate financial instruments.

During the rainy season, the stress is greatest on poor families in rural areas. They find it increasingly difficult at this time to find remunerative work, and they run down their food supplies and begin undereating. Undernutrition combines with infectious diseases (which are at their peak because of hot and moist weather conditions), making it difficult or impossible to get any of the work that is available. Survival may depend, in some cases, on borrowing, which may lead to an inescapable burden of indebtedness. If the poor are small farmers, this may then affect possibilities for future investment and farm productivity. In the worst case, they may even lose their land altogether.

Because of some or all of the above considerations, small farmers are generally not in favor of taking significant risks, including adopting new practices that have considerable risk of failure attached to them. This means that research must produce new technologies that are either relatively safe or have a payoff sufficiently high to compensate a farmer for risks taken in adopting them. Farmers will generally not adopt practices that threaten to jeopardize next year's food supply.

The point in sketching the interlocking systems that make up rainfed agriculture is to emphasize that attempts by outsiders to change and improve this kind of agriculture need to be made with the knowledge that the full implications of any particular change have to be thought through and understood if progress is to be made. Frequently interventions fail, and innovations that scientists have devised after considerable expenditure of time and money are not adopted by farmers because they simply do not address the real constraints farmers face and the decisions they have to make. In recent years, researchers have become more aware of this and have increasingly incorporated a "farming systems" perspective into research (see Caldwell in part II).

Such a thorough understanding of the farming system by researchers is vitally important, since from this may come both improvements within an existing system and entirely new systems that could completely replace the old. The latter may be appropriate in situations where the present system is overstressing an environment or where a completely new system represents a highly profitable alternative opportunity.

Generation of New Technologies

Research is not the only source of new technologies, but it is the major source in the modern world. In earlier times, farmers themselves were the originators of most of the technical advances. Such on-farm innovation continues, but the process of generating technical advances has accelerated markedly and become much more knowledge- and capital-intensive, requiring a thorough research effort. Today's research is conducted mainly by publicly funded agricultural research centers and by agribusiness concerns. The latter are involved in research when they can capture a large share of the economic return from their investment, such as in hybrid seeds, chemical technology (herbicides, insecticides, and drugs), animal feeding, and agricultural machinery and equipment. In other areas, research investments must be carried out by the public sector.

Global statistics and country sector studies suggest that national agricultural research is underfunded in many developing countries. On average, developing countries spend only one-third as much of their agricultural GDP on agricultural research as do developed countries, although agriculture is more than six times as important as a proportion of their overall economies (an average 20 percent of GDP versus 3 percent for the industrial countries) and investment in agricultural research has the highest rate of return among investments in the agriculture sector. The UNDP and the FAO recommend that agricultural research expenditures should reach 10 to 20 percent of total funds for agricultural development and at least 1 percent of agricultural GDP (UNDP and FAO 1984). Countries should give the highest priority to building national research systems with enough basic scientific capability to be able to borrow carefully both from other national systems and from the international institutes. Continued commitment to research over long periods of time is essential, and it is important to build up domestic support on a sustained basis, a difficult task in practice. In some past projects, the abilities of countries to sustain such expanded research through internally generated resources has been overestimated. In these cases, the long-term benefits from external assistance have been much lower than anticipated.

The shortage of human resources is at least as important a weakness as lack of funds in national agricultural research programs. The problems most often encountered are extreme fragmentation of research programs coupled with the absence of a coordinating body and the lack of qualified staff. The latter problem is pervasive and has received inadequate attention. Another major weakness of national agricultural programs, and the one that is also most widely acknowledged, relates to deficient links between research and extension. Effective links are essential not only to communicate research results but also to obtain feedback from farmers, thus putting pressure on research to be more responsive to farmers' needs. Links between research and extension have not been present traditionally in most countries. The two functions are commonly performed by widely separated organizations between which effective links are not easily or rapidly established. So-called "extension services" are too frequently absorbed in policing government regulations or collecting statistics to develop necessary ties of trust to farmers. Studies show that the closer the integration of research and extension, the more appropriate the final technological packages are likely to be.

Wheat, rice, and maize account for about 80 percent of the cereals eaten by humans and are therefore crops of paramount interest to low-income producers. Usually what people have in mind, however, when they speak about crops grown by low-income producers are the coarse cereals, especially sorghum and millets, the starchy roots, especially cassava, and the rather wide range of food legumes, which include many varieties of beans, peas, and lentils. Although much less concentrated research has been devoted to these than to wheat, rice, and maize, with a consequent lack of technological advances, in recent years all have been incorporated into serious international programs.

Another avenue of research aimed at low-income groups is that of encouraging and improving home gardens. Among the most interesting recent work at the Asian Vegetable Research and Development Center (AVRDC) has been the Nutrition Garden Program, on which research commenced in mid-1981. The AVRDC is studying four types of gardens: school (10 meters × 18 meters), home (4 meters × 4 meters), market (10 meters × 18 meters), and processing (10 meters × 18 meters). The achievement so far for home gardens is an output of 1.5 kilograms per day, giving a family of five the following percentages of recommended daily allowances: calcium 72 percent, iron 100 percent, vitamin A 128 percent, vitamin C 500 percent, and protein 21 percent. Effective home gardens with vegetables acceptable to consumers have been developed so far for Indonesia, the Philippines, and Thailand (Gershon 1983). The explicit aim of these programs is small-scale vegetable gardens for unemployed or very low-income people who nevertheless have access to small plots of land.

Throughout farming history there has been a need for periodic replacement of "worn-out" crop varieties as they succumb to pests and diseases that are themselves continuously adapting to circumstances. Farmers have always understood this and have traditionally selected strains and varieties to replace worn-out plants. They have been able to do this because there has been a wide range of strains to choose from and great genetic diversity even within their own fields. If they visited other villages, they were able to broaden the diversity from which to select. With modern plant breeding, however, new varieties with uniform genetic material have been introduced across large areas. This means that replacing worn-out varieties becomes a significant scientific task, since the new plants also have to have many desirable pest- and disease-resistance characters engineered into them at each replacement. The problem is heightened by the use of hybrids, for which new seeds must be developed every year. The maintenance process has been transferred, in effect, from farmers to scientists. As new, more uniform varieties become even more widely used and as agriculture continues to become more sophisticated, expenditure on maintenance research will need to be increased. It will be important to ensure that research designed to continue the technological advances (and not merely maintain them) does not suffer as a result.

Diffusion of New Technologies

The essential components of getting farmers to take up new technologies are transfer of knowledge, distribution of agricultural inputs, availability of credit and other agriservices to improve farmers' access to modern inputs, the existence of market outlets, and good incentive structures.

Four broad sets of activities are needed in the supply of farm inputs: seed breeding, certification, and multiplication; fertilizer mixing, compounding, and marketing; provision of crop and animal protection chemicals and services; and the supply, maintenance, and repair of farm equipment. Each of these needs a framework of regulations, standards, adaptive research, trials, and testing, as well as storage, transportation, and distribution arrangements that ensure timely supplies and services. The development of skilled people to manage and implement these activities may take considerable time. Diffusion of new technology is a matter of policy concern for governments, especially as it affects small farmers who do not always have equal access to the knowledge necessary to use new technology or to the agricultural and financial resources to make it productive on their own farms.

However, governments need not become directly involved in all components of the diffusion process. Truly profitable innovations often spread quickly, no matter what the government does, as long as the economic environment permits it. If the latter condition is not present, even though the government has made sure that extension, distribution, and credit are all available, a technical innovation may be halted in its tracks. When this occurs, government agents are quick to blame farmers for their resistance to change, but close analysis usually shows that the technical innovation is not financially worthwhile to farmers.

The components that make up the process of technology diffusion are interdependent and the absence of any one may impair the adoption of new techniques. Improving farmers' knowledge is not enough. If inputs or credit are not available, a government may have to organize input distribution programs and rural credit schemes, or modify the structure of incentives to ensure that provision of inputs and credit can be profitably carried out by the private sector.

Sometimes, the whole process of technology adoption among small farmers is effectively carried out by a commercial organization. This tends to occur when the technical change affects one particular commodity whose marketing through that organization is obligatory, thereby allowing it to recover costs from farmers' deliveries and to reap the benefits from production expansion. Successful examples of technology diffusion in the commercial realm include dairy improvement by the Indian dairy cooperatives, assistance to cotton growers by the Compagnie des Textiles in several Sahelian countries, and development of tree crops, especially oil palms, by large plantations. In such cases, the commercial entity usually ensures delivery of all three components: knowledge, inputs, and credit.

Although the public role in the diffusion of new technology can be and often has been overemphasized, evidence exists that where government extension services effectively transmit relevant information to farmers, they are an important complement to national research programs. The provision of inputs and agriservices through public sector programs is sometimes a useful, if less than ideal, means to promote technology adoption if the private sector fails to provide the necessary service for lack of incentives or for other reasons.

The training and visit extension system (T&V) deserves special mention because it has embodied many of the lessons of experience with agricultural extension. Recognizing that an extension service can be effective only if there is something useful to extend, T&V provides for strong links with research. These links are forged in various ways, including the conduct of monthly training for subject matter specialists, shared responsibility for adaptive research, and systems that ensure rapid feedback from farmers. The relevance and effectiveness of extension messages revolve around well-chosen impact points. Careful monitoring of these impact points and of whether they continue to develop over time is of key importance in measuring performance and ensuring that the system remains dynamic.

Since participation of the beneficiaries themselves is important to ensure success, T&V places importance on contact farmers as agents of dissemination and change in their own community and on using group structures whenever feasible. To improve the quality of the field extension work, enforcing visit timetables, focusing on impact points, and training the agents themselves are important features of the system. To ensure extension agents' practical understanding of local farming practices and farming systems, they are recruited as much as possible from among local farmers.

Lessons learned from T&V implementation in several countries have accumulated. Planners now recognize that although useful productivity improvements are quickly achieved, it takes 10 to 15 years to establish a fully effective T&V system of extension with the capacity to generate major, sustainable productivity improvements. The long development period is needed to achieve all the changes in procedures, attitudes, incentives, and interrelationships that the system typically requires. Good leadership from key staff introducing the system is a central ingredient of success. Improved supervision of all grades of staff is also important. Finally, effective monitoring and evaluation are essential to ensure that the system is effective and remains dynamic.

Researchers are well aware that the average yields in farmers' fields are far below those obtained on research plots. It is important to know the reasons for this, and one way to investigate the difference is to divide the yield gap into several components.

First, the technical possibilities are usually fewer on a farm than at a research station because the latter has a degree of control over key factors, especially good soil and reliable water supply, that farmers may never enjoy. The main ways to close this gap are investing in water control (irrigation, flood prevention) and doing the research under on-farm conditions.

Second, the economic possibilities may be much lower than what would be technically possible. It is often possible, for example, to obtain higher yields by continuing to apply fertilizer, even beyond the level at which the additional output from the crop pays for the additional input. A farmer will not usually attain absolute maximum yields but will aim for the highest economic return.

Third, the actual attainments on farms may fall far short even of the economic possibilities, for reasons that include adverse and unreliable weather conditions, lack of knowledge or husbandry skills, shortages of key inputs such as fertilizer, water, and labor, and fluctuating or inadequate output prices and other economic incentives. It is in this group of reasons that the most "gap-closing" can be achieved, through agricultural extension, input supply, and good incentive policies.

Many researchers have observed the wide range of achievement between the best farmers and the worst. The two main aims of extension are to improve the performance of the best farmers and narrow the gap between the best and the worst. Worldwide experience suggests that agricultural extension services are most effective when they support a profitable risk-free or low-risk technology, when key inputs such as fertilizer and high-quality seed are available at the right time, and when farmers have ready access to markets for their additional production.

As has been suggested many times in the discussion above, introducing new technologies and moving from a subsistence to a commercial economy is a very complicated, messy process. Policymakers cannot expect to be able to control it, but they can take broad steps to make the transition as smooth as possible and above all to try to protect those most adversely affected by the process. They must not make a distinction between "cash crops" and "food crops," for two reasons. First, farmers often enter the cash market initially by selling food crops, and a very significant proportion of the world's food crops is commercialized. Second, the prime consideration in looking after people's food (and nutrition) security is income. This is especially the case for the small farmers and landless laborers who make up the bulk of the rural poor. Food insecurity is primarily a matter of inadequate income, not inadequate food supplies. It is not as crucial that a small farm family produces enough food for its own home consumption as that it has enough income to secure its food needs.

When a farm is moving into commercial production—be it of long-gestation tree crops or slowly moving livestock development, of fiber or other nonfood crops, or of surplus food crops for sale—the vital thing is to keep income levels high enough to maintain family nutrition during the transition. This means paying attention to the employment situation of all working members of the farm family, the labor demands made upon various people and the returns to this labor, and who receives and controls cash income in farm families. There are risks inherent in adopting new technologies, especially in rainfed agriculture, that must be acknowledged and dealt with; these include the mistakes and miscalculations that farmers may make in doing things that are new to them. The availability of adequate credit at reasonable prices, whether from formal or informal sources, will help support producers in risky situations or where they are waiting for long-gestation investments to come to fruition. Input and output prices must reinforce new technical possibilities rather than make them infeasible. Welfare provisions must be made for those who, in spite of all care in designing development programs, are still adversely affected in avoidable ways. Finally, development programs should be closely monitored, especially from the nutrition viewpoint, to take account of the multiplicity of possible side effects and to allow remedial measures to be taken as quickly as possible.

7

Women in African Food Production and Food Security

Food and Agriculture Organization

Research in most of sub-Saharan Africa shows that the activities of women in support of their families usually determine how much food is available for family consumption and hence the nutritional status of family members living at home. Women make their most effective contribution to family nutrition chiefly as food producers, by means of small-scale farming and livestock raising, but they also buy food with cash that they earn.

Women are generally responsible for providing certain foods for the household that complement the foods and other goods for which men are responsible. Women provide these foods either by producing them in their separate fields, gardens, or livestock concerns, or by selling or exchanging some of their produce to obtain the foods they need. The returns from women's particular activities, in the form of foodstuffs or cash, are therefore a contribution separate from the results of their husbands' activities. Furthermore, men's incomes are not often used to make up a shortfall in women's production. Thus, in much of Africa, thinking in terms of a total household production or total household income is inaccurate. Two sets of activities, men's work and women's work, generate the household's wealth and meet different obligations to the household, and the two sets of household "economies" are not perfect substitutes.

Minor Crops

African women farmers produce their own crops, garden vegetables, livestock, and poultry. The crops and vegetables cover a wide

Excerpted from "Women, Food and Nutrition in Africa: Economic Change and the Outlook for Nutrition," by the Food Policy and Nutrition Division and the Human Resources Institutions and Agrarian Reform Division, FAO. Published in *Food and Nutrition*, vol. 10, no. 1 (1984), pp. 71–79.

range of grains, tubers, legumes, garden vegetables, and fruits that are often referred to as secondary or minor food crops, as distinct from major or staple crops. These minor crops are usually cultivated by women in separate fields or in gardens, often near water (Long-hurst 1983).

Minor food crops may provide up to 15 to 20 percent of the family's total energy intake. More importantly, however, women grow them because of their timing and their variety. Some of the foods are produced for consumption when the main household food stocks are low—an important aspect of household food security. Examples are early-maturing cereals such as "findi" (*Digitaria exilis*), or the plots of maize that women plant early in Zimbabwe so that they are ready for consumption three months before the main food crops. Women also gather some foods at this time of low stocks, such as the starchy fruit pulp of the baobab tree.

The variety of minor crop foods is important for the range of nutrients they encompass as well as the palatability afforded to the diet; both are important for nutritional status. They include fruits and nuts, which are important sources of oils, minerals, and vitamins, especially as between-meals snacks for children. Some of the eggs, milk and other dairy products, and poultry meat that women produce may be consumed by household members, thus adding to the range and pleasantness of their diet and particularly to their protein consumption.

In spite of their importance in nutrition, minor crops are vulnerable to being pushed out of the farming system. Little scientific research and development has been devoted to these crops. Extension workers usually do not promote cultivation of minor crops to the extent that their value warrants. The productivity of most minor crops remains low in terms of returns to land and labor, compared to those of food and nonfood cash crops. With increasing pressure on land and limited labor resources, farmers tend to concentrate on staple food crops and cash crops. This tendency is reinforced if a family is struggling to supply its basic food energy needs on a small land base.

The cumulative impact is that women's crops, both staple and minor, are planted on smaller and smaller acreages as the other crops impinge, which reduces women's ability to meet their food obligations, either from their own production or from some cash income from small sales of their crops. The possibility of investing in fertilizers or other technical improvements for their crops and livestock concerns, where such technical improvements exist, is low. Women may also not be able to buy insecticides to protect their stored crops. Their lack of cash in hand reduces the possibility of buying foods when they are most needed to cover lean periods.

The loss of income for women is sometimes aggravated by the loss of income from an activity that they continue to carry out. This is a well-documented aspect of attempts to raise yields of milk for sale. Women are generally expected to provide the extra time and other resources in projects to raise milk yields, but the dairies usually pay the extra earnings to men, the nominal owners of the cattle. In other words, women have had to work more but have lost the income from the occasional sale of milk and milk products that had previously accrued to them (Chavangi and Hanssen 1983). Another result may be a loss of milk for family consumption. An interesting side effect of this loss of control is that if the dairy raises the milk price to encourage higher levels of marketed production from small farm producers, the desired supply response may not occur because the price incentive does not reach the women who are the actual producers.

The Time Factor

Rural men and women also work within different sets of time constraints. Women's time constraints and the other constraints on their productive activities have major implications for food production and family nutritional status (see Huffman in part V).

Although in general men and women manage their own crops and livestock concerns separately, certain tasks on all crops are usually considered women's work, while other tasks are men's (table 7-1).

Table 7-1. *Time Spent by Men and Women on Agricultural and Subsistence-Related Tasks, Africa*
(percent)

Task	Men	Women
Clearing forest and staking out fields	95	5
Turning soil	70	30
Planting seeds and cuttings	50	50
Hoeing and weeding	30	70
Harvesting	40	60
Transporting crops home from fields	20	80
Storing crops	20	80
Processing food crops	10	90
Marketing surplus crops	40	60
Carrying water and fuel	10	90
Caring for domestic animals	50	50
Hunting	90	10
Feeding and caring for family	5	95

Source: UNECA, Women's Programme (1975).

Typically, women transplant seedlings, hoe, and weed, which can be the most time-consuming tasks. Often women also provide some care for all the family livestock and process livestock products—for example, they make cheese or ghee.

Technical changes in agriculture tend to add disproportionately to the labor demands on women. For example, the use of a plough or of fertilizer requires additional weeding of fields if the gains are to be fully realized. When such technical improvements are applied to men's crops, one result has been that time available to women for their own productive activities and their other household and food-related tasks has been reduced.

On average, women work long hours throughout the year and even more at seasonal labor peaks. Inevitably they cannot cover many tasks well and must take shortcuts. Since most household activities relate in some degree to nutrition, family nutritional status can suffer in a variety of ways. A common time-saving shortcut is to reduce the frequency of cooking meals, which, among other things, reduces the time spent collecting fuelwood. However, children are adversely affected by longer gaps between meals. Furthermore, if cooked food is kept for several hours to be eaten at the following meal, this increases the risk of spoilage and food-borne infection. Another shortcut is the consumption of nonboiled water. The nutritional status of all family members is thus threatened, but the consequences are usually worst for preschool children with immature immune systems. Time pressures and fuelwood limitations also encourage women to use foods that can be cooked more quickly. This is likely to reduce consumption of energy-rich and protein-rich pulses, for instance, since these may require several hours of cooking. Such pressures may also cut down on the preparation of special weaning foods, as these must be prepared in addition to family meals. Nutrition education has a limited scope for success here until the time constraints are reduced (see Hornik and Manoff in part V).

Time constraints imposed by the effort to maintain food production can also affect childcare and women's attention to their own needs. Weight losses have been reported for pregnant and lactating women at times of peak labor demand, for example, among rice growers in The Gambia. The nutritional requirements of this vulnerable group are higher than normal, and working hard in the fields may negatively affect their nutritional status during these critical periods. Breastfeeding may be curtailed if it is difficult for women to take young children to the fields or to other places of employment. Thus infants and young children may achieve lower than normal weight gains. Rest and leisure are usually cut to a minimum during such periods, and attendance at clinics is greatly reduced.

To release time for themselves, women in some countries have begun cultivating crops that require relatively less time and effort, for example, cassava instead of yams and maize. This switch has costs, not only because cassava is low in protein and is thus a poorer family food source, but also in terms of reduced soil fertility. In other places, women have withdrawn some of their labor from men's crops.

Women who take wage employment in agriculture, for example in plantations, are often associated with the families of the lowest nutritional status. This is partly because such women come from the poorest families to begin with. Working conditions may also aggravate the decline in nutritional status—for example, when employers do not permit breastfeeding at work. Childcare in general may be reduced unless others are available to perform the necessary tasks. The incomes, however, do contribute to provision of food supplies, subject to the purchasing power of the low wages generally paid to women.

Since time constraints are a major factor limiting women's ability to maintain their incomes through agricultural and other enterprises and in wage labor, improvements in productivity over the whole range of their activities—even improvements in any one, which will reduce the stress on others—will improve the outlook for family nutrition in a variety of ways.

Implications of Production Patterns

The basic pattern of men and women producing different foods for family consumption has been greatly modified all over Africa during the past 100 years. As different areas have become incorporated into the world market economy, most small farms have added some cash crops to the farming system. Many men have migrated to find wage employment for shorter or longer periods, leaving their wives and families to manage the farm production. Almost everywhere population pressure has cut down access to land, a phenomenon that has been exacerbated in several countries of eastern and southern Africa where much of the best land has been appropriated by immigrants' enterprises.

On small farms, the main cash crops have almost always been regarded as men's crops, and income from them has accrued to men. Sometimes men have continued to manage the main staple crops as before. At other times, the production of these crops has passed to women, who then manage all the on-farm production. Women everywhere have continued to be responsible for their own crops and their own livestock concerns and have continued to be expected to meet their food production obligations for the household. Men's income is rarely used to meet these food needs. It is spent on items that are considered their own obligations, such as school fees and housing. The fact that the income from crop sales comes at one or a few times per year has also encouraged the consumption of expensive consumer items in place of day-to-day food needs. Furthermore, increasing numbers of men eat some meals out, for instance, at places of employment, which biases their perception of family needs for purchased food. There is thus a redistribution of consumed food in the household, since men have access to external, often relatively expensive sources (see Lipton in part V).

Women therefore need to maintain their food production for family consumption even when aggregate family income is high because of cash crop sales or the husband's wages. Women also often need a cash income to buy foods to supplement what they produce themselves. Cash income is also needed to provide capital for their income-earning activities. In the past, they might have obtained this from sales of small surpluses, such as some eggs, milk, or vegetables. Both maintaining production and maintaining a cash income can be difficult in the face of current trends.

In spite of these generalizations, not all women face the same kinds of difficulties. Major differences come from the stage of the life cycle of the family, such as whether there are young children to be cared for. The type of family system—for example, nuclear or extended—influences the woman's role, and so does the type of marriage—for example, monogamous or polygamous. In particular, the problems of women who are household heads and those of women working smallholdings with their husbands are different. The proportion of families with women heads reaches 60 percent in some areas of sub-Saharan Africa.

Labor allocation strategies by women in households with male and female heads may be different as a result of their different needs. In Cameroon, for instance, women heads of households allocated labor between their own food crops and the cash crops, in this case rice, to maximize total agricultural income. Women whose husbands managed the rice crop preferred to allocate more time to the sorghum crop and less to rice. This evidently did not produce the maximum aggregate household income but did increase the amount of sorghum consumed by the family (Jones 1982).

Some trends affect all women. There has been a tendency for all women farmers, whether household heads or not, to lose customary rights of access to land. Most legislation has not promoted women's legal ownership and inheritance rights and has at times undermined their use rights under customary land tenure systems by registering land in the name of the husband or first son. Increasing population pressure has reinforced this trend. And paradoxically, almost all rural development and irrigation schemes aggravate the problem, since they rarely take women as tenants or provide land for growing food to the wives of tenants. Men who grow cash crops and are keen to expand production also sometimes take over some of their wives' holdings. Women's production is threatened because it is on a smaller and poor land base, and this is made worse by little access to other agricultural resources, such as draft power and equipment and cash for investments and inputs.

Another difficulty faced by all women food producers is poor access to official resources. Channels of information, credit, inputs, and access to markets have frequently been aimed at men on the implicit assumptions that men are heads of households and that heads of households produce the food crops. This difficulty is worsened because women, with their daily domestic and childcare tasks, often cannot spend the hours required to go to distant offices to obtain assistance. And extension assistance has far more often gone to male farmers than to women.

Approaches to Strengthening Women's Roles

Many of the forces working against women's agricultural output— and thus against Africa's food production—are not being directly faced. Women have not been asked how much work they do and what their constraints are. They have not been asked what technologies must be developed to help them. They have not been asked what makes their access to farm resources and to official channels for support so difficult. These omissions are not usually deliberate but have resulted because of the mistaken perception of women's roles in food production and household nutrition. Much can be done to obtain a more precise assessment of rural conditions and to buttress women's roles, but in the first place the women themselves must be asked what they need. This requires strengthening women's cooperatives and savings clubs so that these may give voice to women's needs for assistance from extension services, credit services, agricultural research stations, and government units that can do much to legislate women's access to land and officialdom.

Women farmers need new appropriate technologies for their farm and domestic tasks. With recognition of their importance in food security and nutrition, farming systems research is likely to seek ways to improve the yields of secondary crops and small livestock concerns. On the farm, women need improved small-scale equipment to process food crops, such as hand shellers for maize. They need much better storage facilities, again on a small scale, to reduce the substantial proportion of crops lost in Africa each year to disease, insects, and animals (see Pariser in part IV). They need labor-saving technologies for the tasks considered women's work. For weeding, for example, this might be use of ox-drawn equipment or intercropping techniques that increase ground cover and reduce the need for cereal weeding. Some of the desired technologies may already exist—many small maize shellers are illustrated in appropriate publications, for instance—but they are not widely available in rural areas. Women badly need access to information about how to acquire or make the improved devices.

In extending information, training, and other services to women, agents of nutrition education and health care, as well as agricultural extension, should work within the constraints on women's time imposed by the daily needs for childcare and other domestic and farm tasks. Such services may need to be concentrated in the agriculturally busy seasons and to take place as near to farms as possible. Child daycare centers can relieve working mothers of childcare chores as well as provide health and nutrition education services for both parent and offspring. Working mothers in both urban and rural areas can benefit from such services.

In the past, projects specifically designed to aid women's role in nutrition often have not attempted to calculate profit and loss in the projected enterprises, nor the time costs, which would lead to losses in other activities. The FAO is increasingly using time allocation surveys as a tool to find the major constraints on men and women in the farm sector (Lunven 1983). If used with economic estimates of costs and returns, they can show the differential impact of rural development projects within the household so that such projects can be better designed to meet food and nutrition needs (Burfisher and Horenstein 1982).

The trends described in this paper are not unique to Africa. A similar undercutting of women's economic position within the household has been described for other regions. But in spite of the great diversity within the African continent, the trends are sharpest there because of the pattern of different activities and separate purses within the household. It is also in Africa that food production is failing, in most countries, to keep up with the growth in population and the growth in demand in urban areas. It is in the rural areas where the greatest poverty and lowest general levels of nutrition can be found and where dietary intake based on own production of food crops must be greatly increased. This goal will be approached most effectively by gaining an understanding of the major constraints on food output in each area. Greater involvement of women in planning, at community and family levels, is the most appropriate and effective means to chart the way for interventions aimed at African nutrition and development goals.

8

Food Policy Options
for Secondary Regions:
A Framework for Applied Research

Bruce M. Koppel

National and international actors in the food system still focus most of their attention on enhancing the production of major cereal grains, but increasingly they are also giving attention to the development of secondary regions. Secondary regions are those where the land could be better used for crops other than basic cereal grains; where large-scale irrigation infrastructure is not technically or economically feasible, where the role of animal and fish production in local food systems is often significant, and where wild ecosystems and shifting cultivation may represent significant portions of regional land use.

Characteristics of Secondary Regions

Secondary regions are most often associated with substantial amounts of arable land classified as "marginal." That classification, however, is crude. Determining precisely how much of the world's potentially arable land is marginal is difficult. The criteria include measures based on land use, soil capability, opportunity cost, ecological degradation, market system performance, accessibility, geographic location, and urban functions (Morgan 1978; Eckholm 1976; Sanchez and Buol 1975; Johnson 1970; Kellogg and Orvedal 1969; Troll 1966). Each criterion represents a different assumption about what marginality is. In addition, each is sensitive to assumptions about the technology and levels of production needed.

Excerpted from "Food Policy for Secondary Regions: A Framework for Applied Research," *Food Policy*, vol. 6, no. 1 (February 1981), pp. 33–46.

In agroeconomic terms, marginal refers to limited land capability and the levels of technology and management needed to compensate for soil deficiencies and climatic liabilities. It is a characterization that is relative to specific land uses. What is marginal for rice may not be marginal for cassava. What is a profitable application of inputs for one crop may be a losing proposition for another crop. Marginal can also mean that a region is not well integrated into a larger political and economic system, limiting local government initiatives, restricting financial markets, and so on. An area may be marginal in geographic terms because of limited accessibility.

Instead of the term marginal, a term such as secondary may be more useful for referring to areas that combine mixes of agroeconomic, institutional, and spatial marginality. Marginal areas are not necessarily unimportant, particularly to the people directly dependent on them. In many developing countries, secondary regions may contain most of the land and water used for food production under available technology. This is the case for most of Africa, a major portion of the Indian subcontinent, a large portion of Southeast Asia, and significant areas of China.

What are the challenges facing development of the food systems in secondary regions? To begin with, we must realize that the motivation to develop the food systems in secondary regions comes when major food requirements can be met through basic grain production and cereal imports. A strategy then emerges that uses the mineral resources and possibilities for export agriculture in marginal areas as a basis for generating foreign exchange.

With increasing energy import bills, developing countries' capacity to cover food deficits through imports will be strained. At that point, the strategy of using marginal areas to earn foreign exchange will be challenged by the need to use marginal areas for food as well as fuel production. To date, agricultural production and food distribution strategies in secondary regions have been oriented more toward the consumption and foreign exchange requirements of large urban centers and primary regions than to the equity or sustainable growth objectives that one might wish to set for secondary regions.

In many cases, the ecology within which agriculture in secondary regions functions is both more complex and more delicate than the ecologies that have seen the major development of cereal grain production. The complexity arises because production tends to be based on diversified ecosystems in contrast to the generally monocultural ecosystems characteristic of more developed primary agricultural areas. But it is this complexity that ensures the relative stability and resilience of such systems. The delicacy of secondary regions refers to the agroclimatic environment: drainage properties of marginal area soils tend to be problematic, topsoil is often very thin, water and weather erosion are often advanced, micronutrient composition is often seriously deficient, and soil compaction is often well advanced.

Because of this fragility, the lessons from agricultural development in primary agricultural regions cannot simply be transferred to secondary regions. In these situations, tillage practices and cropping choices, for example, can be crucial. Once the topsoil is lost, or once significant changes take place in the soil—for example, hardening of some tropical soils from exposure to the sun, or depletion of minerals—maintaining production can be expensive, if not impossible. Stability and resilience often depend on carefully developed and continuing adaptations to difficult conditions, which generally means not establishing monocultural patterns of production but maintaining some diversity in the system. A trade-off is involved here, as Snaydon and Elston (1976, pp. 54–55) observe:

> There is no single optimum level of species or genetic diversity in agricultural systems. Farming systems depend upon controlled diversity. But the ease of management of homogeneous communities of plants or animals, with their resultant high production under uniform controlled conditions, must be balanced against the greater yield stability of heterogeneous communities and often greater production in suboptimal conditions.

Such choices are rarely evaluated. Instead, the extension into secondary regions of estate-type agriculture (often not for food production) and large-scale monocultural food production continue to be implemented. There are also attempts to replicate in marginal areas the technoeconomic package programs developed originally for the green revolution. Such schemes reflect the belief that strategies gleaned from several decades of experience in institutionally better-endowed cereal grain production areas are applicable to secondary regions.

Because only a small proportion of the available agricultural land in marginal regions is planted to crops and varieties covered by the green revolution, some people have suggested that the potential for a second green revolution in so-called secondary crops is present (NAS 1977; Hanrahan and Willet 1976; OTA 1976; Warley 1976). That potential, however, will be difficult to realize because for many of the crops and varieties involved, there is limited technological research backup (Jennings 1976; Greenland 1975; Pinstrup-Andersen and Hazell in part II).

Documenting large numbers of secondary crop species, a necessary step in building a significant research program, is expensive and has hardly begun, except for cassava, potatoes, and a few legumes. Considerable work remains to be done before even the basic characteristics and production possibilities of most secondary food crops are understood (Ker and IDRC 1979; Ritchie 1979; NAS 1975, 1979). Evidence exists that many secondary crops may be more robust than major cereal grain varieties, but making the effort to capitalize on this characteristic to create more productive varieties will be a large step. Crop breeders have only recently begun serious efforts to produce varieties of the major grain crops that will give high and stable yields in secondary environments. To date, the major successes with high-yielding varieties have been in areas with at least fairly good soils, either reliable rainfall or irrigation, and use of modern inputs. The idea of high-yielding varieties of secondary crops that are well adapted to the more difficult environments is appealing, but as yet very little has been done. Researchers also do not know yet whether such efforts will really pay off.

A high-yielding-variety technology is, in general, a high-input technology. Varieties were crossed to optimize responsiveness to higher levels of nitrogen fertilization and careful water management. Plant architecture was altered to allow heavier grain loads. However, given the large petrochemical content of many of the agricultural inputs, current yield levels will not be maintained easily. Alternatives for the future include breeding programs based on line selection for adaptability, low-input regimes, more exotic approaches that improve the efficiency of carbon and nitrogen cycles, and ecosystem management approaches such as minimum tillage and biological pest control.

Many secondary food crops are grown in highly diverse environments. These environments are not significantly modified in comparison, for example, with the modification of natural ecosystems for wet rice culture. Devising improved production schemes without resorting to high-input technologies will be particularly difficult. One implication is that breeding for generalized environments will be only a limited possibility. If reducing variability in agricultural environments through physical modifications is not feasible, increasing productivity in a manner consistent with ecosystem stability and resilience will require fresh research strategies.

Little is known about either the production patterns or the consumption profiles of many secondary crops. In some instances, plants are seen as nuisances by agriculturists or planners when they in fact have crucial roles in local ecosystems and marginal-area economies. Two examples are sago and mangrove forests (Philippine Council for Agriculture and Resources Research 1978; Ruddle and others 1978). Furthermore, the scope for combining diversified food production with export crop production is underestimated, a misperception that can lead to many of the social costs of marginal area development strategies.

Appropriate Strategies

Formulating feasible, sustainable options for secondary regions involves three complex analytical concerns: farming systems research as a core of regional analysis, technology support system analysis, and administrative capacity analysis.

Programs are needed that combine research, institutional design, and policy evaluation. Such programs would seek to demonstrate that the application of science and technology to difficult production issues can result in an appropriate payoff, that a more differentiated policy environment to deal with food systems can be developed and sustained, and that an integration of ecological and social science analysis is feasible and indeed necessary to identify appropriate food system development strategies.

Farming Systems Research

The rationale of farming systems research dictates that practitioners see agricultural production in a very broad context. While this is increasingly acknowledged in principle (Blackie and others 1979, 1980), much remains to be put into practice. Issues that need to be examined include the following:

Household demographics, especially labor patterns, dependency ratios, and fertility. How many mouths need to be fed now and in the future? What capacities do households have to grow their own food? What is and will be the capacity of marginal area households to purchase food?

Migration behavior and migration circuits, particularly for seasonal employment in nonagricultural enterprises within and outside the region, between cash and subsistence food production activities, and between food and nonfood agricultural activities. What is the role of the food system in supporting income and employment in secondary regions relative to other sectors? How do changes in employment opportunities and wage levels in nonfood sectors affect agricultural productivity, labor absorption, and wage rates in the food system?

Consumption elasticities and intercommodity substitutabilities between and among secondary crops and primary cereal grains and between and among locally produced and imported foods, with special attention to comparisons within as well as between households. How do marginal-area households adjust to changes in relative prices or availability of different foods? Are there social status effects in food preferences among secondary-region populations? If so, what are those patterns and how might they affect local food systems as economic development and seasonal employment in urban areas grow?

Interrelations between villages, and intravillage organizational patterns and production, storage, and consumption patterns. How do marginal-area communities deal with food security and localized variability in food supplies? What relationships are there between the distribution of power, prestige, and access to productive assets in the village and decision making within households about food production, storage, marketing, and consumption? What are the characteristics of socioeconomic inequality? What are the relationships of inequality to patterns of resource use and management?

The characteristics of the market system and, more broadly, the exchange system. There appears to be a renaissance in rural marketing studies (Harriss 1979; Smith 1975, 1976; Johnson 1970) following the recognition that, in many instances, rural market systems tend to act as siphons in secondary regions, extracting surpluses rather than stimulating investment and employment. An example of topics that need to be explored is the effect on secondary and poor people's crops of the market system for primary food crops, export agricultural crops, and secondary-region mineral resources.

The impact of the distribution of urban functions in tertiary market centers. In many instances, secondary regions have neither a major nor a secondary city. Instead, they have a number of smaller market towns with limited storage, transport, processing, and administrative functions. Such towns often have fragile economic connections with surrounding rural areas. However, it is on the basis of just such towns that policy hopes for stimulating occupational diversification, occupational mobility, and nonagricultural development will rest.

The degree of ecological degradation that has already occurred or is in the process of occurring. Determining this will be important for evaluating not only the significance of various tillage patterns but also the sustainability of existing biomass-based rural fuel systems.

Interrelationships between the organization of renewable fuel systems and the characteristics of food systems. How are joint demands for food and fuel from biomass organized? Are there existing or potential problems in managing renewable resources? What are the impacts of demands for biomass produced in the secondary areas to satisfy energy needs outside these areas?

All of these issues would need to be examined to respond to what appear to be relatively simple questions. What is the capacity of the existing food system to meet the income, nutrition, and employment requirements of a local population as well as the demands placed upon the system from outside the region? To what degree is the production problem technological, and what administrative, organizational, and policy problems exist? How would changes in these areas affect the farming system? The last question is especially significant. It requires determining how vulnerable the existing farming patterns are to the instabilities and uncertainties resulting from change in social, economic, and institutional environments.

Technology Support Systems

Many people are calling upon the international agricultural research centers to play crucial roles in generating technologies for marginal-area cropping systems (NAS 1977). In some instances, by responding, the international centers may be attempting to offer more than their capabilities permit.

At high levels within national agricultural research systems, within international centers, and within the donor community, people are seriously rethinking the criteria for allocation of research resources and the appropriate role of international centers. The discussion is complex, but one way to summarize it is to distinguish between efficiency (investment in rice research has led to higher average rice yields) and effectiveness (poorer farmers have not always had access to the new rice technology). It is in this context, for example, that discussions are proceeding on the role of the centers in generating low-input technologies, ways of using genetic material collections maintained by some centers, and appropriate relationships between the centers and national programs.

The centers basically operate as individual entities, but an alternative arrangement would see the centers as a combined resource available to be tapped and used in the context of problem definitions developed within national programs. A promising recent development is the formation of the International Federation for Agricultural Research and Development (IFARD), an association of national research systems (Philippine Council for Agriculture and Resources Research 1977).

Often, the domestic political organization of commodity groups; the subordinate status of research support in relation to other approaches to rural development, such as land reform, infrastructure, food distribution, and price supports; the thrusts of international financial, technical, and educational assistance; relations with agribusiness and privately financed agricultural research and technology support systems; and the operations of the international centers themselves combine to make research concerns for marginal areas and secondary food crops a low priority (Koppel 1978). However, the broad mandates of national agricultural research systems can often spawn—or at least allow room for—significant organizational and programmatic innovation. Limited efforts to engage new areas of concern can develop with considerably more ease than might be possible at the more well-endowed, but also more narrowly focused, international agricultural research centers.

Unlike international centers, national systems must accept more demanding forms of political and social accountability for technology impact. In addition, national research systems have to interact more intimately with rural development institutions. The outreach programs of an international center often have the benefit of demonstration status, with the allocation of special resources that usually entails. Most efforts to verify and transfer technologies by national agricultural research systems proceed under more routine conditions, with shortages of support, cooperation, and commitment.

Under the best circumstances, the skills and attention of national system management are focused on coordinating diverse capabilities present in the system, responding to a variety of often inconsistent pressures for priority research directions, and building patterns of international cooperation that do not excessively deflect the system's goals (Drilon 1977; Hargrove 1977; Pinstrup-Andersen and Franklin 1977). The capability of national agricultural research systems to respond to marginal-area development will be at least partly dependent on the systems' capacities to deal with these issues.

Administrative Capacity

This, in many ways, is an overarching category. Even after technological and nontechnological conditions are specified and ecologically viable technological options are identified, implementing such options is still extremely difficult. One problem is that although most food policy operates through the market system and assumes that the market, through its price and stock allocation mechanisms, will signal various incentives and disincentives to producers and consumers, market systems in secondary regions do not always transmit undistorted versions of such signals to producers or policymakers. The modernization of marketing organization away from multipurpose periodic markets to more firm-centered organization can especially weaken the bargaining power of buyers and sellers in marginal areas. However, the firms may be more efficient at assembling products destined for urban markets.

While most policy interventions in market exchange systems of developing countries are based on an implicit assumption that the systems can function simultaneously to allocate resources (through relative prices) and extract resources (through mediating internal terms of trade), the actual patterns of resource allocation and extraction are not always as anticipated or desired. It follows that food policy must not only be more sensitive to regional and subregional variations in market system operation but must also seek alternative instruments to communicate incentives and disincentives. Cooperatives and other forms of organizational strategies are one example, but there are several others ranging from adjusting local government powers to modifying landholding systems.

In dealing with these issues, it is important to consider the alternatives to standard public approaches to developmental objectives in the village and the region. How can public administration be improved or privatized? How does government affect transaction and information costs in the village? How are linkages between marginal and primary regions institutionalized in commodity, capital, and labor markets? What are the implications for the optimal organization of public intervention and the risks of private investment? What assumptions are made about investment and behavior outside the public sector and what capacity is actually present? What are the existing organizational and administrative capacities, and are the advocates of various strategies being realistic about them?

The questions are not unique to marginal-area development. That they have not been satisfactorily answered in general, however, only underlines the thin basis that exists for generalization of "lessons" from primary-area development experience.

Integrating the Dimensions

Programs combining analyses of farming systems, technology support systems, and administrative capacity would begin with research that builds sufficient understanding of regional systems to yield specific technological, institutional, and policy options. The programs would then move to an active involvement of the international centers working through the national program with backup from IFARD to refine and test productivity-enhancing technological options. At the same time, the organizational and policy issues involved in the longer-run feasibility of such options, especially extension systems, credit programs, and marketing arrangements, would need to be evaluated through active experimentation and training, with principal attention to both efficiency and effectiveness criteria.

After a few years, it should be possible to answer the following questions. Does investment for farming systems research in secondary regions pay, or is it, as many claim, a high-risk, low-payoff proposition? Must cropping system development proceed from an understanding of the dynamics and possibilities of specific existing farming systems, or is such a path unnecessary? What are the long-run manpower and institutional requirements for generating the skills and organization needed to sustain food system development in secondary regions?

An attempt to define a program could take several forms, depending on the manpower and resources available. It could focus on a specific region and conduct the full range of research and applied activities outlined. This is the most ambitious option, and it is also the one that most clearly links farming systems, administrative capacity, and technology support system issues. Second, a program could develop a regional ecological and socioeconomic data base to permit the modeling of food system development in marginal areas. Sensitivity analyses of such models can provide an important mode of policy analysis. Third, some limited generalizations can be generated through careful comparative analyses of current or completed attempts at food system development in marginal areas. Examples include programs for integrated area development, transmigration, road and irrigation projects in marginal areas, estate and cash crop projects, and attempts by national and international agricultural research systems to do cropping systems research in marginal areas.

For particular countries, specific components of the approach outlined may represent such crucial or large areas of uncertainty in marginal-area development that to focus on those alone is a satisfactory step. The following eight issues fall into that category:

o Developing nutrition and food consumption baseline studies for populations in marginal areas
o Understanding the social and economic organization of specific agricultural ecosystems common in marginal areas
o Describing current and likely interactions between food and fuel systems in marginal areas
o Evaluating the effects of public intervention on transaction and information costs in the village
o Measuring the effectiveness, as well as the efficiency, of rural marketing systems in marginal areas and secondary regions
o Examining resource management practices in marginal areas, with special emphasis on water and soil
o Developing, possibly with the assistance of remote sensing technologies, more detailed land use, land capability, and demographic maps for secondary regions and marginal areas
o Assessing the relationships between existing and potential sys-

tems of property rights and the trade-offs between conservation and production objectives.

An important area for research concerns the kind of technology support systems needed to support marginal-area development. Part of that issue is refining methodologies that can incorporate effectiveness criteria into research investment decisions. If technology support systems continue on their current track, outcomes strongly reflecting biases toward shorter-run efficiency considerations are likely. Alternative paths are possible (Wittwer 1979).

Finally, there is a class of educational issues that follow from the overall problem. To what degree is it important to develop new training programs for researchers and project managers who will work on secondary-area development problems? In the longer run, can contemporary formal education provide the manpower needed to engage the complex technological, administrative, and organizational issues involved in secondary-area development? What are the linkages between the formal educational sector and the less well defined cluster of on-the-ground, informal educational processes in secondary regions? What new configurations might be needed to confront food system development problems in secondary regions?

The ultimate challenge of food system development in marginal areas is educational in the broadest sense. If, in fact, area development in secondary regions is not "business as usual," then where are the people who can engage in "business not as usual"? Specifically, how are such capabilities to be developed, and what different institutional arrangements may be needed? Answering those questions should be the principal long-term objective of applied research on food system development in secondary regions.

Conclusion

A program for food system development in secondary regions must develop options that will increase food system productivity, improve local consumption patterns, generate income, and enhance labor absorption in the local food system economy. It is important that production strategies protect water resources, soil fertility, and local ecosystem diversity. The inputs required must be affordable and available and not too vulnerable to changes in external markets. Management must be consistent with the income and technological levels of the majority of cultivators and with the level of external technological support likely to be available to the broadest group of the producing population. Policymakers must explore whether the complex issues involved in marginal-area development can be best dealt with by national agricultural research systems and international agricultural research centers as they currently operate. It may be that alternative modes of problem definition and project implementation are more desirable. Finally, decisionmakers must provide guidelines for the allocation of resources for manpower development for longer-run strengthening of national capacities to effectively meet development issues in secondary regions.

9

The Nutritional Impact
of Agricultural Projects

Shlomo Reutlinger

To discuss how agricultural projects affect the nutritional status of a local population, one must first state some basic propositions about the relationship between agricultural projects and nutrition: (a) agricultural projects cannot be expected automatically to convey nutritional benefits simply because they increase food production; (b) not all agricultural projects need to convey direct nutritional benefits, nor should nonagricultural projects be expected not to convey nutritional benefits; (c) agricultural projects may convey positive nutritional benefits to some people and lead to nutritional deterioration among other people; and (d) adequate nutritional well-being cannot be defined precisely, but nutritionists can relatively easily determine whether groups of people have, on average, an adequate amount of income and consume an adequate amount and quality of food, and hence whether many individuals in the group are likely to be malnourished.

One central issue with many ramifications is the interaction between project-related interventions and countrywide policies. In many instances, projects may lead to negative nutritional consequences only because governments implement certain trade and taxation policies. To implement the project, it is then necessary either to change the policies that lead to the divergence between market and shadow prices received by the participants in the project or to modify the project or the portfolio of projects in conformity with the nonoptimal price structure in the country. Analogously, it may be valid to argue that certain nutritional objectives are better served by changing countrywide policies but that in the absence of such modifications projects should be designed to achieve nutritional objectives in spite of or because of nonoptimal country policies.

Excerpted from *Nutritional Impact of Agricultural Projects*, a paper prepared for an ACC/SCN workshop, World Bank, August 1983.

This paper presents and discusses five cases describing the potentially most important features of agricultural projects that might lead them to have adverse nutritional effects or positive effects that are less than desired. To what extent these features are present and with what intensity must be determined during the design stage of each individual project. It might be questioned whether it is possible to identify these features and related outcomes with sufficient accuracy to provide a basis and justification for remedial action. Undoubtedly experience will tell whether projecting nutrition-related outcomes is more or less hazardous and reliable than projecting other project outcomes such as rates of adoption of new technology, the use of inputs, yields, and prices. The aim here is to assist in asking the right questions, to identify what data are needed, and to recommend possible courses of action once the problem has been identified.

Case 1: Insufficient Increased Income

The project fails to provide sufficient (or any) increased income to many households potentially facing a nutritional risk in the project area. This is a common feature of projects. It is widely recognized and has received much attention in the governments of developing countries and in the general development community. To the extent that assisting small farmers and the landless can be shown to produce incremental increases in the value of production that exceed incremental costs, efforts are being made to include them in projects. This still leaves many outside projects. What more can be done? If poverty alleviation and improved nutrition are explicit objectives, we obviously cannot stop here.

Only two options exist. One is to provide the left-out small farmers with project interventions, such as capital goods, working capital, or human capital, whose costs exceed the incremental value of production. The second is to provide the left-out farm and nonfarm households with monetary or food aid and public health services. The advantages and disadvantages of these two options are not easily determined. Undoubtedly, small farmers whose command over agricultural and human resources is only marginally below the point at which development has a satisfactory benefit-cost ratio are more "efficiently" assisted by including them in the development project. At the other extreme are the farmers whose land is very poor and limited and who themselves are very poorly prepared to make use of modern inputs. For them, the costs would be far in excess of any projected incremental value of outputs and it would be much less costly to provide them with welfare payments.

According to the view presented above, projects would become instruments for achieving distributional objectives as well as development objectives. This is, of course, not an original proposal. Development theorists have proposed on several occasions how project appraisal procedures might be modified to do just that. Squire and van der Tak (1975) provide a very detailed discussion of the theoretical underpinnings of attaching differential weights to the incremental incomes generated by a project for different income groups. Harberger (1978) and Scandizzo and Knudsen (1980) make the case for assessing the incremental value of selected foods in accordance with the value society (not just the market) places on various amounts of food consumed by each of its members. The good feature of the methods proposed by theorists is that they could be uniformly applied to all projects in a country's project portfolio and to all aspects of each project. They provide therefore for an optimal, that is, least costly, way to attain distributional objectives. The problem with these theoretically preferred approaches is that they require the use of many calculations and the use of decision parameters that are highly unstable and subjective.

In reality, these methods have not been used to justify project elements that would not be justified under the traditional benefit-cost criteria. Yet projects sometimes do include features and beneficiaries that would be excluded if it were not for an implicit desire to use projects as instruments to attain income distribution objectives. The practical method consists, then, of averaging the benefit-cost ratio (or rate of return) from various components of the project. While tactically this practical approach has obvious merits in eliciting agreement from those who may not approve the inclusion of poverty alleviation features, the obvious shortcoming is that it limits application to only those cases in which a project is expected to have high rates of return on other accounts. Moreover, it would be surprising if during implementation the primary focus of attention were not on the elements of projects that have high rates of return. If these failed to materialize, the poverty-focused elements would be the first to be eliminated.

An alternative to the theoretical approaches, which have been rarely adopted, if at all, and to the present approach of indirectly introducing poverty-focused elements into some projects, is explicitly to develop projects or components of projects that have a less than acceptable rate of return but provide income to poor people for a reasonable per capita subsidy cost to the government.

The cost-effectiveness of a project for transferring income depends on its social rate of return and on the extent to which the government chooses to recover its cost for such inputs as extension services and roads. In a project that has a benefit-cost ratio of higher than unity, the government can recover its full cost or even realize a surplus while the incomes of farmers are raised. For instance, if the annualized net present value of such a project is $20 per capita, the government can recover all its cost while the farming households' per capita income rises by $20. If this is regarded as an insufficient transfer, the government can choose to forgo the full recovery of its costs on the project (say, for extension services) and thereby achieve additional income transfers dollar for dollar.

In a project that has a benefit-cost ratio of less than unity, a full recovery of the government's costs is of course out of the question. For instance, if the annualized net present value of a project is minus $10 per capita, the project is implementable—that is, it will solicit farmers' participation—only if the government is willing to make subsidy payments on the order of at least $10 per capita. The government can then use the project as a vehicle for transferring income to farmers only by further reductions in cost recovery. For instance, by incurring a cost of $20 per capita, a transfer of $10 per capita to farmers could be realized. This may be judged to be quite cost-ineffective—that is, it would cost the government $2 to convey $1 of income to farmers. However, if the government is willing to forgo an additional $30 per capita of cost recovery, the cost-effectiveness of the income transfer would be improved substantially. The cost would then be $50 per capita and the income being conveyed to poor farmers would be $40 per capita. It would cost the government $1.25 to deliver $1 of income to the participating farmers.

There are few known income transfer schemes, including subsidized food distribution policies and public infrastructure programs in urban areas or public works schemes in rural areas, that deliver a dollar's worth of benefits to the poor for as little as $1.25, or even $1.50. So, while an agricultural project or component of a project with a benefit-cost ratio of less than unity is suboptimal in terms of directly contributing to growth of GNP, it may save the government expenditures for transfer schemes. If poverty and nutrition objectives have any weight, a suboptimal agricultural project may well be an optimal and superior undertaking, as long as it can be shown to be a substitute, at an equivalent or lower cost, for other measures to save lives and improve health.

Finally, what is an acceptable price tag for achieving nutrition and poverty objectives? At one level, the answer is highly subjective, involving political judgments of individual governments and external aid donors. At the practical level, external funding agencies, irrespective of their own preferences about poverty alleviation and nutrition, should ask themselves whether by addressing these issues via projects they could "save" the government resources committed to re-distributive measures. If the government is committed to alleviating hunger, the question of whether this is to be accomplished through extension services and fertilizer or through subsidized food distribution can and should be addressed through hard-headed conventional analysis, if for no other reason than to save scarce resources for development.

Case 2: Reduced Production for Own Consumption

The project results in reductions in farmers' production of foods for their own consumption. Projects that selectively improve the productivity of cash crops—through improved seeds, specialized know-how, or a higher farmgate price—can generally be expected to reduce the production of crops (or livestock) normally produced only for home consumption. Moreover, even projects that augment the overall supply of resources available to farmers may lead to a decline in production of foods for home consumption because the relative productivity of cash crops rises in the process. The yields of cash crops are usually more responsive to water and fertilizers; hence, the productivity of land and labor is also increased when these inputs are allocated in increasing proportions away from the production of traditional, often home-consumed, foods and toward the production of cash crops. However, a failure to recognize reduction in food production for home consumption and to correctly value the forgone food would result in an over-estimation of income changes and nutritional benefits. The correct value of the forgone production is the cost of the food if it had to be purchased.

Given the importance of correctly anticipating the incremental income from projects, it is surprising that few project appraisal reports make mention of potential declines in the production of foods for home consumption. Is this an indication that no changes are anticipated? Or is it that these changes are difficult to anticipate? In any case, the inclusion of nutritional considerations in the assessment of agricultural projects requires more attention to this feature of projects.

Improper evaluation of changes in the value of food production for home consumption may be only one reason why income and nutritional benefits are often overestimated. The other reason is an under-estimation of the cost incurred by farmers in conjunction with cash crops, particularly the cost of working capital. For instance, we hear a lot about the high interest rates small farmers have to pay when they borrow money (because they are high-risk customers and the cost of administering very small loans is high), but rarely do we assess the full cost of borrowing incurred by farmers in conjunction with the use of modern inputs.

The reason for suggesting that more explicit attention should be paid to these apparent biases in evaluating projects' benefits for small farmers is not to discourage cash crop projects but to encourage more selectivity. Not only is overestimation of the positive income effects a danger to the nutritional well-being of participating farmers; it may also explain why some projects fail to realize their stated objective.

Even if total income is correctly estimated, a shift from food production for home consumption to cash crops can lead to less food consumption. One, possibly major, explanation may be in the difference between the bulk price of food at harvest time and its retail price in subsequent periods and the different propensities of the food producing and the nonfood producing farmer to trade food in bulk.

Unless severely cash constrained, food producers usually keep the food they expect to consume from one harvest to the next. Their decision on how much to keep and to consume is likely to take account of the bulk price of food (at harvest time) relative to the cost of acquiring other commodities at their retail prices. The decision made at harvest time on how much food to retain is not likely to be revised later in the year, because selling in small quantities is not likely to be very remunerative.

However, farmers who do not produce food usually do not acquire food in bulk at harvest time. This being the case, their choice between food and other purchases will be based on the retail prices of food as the season progresses. Hence, in spite of the small difference between the selling and buying prices of food in bulk at harvest time and the positive income effects of shifting from subsistence to cash crop production, we can confidently predict less food consumption in the household that does not produce food for home consumption and fails to secure the bulk of its food requirements for the year at harvest time. Food retail prices are notoriously higher than wholesale prices and in many cases increase drastically as the season progresses.

There are many possible explanations why food producers store large quantities of food while nonfood producers fail to do likewise. Transaction costs (psychic and effort), exposure of the cash earner to the marketplace and therefore awareness of the many ways in which money can be spent, traditions about the division of food and money responsibilities in the family, and perceptions about the nutritional value of foods are only a few possible explanations.

This single difference in the way food producers and nonfood producers secure their food can have severe implications for nutrition.

Obviously, if the income gains from a shift to cash crops are very large, this need not be the case. Perhaps in some societies it can be safely predicted that households with cash income will secure their annual food needs through purchases of food in bulk at harvest time. Otherwise, though, projects would need to be modified or special educational programs added to avoid negative nutritional consequences.

So far we have assumed that only selected, and perhaps few, farmers are encouraged to shift from producing foods to cash crops. If an entire community or region is scheduled to participate in such a shift, we should anticipate a rise in food prices at the wholesale and retail levels as the community or region is transformed from being self-sufficient to being food importing. This will reduce the community's incremental income gain, since the lost food output for home consumption has to be valued not at the current price of food (without the project) but at the higher projected price (with the project). The other implication is that we can expect a lower share of a constant level of income to be allocated to food consumption as the relative price of food rises as a consequence of the project.

To sum up, there is good reason to believe that current project appraisals overstate the incremental income gains obtained by semi-subsistence farmers from the introduction of cash crops. This bias should be eliminated for a number of obvious reasons. There is also good reason to anticipate that projects that reduce the supply of food and do not yield large incremental income gains to farmers may in fact reduce food consumption for the reasons stated.

Case 3: Higher Food Prices in the Project Area

The project results in higher prices of food in the project area. For the reasons explained in the previous section, projects that encourage the production of major traded crops—be they food or nonfood for the national or the international market—are likely to result in reduced production of nontraded food consumed on the farm and/or sold in local markets. By nontraded food we mean any food that is not traded in national markets, because it is a preferred food only in a particular region of the country, because it is highly perishable and costly to transport, or because it cannot be easily produced to acceptable uniform standards of quality. A declining supply of such foods leads to increasing nutritional risk among people whose income is low and is not raised by the project.

Moreover, projects that are specifically designed to increase the marketed surplus of nationally and internationally traded foods, such as wheat, rice, and maize, often include interventions that increase the farmgate price of these foods. These interventions may consist of measures to reduce the marketing costs, such as improved roads, or government procurement at higher than prevailing prices. While a higher farmgate food price provides substantial benefits (income gains) to the farmers who produce the marketed surpluses and possibly leads to increased food availability and consumption in other parts of the country, people who live in the project area and do not sell food and/or do not gain income from the sale of their services or labor as a consequence of the project are negatively affected. As these are the people most likely to be at nutritional risk, this feature of many agricultural projects deserves particular attention when nutritional considerations are a concern.

One possible implication is that neglect of proper accounting for the rise in food prices in the project area leads to the development of projects, or components of projects, that should not be undertaken. As an illustration, we will assume that farms in a region in which a new project is planned supply its 10 million inhabitants with an average of 100 kilograms of maize per annum, or with a total of 1 million tons. We further assume that as a consequence of introducing a cash crop project, the area's farms would reduce their production of maize by one-half, that maize is subsequently imported into the region from another country, and that, due to transport costs and so on, the price of imported maize in the project area is $20 per ton above the price that prevailed when the region produced all its maize supply. For simplicity, we will also assume that maize consumption does not decline.

This feature of the project would cost the consumers in the project region $20 million. The farms in the project area will by the same token gain $10 million due to the higher price of maize. The net loss to the economy is $10 million per annum. In other words, the added transportation cost due to the need for increased trade is not negligible. In cases in which the compensating gain from the cash crop does not outweigh this loss, some projects might be better left undone, or the project might be better if redesigned.

The implications of higher food prices for income distribution and, even more so, for food consumption deserve more attention. It may well be that the net gains of the project in the aggregate are still clearly positive. However, a project that results in higher prices of basic staples in the project region will definitely have a negative nutritional impact unless the incomes of net purchasers of food rise commensurately, either as a consequence of additional employment generated by the project or through compensatory redistributive policies.

Case 4: Changed National Food Availability and Prices

The project affects food availability and prices in the country. This is unquestionably the most controversial nutritional feature of agricultural projects. The heart of the question is whether a project that results in higher domestic food production is good for nutrition, or, conversely, whether a project that increases the supply of nonfoods (or "luxury" foods) rather than or at the expense of the supply of food is bad for nutrition.

The question is best broken down into two parts: (a) will the increased food production from the project result in an increased food supply and a lower food price in the country? (b) will a lower food price improve nutrition? Similarly, for a nonfood project, the questions are: (a) will the increased production of a nonfood in the project result in a decreased food supply and a higher food price in the country? and, (b) will a higher food price harm nutrition?

On the first part of the question, most economists will advise that whether a project produces foods or nonfoods should not affect the supply and the price of foods. The decision of what to produce in a project and what to export or import should be formulated on the principle of comparative advantage. Perceptive economists will slightly modify their conclusions to the extent that there is a large difference between the export and import prices and that decisions about production would move the country from being an importer to being self-sufficient or being an exporter or vice versa. The same consideration applies also when marketing costs are high and the project's output changes the trading position of the region in which the project is located.

On the other side of the fence, there are those who argue that a country should minimize food imports, no matter what. In this case, it is clearly important whether agricultural projects produce foods or nonfoods.

No conciliation between these two extreme views is possible. They reflect different subjective views about the goals of economic development and assessments of how well international trade performs. What the two views have in common is that they would have us make project decisions on the basis of how, in the proponents' view, decisions about trade should be made.

In the real world, governments intervene in trade, but not in the way suggested by either of these extreme views. They often do not permit such free trade that domestic prices of food and nonfood products conform to their international prices. But they also do not close their borders. In reality, therefore, more food production in the country does increase food supplies and reduce food prices, but not as much as the self-sufficiency advocates think. This being the case, what, if anything, can we say about the effect of introducing nutritional considerations into the design of agricultural projects?

One approach is to continue to insist that decisions on the output mix of projects must be made on the basis of the principles of comparative advantage. If it is more profitable to produce cotton or beef than maize when border prices are used in the analysis, let the project produce cotton or beef. We would recognize, of course, that this has negative nutritional consequences in the country that makes its decisions on anything other than the principles of free trade. But we would place the blame for the decline of food availability on faulty trade policies rather than on the choice of commodities in the project.

Another approach is to bring about greater harmony between decisions about projects and the government's handling of trade. From the point of view of improving nutrition, this is clearly a more promising route, but it is also very difficult to implement. Ideally, there would be some combination of recognition on the part of the government of the desirability of free trade and willingness to actually move in the direction of more free trade policies, and on the part of project planners, recognition of the forces that will prevent anything like completely free trade from being realized.

So far in this discussion, it has been implied that a larger food supply and a lower food price, whether achieved through food projects or through trade if the country has a comparative advantage in nonfood projects, is desirable from the point of view of nutrition. In contrast, there is the view that a reduced supply of food and a higher food price are what is needed at some stage, because low food prices are the primary reason why rural incomes are low.

If, for a moment at least, we accept the validity of the contention that a reduced national food supply (not production) and higher food prices are nutritionally beneficial, what is the implication for projects? As stated earlier, the answer depends primarily on how we view the role of trade. Those who believe that the burden of adjustment in supply should be entirely on trade would, in any case, use shadow border prices (prices based on international prices) to determine whether more or less food should be produced. To implement the project, the government would then have to procure the food from the farmers at a higher price than the prevailing market price, if that price is below the shadow price. Those who believe that the government cannot or should not be persuaded to adjust its import policy would have to argue for a more cautious expansion of food production to keep down supply and exert upward pressure on prices. This kind of reasoning lies behind accusations that the green revolution is to be blamed for aggravating poverty and malnutrition among farmers whose productivity did not rise commensurately.

There are two major problems with the contention that higher food prices should be encouraged. One is that there are many poor—the landless, the small farmers, the urban poor—whose incomes are not likely to rise with higher food prices. The other is that in many cases the incomes of poor farmers can be raised with a higher price for their nonfood outputs. Only if most of the poor are small farmers producing primarily marketed surpluses of food might it be nutritionally advantageous to raise food prices. In most cases, it is probably best for nutrition, on balance, to advocate a rise in the farmgate price for nonfoods (or foods that are not the main staple in poor people's diets) and the maintenance of low prices for staple foods.

In reality, it will be difficult to move in that direction. Taxes on export crops are major sources of government revenues. Therefore, it is politically easier to keep the price of export crops low. Downward pressure on food prices is likely to continue because of the "urban bias." At the same time we are likely to see an increasing emphasis on expanding the domestic supply of food (to conserve foreign exchange and decrease food "dependence") through measures other than raising the price of food. From a nutritional perspective, this combination of policies—low prices for export crops and measures to increase the domestic supply of food through subsidized inputs used by the commercial farm sector and for parastatals—may well continue to leave the small farmers among the most disadvantaged segments of the population.

Case 5: Increased Variability of Annual Income

The project increases average incomes and even average food consumption over good and bad seasons and years, but in some seasons and years the farmers are worse off. Some project designs, particularly if they reduce diversification in sources of income, in money and in kind, may raise the risk of an occasional failure. This has been widely recognized, particularly in explaining why farmers have been reluctant to participate in what seem to be otherwise attractive projects. If project planners are to pay more attention to nutrition, the risk problem takes on added dimensions.

It is important that risks be assessed not crop by crop, but for alternative crop mixes. In general, a mix of crops is likely to reduce the risk of insufficient income and food consumption, particularly if the sources of the risk are diversified. Thus for instance, the risks associated with the production of foods for home consumption are entirely production risks, whereas in cash crops the risks are associated with market as well as production risks.

A peculiar aspect of the risk problem is that casual observers often misjudge its time dimensions. When the price of a cash crop drops precipitously on occasion, as expected, people quickly jump to the conclusion that the crop should be discarded. Forgotten are all the good years. Forgotten also are the production risks and the famines that occurred prior to the introduction of cash crops. In general, the preferable way of dealing with variability in output, prices, and income is through financial means rather than through adopting farm plans that have less variable outcomes but are on average less productive.

Clearly, if average incomes were equivalent, farming systems that provide more stable incomes year after year would be more attractive than boom and bust systems. Inevitably, the cost to small farmers of borrowing funds against future receipts exceeds the earnings on savings stashed away after a good year, particularly if financial intermediary institutions in rural areas are underdeveloped.

Yet when new farming systems are expected to be significantly more remunerative, on average over good and bad years, than existing systems, they should be adopted. They will be adopted, and from the institutional point of view should be adopted, only if participating farmers in projects can be assured satisfactory "safety nets." The appropriate safety nets will vary with circumstances.

In practice, this means that during the appraisal of projects, the probabilities that farm households will receive varying levels of annual income should be explicitly estimated. To the extent that incomes are highly variable, financial arrangements such as flexible credit provisions, including credit for survival in bad years and income insurance plans, should be planned to facilitate the adoption of the new farming system and to prevent nutritional problems.

10

An Overview of Farming Systems Research and Development: Origins, Applications, and Issues

John S. Caldwell

Farming systems research and development (FSR&D), is the term used to describe an approach to the generation of new agricultural technology for family farms with limited resources.

Farms can be classified based on labor and product use, as shown in figure 10-1. Farms that hire less than 50 percent of the labor they use are termed family farms. Family farms that sell less than 50 percent of their production, and therefore retain more than 50 percent for family consumption, are family subsistence farms (shown in the lower left-hand quadrant). Over half the world's farms may fall in this quadrant (Harwood 1979). However, most of these farms are not purely subsistence farms but sell a portion of their production to meet other family needs for goods that must be purchased from markets.

Family farms that sell more than 50 percent of their production are family commercial farms (upper left-hand quadrant). Most of these farms do not sell all their production but retain a portion for home consumption. Thus, on both types of family farms, the household and the farm business are not sharply distinguished in the minds of family members because family labor is the main basis of agricultural production, some of which is consumed and some sold. It is these types of farms for which FSR&D is designed.

In contrast, in the upper right-hand quadrant are farms that hire more than 50 percent of their labor and sell more than 50 percent of their production. These are agribusiness farms. On these farms, the

Excerpted from "An Overview of Farming Systems Research and Development: Origins, Applications, and Issues," in Cornelia Butler Flora, ed., *Proceedings of Kansas State University's 1983 Farming Systems Research Symposium: Animals in the Farming System.* Farming Systems Research Paper No. 6. Manhattan, Kansas: Kansas State University, 1984. Pp. 25–54.

Figure 10-1. *Farm Typology*

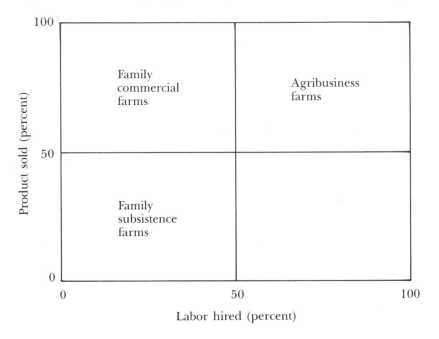

Sources: Vincent (1982); Nakajima (1969).

link between the household and the farm business is weaker. Typically, one family member, usually male, manages agricultural production, which family members generally consider to be a sphere of activity separate from the household and family life. It is these types of farms on which agricultural research and extension in developed countries have tended to focus.

Several characteristics of family farms must be understood by those trying to introduce technical change. First, the family farms, the clientele of FSR&D, are limited-resource farms. Land parcels are small, and families have to make do with what they have, such as a hand-made sugarcane press in the Amazon basin, simple seed storage inside the home in Ecuador, or a homemade tobacco transplanter in the Appalachian mountains of the United States.

Second, because family farms use their limited resources to produce for both home consumption and sale, they use different production strategies than do agribusiness farms. One of those strategies is diversification to reduce the risk associated with dependence on only one or a few types of production (Hildebrand and Luna 1983). Thus, for example, intercropping, as shown in a crop association of mungbeans and maize in the Philippines, is more common on family farms than the monocropping that is typical of agribusiness farms.

Third, the market is also important because family farms around the world have needs that cannot be met solely by their own production. This is as true in Latin America as in Asia and Africa.

Fourth, on family farms everyone in the family plays a role in agricultural production. For example, in Ecuador and Taiwan, not only adult men and women, but also the elderly and children participate. All these family members supply labor and take part in decisions about what to produce and how to use it.

Fifth, because family farms have limited resources, they must frequently share them at critical points in the production cycle. For example, in the Philippines, when the rains come all farms need to prepare land for rice at the same time. Labor sharing for plowing is a typical practice. This in turn means that farm-household and community links are stronger among family farms than among agribusiness farms, which depend mostly if not entirely on the market for additional resources.

Sixth, current production practices reflect the knowledge acquired and shared by farms on how best to use the limited resources of the community with existing technology. This shared knowledge of the basis of the community's livelihood is often expressed through religion and customs, such as in the names of planting dates (Caldwell and Newsom 1984) or in the belief that all maize plants, even volunteers (plants that come up in unexpected places from previous years' seeds, dropped fruit, and so on), are children of God not to be pulled. Strong community links and shared knowledge in turn mean that decision making often involves informal group discussions before individual farms change their production practices (Goodell 1980).

Finally, production changes need to be consistent with overall family goals, which are complex and changing. Changes in resource and time use by family members due to changes in farm production patterns must also be balanced against household production and consumption needs. (See Donovan in part II for a further discussion of family farms and decision making.)

Farming systems research and development reflects the evolution of postwar agricultural development strategies for family farms around the world. Initially, in the 1940s and 1950s, those involved in development tended to compare traditional production practices with production technology developed primarily for agribusiness farms in developed countries. The dominant theses of this period were that limited-resource family farms were characterized by tradition-bound inefficiency, and that families needed to be educated to use existing resources more efficiently and to adopt the technology of developed countries. Thus, community development and transfer of U.S. technology were dominant strategies of this period (de Janvry 1981; Ruttan 1975; Rogers 1969; Schultz 1964).

By the 1960s, however, it became clear that a redistribution of existing resources was not an effective solution. From the practical standpoint, community development efforts were by and large not greatly successful (Ruttan 1975). In addition, studies by Schultz (1964) and others (Sahota 1968; Chennareddy 1967; Hopper 1965; Welsch 1965) showed that limited-resource family farms were not inefficient but were generally making the best use of resources, given available technology. The problem was that they were efficient but poor (Schultz 1964). At the same time came the realization that technology developed in temperate countries with abundant land could not be directly transferred to tropical countries with small landholdings.

The dominant strategy then changed to an effort to provide limited-resource family farms with new resources in the form of new factors of production, primarily high-yielding varieties of wheat and rice, together with fertilizer, in what came to be called the green revolution. The content of technology had changed, but the strategy was still to try to transfer the "right" technology.

By the mid-1970s, it had become apparent that the green revolution strategy also had limits. First, the green revolution had more impact where inputs such as irrigation, fertilizer, and chemicals were available (Ruttan 1977), but such inputs were not always available to smaller family farms with more limited resources (Whyte 1975). In other words, there were differences among family farms that nationwide or even regionwide green revolution technology packages did not take into account.

Second, after the initial impact due primarily to substitution of high-yielding varieties for traditional varieties was achieved, subsequent increases in productivity required more complex and more fundamental changes in production practices, such as more precise timing of planting or preventive control of rats (Goodell 1980). These changes, in turn, required a more complex learning process by farm household members. Without more active involvement of farm household members in this learning process, they would not easily adapt and fully use all the technology now made possible through the advances of component research. Thus, technical inefficiency resulted (Pachico 1980).

Third, in Africa, production systems were even more complex, and research had not generated as much of a backlog of technological possibilities as in Asia, where the green revolution was more prominent.

For these reasons, in locations such as Guatemala, Nigeria, and the Philippines (Plucknett 1980), different attempts were begun to tailor technology generation to smaller, more homogeneously defined groups of family farms, and to involve family farm members more directly in a learning process of technology generation. By the 1980s, these approaches had acquired the generic term "farming systems research" (Hildebrand and Waugh 1983).

Applications of FSR&D

The objective of FSR&D projects is an agrosocial response—not simply to demonstrate a yield response, but to work with farm household members in a learning process of technology generation, adaptation, and adoption. To achieve this objective, it is necessary to establish research priorities that will generate technology that family members both can adopt and are willing to adopt (Norman 1983). The "can adopt" is the necessary condition, which requires an understanding of the biological, social, cultural, economic, and institutional environments in which the farming system operates. This understanding in turn requires insights from disciplines in both the technical and social sciences. Research priorities are therefore identified by multidisciplinary teams through informal survey approaches termed "sondeos" (sounding out), or rapid rural appraisal for groups of farms in similar environments, called "recommendation domains."

The "willing to adopt" is the sufficient condition, which requires an understanding of the goals and constraints of the household in each recommendation domain. Research priorities identified by multidisciplinary teams are therefore based on household goals and constraints. This is in contrast to the traditional commodity approach, where technology is developed by laboratory and experiment station research based on individual researchers' priorities, usually reflecting where they see the frontiers of science advancing. This technology is then transferred to extension for areawide dissemination. Social science, if used at all, is typically brought in only at this point to help "sell the technology" (J. C. Jones 1983).

Thus, diagnosis is the first activity in FSR&D, and the first product of a multidisciplinary FSR&D team is frequently a qualitative description of the farming system managed by the household, including interactions among crop, animal, and household subsystems, and of the various environments in which the farming system functions (Hart 1983). Frequently, this description takes the form of a model, as of a humid upland farming system in Asia (figure 10-2), which includes

Figure 10-2. *Model of a Humid Upland Farming System in Asia*

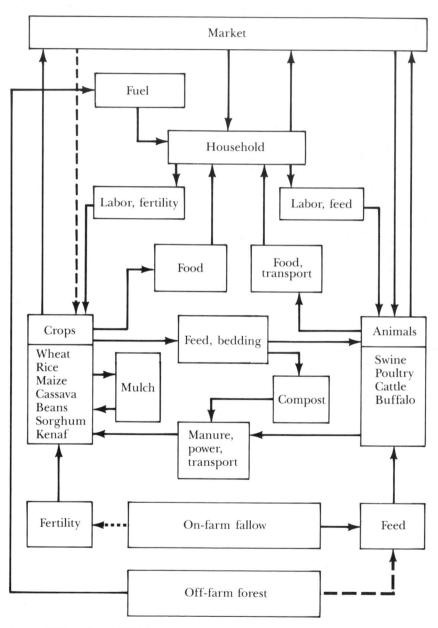

Source: McDowell and Hildebrand (1980)

interactions with the product market environment. These models are not exhaustive quantitative descriptions of the operation of the entire system but qualitative guides that serve to orient the work of the multidisciplinary team.

On the basis of the results of the initial qualitative description of a farming system, the multidisciplinary team can then undertake two complementary types of activities. The first is called farming systems research and extension, or FSR/E (Hildebrand and Waugh 1983). This involves development of applied modifications of farming practices. Because this is a learning process both for the team and for the farm household members, farmer participation in design and testing of the modifications is a key element. Trials are placed on farms with poorer environments as well as on better farms and experiment stations, so that the total survey of environments in a target area is covered. Experiment station research is, therefore, a critical input in FSR/E to measure the full range of responses.

Response is evaluated on multiple bases. For example, yields from alternative technologies can be converted to net economic benefit (Arauz and Martinez 1983b) or nutritional impact can be assessed (Smith 1984). Correspondence among these measures can be compared to assess potential impact of alternative technologies on different measures of farm family well-being.

Ultimately, response to a given new technology is evaluated on the basis of acceptability by representative farmers who have tested the technologies, as measured by the acceptability index (Waugh 1982). This index is calculated as the percentage of representative farms using the new technology times the percentage of the crop for which the new technology is used, divided by 100. For example, if 80 percent of the representative farms use the new technology on 35 percent of their crop, the index equals 28. This is a likely case if the technology is appropriate for most farms, including those with the greatest resource limitations, in the recommendation domain. Also, if 35 percent of the representative farms use the new technology on 80 percent of their crop, the index again equals 28. This is a likely case if the technology is more appropriate for farms with relatively fewer resource limitations in the recommendation domain. In either case, the index is a measure of the learning response of representative farms.

On the basis of the learning responses of representative farms to different technologies, researchers can decide which technologies to promote to other farms in the target area through more traditional extension efforts of mass dissemination. In addition, the team may identify technologies that would have greater potential for adoption or greater potential positive impact on farm family well-being if environmental constraints were changed through improved infrastructure or policy support. The team may make recommendations to policymakers based on the predicted responses of farm households to such changes. To more accurately predict such responses, the FSR&D team may also recommend that more involved and formal directed surveys of selected aspects of the system or its environments be carried out in the target area. This second type of activity in FSR&D is called farming systems infrastructure and policy support, or FSIP.

Because testing modifications of the farming system leads to better understanding of it, FSR/E can contribute to more effective FSIP. Likewise, policy changes resulting from FSIP can expand alternatives to be tested through FSR/E. Together, both activities of FSR&D form an integrated approach to the institutionalization of technology generation in the research-extension linkage (McDermott 1983).

As Flora (1983) explains, this linkage has been weaker in developing countries than during the early stages of the development of the U.S. land grant system, due to several factors. In the United States, male agricultural research and extension personnel came from family farms and understood from personal experience the goals of farm family members. In contrast, developing country research and extension personnel tend to come from urban backgrounds and have less appreciation for the goals of limited-resource farmers, particularly when these are tenants, near-landless, and/or female. Thus, FSR&D attempts to create a mechanism for strengthening the research-extension linkage under social, economic, and institutional conditions where the linkage has not been strongly self-generating.

An Example of FSR&D Application in Panama

FSR&D has been successfully applied in places such as Guatemala (Hildebrand 1983a), Indonesia (Effendi and McIntosh 1983), Malawi (Hildebrand 1983c), Panama (Arauz and Martinez 1983a, 1983b), and north Florida (Hildebrand 1983b). An example from Panama (Martinez and Arauz 1983; Arauz and Martinez 1983a, 1983b) shows how FSR&D is applied to a specific situation. The example is from the Caisan area of Renacimiento District, Chiriqui Province, in the central (interior) part of western Panama. The Caisan area was chosen as the target area (Shaner and others 1982) for the first test of area-specific FSR&D by a new national institution, the Agricultural Research Institute of Panama.

The target area consisted of about 10,000 hectares, divided among some 300 farms in nine communities. Predominant farming systems were:

○ In areas with land of irregular elevation: perennial crops or livestock

○ In areas with flat or slightly hilly land in western Caisan: arable rainfed maize-bean rotation-based farming. This farming system was the one on which the project focused.

The target area was then partitioned into two recommendation domains, based on access to market. An informal survey was followed by a formal survey focusing on maize production. This survey confirmed that there were marked differences in the use of inputs in maize production between the two recommendation domains. Recognizing that different technologies would be needed for farms in the two recommendation domains, and given the project's limited resources, efforts were focused on the recommendation domain with good market access.

The formal survey identified several major problems of the sample farmers. The most serious problem was both biological and socioeconomic in nature: good natural soil fertility, adequate rainfall, and a labor shortage combined to create a weed control problem that could not be solved by hand weeding.

The survey also indirectly revealed a second major problem that illustrates the linkage of FSR/E and FSIP. The government credit program emphasized fertilizer use, but 42 percent of the sample farmers did not use fertilizer, and the remaining farmers applied it at rates considerably below the recommended rate.

Based on the above needs and constraints identified in the diagnostic phase, the project established a research design that included short-, medium-, and long-term strategy components (table 10-1). During the initial phase of the project, on-farm trials in six locations were planned to investigate the benefits of improved plant spatial arrangement, allowing for higher plant density and better chemical weed control, in combination with different herbicides. This research was expected to produce the most rapid benefits to farmers. On-farm trials were also initiated to test the effects of nitrogen and phosphorus application, used in conjunction both with current plant density and weed control practices and with the improved plant density and weed control practices.

The local tall maize cultivar was susceptible to lodging (falling over) but was otherwise well adapted to the area, whereas previously introduced new shorter cultivars were not resistant to the high humidity of the region. Therefore, a breeding program was simultaneously instituted to reduce the height of the local cultivar. This illustrates how FSR&D and experiment station research can complement each other.

Finally, longer-term objectives centered around the problems of land preparation and insects. Zero tillage was proposed as an alterna-

Table 10-1. *Design for Farming Systems Research*

Problem	Time frame for completion	Strategy
Weeds and labor	2 years	On-farm trials: plant density × herbicide
Fertilizer and credit	3–5 years	On-farm trials: nitrogen × phosphorus × (plant density × herbicide)
Lodging	3–5 years	Breeding program to reduce local cultivar height
Erosion, labor, and machinery	Long-term	Zero tillage
Insects	Long-term	Clarify magnitude through observation before beginning research

Sources: Adapted and augmented from Arauz and Martinez (1983b).

tive to conventional tillage, which was associated with both an agro-ecological problem (erosion) and socioeconomic problems (shortages of labor and machinery). The linkage of FSR/E and FSIP was again present here because the credit program had also emphasized mechanized land preparation. On-farm tillage trials were planned to follow the initial trials on the basis of their results. The investigators also expected that observations during the initial trials would help clarify the magnitude of the insect control problem before research on this problem began.

After on-farm trials and an economic analysis of the results, two activities resulted from the first year's experiments. First, new herbicide and plant density recommendations for area farmers were formulated. Second, decreased emphasis on fertilizer use in the credit program was recommended and was instituted beginning in 1980.

The second and third years of researcher-managed trials introduced new variables, including herbicide residue, zero tillage, insect control, and medium-term fertility studies. The key element in the third year was the shift from researcher-managed trials to farmer-managed verification trials on larger fields for the three variables established by the researcher-managed trials as having high potential return. As anticipated, the alternative of using the new weed control, plant density, and zero tillage practices, but eliminating fertilizer use, proved superior to either current farmer practices or the new practices with fertilization.

Finally, a survey in 1982 indicated a high degree of acceptance for the new practices and recommendations. This reflected the application of basic characteristics of FSR&D: selection of research priorities based on system diagnosis; participation by farmers in the design and testing of applied modifications (both the herbicide applicator and minimum tillage light harrowing were ideas suggested by the farmers themselves); and linkage of on-farm trials (FSR/E) with policy recommendations (FSIP).

Issues

The example from Panama demonstrates the strength of the current state-of-the-art of FSR&D in generating new agricultural technology that limited-resource farmers can adopt and are willing to adopt. However, the state-of-the-art of FSR&D is by no means perfect or complete. Implicit in the example from Panama are also several issues that indicate both the limitations of current FSR&D methodology and opportunities for its future advancement.

Diagnosis of the farming system in FSR&D is comprehensive, taking into account crop, animal, and household subsystems and interactions of these subsystems with economic, social, and institutional environments. However, solution design has been more specific. Most FSR&D programs, like the Panama program, have focused on the crop subsystem. Researchers recognize the need to include the animal subsystem in potential solution design, but actual implementation has been limited by methodological difficulties and the scarcity of researchers with experience in on-farm livestock trials (Shaner and others 1982; Gilbert and others 1980).

In contrast to the animal subsystem, the place of the household subsystem in FSR&D has been more ambiguous. Researchers recognize the importance of the household as the "integrating unit" for the crop and animal subsystems. However, nonagricultural family priorities and the impact of change in agricultural technology on family welfare defined more broadly than economic benefit have not been the main concerns to date of FSR&D (Hildebrand 1982; Whelan 1982).

A recent paper by Behnke and Kerven (1983) points out for Botswana, however, a trend apparent in other countries as well: nonagricultural family priorities are often more important than agricultural priorities. Less than one-quarter of all farm dwelling units in Botswana in a 1979 study depended solely on agriculture. Moreover, two-thirds of all rural dwelling units in a 1976 study obtained more than 40 percent of their total income from off-farm employment. Diagnosis of such systems may suggest that innovations in the household subsystem could produce more rapid and more useful benefits to female farmers, who comprise over 40 percent of the official agricultural labor force in 60 countries and may account for as much as 80 percent of the agricultural labor force in African countries with substantial out-migration (Finney 1983; see also FAO in part II). For example, culture-specific home and market gardens, like those being developed for Asian countries by Gershon (1982), or improved methods of using agricultural waste biomass, such as in biogas production for cooking with reduced pollutant emissions (Smith 1983), can be linked to intensified crop and animal production.

Obviously, including the household subsystem as a potential focus of solution design would increase the complexity and cost of FSR&D. This is nonetheless worthy of testing, especially if the welfare of all family members is the measurement of the benefits of FSR&D.

Conceptual models of farming systems by Hart (1983), Norman (1983), McDowell and Hildebrand (1980), and Zandstra (1980) define farming systems' boundaries around the family farm. As Behnke and Kerven (1983) point out, this reflects the need for a clearly defined unit on which to base economic analysis. In contrast, they present two concrete examples from their own research and cite other studies that demonstrate that limited-resource farm household members have evolved complex patterns of animal, labor, and cash exchanges to compensate for inadequate resources at the command of each individual household. The result is the multihousehold farm.

McMillan (1983) has also demonstrated that there are differences in land tenure and crops grown by different members of farm households, depending on gender. Indeed, in parts of Africa, the typology of farms presented earlier in figure 10-1 may need to be disaggregated by gender, placing female farmer groups in the lower left-hand (subsistence family farm) quadrant, and males in the upper left-hand (commercial family farm) quadrant.

The focus of solution design and the diffusion of boundaries among farm households are tied to a third issue: the goal of FSR&D. Norman (1983) states that the primary aim of the farming systems approach to research is to increase the overall productivity of the farming system and therefore, it is to be hoped, the welfare of individual farm families.

To move beyond just hoping that there will be a link between farm income and welfare, an expanded model can be used (figure 10-3) in which crop and animal production activities compete with nonfarm production activities for the allocation of resources and management by household members. These three types of production activities

Figure 10-3. *A Progression of Conceptual Models for Farming Systems*

MODEL A

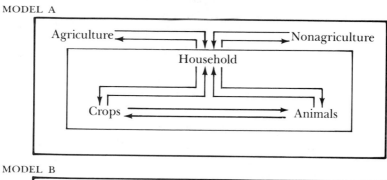

MODEL B

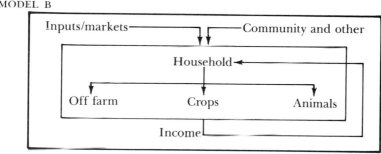

MODEL C

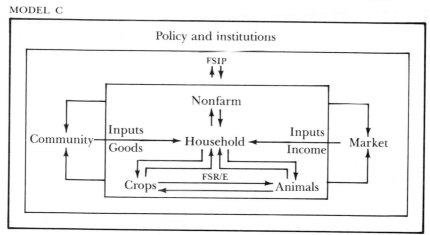

Sources: Key elements and interactions in Model A are abstracted from models by Zandstra (1980), McDowell and Hildebrand (1980), and Hart (1983); in Model B, from a model by Norman (1983).

yield not only income and inputs to the household through interactions in the formal market environment but also nonmonetary inputs and tangible and intangible goods. Moreover, perceptions of welfare affect the goals of farm household members and therefore their allocation of resources and management. In terms of general systems theory, the farming system is characterized by feedback and circular causation: welfare is not only a function but also a determinant of the management of agricultural productivity.

The challenge that these issues present is to advance the state-of-the-art of FSR&D so that we can evaluate the contribution of agricultural productivity to the welfare function without increasing the complexity or cost of FSR&D beyond the capabilities and resources of national institutions. Ultimately, the success or failure of FSR&D depends on its usefulness in strengthening the link between family farm household members and their national institutions.

11

Cash Crops versus Subsistence Crops: Income and Nutritional Effects in Developing Countries

Joachim von Braun and Eileen Kennedy

A crucial food security policy choice facing many low-income countries, especially in Africa, is whether to encourage subsistence crop production or to promote production of cash crops, both food and nonfood, for the domestic market or for export. Many developing countries are choosing export crop production to generate foreign exchange and fiscal revenue, increase the incomes of small landholders, and provide employment for the landless rural poor. Critics of policies to promote cash crop production argue that the potential benefits have never materialized and, more important, in areas where cash crop production has increased, food consumption of the poorest households has declined and their nutritional status has deteriorated. The following evaluates what is known about the income and nutritional consequences of increased commercialization of subsistence agriculture to identify both those factors that enhance positive effects and those that contribute to potential adverse effects.

Extent of Cash Cropping in Developing Countries

To identify the importance of cash cropping in developing countries, we estimated the share of cash crops in the total cropping pattern relative to basic staple foods. Cash crops were generally taken to be those that require substantial off-farm processing (for example, sugarcane), are usually exported (for example, coffee and tea), or are

Excerpted from *Commercialization of Subsistence Agriculture: Income and Nutritional Effects in Developing Countries,* IFPRI Working Papers on Commercialization of Agriculture and Nutrition No. 1. April 1986.

Table 11-1. *Importance of Cash Crops for Land Use in 78 Developing Countries, 1982*
(number of countries)

Share of cash crop area in total crop area	By income[a]			By region			Total
	Low	Lower middle	Upper middle	Asia and Pacific	Africa	Latin America and Caribbean	
Below 10 percent	10	6	0	5	10	1	16[b]
10–30 percent	15	12	7	12	15	7	34[c]
More than 30 percent	8	16	4	6	10	12	28[d]
Total	33	34	11	23	35	20	78

a. Classification follows World Bank (1983b).
b. Afghanistan, Bolivia, Burkina Faso, Congo, Ethiopia, Kampuchea, Laos, Mauritania, Morocco, Nepal, Niger, Sierra Leone, Somalia, Togo, Yemen Arab Republic, and Zambia.
c. Angola, Bangladesh, Burma, Burundi, Cameroon, Central African Republic, Chad, Guinea, Honduras, India, Jordan, Democratic Republic of Korea, Republic of Korea, Madagascar, Malawi, Mali, Mexico, Mozambique, Nicaragua, Nigeria, Pakistan, Panama, Peru, Senegal, Sudan, Syria, Thailand, Turkey, Uruguay, Venezuela, Vietnam, Yemen Democratic Republic, Zaire, and Zimbabwe.
d. Benin, Brazil, Colombia, Costa Rica, Côte d'Ivoire, Cuba, Dominican Republic, Ecuador, Arab Republic of Egypt, El Salvador, Ghana, Guatemala, Haiti, Indonesia, Jamaica, Kenya, Lebanon, Liberia, Malaysia, Papua New Guinea, Paraguay, Philippines, Rwanda, Sri Lanka, Tanzania, Trinidad and Tobago, Tunisia, and Uganda.
Source: FAO production and area data tapes.

mostly domestically marketed (for example, vegetables). Using these criteria, six groups of cash crops were identified: (1) sugar crops— cane and beet; (2) oilseeds—soybeans, groundnuts, castor beans, sunflower seed, rapeseed, and safflower seed; (3) fiber crops—cotton, flax, hemp, sisal, and jute and jute-type fibers—and (because of a similar off-farm processing pattern) tobacco; (4) vegetables— cabbage, artichoke, tomato, cauliflower, pumpkin, squash, gourds, cucumber, eggplant, chili, pepper, onion, garlic, watermelon, cantaloupe and similar melons, and several minor vegetables; (5) beverage crops—coffee, cacao, and tea; and (6) treecrops (other than beverage)—fruit, oil palm, and rubber. Basic staple foods were taken to be cereals, pulses, and roots and tubers.

The share of the crops identified as cash crops in land use, however, underestimates the importance of cash cropping, since the basic staple foods are also often marketed. For example, the share of all foodgrain production marketed by Egyptian farmers was 34 percent in 1981–82 (Alderman and von Braun 1984). Thai farmers sold, on the average, 39 percent of their rice in 1975–76 (Trairatvorakul 1984) and farmers in Bangladesh sold 22 percent of theirs in 1977–78 (Ahmed 1981). Farmers in the Eastern Province of Zambia sold 23 percent of their maize production (Kumar 1986). Not surprisingly, small farmers sell a smaller proportion of their produce than do large farmers. In Egypt, the farms below 0.4 hectares sell about 15 percent of their grains while those above 2.0 hectares sell about 48 percent (Alderman and von Braun 1984). In Thailand, farms between 0.3 and 1.5 hectares sell about 12 percent of their rice, while those above about 15 hectares sell about 67 percent of their produce (Trairatvorakul 1984).

Cash Crop Area

The area devoted to each of the crops defined as cash crops in 78 developing countries was computed as a proportion of total cropland, taken to be the sum of arable land plus land under permanent crops (FAO Production Yearbook tapes, various years). The 78 countries were grouped by region and by income level following the World Bank classification of "low-income," "lower-middle-income," and "upper-middle-income" countries (World Bank 1984b). The results are summarized in table 11-1.

A striking impression from this computation is the high share of cash crop area as a proportion of total cropland as well as the high degree of variance between countries.

- Only 16 of the 78 developing countries devote less than 10 percent of their cropped area to typical cash crops, and those are mostly low-income countries in Africa.

Table 11-2. *Change in Position of Cash Crops in Land Use in 78 Developing Countries, 1968–82*

Average annual percentage change in share of cash crops in land use[a]	By income			By region			Total
	Low	Lower middle	Upper middle	Asia and Pacific	Africa	Latin America and Caribbean	
Number of countries	32	35	11	23	35	20	78
Major cash crops[b]							
Stable (+ or −1 percent)	12	19	7	11	14	13	38
Moderate increase (1–2 percent)	5	7	2	5	6	3	14
Rapid increase (more than 2 percent)	2[c]	6[d]	1[e]	3	4	2	9
Moderate decrease (−1 to −2 percent)	9	2	1	4	6	2	12
Rapid decrease (more than −2 percent)	4[f]	1[g]	0	0	5	0	5
Nonfood cash crops (export crops)[b]							
Stable share (+ or −1 percent)	12	13	0	7	12	6	25
Moderate increase (1–2 percent)	3	4	1	3	3	2	8
Rapid increase (more than 2 percent)	2[h]	9[i]	1[j]	4	6	2	12
Moderate decrease (−1 to −2 percent)	3	1	5	2	3	4	9
Rapid decrease (more than −2 percent)	12[k]	8[l]	4[m]	7	11	6	24

a. Land use refers to the sum of arable land and land under permanent crops.
b. Includes the six aggregate groups of cash crops.
c. Laos and Sudan.
d. Congo, Costa Rica, Mauritania, Paraguay, Philippines, and Zimbabwe.
e. Syria.
f. Chad, Mozambique, Niger, and Uganda.
g. Nigeria.
h. Kenya and Vietnam.
i. Ecuador, Indonesia, Liberia, Mauritania, Papua New Guinea, Paraguay, Senegal, Zambia, and Zimbabwe.
j. Malaysia.
k. Bangladesh, Benin, Central African Republic, Chad, Ghana, Kampuchea, Mozambique, Nepal, Niger, Sudan, Tanzania, and Uganda.
l. Angola, Costa Rica, Haiti, Jamaica, Lebanon, Morocco, Peru, and Thailand.
m. Brazil, Jordan, Syria, and Uruguay.
Source: FAO production and area data tapes.

○ Twenty-eight countries have more than 30 percent of their cropland allocated to cash crops, and those are mostly middle-income countries, to a large extent in Latin America and the Caribbean.

○ A great variety of cash crops contribute to the high shares in countries with more than 30 percent of the area in cash crops. The more traditional nonfood cash crops that are mostly export crops—cotton, tobacco, tea, coffee, and cacao—figure prominently in some countries. Yet in only 3 countries are they more than 30 percent of the cropped area, and in only 20 countries more than 10 percent.

Since the marketed surplus of basic staples tends to range between 20 and 40 percent of gross production in low-income countries, a corresponding share of the basic staple crop area is, in fact, cash crop area. This further increases the ratio of cash crop area to total cropland.

Changes in Cash Crop Area

Production patterns for cash crops in developing countries are not at all stable over time, as table 11-2 shows. From 1968 to 1982, in 38 countries, or about half the total studied, the share of land devoted to cash crops was growing or shrinking by less than 1 percent. However, the other countries are divided into two groups of roughly equal size, 23 with more or less rapid expansion of cash cropping, and 17 with a reduction of cash cropping.

It is evident from table 11-2 that the proportion of cash crops is much more stable in middle-income than in low-income countries. One might expect that the low-income countries would be more rapidly moving into market-integrated agriculture with relatively more cash cropping. This is not supported by the evidence. More countries in the low-income group show decreased than increased cash cropping. Most of the countries that moved away from cash cropping as defined for these tabulations are in Africa, while a majority of Asian and Latin American countries show stable or increased shares for cash crops in land use. The decrease in the share of the traditional nonfood cash crops—fiber crops, tobacco, coffee, tea, and cacao—is particularly striking. Twenty-four countries, mostly low-income countries in Africa, show a rapid decrease, while only 12 show a rapid increase. Also, the upper-middle-income countries have been moving away from traditional nonfood cash crops. Nine of the 11 countries in that group reduced their shares significantly. The position of the nonfood cash crops shows more marked change than cash cropping in general.

The shift of cash crop production between countries of different income levels seems to follow a pattern of reductions in the low-income and upper-middle-income countries and increases in the lower-middle-income countries. The low-income countries seem to have moved more toward basic staple foods. The main conclusion of this overview is that the move into cash cropping is not a one-way street.

Competition between Staple Food Crops and Cash Crops

Cash crops and subsistence crops compete for the scarce resources of the farm household—labor, land, water, and capital. However, cash crops do not always compete for all resources with subsistence crops. They may be grown in a different season or in locations with soils or altitudes inappropriate for subsistence food crops.

Competition between cash crops and subsistence crops does not imply that expanded cash cropping necessarily reduces food availability. Expanded export crop production, for instance, need not reduce overall food availability in the exporting country. If agricultural exports conform to existing comparative advantage, the foreign exchange generated should be sufficient to import more food than the amount that could have been produced by the resources used for export crops.

A key issue, however, is what is actually done with the foreign exchange generated from agricultural exports. The extent to which foreign exchange will in fact be used for food imports depends on a number of factors, including internal food demand, national development policies, and the demand for foreign exchange from other sources (Pinstrup-Andersen 1983). The extent to which scarce foreign exchange is allocated to food imports is very much a political question that, at least in the short run, may not be dictated by economic considerations. The malnourished may exercise little political power. This tends to be particularly pronounced in countries where malnutrition is found primarily in rural areas, because the rural poor generally possess less political power than the urban poor.

The data base compiled about cash crop production in the 78 developing countries discussed earlier permits further statistical evaluation. Correlations were computed relating variables indicating patterns and changes in cash cropping, on the one hand, with country-specific indicators of levels and growth of food production and per capita income, on the other hand. The major findings are as follows:

○ Growth in the area allocated to cash crops is positively correlated with growth in staple food crop production (correlation 1, table

11-3). This probably reflects the fact that conditions favoring agricultural growth, including appropriate economic policies, encourage both cash crop and basic staple food crop production.

○ Growth in the share of cropland allocated to cash crops, was, in general, positively (however weakly) associated with increased staple food crop production per capita (correlation 2, table 11-3). This means that even if relatively more land was devoted to cash crops out of total land available, per capita food production tended to keep growing.

○ The share of cash crops in land use is higher in countries with higher GNP per capita (correlation 3, table 11-3). Also, growth in the relative position of cash cropping is positively associated with growth in per capita income (correlation 4, table 11-3). This should be expected, as the degree of specialization and market integration increases in the process of economic development.

Increased cash cropping may have positive, negative, or neutral effects on national food availability. The effect mainly depends on whether government policies encourage productivity in the subsistence food sector at the same time that they promote cash crops, and on the trade policies of the country. The analysis demonstrates that

Table 11-3. *Cash Crops and Staple Food Production*
in 78 Developing Countries, 1968–82: Selected Correlation Results

Correlation	Variable A	Variable B	Correlation coefficient	Level of significance (percent)
1	Growth of cash crop area	Growth in staple food production, (grain equivalent)	0.32	99.7
2	Growth in share of cash crop area	Growth in per capita staple food production, (grain equivalent)	0.13	86.9
3	Share of cash crop area in total crop area, 1982	Per capita GNP, 1982	0.33	99.8
4	Growth in share of cash crop area	Growth in per capita GNP	0.26	98.6

Source: FAO production data; World Bank (1984b).

growth in cash cropping is not mutually exclusive with growth in per capita food production. In fact, more countries with positive growth in per capita food production have simultaneously expanded the proportionate area devoted to cash crops than have reduced it. Unfortunately, the opposite combination stands out in low-income countries and in Africa: constant or shrinking per capita food production is frequently combined with a constant or shrinking allocation of land share to cash crops. The general message of these analyses is that failure in agricultural policy affects both subsectors alike.

Competition between Food and Livestock Feed

In 1981, about 600 million tons of cereals, almost 40 percent of the world harvest, were fed to animals (FAO 1983). This implies that at the global level there is certainly competition between food and feed use of cereals, and this may affect cereal prices. The nature of the food-feed competition is quite complex, however, and for the developing countries is not as significant as it might appear from global feed use. For 1981, the following situation existed (Sarma 1986; FAO 1983).

- About 73 percent of total global feed (in grain equivalent) was from roughage, of which only a minor share may compete for resources that could also be used to produce basic staple foods.
- Of the remaining 27 percent of feed, about one-third was comprised of milling by-products, including oil meals. The share of cereals in global feed use was about 17 percent (the 600 million tons previously mentioned).
- From the approximately 600 million tons of cereals fed to livestock, only about 22 percent (or 130 million tons) was fed to livestock in developing countries. These 130 million tons correspond to about 15 percent of the total staple food consumption (in grain equivalent) in developing countries.
- The 130 million tons of cereals fed to animals in developing countries are distributed as follows: China, 40 percent; Latin America, 33 percent; Near East, 14 percent; Far East (excluding China), 10 percent; and Africa, 3 percent.

While the current patterns of food versus feed competition do not appear to be an issue of concern for food availability in the developing countries, recent changes in the structure of feedgrain consumption in developing countries do.

- The use of cereals for feed in developing countries increased by about 8 percent a year over the past decade, in contrast to only about 1 percent in developed countries.

○ This increase was particularly dominated by growth in feed use in middle-income countries and the newly industrialized countries in Asia and Latin America, as well as in the oil exporting countries.

○ The rapid growth in poultry industries is a major factor behind the increased feed demand in these countries (Sarma 1986).

There are indications that the income elasticities of total demand for cereals tend to fall and then rise as per capita incomes rise. Mellor and Johnston argue that this shifts the rate of growth in demand for cereals above even the production growth rates achieved by countries highly successful in accelerating food production. Net imports may then have a period of explosive growth, and "given the diminishing returns to limited land area, plus the great difficulty and lack of experience with increasing the yield per unit of land by more than 2 percent per year, we can expect this phase to be one of rising real prices or rising imports of food." (See Mellor and Johnson in part I.) In this process, the nature of competition between food and feed utilization of basic staples may at times result in an adverse effect for food consumption of the poor, especially in countries whose growth path is combined with a skewed income distribution. This is possible because the derived income elasticity for feed due to increased demand for livestock produce may be higher in the middle- and high-income groups than the income elasticity for direct cereal consumption among the poor. Rising incomes in such a pattern could then result in upward pressures on cereal prices, depending on whether that country increased cereal imports and on the local market infrastructure. These higher prices would largely affect the poor, who tend to be more price-responsive in demand for basic food. Increased purchasing power in the hands of the poor is the most desirable assurance that the poor do better than animals in the competition for basic staples.

Relationships between Cash Cropping and Nutritional Status

While important variables affecting the impact of increased commercialization on nutrition are determined at the national and local levels, their actual outcome depends largely on household- and intra-household-level relationships between agricultural production, income generation, and food consumption and nutrition.

Several recent reviews have suggested that expansion of cash crop production may adversely affect nutritional status (Dewey 1981; Fleuret and Fleuret 1980). However, the studies that have looked specifically at the income and nutritional results of cash crop production provide mixed results. Some studies show a positive effect of cash cropping on family food consumption (Harvey and Heywood 1983; Lev 1981). An equal or greater number of studies show a negative impact of cash cropping on the household diet (Lambert 1978; Ogbu 1973; Gross and Underwood 1971). Even in a given country such as Kenya, no consistent positive or negative effect was observed across the different crops (Hitchings 1982).

The studies that have used a cross-sectional design to evaluate the effect of cash crop production are difficult to interpret. Many alternative explanations other than cash cropping could account for the observed differences in income and consumption. The most important limitation of these studies is that their design does not allow explanation of why the reported outcomes are observed.

Income Effects of Cash Cropping

In societies where farmers are free to make their own production decisions, farmers are very unlikely to produce cash crops unless they expect them to yield higher economic gains than any other realistic production option.

There is some evidence to indicate that cash crop production has resulted in significant gains in nominal income. In Kenya, the cash income of farmers participating in a sugar outgrowers scheme was approximately twice the level of nonscheme farmers (Kennedy and Cogill 1985). Additional data from Kenya indicate that income of farmers producing tea also increased (FAO 1984b).

The literature is less revealing about what is happening to real income. The gains in nominal income could be entirely offset by increases in the price of food and nonfood items. If a nonfood cash crop displaces food crop production, food supply and, in turn, local food prices could be affected. This need not happen if local markets are functioning effectively. If food supplies can move freely throughout a country, cash crop production would not affect local food prices beyond the effect of marketing costs. However, if markets cannot respond to decreased food supplies due to administrative or logistical barriers, then real incomes may not increase and in an extreme case could decline as a result of an increase in commercial agriculture.

Commercialization of agriculture may have a substantial impact on the demand for labor. If the cash crop production increases, the need for hired labor and the income of laborers, particularly landless laborers, may increase. However, if the cash crop is less labor-intensive than the subsistence food crop it replaces, then the demand for hired labor may decrease and the income of this group will decline. Ahmed

(1981) has examined this issue in Bangladesh and found that jute production is twice as labor-intensive as traditional rice production in the country. In countries where agricultural land is very limited, increased production of labor-intensive crops is an attractive way of reaching the landless poor who are often not reached by other development activities.

Consumption Effects of Cash Cropping

Conclusions about the nutritional consequences of cash crop production depend, in part, on which indicator is used to assess the impact. Household food expenditure, family energy and other nutrient consumption, individual dietary intake, growth, morbidity, and mortality can all be potentially influenced by the entry of households into commercial agriculture.

In general, as income increases, at least a part of the incremental earnings is spent on food (Mellor 1978; Reutlinger and Selowsky 1976). However, the additional energy consumed as a result of additional income can be quite small and varies widely among groups of households with similar levels of energy deficits. Even at fairly low levels of income, families appear to devote an increasing portion of income to more variety in the diet rather than simply augmenting the energy intake of the household. For example, in one maize-producing village in Tanzania, total income was related to food expenditures but had no effect on energy adequacy (Seshamani 1980). Results from Colombia and Nicaragua show only a weak income-calorie relationship (Goldman and Overholt 1981; Behrman and Wolfe 1984).

Impact of Timing and Form of Cash Crop Income

If household income declines, a decrease in energy consumption or a deterioration in nutritional status is not surprising. But why would increased income be associated with a deterioration in nutritional status? Part of the explanation may be related to the frequency with which the income is received. Lump sum income appears to be associated more with the purchase of consumer durables or investment while continual forms of income are more likely to be spent on food (Korte 1981). Lev (1981) found this in Tanzania; increased income that came in lump form, such as remittances and payment from the coffee crop, influenced wealth in such forms as housing or land ownership but had little effect on the adequacy of the household diet. There is nothing inherent in lump sources of income to account for this. Presumably a portion of these large payments could be saved for purchase of food and other basic items at a later time.

Part of the explanation as to why lump sum payments are typically used differently than more periodic forms of income may be because of who controls the income. The concept of a household as a homogeneous decision-making unit maximizing a common set of objectives and pooling income may be inappropriate. In many cultures, men control cash income and women control food income. This is particularly true in Africa. Cash crops are viewed as men's income. This is clearly illustrated by data from a sugarcane-growing area of Kenya. The responsibility for the cash crop as well as income received from the cash crop is overwhelmingly seen as falling under male control (Kennedy and Cogill 1985). For cases in West Africa, Guyer (1980) pointed out that the level of nutrition depends more on women's than on men's income. The women earn small amounts of money at regular intervals and tend to be responsible for small, regular purchases such as food (see also Tripp 1982).

The form in which income is received is another factor that could affect consumption and nutritional status. Evidence from India suggests that in-kind income is more likely to be used for family consumption than cash income (Kumar 1978). Income from home gardens and home production is more likely to increase household food intake than an equivalent amount of cash income. Food consumption in Kenya is positively associated with farm income and negatively associated with off-farm income (Greer and Thorbecke 1983). This finding suggests that increased agricultural productivity may be a more effective measure to improve household food consumption (and in turn child health) than simply increasing total family income.

One explanation of this outcome may relate to the short-term versus the long-term effect of cash cropping. Cash crops that require a long lead time between initial planting and harvest, such as coffee, tea, or sugarcane, may precipitate temporary food insufficiencies within the household. In Malawi, farmers who planted coffee but who did not have other sources of income prior to the coffee harvest did experience some temporary food shortages (Ogbu 1973). This would also explain why households whose income is generated from a mixture of cash crops and food crops tend to have more adequate food consumption. In addition, it would explain some of Hitchings' (1982) findings in Kenya. Using a long-term measure of preschooler nutritional status—height for age—he found a neutral association between cash crop production and nutritional status for most cash crops. The adverse effect of cash cropping may be only a short-term phenomenon. In the longer term, the gain in income generated from cash cropping may rectify adverse nutritional effects. The short-term adverse nutritional effect of increased cash cropping could probably be largely avoided by appropriate program implementation.

Impact of Changes in Household Relationships due to Cash Cropping

Cash crop production may have significant nutritional effects by altering the internal dynamics within the household—allocation of time and other resources, intrafamily distribution of food, and the health and sanitary environment. Commercialization of agriculture may affect not only women's income but also their time allocation. In many cultures, particularly in Africa, men and women have different responsibilities for crops, labor, and support obligations (Garfield 1979). Frequently men are responsible for land preparation and women are responsible for the other aspects of crop cultivation. The manner in which commercial agriculture is implemented may affect this intrafamily distribution of labor. For example, introduction of mechanical technology for swamp rice production in Sierra Leone decreased the mean hours for men slightly, while the amount of time required for female labor increased by 50 percent. Such effects obviously have an impact on women's household activities such as food preparation, childcare, and other nurturing activities (Popkin 1983; Garfield 1979).

Even if cash crop production were known to increase family income and consumption, it could not be assumed that the food intake and nutritional status of each household member would improve. If family food consumption increases as a result of cash crop production, individual energy intake will increase only to the extent that a part of this is passed on to family members. The literature on intrafamily distribution of food is limited. The allocation of food to children versus adults may be mediated in part by the sex of the child. In one study in Asia, male children were favored in the distribution of food and use of health care over females (Chen, Huq, and D'Souza 1981). Tripp (1982), in a study in Ghana, found that male children tended to be better nourished, as measured on the basis of weight for age. Certainly cultural differences are very significant in determining the intrafamily food distribution.

Food Policy Implications

In the great majority of developing countries, the agricultural sector is already highly integrated into the exchange economy, both at the national level, as indicated by the share in total production of major cash crops, and at the international level, as indicated by export crop production. Direct or indirect promotion of cash cropping is also an element of cooperation with donor agencies. At the program and project levels, many donor-sponsored projects aim at increased market integration of subsistence food crops and promotion of cash crops both for domestic use and for exports.

Autarky Policies

Given the potential problems of increased cash and export cropping for income distribution and nutrition of the poor, some have advocated radical dissociation of developing countries' agriculture from the exchange economy (Dinham and Hines 1983; Senghaas 1983). Not only would such an autarky policy forfeit long-run economic gains by failing to maximize comparative advantage, but there would be short-term problems too. Withdrawal from the international exchange economy would entail substantial domestic short-term adjustments that would adversely affect those rural and urban poor whose employment is linked to cash cropping. However, it is also evident that adverse effects on the poor could occur from a rapid move into export cropping in countries with a mainly subsistence-oriented farming community. Therefore, not only should policies seek a balanced approach to a long-term development of subsistence food and cash crop production that is appropriate for a country's resource base, its comparative advantage, and consumer needs (including the needs of the farm population), but policymakers should also consider the short-term effects and the time path of implementation.

A Checklist for Policy and Program Design

Policymakers considering a strategy for balanced promotion of subsistence food crops and cash crops that takes nutritional effects into account should not ask only, "Is there a national food gap?" or "Are there malnourished people in rural areas?" Rather, they must ask, "Who are the malnourished? How are they affected by alternative production policies such as increased cash cropping? How can their nutritional situation be effectively improved at the same time as economically viable policies for agricultural development are pursued?"

Without a clear understanding of the nature and causes of rural malnutrition and hunger, the choice of subsistence food crop or cash crop promotion may turn out to be inappropriate in the light of nutritional improvement objectives. Understanding the impact of changes in food and nonfood agricultural production on consumption and nutrition is, therefore, a precondition for finding appropriate and efficient solutions to existing nutrition problems as well as for preventing future nutrition problems.

A checklist for policy and program design is given in table 11-4. The checklist shows that in many instances the potential adverse effects of increased cash cropping for food consumption and nutrition may be avoided at little cost by appropriate design of policies and projects. In other circumstances, resources will be needed during an initial period to avoid adverse effects from increased cash cropping. The more cash cropping leads to unfavorable income distribution and carries a potential for adverse nutritional effects for the poor in a particular case, the more targeted subsidies should be extended to compensate for those effects. These must be subsidies that lead to productive employment and steady, unsubsidized income streams for the poor in the long run. The policy measures listed in the checklist basically follow this premise. This review and the checklist make it apparent that policies and programs leading to increased commercialization of subsistence agriculture need to be carefully designed and implemented if they are to assure positive effects for income and nutrition among small farm households. Particular attention should be paid to the effect on real income, employment, and household decision making about income use.

Table 11-4. *Checklist: Potential Adverse Effects of Cash Cropping for Food Consumption and Nutrition*

What are the potential effects?	Selected possible actions
National and regional level (issues for policy dialogue)	
1. Are such resources as land and labor for cash crop production withdrawn from subsistence food production?	Action (as in 2) required only if answer to question 2 is yes
2. Is national or regional food supply from domestic production reduced because of cash crops?	Increase in food imports, including temporary food aid; promotion of interregional trade within the country; promotion of subsistence food production along with cash crops
3. Are local food prices rising as cash crop production increases?	Improvement of rural infrastructure, for example, transport and market infrastructure for basic foods; also actions as under 2
4. Is there an increase in seasonal and irregular fluctuations of food supply and prices?	Intervention for stabilization of markets or of incomes of the poor
5. Is demand for hired labor reduced by increasing cash cropping?	Employment generation in rural areas
6. Is control over land and other resources such as water becoming more concentrated?	Land tenure policies; regulations for access to resources
7. Are local markets for food becoming monopolized as cash cropping increases?	Improved competition in food markets; establishment of public sector food outlets; consumer cooperatives

(Table continues on the following page.)

Table 11-4 *(continued)*

What are the potential effects?	*Selected possible actions*
8. Are public sector companies and parastatals that handle cash crop marketing and processing acquiring an undue share from cash crop returns (without transfers back to the farm sector through such indexes as investment in agriculture)?	Improved efficiency of public sector companies; assistance in building up cooperative schemes handled by farmers; extended role of private sector in marketing and processing, with control over concentration and monopolistic tendencies if necessary

Program and household level (issues for program design and implementation)

9. As cash cropping increases, are the real incomes of the poor and malnourished: a. Decreased temporarily? b. Decreased for an extended time?	a. Temporary income support schemes, including public works; slower program implementation b. Additional program component to generate long-term income for the poor (if this is not effective, program may be rejected)
10. Do the cash crop in question and the related production and processing technology significantly degrade the resource base and the ecology, thereby negatively affecting long-term food and agricultural production and the income-generating capacity of the location?	Identification of alternative crop or technologies, or rejection of program
11. Is increased commercialization destroying local welfare and food sharing systems?	Reactivation of existing traditional systems; possible addition of new components such as grain banks and credit and savings facilities
12. Is the income stream in cash more irregular (lump form) than the earlier flow of subsistence food income?	Activities under 11 and cash management education; more gradual phasing in of cash cropping; periodic payments on basis of estimated value of production
13. Is control over income within households shifted to members less concerned with food and nutritional needs (for example, from women to men)?	Provision of access to cash crop income for women; promotion of subsistence crops to increase marketable surplus, which is more likely to benefit women
14. Is cash crop production increasing the demands on women's time, with negative effects for childcare and health environment of children?	Measures to alleviate pressure on women's time, such as mechanization of production and processing activities; nutrition education; nutritional surveillance with intervention programs
15. Is increased cash cropping raising demand for child labor in field and household activities?	Measures, including mechanization, to reduce labor demand for related activities of children; incentives for school attendance

PART III

Food Security, Trade, and Aid

Policymakers and specialists increasingly understand food security as "access by all people at all times to enough food for an active, healthy life," as Shlomo Reutlinger, whose work has been central in articulating the concept, puts it in this section. Since the early 1970s, the focus has shifted from an aggregate, national perspective to one centered on "entitlement" to adequate food at the household or individual level, to use Amartya Sen's term.

The authors in this section explore the nature and extent of food security problems in developing countries and the policy alternatives available to governments to assure adequate food for all people at all times. The authors' fundamental thrust is that food security problems are not necessarily the result of insufficient food production, as has been widely believed, but instead are due to a lack of purchasing power of households or nations. The roots of food insecurity "range from improper macroeconomic policies to the economic and political structures of local societies that inhibit the ability of many households to procure enough food," as Reutlinger observes.

Economic growth, if it is associated with an equitable distribution of income, may ultimately provide most households with sufficient income to acquire enough food. There are, however, three well-known difficulties. First, economic growth takes time. Second, the current distribution of assets and opportunities means that many poor people may increase their purchasing power only slowly. Finally, there likely will always be some people who will not have the earning capability or asset ownership to enable them to have access to adequate food.

Sen's concept of entitlement clarifies the relationship between food supply and people's ability to obtain food by looking at various bases for the ownership and exchange of food. Focusing on entitlement helps to clarify what causes lapses in food availability for a family or for a segment of society. Sen warns that if policymakers inaccurately assess the causes of inadequate food for a group of individuals, the measures they take to improve the situation may well be ineffective.

Reutlinger estimates that some 730 million people worldwide, mostly in Asia and sub-Saharan Africa, have diets that are insufficient to support an active working life. Although the proportion of people with inadequate diets declined between 1970 and 1980, the absolute number has increased because of population growth. Reutlinger focuses on the household level, drawing a distinction between chronic food insecurity and transitory food insecurity, since these have different policy and program implications.

Improving food security is an investment in human capital, as it leads to improved nutrition, health, and learning capability. However, Reutlinger notes that the significant program resources committed to food security in many countries are often used in ways that are counterproductive to longer-term growth. Hence, it is as important to consider what policies should be avoided as it is to consider what should be done. The benefits of improved human welfare and productivity, Reutlinger cautions, must be weighed against the economic cost of interventions to improve food security, particularly in the current resource-constrained environment. Each country has to decide for itself where to strike the balance; it cannot be imposed from outside.

Policymakers often link national food security to buffer stocks, partly because of a concern that global supplies might prove inadequate or, if adequate, might be high in price or be blocked by political embargoes. Graham Donaldson suggests that holding buffer stocks beyond the minimum required for operational purposes "is expensive, and the benefits are often more psychological than economic." After reviewing major developments in the world grain market during the last 15 years, he concludes "that countries can, with some confidence, make use of the international grain market as a residual source of supplies." They should, however, do this judiciously and as part of a balanced production and marketing strategy.

Another means by which the international community has tried to improve food security is through food aid. Barbara Huddleston traces the trends in food aid as part of the broader growth in world cereal trade and suggests an order of magnitude for future food aid needs. Reutlinger and Judit Katona-Apte propose a controversial formula to decide which food aid commodities to distribute so that the maximum economic benefit may be realized by the recipients. Food aid is a resource that has financial value, since providing food to a family generally means that some other food can be sold or now need not be purchased. Their premise is that the greater the value of the resources saved by the family due to food aid, the more food and other goods the family can purchase, and therefore the choice of commodities should be based on the local market value of the food. In the final selection in this part, Raymond F. Hopkins looks at the evolution of food aid: what its original goals were, how these have changed over the years, and how a synthesis of goals could give rise to a "development-first food aid regime."

12

Poverty and Entitlements

Amartya Sen

Starvation is the characteristic of some people not having enough food to eat. It is not the characteristic of there not being enough food to eat. While the latter can be a cause of the former, it is but one of many possible causes. Whether and how starvation relates to food supply is a matter for investigation.

Food supply statements say things about a commodity (or a group of commodities) considered on its own. Starvation statements are about the relationship of people to the commodity or commodity group. Omitting cases in which an individual may deliberately starve, starvation statements translate readily into statements of ownership of food by people. Therefore, to understand starvation, the structure of ownership must be examined.

Entitlements and Ownership

Ownership relations are one kind of entitlement relation. An entitlement relation applied to ownership connects one set of ownerships to another through certain rules of legitimacy. It is a recursive relation and the process of connecting can be repeated. Consider a private ownership market economy. I own this loaf of bread. Why is this ownership accepted? Because I got it by selling a bamboo umbrella owned by me. Why is my ownership of the bamboo umbrella accepted? Because I made it with my own labor using some bamboo from my land. Why is my ownership of the land accepted? Because I inherited it from my father. Why is his ownership of that land accepted? And so on. Each link in this chain of entitlement relations "legitimizes" one set of ownerships by reference to another, or to some basic entitlement in the form of enjoying the fruits of one's own labor.

Entitlement relations accepted in a private ownership market economy typically include the following:

○ *Trade-based entitlement.* One is entitled to own what one obtains by trading something one owns with a willing party (or with a willing set of parties).

○ *Production-based entitlement.* One is entitled to own what one produces by using one's own resources, or resources hired from willing parties meeting the agreed conditions of trade.

○ *Own-labor entitlement.* One is entitled to one's own labor power, and thus to the trade-based and production-based entitlements related to one's labor power.

○ *Inheritance and transfer entitlement.* One is entitled to own what is willingly given to one by another who legitimately owns it, possibly to take effect after the latter's death (if so specified by the owner).

These are some entitlement relations of a more or less straightforward kind, but others exist, frequently a good deal more complex. For example, one may be entitled to enjoy the fruits of some property without being able to trade it for anything else. Or one may be able to inherit the property of a deceased relation who did not bequeath it to anyone through some rule of kinship-based inheritance accepted in the country in question. Or one may have some entitlements related to unclaimed objects on the basis of discovery. Market entitlements may even be supplemented by rationing or coupon systems, even in private ownership market economies, such as in Britain during the last war.

The scope of ownership relations can vary greatly with economic systems. A socialist economy may not permit private ownership of "means of production," thereby rendering "production-based entitlements" inoperative except when just one's own labor and some elementary tools and raw materials are involved. Not only will a capitalist economy permit the private ownership of means of production; that is one of its main foundations. However, a capitalist economy, like a socialist one, will not permit ownership of one human being by another, as a slave economy will. A socialist economy may restrict the employment of one person by another for production purposes, that is, constrain the possibility of private trading of labor power for productive use. A capitalist economy will not, of course, do this, but it may impose restrictions on binding contracts involving labor-power obligations over long periods of time. Such contracts, however, are the standard system under some feudal practices involving bonded labor, and also in some colonial plantations.

Ownership and Exchange

In a market economy, people can exchange what they own for another collection of commodities. They can do this exchange through trade, production, or a combination of the two. The set of all the alternative bundles of commodities that they can acquire in exchange for what they own may be called the "exchange entitlement" of what they own.

"Exchange entitlement mapping" (E-mapping) is the relation that specifies the set of exchange entitlements for each ownership bundle. This relation defines the possibilities that would be open to an individual corresponding to each ownership situation. A person will be exposed to starvation if, for the ownership that he or she actually has, the exchange entitlement set does not contain any feasible bundle including enough food. Given the E-mapping, it is possible to identify those ownership bundles—call them collectively the starvation set—that must, thus, lead to starvation in the absence of nonentitlement transfers (for example, charity).

Among the influences that determine people's exchange entitlements, given their ownership bundles (including labor power), are the following:

- ○ Whether they can find any employment, and if so, for how long and at what wage rate
- ○ What they can earn by selling their nonlabor assets, and how much it costs them to buy whatever they wish to buy
- ○ What they can produce with their own labor and resources (or resource services they can buy and manage)
- ○ The cost of purchasing resources (or resource services) and the value of the products they can sell
- ○ The social security benefits they are entitled to and the taxes and so on they must pay.

People's ability to avoid starvation will depend both on their ownership and on the exchange entitlement mapping that they face. A general decline in food supply may indeed cause them to be exposed to hunger through a rise in food prices that has an unfavorable impact on their exchange entitlement. Even when starvation is caused by food shortage in this way, the immediate reason for starvation will be the decline in their exchange entitlement.

More importantly, their exchange entitlement may worsen for reasons other than a general decline of the food supply. For example, given the same total food supply, food prices may rise because other groups are becoming richer and buying more food, causing a worsening of exchange entitlement. Or some economic change may affect their employment possibilities, also leading to worse exchange entitlement. Similarly, their wages can fall behind prices. Or the price of necessary resources for the production they engage in can go up relatively. These diverse influences on exchange entitlements are as relevant as the overall volume of food supply in relation to population.

Modes of Production

People's exchange entitlements depend, naturally, on their position in the economic class structure and on the modes of production in the economy. What they own will vary with their class, and even if exactly the same E-mapping were to hold for all, the actual exchange entitlements would differ with their ownership position.

But even with the same ownership position, the exchange entitlements will be different depending on the economic prospects available, and that will depend on the modes of production and people's position in terms of production relations. For example, while a peasant differs from a landless laborer in terms of ownership (since the peasant owns land and the laborer does not), the landless sharecropper differs from the landless laborer not in their respective ownerships, but in the way they can use the only resource they own, their labor power. The landless laborer will be employed in exchange for a wage, while the sharecropper will do the cultivation and own a part of the product.

This difference can lead not merely to contrasts in the levels of typical remuneration of the two, which may or may not be very divergent, but also to sharp differences in exchange entitlements in distress situations. For example, a cyclone that reduces the labor required for cultivation by destroying part of the crop in each farm may cause some casual agricultural laborers to be fired, leading to a collapse of their exchange entitlements, while others are retained. In contrast, the sharecroppers may all operate with a lower labor input and lower entitlement but may not become fully jobless and thus incomeless.

Similarly, if the output is food, such as rice or wheat, the sharecropper gets returns in an edible form without going through the vagaries of the market. In contrast, the agricultural laborer paid in money will have to depend on the exchange entitlement of the money wage. When famines are accompanied by sharp changes in relative prices—and in particular a sharp rise in food prices—there is much comparative merit in being a sharecropper rather than an agricultural laborer, especially when the capital market is highly imperfect. The greater production risk of the sharecropper compared with the security of a fixed wage on the part of the agricultural laborer has been well analyzed; but a fixed money wage may offer no security at all when food prices fluctuate sharply (even when employment is guaranteed). In contrast, a share of the food output does have some security advantage in terms of exchange entitlement.

Similarly, those who sell services (for instance, barbers or rickshaw pullers) or handicraft products (for instance, weavers or shoemakers) are, like wage laborers, more exposed, in this respect, to famines involving rises in food prices than are peasants or sharecroppers who produce food crops. This is the case even when the average standard of living of the latter is no higher than that of the former.

To understand general poverty, regular starvation, or outbreaks of famines, analysts must look at both ownership patterns and exchange entitlements, and at the forces that lie behind them. This requires careful consideration of the nature of modes of production and the structure of economic classes as well as their interrelations.

Social Security and Employment Entitlements

The exchange entitlements depend not merely on market exchanges but also on any exchanges that the state provides as part of its social security program (where such programs exist). Given a social security system, unemployed people may get relief, old people a pension, and the poor some specified benefits. These affect the commodity bundles over which people can have command. They are parts of people's exchange entitlements and are conditional on the absence of other exchanges that people might undertake. For example, people are not entitled to unemployment benefits if they exchange their labor power for a wage, that is, become employed. Similarly, exchanges that make people go above the specified poverty norm will make them ineligible for the appropriate relief. These social security provisions are essentially supplements to the processes of market exchange and production, and the two types of opportunities together determine people's exchange entitlements in a private ownership market economy with social security provisions.

Social security arrangements are particularly important in the context of starvation. The reason why no famines occur in the developed countries is not because people are rich on average. Rich they certainly are when they have jobs and earn a proper wage; but for many people this condition fails to hold for long periods of time, and the exchange entitlements of their endowments in the absence of social security arrangements could provide very meager commodity bundles indeed. With the proportion of unemployment as high as it is, say, in Britain or America today, but for the social security arrangements there would be widespread starvation and possibly a famine. What prevents that is not the high average income of the British or the general opulence of the Americans, but the guaranteed minimum value of exchange entitlements owing to the social security system.

Similarly, the elimination of regular and persistent starvation in socialist economies, for example in China, seems to have taken place even without a dramatic rise in food availability per head, and indeed, typically the former has preceded the latter. The end of starvation reflects a shift in the entitlement system, both in the form of social security and, more importantly, through systems of guaranteed employment at wages that provide exchange entitlement adequate to avoid starvation.

Food Supply and Starvation

There has been a good deal of discussion recently about the prospect of food supply falling significantly behind the world population (see Brown in part I). However, little empirical support exists for such a diagnosis of recent trends. Indeed, for most areas of the world, with the exception of parts of Africa, the increase in food supply has been comparable to or faster than the expansion of population. But this does not indicate that starvation is being systematically eliminated since, as discussed, starvation is a function of entitlements and not of food availability as such. Indeed, some of the worst famines have taken place with no significant decline in food availability per head. (See, for example, the analyses of the Bengal famine of 1943, the Ethiopian famine of 1973, and the Bangladesh famine of 1974 in chapters 6, 7, and 9 of *Poverty and Famines,* from the first chapter of which this extract is taken.)

To say that starvation depends "not merely" on food supply but also on its "distribution" would be correct, though not very helpful. The important question then would be, what determines distribution of food between different sections of the community? The entitlement approach directs one to questions dealing with ownership patterns and, less obviously but no less importantly, to the various influences that affect exchange entitlement mappings. Insofar as food supply itself has any influence on the prevalence of starvation, that influence is seen as working through the entitlement relations. If one person in eight in the world is starving, this is seen as the result of his or her inability to establish entitlement to enough food. The question of the physical availability of the food is not directly involved.

The approach of entitlements is very general and, I would argue, quite inescapable in analyzing starvation and poverty. If, nevertheless, it appears odd and unusual, this may be because of the hold of the tradition of thinking in terms of what exists rather than in terms of who can command what. The mesmerizing simplicity of focusing on the ratio of food to population has persistently played an obscuring role over centuries and continues to plague policy discussions today much as it has undermined antifamine policies in the past.

13

Food Security and Poverty in Developing Countries

Shlomo Reutlinger

Malnutrition persists despite economic growth and increased global food supplies. What policies can alleviate the situation over the short and the long term? The world has ample food. Global food production has grown at an even faster rate than the unprecedented population growth of the past 40 years. Prices of cereals on world markets have even been falling. Yet many poor countries—and hundreds of millions of poor people—do not share in this abundance. They suffer from a lack of "food security," mainly caused by a lack of purchasing power.

Food security, though interpreted in many ways, is defined here as access by all people at all times to enough food for an active, healthy life. Its essential elements are the availability of food and the ability to acquire it. Conversely, food insecurity is the lack of access to sufficient food and can be either chronic or transitory. Chronic food insecurity is a continuously inadequate diet resulting from the lack of resources to produce or acquire food. Transitory food insecurity, however, is a temporary decline in a household's access to enough food. It results from instability in food production and prices or in household incomes. The worst form of transitory food insecurity is famine.

The costs of inadequate diets to individual families and to nations as a whole can be enormous. Inadequate diets increase people's vulnerability to diseases and parasites, reduce strength, curtail the benefits of schooling and training programs, and result in a general lack of vigor, alertness, and vitality of the affected groups. Low productivity, due to inadequate "human capital," depresses output and hence in-

Excerpted from "Food Security and Poverty in LDCs," *Finance & Development*, vol. 22, no. 4 (December 1985), pp. 7–11. The paper summarizes the contents of World Bank, *Poverty and Hunger: Issues and Options for Security in the Developing Countries* (Washington, D.C.: 1986), prepared by the author with the assistance of other World Bank staff.

come, making it more difficult for families and nations to extricate themselves from the cycle of poverty.

The level of food security to be achieved must be determined by individual countries. Their choice will be influenced by many, often conflicting, factors. For example, cost-effective food security interventions can accelerate the rate of human capital formation required for economic growth. But attempting to reach the entire malnourished population too rapidly may entail such large costs and losses in resource efficiency that it will impair food security in the future. This article surveys the extent and nature of food security, and examines ways in which more food can be secured by people who lack it.

Chronic Food Insecurity

In 1980, somewhere between 340 million and 730 million people in the developing countries (excluding China) had incomes too low to provide adequate nutrition. The estimate of 340 million is based on a caloric consumption that would prevent serious health risks and stunted growth in children. If the consumption standard used is enough calories for an active working life, however, the estimate of those with chronically deficient diets rises to 730 million (see Beaton in part V). This higher figure is probably a better indicator of the extent of chronic food insecurity and the harm done to development by inadequate diets. About two-thirds of the undernourished live in South Asia, and one-fifth in sub-Saharan Africa. In all, four-fifths of the undernourished live in countries with very low average incomes.

Under the rather optimistic assumption that income distribution did not worsen during the 1970s, it can be surmised that the share of people with inadequate diets declined between 1970 and 1980. But because of population growth, the number of people with energy-deficient diets appears to have increased under both standards of nutritional requirements. The largest declines—both in shares and in numbers—were in East Asia and the Middle East, regions that enjoyed rapid economic growth during this period. South Asia and sub-Saharan Africa, however, had slight increases in the share of the population with energy-deficient diets, but large increases in absolute numbers.

Barring major changes in the distribution of income and in the price of food in developing countries, chronic food insecurity will probably continue to fall as a share of the population of developing countries but continue to rise in terms of the number of affected persons in the 1980s. The changes in the 1980s are likely to be less favorable than in the 1970s because average incomes are expected to grow less rapidly. Even modest improvements may not be realized, however, if governments in low-income countries pursue policies that make the poor bear the brunt of adjustments needed to cope with rising budget deficits that result from balance of payments problems.

While far too many people have energy-deficient diets, the aggregate energy deficit in their diets amounts to only a small fraction of the total national food supply in many countries. In a sample of 35 developing countries, the aggregate deficit amounts to no more than 3 percent of current aggregate consumption even when the higher adequacy standard is applied. The clear implication is that the inability of people to buy food, rather than overall scarcity of food, is the central food problem.

In some of the poorest countries, however, the aggregate food supply also needs to be greatly increased to alleviate chronic food insecurity. For example, if consumption by malnourished people were increased through redistributive measures and added to the extra demand caused by population and economic growth, the required amount of food could not be supplied in such countries as Bangladesh and many African nations without significant international assistance. These countries would need to realize unprecedented growth in both agricultural production and export earnings, as well as high levels of food aid.

Countering Chronic Insecurity

Clearly, the ultimate solution is to provide people facing chronic food insecurity with opportunities to earn adequate incomes and to assure an abundant food supply from domestic production or imports. It is now widely recognized that in countries that account for large segments of the undernourished (for example, Bangladesh and India), the basic causes underlying food insecurity can only be addressed by accelerating the growth of agriculture. The agricultural sector in these countries is so large that its neglect would jeopardize overall economic development and with it the possibility of providing gainful employment to the growing population and the ability to provide all households with access to adequate amounts of food.

Any policies that raise the incomes of the poor while increasing overall economic growth should obviously be given high priority since they would reduce, or even eradicate, chronic food insecurity without imposing a cost on the economy. However, in many developing countries, even under the best of circumstances, economic growth cannot be expected to proceed fast enough to eliminate the chronic food insecurity of some groups in the foreseeable future. Moreover, long-run economic growth itself is often slowed by the deleterious effects of widespread chronic food insecurity. In these cases, policymakers may want to consider interventions that would speed up the achievement of food security for undernourished groups without waiting for the general effects of growth to reach them.

Many national governments place a high priority on reducing chronic and transitory food insecurity but often use measures that adversely affect economic growth and food security in the long run. These include persistent overvaluation of national currencies, large expenditures on consumer food subsidies, low procurement prices for domestic producers, construction of costly storage facilities, and the holding of excessive stocks of food grain. Such measures are often counterproductive since they result in significant economic wastage and draw resources away from more productive activities.

Most specialized interventions against chronic food insecurity involve weighing the costs and benefits of three approaches:

○ Sharply targeted interventions, involving income or food transfers, with high costs of delivery and administration but reasonably low fiscal costs

○ General consumer subsidies, which are sometimes easy to implement and do not distort producer prices but have high fiscal costs

○ Food supply policies, which are easy to implement and have low fiscal costs but distort producer prices and therefore may create inefficiencies in agriculture.

The appropriate mix of policies has to be determined by each country according to local circumstances.

Income Transfers

In principle, transfer payments in cash or in kind to the poor, who are at high risk of food insecurity, are the most efficient way of increasing the real incomes of the poor and giving them the means to increase their food consumption. A well-known way to transfer income is to ration food to a target group at below-market prices through "fair-price shops," or distribute food free at health centers. Such interventions mostly aid urban dwellers and households that normally buy their food, or that have easy access to such centers. But there is no reason, in principle, why income could not also be transferred to rural households—either in cash or in subsidized rations of consumption goods or farm inputs. The difficulty with this form of intervention, however, is in avoiding "leakage" of the transfer payments to unintended beneficiaries. Efforts to direct the benefits more sharply to the poorest will reduce the fiscal cost of the transfers but raise, often steeply, the administrative costs of the intervention, particularly in less densely populated rural areas.

Some governments have successfully raised the incomes of the poorest people through public employment programs. These are attractive because only the poorest and the most frequently unemployed are targeted for jobs. But such programs can sometimes be inefficient in transferring income to the poor for two reasons. First, they may convey little additional income to workers if the wage offered is only slightly higher than the "opportunity" wage, that is, whatever the workers could earn elsewhere. In addition, the workers may have extra travel costs in reaching distant project sites. Second, the projects may create assets whose value is much lower than the cost of producing them.

Subsidized Food Prices

One way to overcome difficulties in directing subsidies to the poorest and the needy is to reduce prices of selected foods to all consumers without reducing the price paid to producers. The government then finances the difference between the two prices. Even when the foods being subsidized are consumed by poor and rich alike, the subsidies tend to benefit the poor more than the rich, in a relative sense, by increasing the incomes of the poor by a higher percentage than the incomes of the rich. Moreover, the administrative cost can sometimes be much lower for a marketwide food subsidy than for an income transfer program aimed at specific target groups, and a mass subsidy reaches more of the target population.

Subsidizing food prices for all consumers is clearly more costly for the government budget than subsidizing food prices for target groups. Such policies generally require heavy involvement of the government in the wholesale food trade. The government must manage a two-tiered price scheme—a higher price for producers and a lower price for consumers—and be able to identify and keep separate the food sold to consumers and the food bought from farmers (flour versus wheat, for example). Otherwise, the subsidized food may be misused. Farmers, for example, may find it profitable to buy grain from the government at cheaper prices for other purposes, such as feeding livestock or making alcohol.

The efficiency of consumer food subsidies varies according to the foods chosen. In Brazil, for example, one dollar spent on subsidizing bread transfers about 18 cents to the low-income population; in contrast, one dollar spent on subsidizing legumes transfers about 39 cents to this group. Consumer food subsidies can be even more efficient if further selectivity in the foods being subsidized is introduced, for example, by subsidizing inferior grades normally consumed by the poor.

Food Supply Policies

The fundamental question about policies designed to change the national food supply (production plus imports) is whether they increase the real income and food consumption of the undernourished population. The answer depends on how these policies affect food prices and the nominal incomes of the poor.

In discussing food supply policies, it is important to distinguish between foods that are internationally traded—the prices and level of supply of which are largely determined by world prices and the exchange rate—and nontraded foods—the prices of which are determined by domestic demand and production. The domestic supply of traded foods can be increased only by deliberate measures to increase imports or restrict exports. The supply of nontraded foods can be increased only by increasing domestic production.

Increasing the supply of a traded (imported) food will lower its price and decrease its domestic production. This will help the poor only if they are net buyers. They will be able to afford more of the food and will be encouraged to buy more because it is cheaper. These benefits can be considerable, since the poor typically spend one-half to three-quarters of their income on food and only slightly less on basic staples. If the net sellers of food are low-income farmers, they will suffer through a fall in the price. If the poor are primarily subsistence farmers—that is, they are neither net buyers nor net sellers—an increase in the supply of a traded food will have little immediate effect on them.

An increase in the domestic production of a traded food need not affect its price. The increased supply can be offset by reductions in imports or by increased exports. The sole beneficiaries will be the farmers who produce a net surplus of the food.

Abstracting from the indirect effect on food prices of changes in income resulting from changes in production (income effects are not unique to changes in the production of the food in question), an increase in the production of a nontraded food will increase its supply and reduce its price. The net buyers of the food—often the poorest— will definitely gain. Net sellers of the food, however, might gain or lose, depending on the extent to which the lower food price is offset by increased sales and lower production costs.

The choice of interventions needs to be based on a balanced concern for budgetary and economic costs, the administrative and political feasibility of different interventions, and their expected benefits.

Apart from cost considerations, the choice of proper food supply policies for food security objectives obviously depends greatly on commodity characteristics and the circumstances of the individual countries. If the poor are primarily net buyers of food—as is the case in countries with widespread urban poverty or a high proportion of rural landless—increasing national food supplies and lowering food prices is an effective way to enhance food security. If the poor are primarily net sellers of food—as is the case in many sub-Saharan African countries and in Bangladesh—food security may be enhanced by increasing food prices and by measures that lead to a substitution of domestic foods for food imports.

Transitory Food Insecurity

Short of outright famine, temporary disruptions in the ability of households to acquire food are difficult to quantify in the absence of data on short-term fluctuations in food consumption. Yet from what is known about the instability in international prices, food production, and export earnings during the 1970s, it can be surmised that the real incomes of a large number of households can be very unstable. During 1968–78, the coefficients of variation (the standard deviation of the difference between observed and trend values) of international prices ranged from about 20 percent for maize to 30 percent for wheat and 35 percent for rice. Variability in domestic production of cereal crops was very high during this period, with the coefficients of variation in the developing countries averaging 18 percent for wheat, 14 percent for maize, and 8 percent for rice (globally, the respective coefficients of variation were 5 percent, 4 percent, and 3 percent). Finally, the coefficient of variation of export earnings in developing countries—an indicator of a country's ability to import food—was about 15 percent, almost double the instability of export earnings in industrial countries.

Aggregate data usually hide more than they reveal about how transitory food insecurity affects individual households because increases in food production or incomes in one part of a country offset declines in another. In India in 1968–70, for example, aggregate national income, food production, and consumption were fairly stable. Yet survey data on per capita income and expenditure of 4,000 rural households showed considerable year to year instability. Nearly half the households surveyed experienced at least one year in which their income fell below 70 percent of their three-year average.

Famines are the most severe form of transitory food insecurity. They can have several causes, including wars, floods, crop failures, the loss of purchasing power by groups of households, and—sometimes, but not always—high food prices. A decline in the general supply of food is not necessarily a primary cause of famines. Indeed, by paying excessive attention to changes in the aggregate food supply, governments and other organizations have sometimes failed to recognize the other causes of famine.

The loss of real income better explains why famines occur and who is hurt by them. Typically, victims belong to one or several of the following groups:

○ Small farmers or tenants whose crops have failed and who cannot find other employment in agriculture (as in the Wollo Famine in Ethiopia in 1973)

○ Landless agricultural workers who lose their jobs when agricultural production declines (as in Bangladesh in 1974) or who face a rapid rise in food prices when their wages are stagnant or falling (as during the Great Bengal Famine of 1943)

○ Other rural workers (including professional beggars) affected by a drop in real income in the famine regions (this is true in almost all famines)

○ Pastoralists who normally get most of their food by selling their animals. Their herds may be ravaged by the drought itself, or animal prices may collapse relative to food grain prices (as, for example, in the Harerghe region of Ethiopia in 1974 and the Sahelian drought of 1973).

Famines can occur during economic booms or slumps. In Bengal in 1943, the increase in food demand, fueled by gains in urban income, inflated food prices faster than rural wages grew. In Ethiopia, by contrast, a slump (caused partly by the 1974 drought) reduced the demand for food even as food supplies declined, and prices barely rose.

Supply problems, such as those that occur in time of war, can aggravate a famine. But famines happen even when food grain markets are working very well. In several famines, local food prices barely rose and food was continuously available at those prices. But the victims could not buy it; they did not have the income. This underlines the need to focus relief work on groups whose real income has fallen.

Governments that do not prevent transitory food insecurity run big risks. They may face the possibility of disrupting the political order, prolonging human suffering, and losing human energies essential for development. They can reduce these risks by following policies that promote stability in the domestic supply and price of staple foods and that provide vulnerable groups with the financial means to buy enough food as the need arises. These policies, too, must be determined with a clear consideration of their expected cost-effectiveness.

In most countries, the surest and probably the cheapest way to achieve price stability is through international trade. Imports or exports can offset instability in domestic production almost automatically. By using variable levies on imports or exports, for example, domestic food prices can be insulated from changing international prices. But such policies may destabilize the government's budget and balance of payments. Countries may therefore need to hold larger reserves of foreign exchange and rely more on food aid or on international insurance schemes, such as the expanded Compensatory Financing Facility of the IMF, to finance sporadic increases in food imports.

Governments often try to stabilize food supplies and prices through quantitative controls on imports, exports, and the internal movement of foods. However, due to incomplete information on supply and demand conditions, lack of managerial capacity, and frequent political pressures from interest groups, government intervention often aggravates rather than reduces the instability of supply and prices.

Some governments also prefer to keep excessive buffer stocks. Large stocks are seldom cost-effective because of the high storage losses, low capacity utilization of storage facilities, and high interest charges on capital tied up in inventories. Countries with access to foreign exchange usually find it cheaper to stabilize prices by varying imports and exports rather than by using buffer stocks, even if world prices are unstable.

Even if markets are working perfectly and prices are stabilized, the most severely affected groups could still lack the purchasing power to buy food. Such groups include the rural landless whose employment and wages are severely depressed, the small farmer or herder whose marketable surplus has been destroyed or who faces adverse terms of trade, and the artisan or urban worker whose opportunities for work have collapsed. These must be quickly identified and provided with payments in cash or in kind, or—if cost-effective work programs are feasible—given temporary employment. When resources are scarce, special programs are at least needed to preserve the nutritional status of children under five and pregnant and lactating mothers.

External Assistance

So far, much of the foreign assistance for food security has sought to accelerate agricultural development and increase food production. These are important aspects of the problem when they affect the real income of vulnerable consumers and producers. But there has been only modest progress in diminishing worldwide food insecurity, partly because of the widespread misperception that food shortages are the root of the problem. The disturbing fact is that food security problems have become more serious in many countries, despite higher per capita food production.

The international community, in supporting food security, should adhere to the following precepts:

○ The lack of food security is basically a lack of purchasing power of people and nations. The convergence of the objectives of poverty alleviation and of food security is thus strong.

○ Food security does not necessarily derive from food self-sufficiency nor from a rapid increase in food production.

○ Long-term food security is a matter of achieving economic growth with equitable distribution of benefits. Food security in the shorter run is a matter of redistributing purchasing power and resources. By choosing redistribution policies on the basis of cost-effectiveness, governments can play constructive roles in improving the food security of their citizens.

○ Transitory food insecurity—because of fluctuations in domestic harvests, international prices, and foreign exchange earnings—can best be alleviated through measures that facilitate trade and provide income relief to afflicted populations.

International donors can assist nations to apply these principles to their particular food security strategies by helping to identify and formulate appropriate policies to alleviate food security, by providing financing to support these policies, and by improving the external trading environment. Efforts to support food security can be made in three directions: first, by giving priority to lending directed more explicitly to the poor in low-income countries; second, by using trade finance and other international financing arrangements for the alleviation of transitory food insecurity; and third, by better integration of food aid with financial aid.

The often-predicted Malthusian nightmare of population outstripping food production has not materialized. Instead, the world has been faced with the narrower problem of many people not having enough to eat, despite there being enough food for all. This is not a failure of producing enough food and still less a failure of agricultural technology. Its roots range from improper macroeconomic policies to the economic and political structures of local societies that inhibit the ability of many households to procure enough food.

14

Food Security and the
Role of the Grain Trade

Graham Donaldson

Official policy statements from many international agencies and developing countries reveal perceptions about the risks inherent in international grain markets that have not changed significantly since the dislocations of the early 1970s. Policymakers remain particularly concerned that global supplies may prove inadequate to meet needs arising in the event of a poor harvest. And even if global supplies are adequate, concerns remain about the affordability of imports and the possible impact of political trade embargoes. Notwithstanding the large investments required to reduce reliance on international markets, policymakers have made little effort to assess whether, in the light of recent developments in the world grain markets, many of the concerns about the reliability of world markets are justified.

World Grain Supplies and Prices

Although the data on global food trends are poor, they do show that grain production has grown at a generally increasing rate since the early decades of the 19th century and has consistently outstripped increases in global population. In the last 30 years, grain production has grown more than 3 percent per year on average and has grown faster in developing countries than in developed countries. As a result, the price of food grains has declined steadily in real terms, with temporary interruptions in times of civil unrest or war. Economists see no reason why this trend should not continue through the end of this century (Bale and Duncan 1983; Barr 1981; Schuh in part I).

Excerpted from "Food Security and the Role of the Grain Trade," *American Journal of Agricultural Economics*, vol. 66, no. 2 (May 1984), pp. 188–93.

As global grain output has grown, its year to year variability has changed very little. Using USDA data on global production since the early 1960s, our analysis shows that while the absolute size of the annual global variations has increased, so has the production base. The corresponding coefficient of variation was smaller in the 1970s than in the 1960s. Further, the global coefficient of variation is smaller than that for most individual countries. This indicates that production shortfalls in any country or group of countries have tended to be offset by good harvests elsewhere. However, these data do not indicate that national production variability is declining in most countries; in some just the reverse occurred in the 1970s.

Changes in World Grain Markets in the 1970s

Developing countries have increasingly used expanding global markets for grain imports to make up for poor local harvests and to dispose of surpluses. However, reliance on international food markets to stabilize domestic supplies has seemed paradoxical to many governments, since these markets are so widely perceived as unstable. Yet even in 1973, when export supplies were tight and prices high, grain availability was not limited. Developing countries in need were able to import as much grain as they could handle and distribute, although at an increased price. This growth in the global grain trade has continued despite greater price instability. The reasons for this growth range from basic changes in the global monetary system to more mundane technical improvements in grain trading.

Changes in Stockholding and Reserves

The changes in the international markets since 1974 have provided a substantial and effective reserve from which importers may draw. This reserve has three parts. First are aggregate trade flows. These have doubled in volume from some 120 million tons in 1970–71 to over 260 million tons in 1980–81. Second are nongovernmental stocks, currently averaging about 80 million tons, that backstop trade flows and are available for delivery within two to three months. The third—and most important—element in the world's total "buffer stock" is the grain being fed to livestock, which has in the past been diverted to make up for production shortfalls. In the last three years, on average, about 620 million tons of grain per year (including soybeans) were fed to livestock. This equals more than 60 percent of annual human grain consumption and includes large amounts of wheat (about 80 million tons) and soybeans (about 85 million tons), which are important sources of direct human nutrition.

The feedgrain buffer has been tested during the past decade and has provided an effective and surprisingly timely response to production shortfalls. For example, when grain prices rose during 1972–74, the feed consumption adjustment mechanism proved extremely robust and the drop in U.S. feed consumption in 1973–74 was as large as the total global production shortfall (about 30 million tons, or a drop of about 21 percent in U.S. feed consumption). A similar adjustment occurred in 1975–76, when the global grain production shortfall was far larger than in 1973–74 (about 65 million tons below trend) but grain prices remained relatively stable. Experience in 1982–83 provides another example of this grain buffer functioning even in the face of ill-timed government interventions.

Sources of Supply and Competition

The increase in demand for grain imports has been met by a growing number of suppliers in increasingly competitive markets. Important new production areas have opened up in southern hemisphere developing countries, from which grain arrives in world markets well before the North American harvest, thus reducing the need for global stocks. Annual grain exports from South America—mainly Argentina and Brazil—have risen from 10 million tons in the early 1960s to about 40 million tons today. The European Community has achieved production increases of a similar size. While the United States remains the major supplier of grains, it does not exercise monopoly power over the world market. Alternative sources of supply—particularly for rice and wheat, where the U.S. market share is smaller than in other grains—give importers substantial flexibility.

In addition, importing countries are able to deal with an increasing number of major trading companies, including four Japanese firms that handle exports from the United States. Studies by the United States General Accounting Office and independent scholars provide evidence that international grain markets are highly competitive, and that returns to capital of the major traders are comparable with those in other industries (Caves and Pugel 1982). Also, exporting countries have expanded the infrastructure for grain handling and transportation, which now far exceeds the needs of the foreseeable future.

Better Information

Improved information systems, including remote sensing, weather forecasting, and ground surveys, have permitted major breakthroughs in the ability to monitor upcoming harvests throughout the world. This has enabled the world market to know in advance of exceptional crop shortfalls and possible import requirements. As a consequence, major producing countries such as the U.S.S.R. can no longer "surprise" the market as they did in 1972. Substantial improvements have also been made in the mechanisms through which the U.S.S.R. and other centrally planned economies make purchases. Information exchanges between them and suppliers have now been regularized to minimize the risks from unexpected decisions.

Integration of the Global Market

With improved telecommunications and information gathering, the organized grain markets now provide an almost instantaneous and generally accurate reflection of the changing judgments of buyers and sellers throughout the world. Almost all international trade, and the great bulk of marketed production, is priced on the basis of changes in a handful of carefully watched markets. Exporters throughout the world sell at roughly the same world market price even when domestic farmers are paid at a different price (as they are in the EC). And government to government sales agreements—increasingly important in trade—specify quantity ranges, but not prices. Less than 10 percent of current world trade takes place on extramarket terms.

Growth of Futures Trading

The organized grain futures market grew almost 20-fold in the 1970s—the value of total annual transactions is approaching $300 billion—and now provides an immense base for absorbing incremental trading activity that would previously have been disruptive. Even more important, the large volumes of trading permit reliable "hedging," through which trading partners can "lock in" acceptable prices for future cash transactions. This also makes it possible for nongovernmental decisionmakers to hold carryover stocks profitably, reducing the argument for special buffer stocks.

As the futures markets reflect current and expected supply and demand levels, they give clear signals as to when grain should be released into the market or held in stock. In late 1980, for example, when prices rose more rapidly than in 1972, only moderate amounts were released from stocks, which in the aggregate remained sufficient to meet subsequent demand. This was in striking contrast to experience in 1972, when government decisions caused excessive liquidation of stocks.

New "Safety Net" for Poor Countries

Agreements reached by the late 1970s help to ensure that poor developing countries will be able to buy food in the event of local crop shortfalls or high import prices. First, a binding Food Aid Convention guarantees a minimum of 7.6 million tons of concessional deliveries each year. This is double the amount of concessional food aid actually made available in 1974 and is larger than all current net imports of food by low-income countries, excluding China (see Huddleston in part III). Second, the Compensatory Financing Facility of the IMF has been expanded to include concessional medium-term credit for cereal imports. Loans from the facility are made for five years (with two years' grace) at an interest rate of 7 percent. They are not subject to IMF conditions about the borrower's domestic policies. A country cannot draw more from the facility than 100 percent of its IMF quota (which is not static over time), but the maximum is not affected by its drawings on other IMF facilities. A review of the past 20 years' experience shows that in practice this drawing limit should not prove constraining.

Influence of Exchange and Interest Rates

Overall, variations in foreign exchange values during the last ten years have been larger than variations in food commodity prices. As a result, grain traders have resorted to using the same hedging techniques first developed in the grain futures markets to cover foreign exchange and interest rate risks.

In terms of national purchasing power, changes in foreign exchange values have often proved important in determining the relative "affordability" of food imports. For example, the fall in the dollar's trade value helped buffer the rise in dollar-denominated grain export prices in 1972–74 for countries like Germany and Japan. Experience among developed country food importers through 1982 was basically similar. However, in 1983 both the dollar and food export prices appreciated. This created a problem for many food importing developing countries.

Interest rates have also affected commodity prices by raising the cost of holding stocks. Overall, exchange and interest rates have been more variable than food prices (in nominal dollars) and this variability would have made efforts to stabilize commodity prices through interventions such as buffer stocks almost impossible during the past ten years.

Developing Country Food Imports and Related Risks

The food trade dependence of low-income and middle-income developing countries is very different. While the latter have increased imports in line with rising incomes, the former have not, partly because their incomes have grown less rapidly and from a far lower base. In the middle-income countries, where cereal imports grew most rapidly, per capita food production also grew, but in order to meet their "affluence requirements," the middle-income countries had by the late 1970s passed the industrialized countries as the largest importers of grains. Higher incomes, particularly in urban areas, led to changes in the kinds of commodities consumed. Wheat has become more important, as have other higher-value foods such as meat and fresh vegetables.

Among low-income countries too, degrees of dependence on imported food differ widely. Through raising their domestic production, South Asian countries have been able to reduce their dependence on imports to feed the urban poor. In sub-Saharan African countries, the food situation is approaching crisis proportions. Although the share of total foreign exchange that they devote to commercial food imports is quite small and has declined somewhat over the past two decades, their volume of food imports has risen in relation to domestic production.

Food Imports and the Balance of Payments

For the great majority of developing countries, food imports are not a major foreign exchange burden. As always, some countries have fared much worse than the average. When their own harvests have been poor, certain low-income countries have had to forgo planned imports of various kinds in order to buy food. Making these purchases on commercial terms has sometimes been very costly. Certain countries have had to devote, albeit for only one year, almost half of their annual export earnings to buy food. But for developing countries as a group, food imports have constituted only a small and declining proportion of the import bill during the past two decades. The increased pressure of balance of payments—a serious problem for many relatively affluent food importers, including some oil exporters—has come not from food but from oil (the real cost of which increased six-fold while that of grains declined), from debt servicing, and from other imports.

Skill in Trading

The cost of food imports depends to a large extent on the skill of the purchaser. Recent changes in world markets have helped to widen the gap between the more efficient traders and those that have followed inappropriate import practices. Developing countries have not generally taken advantage of mechanisms such as basis trading (negotiating each element of the delivered cost on the most advantageous terms), which can help lower the cost of food imports. The cost of retaining systems appropriate in the 1960s has proven high. Judging from country case studies—which have been confirmed by trade sources—developing countries as a group could save up to $1 billion in foreign exchange each year out of their total commercial grain imports of about $8 billion. The sources of potential savings include freight and handling; purchasing arrangements, including timing, the type and grade specification of the food bought, and its point of origin; financing and insurance; market intelligence; and regularized and open trading procedures. That the potential savings are real is demonstrated by countries such as Chile, China, and Colombia that in tight market situations pay prices similar to those paid by the most efficient traders among industrialized countries.

Reliability of Import Access

Much recent policy debate has centered around the issues of whether countries should risk dependence upon foreign suppliers and uncertain international markets for so vitally important an item as food. Fear that exporters may withhold supplies for political reasons provides a strong impetus for seeking self-sufficiency. However, the last 20 years provide little evidence to justify such a strong concern. Even the U.S.S.R., the world's largest importer and the only country to be subjected to a food trade embargo, has successfully implemented a food security strategy whose viability depends on imports. Nutritional well-being has been raised and consumption has been made less variable. Small countries can also follow such a strategy. And, in emergencies, food need not be purchased directly from exporting countries. It can be bought in entrepôts such as Malta, Rotterdam, or Singapore for only a small premium above the world price.

No developing country has ever been prevented by political action from obtaining needed supplies. For example, Iran continued to purchase U.S. grain all through 1979–80 when almost all its other commercial, financial, and political ties were cut off. In either tight markets or tense political situations when countries have needed supplies quickly (within a few months), they have found sources to meet their import requirements. Premiums for such rapid delivery have been waived by some of the export boards, including the Australian Wheat Board and the Canadian Wheat Board. For straight commercial purchases made through transshipment facilities in third countries—and therefore free of exporters' political control—the net premium above market prices for food imports has not exceeded 10 percent. In recent years, this depoliticization of the food trade has even extended to concessional food shipments.

However, while the international market system offers increasing opportunities for making food more continuously available to all, protectionist policies by major trading countries restrict the opportunities for developing nations to improve their food security. Japan, Western Europe, Eastern Europe, and the United States shelter their agricultural commodities behind often rigid trade barriers. These reduce food security in both industrialized and developing nations by preventing cost-reducing adjustments in rich countries and amplifying production instability in poor ones. More worrisome, however, is the growing agitation for restrictions on nonfood items such as textiles, steel, and simple electronic equipment. Trade restrictions, whether by quota or other barriers, are likely to reduce the export incomes of developing countries. While protectionism can make short-term political sense to beleaguered officials, its long-run effects are to push economies back toward autarky, which inevitably increases food insecurity.

Implications for the Future

This review of the scale and mechanisms of the grain trade suggests that countries can, with some confidence, make use of the international grain market as a residual source of supplies, provided they do so judiciously. However, a grain trading strategy is no substitute for sensible domestic production policies. Internal distribution problems in importing countries make grain imports an expensive and hazardous source of supply for all except those in major cities. Further, since the vast majority of the population in developing countries is in rural areas, and their incomes are dependent on farm production, imports cannot provide a long-term solution to their food security.

Similarly, a grain import strategy is no substitute for a sensible stockholding policy. While the additions to storage capacity can be kept to the minimum required for operational purposes, that is, to keep the pipeline full, domestic political factors may justify the holding of additional reserves of grain, over and above operational stocks. However, such storage is expensive, and the benefits are often more psychological than economic. Since to be useful a reserve stock has to be kept full, even if prices are high, a market advantage to holding reserves seldom exists. The release of grain from official stocks can be effective in buffering short-run price changes, but the amounts of storage required for this purpose are a marginal addition to those required to ensure continuous supply, and such stocks need to be backed by an effective trading strategy.

There is considerable scope for developing country importers to take better advantage of international markets. Doing this requires attention to the overall internal distribution infrastructure, including point-of-entry facilities, storage capacity, and transport systems. It also requires attention to improved information systems, both for internal crop and stock reporting and for monitoring external market conditions, and a system of logistics management, especially for use in emergency situations. Mainly, however, it requires better technical use of the markets for grain, ships, finance, insurance, and risk handling. Often what is needed is not a new organization but a concerted use of hired services to handle these matters. This approach has been used successfully by a wide range of developing countries, including Indonesia, Kuwait, and Zaire.

Finally, the importance of the grain trade for promoting global food security suggests a revised policy agenda, both national and international. This would include greater emphasis on the need to remove trade barriers, and particularly barriers to improving the mechanisms of trade. A high priority is to eliminate policies that protect domestic producers or consumers but dump greater supply or demand instability into the global market. This applies especially to policies of the EC and the United States, but also to those of the U.S.S.R., Japan, and some others. Overall, the most severe shocks to the global food system have been avoidable. Some progress in these areas would diminish the argument for global reserves or buffer stocks, which are very expensive in terms of direct holding costs, reduce the efficiency of the global market system, and are likely to be extremely difficult to manage.

15

Trends in Trade and Food Aid

Barbara Huddleston

The most striking change in the world cereal market since 1961 is the growth in the volume of commodities traded. As table 15-1 indicates, total imports, which include commercial and concessional imports and food aid, have increased from an average of 81 million tons per year in 1961–63 to an estimated 232 million tons in 1981. This growth has been most striking for centrally planned economies, which imported 13 percent of the total in the early 1960s but take 25 percent now. In contrast, Western Europe imported 40 percent of the total in the earlier period but only about 20 percent in 1981.

The share of developing countries in world cereal imports averaged 37 percent between 1961 and 1975 but increased to an average of 40 percent for the period 1976–80 and 43 percent in 1981. As shown in table 15-2, the volume of cereal imports into developing countries has increased from an average of 30 million metric tons per year in 1961–63 to 63 million metric tons per year in 1976–78 and 97 million metric tons in 1981. On a per capita basis, as shown in table 15-3, developing countries as a whole now import 30 kilograms per year as compared to 14 kilograms per year in 1961–63. For high-income developing countries—those with annual per capita incomes greater than $900 in 1976–78—the increase was from 34 to 96 kilograms per year during the past two decades. For middle-income developing countries (annual per capita incomes of $300 to $900 in 1976–78), the increase was about the same as for developing countries as a whole. By contrast, per capita imports of cereals into low-income developing countries (with annual per capita incomes of less than $300 in 1976–78) declined from 10 to 7 kilograms per year during the same period, although within this group the decline is attributable almost entirely to the drop in imports by India and Pakistan.

Excerpted from *Closing the Cereals Gap with Trade and Food Aid*, IFPRI Research Report 43 (January 1984), chapters 1 and 4.

Table 15-1. *Trade in Cereals, by Region, Selected Periods*
(millions of metric tons)

Region or country	1961–63		1969–71		1976–78		1981	
	Imports	Exports	Imports	Exports	Imports	Exports	Imports	Exports
North Africa	2.8	0.6	3.5	0.8	9.9	0.2	15.2	0.1
Sub-Saharan Africa[a]	1.9	0.7	3.1	0.6	5.3	0.5	9.2	0.5
South Africa	0.2	2.0	0.3	1.3	0.1	2.6	0.5	4.5
North America	1.2	45.8	0.9	50.1	1.0	101.8	1.6	136.2
Central America	2.0	0.1	2.8	0.6	5.8	0.1	11.2	0.1
South America	3.7	5.7	5.4	11.0	9.3	14.9	12.1	19.1
Asia and Near East[b]	19.5	6.0	26.6	7.3	37.9	9.9	53.7	12.1
Japan	5.9	0.1	14.7	0.7	21.9	0.1	24.4	1.0
Western Europe	33.1	7.6	40.3	18.6	49.9	26.5	44.1	40.3
Eastern Europe	8.9	1.7	8.6	2.6	14.4	3.7	15.5	3.9
U.S.S.R.	1.6	7.6	2.7	7.9	17.8	3.2	43.7	2.6
Oceania	0.3	6.4	0.3	8.9	0.3	12.3	0.4	13.3
World	81.1	84.1	109.2	110.5	173.6	175.8	231.7	233.8

Note: Data for ranges of years are annual averages.

a. Excludes South Africa.

b. Excludes Japan.

Source: FAO *Trade Yearbook*, various years.

Table 15-2. *Commercial Cereal Imports, and Food Aid Received*
by Developing Countries, by Region and Income Group, Selected Periods
(millions of metric tons, except as specified)

Region or income group	Year	Commercial imports	Food aid[a]	Total imports	Share of food aid in total imports (percent)
Total, developing	1961–63	18.5	11.6	30.0	39
countries	1976–78	55.1	8.0	63.0	13
Region	1981	89.5	7.6	97.2	8
Asia	1961–63	11.4	5.7	17.1	33
	1976–78	22.2	4.2	26.4	16
	1981	33.9	2.5	36.4	7
Latin America	1961–63	3.7	1.9	5.6	34
	1976–78	14.2	0.4	14.6	3
	1981	22.5	0.6	23.0	2
North Africa and	1961–63	1.9	3.9	5.7	67
Middle East	1976–78	14.6	2.5	17.1	14
	1981	26.4	2.5	29.0	9
Sub-Saharan Africa	1961–63	1.5	0.1	1.6	8
	1976–78	4.1	0.9	4.9	18
	1981	6.7	2.0	8.8	23
Income group					
High-income	1961–63	5.6	3.1	8.7	35
developing	1976–78	21.6	1.0	22.6	4
countries	1981	40.3	0.5	40.8	1
Middle-income	1961–63	9.4	3.2	12.6	25
developing	1976–78	26.7	2.7	29.3	9
countries	1981	43.4	3.4	46.8	7
Low-income	1961–63	3.4	5.3	8.7	61
developing	1976–78	6.8	4.3	11.1	39
countries	1981	5.8	3.8	9.6	40

Note: Data for ranges of years are annual averages.

a. Food aid totals for 1976–78 and 1981 do not include approximately 700,000 metric tons reported by the FAO, most of which went to Indochina and Portugal.

Sources: Total cereal imports, FAO (1974); food aid, IFPRI (1981).

Most of the growth in the volume of cereals imported into developing countries occurred in middle- and high-income countries, which took over 90 percent of the total volume imported in 1981. In general, the increase in volume is such that the ratio of cereal imports to total staple consumption also increased. However, for many of the higher-income countries where this occurred, the increase in import dependence is associated with improvements of such economic indicators as per capita GNP, export earnings, diversification out of agriculture, and, in some cases, per capita staple crop production. For this group

Table 15-3. *Per Capita Cereal Imports and Food Aid to Developing Countries, by Region and Income Group, Selected Periods*
(kilograms)

Region or income group	Year	Food aid per capita	Total cereal imports per capita
Total, developing countries	1961–63	5.59	14.49
	1976–78	2.74	21.59
	1981	2.36	30.19
Region			
Asia	1961–63	3.82	11.54
	1976–78	2.06	12.98
	1981	1.13	16.13
Latin America	1961–63	8.31	25.00
	1976–78	1.17	43.26
	1981	1.55	63.47
North Africa and Middle East	1961–63	24.13	35.81
	1976–78	10.22	70.96
	1981	9.77	111.34
Sub-Saharan Africa	1961–63	0.62	7.87
	1976–78	2.89	16.21
	1981	6.02	26.00
Income group			
High-income developing countries	1961–63	12.02	33.73
	1976–78	2.60	58.73
	1981	1.18	96.45
Middle-income developing countries	1961–63	3.27	12.89
	1976–78	2.04	22.10
	1981	2.26	31.13
Low-income developing countries	1961–63	6.34	10.41
	1976–78	3.56	9.19
	1981	2.94	7.42

Note: Data for ranges of years are annual averages.

Sources: Calculated from population figures from FAO (1977b) and from food aid data from IFPRI (1981) or FAO (1981a), whichever is higher. Figures for cereal imports are from FAO (1979).

of countries, increased import dependence is associated with phaseout of food aid and increases in average per capita calorie consumption to amounts that exceed minimum requirements established by a joint expert group of the FAO and WHO. Furthermore, the strong growth in the export sectors of many of these countries meant that the true cost of cereal imports to them remained stable or declined as a proportion of export earnings, despite the tremendous increase in the volume of cereal imports.

Although the rate of growth for cereal imports into many low-income countries is high, particularly in sub-Saharan Africa, the size of the volume increase is small and import dependence is still low, though increasing. Whereas staple crop production in a number of countries with high rates of growth in cereal imports improved, declines in per capita staple crop production are common to many low-income countries. It is primarily in this group of countries that increasing food aid has made the high growth in cereal imports possible, although in many of these countries the amounts are not significant, and they are rarely sufficient to offset inadequate calorie intake.

Food Aid

For all income groups and for all regions except sub-Saharan Africa, food aid per capita declined after the early 1960s. This decline has been particularly pronounced in high-income countries, which received disproportionately high amounts relative to the size of their populations. But note also that food aid per capita in low-income countries is now less than half what it was 20 years ago, and that total imports of cereals per capita declined for this group alone.

The geographic distribution of food aid has shifted because a number of important recipients in the earlier period have since phased out large programs. Particularly notable in this respect are India and Pakistan in Asia; Brazil, Chile, and Colombia in Latin America; and Iran, Syria, Tunisia, and Turkey in North Africa and the Middle East. Although some of these countries still rely on food aid to some extent, the volume received by these nine countries between 1961–63 and 1981 dropped almost 7 million tons. This freed about 3 million tons for distribution to newer recipients, primarily the smaller countries of sub-Saharan Africa and the Caribbean, plus Bangladesh. The remainder of the drop in volume to major recipients in the early 1960s represents the decline in total volume of food aid to developing countries.

While the geographic distribution of cereal imports and food aid in developing countries was shifting, equally important changes were taking place in the exporting countries and the donor community. Whereas the U.S.S.R. and Western Europe each supplied about 10 percent of the world's exports in 1961–63, the U.S.S.R.'s share fell to 1 percent by 1981 while the European share rose to 17 percent. Taken together, the United States, Canada, and Australia had about the same share in both periods—62 percent in 1961–63 and 64 percent in 1981. Similarly, exporting countries in Asia and South America accounted for about 14 percent of the world market in both periods (see table 15-1).

Whereas the United States once supplied nearly all food aid, it now supplies only about 55 percent of the total. Canada, Australia, and the EC are the most important of the other suppliers. Except for the Arab Republic of Egypt, the Republic of Korea, and Morocco, where the United States is the dominant supplier, all food aid donors give more or less proportionate amounts to the top eight recipients. The United States gives a proportionately larger amount to several Latin American countries and relatively less to the Indian subcontinent and Africa, where EC aid is concentrated. Canada and Australia both give to a smaller number of countries, mostly in the Commonwealth, with which they have long-standing ties. Australia has concentrated its aid on Asia and East Africa, though that may have changed since a simple need matrix was introduced into the aid allocation process. Bilateral donors still try to develop markets and gain diplomatic leverage, but there is growing emphasis on using food aid to meet the basic food needs of recipient countries (Wallerstein 1980).

In value terms, about a quarter of food aid is channeled through the WFP. The WFP uses food donations pledged by donor governments to support feeding projects that are considered suitable for multilateral assistance, although the actual food shipments channeled through the WFP are recorded by most donors as part of their bilateral aid to the designated recipients. A small part of the project aid given by the WFP and bilateral donors consists of food items other than cereals, principally vegetable oil, dairy products, and sugar. In terms of food energy content, these items still account for less than 10 percent of the total.

Out of the total increase of 151 million tons in world imports of cereals from 1961–63 to 1981, 40 percent was accounted for by wheat, the same amount by maize, 5 percent by rice, and the rest by other coarse grains. Among developing countries, the proportion accounted for by wheat was slightly higher—about 56 percent— whereas maize accounted for 29 percent and rice and other coarse grains accounted for about 7.5 percent each. The coarse grains other than maize imported into developing countries are primarily millet and sorghum for human consumption. Thus more than two-thirds of the cereals imported into developing countries are used as food. Nevertheless, the growth in the amount of maize imported for use as animal feed is striking, particularly in Asia and to a lesser extent in Latin America. Imports of maize into these two regions totaled less than 1.5 million tons in 1961–63, or about 8 percent of the world total of nearly 18 million tons. By 1981, maize imports into Asia and Latin America had grown to 17 million tons, or 22 percent of the total import volume of 79 million tons (CIMMYT 1981).

Whereas the total value of cereal imports into developing countries nearly doubled between 1961–63 and 1976–78, the value of a ton

Table 15-4. *Value of Commercial Cereal Imports and Food Aid to Developing Countries, and the True Cost of Imports, by Region and Income Group, 1961–63 and 1976–78* (millions of 1977 U.S. dollars)

Region or income group	Year	Total cereal imports	Food aid	Commercial cereal imports	True cost of cereal imports
Total, developing countries	1961–63	6,399	2,233	4,165	5,080
	1976–78	10,558	1,172	9,457	9,825
Region					
Asia	1961–63	3,752	1,150	2,602	3,022
	1976–78	4,385	603	3,782	3,969
Latin America	1961–63	1,158	366	791	998
	1976–78	2,136	47	2,089	2,108
North Africa and Middle East	1961–63	1,078	687	391	669
	1976–78	2,923	445	2,546	2,700
Sub-Saharan Africa	1961–63	411	30	381	391
	1976–78	1,114	77	1,040	1,048
Income group					
High-income developing countries	1961–63	1,918	578	1,340	1,595
	1976–78	3,679	148	3,531	3,593
Middle-income developing countries	1961–63	2,492	583	1,908	2,175
Low-income developing countries	1961–63	1,989	1,072	917	1,310
	1976–78	2,189	641	1,618	1,762

Note: True cost is the c.i.f. value of commercial imports plus the discounted value of the part of concessionally financed food aid that the recipient must eventually pay. Data for ranges of years are annual averages.

Sources: Figures for total cereal imports are from FAO (1974, 1979). Figures for food aid, commercial cereal imports, and the true cost of cereal imports are from IFPRI (1981).

declined from $213 to $168 in 1977 U.S. dollars. Thus the increase in the total cost of cereal imports was less pronounced than the increase in the volume for developing countries as a whole. This may be attributed partly to the fall of the real price of wheat over the past two decades and partly to the increasing proportion of lower-priced maize in the total import mix.

The extent to which food aid contributes to a reduction in the cost of cereal imports depends on the terms on which it is given. Food aid given on a grant basis reduces the foreign exchange cost of imports to zero. Food aid given on a concessional basis reduces the cost by the amount of the grant element in the loan. The true foreign exchange cost of cereal imports to a country that receives food aid is represented by the cost of commercial imports plus the cost of food aid after deducting grant and grant-equivalent portions (see table 15-4).

The ratio of total cereal import costs to export earnings has dropped from 7 to 3 percent for developing countries as a group, indicating that the growth rate of exports (including goods, services, and private remittances) was strong enough to more than cover the increased cost of cereal imports, even if food aid had not been available. Of course, this average masks considerable differences between countries. It also masks year to year variation in the ratio of cereal import costs to export earnings, which is quite large for some countries.

The data indicate that because of poor export performance, the total cost of cereal imports would cause greater strain on the balance of payments for low-income countries were it not for food aid. Since the volume of cereals imported by low-income countries was much lower than the volume imported by middle- and high-income countries, the higher proportion of low-income countries with high ratios of cereal import costs to export earnings apparently reflects the poor export performance of these countries. Food aid reduced the cost for most low-income countries with high cereal import bills, but cereal imports still represented more than 4 percent of exports. Furthermore, the data show that although cereal imports may not seriously strain the balance of payments overall, there may be problems for many developing countries in certain years, even though the trends for both the total and true costs of their cereal imports as shares of export earnings have fallen.

In all, 27 countries had seriously inadequate per capita food supplies in 1977–79. For all of them, current consumption is less than it was in 1961–63. During the past two decades, per capita consumption fell in only one other country, Uruguay, but food energy intake is still more than adequate there.

Generalizations

In looking at the relationships between trade growth, import dependence, food aid, and food supply adequacy in developing countries, several generalizations appear valid. First, countries in which food availability appears adequate tend to be middle- or high-income countries, highly reliant on the world market, and with little need for food aid. Second, on the whole, food aid is not a major factor explaining cereal import dependence. On the contrary, countries tend to become more dependent on cereal imports as income grows and food aid is phased out. Third, in most low-income countries that rely primarily on agriculture for GNP growth, domestic staple crop production has not grown rapidly enough to provide an adequate food supply, and not enough is earned from exports to pay for the necessary imports. These countries are less dependent on imports than most higher-income countries, but they receive a larger share of total food aid flows, both on a per capita basis and in absolute amounts. Finally, the low-income countries whose per capita production of staple crops is below average and whose average per capita energy intake is inadequate are receiving increasing amounts of food aid. However, a few middle- and high-income countries that have more than adequate per capita supplies of food still receive a disproportionate share. If some of the food aid now going to these few countries could be redirected to those with greater need, the nutritional status of underfed groups could be improved without increases in the total volume of food aid.

It is not possible to predict accurately how much food aid will be required in some year in the future. Too many uncertainties influence the final outcome, including world economic conditions, fluctuations in world cereal markets, and variations in the growth rates of key variables. Nevertheless, some general principles may be used to determine how much food aid a country needs. Using these principles and projecting past trends under alternative scenarios, the approximate future requirements of all developing countries can be estimated, although such estimates do not precisely indicate what individual countries are likely to require. If present trends continue, the number of high-income developing countries will increase and the number of middle- and low-income developing countries will drop from 73 to 57 by 1990. Nearly 15 to 30 million metric tons of food aid would be required by these 57 countries under three alternative scenarios based on estimating the probable effective demand for cereal imports. Under a scenario that looks at the imports required to provide enough food to supply market demand and fill an estimated dietary energy gap, the food aid requirement is 22 to 34 million metric tons. Under this scenario, countries with particularly large nutrition requirements in 1990 include Bangladesh, Ethiopia, Tanzania, Zaire, and the land-locked countries of the Sahel.

Quantification of the food aid requirement provides an upper limit to the amount that can be used effectively. However, the actual demand for food aid in most countries is lower because economic conditions and management constraints restrict the amount that can be put to good use. Some economic environments are more hospitable than others to food aid programs that reach the poor. In hospitable environments, food aid can be used in two ways. First, it can be used to create additional demand, thus avoiding disincentive effects for domestic agriculture. However, the administrative costs of demand-creating programs are usually high. Either countries must provide scarce management skills themselves or rely on expatriate voluntary agency personnel. This imposes one kind of constraint on the quantity of food aid a country can use effectively.

Second, food aid can be sold on the open market, perhaps at subsidized prices for consumers, and the proceeds used to support farm prices or otherwise contribute to agricultural development. Although disincentives resulting from open market sales can be avoided if the right policies are adopted, such as a dual pricing system, for example, changing economic policies that use imports to support a cheap food policy while taxing domestic agriculture is often politically difficult. From the donor's standpoint this imposes a second kind of constraint on the quantity of food aid a country can put to good use, even though there may be strong political pressure to increase the flow of food aid before policy changes favorable to domestic agriculture have been initiated. As a practical matter, therefore, increases in food aid are likely to be phased in gradually, in accordance with a recipient country's strategy for using it effectively.

16

The Nutritional Impact of Food Aid: Criteria for the Selection of Cost-Effective Foods

Shlomo Reutlinger and Judit Katona-Apte

One important reason that aid programs sometimes provide people in need with food rather than cash is that governments acquire food as a result of programs designed to support farm incomes. Another is that planners often allege that food aid is preferable to cash aid because the former is nutritionally more effective. This belief requires close scrutiny. Is it true that food aid is nutritionally more effective because it leads recipients to allocate a larger share of their total expenditures to food than they would allocate when provided an equivalent amount of cash aid? Alternatively, is it presumed that the recipients will consume the particular foods delivered in the programs in addition to their existing diets?

The answers to these questions have profound implications for the way food aid should be administered. Acting on the basis of how aid givers would like recipients to use the aid rather than on how recipients actually use the food aid can be very costly in terms of the intended outcome. The nutritional content of the food aid commodity must not be confused with its nutritional effect. Most importantly, accurate perceptions about the effects of food aid can lead to criteria for selecting implementation procedures that will increase potential benefits. The purpose of this article is to sharpen these perceptions and to suggest appropriate criteria for the selection of commodities to be used in some food aid programs.

Excerpted from *Nutrition Today*, vol. 19, no. 3 (May–June 1984), pp. 1–10.

The Two Pathways by Which Food Aid Effects a Change in Nutritional Status

Recipients of food aid have essentially two options for using the provided food. The first is that they may use it as a net addition to the food they are already consuming. This happens in the case of emergency feeding or disaster relief when the recipients have very little food from any other source. Pathway A in figure 16-1 is a diagram of this kind of use of food aid. The nutritional effect stands in direct proportion to the nutritional content of the foods provided through aid. Similarly, the nutritional cost-effectiveness of different foods is directly related to the nutritional value per unit cost of the different foods. Since a nutritionally effective diet requires an appropriate mix of energy and specific nutrients, the most cost-effective mix of foods is the one that supplies all the nutritional needs of the recipients at the least possible cost.

The second option is for the recipients to substitute all or some of the food supplied in the aid program for the same or similar foods they would be purchasing otherwise. The impact of the food is then determined by the size of the potential savings realizable as a consequence of the aid program's distributed food and by what the recipients choose—or are able—to purchase with the added purchasing power. This option is described as pathway B in figure 16-1. The important feature about this pathway is that the amount and composition of foods consumed as a result of the food aid may or may not bear any resemblance to the food aid package provided. The net addition to energy or protein intake may be more or less than that contained in the provided foods, and some of the additional purchasing power is likely to be used for other than added food consumption. However, it is not at all clear that the recipients' nonfood expenditures (that is, for housing, clothing, and education) indirectly made possible by the added purchasing power released as a consequence of the food aid are necessarily any less important to the improvement of the recipients' nutritional status than added food consumption.

This second pathway of nutritional effect suggested here may appear innovative. However, many studies have suggested that the nutritional effect of food aid is not necessarily caused by the nutritional content of the food aid package but by its income transfer potential (Overholt and others 1982; Herrera and others 1980; Delgado and others 1979; Mora and others 1978; Anderson 1977). A comprehensive recent survey of supplementary feeding programs for young children in developing countries by Beaton and Ghassemi provides the most persuasive evidence in support of the existence of the second

Figure 16-1. *Pathways of Food Aid into Nutritional Status*

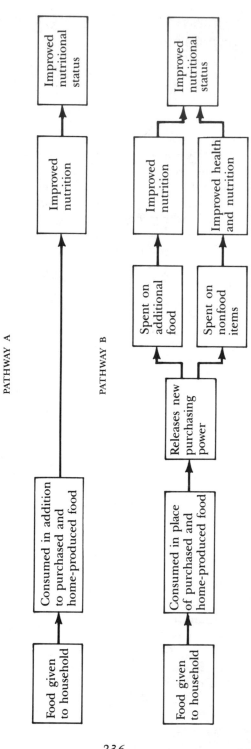

PATHWAY A

PATHWAY B

pathway. They report that in the 8 supervised feeding and 13 take-home food programs for which they had data, ". . . the net increase in intake by the target recipient was 45 to 70 percent of the food distributed, with one program showing a net effect of only 10 to 15 percent . . ." (Beaton and Ghassemi in part V). They speculate that the "leakage" must be due to sharing of the food with other members of the households (in the case of take-home food programs) and to displacement of foods in the existing diets of the target recipients. In some studies, total energy intake actually remained the same, but foods of higher nutritional value were replacing foods normally consumed.

Some researchers have suggested, but without much empirical evidence as yet, that the marginal propensity to spend on food is higher for additional purchasing power conveyed through food aid than for increases in ordinary income. One explanation offered is that women may influence the allocation of food aid more than the allocation of additional income acquired in other ways, and indications exist that when women have control over household budgets, more food is purchased, especially for children. There is also some evidence that the propensity to spend on food can be influenced by nutrition education, particularly if households are provided at the same time with additional purchasing power.

In any case, how much of the food aid will be used to increase food consumption and how much will be used to reduce other deprivations will vary a great deal from one population to another and among households in the same population. If we accept that people do not behave arbitrarily but in their best interest, this might in itself be a good reason for providing food aid in a form that allows the recipients to use it in ways suited to their particular circumstances.

A New Approach to Nutritional Cost-Effectiveness

Once people accept that under certain conditions the changes in quantities and kinds of foods consumed by the recipients of food aid bear little resemblance to the contents of the food aid package, it becomes clear that criteria for selecting foods that are based exclusively on the nutritional contents of the food aid commodities are erroneous. An entirely new approach is needed to achieve the best possible nutritional cost-effectiveness in food aid programs.

The new approach discussed below is applicable wherever food aid provides households with a relatively small, rationed amount of food that is taken home to supplement the existing diet. Under these circumstances—in contrast to food aid programs that provide disaster relief—foods are available in the local market, and if households are not consuming enough, it is for lack of sufficient purchasing power. In this case, the household will generally substitute the food aid commodity for all or part of the foods in the existing diet and use the "savings" for the purchase of other food and nonfood items. To know the precise nutritional cost-effectiveness, we would need to know the household's marginal propensities to spend the saved purchasing power (what they will do with the additional cash, which will vary depending on current income level relative to needs, personal tastes, beliefs, and so on). Fortunately, however, in many circumstances it is not necessary to know these propensities to determine the relative nutritional cost-effectiveness of different food aid commodities. It is then quite easy to select the commodities that maximize the nutritional cost-effectiveness of the program.

First, let us consider the case of a commodity that is identical to a food in the existing diet of the recipient household. In this case, the cost-effectiveness of the commodity i in respect to nutritional unit j (calories, protein, and so on), e_{ij}, is simply:

$$(16\text{-}1) \qquad e_{ij} = (V_i/C_i)\, m_j$$

where

V_i = monetary value per unit of food i to recipient
C_i = cost per unit of food i (including the cost of delivery) to the program
m_j = the household's marginal propensity to spend on nutritional unit j.

The appropriate monetary value of the commodity to the recipient depends on the food in the existing diet likely to be completely or partially replaced. It could be the food supplied by the program or a similar food. Its value would be the retail price, if it is normally purchased in the open market. If the food aid commodity potentially replaces a food obtained at a concessionary price in a food ration shop, the concessionary price would be the appropriate value. If the food aid commodity is supplied to a farming household and is used to replace a food that is in marketable surplus, the appropriate value is the price the farmer receives for the additional food sold.

Since the marginal propensity (m_j) to spend on nutritional unit j is independent of the food aid commodity, the relative nutritional cost-effectiveness of a food aid commodity that replaces the same food (or another food that is the same in regards to the nutritional unit) in the existing diet is simply:

(16-2) $$a_i = V_i/C_i$$

An alpha-value of 1.00 means that a dollar spent by the food aid program on the commodity is worth a dollar to the recipient. Similarly, an alpha-value of 0.50 means that a dollar spent on that commodity is worth only 50 cents to the recipient. If the alpha-value of a commodity is twice the alpha-value of another commodity, it is twice as nutritionally cost-effective with respect to any nutritional unit, provided that the marginal propensity of the recipient to spend additional income on the nutritional unit remains positive.

The second important case involves the substitution of a food aid commodity for another food in the existing diet. This would occur when the commodity supplied by food aid is not part of the existing diet. To the extent that the nutritional units in the two foods differ, the nutritional cost-effectiveness would then be as follows:

(16-3) $$e_{ij} = \frac{N_{ij} - N_{sj}}{C_i} + \frac{V_s}{C_i} m_j$$

where

N_{ij} = nutritional unit j in a unit of the delivered commodity i
N_{sj} = nutritional unit j in a unit of food replaced by commodity i
V_s = value of food replaced by commodity i.

The first term represents the difference in protein, energy, vitamin A, or whatever the targeted nutritional unit, divided by the cost. This represents the nutritional cost-effectiveness of the food aid commodity itself as it is consumed. The second term represents the part of the nutritional cost-effectiveness that comes from the fact that some of the resources saved because the food aid recipient got the free food will be spent on more food. The more the freed-up resources and the higher the marginal propensity to spend on the targeted nutritional unit (and the lower the cost of the commodity to the donor), the greater this term will be.

Some Empirical Illustrations

The reasons that alpha-values and therefore cost-effectiveness can vary greatly among commodities and food aid programs are many.

First, the recipients of food aid may live under a regime of relative food prices that bears little resemblance to the relative prices paid by the food aid donor. This is particularly relevant to international food

Table 16-1. *Imputed Retail Prices, PL 480 Title II Costs of Selected Commodities, and Alpha-Values, 1981*
(U.S. dollars a metric ton)

Item	Wheat	Maize	Rice	Oil	Milk (fluid)
Retail price					
Egypt	94 (0.25)	105 (0.32)	370 (0.58)	763 (0.76)	624 (5.20)
India	187 (0.50)	213 (0.65)	328 (0.51)	1,889 (1.89)	403 (3.36)
Pakistan	178 (0.48)	185 (0.56)	451 (0.70)	873 (0.87)	332 (2.76)
Average	153 (0.41)	159 (0.51)	383 (0.60)	1,175 (1.17)	453 (3.78)
Cost of food aid[a]	370	330	640	1,000	120

Note: Numbers in parentheses are alpha-values.

a. The costs of food aid for the commodities are the acquisition and average shipping costs to the PL 480 Title II program. The cost of milk is based on the concessionary price charges for nonfat dry milk (60 cents a kilogram inclusive of shipping charges) and a conversion ratio of 5 liters fluid milk to 1 kilogram nonfat dry milk because it is presumed that nonfat dry milk has a lower value to the recipients than does fluid milk.

Source: National Research Council (1982).

aid programs. The governments of countries in which the food aid recipients live will often use trade restrictions and selective taxes or subsidies to hold the prices of some foods below and the prices of other foods above international prices. Moreover, domestic food prices may differ from international prices depending on whether the country or a particular region in the country is deficit, self-sufficient, or surplus in a particular food. Second, as mentioned earlier, some commodities may be considered as surplus by the government providing food aid and charged to the food aid program at far below market prices, while others are charged at their full market price. Third, the relative cost of delivering commodities for food aid may be quite unlike the relative cost of handling commodities in commercial channels. For instance, the cost of shipping wheat in bags for food aid to Asia is about $150 per ton, while the cost of shipping wheat in bulk for commercial transactions is $50 per ton. However, the mode and cost of shipping vegetable oil is roughly the same in commercial and food aid transactions. Finally, as mentioned above, some foods may be available to food aid recipients at their normal retail value and some at a concessionary price, while others should be valued at their farmgate selling price.

Table 16-1 shows retail prices of selected foods for 1981, imputed from data reported for 1975 in Egypt, 1980 in India, and 1979 in Pakistan and adjusted for inflation. The costs of the same commodities to the PL 480 Title II program shown refer to acquisition costs plus average ocean shipping charges to the three countries. The alpha-values shown in parentheses are the ratios of the retail prices to the costs of the commodities in the PL 480 Title II program.

Table 16-2 shows the relative monetary and nutritional cost-effectiveness of the different commodities based on their alpha-values and

Table 16-2. *Indexes of Cost-Effectiveness of Commodities*
(wheat = 100)

Index	Wheat	Maize	Rice	Oil	Milk
Alpha-values					
Egypt	100	128	232	304	2,080
India	100	130	102	378	672
Pakistan	100	117	146	181	575
Average	100	125	146	285	922
Energy per dollar in food[a]	100	114	59	95	63
Protein per dollar in food[a]	100	83	32	0	190

a. Derived from energy and protein content, respectively, per kilogram and the costs reported in table 16-1.

compares them with the relative energy and protein cost-effectiveness of the commodities when imputed from their energy and protein contents. By the alpha-value criterion, a dollar spent on nonfat dry milk in a supplementary food aid package provided by PL 480 Title II to consumers in Egypt is 20 times more cost-effective and a dollar spent on oil is 3 times more cost-effective than a dollar spent on wheat. In a similar program in India, milk would be six times more and oil four times more cost-effective than wheat. Such dramatic differences are not common, but they do illustrate the point. Milk has a high alpha-value because it is a genuine surplus commodity for which the PL 480 Title II program is charged far less than its market value. Moreover, in Egypt basic staples are highly subsidized and in India the oil/wheat price ratio is far above the international ratio.

Note how the ranking of commodities would be different if the (incorrect) nutritional unit per dollar in food criterion, rather than the alpha-value criterion, were used. Even with the highly concessionary cost of milk, wheat rather than milk would be supplied if the program's primary objective were to enhance the energy supply in the diet. Obviously, oil would be the least desirable commodity if the program's primary objective were to improve the protein content of the diet.

The empirical evidence provided here illustrates that the alpha-values of commodities can range from far below to far above unity. They are likely to be different among countries and even among different regions within countries, and they will also change over time as relative prices change. We have not considered the costs of distribution within the country or of the handling of the commodities by the recipient households. To the extent that these additional costs are included, all alpha-values will be lower. Moreover, the relative alpha-values of the commodities may be different if the left-out costs are not in the same proportion to the included costs for all commodities.

Further Illustrations of Appropriate Applications of the Nutritional Cost-Effectiveness Approach

As noted previously, whether or not the alpha-value criterion can be used and how the alpha-value is to be imputed depend on the nature and objectives of the food aid program and the available commodities.

The most straightforward application is where the objective of the program is to convey maximum flexibility to the beneficiaries to use the food aid in ways that best suit their individual preferences and circumstances. In this case, the food package that maximizes its weighted alpha-value is best. The appropriate alpha-value of each food depends on what expenditures are displaced by the food. If the quantity of the food supplied is less than the amount (of the same food) currently purchased, its value would be the price at which the food is purchased. If the food commodity is not in the current diet or to the extent that it is supplied in excess of its current consumption, its value is equivalent to the price of the food it displaces in the current diet.

For example, if one kilogram of maize is supplied at a cost of 20 cents a kilogram and the household currently consumes two kilograms of maize at a price of 20 cents a kilogram, the alpha-value is 1.0. If three kilograms of maize are supplied in the food aid package, the alpha-value of the first two kilograms is 1.0, but the value of the third kilogram depends on what food is replaced in the current diet. If it is rice, which the household currently purchases at 40 cents a kilogram, the alpha-value of the third kilogram is 2.0. If sorghum, which is purchased by the household at 10 cents a kilogram, is replaced, the alpha-value of the third kilogram is 0.5.

To estimate the nutritional cost-effectiveness of commodities that are not in the current diet of the beneficiaries and to compare their cost-effectiveness with other commodities requires knowledge and judgments that go beyond alpha-values. The most common case is the inclusion of fortified and blended foods in supplementary food aid packages. The objective is then usually to correct for particular nutrient deficiencies in the diets of the recipients. Several considerations are relevant. First, will the "new" foods be acceptable, that is, will recipients consume them and substitute them for other foods in the existing diet? Second, if they are consumed, their alpha-values will be lower, which means that they will confer less monetary value and probably less energy augmentation of the existing diets per program dollar. Will they on balance sufficiently increase the consumption of the intended nutrients? What is the size of the trade-off, and does sufficient evidence exist that, say, the added cost-effectiveness on protein more than compensates for the reduced cost-effectiveness on energy?

A fortified wheat flour always costs more than nonfortified wheat. If, on top of reducing the supply of wheat from each program dollar, the fortified food is not acceptable for reasons of taste or unfamiliarity, its value, and hence its indirect impact on nutrition, will be further reduced. When fed to animals, for instance, it would have much less value than when it is substituted for a food in the existing diet. Clearly, the reduced alpha-value is the appropriate criterion for comparing the nonconsumed food with other commodities.

Table 16-3 illustrates the cost-effectiveness comparisons of wheat flour with fortified wheat flour when the latter is substituted for the

Table 16-3. *Cost-Effectiveness of Fortified and Nonfortified Wheat Flour and of Oil*

Item	Wheat flour	Fortified wheat flour	Oil
Alpha-value	0.6	0.5	2.0
Index of energy cost-effectiveness[a]	100	80	333
Index of protein cost-effectiveness (marginal protein propensity = 150 grams per dollar)	100	185	333
Index of protein cost-effectiveness (marginal protein propensity = 75 grams per dollar)	100	284	333

a. The index of energy cost-effectiveness for all three commodities and the index of protein cost-effectiveness of wheat and oil are straightforward functions of the alpha-values. The protein cost-effectiveness of the fortified wheat flour is calculated in accordance with equation 16-3, given that the difference in protein content between the fortified wheat flour and the unfortified variety is 40 grams per kilogram.

former in the diet of the food aid recipients. The additional protein consumption induced by a fortified food derives from two sources: the higher protein content in the fortified food and the increased consumption of food made possible by the additional purchasing power conveyed by the commodity. The latter depends foremost on the recipients' propensity to increase the consumption of protein out of an additional dollar of purchasing power. (The indices shown in table 16-3 are calculated on the basis of equations 16-1 and 16-3, discussed earlier.)

As expected, the fortified wheat flour delivers a larger increase in protein consumption per program dollar than the unfortified flour. But there is a trade-off with energy and, of course, with purchasing power that the household can use for nonfood expenditures. The comparison with a commodity of high alpha-value is, however, particularly noteworthy. When the alpha-value of oil, for instance, is much higher than the alpha-value of the fortified food, it can lead to more additional protein consumption than would be obtained from the protein-fortified food per program dollar, although oil per se contains no protein!

Examples of the application of this analytical approach to four WFP projects are given in Katona-Apte (1986).

Summary

Our theoretical and empirical analysis leads us to suggest the following propositions:

o Food aid is more nutritionally cost-effective than money aid whenever the alpha-value of the commodity is greater than unity. This is the case whenever the value of the commodity to the recipient exceeds its cost to the aid providing agency and the marginal propensity to consume it is greater than zero.

o We do not know whether food aid is more or less cost-effective than money aid if the alpha-value is less than unity. The marginal propensity to spend on better nutrition may be higher for food aid than for money aid. If such differences do not exist, or if they could be eliminated with nutrition education, nutritional cost-effectiveness could be enhanced by converting commodities that have an alpha-value of less than unity into cash.

o For foods that are found in the diets of the recipients in excess of the amounts supplied through the supplementary food aid package, the relative nutritional cost-effectiveness of commodities is always in direct proportion to their alpha-values.

o The precise nutritional impact of any commodity depends on the marginal propensity of the recipients to allocate additional income (conveyed through the food aid) to improving their nutritional status. If the recipients' response is judged to be unsatisfactory with respect to energy (calorie) cost-effectiveness, the only possible remedy is to provide nutrition education. The cost-effectiveness of food aid in terms of protein, or any other specific nutrient, might also be increased by supplying a suitable commodity (such as a fortified food) that will be consumed instead of another commodity in the current diet. In this case, there is likely to be a trade-off of, say, more protein for less energy as a consequence of selecting the commodity with the lower alpha-value. This is sensible only if protein content is judged to be more deficient than the energy content in the recipients' diets.

o Selection of commodities on the basis of the alpha-value criterion is particularly important when the intent of the program is to improve nutrition indirectly through providing the beneficiaries with an incentive to participate in nutrition education or work programs.

o Substitution of the new commodity selection criteria for those currently in use in food aid programs could bring about a large increase in nutritional cost-effectiveness. Moreover, the data requirements are low and could be met at minimal cost.

17

The Evolution of Food Aid: Toward a Development-First Regime

Raymond F. Hopkins

Two major political forces in the early 1950s led to the creation of permanent food aid programs. First, agricultural groups in the United States and Canada promoted food aid as a way to expand trade and reduce burdensome grain surpluses. Second, humanitarian and internationalist sentiments, expressed in part through voluntary agencies such as CARE, had an interest in ending famime through government funding of permanent overseas relief. The result was a marriage of surplus disposal and humanitarian relief as a successor to the American food relief efforts in Europe following World War II. In the 30 years since then, food aid has become institutionalized as a familiar international transfer mechanism.

Four Founding Principles

At its founding, four basic principles governed food aid activity. Food aid should:

o Be provided from the donor's surplus stocks
o Be additional food to recipient countries
o Be given under short-term commitments sensitive to the political and economic goals of donors
o Directly feed hungry people.

This initial package of principles rested on the theoretical supposition that food production—largely wheat—in certain rich exporting states was in excess of their socially useful consumption and commer-

Excerpted from "The Evolution of Food Aid," *Food Policy*, vol. 9, no. 4 (November 1984), pp. 345–62.

cial export needs and that hence some stocks could be transferred by "special transactions" to recipients in countries where production and imports were below socially useful levels of consumption (Cathie 1982). The purpose of this food channel was to expand consumption beyond existing effective demand and simultaneously to serve the diplomatic, market, or humanitarian purposes of the donors.

Ever since the enactment of the PL 480 legislation in the United States in 1954, food aid has drawn criticism. At the time of its passage, for example, it was opposed by the State Department and by other exporting countries because of its potential to create enmity and violate liberal trade principles. Others lamented the failure of food aid to involve multilateral agencies such as the FAO, which for years had been discussing its potential role in managing surpluses.

The most enduring challenges to food aid have come from criticisms directed toward one or more of the founding principles. The first principle was challenged on two counts. Initially, domestic U.S. interests opposed policies creating permanent surpluses. Beginning in the 1960s, the United States and some other countries adopted acreage reduction policies to end the surpluses. This policy change in Australia, Canada, and the United States weakened one set of interests supporting food aid. Later, it also prompted concern about ways to achieve supply reliability of food aid if surpluses disappeared. In the second place, as U.S. hegemony declined, the United States and other grain exporters promoted burden sharing among industrialized states. The World Food Program in 1963 and the Food Aid Convention in 1967 were responses to the notion that the rich importing nations of Europe and Japan should also support food aid.

The second wave of criticism addressed the additionality principle. As development objectives came increasingly to the fore, and as desperately poor recipients, such as those in Bangladesh in 1974, came to be favored recipients, the rationale for additionality weakened. First, balance of payments support to aid development investments could not be realized by a country if it had no savings of foreign exchange from displaced food imports. Unless food aid displaced commercial imports, it did little to help desperate governments who were going to feed their populace in any case. Second, criticisms that food aid depressed local food production by lowering prices paid to producers forced food aid managers and supporters to seek devices to prevent the perverse "disincentive" effect. If food aid were a pure substitution, then the disincentive effect via its market effect would vanish—a point in which food aid defenders increasingly took comfort (Stevens 1979; Sverberg 1979).

A third criticism arose over the principle of the short-term and hence unreliable quality of food aid. India became particularly disenchanted with dependence on food aid following the "short tether" tactics of the Johnson administration's provision of food aid in 1965–66 (Bjorkman 1975). When recipients felt that political and market development objectives dominated allocations, little incentive was created to worry about development or domestic food policy when negotiating for food aid. Concerns about short-term allocation and reallocation arose from the way the United States government cut off aid to Chile in 1971 and Mozambique in 1981 while building it up to Southeast Asia in the late 1960s (the so-called "food for war" operations) and to Egypt and Syria in 1974. Even governments that strongly supported emergency uses of food aid, such as Sweden, also firmly endorsed the multiyear principle.

Finally, criticism of the feed-the-hungry principle surfaced. This has been the most muted and cautiously worded attack on the founding principles. Who, after all, would deny food to starving babies? Hunger is a potent symbol, mobilizing political support. Nevertheless, criticisms have grown that, aside from dire emergency situations, delivering food directly to the hungry is a suspect principle for three reasons: transport costs to projects can be excessively costly, amounting to 100 to 200 percent of the food costs in Africa (Williams 1982); small projects may disrupt local food systems, even if the amount of food is small on a national scale; and food targeted for consumption may reinforce excessively expensive subsidy programs, as in Egypt or Sri Lanka in the 1970s (von Braun and de Haen 1982; Timmer and Guerreiro 1981), or create administrative nightmares and invite corruption, as in Zaire (Murdoch 1980; GAO 1979). Food aid critics want the food to be rationed for development ends and not expended for consumption that may even reduce pressure on governments to address rural development (see Mellor and Johnston in part I).

Newer Competing Principles

The criticisms just reviewed have given rise to an evolutionary change in food aid. New principles, largely contradictory to the founding ones, have arisen. The new formula, reflecting principles of market efficiency and development gains rather than exceptionalism and diplomatic gains, states that food aid should:

○ Be supplied most efficiently
○ Be a substitute for a recipient's food imports
○ Be given under longer-term commitments
○ Provide development investments for recipients.

Each of the four new principles has challenged the old ones without displacing them. Each has been embedded in some institutional practices of bilateral donor agencies, especially those of the WFP. With the reformulation of the WFP after 1974, the governing council, the Committee on Food Aid Policies and Programs (CFA), has approved a number of specific guidelines for food aid directed to all donors. In some cases, as with long-term commitments, a new principle has been openly advocated by food aid specialists, even though it is not well received by national budgetary authorities or diplomats. In other cases, such as supplying nonsurplus food, specific new practices have not been given much publicity, since a distinct possibility exists that this could mobilize opposition to them. Nevertheless, each of the principles has achieved a firm base in the food aid regime of the 1980s.

Efficiency of Supply

With the establishment of donors who were not food exporters, the surplus disposal rationale was attenuated. Furthermore, a new rationale arose when it was perceived that countries such as India, Thailand, and Zimbabwe, clearly too poor to be significant donors, could improve their own economies if they became occasional suppliers of food aid. Countries such as Saudi Arabia and the Federal Republic of Germany, therefore, found they could be doubly helpful if they used cash to secure food from one of these developing countries and gave it to another. This would promote regional trade, reduce transport costs, and stimulate development for two countries. "Triangular" supply arrangements, in which neither the food donor nor the recipient is the source of supply, have been encouraged by the CFA and facilitated by the WFP management. The WFP had encouraged the "efficiency" principle both in its own food purchases and as a broker for other bilateral donors. Even the United States, the premier food-supplying nation, has entered into triangular supply arrangements, shipping wheat to Zimbabwe so as to supply white maize to Zambia as food aid.

Substitution for Commercial Imports

In general, food aid has become such a small part of world trade that worry over its market distorting effects has declined. The substitution principle is a logical device to offset market disincentive effects (Schultz 1960) and is also widely upheld whenever food aid is justified as balance of payments support. The conflict with the additionality principle is largely ignored in such cases, almost as if the two could exist simultaneously. Both principles exist as part of the current food aid regime, and efforts are made to satisfy one or the other, or, occasionally and inconsistently, both.

Long-Term Commitments

The rise of development priorities clearly favors the multiyear approach as a way to lend greater stability and reduce risks to development undertakings. The budgeting and planning process in the United States and Canada and for the Commission of the European Communities have reinforced the tendency to allocate similar amounts to similar countries over several years. Budget officials, however, have tended against formally committing their governments to food aid for more than a year at a time. Nevertheless, most aid, especially project aid, is planned on a multiyear basis.

Development Investment

At some point, trade-offs exist between short-term nutritional objectives and long-term strategic ones. The desirability of emergency feeding for people displaced by drought or civil unrest, and of nutritional programs for vulnerable groups such as young children, pregnant women, and lactating mothers, is not challenged by this principle. Rather, it suggests that these priorities, and probably only these, meet the standards of using food directly to promote sustainable development, especially rural development (Johnston and Clark 1982). Even here, efficiency would dictate using local foods in feeding programs when effectiveness did not suffer and no negative externalities were created.

Emphasizing development rather than nutrition as a principle entails looking at the investment prospects and returns from a food resource. Food as such is seldom a serious constraint holding back long-term enhancement of rural productivity and domestic food supplies. More often, constraints lie in hard-to-change government policies which either strangle incentives or provide inadequately for human and social capital. In particular, education, health care, extension services, roads, and market enhancing regulations would greatly add to the accumulation of capital and technological change central to rural development. The emerging food aid principle holds that the criterion for allocating food—directly or indirectly—to nutritional improvement programs should be developmental effectiveness, and according to this standard, many food subsidization and feeding programs are cost-ineffective. They turn out to be welfare consumption items, relating perhaps to immediate quality of life considerations, but are also more accurately explained as implicit political compacts betweeen a shaky government and key support groups, rather than as part of a development scheme.

The challenge for food aid is to reconcile the conflicts between old and new interests reflected in the incoherent principles of the current regime. The next section of this article attempts to justify support for newer, challenging principles formulated as a "development-first" regime.

A Development-First Food Aid Regime: A Synthesis for the Future

A development-only orientation that ignored important political interests of donors and recipients would invite a slow death from resource shrinkage. As powerful interests supporting food aid waned, resources would dwindle. Emphasizing development to the exclusion of all other interests, therefore, is self-defeating. A development-first regime, however, is possible. American and other agricultural export interests no longer find food aid an efficient tool for surplus disposal. Food aid has become too bound by development rules that require targeting of poor countries, concern over disincentive effects, and complicated procedures to reach allocation decisions. These make it unattractive to government officials responsible for surplus stock management, especially in contrast with intermediate credit and bilateral commercial trade agreements, which have proved more attractive mechanisms for expanding exports.

Many of the conditions that would allow food aid to be governed by a synthesis of old and new principles are in place, such as the growing universalism of the donor recipient network and the creation of a 4 million ton wheat reserve as a backup for U.S. food aid. The new approach would be able to be development-first because all participants had either an immediate or a long-term structural interest in it, while surplus disposal problems would return to the general trade regime to be resolved under the auspices of the General Agreement on Tariffs and Trade or, if all else failed, through trade wars (Fribourg 1983).

Institutional devices to achieve the development-first approach are diverse. They range from pressure by domestic interests on the national policies of food aid participants, to continued international policy dialogues within existing frameworks, such as the CFA, and finally to a major new treaty undertaking under the auspices of the UNCTAD, the FAO, or the United Nations General Assembly, analogous in scope to the World Food Conference that encouraged a new approach.

In a crude parallel with the two sets of competing principles outlined earlier, four synthesis principles emerge from the contradictions of current competing ones. The ideas expressed can already be found in the analyses, prescriptions, and undertakings of a variety of individuals and institutions (WFP/CFA 1979, 1983). The purpose here is to consolidate them into a more coherent statement of principles that can engender a reconstellation of interests supporting food aid, use learning from experience and research, and complete the transformation of the approach. The proposed four principles are that food aid should:

- Be linked explicitly to the food policy of participants, requiring efforts for efficiency and stabilization
- Be transferred so as to maximize economic gains
- Be given under long-term contracts
- Be used for human capital investment, food policy costs, and research.

Food Aid Linked to Food Policy

This principle really combines two broad norms. First, it assumes that donors and recipients should lose some sovereignty over their food policy as a cost of participating in a food aid relationship, and second, it asserts that the goals of efficiency and stability should be the limiting factors on policy. Emergency food aid should not be confused with or allowed to displace policy-linked food aid. Rather, food aid should create opportunities for national and international food officials to improve critical national policies, especially food sector policies. These policies ultimately determine long-run food security. Of course, food aid itself is not a sufficient resource for controlling this policy, but its very existence creates presumptions for transparency of action and for international review and prodding.

This principle suggests a number of specific steps. First, rules and procedures for domestic food policies need to be agreed upon as germane to a country's status as either a provider or a recipient of food aid (or both). The CFA has already proposed norms strictly for food aid policy, some of which have been reflected in changes in donor country policies, as the trend toward grants rather than soft loan aid shows. Drawing up norms for donor performance, with strong donor participation and control, is likely to give evaluative criteria for national food policy performance more credibility and to have an impact on donors and recipients.

Part of the procedure for linking food aid to food policy could be an annual review by the CFA of a select few donor and recipient countries, an idea approved at the 1982 CFA meeting (15th session) and implemented with Bangladesh, Sweden, and Tunisia since then. Currently, the WFP reviews and evaluates its own projects. The evaluation and policy units of the WFP would need additional or external resources to undertake more extensive country reviews.

Relevant criteria for evaluation would arise from the various principles discussed here. For example, a review of a donor could assess whether that donor's food aid contributions are adequately assured, so as to allow the food aid system to help stabilize the food systems of recipients. The review process would also provide the opportunity to commend countries that lived up to their FAO commitments during difficult times, as Australia did by buying food abroad after experiencing a drought and wheat crop failure in 1982.

Recipient country reviews would function in similar ways. They could reinforce the tendency already under way to use food aid to improve the food policy framework in recipients, thereby aiding their development of a strong agricultural base and an efficient, robust system of distribution and consumption.

A code devised by developing countries for application to themselves should be more palatable for this purpose than donor-initiated conditionality. A country's standing relative to desired policy conditions could be used for recommending priorities for food aid. In this way, food aid allocations could be turned toward an incentive for policy reform rather than a disincentive. The recent multiyear food aid program to Mali could serve as a model for this approach. The desirability of tightening the link between eligibility, improved terms, and longer commitments for food aid and improved policy frameworks has been suggested in many studies and international reports (Nelson 1982; Timmer and Guerreiro 1981). The next step is to identify appropriate local uses of food aid within a reformed food policy context.

Finally, the interdependence of the world food system suggests that all countries with food policies that affect trade and food aid flows should bear some responsibility for aid. This move toward greater universality appears in the new 1980 Food Aid Convention, which explicitly seeks additional donor pledges. The United States, which supplies about half the world's trade in grains, also supplies about half the world's food aid. This seems reasonable. The responsibility of importing countries arises thanks to this principle of interdependence, although the food importers' role as donors was not initially based on such a broad principle.

The link of the interdependence phenomenon to the food policy principle should now invite other countries to assume donor responsibility. The U.S.S.R. and the richer countries of Eastern Europe are particularly due invitations. The U.S.S.R. is already a member of the International Wheat Convention and has given food aid on an ad hoc basis. Brazil, Portugal, and other rapidly industrializing states should also become significant donors. Greater universality will expand the ability to deliver food aid in a more reliable and efficient fashion. These are the two qualities the system needs if it is to serve development first.

Maximizing Transfer Gains

This principle requires taking into account relevant prices in donor and recipient countries. The information derived from ongoing appraisals when food aid is linked to food policies, as suggested above, makes this task easier. The maximization principle also allows the controversy about whether aid is (or should be) additional to or a substitute for commercial imports to be a moot matter. If a country were generally and heavily subsidizing a food commodity while paying producers well below the import parity price, then the potential recipient might well be substituting food aid for commercial imports, but only in the short run. In the longer run, it really is substituting food aid for domestic production while continuing urban-biased policies. Under the conditions for priority established with the first principle, however, such a country might not be eligible for food aid. Thus, the second principle's major implication is that food aid should aim toward providing balance of payments support (import substitution), but with priority for aid given to those countries where the food policy framework has already met general conditions for effective development as worked out in a recipient and donor country forum.

The maximization principle would entail another set of changes. In general, it would be assumed by all that food aid must be put into recipient country market channels so as to minimize transport costs. Furthermore, self-targeting commodities, such as sorghum in Bangladesh or wheat in Sri Lanka, would not be chosen unless they yielded the highest economic gain to the international transaction, something developing country importers should be able to judge. The idea of food aid supplying a nutritionally self-targeting food has considerable merit, but there is no special reason to use imported foods for a nutrition program of this type.

In countries like Indonesia or Tanzania, raising consumer rice prices and targeting maize or cassava for expanded consumption by the poorest, least nourished population may, for example, be a better way to improve the food system than requiring food aid to be a grain preferred by the poor. Often U.S. maize and sorghum is used for animal feed and is not of good quality compared with the locally produced crop. Indeed, it would be desirable that if a government decides to use a subsidy wedge between production and consumption of a food to improve nutrition, it pick a locally produced crop, one already in the diets of the poorest (Jackson 1983; Levinson 1982). This view implies that high-value commodities, such as wheat, oil, and dry milk, may be the best food aid commodities, even though these are actually consumed by middle-income and upper-income people (see Reutlinger and Katona-Apte in part III). In this sense, the maximization principle is an extension of the efficient supplier principle that was discussed earlier and has already been partly established.

The nutritional and developmental goals in the food aid system can be achieved more efficiently through the policy link between food aid and food policy. The food aid, then, whether donated or sold concessionally and whether linked to a specific project or not, should generally be expected to be sold in the recipient country at a reasonable price (certainly not much below import parity and perhaps even approaching export parity). When the food aid is linked to a nutritional undertaking as part of the overall development it seeks to support, resources from the sale can be used to pay for food rations or subsidized ration shop commodities targeted for special populations. Normally, these would be procured from local production. This reduces transport and storage costs and raises demand for local food production. The current "normal" requirement of free gifts, distributed directly, would be limited to emergencies or unusual cases where local foods would be inefficient or nutritionally perverse for the targeted group. Such a rule, based on the maximization principle, will obviously require some important changes in the rules and procedures of the current approach and development of satisfactory oversight mechanisms to be sure the policy link works.

Long-Term Contracts

The third principle of the proposed development-first regime would make long-term, flexible commitments a standard procedure. Under the current system, even with multiyear commitments, the commodities and approximate delivery schedule are negotiated in advance. Adjustments during a budgeting period require special approval. Although in practice some swapping and flexible use of stocks occur in projects, especially multilateral ones, the food availability commitments are normally quite short-term ones. This principle would change this practice, at least for food policy priority countries. For such countries, I propose that three-to-seven-year food aid contracts be reached under which one or more donor agencies would pledge a substantial total commitment to a recipient. Developing country food officials would be given considerable flexibility to decide the timing of food imports and the commodity mix chosen. Such a contract could combine the features typical of bilateral grain trade agreements, which give only an annual range of commodities to be exchanged, with those typical of credit lines that banks extend to large customers. A recipient country, in return for undertaking or main-taining specified agricultural food policies and projects, such as those affecting production, trade, and/or nutrition, would be given a line of credit for aid imports to be used largely at its discretion.

The advantages for recipients would be numerous. Such a proce-dure would encourage food policy officials, rather than trade and treasury officials, to negotiate food aid. It would, however, give trade officials much greater assurance of meeting possible import needs as the policy changes occurred. Officials could even enter grain futures markets, for example, to procure food aid several years in advance at favorable prices and with lower storage costs, rather than build addi-tional storage in their own countries (Peck 1982; Donaldson in part III). A country like Kenya could use such a facility. Kenya has had periodic maize crop fluctuations during which its Cereals Board ei-ther could not absorb the crop as expected because it ran short of storage facilities and money or could not procure sufficient amounts locally and had to resort to large-scale imports. In 1979, Kenya ex-ported maize at a loss and then in 1980–81 paid nearly $100 million for commercial maize imports. Subsequently, it received large-scale food aid, some of which then had to be stored for a year or more. Hedging risks of probable import costs is typical in industrialized countries. Futures markets offer a "collective good" that reduces risk. With longer-term food aid contracts, developing countries would be encouraged to use hedging more effectively to lock in acceptable prices well before they were sure when the aid was needed.

Under the long-term arrangements envisaged, training and tech-nical assistance would also be in order. One major area of weakness in the food systems of many countries, African countries in particular, is the low competency and inefficiency of marketing boards. Typically, these boards are the effective managers of food aid imports. Often, morale and professional expertise are low in such operations and they are frequently subverted to political purposes. Since food aid directly touches these marketing board operations, donors—relying on the development-first approach's initial principle—should link enhanced performance by these boards to food aid. Food aid and other re-sources should be used to strengthen board members' management capacity, international market sophistication, and career incentives. Increasingly, such technical assistance must be long term, especially in Africa (Leonard 1984). Food aid officials also need to work for longer periods on particular projects and/or country policies—at least five to seven years. The marketing boards can play an important role in improving the framework for food production, including acting as a buffer stock operation and helping to "perfect" markets (Jones 1984).

Human Capital, Food Policy Costs, and Research

The final principle of the development-first approach attempts to resolve the tension between using food directly to reduce hunger (consumption) and using it for development (investment). What is needed in giving priority to development is to relate food aid in this enterprise to nutrition and food production "investments." G. Edward Schuh has identified the concept of human resource and capital formation as one major focus by which to allocate food aid uses within a recipient country (Schuh 1981). As appropriately determined by the food policy commitments of recipients, food aid would be linked to a variety of human capital investments, beginning with nutrition programs to reach the vulnerable groups in society, but also including health, extension, and nutrition education programs. The stress on these human capital investments is in keeping with the implications of the food transfer, even if the actual food transferred can only occasionally be efficiently used in feeding programs. This principle entails policy shifts in the project design and priorities of organizations managing projects.

Apart from emergency feeding of refugees or disaster victims, a country's broad food policy is more important in alleviating hunger than a series of particular feeding projects. If poverty is the basic cause of hunger, as most believe, then development first rather than food first is the appropriate maxim.

Food aid can also be a resource for food policy expenses. Funds from the food sales can be used to support buffer-stock and reserve operations and training of government food officials. The aim would be to promote the reliability of national markets for producers and consumers and to meet national food security goals. In doing this, food aid itself could be stored, if it is for reserve program use, or funds from sales could be used, for instance, for the local construction costs of new storage facilities. The sales revenue raised could also help a government meet other food policy costs, such as extension programs to encourage more efficient domestic food production. Realistically, food aid used in these ways should not be double counted as directly improving nutrition, development, and food policy at the same time.

Many recipient government officials simply do not treat food aid as a serious resource, especially concessionary sales aid as in PL 480 Title I, when accounting by donors asks them to celebrate multiple benefits

of the same aid, especially if at the same time the donor is using hard
currency repayments to finance new concessional food sales. Agreeing
upon fewer and more focused consequences for food aid resources
should actually improve respect for it in the eyes of many recipient
government officials.

Finally, greater use of the food resource should be made for research experiments, pilot projects, prototypes, and demonstrations.
This emphasis would reinforce the principle of linking food policy to
food aid by improving the understanding of a country's food system.
Food managers need to learn how to improve food systems, using an
understanding based on international experience, blended with the
subjective preferences of those whose lives are to be transformed.
Furthermore, research would provide greater opportunities for learning from feedback, which could modify a project and even change its
goals. The food domain provides many opportunites for diverse experimentation and prototyping. There is a paucity of studies on the
impact of food aid. Almost no feeding projects have been designed as
experiments or even with a view to eventual impact assessments (Maxwell 1983).

Food and nutrition projects are sure to continue, especially since
food for work schemes and mother and child health centers are
usually given high marks as very effective and efficient devices to
improve human capital and create development investments. Increasingly, the development-first regime recommendation would be
that these should acquire a greater role as research and learning
devices and mechanisms to enhance the careers and management
abilities of their staffs and of national leaders, in addition to their
direct value to targeted participants.

Conclusion: Linking Food Security, Food Policy, and Food Aid

The world food system has increasingly accepted a responsibility to
end famines and alleviate hunger—a responsibility regularly re-
affirmed in speeches and actions. Beyond this, the food crisis years of
1973–74 and the World Food Conference held then set in motion
initiatives and institutions that continue to seek greater world food
security through development and redistribution. Food aid has been a
mechanism designed to serve both ends, but not without considerable
controversy about the specific norms, rules, and procedures that
should govern its use. The food aid regime has reflected this controversy through evolutionary change of the principles governing it.
Roughly 30 years after its formal beginning, 20 years after the found-

ing of wfp as a multilateral institution, and 10 years after the World Food Conference, the time has come to resolve conflicting principles and redesign the regime to serve development as a first priority.

Whatever its principles, food aid is critically dependent upon the national food policies of its participants. To serve development or other ends, officials who determine the allocation of food aid and negotiate conditions for its use must make food policy their major target if they are to realize results. The ultimate goal is to make food aid a component in achieving universal food security in a world in which trade plays a central role. Food aid, therefore, strongly needs principles that will make it a reliable backup for those receiving it, as well as a cost-effective contribution by those providing it.

Leadership is needed to help governments find policies that allocate food aid in the right kind of commodities, at the right time, with sufficiently long-term assurances, so that it provides a real benefit to both food production and nutrition. Food aid should help shift the burden of adjustment to food trade instability away from the world's weakest states and poorest people and encourage food policies in recipients and donors that promote agricultural development and improve nutrition. The task before food aid participants, especially major donors such as the United States and the central coordinating institutions of the cfa and wfp, is to provide leadership for change that will realize potential institutional improvements.

Studies by the United States, the fao, and the wfp have predicted a need for more, not less, food aid in the late 1980s and beyond. The existing food aid regime has proved adaptable and increasingly complex in its evolution to date. However, with changing international political and economic forces, substantial criticism by scholarly observers, and the decline of the special farm sector support in donor states, a real challenge lies ahead for food aid officials. Food aid could decline further as an international resource transfer. Food aid managers, whether in national governments or international organizations, need to reconfigure the main emphasis of food aid so as to engender renewed and even greater support. Development first—not the status quo and not a purist's development approach—is the regime design recommended to accomplish these goals.

PART IV

Domestic Marketing, Price Policies, and Subsidies

A "fundamental dilemma" of food policy, as Paul Streeten terms it in this part, is that between food prices high enough to encourage agricultural production and low enough to protect poor food buyers. In another chapter, Per Pinstrup-Andersen points out the obvious reality that "policies that attempt to strengthen incentives to expand food production through higher food prices may result in reduced incomes and severe hardships for the poor."

The selections in this part explore this fundamental dilemma with which policymakers must wrestle as they design domestic marketing policies for food. All governments must intervene in their economies, as C. Peter Timmer observes. The challenge is to identify ways in which governments can formulate their food interventions to assure equity and to protect the poorest consumers. As noted earlier, one of the significant changes in thinking about food policy in recent years has been a growing consensus among policymakers and specialists that this dilemma must be addressed from the very beginning of food policy formulation. Looking only at production incentives, under the now widely accepted assumption that farmers are price responsive, and failing to consider the impact of higher prices on low-income consumers is "to ignore political realities and short-run welfare goals," as Pinstrup-Andersen puts it. Addressing the dilemma is a compelling reason for policymakers and analysts to integrate supply, distribution, and consumption.

Recognizing the dilemma and doing something about it, however, are two quite different things. The authors in this section share their insights by examining the underlying price theory as a means of providing policymakers with a better understanding of the impact of proposed policy changes; by looking at alternative formulations of interventions to reduce the impact of higher food prices on low-income consumers through such devices as targeted food subsidies; by suggesting ways to realize marketing efficiency gains and thus reduce the gap between offering higher incentives to producers and maintaining or improving availability of food to vulnerable consumers; and by pointing out the importance of building a political consensus, which will permit rational policy formulation and implementation.

Timmer succinctly lays out the major considerations in using price theory to analyze food policy. He notes that a rather simple theoretical formulation can give powerful insights into the likely effects of any chosen policy instrument—although policymakers cannot stop at such an elementary level but must also consider the broader ramifications of any food price intervention for the overall pattern of production and consumption and the long-term growth of food production.

In a later chapter, Timmer focuses on the relationships between food price policy and the functioning of the grain market. "Markets," he notes, "are the most effective way governments have to reach the multitudes of decentralized decisionmakers whose day to day decisions dictate whether an economy develops or not." Indeed, many may be surprised at how extensive the marketing activities of low-income households in developing countries are. Benson Ateng details some of that activity as reported from Kenya and outlines some of the important marketing activities commonly found among low-income groups in developing countries. Timmer comments that policymakers must determine the impact of food price policies on various classes of producers and consumers, must evaluate the border prices that serve as the standard for welfare comparisons, and must consider the broader macroeconomic and long-term effects of food price policy. Not surprisingly, such a broad approach "creates a problem for policy analysts, for it asks them to be aware of the indirect consequences of price policy for the agricultural marketing system." Timmer suggests, however, that a good starting point is the six price ratios he identifies; more complex analyses can follow.

To implement a price policy requires more than being able to analyze the outcome of alternative formulations or even finding ways to protect the welfare of the poorest groups in the society. The policymaker must also find a means to "shape reformist coalitions or alliances between groups whose interests can be harnessed to the cause of reform," as Streeten comments, noting also that too little is known about the links between politics and food policy and that more research is needed.

One obvious way to resolve the dilemma between offering prices high enough to encourage agricultural growth and meeting the food needs of low-income consumers, Pinstrup-Andersen notes, is "by driving a publicly financed wedge between consumer and producer or import prices." The problem is that the wedge may be costly and is likely to grow over time. Pinstrup-Andersen briefly reviews some of the ways the wedge may be designed to help contain the cost. He also notes recent research on Argentina that shows gains from trade liberalization and exchange rate management to be more than enough for compensation to consumers in the form of subsidies that could maintain their ability to purchase food. He notes that this is an extremely important finding, particularly if it can be generalized to other cases, because "it implies that current pressures in many developing countries to increase food prices to provide producer incentives need not conflict with short-term welfare goals, because economic gains would exceed the cost of full compensation to the poor."

Contrary to what many people assume, Pinstrup-Andersen notes, increased food prices may not be particularly favorable for the rural poor. He cites research indicating that the poorest 20 percent of the rural population in India would lose from increasing food prices, and that in Sri Lanka, only 3 percent of the rural poor (taken to be the poorest quartile of the rural population) would be better off in the short run from an increase in rice prices. The reason is that many among the rural poor do not earn a large share of their income either from wage labor in food production or from the sale of food. A large proportion of the rural poor are net purchasers of food. As a result, the benefit of price increases tends to go to larger farmers and to a somewhat lesser extent to rural laborers employed in food production. Although keeping the cost of food interventions within bounds and administering them efficiently present difficulties, Pinstrup-Andersen concludes that food subsidies have increased incomes and improved nutritional status among the poor in a number of developing countries.

Another means of reducing the impact of the food price policy dilemma is to increase marketing efficiency. Pinstrup-Andersen notes that in some African countries, producers may receive only 40 percent of the retail or export price of food grain, while in some Asian countries producers receive 80 percent. Recent research on Africa indicates that reducing the price spread by 25 percentage points "would result in a 49 percent increase in farm prices and a 13 percent decrease in consumer prices."

Cutting down marketing losses is another way to reduce the impact of the food price policy dilemma. E. R. Pariser reviews post-harvest losses in developing countries and finds overall losses of at least 10 percent of total grain and grain legume production and 20 percent of nongrain staples, perishables, and fish. As a first step in identifying market improvement measures that could reduce the loss and thereby hold down food prices, he surveys the most common sources of post-harvest food losses in developing countries.

18

Price Policy and the
Political Economy of Markets

C. Peter Timmer

All governments must intervene in their economies to raise resources to carry out even the minimum tasks of government: police protection, road building and maintenance, and other inherently public activities. Taxation is thus the starting point for sheer governmental existence. Wherever the economy is primarily agricultural, direct or indirect mechanisms to tax agricultural income will be essential components of government policy. Given a lack of political desire or bureaucratic capacity to tax agricultural income directly through taxes on land, profits, or personal income, use of commodity taxes as a basic source of government revenue is virtually inevitable. The "need to tax" exists even though taxes distort market signals to producers and consumers, so some balance between the need for revenue and the magnitude and impact of the distortion must be struck.

Quite apart from the need to raise tax revenue, governments frequently intervene in agricultural price formation for other purposes. Sometimes those purposes are narrowly self-serving to those in power and their friends; sometimes the purposes are to serve broader social objectives. Characteristically, these goals include efficient economic growth, improved income distribution, a nutritional floor for all citizens, food security for the country, and political stability—which is probably assured if the first four are achieved.

Most government interventions have at least an indirect effect on food prices facing consumers or crop prices facing farmers. These intricate and roundabout influences on agricultural incentives are an integrating theme of *Food Policy Analysis* (Timmer and others 1983). However, the reverse effect is also important and is not developed in

Written for this collection. Another version of this paper appeared in *Getting Prices Right: The Scope and Limits of Agricultural Price Policy* (Ithaca, New York: Cornell University Press, 1986).

that volume. Agricultural prices have subtle and dynamic effects on the entire economy in addition to their direct and more immediate impact on the agricultural sector itself. Price policy analysis can help identify the trade-offs in given circumstances and may even point the way to more efficient sources of revenue or less distorting interventions that achieve the same social welfare objectives, but the analysis cannot eliminate the distortions or the need for government intervention.

Models for Agricultural Price Policy Analysis

What is the "right" price for an agricultural commodity? Economists have an easy answer to the question that is derived from an economic model that assumes a world of perfect certainty, competitive markets, no other government interventions into the economy, and no political concerns for the impact on income distribution. In such a world, any deviation of the domestic price from the international border price, either import or export, reduces total economic welfare in the country because of efficiency losses in production and consumption. Despite the provisos and restrictions needed for this "answer" to be completely correct, the use of border prices as a guide to domestic price policy remains quite powerful. In practical terms, the border price represents a society's short-run opportunity cost with respect to changed consumption or production of the commodity. Consequently, understanding the logic of the border prices is the essential first step in addressing any further policy concerns about the implementation and impact of changes in domestic prices for food and agricultural commodities.

Partial Equilibrium Models

Understanding the use of border prices and partial equilibrium analysis is the starting point for analysis of agricultural price policy— not the conclusion. All participants in a policy analysis and debate must start at the same point with a common framework and set of assumptions. From the initial point, representatives of different interest groups, ministries, and methodological perspectives can each build toward a more complex understanding of the pricing issues and formulate their concerns about the impact of a pricing change.

Evaluating domestic price policy relative to border prices starts with the supply and demand functions of the national market for a commodity, most commonly pictured as curves on a graph. These curves reflect the initial status of technology and productivity on the supply side, including the cost of inputs and alternative commodities that farmers might grow instead of the commodity being analyzed. On the demand side, the curves reflect the tastes of consumers, the level and distribution of incomes, and the prices of alternative consumer goods, including not only other food items but also nonfood goods and services.

These supply and demand curves represent only part of the reaction to a change in the price of the commodity being considered and so are referred to as "partial equilibrium" models. When the commodity is important to the entire economy, as a staple food grain or major export crop inevitably is to a developing country, these partial equilibrium adjustments provide only an initial glimpse of the full adjustments likely to occur when the price changes. Other, more complicated analytical techniques must then be used to understand the full effects of price policy.

The simple supply and demand model can be used to illuminate basic price policy issues as well as to provide a base from which to identify when more complicated issues are likely to arise. Most likely, a partial equilibrium analysis for a commodity that uses a key input such as fertilizer in its production, or for which many important substitute crops are available, such as sugar, will suggest that changes occurring in this commodity market will spill over into fertilizer or sugar markets. If so, further analysis is required. This may mean analysis of one or more additional markets—fertilizer, sugar, or foreign exchange. It may require modeling the entire agricultural sector to capture the impact of more complicated timing, crop substitutions, labor market adjustments, and volume of marketing within the agricultural sector and on the urban sector. It may ultimately involve at least a simple model that traces effects in the economy as a whole—that is, a macroeconomic model—to ensure consistency in national income accounts, trade flows, and savings and investment patterns.

There is a surprisingly large number of circumstances when the partial equilibrium model needs at least informal macroeconomic modeling and consistency checks to provide confidence in the result. A large price change for an individual commodity, or significant price changes simultaneously for multiple commodities, are likely to cause multimarket spillover effects. Price changes for "important" commodities will affect the whole agricultural sector and, indeed, the whole economy—that is, they will have macroeconomic effects. "Importance" is measured in one of four ways.

○ The commodity is the chief wage good in the society and forms a significant share—20 to 50 percent—of the average consumer's budget. This factor alone often makes food price policy analysis a macroeconomic concern.

o The commodity is a major source of farm income. This is important for two reasons. Changing the price alters farm incomes and hence farm expenditures on goods and services that provide employment to many people. Price changes also cause farmers to change input use and alter their cropping patterns and hence affect national agricultural production.

o The commodity is important in the country's international trade as an export or an import. Either way, changes in domestic prices are likely to alter trade volumes and hence the foreign exchange balance. In extreme cases, such as Ghana's experience with cocoa, domestic price policy can nearly wipe out a country's foreign exchange earnings.

o The commodity is important to the government budget, either as a generator of revenue or as a significant drain because of large subsidies. The inherent need for a government to raise money through taxes has already been noted. Price policy analysis cannot ignore this need in favor of either efficiency or income distribution.

The most difficult examples of agricultural price policy analysis occur when the commodity is important for all four reasons—a common situation in developing countries in which a primary food staple is grown domestically and imported or exported. Rice in Indonesia and Thailand, maize in Kenya, Mexico, and Zimbabwe, and wheat in Pakistan and Egypt, for example, easily meet these criteria. For these countries, the level of employment, the nutritional well-being of the poor, the extent of foreign exchange reserves, and the size of the budget deficit all hinge on the price of one critical food grain. Indeed, as violent political demonstrations in response to high food prices repeatedly make clear, even the existence of the government is intimately tied to price policy for basic foods. Analysis of these commodities extends beyond the boundaries of partial equilibrium models even if the political dimensions remain outside the formal analysis itself.

The full extent of economic adjustments to price changes depends not only on spillovers to other markets but also on the time horizon of the analysis, even when the analysis is restricted solely to the supply and demand curves for a single commodity. Producers and consumers tend to adjust to price changes much more flexibly after several years than immediately after the change. A useful rule of thumb is that about half the likely adjustment will take place in the first year, with the remainder occurring in smaller increments in the following years. In these circumstances the "long run" is likely to be five to ten years.

From Partial to General Equilibrium Models

Agricultural price policy analysis attempts to determine the impact of current prices for food and agricultural commodities on welfare and the effects of any change in these prices. The standard partial equilibrium analysis using border prices as the measure of domestic opportunity cost addresses this question at one level by measuring gains and losses in producer and consumer welfare, transfers to and from the budget, changes in foreign exchange earnings and expenditures, and efficiency losses.

The initial framework to assess the welfare effects of changing price policy is a partial equilibrium analysis that assumes no adjustments in the economy other than those shown by the analysis itself. The broader consequences of price changes that take into account secondary adjustments—so-called "dynamic" and "general equilibrium" effects—are extremely hard to measure or predict since no economy is understood well enough for these effects to be modeled except in the roughest, most intuitive way. Of course, this does not mean the broader consequences are unimportant or may be ignored. Incorporating the impact of changed food and agricultural prices on other markets, on the structure of investment, and on long-run patterns and distribution of economic growth is also an important analytical task, no matter how rough the answers may turn out to be. These issues also take the price policy analyst into the macroeconomic policy debate, this time via budget, fiscal, and monetary issues in addition to the debate about macroeconomic price policy.

All markets are linked together by substitution possibilities in production and consumption. Sometimes individual markets are isolated—segmented from other markets for the same commodity by transportation costs, institutional barriers, or government regulation and activity. Even when rural labor or credit markets seem fully insulated from urban or national economic forces, however, indirect economic activities such as migration or remittances provide roundabout and subtle linkages.

In principle, all analysis of agricultural price changes should be set in a full general equilibrium context, in which the market outcome for any one good or service ultimately depends on the activities in all other markets. As a guide to understanding the impact of policy, however, the pervasiveness of such linkages is immobilizing. Do we really need to know the general equilibrium consequences of a price change for tomatoes in the Philippines? Or for maize in Indonesia? Or for rice in Thailand? It all depends.

The approach to finding out whether general equilibrium consequences are significant is to work from the simple to the complex, starting with a single-market analysis. When this first step is carried out carefully and thoughtfully, it provides clear directions about where to look for the most immediate impact on other markets. "Looking" implies asking how the process of adjustment is undertaken. Exactly what does it mean for a supply curve to slope upward toward the right? What are farmers doing? A policy intervention that lowers the rice price, for example, will lead to a reduction in rice production that, in turn, will be accompanied by diminished use of inputs and by some increased effort on other crops or activities, including greater willingness to enter the rural labor market. Immediately, at least three other markets—input markets such as for fertilizer, alternative output markets such as for cotton, sugar, or maize, and the rural labor market—are identified that have potentially significant links to the rice market and would adjust to a change in rice prices.

These multimarket effects are not easy to calculate even once identified because of the likely spillovers from the initial market intervention. Unlike single-market analysis, there is no simple graphical framework using supply and demand curves. Researchers are forced into numerical calculations even as a rough first step, building a multimarket model with as many interconnections as are necessary or within the reach of available data. Such models are much simpler to build if analysts start from current market environments and calculate approximate changes through incremental adjustments than if they attempt to find globally consistent forms for each market's supply and demand curves (Braverman and others 1983).

Even fairly simple multimarket models can yield important differences from single-market analysis. For example, World Bank economists working on agricultural prices in Malawi analyzed a 14 percent reduction in the price of maize, the country's staple food crop (Kirchner and others 1984). With just the partial equilibrium result, they projected that maize production would decline by 6 percent and farmer income would fall by 29 million kwacha. The multimarket result projected the same decline in maize production, but a switch in resources, especially farm labor, led to an increase of 2 percent in tobacco production and 3 percent in groundnut production. Because these crops are exported, foreign exchange earnings would increase by 7.5 million kwacha. The lower maize price would also cause fertilizer use to drop by 15 percent. After the adjustments included in the multimarket model were accounted for, farmer incomes were projected to drop by only 18 million kwacha instead of the single-market estimate of 29 million kwacha.

To build a realistic multimarket model requires determining how the markets respond to price changes, especially whether they respond largely by adjusting the returns received by farmers and other participants or whether all adjustments are through quantities, as in the Malawi case. The primary application for multimarket models, in fact, is where governments enforce fixed prices in several markets and so must plan for any changes in quantities if price stabilization is to be successful.

Because price policy changes can lead to a complex combination of changes in incomes of agricultural producers and to shifts in use of regional or national resources, such as land, water, or labor, a sector-wide model is required to trace the most important effects (Kutcher and others 1986). Analysts have used agricultural sector models since the mid-1960s to check the consistency of agricultural development plans and to examine the resource requirements of alternative cropping patterns. With the advent of much faster computation methods, efforts have recently been made to incorporate realistic price response relationships in the models.

Unlike single-market or multimarket equilibrium models, sector models contain detailed farm models as the basis for supply response and alternative crop choices in the face of changed prices. In principle, similar detail for differently situated consuming households could also be incorporated.

Just as a price change for a single commodity can spill over into other markets and multimarket effects can have important sectoral consequences, so too can agricultural sector adjustments have significant macroeconomic consequences. The task is to identify those price changes for a single commodity that would have this full cascade of ramifications. The following broad categories of sectoral spillovers require at least a rough effort to model macroeconomic consequences:

○ When projected changes in budgetary revenues and expenditures in response to the policy being analyzed are derived from the model by the estimated relationships between production and consumption but occur in different sectors, as when large food subsidies that draw on general tax revenues are used to implement a price policy

○ When macroeconomic prices are determined on a national level and cannot be understood on the basis of sectoral markets alone.

Rural labor or credit markets that are only weakly linked to urban or national markets can usually be analyzed with sectoral models. However, when wages in national labor markets, foreign exchange rates in currency markets, and interest rates in capital markets for savings and investment resources are affected by a change in the price of a commodity, a macroeconomic model that enforces market clearing and general equilibrium is essential for consistent results.

Computable general equilibrium models are not yet capable of capturing many of the key linkages between individual commodity prices and macroeconomic outcomes. Rapid progress is being made on the technology of these models, however. Already the capacity to build and solve a computable general equilibrium model substantially exceeds our understanding of the important connections that must be built into the models if they are to provide useful insights.

Food and agriculture policy is seldom considered as part of macroeconomic policy, or vice versa, partly because of the lack of general equilibrium models that can provide reliable empirical estimates of the effect of commodity price changes on macroeconomic outcomes. Planning agencies, central banks, and ministries of finance are responsible for macroeconomic policy, whereas food agencies and ministries of agriculture design farm and retail price policies. Because of the consequences of food and agricultural policies for the government budget, the macroeconomic agencies have an input into decisions about farm and retail price policies, which is frequently a veto, but the reverse is seldom true. Few ministers of agriculture contribute to the macroeconomic policy debate.

Market Failure and Government Intervention

The tension between the microeconomic perspective of agricultural ministries and the macroeconomic impact of the sector reflects one of the great paradoxes of modern economic systems. The agricultural and food sector is one of the most "public" in terms of policy and program needs, but at the same time it is one of the most "private" in terms of day to day decision making in production, marketing, and consumption. The paradox is explained by the role of markets and the myriad of decisions coordinated by those markets. It is the well-known instances of market failure where markets do not provide public goods to an extent that is socially adequate or where markets do not perform efficiently that give agriculture its public dimensions. Then the need arises for government to ensure competitive markets; to undertake public investment in agricultural research, road and marketing infrastructure, irrigation, and communication facilities; to establish grades and standards; and even to ensure price stability. Government policies and public investments determine the efficiency and dynamism of a country's agriculture more than almost any other sector. Yet, at the same time, millions of individual households make the day to day decisions that actually generate the efficiency and dynamism.

Significant tension exists between the widespread failure of markets in the food and agricultural sectors of rich and poor countries and the desirability, even necessity, to use markets as the vehicle both to reach individual producers and consumers efficiently and to generate an evolving flow of information about costs and returns in the sector. Schumpeter (1950) predicted that free market economies would decline in democratic countries to be replaced by socialism and political controls because most people cannot understand the complex mechanisms by which the benefits of market systems are generated. This complexity causes political support to wane for the contractual property rights essential for market economies to operate efficiently. Special economic groups then use their political skills to intervene in markets for their own financial advantage, a process that gradually undermines the allocative role of prices.

Schumpeter's vision about the changing nature of the fundamental institutions that define the basic contractual arrangements of societies calls into question attempts by economists and economic historians to model the long-run changes in the structure and performance of national economies in terms of prices and incomes. Precisely because these models hold in abeyance the changing "rules of the game" and ideologies of participants, they cannot capture the complicated evolution of modern economic systems as they respond to external shocks or internal policy changes.

It is not just economic modelers who would like to assume away the complexity of interdependent economic systems. Policymakers and populations at large also seek simple, easily understood answers to the difficult problems of modern economic life. Ever since the debate over the repeal of the English Corn Laws, economists have argued that simple answers frequently make for bad policy and that what is good politics in the short run may be bad economics in the long run. Schultz's (1978, p. 9) comment about economists being "'yes men' in the halls of political economy" shows that the debate is still lively. This is not a reason to keep all prices constant for all time, but rather to understand the impact of price changes on welfare and their political implications. Since the political impact is almost always felt much more rapidly than the full economic impact, the analysis must focus specifically on the dimensions of both and illuminate possible side interventions that will make desirable economic changes politically feasible.

Governments have used two fundamental approaches to resolve the tension between the failure of markets and the need to achieve efficient resource allocation to further food policy objectives. One has been to displace markets from their economic function and rely instead on planning allocations or direct parastatal controls. The more tightly regulated and internally oriented economies, however, have suffered declining growth rates, widespread shortages of consumer goods, and open dissatisfaction among the population. Ironically, the reasons have to do with the complexity of economic systems, the extraordinary amount of information communicated through prices, and the multiple decisions involving vast information-processing capacities required of all successful economies in a globally interdependent world. Most of those decisions simply cannot be made efficiently or effectively by a central planning agency or regulatory control board.

As quantitative controls have become progressively less efficient in a highly dynamic world where opportunities and potential losses are a function of information flows, governments have tried new planning experiments. These have taken many forms: the Hungarian orientation to agricultural exports led by decentralized cooperatives and firms reacting to market signals; the Chinese experiment with the production responsibility system and rural markets; an expanded role for private traders in legal markets as competition for government marketing parastatals in several Latin American and African countries; and withdrawal of parastatals from activities that require direct interaction with farmers and consumers, in favor of a new focus on wholesalers and intermediaries or export markets (Austin 1984).

The alternative approach to resolving the tension between market failure and efficient resource allocation has been to use government intervention to strengthen market efficiency within an overall food policy framework. It is a surprise to many that the agricultural sectors of developing countries are an intimate component of a complex economic system, linked to it through markets and price signals. A vision of largely self-sufficient peasants outside the money economy and heedless of the incentives signaled by changing prices recalls a simpler and nostalgic era, but that era passed a century ago in the United States and is now nearly gone for most farmers in developing countries as well. For better or for worse, agricultural and marketing systems in developing countries are now an integral part, often even a dominant part, of their countries' market economies.

This market approach incorporates investment in public goods and a commitment to solving the problems of poverty and hunger through targeted interventions that reach the poor without seriously distorting the signals generated in the markets. Investments in a marketing system can lower marketing costs directly, thus easing the food price dilemma of providing low prices to consumers but sufficiently high prices to producers, and these investments can also increase the efficiency and competitiveness of the marketing system by lowering barriers to entry.

Changes in food and agricultural prices—often the result of price policy—affect the structure of the economy, and in return, the agricultural economy is influenced in roundabout and dynamic ways. It is difficult for price policy analysts to capture these dynamic effects. If high food prices induce technical change, for instance, static analysis may provide seriously misleading estimates of the actual welfare transfers between producers and consumers and the ultimate impact on the government budget. By changing the opportunity cost of holding land for small farmers relative to large ones, a government can induce quite unknowingly, through price policy, changes in land tenure patterns or in choice of production technology. The distribution of income can change not just between producers and consumers but also within rural areas through indirect effects on hiring patterns and rural wages. These effects on income might then have long-run consequences for nutrition and health not captured by the static analysis (Behrman and Deolalikar forthcoming). Because some outcomes reflect the difference between life and death, actually measuring these consequences becomes a serious responsibility for price policy analysts.

The dynamic effects of food price policy interventions are likely to dominate the static effects, but the main issue is whether they reinforce or cancel each other. Much remains to be learned in this area, and comparative case studies of modern economic history rather than econometric analysis are likely to provide much of that knowledge. These studies require a political economy framework that focuses on the role of prices in the process of structural change and incorporates information on institutional response, creation and reactions of effective political lobbies, and the changing attitudes of society about the fairness and functioning of the economy (Anderson and Hayami 1986; Reich and others 1986).

Price Policy Analysis and Policymaking

Perhaps what emerges most persistently from observing the formal analysis of a country's price policy and the resulting policy decisions is the constant need to make decisions, even decisions to do nothing. Many countries maintain price policies that are patently not conducive to their long-run economic growth, despite rather sophisticated analyses that illuminate the consequences of the policies. Simple inertia may be part of the reason. Bureaucrats receive less blame if something goes wrong from current policy than from a visibly new policy. Part of the reason can be attributed to the tangible political costs of a change in policy relative to the tenuous and widespread dispersion of the economic benefits. However, part of the reason stems from a failure to coordinate analysis and policy making. Analysts may solve problems that policymakers are not interested in; policymakers may be unwilling to think about the potential scope of analysis or may focus solely on its limitations.

This lack of coordination is most apparent when analysts and policymakers fail to recognize three quite different problems with the border price paradigm. First, most economists recognize that the underlying assumptions do not hold precisely in even the best of circumstances and that they are wildly violated in many developing economies where knowledge is highly imperfect, markets are badly fragmented, and there is extensive government involvement, all making piecemeal analysis inappropriate. Consequently, the analysis must be robust enough and based sufficiently on empirical understanding of the actual situation that challenges to the theoretical model can be met with relevant adaptations and facts.

Second, the political concern for income distribution simply cannot be assumed away, whether it reflects powerful vested interests of urban workers and the military or a genuine concern for the nutritional well-being of the poor who depend on access to cheap food for their day to day survival. Price changes for important agricultural commodities inevitably carry visible consequences for the welfare of these groups, and "efficient" compensation programs are never feasible in practice, whatever their theoretical merit.

A third level of complexity and concern comes with problems of implementing price policies. Operational ministries are concerned about administrative procedures to implement price policy and the impact of policy changes on the marketing sector in which prices are formed and communicated. They are also concerned to know what the international price will be for the planning horizon of the price policy. International commodity markets are notoriously unstable; a domestic floor price announced before the planting season, for example, may well reflect the opportunity cost of imports at the time of the announcement but be too low or too high by the time of harvest. Instability in international commodity prices is thus a serious issue for the design of domestic price policy in the short run, whereas long-run structural changes in the world food system affect investment decisions about agricultural research, rural infrastructure, and sectoral priorities.

The goal of this essay is to provide a sense of the ways in which price policy analysis can illuminate how markets will adjust in the short run and the long run to a variety of government interventions designed to alter commodity prices. Price policy analysis has no checklist of the desirable and undesirable attributes of a price intervention and the formulas to quantify them. Instead, the need for flexibility in policy design and a capacity to anticipate and monitor outcomes are stressed.

While the free market model provides a powerful paradigm for understanding the initial impact of government intervention, its results are not sufficiently complete or realistic to provide policy answers. Its power lies not in providing an optimal answer but in identifying alternative costs and benefits of different interventions. The search for the full range of effects of price policy interventions, no matter how far-ranging or complicated, is legitimate and important. Price policy analysis will always be a process that is at least as intuitive as it is quantitative. To treat it exclusively as one or the other is to miss both the strength of the underlying economic models of resource allocation for illuminating important social choices and the necessity for society, rather than analysts, to make those choices.

19

Transitional Measures
and Political Support
for Food Price Policy Reform

Paul Streeten

Policymakers are confronted with a fundamental dilemma. On the one hand, they want high prices for food to encourage agricultural production. On the other hand, they want low prices to protect poor buyers of food.

The dilemma has three origins, each presenting an obstacle to reform. First, agricultural price policies have attempted to pursue many objectives. Not only growth with equity, but many proximate and intermediate objectives have dictated policies. Some of these objectives conflict with one another, and even where they are potentially compatible, it would be surprising if a single instrument—price policy—were sufficient to achieve them all. Where conflict exists, there has to be choice. The test of good policymakers is whether they can reconcile objectives where compatibility exists, make a choice where conflicts arise, and know which is which.

The second origin of the dilemma is that policymakers find themselves with a heritage of complex interventions relating not only to explicit and implicit measures to control output prices but also to input subsidies that attempt to offset the deterrent effects of low output prices, explicit and implicit taxes on the consumption goods bought by farmers, and various direct controls and ad hoc measures to meet specific pressures. Some of these measures sprang from a desire to encourage industrialization by keeping real wages low, some from pessimism about the opportunities of international trade. Although they were not intended to discriminate against agriculture (the contri-

Excerpted from "Food Prices as a Reflection of Political Power," *Ceres*, vol. 16, no. 2 (March–April 1983), pp. 16–22, published by the Food and Agriculture Organization of the United Nations.

bution of which to development was acknowledged by subsidies on inputs, by technical advisory services, and by encouragement of research), the impact of this mixed heritage of interventions is detrimental to agriculture in most developing countries.

The third origin of the dilemma is that these measures have given rise to vested interests, political pressures, and political constraints.

Conditions to Make Price Incentives Effective

Economists now generally accept that farmers are responsive to price incentives and that production will tend to increase when rewards are greater. Yet even the most ardent advocates of higher prices for agricultural producers would admit that many other things are necessary to call forth the extra supply. Among these is the removal of physical, social, and administrative barriers to increased supply. To illustrate: transport bottlenecks must often be broken so that the extra food can be transported from surplus to deficit areas or to ports for export. Consumer goods must be available in the countryside so that rural families can spend their higher incomes on something they want. Agricultural inputs must be available so that the technical conditions for raising output can be met. The marketing authorities or the private middlemen must pay promptly for the crops bought. Institutional arrangements that ensure that the benefits of the higher prices accrue to the farmers and not to monopolistic private middlemen or to inefficient or corrupt public marketing authorities must be in place. New technology must be available so that incentives of higher prices can speed up the growth of production significantly.

Proponents and skeptics differ on whether raising prices without these other measures is better than nothing or whether, by itself, raising prices is futile or even counterproductive. The critics can point to cases where the introduction of higher supply prices without an appropriate scale-neutral technology or without the appropriate institutions has, for example, accelerated the transfer of land from small to large farmers and violated equity and poverty objectives. If the productivity per hectare on the small farms was greater than on the large farms, total output fell. The proposition "other measures in addition to price policies are necessary" is therefore open to two diametrically opposed interpretations. It may mean that while other measures help, getting prices right without them is better than nothing. Or it may mean that the right prices together with the institutional and technological measures will achieve the objective but by themselves will be ineffective.

Transition Measures

Economists often argue that a short-term increase in agricultural prices will in the long term lead to lower food prices than would otherwise have prevailed; the improved short-term incentives to invest, innovate, and adopt technical change will bring about a downward shift of the whole supply curve. This is, of course, perfectly possible and appears to have happened, but two qualifications are necessary. Much depends on the initial system of land distribution and access to agricultural inputs, on institutions, on infrastructure, and on information. (Together with incentives these constitute the five "I's" that are conditions for agricultural growth.) In a society in which power and wealth are very unequally distributed, a rise in the price of food may make the rich richer by leading to transfers of land without leading to a lowering of the supply curve.

The second qualification relates to the period of transition. The impact of food price increases on poor food consumers is highly complex but may be summarized as follows: a rise in the price of food raises the real incomes of food producers and lowers, in the short run, the real incomes of food consumers, since in the short run the supply does not rise. There are some very poor people in both groups. In principle, consumer and producer prices can be separated by a system of taxes and subsidies, but in practice there are severe constraints. In the medium and long run, the detrimental impact on poor food consumers can be mitigated or offset by changing technology, an increased supply of food, increased employment, higher wages, and perhaps reduced rural-urban migration with consequential higher urban income levels.

Keynes said we are all dead in the long run, but this does not mean that we are all alive in the short run. Very poor food buyers may starve to death before the blessings of the medium run materialize. In Bangladesh, high rice prices have led to higher child mortality. Policymakers embarking on a course of raising food prices must therefore pay special attention to protecting the poor in the transition.

It is useful to distinguish among three groups vulnerable to rising food prices:

○ Landless laborers and deficit farmers who have to hire themselves out for some of the time and earn wages. They depend on employment, wages, and the price of food, or, if paid in kind, on the value of the crops they receive.

○ Small surplus farmers who depend on their productivity, the prices of the crops they sell, and the price of food they buy

○ The urban poor who depend on employment opportunities, wages, and the price of food. The urban poor in some countries have rural links and therefore can either return to their villages or get food supplements from the countryside if their access to food in town is reduced.

The impact of a rise in the price of food is different for these different groups, and the short-run, medium-run, and long-run responses are different. The composition of these groups will change as a result of a rise in the price of food so that, for example, deficit farmers may become surplus farmers, landless laborers may become urban poor, and so on.

Policies will have a different impact in Africa, where there are few landless laborers, than in South Asia, where there are many, and in countries of South Asia, where there are many subsistence-oriented farmers who sell only a small share of their crops, than in South America, where the marketed surplus plays a greater role.

One method of protection is to increase the price gradually, in small steps. Very large price increases might even have perverse effects on supply because producers will take out some of the gains in greater leisure. In any case, the large, suddenly higher farm incomes generated would not fulfill any economic function. A second way is to make subsidies as selective as possible by concentrating them either on vulnerable groups or on basic food staples consumed by the poor, such as cassava and maize. A third way is to provide income subsidies to the poor.

Subsidies can be combined with rations so that the very poor are guaranteed a minimum amount of food. The basic difficulty with targeted programs is that they should reach all the poor and only the poor, and that is extremely difficult. Whether the subsidies apply to income groups or to types of goods, there are bound to be leakages and deficiencies. It is particularly difficult to reach poor food consumers in the rural areas, and the benefits of the subsidies will be concentrated on urban populations. If the proportion of poor in the population is large, or if the food staples are largely consumed by the target population, total coverage can be achieved more easily and costs need not be excessive. Generally, there is likely to be a trade-off between complete coverage and cost. A compromise has to be struck in the light of the number of poor and the budgetary constraints.

Research on Building a Political Base

In most cases, the obstacle to "correct" policy making is neither stupidity nor cupidity, neither solely lack of knowledge nor solely political constraints. At the same time, there are large areas in which a better analysis and a clearer sense of direction would help, just as there are areas in which it is fairly clear what should be done but vested interests prevent it from happening. Political constraints should be neither ignored nor accepted as ultimate facts. They too call for analysis. In this case, the problem is how to build a political base for desirable reforms.

Let us assume that policymakers are aware of the correct policies and that it is only a question of implementation. Political scientists have done relatively little research into the question of how to build constituencies for reform, how to shape reformist coalitions or alliances between groups whose interests can be harnessed to the cause of reform. It may be said that people are, on the whole, quite good at discovering and pursuing their self-interest and that not much research is needed to steer them along this path. Although this is true, there are many situations in which individuals are helpless and where procedures, rules, or institutions are needed to give expression to their interests.

The rural and the urban poor are weak and powerless, particularly if not organized. In societies in which power and wealth are very unequally distributed, both low producer prices and high producer prices can reinforce the strength of powerful and rich groups. The interests behind low prices are the urban middle class, including the bureaucracy, the military, the police, and politically active students, who have access to fair price shops and to imported food aid and enjoy the benefits of low food prices. The rich and powerful farmers are often protected by subsidies and special allocations of scarce inputs. If this regime is changed to one of higher food prices, again the rich farmers may benefit, while the urban middle class may be protected by special measures under the pretext of protecting poor consumers.

Research is needed into the links between politics and food policies. It would be interesting to relate, for instance, the removal of food subsidies to riots, disturbances, or falls of governments. It would be useful to trace the groups that have an interest, direct or indirect, in higher food prices. It would be rewarding to trace the interests that can be mobilized for the measures needed in the period of transition.

Until the results of this research become available, however, policymakers will need to shape food price policies and complementary measures on the basis of their own knowledge of their societies, keeping in mind the needs of politically weak vulnerable groups and the need to construct a political base for reform.

20

Food Prices and the Poor in Developing Countries

Per Pinstrup-Andersen

Food prices play an important role in the well-being of the poor. Even relatively small changes in the price of food staples may affect the ability of poor consumers, both rural and urban, to meet their basic nutritional requirements. However, the impact of food price changes differs among groups of low-income people, and the immediate impact may differ significantly from the longer-run impact.

Governments in virtually all countries manipulate food prices, irrespective of their development strategy or political beliefs. In some countries, governments use low food prices to make low urban wages possible, thus extracting real resources from agriculture to support growth in the nonfood public and private sectors. Cheap food policies are sometimes justified on grounds of social justice for poor urban consumers, or governments follow them simply to avoid social unrest in urban areas. Some governments enforce low producer prices to acquire public revenues. Others subsidize food prices to maintain low consumer prices without a corresponding negative effect on farm prices and food supplies. Yet other countries maintain support prices to elevate or stabilize producer prices and to stabilize consumer prices, thereby protecting producers while ensuring ample food supplies for consumers.

The importance of remunerative food prices as supply incentives is not questioned, although price policies are but one of many policy instruments available to governments for expanding food production. What is argued here is that policies that attempt to strengthen incentives to expand food production through higher food prices may result in reduced real incomes and severe hardships for the poor, at

Excerpted from "Food Prices and the Poor in Developing Countries," *European Review of Agricultural Economics,* vol. 12, nos. 1 and 2 (1985), pp. 69–81.

least in the short run. Consequently, to attempt to increase domestic food prices to provide greater incentives to farmers while ignoring the implications for—and the need to compensate—the poor would be to ignore political realities and short-run welfare goals.

The Short-Run Impact of Food Price Changes on the Poor

Low-income consumers typically spend 60 to 80 percent of their income on food. In some countries, one staple may account for 40 to 60 percent of the food expenditure, as does rice in Southeast Asia, while in other areas, as in Latin America, no one staple has such overall importance. Contrary to what might be expected, the budget share spent on high-cost foods may be large even among the poor and malnourished. It is not unusual for the urban poor in Latin America to spend more on meat than on any other commodity. Meat expenditure exceeded cereal expenditure among the poorest quartile of the population in five of the ten Latin American cities studied by Musgrove (1978) and was less than one percentage point below in two of the five remaining cities. Thus, policymakers must know the commodity mix in the diet of the poor when deciding on price policies for individual commodities.

The importance of food prices to household purchasing power is illustrated in table 20-1, which shows the impact of a 10 percent

Table 20-1. *Impact of a 10 Percent Increase in the Price of Food on the Real Income of Low-Income and High-Income Groups*

	Decrease in real income (percent)		
Country	Lowest decile	Highest decile	Source[a]
Egypt	5.6	1.0	Alderman and von Braun (1984)
India[b]	5.5[c]	1.2[d]	Mellor (1978)
India	7.3	2.9	Murty (1983)
Nigeria (Funtua)	7.7	6.5	Pinstrup-Andersen and Uy (1985)
Nigeria (Gusau)	9.0	5.7	Pinstrup-Andersen and Uy (1985)
Sri Lanka	8.5	4.1	Sahn (forthcoming)
Thailand	6.0	2.0	Trairatvorakul (1984)

a. Sources are for the data used for calculations, except for Mellor (1978), who reports the estimates shown.
b. Food grains only.
c. Lowest 20 percent.
d. Highest 5 percent.

Table 20-2. *Price Elasticities of Demand for Rice among Low-Income and High-Income Groups, Selected Countries*

	Low income		High income		
Country	*Percentile*	*Price elasticity*	*Percentile*	*Price elasticity*	*Source*
Bangladesh (rural)	10	−1.30	90	−0.83	Ahmed (1981)
Brazil	15	−4.31	90	−1.15	Williamson-Gray (1982)
Colombia (Cali)	1	−0.43	93	−1.19	Pinstrup-Andersen and others (1976)
India (rural)	3	−1.39	96	−0.39	Murty (1983)
India (urban)	1	−1.23	92	−0.21	Murty (1983)
Indonesia	8	−1.92	55	−0.72	Timmer and Alderman (1979)
Philippines	12	−0.73	87	−0.40	Bouis (1982)
Sierra Leone (rural)	16	−2.16	84	−0.45	Strauss (1983)
Thailand	12	−0.74	87	−0.46	Trairatvorakul (1984)

increase in the price of food on the real income of the poor in selected countries under the assumption of no substitution between food and nonfood. The impact on the better-off population is shown for comparison.

While substitution between food and nonfood products may be low, substitution among individual foods is likely to be higher. Thus, estimates of the impact of price changes of individual foods on the real income of the poor, on their demand for individual foods, and on their energy and nutrient consumption should consider both income and substitution effects. Estimates of price elasticities (including income and substitution effects) for food commodities by income level are of recent origin, and only a few are available. Estimates for rice for various countries are shown in table 20-2, and estimates for various commodities in Brazil are shown in table 20-3. As expected, the poor are more responsive to food price changes than the better-off population groups. Absolute values above one are not uncommon among the poor. Thus the data in table 20-2, for example, show that in Indonesia a 10 percent rise in the price of rice would cause the poorest 8 percent of the consumers to reduce their rice consumption by 19 percent (since for every 1 percent change in price they would reduce their consumption by 1.92 percent). Presumably they would substitute other starchy foods.

Compensation to the Poor for the Adverse Effect of Price Changes

Up to this point, only short-run effects have been considered. The longer-run impact depends on the extent to which higher food prices will lead to higher wages, and whether upward adjustment in food

Table 20-3. *Price Elasticities of Demand for Selected Foods, Brazil, by Income Group*

Commodity	Lowest income (30 percent of population)	Middle income (50 percent of population)	Highest income (20 percent of population)
Rice	−4.3	−3.0	−1.2
Maize	−1.8	−1.1	−0.6
Wheat bread	−2.0	−0.9	−0.7
Root crops	−1.4	−0.8	−0.2
Sugar	−1.4	−1.0	−0.6
Beef	−2.4	−1.3	−0.8

Source: Williamson-Gray (1982).

prices improves the efficiency of resource allocation and use, thereby generating economic growth and increased employment. In a study of Argentina, Cavallo and Mundlak (1982) found that trade liberalization and exchange rate management would accelerate economic growth but would cause agricultural prices to increase faster than nonagricultural wage rates, thus reducing real wages in terms of food. They further demonstrated that compensation could be paid to consumers in the form of subsidies that would keep food wages constant at an economic cost considerably less than the gains from trade liberalization and exchange rate management. Hence, the pursuit of policies reflecting long-term economic efficiency goals without adverse effects on food wages was shown to be feasible.

This is an extremely important finding, particularly if it can be generalized to other cases where food price distortions are hampering economic growth. Taken to its logical conclusion, it implies that current pressures in many developing countries to increase food prices to provide producer incentives need not conflict with short-term welfare goals, because economic gains would exceed the cost of full compensation to the poor. The rate of growth may be lower than if no compensation were made, but the poor would not have to wait for trickle-down incomes to regain their real income level.

The extent to which benefits or costs from food price changes are captured by consumers rather than passed on in the form of lower or higher wages varies among countries, and empirical evidence is scarce. How long it will take wage rates to adjust is also likely to vary depending on institutional and other aspects. Pending additional empirical evidence, it may be concluded only that the long-run negative effect of increased food prices on the real income of poor wage earners who do not derive their incomes from food production will be smaller than the immediate effects and may eventually become positive. However, the long-run effects may be of little or no interest to the poor who are adversely affected in the short run, and uncertain future gains may be insufficient to compensate for immediate losses. Furthermore, a large proportion of the urban poor does not derive any income from wages.

Food Prices and the Rural Poor

The impact of cheap food policies on the real income of the rural poor is not easily determined. Different groups of the poor will be affected differently, the most obvious distinction being whether or not they depend on food production for their income. Furthermore, the immediate impact may be quite different from the impact in the intermediate and longer runs.

The impact of food price increases on those poor who derive their income from food production would be expected to be positive provided the price increase is reflected in higher farmgate prices. Higher prices would add to revenues obtained from marketable surpluses, and labor demand for food production would be expected to increase. However, total demand for rural labor need not increase if the food price increases cause the substitution of less labor-intensive for more labor-intensive commodities as, for example, was the case when rice was substituted for jute in Bangladesh (Ahmed 1981).

Recent research indicates that food price increases may be much less favorable for the rural poor than is often expected. Many of the rural poor do not derive a large share of their income from either wage labor in food production or from the sale of food, and a large proportion are net purchasers of food. Mellor (1978) concludes that the poorest 20 percent of the rural population in India would lose from increased food grain prices. The largest gains, both absolute and relative to the current value of sales, would be captured by the highest income decile. In Sri Lanka, Sahn (forthcoming) concluded that only 3 percent of the rural poor (taken to be the poorest quartile of the rural population) would be better off in the short run from an increase in the price of rice.

A study in Thailand shows that the rural poor would not benefit greatly from increased domestic rice prices (Trairatvorakul 1984). Even though many of the rural poor are rice producers, their marketable surplus is often small and a large proportion are net buyers of rice. Trairatvorakul concludes that increasing rice prices would primarily benefit larger farmers and would create severe hardships among rural as well as urban poor. He estimated that a 50 percent increase in the rice price in Thailand would increase the number of urban households below the poverty line from 8 to 13 percent of the urban population. A slight decrease in the population below the poverty line is likely to occur in the rural areas (from 28 to 27 percent), but the proportion of farm workers below the poverty line would increase from 24 to 34 percent.

The long-run impact of food price increases on the rural poor depends on the supply response and the rural labor market, a discussion beyond the scope of this paper.

Price Increases and Expanded Food Supplies

The importance of increased prices in expanding food supplies has been exaggerated in many developing countries. Current single-minded pressures from inside and outside developing countries to increase food prices to provide added producer incentives tend to ignore the complexities involved and may result in a disappointing supply response while making the poor considerably worse off, at least in the short run. Increasing output prices without technological change in production, improved input markets, and better rural infrastructure may have little impact on total agricultural supply, although the commodity mix may change. Because of market imperfections or government policy, only a relatively small part of the price increase in the final market may be transmitted to the producers (Ahmed and Rustagi 1985). Thus, while the negative effects on low-income consumers would materialize, positive effects on food supplies may not. What is needed is a multifaceted approach properly tailored to the particular situation in which producer prices are but one of a series of policy instruments. Technological change that reduces unit cost plays a particularly important role because it facilitates expanded food supply at equal or lower prices and employment creation in rural areas. Institutional and policy changes may be needed to assure that food price increases are transmitted to producers.

Improving efficiency of food marketing and price transmission may offer opportunities to realize simultaneously both higher producer and lower consumer prices. In some African countries, the producer share of the retail or export price of food grain may be as low as 40 percent, while it reaches 80 percent in some Asian countries (Ahmed and Rustagi 1985). Assuming a supply elasticity of 0.3 and a demand elasticity of −0.5, Ahmed and Rustagi estimated the effect of reducing the price spread for food grain between African producers and consumers by 25 percentage points, less than their estimate of the current difference in the price spread between African and Asian countries. They found this would result in a 49 percent increase in farm prices and a 13 percent decrease in consumer prices.

Regional and seasonal price differences also appear to be much greater in Africa than elsewhere. This may be caused by a variety of factors, such as poor rural infrastructure and the resulting high transportation cost, insufficient price information, low volume, lack of storage facilities, and inappropriate public policies.

Seasonal fluctuations in food prices are likely to be more harmful for the poor than for the better-off population. The poor are less able to carry over stocks or purchasing power from one season to another. For the poor, food and other basic needs occupy a larger budget share, leaving less opportunity to substitute food expenditure for expenditure on other goods during periods of high food prices. Therefore, efforts to reduce seasonal fluctuations in food prices are likely to benefit the rural poor. The impact of reduced spatial price variation on the poor is less clear and could be positive or negative depending on the particular circumstances.

Policy Options

A number of policy options are available to governments to correct the undesirable effects on the poor of increasing food prices.

Explicit General Subsidies

Many countries have attempted to shield consumers from increasing food prices (whether in real or nominal terms) by driving a publicly financed wedge between consumer and producer or import prices. The fiscal cost of such policies can be very high depending on (a) the size of the wedge—that is, the difference between government purchase and selling prices; (b) the marketing cost, if borne by the public sector; and (c) the amount of food to which the subsidy is applied. The wedge may be large, as illustrated by domestic consumer prices fixed by the Egyptian government for wheat, sugar, and beans, which were 28, 29, and 35 percent of the international prices in 1980 (von Braun and de Haen 1983).

The size of the wedge may change considerably over time, either to insulate domestic consumers from price fluctuations in the international market or because of a widening gap between international and domestic price trends. Because of its traditionally large price fluctuations, the sugar market provides a good illustration of the cost of insulating consumers from international price variations. Domestic sugar prices in Egypt were virtually unchanged in nominal terms during 1971–81. However, domestic sugar prices varied from 22 percent of the international price in 1974, to approximately parity in 1977, to 144 percent in 1978, and back to 29 percent in 1980 (von Braun and de Haen 1983).

One of the principal reasons for a widening gap between international and domestic price trends in some countries is a desire to maintain constant or near constant nominal prices for basic food staples in the face of increasing general price levels. The nominal consumer prices for wheat products in Egypt hardly changed between 1971 and 1981. However, since international prices increased in nominal terms and the value of the Egyptian currency fell, the price wedge increased from 44 percent of international prices in 1971 to 72 percent in 1980 (von Braun and de Haen 1983). Devaluation of local currencies is one occasion when the wedge is often increased to insulate consumers from the effect of higher domestic prices of imported foods.

Unless the subsidized quantity is reduced, a larger publicly financed price wedge results in higher fiscal cost. The fiscal cost of the wheat subsidy in Egypt, where wheat products are not rationed and the subsidy is not targeted, increased from 0.05 percent to 3.5 percent of the gross domestic product during the 1970s (Alderman and others 1982).

Rapidly increasing fiscal costs occurred for the Sri Lankan food ration shop scheme up through the first half of the 1970s, reaching 15 percent of total government expenditure in 1975 (Gavan and Chandrasekera 1979). Changes in the subsidy program during the second half of the 1970s, including a shift to food stamps with a fixed nominal value, rapidly increasing food prices, and the exclusion of about half of the population from the program, reduced the fiscal cost of the food subsidies dramatically to the current level of about 7 percent of total government expenditure.

Targeted Food Subsidies

Because of the high fiscal cost of general food price subsidies, governments have tried to target food subsidies to households expected to be particularly vulnerable to high and increasing food prices and to limit the subsidies to specific foods or food rations. If the sole goal of food subsidies is to increase or sustain the ability of the poor to purchase enough food to meet nutritional requirements along with other basic necessities, targeting can greatly reduce cost, provided it is politically and logistically feasible.

The government cost of improving the ability of food-deficit households to acquire food by a certain amount is positively correlated with the degree of targeting up to a certain level. This is because targeting excludes some nondeficit households from sharing in the benefit. However, the administrative cost of operating a food price subsidy program increases as targeting increases, and a point exists beyond which the increased administrative cost exceeds the saving from further reducing benefit leakage.

According to a number of studies, food subsidies have increased incomes and improved the nutritional status of the poor, particularly, but not exclusively, the urban poor. A study of the Sri Lankan food ration shop scheme indicates that the scheme contributed to a better standard of living among low-income groups and a more even pattern of consumption throughout the society. At its peak, the ration subsidy contributed the equivalent of 16 percent of the purchasing power of low-income families in Sri Lanka (Gavan and Chandrasekera 1979).

In Kerala, India, about half the total income of low-income families was accounted for by ration income, and "removal of rationing would have a very serious impact on these low-income consumers" (George 1979, p. 52). The rations supplied the bulk of the rice eaten by low-income groups and the subsidy scheme greatly improved the distribution of income (Kumar 1979). Further, the subsidy program was effective in raising nutrition and consumption levels of the poorest households and was more effective than other forms of direct resource transfers (Kumar 1979).

In a study of the food ration shop scheme in Bangladesh, Ahmed (1979, p. 12) concludes that "rationing has aided the urban poor quite successfully since without it the consumption levels of the poorest 15 percent of the urban population would have been 15 to 25 percent lower in 1973–74 than they were." A strong urban bias was found in food subsidies in Bangladesh. While most of the poor people reside in rural areas, two-thirds of the subsidized grain was distributed to urban areas. (See Jamison and Piazza in part VI for a discussion of the extensive food subsidy program in China, which also focuses primarily on urban areas.)

In Egypt, the absolute value of food subsidies is virtually constant among income groups (Alderman and von Braun 1984). As a result, the poor receive a much larger proportion of total income from subsidies than do the rich. Food subsidies account for about 16 percent of the income of the poorest quartile of the population, but only about 3 percent for the richest quartile. Contrary to common belief prior to the study, no urban bias was found for the food price policies as a whole. However, due to higher consumption of wheat bread in the urban areas, some urban bias was found in the explicit wheat subsidy. This bias was offset by a higher rural consumption of explicitly and implicitly subsidized wheat flour. If other agricultural price distortions—such as the protection of animal production—are included, the rural sector received a considerably larger net benefit than did the urban sector.

Alternative Measures

Food price subsidies are but one of the many ways through which governments may increase the purchasing power of the poor to compensate for losses in real income caused by higher general food prices. Tied or untied cash payments, food transfers, and food for work programs are other policy measures that may be available.

Untied cash payments tend to be less palatable politically than transfers linked in some way to food, such as food stamps, targeted food price subsidies, or food supplement schemes. Cash payment programs require costly control measures to prevent excessive leakage to nontarget groups and to avoid fraud. Self-targeting, which may be possible if food subsidies are aimed at less desired foods, is not possible for cash payment. A direct income transfer does not reduce the price paid by the poor for food relative to other commodities and thus does not encourage substitution of food for nonfoods to the same extent as do food price subsidy and direct feeding schemes. Finally, governments should recognize that food may be available from foreign aid at a cost considerably below its market value, thus making food-related transfer less expensive.

One advantage of cash payments or food stamp programs is that the actual distribution of food need not be undertaken by the public sector separate from other food distribution, as is the case with most ration shop schemes. However, targeted or rationed food price subsidy programs may also be based on private sector food distribution, as is partially the case in Egypt.

To reduce leakage to nontargeted households and to focus more sharply on improved nutrition, some countries have opted for food supplements or direct feeding of individuals deficient in calories and protein, usually children and pregnant and lactating women. Such programs may assure that leakage to nontargeted households is small. However, intrahousehold leakage will still occur through reduction in the food allocation for target individuals, thus reducing household food acquisition from some other sources.

A study by Beaton and Ghassemi that reviewed over 200 reports of past food distribution programs for young children (see part V) found that the net increase in food intake by the target recipients was 45 to 70 percent of the food distributed. Such leakage, however, benefited the households of which the target children were members through added real household income and possibly improved the nutrition of other household members. The leakage is merely a reflection of household preferences regarding expenditure and consumption. Nevertheless, if the purpose is to improve nutrition of certain target groups and not to transfer real income, then these programs have generally not been very successful. Furthermore, administrative costs tend to be large relative to other means of income transfer.

21

The Relationship between Price Policy and Food Marketing

C. Peter Timmer

The links between price policy and food marketing take the food policy analyst to the very core of an economy and the most basic issues concerning the consequences of market organization for economic efficiency and income distribution. Food price interventions are among the most potent short-run policy instruments available to governments to influence consumer welfare, producer income, and the economy of rural areas (Meier 1983; Timmer and others 1983; Tolley and others 1982). Such interventions usually focus on food grains, since they dominate food concerns, especially in developing countries. As a result, food price policy analysis is also generally concerned primarily with food grains.

A major role of markets is price formation, expressed in three important components: (a) the domestic price of a commodity relative to its border price and relative to substitutes and complements; (b) the stability of that domestic price over time, given that border prices for most agricultural commodities fluctuate considerably; and (c) the price margins formed for a commodity between points in time, where storage decisions are affected; between points in space, where transportation decisions are involved; and between forms, where processing is at stake.

Prices also influence allocation of resources in both production and consumption. Indeed, it is the coordinating role of prices determined in competitive markets that is supposed to generate the efficiency claimed for market economies. The empirical record suggests that these claims have substantial merit but that actual market performance and its welfare impact depend critically on just how efficiently

Excerpted from "The Relationship between Food Marketing and Price Policy," in Dieter Elz, ed., *Agricultural Marketing and Pricing Policy* (Washington, D.C.: World Bank, forthcoming).

Figure 21-1. *Links between Food Price Policy and Food Marketing*

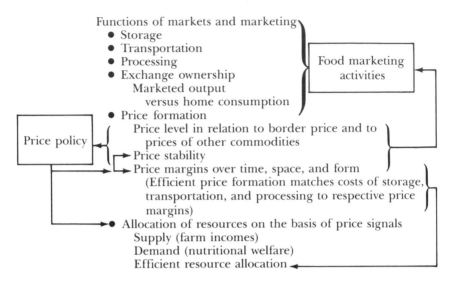

markets generate and transmit price signals and on how efficiently marketing activities are carried out.

Figure 21-1 illustrates issues and connections. Price policy—interpreted as interventions to alter domestic prices relative to border prices and to increase the stability of domestic prices—influences price margins. The price margins in turn influence private and public decisions about food marketing activities. How closely these activities match the costs of storage, transportation, and processing with the price margins actually generated determines whether the allocation of resources in a market economy generates an efficient outcome.

Impact of Price Policy on Markets

Traditional price policy analysis traces the effect of changed price levels, especially of food grains, on consumers, producers, and the government budget, and it calculates the efficiency losses. It is static in that it is short run, generally limited to a single commodity market, and subject to a host of "other things being equal" assumptions. This is what economists mean by food price policy analysis. Two conclusions stand out from this static analysis: (a) changing prices from their border price equivalent results in income transfers between producers and consumers, and (b) allocative inefficiencies always result—the aptly named "deadweight" losses. Price policy issues raised by interventions are reviewed in Timmer (1983) and in my article on price policy analysis in this collection.

If this static, aggregative analysis is not to be seriously misleading, four other aspects of price policy analysis need to be incorporated. First, the impact of price manipulation must be disaggregated to determine the impact on various classes of producers and consumers. Second, the border prices that serve as the standard for welfare comparisons must be considered. Border prices fluctuate widely from month to month and year to year. A strong rationale exists for not letting domestic prices follow these fluctuations too closely. Third, the broader macroeconomic effects must be considered, especially the impact of food price interventions on the government budget, on foreign exchange, and on employment if rising food prices force consumers to increase the share of their budget devoted to food at the expense of goods and services supplied by domestic industry and workers. Fourth, the longer-term, dynamic impact of price policy must be assessed. Higher food prices may induce investments and technological change, cheap food may improve the health and nutrition of lower-income groups, direct government involvement in food marketing may alter the capacity of the system to provide efficient price signals about long-run opportunity costs of production and consumption, and so on. For such reasons, the dynamic effects, and thus the analysis of food price policy interventions, is much more an intuitive and artistic exercise than a scientific process. When price policies are designed in real settings, their implication carries directly into the marketing arena.

Impact of Price Policy on Marketing Activities

Most food price intervention policies are designed to influence price margins as well as price levels, although policymakers usually do not carefully consider the subsequent effect on marketing participants. Each of the three basic marketing activities—storage, transportation, and processing—is influenced by price policy, although storage activities are usually affected the most in the short run.

Storage Activities

A price policy that introduces a ceiling price for a food grain obviously affects the private trade's expectations about future prices. Without a ceiling, seasonal prices will continue to rise in step with storage costs until the new harvest begins, and normal costs of marketing will keep urban prices higher than rural prices all year long.

The private sector will carry the full burden of buying and storing grain, and will recover its full cost of storage, including return to capital, risk, and managerial skill. Competition among private traders is required to prevent monopoly profit and exploitation of farmers and consumers.

Ceiling prices tend to be enforced effectively only in urban markets, frequently by using imported grain distributed by the national food agency. The private trade will cease supplying urban markets once the procurement cost plus the storage cost plus the marketing margin exceed the urban ceiling price—which may be much of the year. In rural markets, the price of grain will continue to rise to cover the full cost of storage, even when it exceeds the urban ceiling price. If it rises far enough, private traders find it profitable to ship grain from urban markets back to the rural areas. In this setting, the urban ceiling price sets a rural ceiling price higher by the marketing margin rather than lower by the marketing margin. The price policy thus has a dramatic impact on the structure of grain marketing. It changes the participants in urban marketing from entirely private to significantly public, and it reverses the traditional rural-to-urban grain flow.

Governments can also implement a price policy that sets both a floor and a ceiling price in an attempt to benefit producers as well as consumers. The floor price can be higher than the previous harvest price and the ceiling price can be kept lower than the previous preharvest price. Two important consequences flow from implementing such a floor and ceiling price policy. First, since the permitted seasonal price rise is less than the full competitive cost, the private sector will no longer provide all the marketing services without government assistance. This means a government agency must itself engage in marketing activities—directly, or indirectly by subsidizing the private sector. The volume of grain handled by the government agency is directly proportional to the squeeze on the price margin enforced by the ceiling, that is, to the share of marketing costs not covered by the mandated price margin.

Second, since storage uses real economic resources, a government subsidy must be paid to the food agency responsible for carrying out the floor and ceiling price policy. This might be an explicit line item in the government budget, or it might come through subsidized interest rates, access to government-owned warehouses at low rates, and so on. The subsidy can be a quite substantial share of the total storage cost— the total subsidy rises with the square of the squeeze on the margin. Such unexpectedly rapid increases in subsidy costs as a result of policy efforts to benefit both farmers and consumers by squeezing the marketing margin often catch food agencies and finance ministries unprepared. The result is failure to implement fully the announced floor and ceiling price policy. This, in turn, immediately affects the expectations of all market participants—farmers, traders, and consumers—and can rapidly lead to speculative activity that further limits government efforts to set prices. The extent to which the government must become involved in grain marketing to enforce a floor and ceiling price policy and the often unanticipated costs of the policy provide a clear example of the dramatic impact that price policy exerts on food marketing.

Transportation Activities

Ramifications are similar when price policy has spatial dimensions. A floor or ceiling price that is implemented uniformly over a wide geographic region is sure to have direct effects on the role of the private sector in transporting commodities from areas of low prices to areas of high prices and in earning a profit from the spatial arbitrage. With a uniform floor price, the private sector will service the relatively favored areas close to points of final demand and the government agency will be left to handle the more distant areas at high cost. Since the operating cost of a government agency is seldom lower than that of the private sector, these long-distance activities will require subsidies.

Results are similar when the government announces a uniform price floor for all qualities of a commodity but retail prices reflect quality differentials. The government agency will end up defending the floor price by buying the lowest quality offered. It usually incurs higher storage costs than the private trade because low quality is related to high moisture content and insect damage, which cause substantial losses in storage.

Price policy can also affect directly the regions of a country that are competitive with imports. For a given cost of production, the landed import cost (after tariff or subsidy) minus the transportation cost from the producing hinterland traces out a "competition contour" beyond which domestic production incurs higher total costs in supplying consumption needs in the port than do imports. As prices vary because of policy changes, the location of the contour shifts as well. If import prices rise because of policy changes, traders go further inland in search of supplies. If prices fall, they restrict their activities closer to the port.

Some price policies are powerful enough to cause a switch in direction as well as in distance for food marketing. If import prices are low enough or subsidies large enough, it becomes profitable to market grain from the ports to the producing hinterland, thus putting immense competitive pressures on domestic producers. A budget crisis or a currency devaluation can sharply alter these prices, raise incentives to farmers, and provide profitable opportunities to market domestic grain in the port cities. Switching the whole direction of flow for a country's marketing system, however, is no easy task. Considerable adjustment time is needed before efficient marketing can be expected.

Processing

The impact of price policy on processing activities is probably smaller than on storage or transportation, but even here it can have dramatic consequences for rural employment, milling conversion efficiency, and the quality of grain available to consumers. An example showing the effects of price policy on investments in rice processing in Indonesia was cited by Timmer (1972). In the first instance, the absolute price level for the output from the rice mill determines the value of "saving" rice through greater technical efficiency. Greater technical efficiency can be obtained only from more capital-intensive equipment as compared to more labor-intensive traditional hand pounding and small mechanical mills. The higher the relative domestic price maintained by a price policy, the more favorable are capital-intensive processes, which adversely affect employment. Second, the government-determined margin between the farm price and the retail price directly influences which mills can survive. Traditional techniques, with their low technical efficiency, quickly succumb to losses as the margin between the paddy price and milled rice is narrowed. Although the foreign exchange rate is not part of food price policy directly, it too is a key variable. Since more capital-intensive milling equipment is likely to be imported, its cost is a direct function of the exchange rate. Devaluation, for instance, raises the cost of capital equipment relative to labor, shifting investment decisions toward more labor-intensive techniques. The foreign exchange rate also directly affects the price of domestic rice relative to imports. If domestic price policy is influenced by this relative relationship, even in the longer run, offsetting forces will work on choice of technique when the exchange rate changes. The net result is still likely to favor greater labor intensity when devaluation comes, but the effect is clearly quite complicated.

Practical Approaches to the Analysis of Marketing Price Policy

The perspective developed here creates a problem for policy analysts, for it asks them to be aware of the indirect consequences of price policy for the agricultural marketing system. Marketing systems are characterized by complicated links among sectors and participants, many of them based on trust and fragile expectations, with ramifications felt throughout the entire marketing system by all participants— producers, consumers, traders, and the government.

Three responses are possible to such complexity. Analysts could attempt to model the entire agricultural marketing system and capture in quantitative terms all the important behavioral relationships. Data limitations—including the lack of historical parallels—mean that the results are unlikely to have much significance for policy. The opposite approach is simply to let the market operate without interference. Few developing countries are prepared to allow the adverse welfare effects that market imperfections would introduce into such a regime. An intermediate approach recognizes that markets do not work perfectly, but that the world is too complex to model with any precision either. Policy analysis then seeks to find socially beneficial interventions into domestic price formation without attempting to identify optimal policies through quantitative modeling. This approach requires a dual analytical perspective, one coming from the national level where price policy interventions are designed, implemented, and evaluated, the other from the field level where the structure, conduct, and performance of the marketing sector itself are analyzed. The analyst must then merge these two approaches into one that simultaneously provides insight into how marketing participants are likely to respond to a change in price policy and illuminates the broader consequences of price changes for welfare and resource allocation.

This type of analysis is best done by building from simple to complex. Accordingly, the analyst can start by gathering data that permit construction of several key ratios. The price ratios described below reveal the structure of the country's marketing system relative to its price environment. Perhaps more important, assembling a historical record of these ratios shows how the price environment has changed and how the system responded to it. Comparing the ratios across countries or regions shows whether significant differences are related to alternative marketing structures.

The following six ratios, three relating domestic prices to international prices and three comparing internal prices, can serve as a starting point.

○ *Compare the domestic price for a commodity with the border price for the same commodity, converted at the existing exchange rate.* This price ratio, often termed the nominal protection coefficient, provides the easiest and most direct comparison of how competitive the domestic price of a commodity is relative to imports or exports. It suggests whether price policy favors producers or consumers. Large divergences in either direction usually indicate whether the government must play a substantial direct role in marketing the commodity. These simple interpretations can be altered if the current foreign exchange rate is significantly overvalued (an issue for a broader food and macro policy appraisal) or if the structure of input costs for producing the commodity is also out of line with border prices. This is examined in the next ratio.

   ○ *Compare the domestic price for a commodity with the prices for key inputs, especially fertilizer, if the commodity is a food or feed grain.* The grain-to-fertilizer price ratio eliminates the need for exchange rate conversions and thus permits direct comparison across countries. An early example from the 1970s that shows the significance of this ratio is given in figure 21-2. The combination of both output and input prices, as in the ratio above, presents a more complete appraisal of price incentives to producers than the nominal rate and hence comes closer to the effective rate of protection. Accurate effective rates of protection, of course, require full information on the structure of input costs and value added by commodity. Especially for grains, the simpler output-input price ratio provides a great deal of comparative information in a single number.

Figure 21-2. *The Rice-Fertilizer Price Ratio (P) and Fertilizer Application Per Hectare (F/H)*

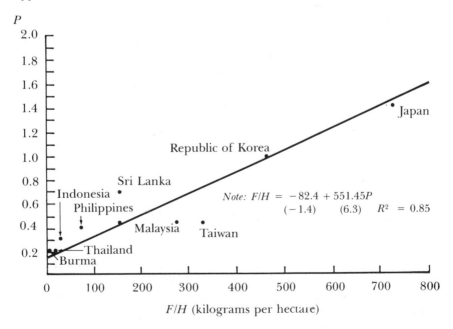

Note: $F/H = -82.4 + 551.45P$
(-1.4) (6.3) $R^2 = 0.85$

○ *Compare the relative domestic prices of two commodities with their relative prices in international markets.* For instance, the analyst could compare the ratio between the domestic prices of wheat and maize to the ratio between the international prices of wheat and maize, or the domestic prices of sugar and rice to their international price ratio. This indicates possible distortions that may be built into domestic food systems, since there is substantial potential for substituting commodities for each other in production systems and end use. Significant inefficiencies in patterns of land use (for example, too much sugar, not enough maize) or in end uses (too much sugar used for alcohol) can sharply affect economic growth rates and patterns.

○ *Compare the average monthly high price to the average monthly low price.* This seasonal price ratio will reveal the size of the margin available to those who store commodities. If the margin is very low—a price ratio of 1.1 or 1.2 over an eight-month seasonal price rise, for example— the government is almost certainly squeezing private traders with its price policy. If the margin is large—1.6 to 1.8 for the same period, for example—either profits or storage costs are high. The analyst can quickly check whether it is the storage cost that is high by determining the interest rate for storage loans to the private sector and the size of physical losses. For example, an interest rate of 3 percent a month plus a storage loss of only 2 percent a month yields a compounded eight-month price rise from these two costs alone of nearly 50 percent, or a seasonal price ratio of 1.5. This ratio provides analysts with important insights about what questions to ask and what data to gather when examining the efficiency of storage activities.

○ *Compare the price of a commodity in rural areas to its price in central markets.* This spatial price ratio gives some indication of how well connected the two markets are and at what cost. Although quite sophisticated models are now available to test the efficiency of spatial market connections (Timmer 1984; Ravallion 1983), this simple ratio, when compared with readily available data on transportation cost, can direct the analyst to important marketing issues. Is there evidence of informal barriers and taxes between rural and urban markets? Are roads in such disrepair that commodity flows are risky and high cost? Is the truck fleet badly maintained or unable to purchase fuel and spare parts? Alternatively, if the ratio is very low, are private market traders being squeezed out of business by government policy?

○ *Compare the price of the raw commodity with that of the processed commodity.* Paddy may be compared with milled rice, wheat with flour, or maize with maize meal. Appropriate ratios for the two commodity forms can be established, at least roughly, by referring to countries where processing is known to be technically efficient and subject to intense competition, for example, the United States, European countries, or Japan. Domestic ratios that diverge widely from such international ratios suggest that high losses occur in processing or that limited capacity and restricted barriers to entry permit high profit rates. As noted earlier, the appropriate degree of technical efficiency is a matter for economic analysis and itself depends on price policy. Barriers to entry in processing, however, are frequently a direct result of government licensing and trade policy. Monopoly profits are often earned where such policies exist, and substantial improvement in economic efficiency and income distribution could result from a policy that promotes more vigorous competition.

Building a Competitive Marketing System with Beneficial Welfare Effects

Prices determined in competitive markets provide the signals that are essential for the awesome task of coordinating millions of otherwise unconnected decisionmakers in an economy. The welfare consequences of all those decisions depend critically on how well the decisions reflect the social opportunity costs of the resources used to implement them. Competitive markets ensure that no price distortions are caused by monopoly profit or manipulation, which frees policymakers to worry about other potential sources of market failure and the consequences of competitive markets for income distribution. Both tasks are easier if high-cost protected producers who are free from competitive pressures are not draining significant resources from the economy, and if the government can exorcise the ghost of monopolistic middlemen by actively promoting a competitive and low-cost agricultural marketing system.

Price policy is a major instrument in designing a competition policy and building a competitive marketing system, but it is an important beneficiary as well. When price policy does not have to enforce competition, it can use competitive forces to achieve goals other than efficiency, especially price stability and better income distribution. Markets are the most effective way governments have to reach the multitudes of decentralized decisionmakers whose day to day decisions dictate whether an economy develops or not. Markets are not ethereal concepts. They are simply the locus of traders' behavior as they respond to the price signals they see and pass on to their fellow participants.

Although agricultural marketing and price policy are separate topics, for traders and marketing agents they are two sides of the same coin. As economies grow and become more interdependent domestically and internationally, the role of prices as signals to coordinate activities among marketing participants becomes progressively more important. The task for the policy analyst becomes commensurately more complicated, but at the same time new options open up to policymakers to provide an economic environment conducive to rapid and equitable growth.

22

Food Marketing Activities of Low-Income Households

Benson Ateng

A major objective of food marketing interventions in developing countries is generally to improve access of low-income households to food. To the extent that low-income rural households do not buy food in the market, however, market-oriented programs cannot reach them. To the extent that market interventions disrupt desirable services supplied by traditional markets, they may actually work against the interests of low-income households.

Low-income households in developing countries are found among the urban poor; among smallholders in rural areas whose holdings are too small to provide an adequate income, whose farms are in areas of low and unreliable rainfall, or who depend on livestock in semiarid regions of low potential; and among rural wage earners, including landless agricultural workers.

Dependence of Low-Income Households on Purchased Food

Low-income urban households buy virtually all the food they consume from the market, but the high proportion of total income spent on food is often not recognized. In Recife, Brazil, for example, the poorest 60 percent of families spend 70 percent of their income on food. In Cali, Colombia, the poorest quartile of families spend 82 percent of their income on food. In La Paz, Bolivia, the poorest third of families spend 66 percent of their income on food. In these three

Excerpted from "The Marketing Activities of Low Income Food Insecure Households in Developing Countries: A Background Paper," Economics and Policy Division Working Paper 52 (Washington, D.C.: Agriculture and Rural Development Department, World Bank, 1981).

cities, more than half the families spend more than 60 percent of their incomes just on food (Harrison and others 1975). These same households are very sensitive to the price of high-quality foods, and any price reduction causes a proportionately high increase in consumption. That is, they have a high income elasticity for high-quality food (Riley and others 1970). If greater efficiency reduced food production and marketing costs, the lowest-income consumers would benefit the most.

Many people do not realize the extent to which poor rural households depend on purchased food. An example from Kenya is typical of many developing countries. On the average, Kenyan smallholders buy at least 50 percent of their food from the market (Kenya 1977). Furthermore, dependence on the market for food in the rural areas is not confined to a particular income group, administrative region, farm size group, or agro-ecological zone. All rural income groups depend on the market for at least one-third of their food. As table 22-1 demonstrates, it is the poorest rural households in Kenya that are most dependent upon the market for food, whether they are classified by income or by size of holding. Low-income rural households are dependent on the market for food mainly because their own farms do not produce enough food for the household and because they contain a high proportion of rural wage earners.

Studies in Kenya also show that small-scale farmers usually sell part of their output of grain and other food even though they subsequently buy back the same commodities later. They do this for various reasons, for example, to meet cash obligations, because they lack adequate storage, or to pass the cost of storage to someone else (Schmidt 1979).

Table 22-1. *Proportion of Household Food Purchased, Rural Kenya*

Group	Food purchases as proportion of total food consumption (percent)	Group	Food purchases as proportion of total food consumption (percent)
By income (Kenya shillings)		*By size of holding (hectares)*	
Under 0	61	Under 0.5	57
0–999	63	0.5–0.9	53
1,000–1,999	56	1.0–1.9	52
2,000–2,999	54	2.0–2.9	51
3,000–3,999	55	3.0–3.9	44
4,000–5,999	48	4.0–5.9	43
6,000–7,999	45	6.0–7.9	48
8,000 and over	36	8.0 and over	44

Note: Excludes pastoral and large farm areas.
Source: Kenya (1977).

These studies show that rural Kenya is largely an exchange economy as far as food is concerned. This is not unique to Kenya. Any policy that improves the food marketing system in the developing countries will have a desirable impact on low-income households, both urban and rural, since these households already depend on the market for their food requirements to a sizable degree.

Food Marketing Structures Serving Low-Income Households

Food marketing systems serving low-income households in developing countries have many characteristics in common and differ mainly in detail. In Latin America, although many commercial farmers sell to large assemblers, the majority of small farmers sell their marketable surpluses to small assemblers who resell to larger assemblers or retailers in nearby towns (Harrison and others 1975). These arrangements are comparable to what Jones (1972) calls "big trade" and "small trade" in Africa. Similar marketing arrangements exist in Asia, where the small assemblers are referred to as "village dealers," "commission traders," and so on (Holmes 1971).

Low-income rural households mostly depend for their food purchases on small traditional markets where little direct government influence on prices exists. Few empirical studies of these traditional food marketing systems have been carried out. What follows is mainly from personal observation and discussion.

The primary function of traditional rural food markets is to provide an opportunity to exchange locally produced agricultural products, and a substantial amount of the activity is horizontal exchange. In addition to the normal determinants of market supply of agricultural products, the supply of food in traditional markets is also influenced by the cash obligations of the smallholders and accessibility of the market to nonfarmer traders and part-time farmers who may bring some commodities from surplus to deficit areas. The determinants of demand apply in these markets. However, time is a crucial variable as far as demand is concerned. During and a few months following harvest, rural households are on the whole self-sufficient in food. Later in the year, pressure on the market increases as most households exhaust their own output and begin to depend increasingly on the market.

These markets are fairly competitive. In most cases, no one single buyer or seller controls a significant proportion of the market. Prices are determined largely by the forces of supply and demand, actual or anticipated. The flow of information in these markets is intricate, but both buyers and sellers appear to know market conditions.

A given marketplace may exhibit marked price differentials for the same commodity at different times of the day, especially for the more perishable foods such as fish, vegetables, and fruit. Prices tend to be high in the morning, since the commodities are still fresh, and demand is expected to continue rising as more prospective buyers arrive at the marketplace. Demand reaches the highest level by early afternoon. This is the time when consumers who have come a long way wind up their purchases and start home. Also, consumers with high opportunity cost in terms of time do not normally stay in the marketplace beyond this time. Demand begins to fall as late afternoon approaches and some of the highly perishable commodities begin to deteriorate. Little is wasted, however, as a traditional way to preserve what is not sold by the end of the day is usually available. For example, fish that is not sold is either smoked or dried in the sun for later sale.

Demand and supply conditions are the main determinants of price in these traditional markets. The degree of collusion among traders is minimal. In India, Holmes found that "all village dealers reported that the basic guide to their determination of purchasing price was the price that they in turn get when reselling, minus direct cost of marketing and an allowance for profit. In addition, their offering price was also influenced by the desire to be competitive with rival dealers" (Holmes 1971, p. 55).

Commodity grading in traditional markets is minimal and usually is done visually. Holmes (1971), for example, found in the Indian study that except for rice sale through commission agents and marketing cooperatives, no formal grading of grain was done. Visual inspection on the basis of a sample was used to determine quality price differentials.

Normally, small traders in the marketplace or village dealers are willing to buy or sell food in any quantity, thus providing a real and desirable service to both producers and consumers in spite of the usual complaints about them. They are unlike cooperatives or agents of marketing boards who specify minimum amounts that they will buy or sell. Selling in small amounts suits the purchasing power of low-income consuming households. Small producers sometimes wish to sell only small amounts to enable them to satisfy immediate cash needs. Small-scale traders who go around villages soliciting supplies provide a welcome opportunity to farmers to sell whatever quantity they wish. Thus small traders allow flexibility in time, place, and quantity. This flexibility tends to be eroded when the middlemen are replaced by parastatal organizations that buy and sell in specific locations and quantities.

Low-income urban households tend to buy mainly from a large market or a bazaar where locally grown grain, fruit, and vegetables (as well as other local and imported goods) are offered for sale in a traditional context, or else from mobile hawkers. Some low-income households take part in the hawking business themselves.

Hawkers buy from wholesalers or even big trade retailers in the large market or bazaar and then resell at the retail level mainly in the low- and middle-income residential areas and along streets with many pedestrians. Mobile hawkers cut down on overheads such as rent and power by operating from public streets and can thus charge relatively low prices. They work where and when they have maximum contact with customers. They can adjust quickly to changes in the market situation, weather conditions, or the arrival of law enforcement authorities who harass them from time to time. They know what to sell where and when. They usually offer cooked foods in urban low- and middle-income residential areas, near construction sites, and along streets with heavy pedestrian flow. Prepared foods are useful for low-income urban workers who would otherwise go without lunch since they cannot afford to eat at restaurants and hotels.

Hawkers' low overheads and adaptability enable them to provide a useful service to their customers, as their goods are cheaper and available at convenient locations and times, even though they cause both traffic and pedestrian congestion and some city authorities consider them a health hazard. Because of their services, especially to low-income households, hawkers should be accommodated in city planning and space should be set aside for them instead of their being declared illegal and harassed by city authorities.

As economic progress occurs, technological breakthroughs lead to increased output, which in turn leads to increased demand for marketing services. Industrialization and urbanization contribute toward greater division of labor. This process gives rise to the need for "new technologies for processing and distributing food, more complex logistical and institutional arrangements and increased participation by government agencies in planning and carrying out market programs" (Riley and Weber 1979, p. 15). However, increasing government participation in food marketing in developing countries through market regulation and parastatal organizations appears to be based more on feelings about private traders than on solid economic arguments. Restricting traditional markets or replacing them with cooperatives or agents of marketing boards means the loss of a significant service to low-income households and has adverse employment effects. Low-income consumers and producers would be better served by fostering competition among private traders and with marketing boards. Public programs could then focus on reducing the undesirable aspects of traditional markets through market improvement, education, technical assistance, and economic incentives.

23

Post-Harvest Food Losses
in Developing Countries

E. R. Pariser

The aggregate quantity of food lost and wasted in developing countries is huge. Estimated minimum post-harvest losses of food grain and grain legumes in developing countries are about 10 percent of total production. For starchy staples and for other perishables and for fish, the losses amount to at least 20 percent of production (National Research Council 1978; Green 1977; James 1977). Only recently have planners and food specialists begun to pay adequate attention to this issue.

This survey focuses on post-harvest losses of the major food crops—cereal grains and grain legumes, nongrain staples, and other perishables such as fruits and vegetables—and of fish. Beverages and plantation and export crops such as bananas and sugarcane are excluded. Meat and dairy products are also excluded because they pose special kinds of loss problems related to the storage and distribution system. If such a system exists, it operates more or less efficiently; if it does not, farmers have little incentive for production beyond their immediate needs and the products are consumed quickly with minimal loss.

Determining Food Loss

Defining post-harvest food losses and determining their extent are location- and culture-specific. The perception of what is food and what is food loss or food waste is highly subjective. Food is taken here to be simply those commodities that people normally eat. Post-harvest loss begins when the process of collecting or separating food of edible

Excerpted from "Post-Harvest Food Losses in Developing Countries," in Nevin S. Scrimshaw and Mitchel B. Wallerstein, eds. *Nutrition Policy Implementation: Issues and Experience* (New York: Plenum Press, 1982).

quality from its site of immediate production is complete and ends when the food enters the mouth (Bourne 1977). Loss means any change in the availability, edibility, wholesomeness, or quality of food that prevents it from being consumed by people. Food losses may be direct or indirect. A direct loss is disappearance of food by spillage, or consumption by rodents or birds. An indirect loss is the lowering of quality to the point where people refuse to eat it. If the food is consumed by people, it is not lost; if it is not consumed by people for any reason, then it is considered a post-harvest food loss.

The nontechnological, subjective, culture- and society-related dimensions of the post-harvest food loss problem make it extremely difficult not only to identify and assess the extent of food losses in a particular community but also to plan and implement an intervention without violating food habits and systems. If one adds to these cultural and psychological problems those that are directly related to the particular political system of a society and begins to consider food losses induced by, for instance, marketing, taxation, and import regulations, the range of issues to be considered becomes even more complicated.

The more loss estimation is analyzed, the clearer it is that there neither is nor can be a simple methodology that can be universally applied. The movement and storage of commodities between production and consumption is seldom an easily analyzed flow. Irregular movement and mixing of various batches in post-harvest operations, for instance, make sampling procedures and generalizations difficult.

More techniques have evolved to estimate grain losses than for any other major food categories, reflecting the importance of grains as staple foods, their relative physical uniformity, and the comparative ease with which they can be stored. Grain loss estimation methodology is the subject of a manual prepared by Harris and Lindblad (1978) and designed to be widely used in developing countries to encourage standardized loss assessment procedures.

Overall loss assessment is the first, and in many cases the most important, of a series of steps leading to estimation and possible reduction of losses. Overall assessment of the commodity movement system involves a search for the points where the most acute food loss occurs. It implies study of the whole physical and social system in which food moves from producer to consumer and identification of how the commodities are handled and the number of participating middlemen. The objective of this assessment is to permit judgments to be made about possible loss reduction interventions. It is helpful if a national policy body exists to deal with post-harvest loss, to coordinate the efforts of national and international assistance agencies, and to gather and analyze loss information. Relevant information can be obtained from a variety of sources: ministries of agriculture and economics, transportation agencies, marketing boards, commercial organizations, and farmers' cooperatives. Despite the complexities of the commodity movement system, experienced professionals can make useful loss estimates and identify possibilities for loss reduction.

Causes of Post-Harvest Loss

Bourne (1977) differentiates between primary and secondary causes of food loss. Taking primary causes first, biological and microbiological damage is consumption or damage by insects, mites, rodents, birds, and large animals and by microbes such as molds and bacteria. Chemical and biochemical losses are undesirable reactions between chemical compounds that are present in the food, enzyme-activated reactions, or accidental or deliberate contamination with harmful substances. Mechanical losses arise from abrasion, bruising, excessive polishing, peeling, or trimming, puncturing of containers, or defective seals on cans or other containers. Physical losses are caused by excessive or insufficient heat or cold or an improper atmosphere. Physiological losses are caused by sprouting of grains and tubers, aging of fruits and vegetables, and changes caused by respiration and transpiration.

Secondary causes are those that lead to conditions in which a primary cause of loss can occur. They include inadequate drying equipment or a poor drying season; inadequate storage facilities to protect the food from insects, rodents, birds, rain, and high humidity; inadequate transportation to move food to the market before it spoils; inadequate refrigeration or cold storage for perishables; and an inadequate marketing system.

Losses may occur anywhere from the point where the food has been harvested up to the point of consumption. They may occur during the preliminary separation or extraction of edible from nonedible animal and agricultural products, such as dehulling of grain, slaughtering and dressing of animals, extraction of sugar from cane, and peeling of fruits and vegetables. There is some room for improvement here to reduce post-harvest losses—for example, by ensuring that grain is not broken or damaged in dehulling, and that as much sugar as possible is removed from the cane. The major emphasis in post-harvest food loss reduction activities in developing countries must be placed on food preservation to prevent losses. This includes, for example, the drying of grain or fruit, the refrigeration or canning of vegetables or fish, and the prevention of the onset of rancidity in oil. Conversion of edible food into another form more acceptable or more convenient to the consumer through processing is another source of loss. Examples include making bread from wheat, brewing beer from barley, making sausages from meat, and making instant coffee from coffee beans.

Food may be lost in storage before consumption. For perishable foods such as some fish, meat, and dairy products, the storage life can be very short—a few hours if stored at ambient temperature, up to a week or longer if properly refrigerated. Staple foods such as cereal grains may be stored for several years. Semiperishable foods such as fresh fruits, most tubers, and oil can be stored successfully for periods of one or two weeks to many months if handled correctly. More storage facilities are needed, particularly for cereals and oilseeds— large storage warehouses in big cities and ports and numerous small-scale, on-farm storage facilities. Most developing countries need an improved transportation system to reduce the time lag between departure from the production site and arrival at the market, which would reduce food losses in transit.

In developed countries, a considerable amount of food is lost during home preparation. These in-home losses are low in developing countries, probably because food accounts for so much of the family budget that it must be of very poor quality to be discarded. In the urban areas of developing countries, the homemaker usually makes frequent trips to the food markets and does not hold any great quantity of food in the house, thus avoiding losses of stored foods. The presence or absence of legal standards can also affect the eventual retention or rejection of a food for human use.

Figure 23-1 depicts simply the food pipeline and the physical and biological ways in which some losses occur. The actual movement of food from harvest to consumer, of course, almost always involves a much more complex process than a cartoon can represent. The real-world pipeline is constructed of a number of different kinds of materials. There are the human and the mechanical parts of the pipeline, the chain of hands, and the line of transport vehicles down which food passes with greater or lesser efficiency, speed, and ease. The food in the pipeline is propelled by socioeconomic and political forces. Regulations and other bureaucratic procedures slow down or accelerate food passage from producer to consumer.

Sources and Magnitude of Post-Harvest Staple Food Losses in Developing Countries

This section draws on figures arrived at by the Post-Harvest Food Loss Group working under the aegis of the National Academy of Sciences (National Research Council 1978) and those compiled by

Figure 23-1. *The Food Pipeline*

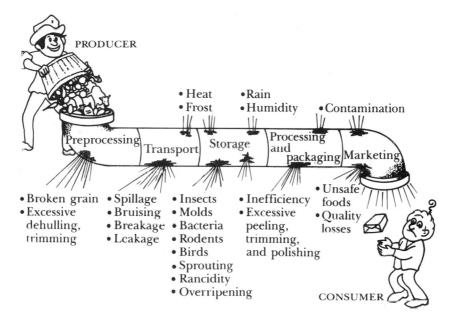

Green for the FAO in worldwide investigations (1977). Because estimation methodologies have, until recently, been accorded little critical attention (with a few notable exceptions), and as the value of published information has been reduced by the absence of standard methods and definitions, the available food loss data are questionable at best and should only be used as rough indicators. The overall results on the magnitude of losses are summarized in table 23-1.

Cereal Grains and Grain Legumes

In most societies, cereal grains and grain legumes are the most important food in terms of quantity produced. The security—even the survival—of a community has depended on keen attention to the conservation of these staples.

The bulk of harvested cereal grain and legumes passes through a fairly well-defined series of steps—the post-harvest system. After harvest, the crops are threshed or shelled, dried, stored, and finally processed. Some commodities require additional steps that enlarge the system—rice parboiling, for example—but there are enough similarities in the flow through the system to permit generalizations about loss problems.

Table 23-1. *Estimates of Minimum Post-Harvest Food Losses in Developing Countries, 1976*

Item	Cereal grains and grain legumes	Perishables	Fish
1976 food production (millions of tons)	420[a]	225[a]	50
Estimated minimum loss (percent)	10	20	20
Estimated minimum loss (millions of tons)	42	51	10[b]
Estimated price per ton[c] (U.S. dollars)	165	25	225
Estimated lost value (billions of U.S. dollars)	6.9	1.3	2.3

Note: Developing market economies are as defined in Green (1977).

a. Production estimates from FAO *Production Yearbook* (1977), assuming 79 percent of grains and grain legumes and 75 percent of perishables are actually used for food (based on Green 1977).

b. Based on James (1977).

c. From Gavan (1977).

Physical damage to the crop during harvest may affect storage. Undamaged cowpea pods, groundnut shells, and paddy grain husks afford the crop a noticeable degree of protection from infestation by most insect species.

Drying is a particularly vital operation in the chain of grain handling, because moisture may be the most important factor in determining whether and to what extent grain will deteriorate during storage. In developing countries, grain is usually dried by a combination of sun and air drying, although supplemental heat may be employed. Overdrying—which can easily occur in arid regions or after excessive exposure to sun or other heat—can cause breakage, damage to the seed coat, bleaching, discoloration, loss of germinative powers, and nutritional changes. Too rapid drying of crops with high moisture content also causes damage. For example, bursting (or "case hardening") causes the surface of the grain to dry out rapidly, sealing moisture within the inner layers. Underdrying or slow drying, a problem in humid regions, results in deterioration caused by fungi and bacteria and, in extreme cases leads to total loss.

The storage environment has much to do with the rate of deterioration and loss. High temperature and humidity encourage mold formation and provide suitable conditions for rapid growth of insect populations. Deterioration is minimal in cool, dry areas, more marked in hot, dry ones, high in cool, damp conditions, and very high in hot, damp climates. Some climates lessen the residual activity of certain pesticides and can reduce the effective life of storage containers and structures. Different structural materials may alter the effectiveness of various formulations of a given insecticide.

Insect pests are a greater problem in regions of high relative humidity, but temperature is the overriding factor that influences insect multiplication. At temperatures of 32° centigrade, the rate of insect development is such that a monthly compound increase of 50 times is theoretically possible. Insect attack on cereal grains and beans can be so severe as to reduce the commodity to empty husks and dust. Large numbers of insects can be expected to produce extensive weight losses, and the resulting contamination by dead and live insects and their excreta can be sufficient to make the commodity completely unpalatable and unacceptable in the market.

Fungal attack in storage generally occurs when drying has been inadequate, when large numbers of insects are present (causing a high temperature rise in the grain), or when the stored crop is exposed to high humidity or actual wetting. When the moisture content of the commodity is in equilibrium with an atmosphere of 70 percent relative humidity, fungal development does not normally take place. Fungal spoilage is more serious in those regions with a permanent high relative humidity, or where a season of high humidity coincides with the time when the grain is being dried or kept in store. Microorganisms may multiply and create heat that can increase in unventilated grain to the point of complete destruction.

Rodent damage to stored grain can occur in a number of ways. The animals not only consume the grain but also foul a large amount with their excretions (which may carry microorganisms pathogenic to humans), destroy containers by gnawing holes that result in leakage and wastage of grain, and paw into and scatter grain while they eat. Damage to grain stored in bulk may be much less than to grain stored in bags because rodents are unable to burrow into the bulk (Hopf and others 1976).

Processing losses occur in threshing and milling, parboiling, and further processing, including baking, brewing, canning, packaging, and the like. Processing losses tend to increase as larger amounts of crop are produced that strain the capacity of the traditional processing system. Maize traditionally shelled by hand, for example, may be placed in sacks and pounded with a stick to detach the grains from the cob. Mechanical processing is generally less efficient than manual processing, both because it is incomplete and because of damage to grains caused by their variation in size or by poor adjustment of the machinery. In many societies, central milling facilities process grain brought in by farmers for a price determined by the initial unmilled volume or weight. Mill operators thus have little incentive to reduce subsequent losses caused by poorly adjusted equipment or leakage and spillage.

To estimate the magnitude of post-harvest losses of cereal grains, grain legumes, and other foods, Green (1977) surveyed 51 member nations, receiving in most cases fragmentary and partial data. The NAS Post-Harvest Food Loss Study Group subsequently made a considerable effort to collect quantitative data to supplement the FAO figures (National Research Council 1978). Tables 23-2 and 23-3 contain loss information for rice and maize based on these and other sources, together with indications of where in the food pipeline the losses occur. The figures for rice are reasonably accurate; those for maize are more difficult to assess.

Perishables

The main perishable staples are cassava, yam, sweet potato, white potato, taro, banana and plantain, and breadfruit. In the developing countries, these staples and the major vegetables and fruits comprise about two-fifths of the food crops consumed.

From the perspective of post-harvest losses, the perishables present a very different set of problems from those associated with the cereal grains and grain legumes. In many developing countries, there has been no need (because of abundant, cheap supply) or no policy (because of a predominant interest in exports, commercial crops, or grains and legumes) to try to reduce these losses. Perishables have a relatively high moisture content—from 50 percent upwards—and are difficult and expensive to dry and hence to store as dry products. Furthermore, the dried product is very different from the fresh and is often less acceptable. Lacking the hard texture of cereal grains, the perishables bruise easily. Although perishables comprise the storage and reproductive parts of plants, even those that are organs of dormancy (such as yams) are metabolically much more active than cereals and seldom have prolonged dormant periods. This limits their extended storage possibilities.

The edible parts of most fruits and vegetables are not the seeds, which are often discarded, but the fleshy tissues whose natural function is to support the germination and growth of the seed where it falls or to attract birds or other agents by which the seeds can be spread. The edible tissue is meant to perform these functions when it is ripe, not to serve as a food store in the dry condition, and its storage life may be only days.

The high moisture content of perishables seriously affects loss estimation because it is difficult to express weight loss on a constant moisture basis and loss of moisture over short periods may be taken to be loss of nutrients. Reports of loss assessment must be meticulous as to the age and state of the commodity.

Perishables are much more susceptible to mechanical injury than are grains and grain legumes because of their shape and structure, the relatively soft texture associated with their high moisture content, and the need for more frequent specialized handling. Injury can occur at almost any point in the post-harvest system and results from poor handling and packaging, from transportation and storage conditions, or from damage in the marketplace.

Physiological losses occur as a result of endogenous respiration or reduction of moisture content from wilting or transpiration and may be abnormally high if the product is exposed to undue heat, cold, or otherwise unsuitable environmental conditions. Possibly the greatest single cause of post-harvest loss in perishable produce is decay caused by microorganisms (Coursey 1972). Attacks by rodents or insects in stored products are usually of relatively minor importance in comparison with decay from microorganisms, although these factors may be important in particular instances.

The main causes of storage loss in perishables include fungal damage, influenced by the lack of rigidity of perishable crops as compared with grains and the ease with which they are damaged during harvest or handling; sprouting at the end of the natural period of dormancy, which affects roots and tubers; and insect damage, which occurs most frequently while the root is still in the ground or the fruit or vegetable is still attached to the plant and is relevant mainly in that it aggravates fungal problems by providing additional points of entry.

Refrigeration is undoubtedly an important way to prolong the storage life of high-quality fresh tropical produce, but it has a number of limitations for reducing food losses in developing countries. Many of the perishables are too low in unit cost to support the expense of mechanically refrigerated storage, while many of the more valuable tropical horticultural products are liable to low-temperature injury— physiological deterioration at temperatures near but above freezing. The capital cost and the not inconsiderable recurring cost and organizational problems associated with efficient and continuous maintenance of significant amounts of mechanically refrigerated storage facilities are likely to continue to be a major limitation for the forseeable future.

A major reduction in perishable losses can be accomplished simply by improving handling and packaging at all stages of the movement from harvest to consumption. Delicate produce is often handled in the same way as grain is, and mechanical damage greatly increases the rate

Table 23-2. *Post-Harvest Losses of Rice*

Country or region	Total weight loss (percent)	Reported national production (thousands of tons)	Remarks (numbers are percentage losses)	Source
Bangladesh	7	18,500	—	Green (1977)
Belize	20–30	2	On-farm storage	J. P. Cal, personal communication (1977)
Bolivia	16	113	On-farm 2; drying 5; unspecified storage 7	Green (1977)
Brazil	1–30	9,560	Unspecified storage 1–30	Green (1977)
Dominican Republic	6.5	—	On-farm storage 3; central storage 0.3	Green (1977)
Egypt	2.5	2,300	—	Green (1977)
India	6	70,500	Unspecified storage	Green (1977)
	3–5.5	—	Improved traditional storage	Boxall and Greeley (1978)
Indonesia	6–17	22,950	Drying 2; storage 2–5	Green (1977)
Malaysia	17–25	1,900	Central storage 6; threshing 5–13; drying 2; on-farm storage 5; handling 6	A. Yunus, personal communication (1977)
Nepal	4–22	2,404	On-farm 3–4; on-farm storage 15; central storage 1–3	Green (1977)

Country				Reference
Pakistan	7	3,942	Unspecified storage 5	Green (1977)
	2–6	—	Unspecified storage 2	H. A. Qayyum, personal communication (1977)
	5–10	—	Unspecified storage 5–10	J. H. Greaves, personal communication (1977)
Philippines	9–34	6,439	Drying 1–5; unspecified storage 2–6; threshing 2–6	Green (1977)
	Up to 30	—	Unspecified storage	FAO and others (1977)
	3–10	—	Handling	Toqero (1977)
Rwanda	9	5	—	Green (1977)
Sierra Leone	10	580	—	Green (1977)
Sri Lanka	13–40	1,253	Drying 1–5; central storage 6.5; threshing 2–6	Green (1977)
	6–18	—	Drying 1–3; on farm storage 2–6; milling 2–6; parboiling 1–3	J. Ramalingam, personal communication (1977)
Sudan	17	7	Central storage	A. H. Kamel, personal communication (1977)
Thailand	8–14	14,400	On-farm storage 1.5–3.5; central storage 1.5–3.5	Green (1977)
	12–25	—	On-farm storage 2–15; handling 10	B. Dhamcheree, personal communication (1977)
Uganda	11	15	—	Green (1977)
West Africa	6–24	—	Drying 1–2; on-farm storage 2–10; parboiling 1–2; milling 2–10	H. van Ruiten, personal communication (1977)

— Not given.

Table 23-3. *Post-Harvest Losses of Maize*

Country or region	Total weight loss (percent)	Reported national production (thousands of tons)	Remarks (numbers are percentage losses)	Source
Belize	20–30	20	Traditional on-farm storage	J. P. Cal, personal communication (1977)
Benin	8–9	221	Traditional on-farm storage; six months improved storage	Harris and Lindblad (1978)
Botswana	—	62	Insect damage	Rawnsley (1969)
Brazil	15–40	17,929	Farm storage	Green (1977)
Côte d'Ivoire	5–10	120	Twelve months stored on cob	Hall (1970); Vandevenne (1978)
Dominican Republic	19	49	Farm storage 15; processing 1	Green (1977)
Ghana	7–14	395	—	Green (1977)
	15	—	Eight months storage	Hall (1970)
Honduras	20–50	289	Traditional storage, poor facilities	A. B. Balint, personal communication (1977)
India	6.5–7.5	6,500	Central storage 7.5	N. S. Agrawal, personal communication (1977)

320

Country				Reference
Indonesia	4	2,532	—	Green (1977)
Kenya	10–23	1,360	Four to six months central storage	Green (1977)
	12	—	Hybrid maize, hotter regions six months	De Lima (1973)
Malawi	minimum 10	—	Hybrid	Green (1977)
	6–14	1,200	Drying 6; on-farm storage 8	Tropical Products Institute (1977); Schulten (1975)
Mexico	10–25	8,945	—	Green (1977)
Nicaragua	15–30	201	—	Green (1977)
Nigeria	1–5	1,050	On-farm storage	Green (1977)
	5.5–70	—	Six months on-farm storage	FAO and UNECA (1977)
Pakistan	2–7	70	—	Green (1977)
Paraguay	25	290	—	Green (1977)
Rwanda	10–20	60	On-farm storage	Green (1977)
Tanzania	20–100	1,619	Unspecified storage	Green (1977)
	9, 14, 67	—	Three, six, and nine months	Mushi (1978)
Togo	5–10	135	Six months central storage	Tyagi and Girish (1975)
Uganda	4–17	623	—	Green (1977)
Venezuela	10–25	532	—	J. Martino, personal communication (1977)
Zambia	9–21	750	On-farm storage	Adams and Harman (1977)

— Not given.

and extent of both physiological and microbiological deterioration. Improvements in packaging and handling often may be accomplished at little cost. They may require nothing more than ensuring that the produce is handled in smaller quantities and put into shallower containers—for instance, in rigid wooden crates or cardboard cartons rather than in sacks or in loose bulk. Proper packaging and handling are so important that they should be among the first aspects of food loss to be investigated. Improved transportation and marketing systems to reduce the time between harvesting and consumption can also greatly reduce loss.

When we look at the loss data for perishables in table 23-1, the very wide range on which the overall estimated loss of 20 percent is based suggests the need for caution. The opinion of a professional group with long experience with perishable commodities in developing countries gives an idea of the wide range (National Research Council 1978). For white potatoes in Chile, Peru, and Venezuela, they estimated post-harvest losses to be 25 to 30 percent. For cassava in Colombia, the Dominican Republic, Ecuador, Venezuela, and Central America, the estimate is 15 to 20 percent. For yams in Ghana and Nigeria, the estimated loss is 10 to 20 percent. In most developing countries, the loss of fresh tomatoes is about 50 percent.

Fish

Post-harvest loss in the production of fish (used here to denote all aquatic animal food produce) is unique among the staples. For no other class of food does so much evidence of serious loss at every stage from harvest to consumption exist, with so little precise knowledge of the overall proportion of losses to the potential harvest or to the food finally consumed. Yet post-harvest loss of fish is of great significance because about 17 percent of the world animal protein consumption comes from fish and fish products (Pimentel and others 1975).

Here we focus particularly on artisanal fisheries that are small-scale, poor, dispersed, and unorganized. In spite of their great importance, two aspects of fishing and fish consumption are not considered here: commercial fishing carried out by large vessels on the high seas and fish meal and fish oil production.

For fish we need an expanded definition of post-harvest food loss. Specifically, post-harvest losses of fish should include fish discarded at sea as by-catch in the harvest of other species such as shrimp. This is justified not only because the by-catch frequently represents a multiple in weight of the principal harvest and often contains a large proportion of locally acceptable food fish, but also because the loss could be identified and research and development could be applied to reduce this loss.

In most developing countries, the market preference is for whole fish. About 60 percent of the world edible fish catch goes directly to consumers in the raw, reflecting their desire to inspect the raw fish carefully for freshness. In countries where Far Eastern fish sausages and sauces are unknown, fish products in which the original identity is not preserved represent only a very small proportion of fish consumed. Under the usually prevailing primitive conditions of preservation and distribution, only small harvests can be rapidly marketed. As a result, most ocean fishing in developing countries is carried out by fleets of many small fishing boats.

Moreover, the entire marine fisheries industry in developing countries is so fractionated by local customs and cultures, and is controlled by so many individual entrepreneurs from harvest to consumer, that losses occur simply as a consequence of frequent handling and transfer of fish from one middleman to another.

The extent of post-harvest losses on board the fishing vessel is likely to be considerable, especially in warm climates, because of spoilage due to poor handling and lack of refrigeration. Actual losses are camouflaged, however, because even stale or spoiling raw fish is later processed.

The simplest and most widely used technique for preserving fish is to spread it on the beach or on a mat and allow it to dry in the sun. Under these conditions, the wet fish are subject to attack by blowflies, mainly *Chrysomyia* species, whose larvae burrow into the fish and cause damage and spoilage. Apart from the physical damage to the fish and the associated spoilage, the blowflies are a serious source of disease because the beaches they infest are widely contaminated with human feces as a result of limited public sanitation facilities. The dried fish is also subject to attack by *Dermestes* beetles. If this infestation is allowed to proceed, the beetles consume the fish.

Preliminary salting is often used to enhance the quality of naturally dried fish. Salting, either by stacking the split fish with dry salt between the layers or, preferably, by immersing the fish in brine, serves to speed up the removal of water from the flesh and to reduce the time necessary for air or sun drying. (In the case of oily fish, such as sardines, prolonged drying leads to discoloration and rancidity.) Salting is also a chemical method of bacterial control. Flies will not attack fish that has been brined before drying, and the rate of attack by beetles is inversely proportional to salt concentration (James 1977). Proper packaging is required to prevent salted, dried fish from reabsorbing moisture from a humid atmosphere.

Smoke drying is widely used in West Africa. Fish is suspended over cooking fires as a means of deterring insect infestation. Smoking, however, offers little defense against insects that deposit their eggs in the flesh before and during drying. During smoking of thick-bodied fish, the insects are deterred by heat and smoke, but the larvae already present in the fish penetrate the deeper parts of the fish where heat and smoke cannot reach. Traditional processing may be responsible for a loss of value as high as 15 percent (Hoffman 1977).

Next to losses caused by insects, the most important physical and economic losses of dried fish result from crumbling during storage and distribution. Poorly dried fish is a fragile product that, if roughly handled or vibrated on overloaded trucks on poor roads, will be reduced to a powder.

James (1977) roughly estimated losses of dried fish to insect infestation at 3 million tons per year (25 percent of 12 million tons produced); discarded edible by-catch from shrimping alone at 5 million tons (five times the total shrimp catch); and loss to spoilage at 2 million tons (10 percent spoilage loss of the 20 million tons estimated to be consumed fresh). These conservative rough approximations give a loss figure of 10 million tons per year—20 percent of the total catch now going to direct human consumption.

These figures are highly speculative because with few exceptions no reliable data are available for any developing country on either post-harvest losses or the harvests caught by unchartered and uncontrolled individual fishermen.

Conclusions

For planning purposes, experts cite minimal overall losses in developing countries of 10 percent of total production of grains and grain legumes and 20 percent of nongrain staples, perishables, and fish (table 23-1), although the overall picture we have today is incomplete. In contrast, we are precisely aware of the most important primary causes of food loss in developing countries. We also have a fairly good idea about where in the food pipeline between harvest and consumption these losses occur. However, we know very little about many of the nontechnological, nonbiological secondary causes that are responsible for food losses in small communities, by individual subsistence farmers and fishermen, and by individual members of a family. We know, finally, much too little about the effects of political pressures, taxation, and other official and unofficial government regulations and actions.

If post-harvest food losses in developing countries are to be reduced, priority attention must be given to training and extension programs to remedy acute personnel shortages at all levels of the post-harvest food system. More systematic approaches to loss estimation in developing countries must be developed and international technical assistance agencies should cooperate to strengthen and expand post-harvest food loss documentation services. Substantial refinement of knowledge about economic cost-benefit factors in post-harvest food loss reduction is needed, and so is research on improvement of the storage and processing techniques and facilities—at both the central and the village levels—and on the effectiveness and safety of pesticides.

This review raises certain questions. In attempts to reduce world food shortages, what is the significance of the quantity of food lost and willfully wasted? Under what conditions is it fair to say that if losses could be reduced, more people could be fed adequately? Assuming that members of a certain community are malnourished because they are unable, for economic or any other reasons, to gain access to sufficient food, does the reduction of food losses in that community mean that those in need can obtain more food or will it simply enhance the consumption of those already meeting their food needs? In other words, what are the conditions that will make it possible for a food loss reduction in one locality to permit people in that or another locality to comsume more food?

PART V

Malnutrition and
Nutrition Interventions

Persisting widespread malnutrition during the decade since the 1974 World Food Conference despite impressive increases in per capita food production has shown policymakers in developing country governments and international development agencies alike that an adequate supply of food alone is not sufficient to assure adequate nutrition. If the common view ten years ago was that we needed more food, the common view today is that we need higher incomes.

It is undoubtedly true that malnutrition has its roots in poverty and that, in the long run, increased per capita income can be expected to bring about improved nutrition. The catch here is "in the long run." Even the most optimistic predictions about economic growth in developing countries foresee that growth in real income, particularly among the poorest segments of the population, will occur only slowly. As Alan Berg puts it in *Malnourished People:* "Even with moderate success in directing general development into accelerated growth in the income of the lowest deciles—combined with a strong effort to increase food production—strong complementary measures will be required to increase the level of food consumption of the poor. The expected course of national growth is not a promising means of meeting this generation's shortfalls" (1981, p. 24).

Reliance on increasing the incomes of the poor as a solution to malnutrition is insufficient, not only because it is slow, but also because income is only one determinant of nutritional status. At all levels, from national to community to household, there are significant differences in the prevalence of malnutrition that cannot be explained solely by differences in income or other measures of economic status. As Michael C. Latham points out in this part, "all four [major] forms of malnutrition are more prevalent among the poor, but a reduction in poverty will have a different impact on the incidence of each disease." Recent experience has demonstrated that social expenditures, community programs, and changes in household practices can reduce malnutrition, even when per capita income remains stagnant.

The nutritional status of a population not only results from but also contributes to national economic development. The most painful loss from malnutrition is loss of life, usually among children. Conservative estimates suggest that malnutrition is a significant factor in the deaths of at least 10 million children a year. Aside from the devastating human consequences of this loss, these children have no opportunity to contribute to their countries' development.

The effects of malnutrition among the survivors also have serious consequences for economic development. In many developing countries, half of all children fail to achieve their full genetic growth potential due to the combined effects of inadequate nutrition and frequent illness. This stunted physical growth is often accompanied by impaired mental development. A small but significant number of children suffer irreversible mental damage before birth due to maternal iodine deficiency. A much larger number of children suffer from protein-energy malnutrition, leading to poor mental development apparently due to the combined effects of insufficient nutrients, low activity levels, and inadequate social interaction.

The synergistic relationship between malnutrition and disease does not cease after childhood but continues among adults. Although their physical and mental development may no longer be at risk, the costs of malnutrition among adults are still enormous in terms of fewer work days, lowered productivity, and less energy to put into the well-being of their families and communities.

That malnutrition is a serious problem affecting a significant proportion of the population in developing countries, and that the problem is unlikely to resolve itself in the near future without specific nutrition policies and programs, seems clear. The selections in this section were chosen to provide a basis for developing these policies and programs.

The opening selection by Latham provides an overview of the prevalence and causes of the four major forms of malnutrition: protein-energy malnutrition, vitamin A deficiency, anemia, and goiter and cretinism due to iodine deficiency. Latham discusses a number of promising approaches to preventing or treating these nutrient deficiency diseases. George H. Beaton then focuses specifically on the functional consequences of inadequate energy intake. After questioning several widespread practices and assumptions among nutritionists, he concludes, "If we accept that our task is to define a level of intake and expenditure at which both energy balance and optimum health are achieved and to define the functional consequences of deviation from that level, then the basis for much of the current controversy over energy in human nutrition becomes clearer."

The next selections discuss three important determinants of malnutrition that are not always taken into consideration. Joanne Leslie reviews evidence showing infectious diseases, particularly diarrhea, to be as significant a cause of malnutrition among preschool children as inadequate food. She points out: "The fact that there are important causal links between malnutrition and infection provides an additional compelling reason for health planners and food and nutrition planners to work closely together." Sandra Huffman describes the dual reproductive and productive responsibilities borne by virtually all women in developing countries. It is important to recognize the heavy demands on women's time not only to understand the causes of child malnutrition but also to allow design of realistic health and nutrition interventions. Michael Lipton's discussion of variable access food focuses first on the contradictory evidence concerning intrahousehold food distribution and then on variations in nutritional risk due to seasonality.

The theme of nutritional risk is further developed by Wendy McLean, who emphasizes the importance of accurately describing social and economic differences among households and communities so as to develop policies and programs to prevent malnutrition. John B. Mason and Janice T. Mitchell describe the growing practice of nutritional surveillance, which can be useful to developing country governments for long-term planning in health and development, program management and evaluation, and timely warning and intervention to prevent critical deterioration in food consumption.

The last three selections focus on specific nutrition interventions. Beaton and Hossein Ghassemi review a wide range of supplementary feeding programs for preschool children and conclude that such programs have been rather expensive for the measured benefits but caution, "we remain unconvinced that the benefit usually measured, physical growth and development, is either the total benefit to the family and community or even the most important benefit." Robert C. Hornik reviews recent encouraging experience with nutrition education, emphasizing that "the trade-off between reaching large audiences, which media-based programs can do, and producing nutritionally significant behavior change, which pilot outreach projects have been able to do, remains the central problem of nutrition education." Richard K. Manoff concludes this section with a distillation of 22 precepts to be followed and pitfalls to be avoided in designing nutrition education.

24

Strategies for the Control
of Malnutrition and the Influence
of the Nutritional Sciences

Michael C. Latham

No accurate figures on the global prevalence of malnutrition exist, and even good estimates are difficult to obtain. To some extent, prevalence estimates depend on definitions. Relatively minor changes in anthropometric cutoff points used to assess protein-energy malnutrition (PEM) or in the recommended minimum requirements for energy or other nutrients can change by millions the estimated numbers of malnourished and undernourished in the world.

The attempt by WHO to provide prevalence rates of the most important forms of malnutrition is shown in table 24-1. These figures are useful, but they are only educated guesses based on insufficient data and should be used with caution.

Table 24-1 suggests that PEM affects about 500 million people, and that some 350 million women of childbearing age have iron deficiency anemia. The other two of the "big four" nutritional deficiency diseases are xeropthalmia, or vitamin A deficiency, which is a leading cause of childhood blindness, and endemic goiter and cretinism due to iodine deficiency. The immediate cause of each of these four prevalent forms of malnutrition is a nutrient deficiency, but the solution involves social, economic, agricultural, and political actions.

PEM and vitamin A deficiency are largely confined to the poor segments of the population. Therefore macro policies to improve food intakes and reduce poverty will greatly reduce the incidence of both PEM and xerophthalmia. Nutritional anemias, while considerably more prevalent in poor communities, are not uncommon in industrialized countries. Endemic goiter is mainly related to low intake of

Excerpted from *Food and Nutrition*, vol. 10, no. 1 (1984), pp. 5–31, published by the Food and Agriculture Organization of the United Nations.

Table 24-1. *Estimated Numbers of People Affected by Preventable Malnutrition, Worldwide*

Deficiency	Morbidity owing to malnutrition	Prevalence of morbidity[a]	Group most affected	Mortality per year
Protein and energy	Stunted growth[b]	500 million	Ages 0–6	—
	Clinical cases of kwashiorkor and marasmus[c]	1 million	Ages 1–4	10 million[d]
Iron	Anemia[e]	350 million	Women 18–45	—
Vitamin A	Blindness[f]	6 million	All ages	750,000[g]
Iodine	Goiter[h]	150 million	All ages	—
	Cretinism[i]	6 million	All ages	—

— Not applicable.

a. The estimates are gross and do not express the significant variations occurring not only from country to country but also within countries.

b. Stunted growth is defined by weight below the 2.5th percentile of the WHO growth standards. This figure includes mild malnutrition and is therefore higher than the usual estimate of 200 million moderately to severely malnourished. The first manifestation of stunting appears at birth and is defined by low weight for gestational age. The rough estimate of 22 million live-born low-birthweight infants is equivalent to one-sixth of the total number of births. If one-third of these cases are a result of other factors, at least 14 million babies with nutritionally related stunting are born each year. Some evidence suggests a higher mortality for these babies than for bigger babies.

c. About 1.5 percent of those with stunted growth are so malnourished that they will show the life-threatening symptoms of marasmus and kwashiorkor within the year (about 7.5 million cases a year). The mean duration of kwashiorkor is about a month, of marasmus, about three months, for an average of two months. The prevalence at any given time is thus over 1 million.

d. Diarrhea is often the proximate cause of death. Most cases of death by diarrhea (about 1.5 percent of children aged one to four years, or 4.6 million a year) are associated with stunting and wasting. Of the 7.5 million cases a year of kwashiorkor and marasmus, 7 million die; of these many die with diarrhea.

e. Fifty percent of these women have hemoglobin values below the 17th percentile of the WHO standards; that is, 33 percent of women aged 18–45 years are anemic.

f. This is an underestimate of persons affected because it includes only cases in Southeast Asia. This area does have the highest prevalence in the world, but further cases should be added from Africa and the Americas. Of a million new cases of blindness each year, 25 percent survive that year, so there are 250,000 blind survivors each year. These probably have another 40 years of mean life span, resulting in a prevalence of 6 million.

g. Deaths are caused by reduced resistance to disease as a result of vitamin A deficiency.

h. An estimated 200 million in 1960. We estimate that successful campaigns against goiter have reduced the prevalence to 150 million today.

i. In goitrous populations 1.5 percent of the children born have severe mental and physical retardation (cretinism); 750 million people live in goitrous areas (overall prevalence of 20 percent goiter in such areas). Thus about 250,000 cretins are born each year in these areas. Even if their life span is half that of noncretins, 6 million persons living today are mentally deficient because of maternal iodine deficiency.

Source: Latham (1984).

iodine, which in turn is influenced principally by the iodine content of the soil in which the crops are grown. Iodine deficient soils tend to be found in mountainous or inland plains regions. In coastal regions, goiter and cretinism due to iodine deficiency are virtually unknown even among the poor. In areas with iodine deficient soil, those who are better off avoid developing goiter because they consume a varied diet, including food imported from other areas, while their poorer neighbors, who subsist on locally grown crops, remain iodine deficient. In brief, all four forms of malnutrition are more prevalent among the poor, but a reduction in poverty will have a different impact on the incidence of each disease.

Protein-Energy Malnutrition

PEM is the most prevalent form of malnutrition in almost all developing countries. In recent years, an apparent reduction has occurred in the overall incidence of the severe clinical forms of PEM: kwashiorkor, caused by severe protein deficiency and characterized by retarded growth, apathy, loss of appetite, fluid accumulations, and loss of pigment in the skin and hair; marasmus, caused by a severe deficiency of both energy and protein and characterized by retarded growth and extreme thinness; and marasmic-kwashiorkor, a mixed state showing signs of both kwashiorkor and marasmus.

However, mild or moderate PEM does not seem to have decreased as much. Three recent scientific advances in the field of public health have important implications for policies aimed at reducing the prevalence of mild to moderate malnutrition: (a) a growing recognition that when commonly consumed cereal-based diets meet energy needs, they usually meet protein needs as well; (b) the development of appropriate ways to use anthropometric measurements to monitor growth; and (c) new techniques to control parasitic infections and to treat diarrhea with oral rehydration therapy. (Oral rehydration therapy involves the use of prepackaged or home prepared mixtures of water, salt, and sugar in specified proportions to replace the fluid lost during diarrhea.)

Energy and Protein Needs

In the early 1970s, a series of influential articles pointed out that nutritionists had overemphasized the protein problem, that protein deficiencies were less prevalent than energy deficiencies, and that major efforts to increase the consumption of protein-rich foods were likely to have a rather small impact on the prevalence of PEM (Waterlow and Payne 1975; McLaren 1974; Sukhatme 1972).

This new appreciation of the relatively greater importance of dietary energy has led to major changes in our thinking and in policies to control PEM. We no longer see major emphasis placed on amino acid fortification of cereals, on single cell protein or fish protein concentrate, on high protein weaning foods, or on the consumption of meat, fish, and eggs. Instead we see more efforts to promote breast-feeding; to increase consumption of cereals, legumes, and locally produced weaning foods; to control infections and parasitic diseases; to increase meal frequency for young children; and to encourage a higher consumption of oil, fat, and other items that reduce bulk and increase the energy density of foods fed to children at risk.

However, we should not forget the importance of dietary protein. In particular, we must remember that the protein requirements of children are proportionately higher than those of adults, and that infections result in increased urinary nitrogen losses, which raise protein needs. Nutritionists also accept that diets based on some noncereal staple foods such as cassava, plantain, and sugar are more deficient in protein than are cereal-legume-based diets and put children at particular risk of developing kwashiorkor.

Anthropometric Measurements and Growth Monitoring

During the 1950s and 1960s, weight for age based on the use of the Gomez classification was the main method used to assess nutritional status, both of the individual child and of the community (Gomez and others 1955). In the early 1970s, this author and a colleague suggested that it was important to distinguish three different categories or types of malnutrition using weight and height measurements of children (Seoane and Latham 1971). The suggested categories were the following:

○ Acute, current, short-duration malnutrition, where weight for age and weight for height are low, but height for age is normal
○ Past, chronic malnutrition, where weight for age and height for age are low, but weight for height is normal
○ Acute on chronic or current long-duration malnutrition, where weight for age, height for age, and weight for height are all low.

Waterlow (1972) discussed this new classification in an influential paper in which he suggested that acute malnutrition be termed "wasting," that chronic malnutrition be termed "stunting," and that the combined condition of acute on chronic malnutrition be labeled "wasting and stunting." Although nutritionists have not reached firm agreement either on the terms to be adopted or on the cutoff points for low weight and low height, this classification system is now widely used.

Policymakers must also decide which growth standards to use as a reference for assessing malnutrition. In recent years there has been increasing acceptance of the National Center for Health Statistics (NCHS) growth standards (Hamill and others 1979). WHO strongly urges adoption of the NCHS reference population data because interpretation of comparisons made to the NCHS standards is clearer than earlier standards used, such as the Harvard standard (Griffiths 1981). An editorial in the *Lancet* (1984) discusses the use of international growth standards in developing countries, particularly the WHO/NCHS standards. The article concludes that the growth of privileged groups of children in developing countries does not differ importantly from these standards and that the poorer growth so commonly observed in the underprivileged is due to social factors—among which the malnutrition-infection complex is of primary importance—rather than to ethnic or geographic differences.

Some people still suggest that the low anthropometric measurements found in groups of children in developing countries may be "normal" or that "smallness" may be advantageous. This view is not supported by the evidence, as has been convincingly argued by Gopalan (1983). Recent data strongly support the view that ethnic differences are much less important than other factors as causes of growth failure in children (Stephenson and others 1983; Habicht and others 1974). Inadequate food intake, infectious and parasitic diseases, and adverse environmental factors often associated with poverty combine to prevent children from realizing their full growth potential. Certainly ethnic factors influence achieved body size and especially stature, but in prepubertal children, heredity seems to be a much less significant cause of below-average growth than other factors. In adults, both environmental factors in childhood and heredity affect stature.

The research on anthropometry and the new knowledge about the appropriateness of international standards have assisted greatly those conducting nutritional surveys, surveillance, or growth monitoring. In the last decade the use of weight charts as a way to monitor nutritional status has greatly increased, and mothers are more involved in maintaining good nutritional status in their children and in rehabilitating children who have become malnourished. The advantages of weight charts include their inexpensiveness, their practicality, and their use as a powerful tool for nutrition education. This is one of the four activities that UNICEF is emphasizing in its approach to improving the state of the world's children (Grant 1984). In addition to growth monitoring, UNICEF is emphasizing oral rehydration, breastfeeding, and immunization in what has come to be known as the GOBI approach. The numbers of children whose growth is being monitored worldwide is now in the tens of millions.

Nutrition and Infections

Our knowledge of immunology has advanced markedly in the last ten years. This chapter will not review either this new knowledge or what is now known about the relationship between nutrition and infection (see Leslie in part V). Instead, the discussion will be limited to three strategies for the control of infections, all of which have important implications for nutritional status, namely, immunization, the treatment of certain parasitic infections, and oral rehydration therapy for diarrhea. Recent scientific knowledge suggests that a much wider implementation of all three could, in a very few years, greatly reduce morbidity, mortality, and malnutrition related to several of the most prevalent infectious diseases of childhood.

We are now on the threshold of major new advances in our ability to immunize people against a whole range of diseases. In the 1970s, we saw the last case of naturally transmitted smallpox. International and national actions had harnessed a technology introduced by Jenner in England in 1796, and humanity had conquered a deadly epidemic disease.

If we had the political will and were provided with the rather modest required financial means, we could probably conquer measles in the same way. The task would be more difficult because measles is more contagious than smallpox, it usually strikes children at an early age, and the current vaccine is more sensitive to adverse conditions than is smallpox vaccine. But measles does not have an animal reservoir (that is, it can only be transmitted from one person to another), immunization is highly effective, and several industrialized countries have demonstrated that the disease can be controlled. Measles in childhood contributes significantly to malnutrition in developing countries, and some studies have found case fatality rates from measles to be many times higher in malnourished children. Measles immunization can therefore both reduce malnutrition and greatly lower infant and young child mortality rates. A serious attempt should be made to obtain universal or near universal immunization against measles in children before the turn of the century. Perhaps one of the industrialized countries in the East or West could forgo the building of one large warship or the construction of one set of atomic weapons and use the funds saved to finance the eradication of measles from the world.

Common parasitic infections in children also have an impact on their nutritional status. The common roundworm (*Ascaris lumbricoides*) is estimated to infect 1,000 million people in the world, and studies show that it contributes to poor growth and to malnutrition in young children (Stephenson and others 1980). Hookworm infections are a major cause of iron loss and anemia (Crompton and Nesheim 1984).

A new study in progress by L. S. Stephenson and Latham suggests that schistosomiasis (*Schistosoma hematobium*) contributes to anemia, retarded growth, and low physical fitness in Kenyan schoolchildren.

These three parasitic infections, plus several other worm infestations, can now be easily treated with drugs that are cheap, effective, and safe. In many poor countries, only slow progress is being made to make safe water supplies available to all households, to improve sanitation, and to increase health knowledge—measures that in the long term are needed for permanent control of these parasitic diseases. Therefore, at least in the short term, serious consideration needs to be given to routine deworming of infected populations. Such action would have important nutritional implications.

The last decade has seen a revolution in the treatment of diarrhea. Oral rehydration therapy (ORT), often given in the home, has reduced deaths from dehydration caused by diarrhea in many parts of the world and has largely displaced intravenous therapy. Some evidence suggests that ORT may shorten the duration of diarrhea, or at least promote an earlier return of the child's normal appetite. In 1978, an editorial in the *Lancet* stated that the basic scientific discovery that led to the development of ORT—the discovery that sodium transport and glucose transport are coupled in the small intestine, so that glucose accelerates absorption of solute and water—was potentially the most important medical advance in this century (*Lancet* 1978). Now many countries have major programs to expand the use of ORT, and this has become a major focus for actions supported by both WHO and UNICEF.

Gastroenteritis, often due to infections with rotaviruses, is such a common cause of morbidity, of malnutrition, and of deaths of infants and children in developing countries that this new form of therapy deserves major support. This is an example of scientific research that has led to a practical means to deal with an extremely prevalent childhood disease that is known to be an important cause of malnutrition. We should remember, however, that ORT is a treatment, not a prevention. Other steps must be taken to prevent diarrhea, such as provision of adequate water and sanitary facilities.

Xerophthalmia and Vitamin A Deficiency

In many developing countries, xerophthalmia due to vitamin A deficiency is the most important cause of childhood blindness. Yet treatment and prevention of this condition are relatively cheap and easy. In recent years, there has been an increasing appreciation by governments and international agencies, and to some extent also by physicians and nutritionists, of the magnitude of the problem and of the means available to deal with xerophthalmia.

The establishment of the International Vitamin A Consultative Group (IVACG), which grew out of a small meeting of concerned nutritionists, physicians, and ophthalmologists in 1974, was a signal event. IVACG, with a tiny budget, has helped focus attention on the problem and has guided international activities to reduce vitamin A deficiency worldwide, and its members have been innovative in applied research and in instituting control programs. IVACG has also prepared a series of guidelines and other publications relating to vitamin A deficiency and its control which have helped systematize and standardize activities related to xerophthalmia.

Recent research has considerably advanced our knowledge of the biochemistry and physiology of vitamin A, particularly the important relationship between vitamin A and protein. When kwashiorkor is treated with a diet high in protein and energy, but without added vitamin A, there is an increase in the special retinol-binding protein with which vitamin A forms a complex. However, only after the administration of vitamin A do circulating levels of retinol (vitamin A) increase (Reddy and others 1979).

Our understanding of the interrelationship between vitamin A deficiency and infections has also increased in recent years (WHO 1982). Many reports show a drop in serum vitamin A as a result of infections. But we still do not adequately understand the relationship of measles to xerophthalmia, or whether blindness following measles, which is frequently reported in Africa, is due mainly to vitamin A deficiency or to other causes.

In the majority of countries where xerophthalmia is prevalent, most of the dietary vitamin A comes from carotenes in nonanimal foods. The use of more sensitive methods of nutrient analysis of foods has demonstrated that the older methods used tend to grossly overestimate the carotene content of such foods, and therefore that most food composition tables have major errors. This has important implications for applied programs that aim to improve vitamin A nutritional status through raising intakes of vegetable sources of carotene.

Long-term studies in Central America, India, Indonesia, and the Philippines have in recent years greatly extended our knowledge of xerophthalmia and its control. An INCAP project in Guatemala demonstrated that fortification of sugar with vitamin A significantly improved serum vitamin A levels in the community (Arroyave 1983).

The continuing work in the Philippines has been unique in that it has been the only major study to compare the relative effectiveness of three widely suggested strategies for controlling vitamin A deficiency

(Solon and others 1979). The three actions were (a) the provision every six months of a capsule containing vitamin A, (b) the fortification of monosodium glutamate (MSG) with vitamin A, and (c) a public health and horticulture intervention to improve curative and preventive health services and to increase local production and consumption of foods containing carotene. The results of the research showed a reduction of xerophthalmia in children in all three intervention areas, but fortification proved to be the most cost-effective and to result in significant rises in serum vitamin A levels, particularly in the children at greatest risk of developing serious xerophthalmia. Recently, MSG fortification has been undertaken in two whole provinces in the Philippines, with a third province serving as a control and using normal marketing channels for fortified MSG.

In Indonesia, a detailed study of xerophthalmia demonstrated that a history of night blindness was a reasonably useful screening tool for xerophthalmia (Sommer 1981). Indonesia has had experience with a limited use of high dose vitamin A administration but, influenced by the experience with this procedure in the Philippines, is now seriously considering fortification of MSG with vitamin A. A large proportion of Indonesians, including children and the poor, like many other Asian peoples, use MSG regularly in foods.

India has had the most extensive experience with periodic dosing of children. The national vitamin A prophylaxis program instituted in the early 1970s now covers over 50 million children. Unlike most other countries, where high dose capsules are used, India uses a locally manufactured liquid vitamin A preparation provided every six months. Several evaluations (for example, National Institute of Nutrition 1981) indicate that the program has been effective but has some logistical problems.

Most nutritionists now agree that, if an appropriate vehicle can be found, fortification is the cheapest and most effective means of controlling xerophthalmia in most countries. The use of periodic high dosing is effective, but it requires a delivery system that can be expensive, and it necessitates locating all children at risk every six months. Often the most vulnerable children are the most difficult to reach and therefore are easily missed.

In the long run, means other than fortification or dosing with vitamin A are needed and can be effective. These involve horticultural and related activities to increase the availability of carotene-rich fruits and vegetables; nutrition education to ensure that diets contain adequate quantities of carotene and vitamin A; actions to reduce the prevalence of various health and nutritional problems that are related to xerophthalmia; the provision of services for early diagnosis and treatment of eye and related diseases; and steps that will reduce poverty and allow families to grow or purchase an adequate diet.

Iron Deficiency Anemia

Nutritional anemias are among the most common deficiency conditions in both developing and industrialized countries. Iron deficiency is by far the most prevalent form, although folate (one of the B vitamins) deficiency is also quite widespread.

The problem of iron deficiency is complex, and control of anemia is not as straightforward as people used to think. Recent studies have shown that the form of iron consumed is at least as important as the amount (Dallman and others 1979), and that substances exist that enhance or retard iron utilization or absorption. Most dietary iron comes from cereals and legumes (nonheme iron) and is relatively poorly absorbed, while a smaller amount of better absorbed iron (heme iron) comes from animal products. The body handles these two forms of iron quite differently. Factors that decrease the absorption of iron from cereals and legumes seem to have less effect on the iron from animal products.

The question of iron nutritional status in infancy has been perplexing because breast milk contains only a small amount of iron per liter. However, studies have shown that 49 percent of the iron in breast milk is absorbed compared with 10 to 12 percent from cow's milk or from unfortified formula (Saarinen and Siimes 1977). The mechanism that allows such high absorption of iron from breast milk is not fully known, but this finding provides further support for the superiority of breastfeeding.

Women during pregnancy, especially in the last trimester, are at an increased risk of developing both iron and folate deficiency anemia. It is now known that the adverse consequences of this anemia are mainly to the mother, not the unborn child. At birth, and throughout the first year of life, hemoglobin concentrations in infants born to both anemic and nonanemic mothers are very similar (Dallman and others 1979).

It is well established that anemia can adversely affect worker productivity (Basta and others 1979; Brooks and others 1979). This is probably due mainly to the reduced oxygen carrying capacity of the blood in anemic, compared with nonanemic, workers. However, iron deficiency may also result in muscle dysfunction.

The relationship of iron nutritional status to infections remains controversial (Bothwell and others 1981). Of particular concern is the evidence suggesting that providing iron therapy in malarial areas may precipitate attacks of malaria. At present this is far from proven, but appropriate interventions to control anemia in malaria endemic areas have been thrown into doubt until more definitive research is completed.

For many years, physicians have known that hookworms suck blood and that heavy and even moderate loads of hookworms are an impor-

Table 24-2. Characteristics of Intervention Programs for Control of Iron Deficiency

Type of intervention	Population coverage	Time required to achieve benefit	Focus	Initial costs	Continuing costs	Public participation	Personnel requirements	Degree of expertise	Initial effect	Continued effect	Complexity of monitoring
Supplementation	Individual	Relatively short (months)	Single or multinutrient	High	High	Very active	High	Low	High	High	Difficult
Fortification	General or target	Medium (1–2 years)	Single or multinutrient	Moderate	Low	None	Low	High	Medium	Low	Simple
Food education	General	Long (years)	Multinutrient	Moderate	Moderate	Active	Variable	High	High	Medium	Difficult
Socioeconomic	General	Long (years)	Multinutrient	Variable	Variable	Active	Variable	High	Variable	Variable	Variable
Parasite control (hookworm)	General	Long (years)	Single nutrient multifaceted	High	High	Very active	High	Medium	High	High	Simple

Source: INACG (1977).

tant cause of iron deficiency anemia. An estimated 900 million people in the world harbor hookworms, and so this remains an important cause of anemia. Many of those infected with hookworms are poor and malnourished and have other reasons for being at high risk of developing iron deficiency. Other parasites may also play a role in anemia by causing blood loss or for other reasons such as hemolytic anemia resulting from malaria. Recent research has shown that schistosomiasis may also be a cause of anemia. Drug treatment for *Schistosoma hematobium* infections in Kenyan children resulted in a significant rise in hemoglobin levels (Stephenson and others 1985). Up to now, those concerned with the control of anemia have given inadequate attention to treating and preventing parasitic infections. Yet millions of people worldwide would benefit from such actions.

Although researchers have known for a long time that ascorbic acid (vitamin C) enhances iron absorption, it is only recently that this knowledge has been applied to improve iron nutritional status, and then in very limited trials. Ascorbic acid is a very powerful enhancer of absorption of iron from nonanimal foods, apparently by increasing its solubility (Cook and Monsen 1976). Many studies have shown that ascorbic acid or foods rich in this vitamin, such as fruits or fruit juices, will increase the absorption of both iron supplements and the iron present in foods consumed at the same time as the ascorbic acid, which suggests that vitamin C supplementation should be considered (Aguilar and Latham forthcoming). This knowledge has important implications because, as stated earlier, most of the world's population have fairly high iron intakes, but this is mainly from cereals and legumes.

The strategies available to prevent and treat iron deficiency anemia are summarized in table 24-2. Such strategies include supplementation (iron provided to the individual on a curative basis), fortification with iron or with ascorbic acid to enhance iron use, nutrition and health education to improve dietary intake of foods rich in iron and ascorbic acid, reduction of the consumption of interfering substances and protection of the individuals from conditions that lead to bodily iron losses, and control of parasitic diseases known to be a major cause of anemia in certain areas.

In countries or communities with a high prevalence of iron deficiency anemia or in groups of the population at especially high risk, such as pregnant women or young children, therapeutic or prophylactic supplementation programs are indicated at least until such time as fortification or other steps can be taken to provide long-term control. However, such supplementation programs require an adequate, often expensive, delivery system.

Fortification has considerable advantages over long-term supplementation and must surely provide the best hope for long-term control in populations in both developing and industrialized nations (Finch and Cook 1984). Where the difficulties can be overcome, it is cheaper than supplementation, it does not require a separate delivery system, and it reaches many more people. But a suitable carrier has to be found, an effective compound has to be added, and other difficulties need to be overcome. These have been discussed in detail elsewhere (INACG 1977). The evaluation of salt fortification in India and the use of sugar fortification in Guatemala (Baker and DeMaeyer 1979) have increased our knowledge and indicate the possibilities of control. In the decade ahead, fortification of foods with ascorbic acid, with or without added iron, deserves serious consideration and trials.

The reduction of iron losses from the body, where these are an important cause of anemia, deserves more attention. Where hookworm infections are prevalent and heavy worm loads are found, periodic deworming would unquestionably reduce iron losses. Similarly, where *Schistosoma hematobium* infections are endemic, regular treatment would reduce urinary blood loss, help control anemia, and reduce morbidity. Of course, in the long run, improved sanitation, better water supplies, and health education will all help reduce parasitic infections, but progress in these fields is often slow.

The establishment of the INACG in the 1970s, modeled on IVACG, has served to bring experts concerned with control of anemia together with clinicians and scientists studying iron metabolism, pharmacology, and other related topics. INACG, mainly through its annual meetings and its publications, has been a potent force in guiding international activities aimed at reducing nutritional anemias worldwide.

Although more research would be useful, we do have enough knowledge to enable us to take steps to control nutritional anemias. Countries now need to determine the nature and extent of their anemia problem and the best methods of control under their own circumstances. International and bilateral agencies should give high priority to assisting the poorer countries with their efforts to control iron deficiency anemias. Such help should include support for the first steps, which might include surveys and experimental studies to find the optimal control measures.

Endemic Goiter and Cretinism

Of the big four nutritional deficiency diseases, it is perhaps most disappointing that goiter, often accompanied by crippling endemic cretinism in the community, still affects so many people in the world, particularly as recent research suggests that in iodine deficient areas mental retardation (apart from cretinism) is more prevalent than elsewhere. Since the turn of the century, we have known how to control this condition. A relatively small expenditure internationally together with proper local implementation of programs could reduce the total world prevalence of goiter to relatively small numbers. Endemic goiter and cretinism are due mainly to iodine deficiency, and for years we have had at our command simple, cheap, and effective methods of providing iodine to populations.

In the industrialized countries, control of iodine deficiency has generally come about by means of mandatory or voluntary iodization of salt, or occasionally of other foods, improved economic status leading to more varied diets, and a greater movement of food so that those living in an iodine deficient area are now consuming many foods produced in iodine sufficient areas. Recent scientific research does not suggest that we need to change significantly the well-tried strategies for goiter control, although some nations or certain communities within developing countries appear to have no suitable vehicle for carrying iodine to the population.

Certain developing countries have shown progress in the control of goiter. A recent review (Stanbury and Querido 1983) suggests considerable progress with control in several Latin American countries. Iodization of salt in Argentina, Colombia, Guatemala, and Mexico has greatly reduced goiter prevalence. But in certain parts of Bolivia, Brazil, Ecuador, and Peru a high prevalence of goiter persists, and cretinism remains endemic in much of the high Andes.

Where iodization of salt or another food is impossible or difficult, researchers have shown that injections of iodized oil are effective in preventing goiter and cretinism. Programs to prevent cretinism have concentrated on injecting women of childbearing age. Evidence suggests that a single injection of iodized oil will prevent the birth of an iodine deficient cretinous infant for at least three and possibly five years. However, the new experience with iodine injections should not allow this method to take precedence over salt iodization, which is so much cheaper, is effective. and has a simple delivery system.

When iodized salt is introduced into a community, often a few individuals will develop problems of excess iodine intake. But evidence suggests that the incidence is always extremely low (Stanbury and Querido 1983), and this concern should not be allowed to prevent salt iodization programs, as the benefits will greatly outweigh the costs.

Conclusions

Scientific knowledge and the results of various nutritional studies, many conducted in the last ten years, show that xerophthalmia, iron deficiency anemia, and endemic goiter could all be largely controlled in a few years if we were to use this knowledge and were provided with the necessary, rather small, resources. Protein-energy malnutrition is considerably more difficult to prevent and will not be markedly reduced without attention to improved agricultural production, to better food distribution, and to control of a number of infectious and parasitic diseases. The prevalence of all of the big four nutritional diseases could be greatly reduced by a reduction in the extent of poverty and by proper attention to food distribution, both among and within households.

The 1974 World Food Conference emphasized that the relative neglect of agriculture was at the heart of the slow pace of development and the extent of hunger in many developing countries of the South. The answer to the problem was seen as a major emphasis on increased food production, especially in the food-deficit countries.

We find in 1984 that the world has good supplies of cereal grains; their prices are moderately low; and that supplies exceed demand for grain produced in North America, Western Europe, and certain grain exporting countries. It was unexpected, and is highly commendable, that world food production per capita has increased during the decade and that even in the poor countries it has declined only slightly. Nonetheless, the hopes of a major reduction in the extent of hunger and malnutrition between 1974 and 1984 were not realized (see Berg and Austin in part VI). Nutritionists and food economists now accept (though many agronomists do not) that important as food production is, it does not solve hunger if we do not deal with problems of adequate access to and appropriate use of food.

The world deals better now than in the past with famine relief, and this has reduced deaths due to starvation. Actions now need to be taken to address the problem of the chronically undernourished, whose malnutrition is less dramatic than starvation but among whom many millions of deaths a year are due to the synergism of malnutrition and infections. In addition to continuing efforts to increase agricultural productivity, attention must now be focused on the demand aspects of food security (see Sen in part III).

Certain actions by the industrialized countries of the North could assist the poor countries of the South. The most important of these would be acceptance of a new economic system that would ensure fair prices for the agricultural and other products now produced mainly in the South. The elimination of a number of "unfair" or "undesirable" practices of the industrialized countries would also help the economies of the South. For example, the "uneconomic" production of sugar beets in the United States and Europe could be phased out, leading to increased sugar exports by countries of the South.

In 1974, there was concern that there might not be adequate food in 1984 to feed the increased world population. The world does produce enough food now to feed all its people and in the year 2000 will still be able to do so. The problem is one of chronic undernutrition for millions of people, not a world food shortage. The present distribution of food in the world is unacceptable because it keeps a large proportion of the world's population living with poor nutritional status, with a constant threat of hunger, and with ill health. Changes are needed in the present economic order, in the empowerment of poor peoples and nations, and in the attitudes and practices of the rich toward the poor.

25

Energy in Human Nutrition:
A Reconsideration
of the Relationship between Intake
and Functional Consequences

George H. Beaton

At the turn of the century, W. O. Atwater and his colleagues E. B. Rosa and F. G. Benedict made a monumental contribution to the study of the physiology of energy metabolism and related aspects of human nutrition (Atwater and Rosa 1897; Atwater and Benedict 1899). They constructed a human calorimeter and then conducted painstaking experiments to establish, using very precise measurements, that the law of conservation of energy applies to humans as well as animals. This may seem obvious now, but it was not obvious then. This observation gave us the basic tenet of the nutritional aspects of energy metabolism.

Energy intake = Energy expenditure

+ Change in energy content of body

Many may argue that in the three-quarters of a century since then we have hardly progressed farther, not because we have not learned much more about energy metabolism, its regulation and aberrations, and the components and costs of energy expenditure, but rather because we have learned so much. While we still accept and keep returning to the concept established for humans by Atwater, we continue to be confused and confounded in attempting to appreciate some of the practical implications of this relationship as it relates to the definition and description of energy requirements.

Excerpted from "Energy in Human Nutrition: Perspectives and Problems," *Nutrition Reviews*, vol. 41, no. 11 (November 1983), pp. 325–40.

Atwater's equation has evolved in the past 50 years. Those interested in obesity (and underweight) see this equation as:

Change in body weight = Energy intake − Energy expenditure

in which expenditure is almost taken as a given, albeit correlated with the existing body mass.

Those interested in child growth fall into the same pattern of thinking, expressing the equation as:

Child growth rate (or, pregnancy weight change)

= Energy intake − Maintenance energy expenditure

Although nutritionists recognized from the beginning that if physical activity differed, this would affect the position of the balance or the magnitude of the numbers, these reformulations of the energy equation have led us into a way of thinking that has potentially serious consequences.

Nutritionists have come to accept that the ultimate measure of the adequacy of energy intake is an anthropometric index, that is, a measure of body size such as height or weight. For adults, we consider whether they are underweight or overweight, expected weight being adjusted for height. For children, we use indicators such as weight for height and weight for age or, if the data are adequate, we use growth measures such as change in anthropometry over time. We have coined names for deviations from the anthropometric norms, such as protein-energy malnutrition (PEM). We have undertaken many studies of children and adults to look at the association between anthropometric parameters and health outcomes: birth weight and childhood mortality; growth rate or weight for age or height and childhood mortality; obesity and cardiovascular disease; and so forth. We have then inferred that we have measured relationships between nutrition and outcomes. Perhaps we have. But have we missed other relationships?

In effect, we have fallen into a trap of assuming that anthropometry is an adequate proxy for "nutrition" rather than an index of one aspect of nutritional status. Our current mode of thinking goes along the following lines:

Inappropriate energy intake → Deviant anthropometric status

→ Functional abnormality

In our analyses, we have tended to accept anthropometric status as a proxy for adequacy of food intake in looking at functional outcomes, such as worker productivity or cognitive development, and as a proxy for functional status in evaluating the effect of change in food intake.

Achievement of appropriate anthropometric parameters has become the central goal of most nutrition policy and interventions.

This could be very misleading. Do we really have any sound evidence that body size and composition are intermediary variables in the linkages between intake and function? Do we even have clear evidence that deviation in anthropometry will necessarily accompany a deviation in function? I think that the answer to both questions has to be no.

A model of the relationships could be as portrayed in figure 25-1 without interdependence of pathways. This model suggests that food intake may relate to activity or to immunologic competence or to other functional outcomes in a manner that does not involve intermediary change in anthropometric status. By the same token, it suggests that anthropometric status may differ without implying that other functions are affected.

The existing evidence suggests that in the presence of major deviations in anthropometry toward the low side, many other functions are compromised. These are the studies that give rise to the assertion that severe malnutrition has measurable functional effects. However, evidence also exists that food intake has effects on functions that are not associated with changes in anthropometry.

When we see major deviations from expected body weight, it is reasonable to accept that a nutritional variable is involved. It is fair to describe a child with abnormally low weight for height or weight for age as probably undernourished or malnourished. It is also reasonable to suggest that when morbidity and mortality correlate with this very low weight status, an association between malnutrition and disease exists. I do not challenge this conclusion.

Figure 25-1. *Components of the Energy Balance Equation*

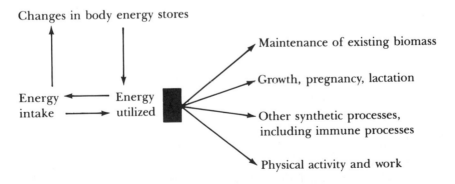

Source: Based on Beaton (1983).

Chen and his colleagues (Chen, Chowdhury, and Huffman 1980, 1981) demonstrated the predictive relationship between depressed anthropometric status in young children and mortality. Their data showed that children who were severely malnourished according to all anthropometric indices experienced markedly higher mortality risk, whereas normally nourished and mildly and moderately malnourished children all experienced lower but similar risks. However, in a subsequent note, Chen (1982) took issue with the manner in which some had interpreted these findings. He noted that the original intent was to ask whether anthropometric criteria could be used to identify children at risk of death, not to define malnutrition. He noted also that although normal, mild, and moderate malnutrition classifications did not offer differential predictions of mortality, the mortality rates in these children were approximately ten times higher than those among more privileged children in both rich and poor countries (Chen, Rahman, and Sarder 1980).

Chandra (1983) has repeatedly made the point that much less severe depressions of anthropometric indices than suggested above are associated with disturbances of the immune system, although how these relate to either susceptibility or response to infection is not entirely clear. Chen (1982) points out that at least one role of "nutrition" may be to ameliorate the debilitating effects of infection or, phrased another way, to facilitate the recovery from infection and to foster "catch-up growth" between periods of infection. Martorell, Klein, and Delgado (1980) make the additional point that food intake is depressed by disease, further confounding the situation.

What about the other outcomes of undernutrition? Are these necessarily mediated through, or even indicated by, anthropometric status? In the realm of physical activity, we have evidence that the relationship between intake and activity can be independent from that between intake and anthropometry.

Rutishauser and Whitehead (1972) described a Ugandan child population in which physical growth rates had been maintained at reasonable levels in the face of apparently low food intakes. Further examination of the community suggested that one way in which the children had achieved this was by a very low level of active play. Chavez and colleagues (Chavez and Martinez 1975, 1983; Chavez and others 1972) demonstrated that supplementary feeding increased physical movement among children in a Mexican community. It has been reported anecdotally that a common finding in food distribution programs is that the children become a nuisance, implying perhaps that they exhibit increased and socially atypical patterns of physical activity, even though these same programs may have minimal effects on anthropometric indices (see Beaton and Ghassemi in part V).

Viteri and Torun (1981) reported a series of studies of children that strongly suggested an additional and potentially important relationship. Reduced physical activity was a response to reduced food intake in keeping with the other studies cited. However, physical activity level, independent of food intake, seemed to have an important influence on height. This suggests that in some cases, physical activity may be an intervening variable between intake and anthropometry.

While the above studies are only suggestive, they do raise the possibility that we may be misled by thinking of anthropometry as the intervening variable between dietary intake and functional effect, or in accepting too literally the various anthropometric criteria and the designations normal, mild, moderate, and severe malnutrition as descriptors of nutritional status rather than, at most, indicators of one dimension of nutritional status.

We must also recognize that if variation in physical activity is part of the mechanism of adjustment of energy balance, it can lead to other effects, as suggested in figure 25-2. Thus, for example, if it is valid to assume that a child's cognitive development is influenced by interaction with its physical and human environment, two distinct paths of effects are possible. The child's energy intake and activity are associated; his or her activity level affects the child's exploratory behavior and that aspect of environmental interaction. This is a potential direct pathway of effect. The second pathway is indirect. The energy intake of the child's caretaker associates with the activity level of the caretaker; in turn this influences the caretaker's response to the child's signals and thus influences the interaction between child and environment. Similar examples might be hypothesized about other aspects of childcare, such as sanitation and care during illness.

Although researchers have studied the relationship between intake and functional activity measured as "productivity" in a narrow economic sense, results have suggested that supplementary feeding has little or no operational significance unless the original level of deprivation was severe. Rather, incentives for production seem to have more influence, albeit carrying with them a need for additional food. However, studies to date have not included systematic examination of the levels of "nonwork" activities that associate with changes in intake, nor has there been adequate consideration of the potential significance of these activities, sometimes termed "discretionary activities" (UNU 1981).

The FAO/WHO (1973) report on energy requirements recognized the inherent issue. The report cautioned that while activity was customarily classified in terms of occupations, a major variable might be what people did when they were not working. The issue was raised again in a review of that report. The reviewers expressed concern about the

Figure 25-2. *Some Functional Implications of the Energy Balance Equation*

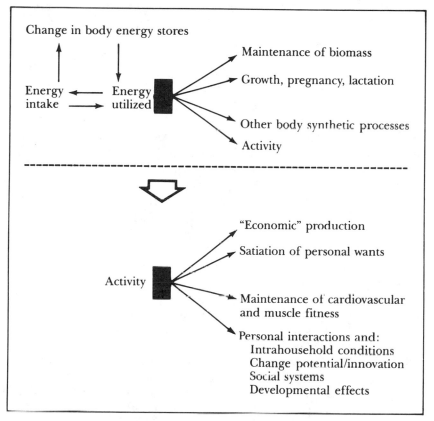

Source: Based on Beaton (1983).

dangers of accepting low levels of energy intake that might be achieved by reduction in physical activity (FAO/WHO 1975). A UNU workshop (1981) emphasized this point and urged that nutritionists recognize the importance of "discretionary activity." Recognition of this factor is also reflected in a recent report on energy and protein requirements (FAO/WHO/UNU 1985).

Where does this leave us? Durnin and colleagues suggested that these uncertainties meant simply that we cannot describe human energy requirements (Durnin and others 1973). I believe that we can describe human energy requirements, but that we must first answer the question, requirements for what? As a starting point, I suggest that we view energy requirement as the level of energy intake and expenditure at which a balance is established. In itself such a view makes no assumption about whether food intake restrains expenditure or whether external influences of society establish expenditure levels that in turn limit intake. Rather, it addresses the overall level and its functional significance.

Consider what we have learned from recent studies and the focus of current debate at the international level. At the level of populations, if we set aside the famine areas and the natural or man-made disasters, it is clear that existing populations are in some sense in energy balance. If we accept maintenance of energy balance as a criterion of requirement, then we must conclude that all populations are currently meeting their energy requirements. Certainly within populations there are individuals who do not manage to maintain long-term energy balance and who die of protein-energy malnutrition or starvation. However, the number of such individuals is small in comparison to the usual estimates of the size of the nutrition problem (see table 24-1 in Latham, part V). If severe malnutrition leading to death is the problem that concerns us, then we would be well advised, as many advocate, to focus upon those individuals with treatment and specific intervention programs.

But are we really prepared to say that being in energy balance means that these populations are healthy in the sense that the energy flux is at an appropriate level? Let me cite two examples of contrasting situations to make my point.

Reported energy intakes in North America are below the FAO/WHO (1973) or FAO/WHO/UNU (1985) requirement estimates, and even below intakes reported for some developing countries. Yet few would say these populations, with their high prevalence of obesity, are undernourished. This would seem to be a sound criticism of our present mode of thinking about requirements. However, most nutritionists would agree that these populations are underactive and that this underactivity carries an associated risk to health. The FAO/WHO/UNU (1985) report makes that suggestion. It states that the North American population has established energy equilibrium at a level below that required for good health and, hence, good function.

For my second example, I draw upon recent studies of pregnant and lactating women conducted in The Gambia. In The Gambia, women can exist on very low intakes of food and can produce viable infants and nourish these infants adequately at the breast. At three months of age, the infants' weights are reasonable, albeit a bit low by British standards (Prentice 1983; Prentice and others 1981). At one season of the year, the women's food intake was reduced still further, and depression of birth weight was seen. However, subsequently, when food intake improved, these infants were nursed at a level that permitted a higher growth rate. There was no evidence of a progressive loss of maternal weight across successive pregnancies. The provision of supplemental food did not appear to influence either the mothers' or infants' anthropometry (Whitehead 1983). A reasonable conclusion is that the women maintained long-term energy balance. There was no suggestion that this was achieved by less participation in agricultural work. While one may challenge the estimates of food intake, as they were not validated by estimates of energy expenditure, it is difficult to challenge the conclusion that these women achieved energy balance on intakes well below current requirement estimates (Beaton 1983). Again we are faced with published requirement estimates that seem too high.

However, after using these data to demonstrate that Gambian women may be typical of many people living in developing countries in making more efficient use of their energy intake, Prentice (1983) concluded that although it may be possible to survive on much lower intakes than considered possible hitherto, such dietary conditions are almost certainly not compatible with optimum quality of life. Speaking of the same women, Whitehead (1983) reported that the first reason given by pregnant and lactating mothers for the popularity of the supplement was that it gave them "power" for work. On another occasion, Whitehead reported that the supplemented women sang while they worked. Are these suggestions of effects of food intake on affective behavior? Are they hints that there are other effects, lying in the social domain, that we have failed to measure in our studies? Can we really say that in these women the level of intake that is sufficient to maintain energy *balance* meets their energy *requirement*?

The question, energy requirement for what, emerges as the core issue in a comparative examination of different approaches to estimates of the magnitude of the nutrition problem. It is also the core issue that must be faced in designing nutrition interventions. It is much more than a methodological question.

If we accept that our task is to define a level of intake and expenditure at which both energy balance and optimum health are achieved and to define the functional consequences of deviation from that level, then the basis for much of the current controversy over energy in human nutrition becomes clearer. The issues we now face combine the domains of biological and psychosocial sciences. Although physiologists will help to find the answers, only a multidisciplinary approach to understanding energy requirements will suffice in the future. It is this new perspective on energy balance and its functional dimensions that has driven the design of the USAID-funded Collaborative Research Support Program on Nutrition and Function (Nutrition CRSP), which is administratively based at the Berkeley campus of

the University of California and involves several U.S. institutions and
collaborating national institutions in the Arab Republic of Egypt,
Kenya, and Mexico.

What is at risk? What is the import of an improved understanding?
I suggest that at least one thing at risk is the definition of our goals for
development! Depending upon how we choose to interpret and extend the Atwater energy balance equation, we are likely to conclude
either that there are major problems in meeting energy requirements
in virtually all countries, developed and developing, or that there are
relatively few people who do not meet their energy needs.

26

Interactions of Malnutrition and Diarrhea: A Review of Research

Joanne Leslie

Nutritionists and non-nutritionists alike have had little difficulty in recognizing the importance of lack of food as a determinant of malnutrition, although controversy remains about the relative importance of specific nutrients, particularly their effect on the growth and development of children (see Latham in part V). In contrast, the role of infectious diseases, particularly diarrhea, as a cause of malnutrition is as important as inadequate food but has been less widely recognized, particularly outside the public health and nutrition community.

The mechanisms by which infectious disease may directly cause malnutrition can be summarized as follows: (a) nutrient consumption is reduced due to loss of appetite and/or vomiting; (b) nutrient absorption is reduced due to mucosal damage, impaired production of digestive enzymes, and rapid transit through the gut (especially true of infectious diarrheas); and (c) nutrient wastage occurs due to fever and other metabolic processes. At the same time, malnutrition may impair one or more aspects of the immune system, thus increasing the risk of infection or the severity and duration of the illness once it has begun.

The relationship between malnutrition and infectious disease in general and diarrhea in particular has been the focus of investigation throughout the developing world for the past 20 years. By now sufficient evidence has accumulated to allow us to draw some conclusions with reasonable confidence. This brief review of the research addresses three issues. It looks first at the nature and strength of the evidence that malnutrition and diarrhea are associated in developing countries, at least among the substantial majority of the population

Revised and updated from "Child Malnutrition and Diarrhea: A Longitudinal Study from Northeast Brazil," D.Sc. thesis (Johns Hopkins School of Hygiene and Public Health, 1982), chapter 2.

who live in poverty. Next, it considers the evidence that diarrhea is a direct cause of malnutrition. Finally, it considers the effect of malnutrition on the incidence and duration of diarrhea. The review is intended both to establish the public health significance of the interaction between diarrhea and malnutrition and to suggest how an understanding of this interaction can contribute to a broad-based strategy to reduce malnutrition. Readers interested in a more detailed discussion of the issues should refer to Martorell and Ho (1984) and Chen and Scrimshaw (1983).

Establishing the Association

One of the earliest field studies specifically designed to study the relationship between infections and malnutrition was undertaken in the Punjab region of India in the late 1950s (Gordon and others 1963). The researchers gathered data during a four-year period on all children born in the study area. They visited participating households monthly to determine illness history and diet but did not make any anthropometric measurements. The study concluded that, irrespective of age, weaning increased a child's risk of diarrhea. One particularly interesting finding was that children receiving breast milk plus other milk had diarrhea rates intermediate between those of children exclusively breastfed and those who were fed with other milk plus solid foods. (These and similar findings have led to the current emphasis on the importance of breastfeeding in protecting children's health in developing countries.)

An associated group of researchers in Guatemala undertook a parallel study between 1958 and 1964 and found the same strong association between weaning and diarrhea (Gordon and others 1964). In Guatemala, mothers introduced supplementary foods at a later age and completed weaning at a later age. Diarrhea attack rates were somewhat higher than in the Punjab but, perhaps because the children were older, death rates from diarrhea were lower. In the Guatemala study, researchers obtained data on the children's nutritional status as well as on their diet and found that the more malnourished children, using weight for age as a measure, had more diarrhea.

Based on these pioneering field studies in India and Guatemala, and drawing in addition on extensive laboratory and clinical research, in the late 1960s WHO published a monograph entitled *Interactions of Nutrition and Infection* (Scrimshaw, Taylor, and Gordon 1968). This publication served not only to document the scientific understanding up to that time of the synergistic relationship between malnutrition and infectious disease but also to bring this important issue for the first time to the attention of a broad range of researchers and policymakers working in developing countries.

Since the publication of the WHO monograph, research to clarify further the complex relationship between malnutrition and infectious disease has progressed along two main lines. The first has concentrated on exploring the physiological mechanisms by which malnutrition can cause increased susceptibility to infection or increased severity of disease, and the mechanisms by which infectious diseases cause malnutrition. A substantial body of literature now exists based primarily on animal research and hospital (metabolic ward) studies of human populations. The studies define the precise effects of malnutrition on different components of the immune system and describe the effects of infection on the absorption, use, and retention of specific nutrients (see, for example, Taylor and others 1979).

A second line of research has involved field studies to establish the public health significance of the interaction between infectious disease and malnutrition. Because diarrhea is the most prevalent infectious disease, at least among those who are at highest risk of malnutrition—preschool children—field studies have focused on the relationship between diarrhea and malnutrition.

Table 26-1 summarizes the findings of nine field studies that gathered cross-sectional data on both nutritional status and diarrheal disease among children and analyzed the relationship between these two variables. Without exception, the nine studies found a significant negative association between diarrhea and nutritional status. Four of the studies (Leslie and others 1981; Binns 1976; Adelman 1975; Cravioto and others 1967) reported information concerning infectious diseases other than diarrhea. Three found either no association between other diseases and malnutrition or a much weaker association. Binns, however, found an even stronger association between low weight for age and pneumonia than between low weight for age and diarrhea.

In addition to the studies summarized in table 26-1, several researchers from developing countries have investigated the seasonal patterns of malnutrition and illness in developing countries and have frequently found that where there are distinct seasonal peaks, both malnutrition and diarrhea increase at the same time of year. In one of the earliest of these investigations, a clinic-based study of children under three years old in Uganda, researchers found that clinic attendance was higher during the rainy season, with attendance reaching a peak toward the end of the rainy season (Poskitt 1972). The researchers calculated the rates of measles, malaria, lower respiratory tract infections, severe diarrhea, and kwashiorkor for each four-week period during the two years and found that the rates were highest toward the end of the rainy season, with the peak incidence of

Table 26-1. *Summary of Findings from Cross-Sectional Field Studies of the Relation between Malnutrition and Diarrhea*

Location	Sample	Nutritional status measure	Diarrhea measure	Method of analysis	Main findings	Reference
Four villages, Guatemalan highlands, 1964	179 Mayan Indian children 0–4 years	Weight/age (Gomez categories)	Number of episodes and severity, based on semimonthly household interviews	Cross-tabulation	Diarrheal attack rates increased progressively with degree of malnutrition for the sample as a whole and for each one-year age group. Severity was also associated with poorer nutritional status	Gordon and others (1964)
Village, central Guatemala, 1963–64	84 children followed from birth to 6 months. Selection was all live births during a nineteen-month period	Monthly weight gain	Percentage of days ill with diarrhea, based on semimonthly household interviews	Cross-tabulation (Chi square test of statistical significance)	Higher rate of weight gain was significantly associated with lower percentage of days ill with diarrhea	Cravioto and others (1967)
Candelaria, Colombia (semiurban), 1963–64	721 children 0–72 months, from random sample of Candelaria households	Weight/age	Presence or absence of diarrhea during prior week, based on interviews with mothers	Cross-tabulation (Chi square test of statistical significance)	Prevalence of diarrhea was significantly associated with poorer nutritional status	Wray and Aguirre (1969)
Council Housing, Capetown, South Africa, 1965	114 children 3 months to 3 years from a stratified sample of households from four income groups	Weight/age	Number of episodes and duration, based on weekly household interviews	Cross-tabulation	Percentage of children with recurrent diarrhea increased progressively with degree of malnutrition except in the lowest income group, where all children had high diarrhea rates	Wittman and others (1967)

Location, Year	Sample	Anthropometric measure	Measure of diarrhea	Statistical method	Results	Reference
Papua New Guinea, early 1970s	630 children 1–4 years, 30 children from each of twenty-one randomly chosen maternal and child health clinics	Weight/age	Number of episodes during past month, based on interviews with mothers	Cross-tabulation (Chi square test of statistical significance)	Significantly more episodes of diarrhea in the subsequent month were found among malnourished children	Binns (1976)
Kinshasa, Zaire, 1974	4,391 children aged 6 months to 4 years randomly chosen from those attending mobile vaccination clinics	Weight/age	Number of past episodes of diarrhea, based on interviews with mothers	Correlation and regression analysis	Children for whom past diarrhea was reported were significantly more malnourished than others (both nonweaned and weaned children)	Adelman (1975)
Etimesgut District, Turkey, 1975–76	1,237 children 0–4 years	Weight/age	Number of episodes, based on mothers reporting diarrhea and on monthly home visits by mid-wives	Cross-tabulation (Chi square test of statistical significance)	Significantly more episodes of diarrhea were found among malnourished children	Egeman and Bertran (1980)
Terai, Nepal, 1977–78	Two surveys of 341 children 6–72 months from a random sample of households in twelve panchayats	Height/age, weight/height (Waterlow categories)	Presence or absence of current diarrhea or diarrhea in past month, based on interviews with mothers	Cross-tabulation (Student's t test of statistical significance)	First survey found low weight for height and low height for age significantly associated with both more current and past diarrhea. Second survey found significant association only between low weight for height and current diarrhea	Leslie and others (1981)
Four regions, El Salvador, 1978	Two surveys of 3,600 children 6–59 months selected by a two-state cluster sampling procedure	Weight/age, height/age, weight/height, and arm circumference	Number of episodes of diarrhea during the preceding week, based on interviews with parents or guardians	Cross-tabulation	Significant association was found between diarrhea and low weight for height, low weight for age, and low arm circumference. No significant association between diarrhea and low height for age was found	Steler and others (1981)

kwashiorkor occurring about a month after the peak incidence of infectious diseases. Since this was not the period of greatest food scarcity, the study attributed the kwashiorkor directly to the effect of repeated episodes of infectious disease.

A later study undertaken in El Salvador in 1975 and 1976 compared seasonal variation in malnutrition based on an anthropometric survey with seasonal patterns of diarrhea established by health clinic records (Trowbridge and Newton 1979). Researchers found that both malnutrition and diarrhea were most prevalent in the summer.

Another study in Bangladesh used a similar combination of field-based anthropometric data on mothers and children and clinical data on diarrhea—in this case, diarrheal admissions to the Cholera Research Laboratory of the Matlab Hospital (Chen and others 1979). As in Uganda, this study found that September, the rainy season, was the peak month for diarrheal admissions to the hospital and that actual weight losses among both mothers and children also occurred during September.

The studies reviewed so far have confirmed a strong association between malnutrition and infectious disease, particularly diarrhea, across a broad range of cultural and ecological settings. However, the cross-sectional nature of the data leaves the studies open to several different interpretations: infection (especially diarrhea) causes malnutrition, malnutrition makes children more susceptible to infectious diseases, or both infectious diseases and malnutrition are due to some third factor, such as poverty or lack of health care. To allocate scarce resources optimally, government health officials need to know under what circumstances and with how much strength each of these causal factors is operating.

Diarrhea as a Cause of Malnutrition

Several investigators, aware of the difficulty of establishing causality from cross-sectional data, have undertaken prospective studies that included measurement of both nutritional status and disease. Table 26-2 summarizes the findings from seven prospective longitudinal field studies undertaken to determine the extent to which infectious disease, particularly diarrhea, is a cause of child malnutrition in low-income communities of the developing world. Each of the studies used statistical controls to separate the effect of illness from other factors such as age, sex, and sociodemographic variables.

A reasonably consistent pattern of prior diarrhea relating negatively to subsequent nutritional status emerges from these seven studies. In addition to diarrhea, all of the studies considered other illnesses, usually fever and/or respiratory illnesses. Most found that diarrhea was the only illness to have a significant negative effect on growth, although De Sweemer's (1973) research in India found a significant negative effect of total illness days on child growth, and Leslie's (1982) research in Brazil found respiratory illness to have as strong an effect as diarrhea on short-term weight loss.

Although it is difficult to compare the magnitude of the effects reported by the studies in table 26-2, the results suggest that children in the preschool years who have high rates of diarrhea may gain, on average, one-third of a kilo less per year than they would otherwise have gained. During the preschool years, expected weight gain is about 2 kilos per year (after the first year), so this represents a potential loss of 17 percent of expected weight gain each year. Although the evidence on height is even more limited, the studies suggest significant effects, in the range of 4 to 6 centimeters less growth, during the preschool years due to diarrhea.

It seems inevitable that a high prevalence of diarrhea will continue in most poor communities of the developing world for at least some time to come. However, partial reductions may be possible with provision of plentiful water and sanitary facilities, with education to encourage longer breastfeeding (in areas where supplementary food is introduced excessively early), and with more hygienic feeding practices (Guerrant and others 1983; Torun 1983). In addition, the negative effects of diarrhea on nutritional status may be significantly reduced by improved feeding practices. Studies suggest that during the acute phase of the illness, even when food is not purposely withheld from children, their intake will be reduced about 30 percent (Molla and others 1983). However, during the convalescent period, appetite rapidly returns to normal, even supranormal, levels, and evidence exists that provision of an adequate diet for catch-up growth during recuperation from an episode of diarrhea or other infectious diseases may be a key factor in alleviating child malnutrition. Whitehead (1977), from The Gambia and Uganda, and Rohde (1978), from Indonesia, cite findings to show that given adequate food, children are capable of catch-up growth following illness at least five to seven times the normal rates. Rohde and others (1983), in a paper on therapeutic interventions in diarrhea, suggest that if possible, food intakes should be increased 25 to 50 percent above recommended daily allowances during a period two to four times the duration of the illness.

Malnutrition as a Risk Factor for Diarrhea

Among those working in public health in developing countries there is considerable concern that malnutrition may increase a child's risk of getting an infectious disease or may increase the duration or

Table 26-2. Summary of Findings from Longitudinal Field Studies of Diarrhea as a Determinant of Malnutrition

Location	Sample	Nutritional status measure	Diarrhea measure	Method of analysis	Main findings	Reference
Santa Maria Cauque (highland village, Guatemala), 1964–73	45 children 0–3 years representing about half of all children born during 1964–66, selected on the basis of maternal cooperation	Weight growth based on weekly weighings during first year and weighings every four weeks during second and third years	Rates of infection for specific pathogens and percentage of days ill with diarrhea, based on weekly fecal exams	Cross-tabulation and step-wise regression analysis	Diarrheal disease was not a significant determinant of weight growth during the first year of life. During the second and third years, rates of infection with some specific pathogens were significantly negatively associated with weight growth	Mata (1978)
Narangwal, Punjab, North India (rural), 1968–70	494 children 0–35 months from villages chosen as representative of rural Punjab	Weight increments, weight/age, height/age, and weight/height, based on anthropometric measurements made monthly or every three months depending on age	Days ill from gastrointestinal complaints, based on weekly home visits	Analysis of variance	Prior diarrhea was significantly negatively related to weight/age, height/age, and weight/height. The relation between diarrhea and weight increments was mixed	De Sweemer (1973)

Location	Sample	Measures	Illness measure	Analysis method	Findings	Reference
Rural community, southwestern Mexico, 1968–73	276 children 0–3 years representing 85 percent of a thirteen-month birth cohort	Twelve-month weight and height increments, based on monthly height measures and bi-weekly weight measures	Percentage of days ill based on illness histories taken every two weeks	Analysis of variance	Diarrhea had a significant negative effect on weight increments but not on height increments. The cumulative reduction in weight gain over the three years was, on average, 0.72 kilograms	Condon-Paolini and others (1977)
Four villages, eastern Guatemala, 1970–72	716 children 15 days to 7 years, representing all households with appropriate-age children in the four villages	Semestral and yearly length and weight increments	Percentage of days ill with diarrhea, based on fourteen-day interviews with the mothers in the home	Analysis of variance	Both length and weight increments were significantly negatively affected by diarrhea. The cumulative growth difference over the entire age range between those with high- and low-frequency diarrhea was 3.5 centimeters and 1.5 kilograms	Martorell and others (1975)
Candelaria, Colombia, (semiurban), 1970–74	1,270 children 0–6 years from all households with appropriate-age children in the catchment area of the *promotora* program	Weight/age, height/age, and weight/height, based on bimonthly measures of height and weight made at home visits by *promotoras*	Occurrence of an episode of severe or mild diarrhea during preceding period, based on bimonthly home visits	Multiple regression analysis	An episode of severe diarrhea was found to have a significant negative effect on height/age but no effect on weight/height, and a positive effect on weight/height during the first year. An episode of severe diarrhea was found to have a significant negative effect on weight/height and weight/age after age 1 but no significant effect on height/age. No effect of a mild episode of diarrhea was found	Heller and Drake (1976)

(Table continues on the following page.)

Table 26-2 (*continued*)

Location	Sample	Nutritional status measure	Diarrhea measure	Method of analysis	Main findings	Reference
Kenaba, The Gambia, 1977, and Namulonge, Uganda, 1974–75	152 children from Kenaba and 45 from Namulonge 0–3 years who regularly attended village maternity and child health clinics	Weight gain, based on monthly weighings made at routine clinic visits	Percentage of days ill with gastroenteritis for Kenaba; number of episodes during the interval for Namulonge	Multiple regression analysis	In both communities gastrointestinal disease had a highly significant effect on weight gain. Gastrointestinal disease was associated with an average loss of 100 grams of weight gain and 0.5 centimeters of height gain per child per month in Kenaba and an average loss of 14 grams of weight gain per child per month in Nemulonge	Cole and Parkin (1977)
Pactuba (semiurban community, northeast Brazil), 1978–80	174 children 0–12 years from fifty randomly selected households representing three socio-economic levels	Weight/age, height/age, weight/height, and arm circumference/age, based on measurements made every three months over 2.5 years	Number of episodes and percentage of days with diarrhea for each three-month period over 2.5 years	Multiple regression analysis	Controlling for age and socio-economic status, diarrhea during preceding months had a significant negative effect on all measures of nutritional status of children 0–5 years except weight/height, and when nutritional status at the beginning of the period was controlled, significant effects on height/age and arm circumference/age were found. No significant effects were found for children 6–12 years	Leslie (1982)

severity of the illness. This is partially due to the finding of higher death rates among malnourished children. A study in Bangladesh of children aged one to nine years found that poorer nutritional status significantly increased the risk of mortality during the subsequent 18 months (Sommer and Loewenstein 1975). Although the Bangladesh study found a steadily increasing risk of death with poorer nutritional status, a study in Narangwal, India (Kielmann and McCord 1978), found the risk of death among children was primarily increased for those most severely malnourished (less than 70 percent of weight for age). A later study from Bangladesh also found a higher risk of mortality only for the children in the most severely malnourished category (Chen, Chowdhury, and Huffman 1980).

However, the evidence that the risk of morbidity also increases due to malnutrition is less clear. Table 26-3 summarizes eight longitudinal field studies that have examined the incidence or severity of diarrhea by nutritional status. Wray's (1978) documentation of an unanticipated decline in rates of diarrhea during a one-year nutrition rehabilitation program in Candelaria, Colombia, is sometimes cited as evidence that nutritional status is a determinant of incidence of diarrhea. Wray himself, however, does not go this far in his conclusions, in part because the study was not designed to examine this effect and therefore diagnosis of diarrhea may have been somewhat inconsistent.

All the other studies in table 26-3 were designed specifically to measure the relationship between nutritional status and subsequent diarrhea. Most looked only at incidence, but some measured duration and/or severity as well. Five of the seven studies found some evidence of a greater incidence of diarrhea among the more malnourished children, although usually only for some age groups or for some nutrition status measures. Two studies found no difference in diarrheal incidence by nutritional status. However, all three studies that measured duration found that length of time ill with diarrhea was consistently and significantly greater among the more malnourished children. Indeed, a recent review by Sahni and Chandra (1983) concludes that the most prominent effect of malnutrition on infectious diseases in general is on duration and severity rather than on incidence.

Conclusion

It has become standard for a review of research to conclude with a recommendation for further research, and it will be clear to the careful reader that many interesting questions remain to be answered about the interaction of malnutrition and diarrhea. One such ques-

Table 26-3. *Summary of Findings from Longitudinal Field Studies of Malnutrition as a Risk Factor for Diarrhea*

Location	Sample	Nutritional status measure	Diarrhea measure	Method of analysis	Main findings	Reference
Candelaria, Colombia (semiurban), 1963–64	182 children under 6 years of age: regular attenders out of 413 malnourished children registered in a one-year nutritional program	Weight/age categories, based on monthly weights at nutritional rehabilitation center	Number of episodes of diarrhea, based on weekly interviews with mothers at the nutritional rehabilitation center	Cross-tabulation	Nutritional status of the children improved significantly during the year of rehabilitation, and number of episodes of diarrhea declined significantly	Wray (1978)
Low-income suburbs, San José, Costa Rica, 1966–67	137 children under 5 years selected randomly from five low-income suburbs	Malnourished (less than 75 percent weight/age) or normal weight, based on baseline anthropometric survey	Number of episodes of diarrhea, duration, and hospitalization for diarrhea, based on weekly home interview with mother	Cross-tabulation	Number of episodes was significantly greater for initially malnourished children for those 36 months or older. Duration of diarrhea was longer in all malnourished groups except those under 1 year	James (1972)
Narangwal, Punjab, north India (rural), 1968–70	494 children 0–35 months from thirteen villages chosen as representative of rural Punjab	Weight increments, weight/age, height/age, and weight/height, based on anthropometric measurements made monthly, bimonthly, or every three months, depending on age	Days ill from gastrointestinal complaints, based on weekly home visits	Analysis of variance	For some age groups lower weight/age, lower weight/height, and smaller weight increments were significantly related to greater gastrointestinal illness in the subsequent period; effects were stronger for illness during the total period than during a three- or six-month period and for children below 9 months of age	De Sweemer (1973)

366

Location and date	Sample	Nutritional measure	Diarrhea measure	Analysis	Findings	Reference
Candelaria, Colombia (semiurban), 1970–74	1,270 children 0–6 years from all households with appropriate-age children in the catchment area of the *promotora* program	Weight/age, height/age, and weight/height, based on bimonthly measures of height and weight made at home visits by *promotoras*	Occurrence of an episode of severe or mild diarrhea during subsequent period, based on bimonthly home visits	Multiple regression analysis (logit specification)	Children with low height/age were more likely to have diarrhea (both mild and severe) in the subsequent period, but children with low weight/height were only at risk for higher rates of severe diarrhea for the 6–24-month age group	Heller and Drake (1976)
Kirkos, Addis Ababa, Ethiopia, 1972–73	749 children under 12 years	Below or above 90 percent of Harvard median weight/age, based on fortnightly home visits	Proportion of home visits on which child was reported to have gastroenteritis, based on fortnightly home visits	AIT analysis	For children less than 60 months, low weight/age was an important predictor of higher subsequent rates of gastroenteritis, but no relation was found for older children	Freij and Wall (1977)
Matlab Thana, Comilla District, Bangladesh, 1978–79	207 children 0–4 years selected from households in six villages	Weight/age and monthly weight gain, based on monthly weighing at home visits	Number of episodes of diarrhea during the year, based on weekly visits to the household	Cross-tabulation	No significant difference in subsequent diarrhea attack rates was found on the basis of weight/age at the beginning of the study year, nor was any relation found between weight gain during one four-week period and diarrhea during the following period	Chen, Huq, and Huffman (1981)

(Table continues on the following page.)

Table 26-3 *(continued)*

Location	Sample	Nutritional status measure	Diarrhea measure	Method of analysis	Main findings	Reference
Malunfashi village area, northern Nigeria, 1979	343 children 6–32 months selected randomly from demographic enumeration by Endemic Diseases Research Unit	Weight/age, height/ age, and weight/ height, based on baseline measurements	Diarrhea attack rate, percentage of time with diarrhea	Cross-tabulation	Only weight/height was significantly negatively associated with diarrheal attack rate, but percentage of time with diarrhea was significantly greater for malnourished children by all three measures	Tomkins (1981)
Two villages, Matlab field research area of the ICDDR, Bangladesh, 1978–79	125 children under 24 months (approximately 95 percent of age cohort)	Weight/length, weight/age, and length/age at the beginning of each 60-day period, based on monthly measurements made over one year	Duration, incidence, and etiology of diarrhea during 60-day periods over one year	Cross-tabulation and analysis of variance	Children with low weight/length had longer durations of diarrhea than better-nourished children; however, children of differing nutritional status had similar diarrhea incidences. The duration of diarrhea caused by *Ecoli* was more strongly affected by nutritional status than was diarrhea due to shigella	Black and others (1984)

tion would be, does the effect of diarrhea on nutritional status and of malnutrition on susceptibility to disease vary significantly for diarrheal illness caused by different pathogens? The Black and others (1984) study from Bangladesh suggests that this is the case. Another question would be, are there differences between the effects of chronic and acute diarrhea on nutritional status? However useful further research will be, there have been enough studies since the publication of the WHO monograph (Scrimshaw, Taylor, and Gordon 1968), and the findings have been sufficiently consistent to allow some conclusions to be drawn and the implications of these conclusions for food and nutrition planning to be assessed.

First, we can conclude that high prevalences of malnutrition and of infections are found in the same communities, not only because both are a result of poverty, ignorance, and lack of health services, but also because each is to some extent a direct cause of the other. In addition, among infectious diseases, diarrhea is particularly strongly associated with malnutrition, in part because diarrhea is so widespread and in part because it has the greatest direct effect on the intake and use of food. We have seen that diarrhea is consistently found to have a significant negative effect on child growth, accounting for substantial height and weight deficits among preschool children. As far as the other direction of causality is concerned, we find that the major effect of malnutrition on diarrhea is to increase the duration and possibly the severity of the illness. Although there may also be some relationship between malnutrition and diarrheal incidence, the research results so far are contradictory on this effect.

An understanding of the important interactions between malnutrition and diarrhea has implications for food and nutrition planning at all levels, from the national to the household. It is standard, for example, to estimate unavoidable food losses when calculating national food requirements. In addition to losses that occur during harvesting, transportation, and storage, losses due to human diseases, particularly diarrhea, should also be estimated and taken into consideration. Similarly, the need for an adequate quantity and quality of food to allow catch-up growth during recovery from diarrhea potentially creates peaks in food requirements that need to be considered along with seasonal availability and seasonal variability in activity levels. Also, if infectious diseases, such as diarrhea, are particularly prevalent in certain regions of a country, the population there should be considered at greater risk of malnutrition and perhaps interventions should be targeted accordingly.

At the community and household levels, recognition of the interaction of malnutrition and diarrhea has implications for the design of interventions. Since breast milk not only provides a nutritionally appropriate and hygienic food but also carries maternal antibodies that protect infants against the specific infections in their community, promotion of breastfeeding can be expected to directly and indirectly reduce both malnutrition and diarrhea. Education about weaning foods and weaning practices should consider not only the nutritional requirements of the weaning-age child, but also the fact that contaminated weaning foods are frequently the source of diarrheal infections. Oral rehydration therapy for the treatment of diarrhea should be combined with nutritional therapy; both can be done by mothers in the home if they are carefully instructed. If this is done, it will be possible to prevent not only much of the mortality but also much of the malnutrition that currently results from diarrhea.

The fact that there are important causal links between malnutrition and infection provides an additional compelling reason for health planners and food and nutrition planners to work closely together. Combined efforts to improve nutritional status and to reduce the incidence of infectious disease, particularly diarrhea, can be expected to reinforce each other and to produce more improvement in child health and survival than the same amount of money invested in just one effort or the other.

27

Women's Activities and Impacts on Child Nutrition

Sandra L. Huffman

Attempts to improve the nutritional status of children in developing countries have tended to focus on the direct causes of malnutrition: declining rates of breastfeeding, inadequate complementary feeding, and high rates of infection. These problems occur because of poverty and inadequate childcare practices. Although nutritionists have acknowledged the impact of poverty, they have generally assumed that inadequate childcare practices are due to mothers' limited knowledge. While this may be part of the explanation, the competing demands on the poor mother's time that prevent appropriate childcare have not been generally acknowledged. Since the mother has the primary responsibility for childcare, an understanding of her competing roles in providing food for the family, in allocating resources within the family, and in having the time available to provide adequate childcare is paramount to understanding why children become malnourished. Heavy demands on women's time due to both income-producing activities and home production activities limit the time available to prepare special food necessary for the young child, to feed the child, to care for and feed a sick child adequately, or to prevent illness in young children by, for example, good hygiene and timely immunizations.

Development experts have traditionally viewed women as part of a family unit that would automatically benefit from employment opportunities for the male heads of households. This view neglects the high proportion of households headed by females and the need for each member to contribute to the family's survival in poor households (Tinker 1979b). The traditional view also neglects the particular re-

Excerpted from the original version prepared for the Clearinghouse on Infant Feeding and Maternal Nutrition, American Public Health Association, Washington D.C., February 1985.

sponsibility of women as caretakers of children. In some cultures, control of income may be primarily in the hands of the father and increases in family income through increased wages of the father may not necessarily lead to increased food purchasing power for the mother. The woman's status within the household is an important determinant of her control over resource allocation and will affect whether she is able to spend available income on food or health care for the children.

The role of women who are single heads of households most directly affects child welfare because they are responsible for both earning income and providing childcare. Between 25 to 35 percent of households in the developing world are headed by women because of divorce, death, desertion, or long-term migration of husbands or because they were never married (Youssef and Hetler 1983; Tinker 1979a). These female-headed households are among the poorest in every country. Participation in the formal or informal labor force is essential for these women.

In addition, married women are not necessarily released from the responsibility of providing food for their children or from labor force participation. Although often undercounted in official statistics, women play a major role in the economies of developing countries, either by income production through labor force participation or by income saving through home production activities. In many countries, women participate heavily in agricultural production, and in most, women are responsible for many crop processing activities (see FAO in part II).

Africa, except for Muslim countries, has the highest proportion of economically active female labor force participation (defined as provision of labor for production of goods and services in Dixon 1982), with up to 47 percent of women in Botswana and 32 percent in Nigeria active in the labor force. Asia has the next highest level of labor force participation. India, for example, has 27 percent of its female population economically active. Caribbean countries, such as Haiti and Jamaica, whose populace is primarily of African descent, have high rates (46 percent and 26 percent), while Central America (10 percent) and South America (13 to 18 percent) have lower rates. Arab states have the lowest rates, generally around 2 to 5 percent (UNDP 1980).

These rates primarily reflect differential female participation in the agricultural labor force. Using FAO figures, in sub-Saharan Africa, 47 percent of the agricultural labor force are women, compared to 40 percent in Asia, 25 percent in North Africa and the Middle East, 19 percent in Central and South America, and 54 percent in the Caribbean. Comparisons of ILO and FAO statistics indicate that often women's agricultural participation is not counted in the official statistics for overall participation in the labor force (Dixon 1982).

Women's Time Allocation

Village-level studies conducted throughout the developing world reveal that commonly women work longer hours than men. The proportion contributed to family income is highest among poor women (UNDP 1980). Poor women are often those faced with the severest constraints on their time and limited resources for adequate child feeding and childcare.

A study of peasant households in the Sierra region in Peru found that mothers are responsible for 93 percent of agricultural processing and cooking activities, 78 percent of water collection, 58 percent of fuel gathering, and 62 percent of animal care (Deere 1983). In a Tanzanian study, women did 91 percent of the weeding and harvesting, 64 percent of the plowing and hoeing, and 79 percent of the slashing of grasslands (Tobisson 1980). Direct observations of villagers in Burkina Faso showed that women carried out 64 percent of all production and supply tasks (including food and cash crop production, food storage and processing, and water and fuel supply), 23 percent of crafts and other professional obligations, 97 percent of household tasks (childcare, cooking, and cleaning), and 23 percent of community obligations. Overall, women performed 56 percent of all work, compared to 44 percent for men (McSweeney 1979).

Researchers have studied the total time spent per day on agricultural production, income production, and home production in several countries (table 27-1). Rural women worked 10–12 hours per day on home and market production. These figures indicate the large amount of time spent on home production activities, including food processing, cooking, fuel and water gathering, and childcare, which compete with time needed for income generation and agricultural production. Often researchers discount these home production activities, but their importance to the functioning of a household is evident.

Allocation of Resources

When women spend most of their time on activities within the household, they are generally less able to provide additional food or other benefits for their children. As they gain access to cash income, they are increasingly able to allocate such income to provisions for the household.

Table 27-1. *Daily Time Allocation of Rural Women in Developing Countries*
(hours a day)

Country	Food preparation			Gathering fuel	Carrying water	Agricultural production	Childcare	Other	Total	Reference
	Processing agricultural products	Cooking	Total							
Africa										
Burkina Faso	2.2	2.2[a]	4.4	0.6	0.1	3.0	0.3	1.4	9.8	McSweeney (1979)
Tanzania	n.a.	n.a.	2.9	1.0	1.4	2.3	*	3.4	11.0	Tobisson (1980)
Tanzania	1.5	1.1	2.6	1.3	1.5	5.3	*	0.3	11.0	Omen-Myin (1981)[b]
Asia										
Bangladesh	1.3	2.2	3.5	0.4		1.6[c]	0.8	2.1	8.4	Cain and others (1979)
India	n.a.	n.a.	4.0	n.a.	n.a.	n.a.	2.0	n.a.	n.a.	Khare (1984)
Indonesia	n.a.	n.a.	4.3[a]	0.1		1.6	1.2	5.1	12.3	White (1975)
Nepal	1.0	2.0	3.0	0.5	0.7	3.7	0.1	2.8	10.8	Berio (1984)
Malaysia	n.a.	n.a.	2.6	n.a.	n.a.	1.8	4.4[d]	3.0	11.8	Da Vanzo and Lee (1983)
Philippines	n.a.	n.a.	3.4	n.a.	n.a.	2.0[c]	1.6	3.3	10.3	Ho (1979)

n.a. Not available.
* Concurrent with other activities; not reported separately.
a. Includes cleaning and washing.
b. Personal communication.
c. Other income production.
d. For women with children under two years old.

An in-depth study in Nepal illustrated that when women are confined to subsistence production on family farms, they have little influence on how resources will be allocated in the household (Acharya and Bennett 1983). When they participate in the market economy outside the village, their input into all aspects of household decision making increases. Limiting women's involvement to the domestic and subsistence sectors reduces their decision making, regardless of the total number of hours worked, their age, or their socioeconomic status. Earning a cash income, by sale of crafts, for example, allows women to contribute to the household income and enhances the perception of women as equal contributing partners. Studies in Kerala also found that participation in income generation gave women more control over its allocation. This was also true with home garden production, which led to benefits for children's nutritional status (Kumar 1978).

In most parts of Africa, women have traditionally been more involved in subsistence agricultural production, while men have taken over cash crop production. Tobisson (1980) observed that in Tanzania, women, although responsible for agricultural tasks, lacked authority to influence decision making and allocation of resources within the family. With limited access to cash, they were unable to buy additional food for their families and relied on what they produced to feed their families. Increasing use of cash wages in Tanzania has concentrated money in the hands of husbands, who have most of the land ownership rights. In 90 percent of the families studied, spending money is reserved for husbands. This study found that malnutrition is more prevalent in households that depend on wage income than when they cultivate their own crops, presumably because men do not spend the money on food as readily as women. Dey (1981) noted a similar phenomenon in The Gambia, where women are responsible for crop production and for feeding their families. If women make extra cash income through crop production, they will spend it on food, while husbands seldom spend any income they earn on food.

In a study of two villages in Cameroon, researchers found that women provided 57 percent of family cash income, mostly from the sale of their own food production, even though they earned less cash income than men (Guyer 1980). Husbands supplied only 30 percent of cash income used by women. Two-thirds of total expenditures on basic food and supplies were financed by women's self-earned income. As family income increased due to seasonal patterns of work, women spent the same proportion of income on food. Guyer suggests that women used the increased income to buy not only more food, but more expensive, higher-quality food, such as meat or fish oil.

When women participate primarily in the subsistence sector, they view attending health or nutrition activities as a luxury. Unless the time they spend away from chores can buy some visible contribution to family income, neither they nor their households will feel that their time is justified (Acharya and Bennett 1983).

To enhance women's power over resource allocation, they must be provided with cash employment. However, most women in developing countries are already overemployed, with little or no extra time available. Employment policies should therefore emphasize increasing the efficiency and economic productivity of work time. For example, an integrated rural development project in Cameroon is providing increased agricultural extension to women to develop improved cropping systems and animal husbandry methods that will raise their productivity and incomes (Scott 1979). Improved access to transportation in Kenya and Mexico has led to an increase in earnings by rural women (Kneerim 1980; Tinker and Bo-Bramsen 1976). Credit programs have led to increased income for market women in Bangladesh (Chen 1983).

For cultural reasons, production activities for women have often been focused within the household, thus giving rise to the term "cottage industries." Dixon (1978) argues that economic production should be located at a central workplace for the following social and economic reasons:

○ It allows closer supervision, more control over quality of goods, and more protection of working conditions and wages by regulating agencies.
○ It promotes economies of scale and division of labor.
○ It facilitates technological innovation.
○ It draws women out of isolation and the conservatism of the domestic environment and promotes social interaction.
○ It enhances the delivery of special training programs such as literacy, vocational training, and health and nutrition education.
○ It encourages delayed marriage and control of fertility (because of its incompatibility with the family role).

Removing production activities from the home also ensures that women are paid for economic activity directly rather than working as part of a labor unit in which the husband controls the assets.

In addition to the need to provide more economic activities for women, education of women is vital. Studies have consistently found women's education levels, independent of household income, to be positively related to child nutritional status (Ware 1984; Cochrane and others 1982). In the traditional patriarchal family, resources flow from wife to husband—a flow that is reduced when an educated wife demands more equitable treatment or is awarded it because of the way society views the educated (Caldwell 1980). With increasing maternal

education women have more power within the family to allocate resources and will use this on food allocation and other expenditures
for their children. They also are less likely to follow inappropriate
cultural taboos concerning food and are more likely to use health
facilities.

Effect on Children's Nutritional Status

When women have access to resources, generally through earning
income in the market economy, they are more likely to spend their
income on food and other needs for their children. The ultimate
concern, however, is whether children's food intake increases and
whether improvements in nutritional status result. Of special concern
is whether employment—most importantly, that outside the home—
results in improvements over and above detriments that may result
from a reduction in breastfeeding and childcare activities.

The work of Popkin and Solon (1976) in the Philippines was one of
the first studies that attempted to address this issue. In their analysis
of data from Cebu, they found that families with mothers working in
the market economy had weekly food expenditures 1 to 5 percent
higher than those without female labor force participation. Household food energy and protein intakes improved in these households,
but in the rural subsample, vitamin A intake was marginally less, and
for poor families, the rate of xerophthalmia increased among children
of mothers who worked. The authors suggest that this may indicate a
positive income effect associated with cereal and meat consumption
but not with vegetable consumption.

Popkin also analyzed data from rural households in the province of
Laguna, Philippines, and again found significantly higher energy and
protein intakes among preschool children of mothers who worked as
compared with children whose mothers did not work (Popkin 1980,
1983). (Vitamin A intake was not reported for the Laguna study.) An
earlier analysis of the relationship between mothers' work status and
child nutritional status in the Laguna data appeared to show that
mothers' work away from home was associated with significantly
poorer nutritional status among their children (Popkin 1980). However, a later, more rigorous, analysis of the same data found no
significant relationship, perhaps because the positive effect of mothers' work on children's diet and the negative effect on childcare time
cancelled each other out (Popkin 1983).

Kumar's (1978) work in Kerala found that children whose mothers
were in the labor force had significantly lower weight for age than
children whose mothers did not work, even though per capita income
was higher among families with mothers working. In families without

mothers working, increases in family wage income had no incremental benefit on the children's nutritional status. Where mothers worked, their own wages had a positive effect on the nutritional status of their children. These somewhat conflicting results appear to occur because families with working mothers were generally poorer and their children were more malnourished, but within that group mothers' incomes had a positive effect.

Haggerty's (1981) study of poor working mothers in Haiti had similar findings. Mothers working at very low wages, such as those marketing farm goods, were unable to make sufficient money to support adequate nutrition in their children. During the first year of life, children of mothers who worked at home were better nourished than other children. However, factory workers' children in the second year of life, whose mothers made more money, showed better nutritional status than children of nonworking mothers, market women, or mothers working at home. As children grow older, it appears that the income effect of working outside the home is more important than the childcare time mothers are able to provide by being at home.

Studies in Panama found that malnutrition among families was higher when a woman was the head of the household (Franklin and Vial 1981). The number of hours spent working outside the household had a significant negative effect on nutritional status when family income, family food consumption, and education were controlled. Although family income increased when mothers entered the labor market, the increased income effect on food consumption appeared to be insufficient to compensate for reductions in the time available for nurturing activities, including feeding.

With the proportion of female-headed households in developing countries estimated at nearly one-third, concern for the impact of women's work on child nutrition is paramount. As Clark (1981) states, what causes poor child welfare is not women's work but the poverty that is associated with the low wages women earn or that forces them to enter the labor market. The poor need an increased income to enhance food consumption before the benefits of increased knowledge about childcare and nutrition can be seen. Poor women cannot afford the leisure time for education classes, demonstration projects, or attendance at health clinics.

Technologies to Improve Women's Time Allocation

The preceding discussion illustrates the many competing demands on women's time and the importance of all their roles on their children's nutritional status. The amount of time spent on childcare, especially in the first year of life, seems to be an important determinant of child welfare. Participation in agriculture and market activities enhances access to food and cash that women will use to increase food consumption of families. Food processing can be an important source of cash income for poor women and is a prerequisite for food preparation in all families. Time spent gathering fuel and water competes with time available for the other activities. Technologies that can increase the efficiency of or reduce the time spent in some of these activities may help to increase the time spent in other activities more beneficial to child health, such as childcare and market production.

Childcare

Little has been done on a large scale to address the problem of care for the children of poor women in developing countries. Most women rely on their older children or other family members to care for the young children when they are busy with other activities. When women work far from their homes, breastfeeding is often reduced, with negative health effects among children of poor families (Popkin and Solon 1976).

Where community childcare centers have been established, the results have been impressive. In Brazil, neighborhood home care centers with caregivers trained in childcare, sanitation, and nutrition reduced the cost, time, and difficulties mothers previously encountered in finding suitable childcare (Frazao 1982). Mobile creches set up at construction sites in India allowed women to continue breastfeeding their infants during work breaks and provided care and education for preschool children (Mahadevan 1977). In addition to ensuring adequate nutrition and health care for children, such centers also reduce absenteeism by workers and provide additional employment for the low-income women who staff the centers.

Another important element in enhancing the ability of women to improve childcare is weaning foods that do not require extensive preparation time. A major deterrent to proper feeding of young children is the need for frequent feedings of energy dense foods that are free from bacterial contamination. Centrally processed, low-cost, precooked foods have been distributed with success in the Philippines and Sri Lanka, while other attempts, such as that with Incaparina in Guatemala, have been too expensive for the local poor to use on a consistent basis (Gibbons and Griffiths 1984). Weaning foods have been produced locally by village groups such as mothers' clubs in Hyderabad, India, or by cooperatives as part of the Integrated Village Nutritional Applied Program in Thailand. The foods are either provided free or sold to families in the village for consumption by young children. These activities have had the triple benefit of improving child nutrition, reducing the time spent by women to prepare food, and providing income for villagers involved in food production.

Community kitchens are a third way to meet the feeding needs of children while reducing the time requirements of mothers. In the Kamanves project in Maharashtra, India, mothers organized and ran community kitchens in a low-income urban area. The mother who cooked received a free meal and a small payment. Children paid a minimal price for the meal or contributed fuel used in food preparation (Ram and Holkar 1978). Such community kitchens reduce the overall time spent in cooking, as one person is responsible for many children, thus increasing efficiency, freeing up time for individual mothers, and providing a cash income to the woman responsible for food preparation. Because the mothers' time is freed for other economic activities, the benefits from the income-producing jobs should override the small cost of the prepared food.

Agricultural Activities

A major deterrent to improvements in food production in which women are involved is that women generally produce food for consumption and are rarely able to obtain cash or technological advice that would help them improve the techniques used (Boserup 1970). Even when the government provides technical assistance for food crop production, men often receive the assistance in preference to women. In the National Maize Project in Tanzania, 20 percent of the participating women were visited by an agricultural extension agent compared to 58 percent of the men (Tinker 1979a).

When technological interventions have been adopted, often these have led to increased workloads for women. For example, in Tanzania, when plows and tractors were introduced as alternatives to hand hoeing, more land could be cultivated by the same number of men. This however, led to an increased need for weeding, which was traditionally the woman's responsibility (Tobisson 1980). As cash crop production increased, women began to have all the responsibility (previously shared with men) for subsistence crops. Women's workload increased to maintain food availability for the family, while the additional cash income was kept by the men, with women seeing little of it (Tobisson 1980). Similarly, in The Gambia, as improved agricultural methods were introduced, women's work time in agriculture rose by 20 hours, while men's time fell by 10 hours (UNDP 1980).

The same trend was seen in Ghana. Men spent more time in cacao production and had less time to work on raising yams, traditionally their reponsibility, because they were harvested at the same time

(Savane 1981). Women had to take over food production from the men, but because yams require more labor with less yield than cassava, women shifted crop production to cassava. Diet quality therefore decreased, because cassava is lower in protein and vitamins than are yams.

When an irrigated rice scheme was introduced in Kenya, women working on the land received rice as payment. However, since husbands would not eat rice, the women would sell the rice to buy the traditional food at increased prices (because supply was reduced). Although women worked more hours than before on the irrigated rice projects, they could not provide as much food for their families. Since they had less time available, they had to buy more wood for fuel instead of gathering it themselves. While the total income and visible wealth of families (such as radios and bicycles) increased due to husbands' incomes, nutritional levels fell (Palmer 1977).

Another concern with technological change in agricultural production is the displacement of women from traditional roles that provided them with access to food or cash. In Uganda and Kenya, the use of herbicides and knapsack spraying of fields led to an 80 to 85 percent decrease in the number of days needed for weeding on coffee and tea estates (UNDP 1980). Since 75 percent of the weeding was previously done by women, this reduced the women's opportunities to earn cash income. In Java, Indonesia, women had traditionally been involved in harvesting rice on large farms using small *ani-ani* knives and were paid a share of the harvest (Stoler 1977). Now men use large sickles to harvest the rice, which leads to reduced rice wastage but has displaced women from the field (White 1975).

Food Processing and Preparation

Women spend large amounts of time in food processing activities such as hulling rice, grinding maize, and preparing millet, as well as in the actual cooking. For example, in the Congo, researchers estimated that the household processing of tapioca and maize took four times as long as the time spent to cultivate these crops (Boserup 1970). In Senegal, women spend four hours daily converting 5 kilograms of wheat into couscous to feed their families (Scott 1979). Although it would appear that technologies to decrease the time required for such tasks would be beneficial, as poorer women often work in richer households helping with these activities, food processing also offers employment opportunities for poor women.

In Java, traditional home pounding of rice was a major and regular source of income for women in poor households (Stoler 1977). Between 1970 and 1974, rice hullers, imported from Japan, that used rubber rollers spread widely throughout the country. Researchers estimate that 125 million woman-days of wage labor were lost in 1972 because of this new technology, although it resulted in lower consumer prices for rice, which exceeded the value of the lost jobs to the national economy (Tinker 1979a). The impact has been to replace a strenuous but paid job with unemployment, resulting in an increase in rural poverty (White 1975). Although the country as a whole gained, poor women lost a major source of employment that was not compensated for by a sufficient increase in public works programs.

A Bangladesh study observed that 50 percent of female wage employment came from rice husking and processing. Currently, the Bangladesh government is committed to a policy of mechanizing rice processing, which would severely erode the fragile female labor market (Cain and others 1979). Other researchers in Bangladesh have also observed that women's tasks are often displaced by new technologies usurped by men, such as grain threshing and processing technologies (Chen 1983). In Mexico, when mechanical maize grinders were developed, men took over the traditionally female job of making tortillas. To have sufficient cash to buy the tortillas, women had to work more hours making clay pottery. As women's wages were lower than men's, it meant they had to work harder than before the "seemingly beneficial" technology was introduced (Tinker 1976).

In Burkina Faso, mechanical mills were introduced to decrease the time spent by women on food processing activities (McSweeney 1979). These mills ended up being used only when women were tired or busy, because they perceived the taste of grain to be poorer than when hand ground. Since grain could be ground quickly, meals could be cooked even on a busy day, but this required one or two hours of cooking time, leading to a longer workday. This is not to argue against the introduction of labor saving technologies but to suggest that whatever technologies are introduced should not replace female labor but should make the labor more efficient and should remain under the control of those whose labor is being displaced (Tinker 1979a).

Fuel and Water Collection

As illustrated by table 27-1, rural women expend much time and energy on obtaining fuel and water. Fuel, including firewood, charcoal, and crop residues, accounts for two-thirds of all energy used in Africa and one-fifth in Latin America. In Bangladesh, India, and Pakistan, 90 percent of all fuel and 40 to 50 percent of energy used for cooking is from noncommercial fuels, with half supplied by dung

(Tinker 1979a). Enhancing access to inexpensive fuels would be an important means of reducing the time and energy spent by women in non-income-producing activities. Technologies to improve access to fuel, aside from use of animal drawn carts for fetching fuel in rural areas, include (a) planting of quick growing trees and (b) more efficient use of traditional fuels through improved cooking stoves such as solar cookers and lorena stoves, processing of brush and residue for higher temperatures, and development of more efficient methods of charcoal production (Tinker 1979a; McDowell and Hazzard 1976). Examples of improved technology include the introduction of eucalyptus trees as a fast growing fuel source by the Village Technology Unit in Kenya (McDowell and Hazzard 1976) and the introduction of technologies for making fuel bricks from peanut shells in Senegal (Scott 1979).

In many rural communities, fetching water is one of the most tedious, time consuming activities (Briscoe 1984). Water needs are high for cooking, animal and crop raising, and bathing and sanitary needs, but access to water determines the amount used. In Nepal, 40 gallons of water per family per day are used if a convenient well is available, while half that much is used when wells are far from the household (Dixon 1978). Women often spend substantial time and energy obtaining water for household use. Estimates from several African studies show that on average, one-sixth of energy expended is for carrying water (McDowell and Hazzard 1976). Improved water systems would reduce women's workloads significantly and could help increase benefits from income-generating activities where water is needed. For example, when poultry projects were introduced in villages in Zaire, the task of carrying water for the chickens became the responsibility of the women. The increased workload without sufficient compensation caused women to be indifferent or even hostile to the project, whose original intent was to help improve their condition (Dixon 1978).

Water catchment from roofs has been suggested when precipitation is adequate. The most expensive aspect of these systems is the large storage tanks needed (about 700 liters), as inexpensive bamboo gutters can be used (McDowell and Hazzard 1976). Communal societies in Kenya developed rotating credit clubs to help families accumulate cash to buy tin roofs to collect water. With the time saved from gathering water, women increased their production of vegetables and small animals that they sold in urban markets (Tinker 1979b). In Kenya, however, when water was made more accessible, women received less assistance from other family members in fetching it, so results are unpredictable.

Conclusion

Women in developing countries spend most of their waking hours on home production, (including childcare, food processing, food preparation, and water and fuel supply) and on market production (subsistence or cash crops) and other income-producing activities. These two categories of work often compete with each other. Lightening women's work burdens at times of stress is important, but it is essential that in doing so women are not displaced from paid work. Therefore, what is needed are methods of decreasing the drudgery associated with unpaid tasks such as cooking, cleaning, fuel and water gathering, and domestic food processing (Chambers 1983). As well stated by Fagley (1976), the rural housewife invariably works with her hands. If the job were mechanized it would be taken over by men. When employment opportunities for women are offered in conjunction with labor saving improvements, such as centrally located wells, cooking stoves that use fuel more efficiently, hand run machines to grind and hull grain or press oil, and centralized childcare, women will have an incentive to adopt innovations to free themselves for more productive activities (Dixon 1978).

Public policies can influence the availability and characteristics of jobs and help ensure through taxes, subsidies, and regulations that, for example, women will be able to breastfeed at childcare facilities near workplaces (Butz and others 1981). However, in a tight labor market, special regulations for women workers may undercut their ability to compete with men for jobs. In Peru, when legislation was passed providing maternity leave to women and restricting the work week to 45 hours instead of the 48 required of men, many employers stopped hiring women (Newland 1980).

Before women can be expected to take part in literacy or health and nutrition education classes, they must be freed from some of their current time consuming tasks. Few nutrition or health projects have taken into consideration current constraints on women. In the future, the demands on women's time that often put childcare needs counter to equally important income-generating needs must be considered in program planning. However, the delicate balance between providing benefits to aid women, such as childcare facilities, and pricing women out of the labor market needs to be carefully addressed in the promotion of policies that will enhance child welfare.

28

Variable Access to Food

Michael Lipton

The link between poverty and undernutrition is well accepted. However, two additional problems may compound the impact of poverty on nutrition. One is that undernutrition in poor families may be caused partly by inappropriate food distribution within the household. The second is that the "peaky" distribution of nutritional needs over time—seasonally and in the life cycle—may increase the nutritional risk of some members of the household.

Intrahousehold Food Distribution

How valid is the claim that, while some household members—typically adult males—get more food than they "need," others—women, children, and especially girls aged zero to four—are underfed? The evidence suggests that first, families too poor to eat enough tend to have a disproportionate number of under-fives and possibly of women; this observation should not be misread as food discrimination against these groups. Second, the evidence for food discrimination against small girls is quite strong for rural areas of Bangladesh and northern India, weak elsewhere in Asia, and absent or negative in other regions. Third, many apparent cases of discrimination may be explicable in other ways: medically, as a response to the greater ability of underfed groups to avoid damage, or to their lower benefit from extra food; economically, if poor families' medium-term capacity to earn and survive depends on the relative overfeeding of its "stronger" members; or in terms of food habits, preferences, or beliefs that, while harmful, are not in themselves discriminatory. Let us examine each of these propositions in greater detail.

Infants and children aged one to five are significantly overrepresented in poor households (though, interestingly, not more among the

Excerpted from *Poverty, Undernutrition, and Hunger,* World Bank Staff Working Paper 597 (Washington, D.C., 1983).

extremely poor than among other poor). Female heads of households and women as a group are somewhat overrepresented in poorer households (Visaria 1980; Botswana 1976). Women typically spend smaller proportions of their lives in nondomestic work and earn somewhat lower task-specific wage rates; thus Indian rural data show that women's expected lifetime earnings appear to be about half of men's (Rosenzweig and Schultz 1980). A random sample of the population, therefore, could well find worse nutrition among women and children than among adult men and could correctly associate this with lesser poverty among men; but it would be wrong to infer that household food allocations are discriminatory in favor of men.

This effect is compounded by another. Among the poor, those "good at" coping with low dietary energy intakes are likeliest to survive to adulthood. Hence, clinical inspection of poor groups reveals a much lower incidence of clinical symptoms of gross undernutrition among adults than among children. Thus, clinical reports at population level may create an illusion of discrimination against children within the household.

The statistics of overrepresentation of children among the poor, then, mean that discrimination against them is overestimated. But these statistics have their dark side. It is the user's fault if they are misread as indicating discrimination; however, they genuinely point to greater hardship among children. Moreover, it is in early life that the damage done by a given percentage shortfall in dietary energy intake below requirements is greatest and most likely to be irreversible later. Proneness to infection is greatest in the period from about 6 to 18 months after birth. At this time, the child has lost the passive immunity initially acquired from the mother but has not yet gained active immunity through building up antibodies during exposure to infections (Schofield 1974).

We cannot infer simply from the fact that dietary energy deprivation among infants and children is both more and worse than among adults that children are relatively underfed within and by the households to which they belong. A 1969 survey in Calcutta showed no discrimination either against children below five years of age compared with adults or in favor of boys compared with girls. These results have been replicated elsewhere in India (Bhalla 1980). In Tamil Nadu, there was some evidence that families with small or marginal food energy deficits kept children under two on calorie intakes consistent with moderate malnutrition, but the evidence of harm to them was weak. Severe child malnutrition is usually not permitted until the family suffers an average deficit of 40 percent (Chaudhuri 1982), that is, until extreme poverty forces the terrible choice: sacrifice earning power for all or risk the health of nonearners only.

As for Latin America, among low-income groups in Bogotá, Colombia, children in vulnerable age strata, aged below two, were fed at 97 to 100 percent of requirements, while older children received considerably less (Betancourt 1977). In ten African village surveys from the 1950s and 1960s, preschool children met only 80 percent of kilocaloric requirements, as against 94 percent for villagers as a whole, but intragroup variance was great and the differences were not statistically significant (Schofield 1979). Moreover, many parents tend to underfeed sufferers from diarrhea (wrongly regarding less food as a cure), and such sufferers are more likely to be infants and children. Therefore, to the limited extent that parents relatively underfeed children, it is partly due to misinformation rather than discrimination.

As for food discrimination against females, the evidence does not support this except for a short period of life in some parts of Asia. In Africa, a survey in Pangani Basin, Tanzania, in the late 1960s showed girls with a weight for age curve as least as good as for boys, and males in all age groups showed a somewhat higher incidence of protein-energy malnutrition than females. Researchers obtained parallel findings for the Mwea-Tebre settlement in Kenya (Korte 1969; Kreysler and Schlage 1969). In 26 African village surveys, adult females averaged 94 percent of weight for height norms, as against 89 percent for adult males. The respective proportions in 31 Latin American surveys were 101 percent and 93 percent (Schofield 1974). In rural and urban Chile in 1974 "females and children [were] discriminated against in the main meals, [but] when all meals eaten in the home are considered, the bias disappears and is, in part, reversed" (Harbert and Scandizzo 1982, p. 23).

In South India, the Tamil Nadu Nutrition Study confirms that women have a higher ratio of energy intake to requirements, by about 7 percent, than men (Chaudhuri 1982). In some parts of Bangladesh and northern India, however, researchers found some evidence of food discrimination against girls under four. In a large sample surveyed in Matlab Thana, Bangladesh, in 1978, the male-female ratio of energy intake as a proportion of requirements (adjusted for body weight, pregnancy, lactation, and activity) was 1.08 for the age group 0–4, 0.99 for 5–14, 1.01 for 15–44, and 1.03 for those over 45 (Chen, Huq, and D'Souza 1981). As a result, females had a higher mortality rate than males, but only for girls aged 1 month to 14 years. Girls from birth to age 5 were likelier to be severely undernourished—below 60 percent of Harvard weight for age or below 80 percent of height for age—than boys of the same age.

Researchers found similar results in 17 villages in Morinda, Punjab, in the early 1970s. In Laguna, the Philippines, household surveys showed small but significant male excess intake/requirements ratios.

While not all these studies reach firm conclusions on which house-holds place girls at most risk, the Morinda study clearly locates them in the poorest castes, with female infant mortality at 196 per 1,000 and male at 125 (Carloni 1981). At least in rural India, these sex discrep-ancies do not apply to adults (National Institute of Nutrition 1977); if anything there were, in both 1975 and 1976, more households in which women ate adequately while men were underfed (13 percent) than vice versa (10 percent). Moreover, in Sri Lanka, the sex composi-tion of families is statistically unrelated to the share of outlay devoted to food (Deaton 1981), suggesting that sex discrimination in food availability is not very prevalent.

Can "reasonable" medical or economic explanations be found for age or sex discrimination in dietary energy supplies? Medically, data from rural Guatemala suggest that supplementary calories alone have a less significant impact on anthropometric status among girls than among boys (Martorell, Yarbrough, and others 1980). Analysts of these data also argue that "if malnutrition retards mental develop-ment through its effects on brain growth . . . nutritional insults would be felt more keenly by boys, because they appear to be biologically at greater risk" (Engle and others 1983, p. 199). This would "justify" a higher intake/requirements ratio for boys only where severe under-nutrition (such as might retard mental development) is a danger and might explain why a higher ratio is found mostly in the poorest areas of South Asia. If parents were aware of this difference, they could concentrate children's scarce food so as to maximize the medical probability of a surviving, healthy, and mentally developed adult—and thus concentrate upon boys, because the impact of extra food upon that probability is greater for boys than for girls.

Clearly, however, no medical explanation for food discrimination against children as a whole is plausible. Here, a typical economic explanation runs in terms of maintaining a source of income, however low, through allocation of sufficient food to income-earning members even at the cost of malnutrition among small children (Pinstrup-Andersen 1981). However, in a world of certainty, it is hard to explain overallocation of food to men while women go underfed. First, much of "women's work," especially water carrying, is as energy consuming and as necessary to family survival as "men's work." Second, apart from nutrient needs, it is usually women who control the depletion of stores and the allocation of food. Indian and Bangladeshi mothers control many grain stores and should be able to deplete them to feed themselves and their hungry children while fathers are at work.

However, men may have an advantage in meeting their nutritional requirements because a larger proportion of men's time is spent in hired work. Men are thus likelier to be fed by employers, partly perhaps to increase nutrition-linked productivity. Even in poor families—where women are likelier than elsewhere to participate in the labor force, and where the proportion of participants' time comprising work done for hire is greatest due to the family's lack of productive capital or land—men's time remains likelier than women's to be spent in work done for others.

Any extra access to food obtained in this way by men, however, is not correctly seen as intrahousehold food discrimination against women. It is rather the result of employers' preferences for men in the "hire and feed" labor package, and/or of intrahousehold preferences to hire out the men. Such decisions on the part of employers may be profit-seeking, discriminatory, or a mixture of both. Perhaps they are related to the association of women's work with daily, casual labor, so that employers find it harder to "capture" the long-term gains in productivity (associated with providing meals at work) than with generally longer-term male employees. But, whatever the explanation, "intrahousehold food discrimination" is not it.

What happens in employment markets is also crucial to the most sophisticated attempt so far to explain differences between boys' and girls' survival prospects in terms of expected work and income chances, without reference to risk avoidance. Rosenzweig and Schultz (1980) show a strong relationship between sex differences in child survival and in adult employment and wage rates. Among 1,334 rural households in India in 1971, excess death rates among girls were associated significantly only with (a) landlessness in the household, (b) low rainfall—presumably a rough proxy for agricultural "backwardness" and insecurity, (c) paternal lack of education, and (d) low female employment rate (or a high sex gap in expected lifetime earnings). Despite (a) and (b), districts with high proportions of landless people feature significantly lower, not higher, excesses of girls' death rates over boys'.

Where food—or other—discrimination against girls exists, as in northern India and Bangladesh, it may thus be caused by their poorer earning prospects. Indeed, Rosenzweig and Schultz (1980) stress that Muslim villages and households do not show higher excess death rates of girls over boys than would be "predicted," given the greater employment and earnings gaps between women and men that prevail in Muslim areas. However, this analysis simply transfers the quest for the lethal discrimination from food allocation to labor markets. If poor parents act as though they predicted lifetime earnings and adjusted allocation of household resources accordingly, why should they adjust behavior with respect to sex-selective child survival rather than to employability of female labor supply? It is not plausible that the reasons lie entirely on the side of constraints on (or preferences affecting) the demand for labor.

Perhaps adults, especially men, need to be relatively overfed in some circumstances to counter the effects of uncertainty in labor markets. Very poor households are both at most risk of undernutrition and most dependent on income from casual hired employment. Employment uncertainties have little effect on the energy requirements of under-fives, and less on women than on men. Although women have somewhat higher unemployment rates than men, they have much lower participation rates and therefore spend a smaller proportion of time in job search (Lipton 1983). Moreover, the energy requirements of household work, while often heavy, are predictable; the energy requirements of a job search on foot are less certain.

Casual or seasonal employees, in particular, often use much time and energy to move among potential employers to seek jobs. At the start of the day, the family does not know how much energy the job searchers will have to devote to job search. It will thus normally pay the family (if the search is worthwhile at all) to provide its casual employees with enough dietary energy—on the previous evening and for breakfast—to enable them (a) to move around in search of a hiring employer, (b) if one is found, to look alert enough to induce him or her to hire them, and (c) if they are hired, to complete the work and return home. On many days, some of these kilocalories of energy are unnecessary, either because the job search is swiftly successful or because it is altogether unsuccessful. However, up to a quite large "insurance" level of consumption, the family might well maximize the probability of earning enough to feed all its members adequately this week if on Monday and Tuesday some go hungry while the "uncertain" casual workers—most of them adult men—are fed more than their average daily requirements so as to cut the risk that these workers do not on some days forgo earnings because they do not meet conditions (a), (b), and (c) above. Such missed chances might imperil the medium-term nutrition of the whole family, including women and children, even more than does the temporary undernutrition of the latter.

To summarize, it is rare to find food discrimination against adult women in intrafamily food allocation, slightly more common to find it against children, and most common to find it against girls aged zero to four, though even this appears to be typical only in Bangladesh and northern India. Where food discrimination does exist, it may often represent a desperately poor family's last resort, maximizing its prospects of pulling through by feeding members most likely to earn incomes, either currently or when they are older. Intervention in intrafamily food distribution is probably seldom practicable. Where discrimination exists, it is to labor markets—and the power of the poor to employ their own labor, female and male, at a decent return—that one should look first.

Fluctuations in Nutritional Risk

Microsurveys show only that 3 to 5 percent of under-fives in developing countries fall below the critical weight or height limit for "severe" undernutrition (and milder states are not clearly associated with increased risk of death or functional deprivation). However, substantially more of them—probably 10 to 20 percent depending on the country—move in and out of risky states. This is for two reasons. First, the environment changes, both seasonally and from year to year, depending on the harvest. Second, the family cycle alters both the family's capacity to earn income and its exposure to nutritional risk.

Suppose that in a community, 3 percent of persons (and of under-fives) are on a typical day severely undernourished. Seasonal and year to year changes alter, in two ways, the meaning of such an average estimate. First, even if the 3 percent are always the same persons, they are not always equally undernourished. People at risk of undernutrition tend to be at greatest risk, relative to their requirements, in the hungry season. Then, direct nutritional risks, such as infection and inadequate food, interact (Schofield 1974, 1979) and are intensified by the greater tendency of the poorest to be exposed to covariant, and relatively severe, fluctuations in employment and wage rates (Lipton 1983). The greater seasonal variations in death rates among infants and in the poorest groups partly reflect such facts (Crook and Dyson 1981). This means that yearly averages will substantially understate the intensity of periodic severe undernutrition. Proportions with inadequate weight for age, with scanty breast milk, and presenting at hospital with kwashiorkor or marasmus all vary seasonally, tending to rise in the later wet season in most cases (Chambers and others 1981; Longhurst and Payne 1981; Onchere and Sloof 1981; van Steenbergen and others 1981; Cantrelle and Leridon 1971). This seasonal rise in risks for the most exposed groups is possibly related crucially to higher work requirements for—and absences from home among—working mothers who are still lactating (Drasor and others 1981; Tomkins 1979; Kumar 1978; and Huffman in part V).

Second, some people not normally at risk of a given degree of undernutrition move into risk during unexpectedly bad seasons or years. Average estimates, unless they include such times, will altogether omit such people from the undernourished. Since the poor are relatively unlikely either to be able to afford to carry large reserves of cash or food or to be able to borrow, and relatively likely to rely for income on casual employment, which contracts during lean seasons and years, they are doubly exposed to fluctuating undernutrition. Indeed, those near the margin between the poor and the very poor may be less equipped to stand a lean season than families accustomed to generations of extreme poverty. This, too, may help account for the sharply fluctuating infant mortality rates documented in the Punjab (Kielmann and others 1983), Bangladesh (Crook and Dyson 1981), and elsewhere.

To the extent that seasonal and year to year variation in the environment "spreads out" a given average incidence of severe undernutrition over more people (because the victims change over time), it probably saves lives and health. It does, however, mean that the target population, to be considered as very poor and hence at nutritional risk, is larger than such an average incidence suggests. To the extent that the environmental variation for given severely undernourished persons concentrates risk in exceptionally severe periods, it almost certainly increases the risk to such persons. In respect of both effects, surveys that simply average out—or, even worse, omit—lean seasons or years thereby understate the proportions of persons affected by extreme poverty and the risk of hunger. The concentration of under-fives among the very poor (Lipton 1983) increases the importance of both these effects.

It is impossible to state precisely the increase in estimates of proportions at poverty-induced nutritional risk due to seasonal factors. However, in communities where up to 20 percent of people die before their fifth birthday and where food is scarce seasonally, a substantial increase in such figures, above the 3 to 5 percent recorded as severely undernourished in most surveys, is certainly indicated. The increase is, however, extremely unlikely to raise the prevalence to the 40 to 60 percent malnourished sometimes suggested (Reutlinger and Selowsky 1976), even for very poor communities. Most surveys in such communities, however, do report data on both capacity to buy food and economic behavior relating to food that indicate a much severer (and structurally different) problem among the poorest 10 to 20 percent of persons than among others. These are the households apparently unable on average to afford even 80 percent of average recommended daily allowances despite spending roughly 80 percent of their income on food.

29

Nutritional Risk: Concepts and Implications

Wendy P. McLean

In its simplest sense, risk is the chance of an undesirable event occurring. Nutritional risk is the chance of death, ill health, malfunction, poor achievement in body size, or hunger due to insufficient food. All these are manifestations of malnutrition. Malnutrition is undesirable for both individuals and the community to which they belong and its elimination should be a priority for all those concerned with the welfare of society.

Identifying nutritional risk enables governments to take steps to reduce that risk and to prevent malnutrition. If we are to develop or adjust policies and programs to improve nutritional status, we must identify the context in which deprivation occurs and do this in a way that planners can understand and use. Joy (1978) has suggested that nutrition problems should be described in terms of who, where, why, and how. How governments identify nutritional risk depends considerably upon their perceptions of the origin of the risk. These perceptions are also crucial because they determine views about which sectors might tackle malnutrition. Table 29-1 depicts the perceptions of nutritional risk that exist today and the sectors that can play a role in tackling nutrition problems.

An essential feature of multidisciplinary approaches to reducing nutritional risk is the identification of the type of household in which deprivation occurs. Without understanding the context in which nutrition problems arise, governments cannot design strategies to deal with malnutrition. The predominant approach among nutritionists is to identify nutritional risk at the individual level and to focus on young children, in whom malnutrition is most frequently diagnosed.

Excerpted from *The Identification of Nutritional Risk at the Household Level: A State of the Art Review*, Occasional Papers 2 (London: Department of Human Nutrition, London School of Hygiene and Tropical Medicine, 1984).

Table 29-1. *Perceptions Regarding Nutritional Problems*

Who is at risk?	Why?	Strategy	Primary sector or discipline	Example of strategy
Children	Disease	Curative	Medicine	Medical treatment, nutrition/rehabilitation
Mothers and children	Biological vulnerability	Preventive	Health/nutrition	Supplementary feeding, surveillance of growth
Households	Social and economic vulnerability	Preventive	Development planning	Food supply and distribution planning, price and income strategies, public services (for example, education, water, sanitation)
Groups of households within communities[a]	Vulnerability seen as lying in the social and economic relations between households and communities[a]	Preventive	All sectors	Alterations in existing relations and thereby in entitlements to food[b]

a. Communities are defined as population groups at local, national, and international levels.
b. Entitlement is access to food (see Sen in part III).

However, Mrs. Pember Reeves' report from London in the early part of this century provides a clear and still valid example of the importance of knowledge of the household background in tackling nutrition problems.

Mrs. Pember Reeves has ably investigated family budgets among the poor, and has shown how exiguous is the amount usually available for food. She says: That the diet of the poorer London children is insufficient, unscientific and utterly unsatisfactory is horribly true. But that the real cause of this state of things is the ignorance and indifference of their mothers is untrue. What person or body of people, however educated and expert, could maintain a working man in physical efficiency and rear healthy children on the amount of money which is all these mothers have to deal with? It would be an impossible problem if set to trained and expert people. How much more an impossible problem when set to the saddened, weakened, overburdened wives of London laborers (Medical Research Committee 1917, p. 11).

The availability of food to individuals reflects the capacity of the social and economic unit to which they belong to provide for basic needs. In turn, the availability of food to households is related to the food production and distribution system, and thus to the wider social and economic structures of societies.

The term household is defined as the smallest and most common unit of production, consumption, and organization in societies. The rationale for choosing such a unit to identify nutritional risk is that it is there that the many factors operating on nutritional status merge. It allows nutritionists to see the context in which deprivation occurs more clearly and provides a basis for analysis of the origin of the risk. This approach does not preclude intervention at the individual level, but indicates the factors that influence the nutritional status of the individual.

The majority of policies and programs that can influence nutritional status are not designed by nutritionists, nor do they commence with nutrition goals, yet they often have the potential to affect nutritional risk. Thus, policies and programs to alter patterns of crop production, employment possibilities, wages, or prices of basic needs, particularly staple foods, may all influence nutritional status by affecting the availability of or entitlement to food in the household (see Sen in part III). Figure 29-1 illustrates this point through a diagrammatic representation of the components of systems of food acquisition. The outcome, nutritional status, is the result of the sum of processes operating at different points in systems wherein food is produced, distributed, consumed, and used. Table 29-1 and figure 29-1 show

Figure 29-1. *The Food System*

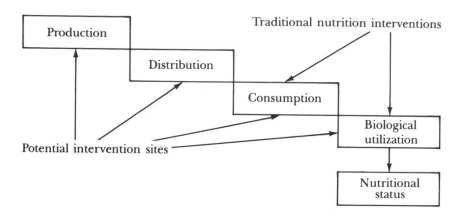

that the multidisciplinary approach to reducing malnutrition is essential.

The Assessment of Risk

No single definition of nutritional risk exists. The undesirable event being considered may be some malfunction or some less than acceptable achievement. As regards malfunction, the risk may be death, illness, nutrient deficiency, or hunger. In considering less than acceptable achievement, the risk may be defined in terms of attained body size, or quantity and quality of diet. Malfunction should be the primary concern, but as conditions improve, the concept of less than acceptable achievement may be used in the definition of risk (see Beaton in part V). Figure 29-2 illustrates the spectrum of risk definition; the gray area denotes where malfunction and acceptable achievement merge. It is important that the type of nutritional risk faced by different households and communities be distinguished to allow governments to develop priorities.

Since nutritional risk results from the interaction of several events, it is rarely constant over time and space (see Lipton in part V). In a drought, households with a resistant crop, such as cassava, may be able to buffer the effects better than households whose crops depend on more rainfall, but who have no access to irrigation. In contrast, in years of reasonable rainfall, cassava growers may face greater nutritional risk than other households if they depend on this one staple, as its nutritional value is relatively poor.

Figure 29-2. *The Spectrum of Risk Definition*

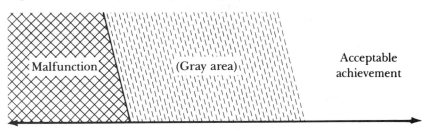

Distribution of the indicator

To establish the nature of a risk we must consider how households obtain their food and how social and economic factors assist or undermine their ability to obtain adequate supplies. Two studies from India illustrate different ways of identifying nutritional risk. They also demonstrate how the prevalence of risk can vary between households within communities. An analysis of malnutrition in a village in the Punjab focused on individual children, but families were classified based on household characteristics associated with economic status (Levinson 1974). Table 29-2 shows how one group of families, the Ramdasia class, experienced significantly higher rates of nutritional deprivation compared with another group, the Jats. Levinson confirmed some potential determinants of nutritional status, such as income, while others, such as beliefs, were found to be unrelated to nutritional status. The results of such analyses help to determine the origins of risk and suggest areas that policies or programs to reduce risk must address.

In the state of Tamil Nadu, two investigators concerned with the effects of a drought revealed the potential nutritional risk to different groups within a village (Moses and Pandian 1983). Using the availability of water resources for agricultural production as a measure to distinguish households, they identified three groups. The first group had pump sets with which to irrigate land and also used the village tank. The second group relied on the tank alone, while the third group depended for their food and livelihood on the need for surplus labor in cultivation undertaken by the other groups. The consequences of the drought differed for each group, as shown in table 29-3. The results indicate that group 3 is at greatest risk, followed by the poorer sections of group 2. The authors' analysis elicits important considerations for the design and direction of drought relief measures by distinguishing the effects of drought on different sectors of the population. Thus, while ensuring that the tank is in good condition

Table 29-2. *Household-Level Variables and Children's Nutritional Status, India*

Gomez group (weight for age)	Number of cases	Percentage Jats	Percentage Ramdasia	Average percentage of caloric allowance	Average family income (rupees)	Average mother's belief index[a]
Normal (greater than 90 percent)	73	54.8	19.2[b]	65.0[b]	285[b]	2.4
First degree (76–90 percent)	181	46.4	37.2	63.1	245	2.5
Second degree (60–75 percent)	202	37.7	44.1	60.4	231	2.4
Third degree (less than 60 percent)	40	20.0	57.5	51.8	192	2.2
All cases	496	42.1	39.1	61.3	241	2.4

Note: Braces indicate pairs of figures that are significantly different at the 0.95 level of statistical significance.

a. 4, beneficial to child's health; 1, detrimental to child's health.

b. Significantly different from the third degree malnutrition figure at the 0.95 level of statistical significance.

Source: Adapted from Levinson (1974), table 23.

Table 29-3. *Effects of Drought on Nutritional Risk in Village Households, Classified According to Water Resources, India*

Water resource	Percentage of normal crop possible in drought	Strategy for survival
Pump set and tank (group 1)	20–25 percent	Keep assets
Tank (group 2)	None until rains come (tank dry)	Richer half keep assets; poorer half sell assets, take loans[a]
None/landless (group 3)	None	15 percent find alternative employment; rest are unemployed, take loans[a]

a. Interest rates are 36–120 percent (highest rates are on smaller loans).
Source: Constructed from data from Moses and Pandian (1983), p. 996.

will aid everybody in the village should rain fall and in the longer term, the priority for reducing nutritional risk would be to find a means for group 3 (and possibly some of group 2) to obtain food—for example, through alternative employment or a ration scheme. Disaggregating data to distinguish types of households reveals the distribution of nutritional risk in a community and provides a basis for looking at the effects both of social and economic factors and of new policies and programs on different groups.

An example of the uses of disaggregated information is given in the data from Mexico shown in table 29-4. The average prevalence figures fail to demonstrate that the rate of severe malnutrition (that associated with the highest risk of mortality) had not altered during an agri-

Table 29-4. *Prevalence of Malnutrition, Mexico, 1958 and 1971*
(percent)

Gomez group (weight for age)[a]	1958	1971
Normal	13.0	30.6
First degree	60.9	46.1
Second degree	21.7	18.4
Third degree	4.4	4.1
Total, second and third degree	26.1	22.5

a. Gomez and others (1956).
Source: Hernandez and others (1974).

cultural development program. Taking these figures, one might assume that nutritional status had improved overall and equally throughout the community. However, when the data are disaggregated, not only is it apparent that the prevalence of severe malnutrition (as indicated by the Gomez third degree category) had not been reduced significantly (either in practical or in statistical terms), but comment in the text also revealed that among the poorest 30 percent of the population, food intake had not increased. Together these data suggest that any improvements in nutritional status that had taken place had eluded those most at risk of malfunction from nutritional deprivation.

Implications for Data Collection

Generally, the more disaggregated the data, the greater are the between-group differences that emerge in the prevalence and nature of nutritional risk (Popkin 1981; Joy 1973). The differences found between groups of households, as in the examples from India and Mexico, both provide information on the location of those at risk and give a basis on which to plan project components that help the households in need. Obviously planners must compromise between planning for specific groups and problems and the number of different groups that can be dealt with. However, if researchers gather the information in a manner that allows disaggregation, planners can distinguish what is happening to different groups and the characteristics of households with and without nutritional problems. Keeping the data in a format that allows different levels and bases of aggregation improves its usefulness (FAO 1982a).

The data needed to plan at the household and community levels come from a wide range of sectors, commensurate with the nature of nutritional risk. Relevant information may come from the fields of agriculture (including marketing, food prices, and elasticities), employment, income and expenditure, housing, food consumption, anthropometry, health, vital statistics, social services, and anthropology. Identifying the location and characteristics of those most at risk must be followed by an analysis of risk that looks for its causes. Both quantitative and qualitative information are relevant to such analyses.

The existence of national information systems may cut the cost of data collection if data are maintained at an appropriate level of disaggregation (preferably at the household level) and if they are suitably updated. Such an information system should be used not to produce an average national statement but to locate nutritional problems (in socioeconomic, ecological, and administrative terms) and establish the nature of the nutritional risk.

Some techniques to speed up and refine data collection and analysis for planning purposes have been explored under the umbrella title "rapid rural appraisal" (Longhurst 1981). The researchers derived suggestions and examples from a variety of disciplines and specific experiences and considered some departure from conventional approaches to surveys. For those involved in planning and in information collection, these ideas provide a basis for discussion of some approaches that have been fruitful in development planning.

Conclusion

Planners know that poverty, in broad terms, is associated with high levels of nutritional risk. However, projects that are appropriate to the nature of nutritional risk cannot be planned on the basis of poverty alone. To prevent the aggravation of nutrition problems and to direct benefits to those at risk, planners must examine the relationships underlying poverty. To design appropriate strategies and project components, they must analyze the risk itself so as to elicit the relationships that influence and determine its existence in different groups. Thus poverty by itself is an insufficient diagnosis because it does not reveal the network within which deprivation thrives.

Reducing the incidence of malnutrition requires a multidisciplinary approach. The first steps could be discussion among those involved in the planning process, including representatives from different sectors, concerning the identification of nutritional risk at the household level. Interdisciplinary discussion should highlight areas where spin-off from activities in other sectors can reduce nutritional risk. The need to tackle the economic and social factors that cause malnutrition has never been more obvious than today.

30

Nutritional Surveillance

John B. Mason and Janice T. Mitchell

Surveillance of infectious diseases by keeping track of disease incidence has supported the health services by allowing timely prevention
and treatment and by permitting assessment of progress. By analogy,
the concept of nutritional surveillance has appeal for preventing malnutrition, particularly in the developing countries.

This idea first came to prominence at the World Food Conference
in 1974, and since that time the concept has evolved and has been
applied in a number of developing countries. Nutritional surveillance
is defined as "to watch over nutrition in order to make decisions that
lead to improvements in nutrition in populations." At present, some
20 or more countries have nutritional surveillance programs, and
consensus on the purposes and means of nutritional surveillance
systems is evolving.

The immediate result of the 1974 World Food Conference's call for
nutritional surveillance was the convening of a joint FAO/UNICEF/WHO
Expert Committee, whose report describing a proposed methodology
was published in 1976 (WHO 1976). By 1979, enough experience had
been gained in the developing countries to justify a review of progress
in nutritional surveillance. The review revealed that governments and
development planners were pursuing three related but distinct objectives. They were developing nutritional surveillance systems

- For long-term health and development planning
- For program management and evaluation
- For timely warning and intervention to prevent critical deteriora-
  tions in food consumption.

Excerpted from "Nutritional Surveillance," *Bulletin of the World Health Organization,*
vol. 61, no. 5 (1983), pp. 745–55.

These objectives are not mutually exclusive, but priorities have to be set because not all the objectives are necessarily appropriate at the same time, nor can they all be met at once.

The 1979 review provided material for two regional workshops: in Cali, Colombia, in 1981, and in Nairobi, Kenya, in 1982. It was also the basis for a book in which more detailed discussion of many of the points covered in this article may be found (Mason and others 1984).

Purposes of Nutritional Surveillance

Decisions that influence the nutritional conditions of populations may be made at several different administrative levels. These decisions may concern policies and programs that can fundamentally affect people's living standards in the long term, programs that provide for more immediate alleviation of hunger and malnutrition, or a number of intermediate possibilities.

The objective of nutritional surveillance is to provide information so that decisions can be more favorable to nutrition. This will lead to the allocation of resources to improve the nutrition of the malnourished. Policies and programs related to nutrition may be classified as follows:

○ National policies
○ Development programs
○ Public health and nutrition programs
○ Timely warning and intervention programs.

Nutritional surveillance systems can provide useful information to these policies and programs, as indicated in table 30-1. Since the purpose of nutritional surveillance dictates how it will be carried out (for example, the data needed for long-term planning differ from the data needed for timely warning), decisions about what data to collect must be linked as closely as possible to the specific policies and programs for which the data are needed.

Whether nutritional surveillance is useful thus depends in the first place on the potential for action to improve nutrition. Realizing this potential depends on the level of commitment at high decision-making levels and a willingness to make available the resources and the necessary trade-offs against other objectives. In addition, it requires suitable institutional arrangements so that decisions can be implemented. Governments have, as yet, very limited experience with all this. However, in a number of countries decisionmakers are committed and resources now exist, and the crucial step required is to feed

Table 30-1. *Policies and Programs That Affect Nutrition*

Policy or program	Relevance of information from nutritional surveillance

National policies
  Resource allocation by area and sector
  Legislative: price policy, commodity flows,
    minimum wages
  Program directions: promoting different crops,
    preventive and curative health
	Planning

Development programs
  Area development
  Commodities
	Planning and evaluation

Public health and nutrition programs
  Environmental health
  Primary health care
	Planning and evaluation

Timely warning and intervention programs
  Famine prevention
  Alleviation of seasonal food shortages
	Initiation of interventions

Source: Mason and others (1984).

realistic options favorable to nutrition into the decision-making process.

Decisionmakers can obtain the information needed for designing national policies and programs from answers to questions such as the following:

○ Do certain population groups have worse nutrition than others, and what are their characteristics?

○ Is the overall nutrition situation deteriorating or improving? Is this the same for all groups? How are groups with particular problems defined? Can these trends be explained?

○ Do indications of specific short-term nutrition problems exist at present? Are there indications of future problems?

To answer these questions, decisionmakers need data on indicators of nutritional conditions disaggregated by relevant groupings, such as area, occupation, and resource endowment, and repeated during relatively long periods of time, usually years.

Most of the nutritional surveillance systems aimed at planning and programming have succeeded in answering only the first question. Studies have generally used cross-sectional data analyses, as, for example, in Costa Rica, Kenya, and the Philippines. In some cases, investigators have collected data over a period of time, but these have still to be analyzed to assess changes in nutrition and their possible causes.

The information required for program management and evaluation is different in terms of the variables measured, the frequency of data collection and analysis, the level of aggregation, and so on. Simple data on program delivery and on nutritional trends in the population concerned would provide the information needed. Investigators should ask two questions.

○ Is the program being delivered as planned to the intended target group?

○ Is the gross change in the group's nutrition adequate?

The data to answer the first question can come from administrative records on program delivery. Matching of data with target groups reveals how far the target groups are included in the program and to what extent those in need are actually recipients. The second question examines the overall trend in the nutritional status of the recipients without taking into account the changes that might have occurred anyway. Often indicators of nutritional status are obtainable through regular service delivery.

Nutritional surveillance programs aimed specifically at preventing short-term food crises include the means to intervene when necessary; hence they are called "timely warning and intervention programs." Such programs aim to give information so that interventions to prevent a serious decline in food consumption can be planned, with sufficient lead time to put the interventions in place. The required indicators will therefore describe the situation prior to the deterioration in nutritional status and will include such factors as rainfall, the area under cultivation, other agricultural indicators, and possibly indicators of early responses to anticipated food shortages. Generally, the administration of such programs should be decentralized. Nutritional status indicators may be included, but more as a fail-safe mechanism than to provide the timely warning itself.

Design of a Nutritional Surveillance System

A nutritional surveillance system includes both decision making and provision of the necessary information to guide decision making, for which data collection, flow, and analysis are required. Clearly the first step in design of the system should be to decide on its purpose, which will establish the specific questions that need to be answered.

*Uses and Users of Nutritional
Surveillance Information*

Potential users of nutritional surveillance information are to be found in various sectors because of the interrelated factors that lead to malnutrition and because of its close relationship with poverty. Although it is unrealistic to expect decisionmakers to base their overall resource allocation decisions primarily on nutritional considerations, they can use nutritional surveillance to analyze policies for their nutritional consequences, to suggest alternative policy options, and eventually to assess the policies' actual nutritional effects (see Pines in part VI).

Some people support long-term nutritional surveillance as a way to influence the fundamental causes of malnutrition. However, the greatest scope for bringing about policy changes that are favorable to nutrition lies in tackling specific issues. While these issues may often be less related to the basic causes of malnutrition, such as the inequitable distribution of resources, decisions on them in reality have a better chance of being influenced by nutritional considerations.

AGRICULTURAL AND RURAL DEVELOPMENT PLANNING. Agricultural ministries view themselves as having a primary responsibility for food—certainly for its supply, if not always its consumption (and sometimes they consider that supply determines consumption). They are in a good position to affect nutrition, as many of the malnourished are the rural poor who depend on agriculture for their livelihood. Since the availability of food to the poor, including the poor farmers, depends on their real income and hence their purchasing power, and since this in turn depends on the profitability of agricultural production, agricultural policies inevitably affect nutrition. These policies, whose objectives may be, for example, food self-sufficiency or export earnings, nonetheless embody decisions that can influence nutrition. Such decisions will be based on issues such as what to produce, who will produce it, who should be helped to produce and by provision of what inputs and services, what price the farmers will be paid, and the like. A second set of decisions, at a policy level, will often depend on the prices set for the consumer; for example, governments often control the prices of staple foods and thus influence food consumption patterns, especially of the poor.

These decisions have far-reaching nutritional consequences, and under certain circumstances (defined above all by political, economic, and institutional considerations), better information may modify the decisions and lead to more favorable effects on nutrition. There are a few examples of progress in this area, such as the increasing attention to the possible deleterious effects of concentration on certain export crops. Appreciation of how difficult it is to reach the small farmer, combined with growing awareness that those with the smallest land-holdings are the most malnourished, is helping efforts to benefit small farmers and landless laborers.

Researchers are recognizing that indicators of the kind used in nutritional surveillance can be used in agriculture and rural develop-ment projects, not only because of their relevance to the quality of life, but also because they are relatively easy to collect. Donor agencies cooperating with governments in agricultural and rural development must also use nutrition information in project planning. The issues are similar to those at the national level, if more restricted. They revolve around such questions as how far the needy can participate in such projects and whether the benefits, usually in terms of income, are in fact likely to improve nutrition. One major reason for the breakdown of the link between income and better nutrition is a change in the source of income, for example, a shift from subsistence to marketed production. A number of projects led by the FAO are examining this matter (Lunven and Sabry 1981).

THE HEALTH SECTOR. The potential users of nutritional sur-veillance data in the health system include those who have to make decisions about the allocation of scarce resources. These range from ministers of health to primary health workers in isolated rural health posts.

At the national level, to introduce or expand primary health care, planners decide where to locate health centers, how many staff to assign, and what services to provide. These decisions can be based on the number of malnourished people and their locations. Nutritional surveillance data can provide guidance on the types of activities needed in the health sector. In a congested urban slum, malnutrition may be secondary to frequent intestinal infections, which suggests the need for environmental health workers to evaluate, correct, and moni-tor the water supply and sanitation facilities. A rural area prone to seasonal food shortages might benefit more from inputs to improve local diets, the introduction of home gardens, and coordination with local agricultural extension agents to promote crops less affected by drought or crops that could be grown in the off-season.

Local clinics can use nutritional surveillance data to identify pockets of malnutrition or times of malnutrition so that they can plan appro-priate interventions. They can also use these data, along with disease surveillance and administrative data, to justify requests for additional personnel, training programs, or supplies.

Nutritional surveillance can provide some of the information needed to evaluate health programs. Anthropometric data collected over months or years indicate whether nutritional conditions have improved or deteriorated. Further analysis, usually with additional data, can then be used to investigate why the program is or is not having the desired impact.

In the uses discussed here, nutritional surveillance has many similarities to health information systems. For use by the health sector, it should not be developed in isolation from health information systems. Depending on the state of development of health information, nutritional surveillance can form part of a broader information system or, in some cases, can take a lead in providing data for this purpose.

NUTRITION AND SOCIAL WELFARE PROGRAMS. Certain countries, notably in Latin America, are adopting large-scale nutrition and social welfare programs. These usually include nutritional surveillance for program planning, management, and evaluation. A well-known example is in Costa Rica, where the nutritional information system has provided important information for the family welfare program and has been used more extensively in development planning. In the Philippines, both central and local authorities use nutrition information to plan and manage nutrition programs.

In this sector again, nutritional surveillance information has been used initially to identify areas or occupational groups in which malnutrition is prevalent and may be useful later to evaluate the effectiveness of programs.

Indicators

For planning, program management, and evaluation nutritional surveillance usually provides one or more nutritional outcome indicators. These nutritional outcome indicators generally include one or more of the following: prevalence of malnutrition among preschool children (for example, proportion of children less than 80 percent weight for age); prevalence of low birth weight infants (less than 2.5 kilograms); prevalence of stunting in school entrants (less than 90 percent height for age); and estimates of infant and/or child mortality rates. Other outcome "status" indicators, generally presented alongside nutritional outcome indicators, may include assessments of quality of housing, water supply, and sanitation, and literacy rates. Initially, such indicators are used cross-sectionally; with progress, researchers can trace changes over time.

The most common classifying or descriptive variable is simply the administrative area, and indeed this is the most relevant for many programs, particularly in the health sector. Beyond this, the appropriate classification depends on the particular use; for example, it may be by ecological zone, cropping area, or farm size for agricultural use, or by accessibility, use of services, endemic disease areas, and environmental factors for other programs.

Timely warning and intervention programs require different indicators, which can often be identified by historical analysis. Here, the objective is to spot signs of deterioration in sufficient time to intervene. Agricultural indicators such as crop damage, food prices, and population responses to shortage—for example, migration and distress selling—may be suitable indicators.

However, the indicators may not fully define the problem, its changes, and its causes. Rather, surveillance information suggests where to look and what to look for. Often further investigation is needed.

Data Sources

Two types of data sources exist, administrative and survey, each with its own advantages. Data from administrative sources tend to be more numerous, making them easier to disaggregate to refer to particular geographic areas, often down to the village level. However, researchers do not usually know how representative the data are. Data often refer to geographic units such as the village, rather than to households. Rarely are more than a few variables available for the individuals referred to; for example, occupation may be recorded at the same time as a disease is reported, but even then this information is seldom passed on.

Some data integration may be possible at the village or district level. Sample survey data, however, are usually available at the household level, provide an integrated data set, often have a wide range of useful variables, and are of known representativeness. But cost usually precludes large sample sizes, so that it is usually not possible to disaggregate the data down to the level of individual villages. Indeed, this is not the purpose of most sample surveys.

Most nutritional surveillance systems depend largely on administrative data, usually from the health system, and often also use sample survey data. Details of both types of data source follow.

ADMINISTRATIVE DATA SOURCES. The commonest sources of administrative data are the health system, schools, and local government records of vital statistics. Health facilities frequently record births, deaths by age and cause, and specific diseases by the numbers of people seen per time period. Sometimes the local health facility records such data but does not report them to the regional or national levels. This is particularly true for anthropometric data. Many clinics record the weight for age of preschool children on health cards kept by the mothers. Tallying of these data may provide useful indicators of current malnutrition. For example, this is done in Colombia for health reporting and in Botswana to monitor the effects of drought.

Home visits by health workers are another source of information on living conditions, as well as on health and nutrition. In Costa Rica, health workers regularly visit a majority of rural households. They collect anthropometric, socioeconomic, and housing data and report them through the health system. A central agency analyzes the data and distributes results to interested agencies and ministries.

In the elementary schools of many countries, children are weighed and measured regularly, particularly at school entry. Often these data are carefully recorded on the appropriate form and just as carefully filed away forever. Retrieval and analysis of these data could give reliable indicators of changes in long-term nutritional status. Surveys using this source of data have been carried out in Costa Rica and the Philippines. In countries with a high rate of school enrollment, this method of long-term nutritional monitoring may become increasingly important.

Local records of births and deaths are probably the least reliable administrative source, but it may be worth the investment to improve them. Infant and child mortality rates are of fundamental concern well beyond the specific interests of nutritional surveillance. Further, many birth and death certificates record additional information, such as occupation or location, and may provide further insights.

Information about rainfall and crop progress is particularly important in nutritional surveillance systems designed to give timely warning of food shortages. Weather stations can collect rainfall data and report it through the ministry of agriculture. Some people have suggested setting up simple rainfall reporting through other means, such as schools or farmers' associations.

Reports from agricultural extension workers on crop progress, yield estimates, production, and/or areas harvested can also be used for early warning. For example, in Indonesia an indicator derived from estimates of the proportion of planted areas subsequently harvested is used to locate areas of potential food shortage and estimate the severity of the shortage. For longer-term planning, estimates of food production by area are in themselves not generally useful because of the difficulty of measuring trade. Estimates of the value of agricultural production by area would provide useful data, although as yet this is not widely done. Reliable data on agriculture more often come from surveys.

SURVEYS. Researchers obtain nutritional data from sample households either by surveys designed for the purpose or by adding a nutritional module onto existing surveys. The latter, which involves training enumerators to measure children and to administer a short questionnaire, as well as supplying relatively inexpensive equipment, has the advantage both of being cheaper and of providing a set of data in which nutritional status is potentially linked to a broad range of variables. When the survey is longitudinal (that is, repeated measurements are made on the same or similar households), periodic nutritional status measurements give time-series data to assess changes in nutritional status. This is how Kenya approaches nutritional surveillance—three rounds of nutritional data have been obtained at two to three year intervals by this means. The United Nations Household Survey Capability Program is supporting the buildup of such continuing survey systems, and this method of nutritional surveillance should become more important in the future.

Ad hoc surveys for program design, monitoring, and quick assessment may form part of a nutritional surveillance system. The capability to carry out such surveys can be established as part of the system. Conversely, some surveillance activities draw on surveys carried out for other purposes, such as labor and employment surveys in Costa Rica.

The FAO has developed a simplified methodology for project assessment, and the U.S. Centers for Disease Control use national survey methods extensively. These methodologies are being published as a series of manuals. However, considerable caution is required before embarking on a sample survey. Researchers must specify the purposes of and need for the survey, down to details of the questions that really need to be answered. Often researchers will find that they can use existing data and achieve much of the purpose at a fraction of the cost. But when justified, a carefully designed survey can give information not otherwise obtainable.

Data Analysis

A key issue in much nutritional surveillance has been who should be responsible for data analysis. Obtaining suitably analyzed data, adequately interpreted, and within a reasonable time, is not easy in many developing countries. In most cases, fairly simple data outputs are sufficient. Tabulations of nutritional and related outcome indicators by suitable groupings presented strikingly to planners can guide decision making. For example, in Costa Rica the demonstration that about 10 percent of the administrative districts had a high prevalence of height retardation led to substantial reallocation of resources to these areas.

A central unit with primary responsibility for designing the system and for analysis and interpretation of the data is the core of most surveillance programs. Gathering enough people with the right skills may require links with other institutions and technical assistance, especially for training and the development of appropriate methods. This capability is generally best located within a government agency, such as the statistical office. A number of full-time staff are assigned to this task in almost all the systems that are running promisingly. The skills required include, but go beyond, health and nutrition and involve statistics and/or epidemiology, some computing ability, economics, and planning. Beyond the primary interpretation of data, substantial benefit can be gained from more detailed analysis, both for policy purposes and for research to develop the system. For this, links with research institutions can be valuable.

Finally, cooperation between those responsible for data collection, for analysis, and for the regular use of information for decision making is essential and requires working institutional arrangements. Generally more data are collected than compiled, more compiled than analyzed, and more analyzed than used. The main constraints are not only technical, but institutional and political. To design and maintain a useful system, much hinges on good working relationships between the different institutions concerned, and the realization that they have common objectives is indispensable.

31

Supplementary Feeding Programs for Young Children in Developing Countries: A Summary of Lessons Learned

George H. Beaton and Hossein Ghassemi

We undertook this review to address the question, what have we learned from past experience that will assist in future consideration of food distribution programs aimed at older infants and young children? This is a planning question. Those involved in food and nutrition planning wish to have information available that delineates situations in which introduction of various types of food distribution programs seems beneficial.

We limited our consideration to programs involving children between the ages of about six months and six years. Thus, we do not discuss the distribution and marketing of breast milk substitutes, or school feeding programs. Although a number of programs examined also included food distribution to pregnant and lactating women, we did not specifically examine this aspect.

We recognize that food distribution programs are but one class of interventions that might be selected for implementation in a particular country. It is the task of national planners to choose among a variety of intervention approaches and to select and develop that combination of programs and approaches that will best meet the goals and circumstances of their country at the particular point in its development. This summary is not intended as an argument for or against supplementary feeding programs. Should planners decide to implement such a program, they will need to examine logistic and other

Excerpted from "Supplementary Feeding Programs for Young Children in Developing Countries," *American Journal of Clinical Nutrition*, vol. 35, no. 4 (April 1982), pp. 864–916.

matters of an operational nature in more detail. (See, for example, Anderson and others 1981.)

We reviewed more than 200 reports, about half of which provided quantitative or qualitative information about particular food distribution (take-home or supervised feeding) programs. Much of the available quantitative data comes from research or pilot projects. This creates a bias in that, in general, such projects were more effective than ongoing programs.

Evidence seems to suggest that food distribution programs directed toward young children, as now being operated, are rather expensive for the measured benefit. However, we remain unconvinced that the benefit usually measured, physical growth and development, is either the total benefit to the family and community or even the most important benefit. Therefore, we judge that it would be unwise to withdraw such food distribution programs until researchers have had an opportunity to assess their true effects and benefits.

Effectiveness of Food Delivery Systems

In evaluations of supplementary feeding programs, researchers have measured the "leakage" of food between distribution and the net increase in intake by the target recipients in terms both of sharing with others and of substitution for food that recipients would otherwise have consumed. In supervised feeding programs, the former was assumed not to occur (in truth some sharing with accompanying family members occurs, but only anecdotal data are available). In take-home distribution programs, sharing may account for 30 to 60 percent of the food distributed. The substitution effect was generally found to be greater in supervised feeding programs than in take-home programs. Overall, the net increase in intake by the target recipient was 45 to 70 percent of the food distributed, with one program showing a net effect of only 10 to 15 percent. Since the participation rate ranged from 25 to 80 percent of the intended level of distribution, the programs providing detailed information suggested that a relatively small part of the apparent food energy gap was being filled.

The determinants of leakage were not specifically identified. It was not clearly related to the apparent nutritional need of others in the family. It may reflect behavioral traits of family units. Also, in part, it may reflect satiation of the expressed demand (hunger) of the target recipient. Sharing was more pronounced when the foods used had wide acceptability for the whole family; however, substitution was not affected by the nature of the foods used.

The results of some take-home programs suggested that the net increase in energy intake by the target recipient was greater than the consumption of program foods. This is interpreted to mean that in some situations, additional foods reaching the family are distributed in a manner deemed appropriate in the family, with the net effect that more of the family food is reaching the target individual, the young child. However, the available data do not provide an adequate base to be certain about this potentially important observation.

We did not find the programs reviewed to be effective in reaching older infants and young children below the age of about two years. One reason for this in certain areas, such as India, from which many studies were reported, may be the pattern of delayed introduction of complementary foods. Most nutritionists agree that breastfeeding is adequate until at least four months, and that supplementary or complementary feeding is essential by six months, although Waterlow and Thompson (1979) have suggested that an earlier introduction of complementary foods may be nutritionally desirable when mothers are malnourished.

If programs are to reach children in the weaning/postweaning period, some major changes will be needed. These may include the use of foods deemed by the community to be appropriate for this age group and educational activities to promote earlier complementary feeding of breastfed infants. Since weaning practices vary across cultures and classes, the approaches will vary (Anderson and others 1981; WHO 1979).

Program Benefits

The measured benefit of most programs was anthropometric change, or difference from a control population. The most common measures were changes in weight or height. Tables 31-1, 31-2, and 31-3 summarize the effects on growth reported in published evaluations of food distribution programs. Not all programs examined had appropriate controls. Most claimed beneficial effects, but for some major ongoing programs, there was no demonstrable increase in anthropometric indices for the program as a whole. Positive effects were reported in some distribution centers and not in others. Close scrutiny of the results of the total experience suggested that anthropometric improvement was surprisingly small. In part, this may be explained by the relatively low levels of average net supplementation.

Not surprisingly, children with the greatest apparent weight deficit at entry into a program tended to show the greatest response to

Table 31-1. *Evaluations of Take-Home Food Distribution Programs*

| Country and region; source | Description of program | | | | | | Description of evaluation | | |
| | Urban or rural | Duration[a] | Target age (months) | Supplement used | | Design type[d] | Criteria used[e] | Reported conclusions[f] |
				Amount[b]	Type[c]			
Colombia, Candelaria (Wray 1978)	Urban	1964	0–72	n.a.	DSM	C	4	Improvement in weight gain and weight distribution
Colombia, (WFP 1972)	Mixed	1972	0–60 Mothers	580/32	DSM, O, W, fish	n.a.	4	Decrease of numbers of children in low weight categories; children selected for participation
Colombia (Mora and others 1974)	Urban	1972–76	Family (0–36)	670–428/ 30–23	DSM, O, W	A	1,2,6,10	Significant improvement in weight; no change in height; significant improvement in cognitive development. Difference due to deterioration in controls
Colombia (Mora and others 1981)	n.a.	n.a.	0–36	n.a.	n.a.	n.a.	4	Significant reduction in moderate and severe malnutrition

Study								Results
Colombia (Anderson and others 1981)	Mixed	1972–76	0–50	305/18.3	B, DSM, LF, O, SFWF	B	1,2,3,4, 6,8	No effect on growth or malnutrition rate overall; some centers had impact
Dominican Republic (Anderson and others 1981)	Mixed	1973–76	0–60	337/17.9	CSM, SFRO, WSB	B	1,2,3,4, 6,8	No significant impact on weight overall; some improvement in weight distribution; some centers had impact
Ethiopia (Hofvander and Eksmyr 1971)	Rural	1965–67	0–132	330/14	B, SM	C	1,2,6	No significant effect on height or weight; significant improvement in upper arm circumference
Ghana (Jacob and Gordon 1975)	Mixed	n.a.	0–72	n.a.	Various	C	1	Some improvement in weight distribution; not significant
India, Poshak (Gopaldas and others 1975)	Rural	1 year	6–36	400/20	CSM	A	1,2,4,8	Significant improvement in 12–36-month weight for regular collectors of food; reduction in morbidity
India, Tamil Nadu (Rajagopalan and others 1973)	Rural	1971–72	6–30 Mothers	350/18	CSM	A	1,2	Significant improvement in 9–24-month weight; no change in height

(Table continues on the following page.)

Table 31-1 (*continued*)

Country and region; source	Urban or rural	Duration[a]	Target age (months)	Amount[b]	Type[c]	Design type[d]	Criteria used[e]	Reported conclusions[f]
		Description of program		Supplement used		Description of evaluation		
India, Bombay (Khare and others 1976)	Rural	1972–74	0–60	335/17	G, GN	C	1	Weight status improved for 75 percent of children; nutritional status improved (internal data)
India (Shah 1976, 1977)	n.a.	1975–76	0–66 Mothers	285/16.4	n.a.	D	1	After one year 50+ percent severely malnourished children improved weight by more than 10 percent above expected growth
Jamaica (Alderman and others 1978)	Rural	1973–76	0–60	n.a.	CSM, DSM	D	4	40 percent decrease in proportion of children below 75 percent expected weight for age; children selected for participation
Lesotho (Cohen and Clayden 1978)	n.a.	1964–74	0–60	430/15	n.a.	C	1	No significant effect
Lesotho (Mackay and others 1974)	Mixed	1966–74	6–72	348/8.5	B, DSM, O	A	1	Significant improvement in weight

Location	Setting	Years[a]	Age (months)/Family	Energy/protein[b]	Food[c]	Control group[d]	Conclusions[e]	Comments[f]
Peru (Baertl and others 1970)	Mixed	1962–69	Family	256/7.5, 12.5	W ± fish protein concentrate	A	1,5,7	Small weight effect, not significant; significant reduction in mortality
Philippines (Asia Research Organization, Inc. 1976)	n.a.	n.a.	6–60	n.a.	n.a.	n.a.	1,4	Some reduction in second and third degree malnutrition; more effective in third degree
Rwanda (Jacob 1975)	Mixed	n.a.	0–48	514/17	DSM, WSB	C	1	Weight improved
Trinidad (Caribbean Food and Nutrition Institute 1975)	Rural	1974	0–60		DSM	B	4	Improvement in weight distribution (no statistical analyses)

n.a. Not available.

a. Duration of program to end of evaluation period; some programs continued beyond that date.

b. Energy content (kilocalories per day)/protein content (grams per day).

c. In tables 31-1 through 31-4: B, bulghur; CSM. corn soy milk; DSM, dried skim milk; G, gram (Bengal, green); GN, groundnuts; LF, local foods; MPF, multipurpose food; O, oil; S, sugar; Saha, local food mix; SB, soybean meal; SFB soy fortified bulghur; SFRO, soy fortified rolled oats; SFS, soy fortified sorghum; SFWF, soy fortified wheat flour; SM, soy milk; W, wheat (and pasta); WSB, wheat soy blend WSDM, whey soy drink mix.

d. In tables 31-1 through 31-4: A, longitudinal data compared with a control group; B, cross-sectional data compared with a control group; C, longitudinal data without a control group; D, cross-sectional data without a control group.

e. In tables 31-1 through 31-4: 1, weight; 2, height, weight for age; 3, weight for height; 4, weight distribution, degrees of malnutrition; 5, growth rate; 6, midarm circumference; 7, infant and child mortality; 8, infant and child morbidity; 9, physical activity; 10, cognitive development; 11, other.

f. Conclusions are those reported by authors of original reports.

Table 31-2. *Evaluations of Supervised Feeding Programs*

Country and region; source	Description of program					Description of evaluation		
	Urban or rural	Duration	Target age (months)	Supplement used		Design type	Criteria used	Reported conclusions
				Amount	Type			
Brazil (Gandra 1977)	n.a.	n.a.	26–84	n.a.	n.a.	n.a.	4	Significant reduction in second degree malnutrition
Costa Rica (Anderson and others 1981)	Mixed	1966–76	0–60	959/30	CSM, DSM, LF, WSB	B	1,2,3,4, 6,8	Third degree malnutrition eradicated; no other overall significant effect; some centers had positive impact
Costa Rica (Vargas 1976)	Rural	1974	27–72	230	n.a.	B	7,8	Significant fall in infant mortality and child morbidity
Guatemala (Behar and others 1968; Gordon and others 1968; Guzman and others 1968; Ascoli and others 1967; Scrimshaw and others[a])	Rural	1959–64	n.a.	n.a.	Incaparina	A	1,2,5,7, 8,11	Increased weight and height; decreased morbidity and mortality
Guatemala (Habicht and others 1972)	Rural	1969–72	9–72	Ad lib	Atole/Fresca	A	5	Significant improvement in growth rate with protein supplement
Guatemala (Freeman and others 1977)	Rural	1977	36–48	Ad lib	n.a.	A	2,10,11	Cognitive development improved; no direct data on growth
India, Hyderabad (Swaminathan and others 1970)	Rural	1968–70	24–72	300/10	G, GN, W	A	1,2	Significant improvement in height and weight in children 3–4 and 5–6 years old; no significant effect for children 2–3, 4–5

Location	Setting	Years	Age (months)	Dose	Supplement	Group	Notes	Results
India, Hyderabad (Gopalan and others 1973)	Rural	1971–72	12–60	310/3	O, S, W	A	1,2	Significant increase in weight and height; reduced clinical signs of malnutrition
India, Andhra Pradesh (Rao and Nadamuni 1977)	Rural	1974	12–60	310/3	n.a.	B	1,2	Severely malnourished benefited most
India, Andhra Pradesh (Rao and others 1975)	Rural	1970–74	6–72	300/3–10	CSM, DSM, MPF, bread	B	1,2	Significant improvement in height and weight
India, Narangwal (Kielmann and others 1983)	Rural	1968–73	0–36	400/11	DSM, O, S, W	A	1,2,7,8	Significant improvement in weight and morbidity. Children were selected on health criteria for direct intervention but treatment population was not selected
India, Tamil Nadu (Anderson and others 1981)	Mixed	1973–76	0–60	383/16	O, SFB, SFS, balahar, W	B	1,2,3,4 6,8	Slight improvement in height; no significant change in weight distribution; some centers had positive impact
Mexico (Chavez and Martinez 1975; Chavez and others 1972)	Rural	1968–72	0–24	Ad lib	Milk formula infant food	A	9	Physical activity increased
New Guinea (Becroft and Bailey 1965)	n.a.	1961–62	6–12	101–284/ 10–11.4	DSM, GN, SB	A	1,2	No significant effect on height or weight

n.a. Not available.

Note: See notes to table 31-1.

a. Scrimshaw, Guzman, and others (1968); Scrimshaw and others (1968); Scrimshaw, Gordon, Kevany, Flores, and Iscaza (1967); Scrimshaw, Guzman, and Gordon (1967); Scrimshaw, Guzman, Kevany, Ascoli, and others (1967).

Table 31-3. *Evaluations of Nutrition Rehabilitation Centers*

Country and region; source	Description of program					Description of evaluation		
	Urban or rural	Duration	Target age (months)	Supplement used		Design type	Criteria used	Reported conclusions
				Amount	Type			
Brazil (Federal University of Pernambuco and Secretary of Health for the State of Pernambuco 1971)	n.a.	n.a.	12–60	100 percent energy requirement, 60 percent protein requirement	Nutrien V, LF	n.a.	1,4	Improved weight for age
Colombia (WFP 1972)	Mixed	1970–71	n.a.	670/34	DSM, LF, W	C	4	Reduced incidence of low weight
Haiti (Fougere 1972)	n.a.	n.a.	12–48	n.a.	n.a.	n.a.	4	Significant reduction in third degree malnutrition
Haiti and Guatemala (Beaudry-Darisme and Latham 1973)	Mixed	1964–66	0–60	1,290/40	LF	A	1,7	Significant increase in weight compared with controls; decreased mortality; difference in weight persisted one year in Haiti, not in Guatemala

India (Venkataswamy and Kabir 1975)	n.a.	n.a.	12–60	n.a.	n.a.	n.a.	4	Substantial reduction in third degree malnutrition; increase in normal status and first degree malnutrition
India (Krishnamurthy and Kabir 1977)	Rural	1973–75	12–60	1,353/48	LF	C	4	Significant weight improvement (internal comparison)
India, Hyderabad (Devi and Pushpamma 1978)	Rural	1968–70	6–30	850/25.7	LF	A	1,2,4,6, 11	Creche. Significant increase in weight, height, and arm circumference; reduction of clinical signs of malnutrition in comparison with controls
Latin America (Beghin and Viteri 1973)	Mixed	1965–79	12–84	n.a.	LF	C	1	Weight status improved in most children (20 percent failure rate)
Philippines (Asia Research Organization Inc. 1976)	n.a.	n.a.	6–60	n.a.	MPF, bread	n.a.	4	Significant reduction in second and third degree malnutrition
Tanzania (Kraut and others 1978)	Rural	1969–71	24–72	1,300/30	n.a.	C	1,2,3	Significant weight improvement (internal comparison)

n.a. Not available.
Note: See notes to table 31-1.

supplementary feeding. Although apparent effectiveness and cost-effectiveness might be improved by selecting only children in the greatest need, this would exclude many children who could have responded and thereby would reduce effective coverage of the at-risk population.

A few studies reported morbidity and mortality data. When food distribution programs significantly reduced the prevalence of severe malnutrition, there appeared to be an accompanying reduction of morbidity or mortality from infectious diseases. The effect of preventing less-than-severe malnutrition is not clear. Indications imply a synergistic effect of combined feeding and health care programs. For example, data from one study suggest that recurrent illness and accompanying anorexia may limit voluntary food intake (Anderson and others 1981; also Leslie in part V).

One study demonstrated that a response of young children to additional food intake was increased activity (Chavez and others 1972). This was reported also for adults (Chavez and Martinez 1975). The other studies reviewed did not examine this possible outcome. Child development specialists have noted that increased voluntary activity in children (play) may affect cognitive development. The data suggest that the observed growth response accounts for only a small part of the net increase in energy intake. The missing energy may be producing unmeasured responses in children, such as physical activity, deadaptation of basal metabolic rate, and body composition changes. Some of these might have greater significance for overall child development than growth per se.

That researchers have seen and measured the leakage of food only as an undesirable aspect of food distribution programs is unfortunate. Researchers have made little or no attempt to trace the effects of this food, which may account for 30 to 80 percent of the food distributed. We cannot assume that there is no effect or that the effect in the family and community is not beneficial. If nothing else, it represents an increase in effective income/buying power. Therefore, we recommend that detailed investigations be undertaken to establish in more detail the effect of supplementary food on the individual and on the family and community. Until such research has been undertaken, the real effects and benefits of supplementary feeding programs cannot be known.

Program Costs and Use of Imported Food

Total reported cost (food and administrative costs) of operational programs intended to provide 300 to 400 kilocalories/day was about

$15-25 per enrollee per year (see table 31-4). In take-home programs, about 70 percent of this was the cost of food. In supervised feeding programs, the total cost (administrative cost in particular) was somewhat higher than in take-home programs. Costs of research and pilot programs were generally higher, reflecting the increased number and training of workers. These programs were also more effective. This may suggest that administrative budgets have been kept too low in operational programs and that additional or better-trained personnel might increase effectiveness.

Most of the programs reviewed made use of imported foods, either donated or purchased by the local government. The reasons stated for use of imported food (other than donated food) included assurance of continuity of supply and potential impact of large purchases on local food prices. There was no clear indication that the use of local foods rather than imported foods would be either cheaper or more expensive. Examples in each direction were found.

With one exception, there was no evidence that the foods used were unacceptable or that the use of local foods versus imported foods affected participation rates. One study demonstrated that when foods available locally were distributed free, participation was high; when a transition to purchase of the foods in the local market by the family was attempted, participation fell to very low levels (Gopaldas and others 1975). Cost to the family rather than source, familiarity, or knowledge of appropriate use was the most important determinant of usage.

Little or no experimental evidence in the studies reviewed related to the potential impact of program purchasing practices on the long-term use of local foods. There was no clear evidence that governments or communities were willing or able to make a transition from imported, donated foods to local, purchased foods.

No specific evidence of either beneficial or detrimental effects of food distribution programs on breastfeeding practices was identified. A number of authors commented that there was no detrimental effect even when the programs distributed such potential breast milk substitutes as milk powder. However, specific analyses to support these assertions were not provided.

Conclusions and Recommendations

Although supplementary feeding programs account for substantial amounts of money (or food equivalents), the present scale of most of them is probably much too small to have a major impact upon total communities or countries. However, if programs are to expand to the

Table 31-4. *Estimated Costs of Selected Supplementary Feeding Programs for Young Children*

Country and region; source	Program description						Cost per child per year (1976 U.S. dollars)[a]		
	Target age (months)	Urban or rural	Duration[b]	Type of food[c]	Target ration[d]	Days of supplementation	Total	Food	Administration
Take-home food distribution									
India, Poshak (Gopaldas and others 1975)	6–36	Rural	1975	CSM	400/20	365	15.00	11.60 (77)	3.30 (23)
Colombia (Anderson and others 1981)	0–60	Mixed	1972–76	B, CSM, DSM, O, SFRO, SFWF, WSB	305/18.3	365	24.75	13.41 (54)	11.34 (46)
Dominican Republic (Anderson and others 1981)	0–60	Mixed	1973–76	CSM, SFRO, WSB	337/17.9	365	15.20	10.34 (68)	4.90 (32)
Pakistan (Anderson and others 1981)	0–60	Mixed	1972–76	M, O, WSDM	298/16.6	365	23.51	16.64 (70)	6.87 (30)
Morocco (Robert Nathan Associates, Inc. 1979)	0–60	Mixed	1979	DSM, WSB	774/33	365	41.90	n.a.	n.a.
Sri Lanka (Robert Nathan Associates, Inc. 1978)	6–60	Mixed	1978	Triposha	185/10	365	11.14	6.68 (60)	4.46 (40)

Supervised feeding

Tunisia (Fox and Gibson 1979)	6–72	Mixed	1979	Milk, Saha, CSM, O, S	560/16.5	300	25.30	n.a.	n.a.
India, Tamil Nadu (Anderson and others 1981)	0–60	Mixed	1973–76	Balahar, O, SFB, SFS, W	383/16	300	14.48	10.69 (75)	3.79 (25)
Costa Rica (Anderson and others 1981)	0–60	Mixed	1966–76	DSM, CSM, WSB[e]	959/30	300	94.54	70.58[e] (68)	23.96 (26)
India, Andhra Pradesh (Rao and Nadamuni 1977)	6–72	Rural	1974	Bread, CSM, DSM, MPF	300/8–10	300	10.70	8.00 (75)	2.70 (25)
India, Narangwal (Kielmann and others 1983)	6–60	Rural	1968–73	DSM, O, S, W	400/11	120	38.70	n.a.	n.a.

n.a. Not available.

a. Cost figures are adjusted on the basis of a producer price index of consumer foods. Numbers in parentheses are percentages.

b. Duration of program to observation period; some continued beyond that date.

c. For definitions, see table 31-1.

d. Energy content (kilocalories per day)/protein content (grams per day).

e. Ninety-five percent of food distributed (including meat, milk, and fresh fruits) was obtained from local sources and purchased by the government. This accounts for the very high food cost.

point where they can exert a real impact, planners must define their true objectives and the programs must be designed and implemented accordingly. The objective might be to use such programs as an instrument for redistribution of effective income/demand and for community development (with the community as the target), or they might be used as a specific form of supplementation targeted toward high-risk individuals. The design would be quite different for these two goals.

If supplementary feeding programs are to continue to operate within the existing definition of their goal of improved growth and development of target age groups, perhaps the greatest impact would follow from measures that would enable the programs to reach children in the 4-to-24-month age group. However, we are uncertain that this can be achieved without directing the program to the family as a unit.

In many if not all of the communities that might be selected for food distribution programs, populations are now in equilibrium with their unfavorable environment (including chronic underfeeding) through social and individual adaptations. A food distribution program may disrupt these adaptations as well as effect an improvement in overall health. If such programs are abruptly withdrawn, the previous adaptations may not be quickly reestablished. Therefore, there is need for reasonable assurance of continuity before food distribution programs are initiated, whether these are experimental or operational programs. Although the programs reviewed do not contribute data about the effect of withdrawal, the literature provides ample evidence that programs have been withdrawn after a year or two of operation.

This review may raise more questions than it answers. Certainly it challenges many widely held assumptions. For this reason, we strongly recommend that additional, intensive studies of the effects of food distribution programs be undertaken. Since such programs are likely to expand—in response both to political pressure and to general scientific opinion that if there is widespread undernutrition, feeding must be good—the questions raised here should be addressed promptly.

32

Nutrition Education: An Overview

Robert C. Hornik

This review asks three questions. What is the potential for educational interventions in nutrition? Do such interventions as have been evaluated have any worthwhile consequences? Is it possible to extend effective programming on a large scale?

Does Education Have a Role?

Few nutritional behaviors are unequivocally open or closed to education. Knowledge of the determinants of particular nutritional practices is thin and is growing only slowly.

Most authors believe that aggregate household nutritional status is largely closed to nonincome interventions but that intrahousehold food distribution and inequity of nutritional status within families is open to such interventions. Although this consensus may reflect less definitive research than one might like, most nutrition education projects act on these assumptions, emphasizing breastfeeding, the feeding of weaning-age children, diarrheal treatment, and special diets for pregnant and lactating women, with some adding activities to improve the balance of meals and sanitary practices. That projects have been developed on this basis is just as well, since the best evidence for the openness of these behaviors to educational interventions is likely to come from evaluations of those interventions, rather than from further basic research on determinants.

Effectiveness of Nutrition Education

While most nutrition education is unevaluated and is probably ineffective, a few projects exist that show substantial effects on behav-

Excerpted from *Nutrition Education—A State of the Art Review,* ACC-SCN State of the Art Series, Nutrition Policy Discussion Paper 1, 1985.

ior and nutritional status. In Morocco, education together with food supplements produced greater nutritional status change than did supplementation alone (Gilmore and others 1980). In Micronesia, promotion of coconut milk as a substitute for imported drinks led to widespread behavior change (Rody 1978). In Indonesia, nutrition education by village volunteers, supported by radio and specially designed "action" posters, produced a significant improvement in nutritional status (Manoff International, Inc. 1984). Media-based projects in The Gambia, Honduras, the Philippines, and Tanzania have reached large audiences who display new knowledge and changed attitudes and report some change in practices (Academy for Educational Development, Inc. and Stanford University 1984; Cooke and Romweber 1977; Mahai and others 1976). For the last two projects nutritionally significant change may be occurring as well (Foote 1983). These successful projects are not representative, nor do they prove that nutrition education is possible on a large scale, but they do show that nutrition education can have a positive effect.

The trade-off between reaching large audiences, which media-based programs can do, and producing nutritionally significant behavior change, which pilot outreach projects have been able to do, remains the central problem of nutrition education. Large-scale expansion of face-to-face outreach projects is difficult. Recruiting, training, and supervising the necessary field workers is likely to be a huge task. Paying them in cash and/or providing them with sufficient incentives to work effectively over the long haul will be expensive and difficult. Agricultural institutions, with a long history of building extension systems and with much larger budgets, have rarely succeeded in reaching the poorest farmers or in changing their practices (Hornik 1982; Orivel 1983). Optimism about the probability of the health system (or a nutrition component) achieving that end must be limited. Few countries will be able to muster the budgets, the management skill, and the long-term enthusiasm required. Nonetheless, building nutrition education onto extended health systems, where they do reach the poorly nourished and have a preventive as well as a curative mission, is surely worth trying.

Perhaps the only way that face-to-face nutrition education will be realized effectively on a large scale will be if communities take administrative and financial responsibility for such programs on their own, depending as little as possible on outside help. If people are paying for a service, they will take full advantage of it. Education can bring about change, and the relevant educational concepts are well within the grasp of at least some members of each community. Theoretically, locally operated education is feasible. If a modest amount of equipment, such as weighing scales, and training were available from outside and sought by the community, effective nutrition education might be realized autonomously. The fundamental constraint would be the willingness of and feasibility for a particular community to organize. In some cultures, shared communal responsibility will be accepted with little outside stimulus. In other cultures it is less likely to appear.

The alternative route is to rely essentially on mass media–based programs, complemented when feasible by face-to-face and other support activities. The central problem of media-based programs will be their tendency to become dissociated from what goes on in the field. Radio broadcasts made by city-based producers without careful and continuous interaction with the target audience are likely to meet with limited success. The critical elements are prior investigation, instructional design, pretesting, information from the audience, and responsive readjustment of messages.

However, stressing careful instructional design and qualitative field research in media-based nutrition education has major cost implications. Budgeting for field activities and for instructional design, as well as for actual production and the purchase of media time, may not be easily accepted. Absolute budgets directly allocated to nutrition education will be much higher than is customary, even if cost per client reached effectively is likely to be lower. The Mass Media Health Practices program in The Gambia and Honduras, even without its technical assistance component, cost $125,000 annually, although the cost per self-reported adopter of the oral rehydration therapy promoted was only $2.50 in Honduras (Foote 1983). Similarly, the cost per beneficiary of the Indonesia Nutrition Communication and Behavior Change Project was estimated to be about $3.90 for the pilot phase (or $9.80 per child with nutritional status improvement), based on estimated recurrent costs of about $100,000 per year, although the cost was expected to fall to about $2.00 per beneficiary (or $5.00 per child with nutritional improvement) if the project were expanded to more areas in Indonesia (Manoff International, Inc. 1984). Yet without these relatively high central costs for broadcast time, for materials preparation, and for field data collection, effective mass media–based nutrition education is unlikely to be effective.

Other questions about the usefulness of the mass media remain open. Some argue that the media are likely to affect superficial knowledge or practices but will not affect behaviors that are more complex or important for an individual. They suggest that the personal support of a trusted friend, given face-to-face, is necessary for change in most circumstances. However, an alternative view may be plausible also. If people are actively seeking solutions for problems, they will make use of any source that responds to their needs. If they are not anxious to change, face-to-face persuasion will be no more effective than mediated communication. That many media-based programs have been ineffective reflects not necessarily an intrinsic weakness but rather the scarcity of programs that have used media well. No evidence exists that sophisticated media-based programs cannot work, and some indications show that they can. Despite potential limitations, a serious look at media-based education can be justified. It may be the only realistic strategy. Any system that reduces the political, financial, and, most of all, the logistical complexities on which projects so often founder is worth a major trial.

Logic and some evidence suggest that a promising approach is to link nutrition education with other resource changes. The logic is that whenever the old rules do not work optimally, people are likely to be open to new information that allows them to adapt. Supplemental food supplies allow different feeding patterns; education can enable consumers to make optimum choices. Moving to a new location where new foods are available or new prices for previously consumed foods are encountered may, similarly, allow dietary change. Education can ease the transition.

Another set of linkages also often recommended is perhaps not as easy to support. The logic is straightforward: agriculture extension agents are already in the field, and it is wasteful to have single purpose agents. Development is multifaceted; focusing on only one problem risks exacerbating others and is parochial. Why not build on what agriculture extension agents do and have them become nutrition agents? Nonetheless, in practice, this is unlikely to work.

Agricultural extension agents rarely get to the poorest farmers and by definition ignore landless laborers. Yet those two groups are among the most malnourished. Women are rarely a direct audience for agents (see FAO in part II). Extension agents in more sophisticated systems, such as the Benor Training and Visit System, are fully laden with specific agricultural tasks and would resist taking on multipurpose roles. While backyard gardens and the raising of small animals for protein fall more directly in their purview, it may be unrealistic to expect agents to take on these tasks. In any case, they are rarely the primary practices recommended in nutrition education programs. As appealing as the idea of linkage with another, richer sector's activities may be, in reality success is unlikely.

Based on experience to date, what can we conclude about the feasibility and effectiveness of nutrition education? The evidence for the potential of education is far from definitive, although for important nutritional outcomes it is clear that income does not account for all variation—a result consistent with investment in education. A number of educational programs using face-to-face methods have had an observable impact on nutritional status. However, organization and maintenance of such programs on a large scale has not been accomplished and may prove difficult. Some recent mass media–based efforts exhibit an ability to reach large audiences and teach new behaviors. They show some promise although, as yet, not unequivocal evidence of affecting nutritional status. The most effective programs integrate broadcasts with content development based on careful field research, continuing field contact, and some incorporation of the health infrastructure.

Implementation and Research: The Next Steps

What are the appropriate next steps for people concerned with nutrition education? How should a national planner considering strategies to combat malnutrition view nutrition education?

The first thing to do is to stop considering nutrition education as it has traditionally been considered—as a minor activity involving a few posters and irregular clinic-based advice run out of a basement office in the ministry of health with no budget or status. If it is to be worthwhile at all, planners must adopt goals of behavior change for large audiences and must allocate the budgets and personnel commensurate with the necessary tasks. Planners need to choose something serious to do and then ask whether nutrition education is a competitive strategy for accomplishing that goal. They ought not be asking what improved consequence can be achieved within current minimum budgets. The answer is likely to be, very little. If it is politically unrealistic to expect larger budgets for nutrition education, it is substantively unrealistic to expect worthwhile consequences.

The next step is to ask whether nutrition education, no matter how effectively implemented, is likely to affect a particular nutritional concern. In some cases, initial research will eliminate education as a useful strategy. For example, if withdrawing the breast during an episode of diarrhea is rare in a particular culture, or occurs because of sick children's lack of appetite and despite mothers' attempts to feed them, it is not likely to be an appropriate target for nutrition education.

If economic circumstances preclude practice change, or a recommended change is likely to produce minimal nutritional status change, there may be little point in addressing it with education. Water boiling, both because of the demands it makes on fuel and time and because it may have little effect on infection in the face of so many other environmental sources of infection, is an example on both counts.

However, if lack of knowledge remains a possible cause of poor nutritional status in a given culture, the next step is to investigate other educational projects that might serve as useful models. Since relatively few projects have been evaluated, and even fewer have done education as well as it might be done, this will be a limited resource. Nonetheless, reviews (for example, the longer version of this chapter; Jenkins 1983; Leslie 1981; Zeitlin and Formacion 1981) may suggest some promising topics and methods and some to avoid.

Next come questions about what is feasible with regard to education. What field structures are in place and reaching the target audience? Is there a saturated network of distribution points for products? How far do agents who might take part in an active educational network reach? What incentives are likely to encourage effective delivery of education? Can backup training and supervision be implemented? Is there a network of agents who could be part of a passive educational system, even if expecting effective and active outreach is unrealistic? What proportion of the audience can be reached by radio, given language and ownership issues? What level of community responsibility for nutritional improvement is likely to be activated? Is there a reasonable possibility of local and autonomous management of education-based change?

Given the experience summarized in this review, the answers to these questions are likely to lead away from face-to-face active outreach education systems. This is particularly likely to be the case if one has to build a network from scratch or depend on people whose salaries are paid by other bureaucracies, and if communities cannot be expected to take long-term financial and administrative responsibility for local activity. The answers are likely to lead either to some skepticism about the viability of educational strategies altogether, because they are so difficult to implement, or to the construction of media-based education systems that promise audience reach, logistic feasibility, and at least a reasonable potential for success.

Such systems should probably assume that people are open to change and are looking for solutions to current problems. The problem for media-based systems is to find appropriate educational messages which reflect solutions that fit the lives and preferences of audiences, and then to communicate them clearly and with enough specificity that they permit action. Broadcasts linked to concomitant resource or environmental change are particularly promising, and such links may be crucial for some areas of change in practices.

Under current circumstances, national planners are best advised to be wary of face-to-face outreach education on grounds of feasibility and may find media-based systems promising. For those in the business of developing yet more informed judgments about the utility of nutrition education, five specific research activities may produce some return.

1. Look at what actually goes on in conventional nutrition programs. What little money goes into nutrition education in many countries may be located in such programs. Is it possible to build an effective program on the basis of what is already done, or is the structure fundamentally inappropriate, as assumed in this review? The tendency to start anew, while understandable, raises difficult issues with regard to long-term survival. Building on existing programs, while it risks opposition from an entrenched bureaucracy, may be an easier administrative route.

2. Look at the Indonesia Nutrition Communication and Behavior Change Project over the long term. Does the volunteerism continue to work and expand? Is it possible that, even if the number of volunteer hours declines, the new practices have taken hold and will diffuse in the community? Or, on the contrary, does the atrophy of voluntary participation mean that even those who improved during the experimental year will backslide? Long-term observation may also provide further information about the possibility of face-to-face outreach on a routine, large scale.

3. Media-based projects deserve further tests. Field-based programs that emphasize careful message design may be the only way to carry out large-scale nutrition education in many countries. They may not be as effective as well-done face-to-face outreach, but they may be logistically feasible and thus the only game in town.

4. For both media-based and face-to-face projects, the development of methods to assess nutritional problems, pretest messages, and gain constant information about audience response and change would be helpful. The need for precision, representativeness, and insight combined with timeliness and low cost make the methodological problems significant. These problems are increased if project staff lack sophisticated methodological skills.

5. Nutrition education would be well served by a far more rigorous cost and financing study than is possible with the limited cost data available for most projects. Uncovering hidden costs, appropriately amortizing technical assistance and other capital expenditures, defining comparable measures of effectiveness, correctly indicating where financial burdens lie, and presenting the absolute budgets likely to be part of a fully operating budget would surely help decision making. Such information is not now available across a range of nutrition education approaches.

33

Nutrition Education: Lessons Learned

Richard K. Manoff

Discovering the lessons learned from experience can be a precarious enterprise if one ventures beyond the limits of documentation into the uncharted waters of insight and interpretation. While it is safer not to do so, there is value to be found in experience that eludes the coarse mesh of numerical measurement. These lessons learned are presented, therefore, with all risks revealed. If many are not documentable, be assured, at least, that all are the product of hard experience, some of it bitter, but all of it unforgettably instructive.

Establishment of nutrition education priorities as a first step is essential to avoid program clutter and diffusion. Nutrition education is a category of subjects of which only some are of pressing concern at a given time. Urgent problems should be dealt with first. When teaching attempts too much, learning suffers. Thus, before we teach, we must determine what most needs to be learned. In this way we achieve the aims of nutrition education in accordance with the needs of the community, not the presumptions of the educator.

Before setting objectives, the behavioral tasks required of the target audience must be analyzed. What must a mother do to prepare a new weaning food? Are the recommended ingredients readily available? What cooking steps, utensils, and fuel are necessary? Objectives must be framed by what is probable, not merely possible. Encouraging the inclusion of dried fish to enrich the infant *lugaw* in the Philippines was preceded by a market analysis to ascertain its year-round availability at an affordable price.

The real decision-making authorities for nutrition education policies and programs must be identified. These are not always the "portfolio officials." Knowing who the decisionmakers are in advance saves time, effort, money, and morale, not to speak of the program.

Formative evaluation of concepts, content, and message design makes a prudent contribution to the nutrition education program. Formative evalua-

Reprinted with minor editorial revisions from *Mothers and Children*, vol. 2, no. 3 (September 1982), Washington, D.C.: American Public Health Association.

tion is essentially an unstructured interview technique designed to uncover questions and attitudes rather than to quantify existing ones. It lends itself to group discussion as well as to individual interviewing. Quantitative research, with its closed-end question design, updates responses to old questions. Formative evaluation enables us to ascertain change and to uncover the new questions uppermost in the minds of the target groups; it minimizes design bias by encouraging expression from those whose attitudes we seek to measure. In Nicaragua in 1975, health authorities in Managua had included bicarbonate of soda in the recommended oral rehydration formula. But formative evaluation revealed how few of the villagers knew of bicarbonate of soda and how sparsely bicarbonate of soda was stocked by local stores.

For a homemade weaning food formulation, the Indonesian Nutrition Development Program (Manoff International, Inc. 1984) employed formative evaluation to involve mothers in the development of the recipe. Parameters were set for the types of food, but the choice was left to the mothers. A return visit ascertained whether the choice satisfied pre-established nutritional values. Thus mothers participated in product development in the same way as manufacturers engage them in product testing and solicit the consumer's likes and dislikes in deciding the final formulation.

Finally, formative evaluation is indispensable to message design and testing. The constraints, the resistance points—the bases for opposing the desired behavior—and the cultural and attitudinal blocks uncovered through formative evaluation provide the key message elements. Continuing formative evaluation provides a review of message design and of the quality of the target audience's response.

Community-based participation in the formulation of concepts and message designs is indispensable. This is implicit in formative evaluation.

The difficulties involved in planning and executing baseline studies limits their usefulness for many nutrition education programs. Baseline studies are expensive and are frequently flawed by "research overkill." In addition, baseline studies are too often hurriedly implemented because of onrushing deadlines. The result is that many baselines are defective, either in questions asked or unasked or in subject matter covered. This may be less true of pilot programs, whose scheduling is more flexible.

A proper baseline cannot be executed until all program elements— the target audience, the messages, the educational channels and media, and other program interventions—are verified. Otherwise, the questionnaire and interviewer training cannot be related exactly to the program. Baseline norms will be either incomplete or missing and therefore inadequate for measuring performance through tracking studies. Researchers may try to compensate for these deficiencies in the tracking studies, but there is no baseline norm. This raises the question, why not use less costly and more flexible research methodologies, such as (a) periodic tracking with formative evaluation (sacrificing exact quantification for prudent trend measurements); (b) delay of the baseline for perhaps two to three months after the program's start (sacrificing the possibility of an exact preprogram situation assessment in return for a more accurate measure of the program's long-term impact); or (c) a control sample for comparison (not ordinarily possible when a program is national in scope); in this case the baseline is dispensed with altogether.

Prudence is a more effective management strategy than exactitude. We cannot know everything before beginning a program. We have to settle for a prudent appraisal of information available. This suggests prudence in research—enough research to support and evaluate our program, but not so much that management and study costs take an excessive share of the program budget.

Nutrition educators often blur the distinction between educational materials and the media for education. Films, slides, posters, reach-and-frequency messages (such as advertising techniques) for use on television and radio, pamphlets, and flipcharts are materials, not media. Media are needed to deliver materials to target audiences. People—health agents and promoters—are a medium. Television, radio stations, and schools are media. Newspapers and magazines, walls for posters, and the people to put them up—these are media. Cinemas and mobile film vans are media. They must be provided for in advance and their costs and capabilities must be calculated. Too many programs are handicapped from the start because messages and materials are ready but there is no media strategy and plan or no personnel and funds to deliver them.

Nutrition education programs must be supported at a sufficient level of effort with adequate time and with money for materials, staff, and media. Since formal and informal delivery systems are essential to deliver messages to target audiences, their costs and personnel must be budgeted and provided for. It is better to know of budgetary limitations at the start and to plan accordingly than to have the program hampered later.

Since budgets are always limited, programs must be scaled to available resources. We must project practical goals and objectives to calculate what we have to work with—the priority problems to be dealt with, the geographic area to be covered; to recognize the constraints of limited money and personnel; and to budget tasks accordingly. It is a tactic of trading time and objectives for money and people. The less we have to work with, the less we should attempt, both in goals and in time. Limited successes are preferable to grandiose failures. A successful, though limited, program can later be expanded.

Pilot projects often fail to take into account the eventual costs and capabilities of the national expansion. Pilot project plans should include the cost of the national expansion. Otherwise, the project is without point. To make a "best effort" in the pilot project without calculating the personnel and funding inputs necessary for its national expansion is to court certain disappointment—a failure to achieve national goals despite successful pilot program results.

Almost without exception, every food and nutrition intervention represents an opportunity for nutrition education. The food supplementation program in Morocco (Gilmore and others 1980) reports better results with a nutrition education component than without it. A similar report emerges from the Nutrition Development Program in Indonesia (Manoff International, Inc. 1984), in which weighing and growth chart interventions were combined with nutrition education, and from the Palawan Integrated Area Development project in the Philippines, which provided for nutrition education by project design. This lesson is part experience, part insight: we know of no food or nutrition project in which nutrition education could not have been an essential element—whether for consumers, farmers, or food processors.

Use all the nutrition education channels and media you can afford and manage consistent with target audience strategy and the messages to be delivered. Nutrition education interventions are rarely mutually exclusive. They are usually complementary and offer reinforcement of the nutrition education messages. Duplication of message delivery is desirable provided there is message harmony. Mass media, for example, are not a substitute for more formal nutrition education systems. If properly harmonized in terms of messages, the one reinforces the other.

The nutritional problems of mothers and children cannot be separated into discrete nutrition education programs. The promotion of breastfeeding is inseparable from the nutrition of the pregnant woman, the nutrition of the lactating woman, the introduction of weaning foods, the prevention and treatment of diarrheal infections, the curbing of deleterious marketing practices for breast milk substitutes, changes in hospital practices, and the need for policy initiatives, such as paid maternity leave and workplace childcare. The effort to deal with any one of these involves consideration of the others, since it is handicapped without them.

There are limits to nutrition education because not every nutrition problem is an education problem; some problems, like bad water, are economic. A water boiling education effort proved almost a total failure in Ecuador in 1972. Potable water is an economic problem requiring a structural change in the system. The same is true of hospital practices. In Recife,

Brazil, eight out of nine maternity hospitals have changed to rooming-in. Breastfeeding in the first 12 hours is now almost 100 percent as compared with 24 percent when infants were separated from their mothers. Diarrheal infections are nonexistent as compared with 15 to 20 percent before. The use of breast milk substitutes is now only 20 percent of what it used to be. Baby abandonment has ceased to exist. Breastfeeding education without this structural change in hospital administration would have been ineffectual by comparison.

Goiter is also an economic, not an educational or medical, problem. Education becomes practical only after salt is iodized and made available at an appropriate price.

To understand in advance the limits of nutrition education reduces the danger of overburdening the target audience, usually women. Behavior modification of the system instead of the individual is frequently the more appropriate objective. Yet on occasion nutrition education serves as an unwitting surrogate for inaction on social policy initiatives. However, in the state of Santa Catarina, Brazil, new legislation in 1979 enabled inspection of business establishments to compel compliance with a previous law requiring childcare. In one year, 85 percent of them had established such facilities. Another example is the regulation of marketing of feeding bottles in Papua New Guinea, which is credited with significantly reducing second and third degree malnutrition.

Before establishing behavior modification objectives, nutrition educators must ascertain possible structural constraints. Furthermore, a task-by-task analysis of the demands imposed by proposed behavioral changes might reveal unreasonable expectations.

Among structural constraints, none has exerted more negative influence on nutrition education programs than antagonistic commercial marketing practices. For example, the overmarketing of breast milk substitutes must be controlled as a matter of policy. Otherwise, even a well-planned and well-executed breastfeeding campaign can be cancelled out to produce a zero-sum effect.

The mass media, particularly radio and television, add a valuable dimension to every nutrition education program. Mass media can extend the reach of health workers, educators, and health systems. Since only a fraction of the population comes to the local health centers, an effort is warranted to bring the health center to the people. Those who do not come may be the most vulnerable—either unmotivated or unaware. Because nutrition education is essentially a preventive health strategy, the mass media can be particularly helpful. Preventive health messages are mostly simple, direct, and nontechnical—ideally suited to mass media delivery. Mass media also help to reduce message dissonance by standardizing nutrition education messages for all nutrition educators (as well as for the public), influencing them to harmonize their messages on the same subjects with those emanating from the mass media.

Design and execution of messages are major weaknesses in nutrition education. There is widespread misconception about what constitutes a nutrition education message—whether delivered one-to-one in a health center, in a classroom, or via the media. A slogan is not a message, nor is a restatement of the objective. Nor does a repetition of the theme, the problem, the desired behavior, or the benefit constitute a complete message in every situation. On the contrary, a nutrition education message must go beyond the problem, the desired action, and its benefits to the resistance points—the behavioral constraints. The discipline of dealing with the resistance points to achieve a desired behavior is the essence of effective message design. Breastfeeding messages that acclaim the superiority of mother's milk do not deal with the heart of the problem. Though almost everyone agrees that breast is best, the use of breast substitutes is becoming universal. Obviously, critical constraints are creating the chasm between belief and behavior. In Brazil, formative evaluation (through focus group discussions) has produced rich insights into the psychological and sociological resistance points among new mothers. These range from her self-doubts and insecurities and her loneliness in the absence of traditional support systems to her practical problems as a working woman. Nutrition education messages that deal with these in an effective mode enable the new mother to realize that she is not alone in her uncertainty and give her renewed assurance and relief from anxiety. Only a message—whether in the health center or other media—that deals persuasively with her fears, real and imagined, offers the possibility of impact.

In much the same way, message delivery systems must be selected carefully. Media need to be viewed for their inherent differences, not summarily lumped together without distinction. No two media are identical, either in their uses, their advantages and disadvantages, or their target audience efficiencies. The modern nutrition educator needs to appreciate media diversity and the special advantages of each medium in terms of target audience and message.

Nutrition education evaluators mistakenly assume that the quality of nutrition education is a constant in all situations. Nutrition education is not of uniform value. Its worth is as variable as the people involved and the inputs they make. Yet evaluations invariably focus only on measuring the impact of the nutrition education component instead of first attempting to assess its quality. What was the content of the education? Was the content relevant to local problems, to the target audience? How well designed were the content messages and how rigorously were they tested? Did the content deal with priorities or with a diffusion of problems? How relevant were its motivational elements to identifiable resistance points? and so forth?

The mass media are similarly stereotyped. The value of radio in nutrition education is automatically presumed to be a constant. Evaluators characteristically proceed to ascertain its impact rather than to analyze how well it was used. Was the radio format appropriate? Did the time periods efficiently deliver maximum shares of the desired target audience? Were the messages effective in content, relevant to priority problems, and motivating in terms of identifiable resistance points?

Nutrition education is an inside/outside responsibility, with nutrition educators requiring continuing education along with the public. In Brazil, few members of the National Working Group responsible for the national breastfeeding program were aware of the successful experience with rooming-in in Recife. Several were unaware of the Santa Catarina experience in setting up workplace childcare. No more than 10 percent of the health professionals we addressed in five different cities knew about the new WHO/UNICEF International Code for the Marketing of Breast Milk Substitutes, even though Brazil voted for it at the 1981 World Health Assembly. If educators are to be effective with the public, they must be adequately informed for their jobs. This requires a system of in-service training and communication at all levels of the health system.

Nutrition education capability must be institutionalized locally. Nutrition education professionals should be placed where they can best respond to demands for their services. They must assess all multisectoral food, health, and nutrition programs to identify the appropriate nutrition education intervention. It is not enough for nutrition education to be an available resource. Nutrition educators must also engage in advocacy for the use of their services.

PART VI

Food and Nutrition Planning

The last decade has seen considerable attention paid to food and nutrition planning. As the emphasis shifted in the mid-1970s from a narrow focus on food supply or technological fixes to a recognition of the complex interaction of a range of economic and cultural causes of malnutrition, there was a surge of optimism that multisectoral or integrated food and nutrition plans would provide an answer to the problem. However, ten years of experience have shown that although malnutrition may have multisectoral causes, multisectoral interventions are not necessarily the solution.

Politically and administratively, large nutrition programs that cut across sectoral boundaries have proven extremely difficult to agree upon and develop, much less implement. These difficulties, as Alan Berg and James Austin observe in this section, have "led the nutrition community to reexamine the possibilities of working within traditional sectors but addressing the problem in several key sectors simultaneously." The current emphasis is less on the need to develop comprehensive and detailed food and nutrition plans and more on the need to build a consensus and to seize opportunities when they arise, be they political, economic, or technological. The selections in this section review recent experience with food and nutrition planning from several viewpoints, including an in-depth focus on China and sub-Saharan Africa.

In the opening selection, Berg and Austin assess the success of the new multidisciplinary approach to nutrition planning. They find that significant progress has been made in terms of higher visibility for nutrition within governments and development agencies, valuable scientific research on the biological bases of nutrition, and the development of more sophisticated methods for examining "the economic and administrative dimensions of the malnutrition problem." On the whole, however, they conclude that the hopes raised at the 1974 World

Food Conference have not been fulfilled. In urging the development community to fulfill its unfinished nutrition agenda, they point out that "malnutrition is, like unemployment, a condition, not a sector. If countries are able to organize their various sectors to produce policies and programs that address unemployment, they should be able to do so for malnutrition."

The selection by James M. Pines on national nutrition planning focuses on an issue also raised by Berg and Austin: that "neglect or inadequate response to political aspects explains much of the multisectoral approach's weakness in affecting policy." Pines points out that not only have nutrition planners frequently failed to build a political constituency, but they also have often been unprepared or unrealistic when given a political opening. "When decisionmakers finally ask, 'What do you want me to do about it?'" Pines says, "planners must be ready with actions intended to alleviate specific nutrition problems that are feasible administratively and financially and are likely to produce visible results within the politically relevant time period."

Dean Jamison and Alan Piazza describe China's encouraging experience in mobilizing physical, social, and political resources to raise the nutritional status of its population and dramatically increase life expectancy in the 30 years since the revolution. The three key features of the government's food policy were implementing an urban food rationing and subsidy system and rural grain transfer programs, favoring direct consumption of grain over the consumption of preferred foods such as pulses, vegetable oils, and animal foods, and moderating local and regional food shortages through international and domestic agricultural trade. Successful as this policy has been in aggregate terms, however, Jamison and Piazza caution that "progress to improve health and nutrition has been far from uniform, and major rural-urban differences and differences among rural areas still exist."

Alain de Janvry analyzes the discouraging decline in per capita food availability in sub-Saharan Africa during the last 25 years. In looking for ways to increase food production in this region in the future, he points out that adequate producer prices are necessary but not sufficient and urges "policies aimed at structural change, even if they are more difficult to manage than price incentives." De Janvry also calls attention to the necessity for a genuine political role for farmers, one that will enable them "to become full-fledged citizens in the political apparatus and to assert their rights through lobbying groups." The same point is raised by Kees Tuinenburg in his review of the experience of four African countries—Kenya, Mali, Rwanda, and Zambia— that have begun to formulate and implement food strategies with assistance from the European Community. Although all four countries have taken encouraging and innovative steps, Tuinenburg's conclusion, which might equally serve as a conclusion for all the selections in this part, is that "food strategy formulation and implementation is an ongoing process that requires patience, since by its nature, results cannot be expected overnight."

34

Nutrition Policies and Programs: A Decade of Redirection

Alan Berg and James Austin

The World Food Conference more than a decade ago signaled a turning point for the international nutrition field. No longer was hunger viewed simply as a food supply problem whose solution rested on the shoulders of the world's farmers. Nor was malnutrition seen as only a health problem within the biomedical domain of the scientists who had traditionally dominated the nutrition field. Rather, the 1974 conference added impetus to a small movement, already under way, aimed at broadening the diagnostic and prescriptive scope of nutrition to encompass other factors and disciplines, particularly economic and managerial.

The new model of malnutrition, with a multidisciplinary focus, was based on four main propositions.

○ Although malnutrition was inescapably entwined with health status, mass alleviation of protein-energy deficiency, the primary nutrition concern, was not likely to be achieved through medical treatment and health systems.

○ Although malnutrition was redefined as a food problem, the key issue was access to food rather than the total supply of food. The focus thus shifted to poverty, income distribution, and employment.

○ Although malnutrition was part of the poverty syndrome, in certain circumstances nutrition improvement was possible without major income increases.

Excerpted from "Nutrition Policies and Programs," *Food Policy*, vol. 9, no. 4 (November 1984), pp. 304–12.

○ Although malnutrition was clearly in the province of the biological sciences, economic and managerial analysis and planning could and should be applied. As malnutrition was now seen as a development problem—as both a contributor to and a consequence of underdevelopment—these development disciplines were relevant and needed to be tried.

The world food crisis in 1973–74 captured the attention of policymakers. With the World Food Conference, which was mounted to discuss ways of dealing with the crisis, an opportunity to try out the new model became available.

Evolution of Nutrition Programs: Expectations and Performance

We can point to some progress since the World Food Conference. Nutrition has received consideration as a development issue, becoming sufficiently respectable to be included on the agenda of many planning ministries. International development agencies have created or strengthened small nutrition units. Cadres have been trained within universities, within ministries, and within international agencies. More sophisticated methods have been developed to examine the economic and administrative dimensions of the malnutrition problem and to devise solutions to the problem. The frontiers of knowledge in the biological sciences have been moved outward. And the experience accumulated in nutrition programs has shed light on the feasibility of various new interventions.

Several countries have mounted impressive and largely successful nutrition programs, but for every country that has made significant progress, there are several where nutrition concerns and actions are not much further along than they were a decade ago. Overall, achievements have fallen considerably short of the expectations raised by the World Food Conference. Globally, nutrition actions have not met the magnitude of the need nor the full extent of the expectations raised.

The sense of urgency created by the food crisis, the intellectual excitement surrounding a new model, and the commitment of those pushing for attention for nutrition put nutrition on policy agendas in the middle and late 1970s. In more recent years, interest has lagged in some quarters. Although nutrition may appear to have taken the path of a rapidly rising and slowly declining star, close examination reveals a more complex pattern of several distinct but overlapping intellectual and programmatic thrusts.

The Technological Fix

Just before the World Food Conference, nutrition had passed through an era of enchantment with technological solutions. Single-cell protein, fish protein concentrate, synthetic amino acid fortification, and oilseed protein isolates were among the magic bullets that attracted attention and resources. Nutritionists saw supply as a problem, protein inadequacy as a crisis. This approach reflected what is now recognized as too narrow a view of the etiology of malnutrition and an excessive belief in the power of technology. None of the technological fixes had much of an impact on the malnutrition problem, and this made nutritionists more willing to entertain a much broader approach to nutrition than they would have traditionally accepted.

Integrated Nutrition Planning

The new model manifested itself first as a movement toward integrated nutrition planning. With recognition of the multiple etiology of malnutrition as a base, nutritionists used systems analysis concepts and techniques to reveal the underlying causes and relative importance of malnutrition problems and appropriate solutions to the problems. They assumed that the national planning process was the appropriate vehicle for applying this methodology. They made efforts to encourage the writing of national nutrition plans and to create inter-ministerial councils to administer them.

Although much activity was generated, with only a few exceptions little progress of consequence resulted. The systems approach was deemed conceptually valid but generally incompatible with administrative and political reality. Integrated nutrition planning threatened, conflicted with, or at least brought pressure for change in governmental organizations firmly defined by sector, professional discipline, and political power base. Responsibility for nutrition was not easily accommodated on the organization charts of governments. When viewed as a health problem to be dealt with by health professionals, nutrition had a logical and appropriate bureaucratic home; but a health ministry was not the appropriate agency to deal with consumer food subsidies, mass media communications, or the nutritional consequences of agricultural planning. Simply finding a home for the new concept of nutrition absorbed much of the energy needed to move programs forward. Nutrition suffered something of an identity crisis, which weakened its momentum. A similar dilemma was created for development assistance agencies, which largely mirror the organization of the governments they are designed to service.

A second debilitating factor was the nutrition community's limited capacity to respond to the demands flowing from the new model. The programs being proposed were untested, the techniques new and crude, and the professionals with the needed broader perspective too few. When in the mid-1970s Arturo Tanco, president of the World Food Council and minister of agriculture for the Philippines, asked for a set of nutrition guidelines for the agriculture ministers of the world, the response from the international nutrition community was meager and largely infeasible. Similarly, a group of senior planners who met in 1977 at the University of California at Berkeley discovered that academia had fewer practicable answers than they had expected.

The inability of the nutrition community to provide workable models and solutions dampened enthusiasm and reduced receptivity to the new nutrition planning, even when the methodological tools and capabilities were subsequently considerably improved. Integrated nutrition planning confronted many of the same barriers and suffered a fate similar to that of integrated rural development, which was in vogue at the same time. (For a detailed analysis of the integrated nutrition planning effort see Pines in part VI.)

Sectoralization

The difficulties encountered in trying to achieve full integration led the nutrition community to reexamine the possibilities of working within traditional sectors but addressing the problem in several key sectors simultaneously.

Health Revisited

Interest turned to health both because of the biological link between nutrition and infection and because health, unlike nutrition, already had an accepted delivery system in place. Moreover, some traditional nutritionists felt more comfortable dealing with medical professionals than with the intruders from other disciplines whom nutritionists perceived as trying to capture nutrition from them.

During the past decade, changes in the health sector toward more primary health care and preventive medicine have provided fertile ground for incorporating nutrition concerns. Certain measures pioneered by nutritionists have been integrated into the standard health care service package, particularly growth monitoring and oral rehydration therapy. Health systems are also more actively addressing the iodine, vitamin A, and iron deficiencies to which the World Food Conference drew attention. Similarly, the health community has responded to the nutritionists' alert concerning the dangers of infant bottle feeding and the importance of breastfeeding.

Certain international agencies are paying greater attention to nutrition in their health agendas. Nutrition has assumed a prominent place in the WHO Health for All by the Year 2000 strategy. WHO and UNICEF have jointly initiated important nutrition undertakings in 17 countries. The Pan American Health Organization in 1983 gave nutrition top priority in its action agenda. USAID and the World Bank are increasing their emphasis on nutrition in health programming.

However, all is not well with nutrition in the health sector. The coverage of national health programs remains extremely limited and inclusion of nutrition in these programs more limited still. Despite worldwide attention to preventive and primary health care, national health programs generally lean toward medically defined services. However, malnutrition, at least protein-energy deficiency, commonly results from both diarrhea and inadequate food. Doctors are comfortable with curative treatments, such as oral rehydration therapy, for the former but often neglect or resist more food-oriented actions because these are not part of their medical training or tools.

There is no question that the primary health care system is an important vehicle for introducing nutrition services, but the health system has significant limitations in scope and coverage. The deteriorating financial situation in many countries in recent years, with obvious implications for the food consumption and nutrition levels of the poor, has generally swamped the capacity of explicit nutrition efforts delivered through health facilities. Expecting the health system to respond sufficiently to accommodate such levels of need will only create disillusionment and risk neglect of needed actions in other areas.

Agriculture Revisited

Nutritionists also eyed the integration of nutrition into agriculture as part of the return to the more manageable scope of a single sector. The idea was that nutrition objectives should be included explicitly in agricultural sector analysis and projects. Rather than simplistically regarding increased output as sufficient to improve nutrition status, the nutrition consequences of agricultural projects would be systematically analyzed (see, for example, Reutlinger in part II).

During the last decade, the FAO and USAID developed and tested guidelines in this area, with IFPRI also making valuable contributions.

IFAD, a creation of the World Food Conference, began to stress nutrition objectives in its lending program, and the network of international agricultural research centers (CGIAR) showed an increasing interest in nutrition in its planning of agronomic research.

Despite these promising steps, the infiltration of nutrition into the agricultural community has gone slowly—excruciatingly so. Few agricultural sector or project documents of international agencies or ministries of agriculture include serious and useful analyses of consumption and nutrition effects. Many agricultural leaders in government and academia do not regard nutrition as their responsibility. They are not trained in nutrition and therefore are not familiar or comfortable dealing with such issues. In many cases they are too busy with what they perceive as higher-priority areas. Their reward systems rarely include incentives for taking on the additional work of dealing with nutrition. Thus, integrating nutrition into the agriculture agenda, as with health programs, is a critically important task that has had some success but remains largely unfinished.

Nutrition Intervention Analysis

The past decade has also seen a move toward analyzing and improving the design and implementation of various kinds of nutrition interventions (Austin and others 1981; Berg 1981). The new emphasis is on understanding and dealing with the administrative, economic, and political realities of such efforts.

Some countries have made significant progress in improving performance in intervention programs. In the south Indian state of Tamil Nadu, a program that focuses on growth monitoring, selective food supplementation, and nutrition communications now effectively covers 7,000 villages. Among the 13-to-36-month old children in those villages, severe malnutrition is 40 percent less common than in control villages, which have higher incomes. By five years of age, the children in participating villages are 1.75 kilograms heavier than those in control villages. The program, which developed out of an integrated nutrition systems analysis and is carefully managed and tightly evaluated, offers an example of how a relatively low-cost delivery system (1.3 percent of the state's revenue budget when fully implemented statewide) can bring about nutritional improvement for children, at an affordable cost, without waiting for major gains in family income.

In Indonesia, nutrition programs that were in place in only a handful of villages at the time of the World Food Conference now cover over 30,000 villages, albeit unevenly. Nutrition has attracted such interest that it is commonly referred to as a "movement." The government has strengthened Indonesia's institutions, developed an elaborate nutrition surveillance system, and carried out training on a scale commensurate with staffing needs. Indonesia has also made important breakthroughs in nutrition education (see Hornik and Manoff, both in part V).

Elsewhere, pilot projects and field research have helped identify design factors that affect the feasibility and desirability of intervention programs. Planners have put greater emphasis on program costs and effectiveness. Consequently, careful scrutiny has been given to ways of more sharply targeting the interventions to the neediest groups. In Brazil's consumer food subsidy efforts, for instance, careful targeting has proved feasible and has lowered costs. Such findings are particularly important, given the increasing fiscal austerity in most countries. While the conclusions of studies of interventions in a number of countries are important for microlevel programs, they have not proven helpful in analyzing or dealing with many of the broader forces that have a major effect on nutrition.

The Macro View: Food Policy Analysis

Incorporation of consumption and nutrition considerations in the analysis and formulation of food policies in some countries is one of the important achievements of the past decade. A prominent example is the overwhelmingly economic approach of Timmer and colleagues (Timmer and others 1983), which focuses on pricing policies and market effects, recognizing that poverty and purchasing power are central to the malnutrition problem. To a certain extent, this approach captures the systems concepts of the earlier integrated nutrition planning approach. Econometric analysis is a key tool in the new approach, and during the past decade, econometric techniques and the methods of applying them to national data have been honed.

Nutrition has been assigned a prominent role in the analysis of macro food policy in the Arab Republic of Egypt, Indonesia, Kenya, the Philippines, Sri Lanka, and Thailand. The World Food Council has promoted the formulation of national food strategies and food policy analysis, and IFPRI has done excellent work in the area. Professional capacity within government planning agencies is increasing. In October 1984, the World Bank's Economic Development Institute organized a special course for country officials dealing specifically with this kind of analysis.

Perhaps most impressive is Indonesia's work on food policy analysis. In the preparation of its latest five-year plan, the attention to and sophistication in food consumption issues were far superior to those in the previous plan. Officials of BAPPENAS, the national planning agency, reported that the section of the plan dealing with nutrition concerns was better prepared and more analytically inclined than the parts on other more traditional sectors, including agricultural production.

Analysis of macro food policy has filled an important void, giving a more concrete and inclusive view of food security (see Reutlinger in part III). Food systems are better understood, as are the advantages and disadvantages of consumer food subsidies. Further methodological refinements need to be made, and so do the hard trade-offs of reconciling the need for high prices for farmers to stimulate output and low prices for consumers to assure access to food (see Pinstrup-Andersen in part IV). Food policy analysis does not eliminate the tough decisions, but it does make possible a more systematic examination of relevant factors. The risk remains, however, that those who view nutrition from the macro perspective will be insensitive to microlevel opportunities.

The Challenges

Nutrition progress during the next decade will require the development community to confront a changed environment and several challenges. The surge of conservative politics in the early 1980s has endangered the opportunities opened by the World Food Conference. Concerns voiced in the late 1970s about basic human needs and human rights, including the right to food, have faded. Consumption and distribution issues do not receive the attention and priority from policymakers that they commanded just a few years ago. The lessened interest in nutrition also reflects the severe economic problems most countries face. Preoccupation with debt and budgetary crises has led many countries to give paramount attention to production of export crops and to cut certain social programs, generally without adequate consideration of the nutrition consequences.

Perhaps the first challenge growing out of the lessons of the past decade is attitudinal. Governments and donors must be realistic about the many barriers to implementation of nutrition policies (see Pines in part VI). At the same time, sufficient examples demonstrate that significant reductions in malnutrition are feasible, even within the current austerity.

The intellectual evolution in nutrition during these past ten years has been significant, with macro food policy work now in the forefront. In this context, a remaining challenge is to construct solid analytical and programmatic bridges between macro policies and microlevel endeavors.

Efforts to institutionalize nutrition objectives within the health and agricultural sectors must also continue. Improvement of nutrition must become an integral part of the missions and methods of these sectors. Because their actions inescapably carry consequences for nutrition, basic changes need to be made in the way personnel in these fields are trained and rewarded. Nutrition considerations must be integrated into the training programs for agricultural economics and extension and for medicine and public health, and government workers in these fields must be evaluated at least partly in terms of their contribution to nutrition.

The sectoralization of nutrition is a pragmatic response to political and organizational realities. It does not invalidate the conceptual view of malnutrition as a systemic phenomenon. Care must be exercised, therefore, that a piecemeal approach does not supplant this holistic vision (see Introduction). The search for a home for nutrition should not be allowed to precipitate another identity crisis, for home is where the action is—whether in agriculture, health, or macro food policy arenas. Yet concern for malnutrition must be strong enough at the highest political and planning levels to ensure that nutrition efforts within the sectors are not neglected or diluted and that coordination exists even without integration. This will require an organizational focal point.

Malnutrition is, like unemployment, a condition, not a sector. If countries are able to organize their various sectors to produce policies and programs that address unemployment, they should be able to do so for malnutrition.

Another challenge is to the development agencies. They must structure themselves, both individually and collectively, to be more creatively responsive to the nutrition problem—and on a scale more commensurate with what the problem requires. As measured by budget, staff, and other indicators, nutrition is a peripheral interest of most assistance agencies, UNICEF being the exception.

Paradoxically, the very international development assistance system that for a good part of the decade had been active in pursuing the alleviation of poverty has, in some countries, been involved in carrying out economic adjustment processes to reduce fiscal and balance of payments deficits that have worsened the nutrition problem. The development economists' explanation is that the food consumption situation has to get worse in the short run if there is any chance of its getting better in the longer run. Granted that economic adjustment is a necessity, the key issue becomes how the burden is to be spread among social groups. The malnourished are the least able to absorb economic adversity; even in good times they exist on the slimmest of margins. Increasingly, the nutrition community is asking whether enough attention is being given to how, within the confines of adjustment policies, the food consumption level of the poorest can be prevented from deteriorating.

Nutrition conditions are, of course, rooted in a country's structure of inequities. Income and land distribution patterns are key determinants. A nutrition community working at full energy may not be able to help many people if the country's political logic is operating in the opposite direction. And in some countries, corruption further erodes those possibilities. Technical issues often pale in comparison with the political and economic influences surrounding nutrition. How to deal with malnutrition in this context remains a fundamental challenge.

One approach for the nutrition community is to concentrate its resources where governments are committed to alleviating the malnutrition problem. Although this may sound like past cries for political will, the fact remains that commitment is necessary if much is to happen. Experience reveals that where a serious nutrition effort exists, dramatic progress can be made. Countries move up the nutrition intervention learning curve. Progress breeds progress.

Meanwhile, countries that lack commitment at the top level need not be neglected by the international assistance community. Few countries offer only one entry point. In most, groups committed to nutrition can be identified and strengthened so that when the political environment changes the countries will be in a position to move forward rapidly. This has already happened in several Latin American countries.

Malnutrition is intrinsically a local problem, affecting the individual, the family, and the community. Thus, a final challenge is to mobilize local efforts and resources to increase people's own capacity to fight malnutrition. Although this is another of those often heard but generally elusive development goals, communities clearly are better able to understand their problems than are outsiders, and they almost always have untapped resources. Empowering communities to become more self-reliant is hard—more so in some cultures than in others—but promoting local solutions reduces the communities' exposure to the vagaries of outside political winds and economic forces over which they have no control.

Much has been written about trends in nutrition conditions since the World Food Conference (see Mellor and Johnston, and Falcon and others, both in part I). The variations are wide, with the number of malnourished up about 20 percent in low-income countries and down about 20 percent in middle-income countries. Sub-Saharan Africa generally is the worst off, perhaps 50 percent worse off in 1980 than in 1970, and East Asia is showing the most progress, about what might be expected given the broad drift of economic circumstances. The severity of refugee and other nutrition relief problems fluctuates, depending on the crisis of the moment. In dealing with nutritional stress in emergencies, the world appears to be better organized than it was a decade ago.

As for the process of bringing about improved nutrition, conclusions probably vary with the vantage point of the viewer. Those in, say, Jakarta, Madras, and Bangkok are likely to have a more positive sense of what has and can be achieved than those sitting in the headquarters of development assistance agencies. Almost everyone, however, would probably agree that during the decade since the World Food Conference, the field of nutrition has undergone a metamorphosis and that there has been progress, albeit well short of the promise held out. The development community still faces an unfinished nutrition agenda.

35

National Nutrition Planning: Lessons of Experience

James M. Pines

National nutrition planning, the general term for all promotion, analysis, and design work preceding activities intended to improve nutrition, experienced an optimistic surge during the 1970s. Ten years later, malnutrition remains as bad as before, or worse. China, Sri Lanka, and the few other countries showing improvement accomplished it without explicit nutrition planning, multisectoral or otherwise. The impacts of inflation, unemployment, international terms of trade, and poor harvests on nutrition have made nutrition planning seem irrelevant and revived interest in macroeconomic solutions, "trickle-down" approaches, and social revolution. Multisectoral nutrition planning, oversold and underpolitical from the start, stands discredited for its failure to bring about the improvement in nutrition that a realistic initial assessment would have shown to be unattainable.

Although this article agrees with many of the doubts about multisectoral nutrition planning, it proposes modifications to make it more practical. If nutrition planners were to use the systems approach, some of the less useful planning and organization tools now associated with multisectoral nutrition planning would be eliminated. However, regardless of improvements, nutrition planners should have no illusions about the potential of their art. The major decisions that affect national nutrition status are well beyond their control, though subject to their influence. Nonetheless, good reasons remain for improving nutrition planning. Done effectively, planning achieves nutritionally favorable outcomes that are otherwise unlikely. The lessons of nutrition planning experience, if applied, support modest optimism that some of these outcomes may yet occur.

Excerpted from "National Nutrition Planning," *Food Policy*, vol 7, no. 4 (November 1982), pp. 275–301.

Accomplishment of even limited nutrition improvement in the highly competitive political environment requires planning geared to these conditions. The planning methods and organizations so far developed from the systems approach failed to equip nutrition advocates adequately. More practical and political models cannot guarantee more action and improved nutrition, but they will ensure better representation for nutrition in the development process.

Political Lessons

Nutrition planning is both an intellectual and a political process. Neglect or inadequate response to political aspects explains much of the multisectoral approach's weakness in affecting policy. Until a government and its agencies take nutrition problems seriously, studies and plans remain ignored. Significant nutrition improvement becomes likely only when commitment generates actions that make it possible. The planners' work achieves impact by stimulating action. Nutrition planners become advocates in the political process that distributes power and well-being in their societies. Their planning must reflect this role or remain ineffective.

A few nutrition planners work in national planning offices, such as Colombia's National Planning Department, or in autonomous multisectoral nutrition agencies like the National Food and Nutrition Institute in Brazil and the Tanzania Food and Nutrition Centre. More often, "nutrition planner" means anyone, regardless of title, doing planning or project design work in agriculture, health, or some other ministry, who is concerned about nutrition problems. Improved nutrition comes less from a national nutrition plan for coordinated activities addressed to a common nutrition goal, or from nutrition interventions, than from a review of the nutritional implications of sector plans addressed to competing goals. The reviewer, who analyzes and influences nutrition consequences, also becomes a nutrition advocate.

However, encouragement of higher priority for nutrition among broad development goals and references to it in national development plans only begin the process. References and statements of aspiration in national plans mean little until translated into detailed designs and action. In Senegal and Thailand, for example, where development plans refer extensively to nutrition goals and action, the influence of competing pressures and the absence of advocacy to counteract them have produced disappointing performance. The competition for attention and resources that makes advocacy essential at the centers of power extends to all parts of government. Nutrition planning, a stage of the political process from which national nutrition status emerges, makes explicit the goals of the advocacy that precedes and follows it.

Nutrition planners must identify the chain of decisions involved in producing desired responses and the people who make them. Questions such as "who decides that nutrition will receive attention?" "who controls design of rural development?" and "who in the health ministry can include nutrition surveillance in the plan?" suggest appropriate action and permit early identification of obstacles. By first identifying those with power over nutrition issues, planners can respond more effectively to their concerns.

Major commitment to nutrition improvement in Colombia, for example, followed the nutrition planning group's recognition of and response to incoming President Lopez's desire for a dramatic initiative in 1974 (Lopez 1978). Tailoring plans to the political circumstances helped nutrition become a successful contender for resources. Substantial Philippine efforts in nutrition stemmed from the interest of the president's wife, encouraged by leaders of the national nutrition community (Solon 1978). Brazil's national nutrition program, including a related $19 million World Bank loan, required approval by the country's "economic czar," for whom the loan may have provided an added inducement. In all three countries, despite increased national commitment to improving nutrition, agricultural policy development continued to neglect nutrition consequences. Continued nutrition advocacy in this sector has produced a better response, though much remains to be done.

Decisions about nutrition activity often need approval by budget offices, finance ministries, planning department economists, and others unfamiliar with or unimpressed by nutrition concerns. Ministers willing to support nutrition improvement may never receive plans for doing it if a principal secretary decides that other matters have priority. Personal predilections of powerful field staff and political leaders may frustrate technically competent nutrition plans unless their interests receive attention.

Determining who has access to and influence with the decision-maker also improves planning. Even in the most centralized regimes, the press and public opinion retain some influence. Food price and subsidy policies cannot rest solely on technical analysis, or public reaction may prevent approval. Nutrition plans that ignore the interests and perceived needs of intended beneficiaries accomplish little, despite support by program decisionmakers.

Within governments, chief executives rely on trusted advisers, ministers look to senior bureaucrats, and legislators respond to tribal chiefs and other political allies. In many developing countries, international aid and lending agencies affect decisions. When the IMF presses for financial retrenchment, planning to prevent accompanying deterioration of nutrition status must satisfy the international advisers who influence national approval.

Politically experienced planners and interest groups in other sectors understand the need to apply marketing principles in seeking action. Nutrition planners need the same skills. Identifying decisionmakers and those who influence them begins the political process of encouraging nutrition action. Their attitudes dictate the content and presentation of the planners' work.

Nutrition specialists frequently lack policy influence because they let technical considerations prevail over the requisites for persuasion. Economists in agriculture ministries, for example, respond more to a showing of nutrition impact on farm labor productivity than to data on severe malnutrition among children. Nutrition recuperation centers receive support in many countries because they are cheaper than hospitals, not because they are more effective at building nutritional independence. Decisionmakers lose interest when well-conceived multisectoral responses will cost more than the country can "afford" or, more accurately, chooses to spend.

Effective nutrition planning requires that feasible responses accompany descriptions of serious nutrition problems. Developing country governments, already burdened with overwhelming problems, show little interest in demands for attention to new ones unless impressive savings or inexpensive visible impacts seem likely.

Political judgment as to whether dramatic evidence of the consequences of malnutrition can stimulate government response must temper this conclusion. In India, for example, allegations that malnutrition would produce "a generation of idiots," though exaggerating the significant impact of malnutrition on mental development, encouraged national attention to the problem. Newspaper articles in Thailand during 1974, when malnutrition raised little concern, publicized evidence that 45,000 to 55,000 infants died annually from it. Despite protests about methodology, the figures helped increase attention to nutrition in the next development plan.

Nutrition scientists shifting to policy advocacy are often unaware of the different ways to use information. Condensation, dramatization, and exaggeration transform scientific conclusions into tools to influence action. Government officials often lack the time, interest, or capacity to read and understand nutrition documents and, if they do read them, lack the patience for the reservations and qualifications necessary in presenting scientific findings. With other sectors exaggerating the seriousness of problems and ease of solutions, nutrition supporters risk being ignored unless they compete effectively. Policymakers often hide opposition to proposed actions behind insistence on rigorous scientific evidence. Less demanding standards of proof frequently suffice for other actions to which they are already predisposed.

Winning political battles, whether for nutrition or less significant concerns, depends on much more than information. Nutrition issues often conflict with economic agendas represented by advocates with more resources and political skills than nutrition commands. Accepting the dominance of power in policy determination still allows influence through nutrition planning.

Effective nutrition planning also requires giving priority to action responses. Planners too often encourage studies and surveys that, although useful, allow governments to postpone feasible action. National meetings to support nutrition, an advocacy technique, make a different mistake by recommending so many governmental responses that none receive serious consideration or concentrated support. When decisionmakers finally ask, "What do you want me to do about it?" planners must be ready with actions intended to alleviate specific nutrition problems that are feasible administratively and financially and likely to produce visible results within the politically relevant time period. This emphasis often involves initial compromise of scientific rigor or technical elegance.

Appropriate responses vary with country conditions and the entity responding, but nutrition planners must anticipate and prepare for favorable opportunities. Recent Costa Rican "glass of milk a day" and Peruvian food stamp programs, for example, offered chances to shape activities in nutritionally favorable ways. Unfortunately, these rapid political initiatives left nutrition planners unprepared, diminishing the likely nutrition impact.

Planners should not assume that funding of nutrition activities emerges from rational consideration of alternatives and review of multisectoral strategies. These tools help planners compete in the political process but cannot substitute for skill in recognizing opportunities and influencing decisions. By overemphasizing the need for multisectoral plans in the past—plans that were elaborate and unrealistic—nutrition planners diverted attention from the practical political requirements for nutrition action. I have observed efforts resulting from this emphasis, and their consequences, during evaluation reviews of nutrition planning in El Salvador, Ghana, Honduras, Liberia, Thailand, and Tunisia between 1974 and 1981. The very limited progress in getting nutrition plans accepted and implemented, and the difficulties in preventing malnutrition in unfavorable economic conditions, even in the best examples of Colombia and the Philippines, emphasize the need to orient nutrition planning more directly to political and economic contexts and opportunities (Sanders 1980; Chafkin and others 1978).

Effective nutrition planning requires subordinating technical differences in favor of common programs and political priorities. Decision-makers complain frequently that nutrition advocates speak with too many different voices and make too many, often conflicting, proposals. Without sacrificing scientific integrity, nutrition experts must learn to compromise and develop shared recommendations. Unless the nutrition community unites to support a few key actions, political opportunities will be lost.

Organizational Lessons

The multisectoral approach to nutrition encouraged the formation of multisectoral nutrition planning and coordination organizations. The Tanzania Food and Nutrition Centre, Colombia's nutrition unit in the planning department, and CANAS, Senegal's nutrition coordination office in the planning ministry, illustrate the diverse responses to this interest. The Tanzanian organization combines research and advocacy. The Colombian nutrition planners coordinate a national program involving several ministries, using control of USAID and World Bank loans to aid them. Although various high-level nutrition commissions in many countries have atrophied, CANAS continues to bring together senior officials from various sectors who decide some nutrition issues. Their support produced a substantial nutrition section in Senegal's current national development plan, though CANAS lacks power to ensure performance.

Though differing country contexts and political possibilities limit the applicability of any single model, experience with multisectoral organizations suggests some cautions and principles that may improve their effectiveness. The distinction between research and advocacy, for example, merits special attention. Nutrition action requires institutions broader than the research organizations previously typical in the field. Though the work of Chilean and Bolivian research institutes, for example, now includes the social and economic aspects of nutrition, the use of findings for advocacy and planning is best done outside the research community. The skills and interests of most researchers, combined with governmental perceptions of their role, give them little leverage and encourage scientific caution.

Current increased interest in research on the nutrition consequences of agricultural and macroeconomic policies illustrates effective research response. The Nutrition Center of the Philippines and

CONPAN, Chile's nutrition agency, soon discovered that their orientation to interventions left them with little influence on critical decisions affecting nutrition, despite the strength and acumen of their leaders. They lacked the research and analysis necessary to question nutrition consequences. While the Philippine nutrition group probably could not have prevented it, its lack of analytical capability left it unable even to contest a decision to export 25,000 tons of rice in the midst of serious national malnutrition. The overwhelming impact of Chilean economic policies on nutrition forced CONPAN to broaden its research priorities. This research did not reverse the policies but enabled CONPAN to participate in nutrition planning and to alleviate further nutritional damage.

The need to influence sector ministries dictates the form and staffing of nutrition planning and coordination organizations. Their work includes education, exhortation, demonstration, financial inducement, and sensitive use of political power. CONPAN abandoned its unsuccessful efforts to achieve goals by political power and built credibility by showing other agencies how to save money. Offering business administration specialists instead of political operators and nutrition planners proved the best way to gain influence. Management assistance, though far from a conventional conception of the nutrition planning role, often initiates the sympathetic engagement that later permits a more substantive impact on agency activities. CONPAN introduced improved targeting of supplementary feeding as a management improvement, simultaneously increasing nutrition impact.

CONPAN and others have also learned the importance of developing innovative activities through ministries rather than relying on separate pilot projects. A promising nutrition-oriented agricultural information system and an impressive sanitation project, developed independently of the relevant ministries, received little attention. By thereafter involving ministries from the start in the planning and execution of new ideas, CONPAN achieved far more impact.

Nutrition organizations gain influence by systematically placing nutritionally sensitive staff in key ministries. This can be done by training people already in the ministries or by assisting newly trained candidates to enter them. Thailand, despite an absence of nutrition planning, benefits from the presence of a few trained and dedicated nutrition advocates in the ministries of health and agriculture. Nutrition planning concentrated on health and agriculture makes significant impact possible, even without a strong multisectoral organization, if both ministries have enough staff interested in nutrition.

Engaging key ministries and building nutrition sensitivity among them can begin before formation of a new nutrition planning office. In Sierra Leone and Swaziland, for example, informal associations of university, private organization, and international nutrition specialists with interested public officials encourage ministry involvement. The multisectoral office formalizes and institutionalizes a process that begins when the nutrition community mobilizes to do something.

In the past, multisectoral planning and the vision of all ministries sharing a coordinated attack on malnutrition diverted attention from the political process of moving toward this idea. Although it is only a small step toward joint planning, bringing agencies together to talk about nutrition problems challenges coordination skills. The organization and staff of multisectoral agencies must reflect this initial task instead of their more typical priority of building the multisectoral information base.

To be listened to, the coordinating agency must first be heard. The Nutrition Center of the Philippines subordinated research and planning to mobilizing ministries. Bringing them together and suggesting that they focus their activities on malnourished families, without seeking to change the activities, sensitized ministries to nutrition problems, benefited malnourished communities, and built relationships useful for future activities.

In Bolivia, the nutrition planning group concentrated on generating the interest and cooperation of a few regional development corporations—decentralized agencies that offered more promise of nutrition action than less receptive central ministries. Colombia started a national nutrition program despite central decisions that supported the ministry of agriculture's refusal to cooperate. The program's political impact later stimulated agricultural involvement.

Lesotho's small nutrition planning group serves interested ministries without pressing for joint planning. Sierra Leone formed the Council of Health and Nutrition Education, which, after several years of coordinating one activity, seems likely to become a multisectoral nutrition agency.

The advocacy role and the gradual emergence of multisectoral linkages dictate flexibility in organization and staffing. Once a group is established, its organization, functions, and staff depend on opportunities. The nutrition planning group's form flows more from political possibilities than from idealized organization charts. A nutrition planning approach directed primarily to health and agriculture ministries guides priorities in establishing credibility, building influence, and engaging agencies in useful ways. Possibilities for integrating agriculture and health in rural development nutrition programming make broader efforts to encourage ministry collaboration less compelling. Attention to individual rural development projects offers more promise.

Nutrition planning means representing nutrition effectively and subordinating studies and plans to that role. Few nutrition planning organizations win many battles in the beginning. Those lacking political sensitivity and skills soon disappear, but the best become a national nutrition conscience that is occasionally heeded.

Lessons of Nutrition Goals

The difficulties of making multisectoral nutrition planning part of government operations emphasize the limitations of nutrition as a separate development goal. For only the most single-minded advocates could nutrition remain an end in itself. Most soon recognized that nutrition goals are inseparable from broader goals related to how societies function and the benefits they provide. Self-reliance, independence, and equity, valued highly by many planners, became explicit social consequences included in nutrition goals.

Because most action to improve nutrition comes from sectors with other primary goals, the separate nutrition goal and related activities can be only an analytical tool and not a description of feasible aspirations. Nutrition planning becomes a process of influencing individual sectors to incorporate nutrition considerations into their primary activities. Accepting the compromises and partial responses inherent in this approach differs fundamentally from seeking specific actions described in a nutrition plan.

The nutrition planner, for example, encourages a shift of agricultural extension toward food crops, or modification of a road network design to improve food distribution, without regard to any multisectoral plan and often without identification of any nutrition-specific activity. Representing nutrition, rather than planning separately for it, the planner confronts the political competition among goals and the multiple outcomes of sectoral activities. The nutrition outcome becomes part of the total development result, with occasional separate nutrition-specific activities.

Integrated rural development and regional development projects illustrate the process. Forced to rely primarily on integrating nutrition into other activities, the nutrition planner joins, for example, the environmentalist, the employment specialist, and the feminist in trying to ensure a pattern of development that gives the priority interest a reasonable position. A victim of its strong multisectoral causation and the single-sector organization of government activities, nutrition must adapt goals and planning to these circumstances.

These adjustments impart a disturbing tension to nutrition planning. Most actions requisite to or consistent with improved nutrition relate first to other goals. Better water and sanitation, for example, improve nutrition incidentally to other purposes. Even increased food production, sometimes viewed as an intermediate goal for better nutrition, primarily serves economic objectives. That these activities are done for other purposes changes, but does not eliminate, the nutrition planning task. Whether and how fast nutrition improves depends on the influence of nutrition planning over other sectors as they pursue their primary goals. If the planner persists in addressing only narrow nutrition goals, feasible actions diminish because of sector resistance and, if achieved, the limited goal raises more problems than it solves.

Conclusion

The lessons of nutrition planning flow from review of the political and operational contexts in which it occurs. Making it a technique to produce effective action requires grounding in the harsh and often unpromising realities of insensitive governments, inefficient bureaucracies, and intractable, malnourished communities. For those whom this confrontation does not drive to more radical solutions, some useful tools for influencing nutrition outcomes remain.

Influence demands engagement—involvement with the governments, bureaucracies, and communities expected to act. Planning, with the studies and analysis that support it, only begins with intellectual output. Planners and analysts must join the political process of seeing things through to effective action, or at least respond to the needs of those who do. Failure to heed the lessons and requirements of the world where nutrition evolves dooms multisectoral nutrition planning to isolation, irrelevance, and disillusionment.

36

China's Food and Nutrition Planning

Dean T. Jamison and Alan Piazza

Chinese development efforts from 1949 to about 1979 emphasized two main objectives: development of a heavy industrial base and elimination of the worst aspects of poverty (World Bank 1983a). In 1949, China's population suffered a crippling burden of disease and premature death. Perhaps the most striking success of China's subsequent antipoverty struggle has been to increase dramatically the level of life expectancy, with an accompanying reduction of illness. Public health measures—combined with reductions in malnutrition, improved water supplies, and close attention to hygiene and sanitation—have contributed to the increase in life expectancy from 32 to 69 years in the period from 1950 to 1982. This level is only about six years lower than that in the industrialized market economies (Hill 1985). Growth in agricultural production and improvements in food distribution have substantially alleviated hunger and contributed to improved life expectancy. Nonetheless, progress to improve health and nutrition has been far from uniform, and major rural-urban differences and differences among rural areas still exist (Jamison and others 1984).

Although China's overall level of living has substantially improved since 1949—indeed, it has improved somewhat more rapidly than levels of living in developing countries generally—improvements in income levels alone can account for only a fraction of China's achievements in nutrition and health. Table 36-1 presents selected development indicators for China and a number of other economies and groups of economies. Columns 1 and 5 indicate that although per capita GNP is low in China, life expectancy is nonetheless high by comparison even with places having substantially higher income lev-

An earlier version of this paper was presented at a Rockefeller Foundation Conference on Research and Education in 20th Century China, Pocantico Hills, New York, May 21–23, 1984. That version will appear in the proceedings of the conference, *Research and Education in 20th Century China,* edited by N. Sivin (Ann Arbor, Michigan: Center for Chinese Studies Publications).

Table 36-1. *Selected Development Indicators, China and Other Economies*

Indicator	Per capita GNP, 1980 (1980 U.S. dollars)	Annual growth rate of per capita GNP, 1960–80 (percent)	Annual population growth rate, 1970–80 (percent)	Total fertility rate, 1980 (percent)[a]	Life expectancy (years)		Daily per capita energy supply, 1979–81 average (kilocalories)	Adult literacy rate, 1977 (percent)
					1980	Gain, 1960–80		
	(1)	(2)	(3)	(4)	(5)	(6)	(7)	(8)
Low-income economies (excluding India and China)	230	1.0	2.5	6.1	57	15	2,066[b]	34
India	240	1.4	2.2	4.9	52	9	2,056	36
Sri Lanka	270	2.4	2.0	3.6	66	4	2,251	85
China	290	3.6[c]	1.8	2.5	67	27[d]	2,525	66
Pakistan	300	2.8	3.0	6.1	50	7	2,180	24
Indonesia	430	4.0	2.2	4.5	53	12	2,372	62
Thailand	670	4.7	2.7	4.0	63	11	2,330	84
Middle-income economies	1,400	3.8	2.4	4.8	60	9	2,593[b]	65
Hong Kong	4,240	6.8	2.5	2.2	74	7	2,771	90
Nonmarket industrial economies	4,640	4.2	0.9	2.3	71	3	3,382[b]	100
Industrial market economies	10,320	3.6	0.9	1.9	74	4	3,415[b]	99

a. Expected total number of births per female reaching childbearing age.

b. Average, 1980–81.

c. Growth rate of GDP minus the population growth rate. For 1960–80, GNP and GDP in China grew at approximately the same rate.

d. The year 1960 and the adjacent years were periods of acute famine and turmoil in China, and mortality rates were substantially elevated. The 27-year gain in life expectancy reported here is therefore based on an imputed 1960 life expectancy that is the average of the 1957 and 1963 life expectancies.

Source: World Bank (1982); FAO (1984a); for China, Jamison and others (1984).

els. Income growth in China has been moderately rapid, but columns 1, 2, and 6 suggest that neither the level nor the growth rate of income explains China's improvement in life expectancy. The 27-year increase in life expectancy between 1960 and 1980 exceeds that of other economies sufficiently to indicate the importance of other factors. Potential other factors, beyond the activities of public health agencies, are education levels (column 8), reductions in the population growth rate (columns 3 and 4), availability of food (column 7), distribution of available food, and improvements in water supply and sanitation. China's achievements in each of these areas, relative to its income level, have undoubtedly complemented the efforts of public health authorities to reduce mortality and morbidity during the past 30 years. (See also Jamison and Trowbridge 1984; Piazza 1986.) Our purpose in this chapter is to review the nature and impact of one critically important factor—food policy and its nutritional outcomes—in China's successful efforts to improve health and life expectancy.

Agricultural Production Control and Food Policy

The Chinese government moved rapidly during the 1950s to establish control over agricultural production and both domestic and international agricultural trade. Control over agricultural production and trade was secured through manipulating agricultural prices, setting quotas for sown area and crop production, and developing a state monopoly of agricultural marketing (Lardy 1983b; Tuan and Crook 1983; Perkins 1966).

The government viewed state control of agriculture as a central feature of socialism. More pragmatically, control was intended to increase foreign exchange earnings from agricultural exports, supply raw materials to light industry, and assure adequate food for the growing urban population. Effective control of food production and distribution having been established, the government food policy consisted of (a) implementing an urban food rationing and subsidy system and rural grain transfer programs, (b) controlling the mix of agricultural production and food consumption, and (c) moderating local and regional food shortages through international and domestic agricultural trade.

Rationing

The urban rationing system was established in November 1953. Under the rationing system, most households receive ration coupons for grain and certain other basic foodstuffs. Approximately 16 percent of China's population benefits from this system (Lardy 1983a). Rations vary by age, sex, occupation, and locality and are heavily subsidized. The rationing system helps ensure that all entitled urban residents receive adequate supplies of food at affordable prices and has helped to reduce greatly urban malnutrition in China, an important accomplishment in contrast to the severe malnutrition of the urban poor in many developing countries. In recent years, the rationing system has also been extraordinarily costly, however, absorbing about 4.2 percent of China's 1981 GNP. The urban food subsidy is estimated to have been worth 96 yuan per urban dweller in that year, or almost one and one-third times total expenditures on health care.

No formal rationing system exists in rural areas, but grain is transferred from surplus to deficit areas as part of the government's effort to maintain a floor level of grain consumption. The floor level of grain consumption varies from province to province and, within provinces, from county to county. Typically, the guaranteed minimum is 200 kilograms of unprocessed grain per annum per person in rice growing areas and 150 kilograms in other areas. (A ration of 200 kilograms of unhusked rice provides 1,400 kilocalories per day of energy and 25 grams of protein—approximately 64 percent and 69 percent, respectively, of the 1979 level of daily requirements in China. A wheat ration of 150 kilograms provides 1,250 kilocalories per day and 35 grams of protein, or 57 percent and 97 percent of requirements.)

Provinces unable to produce enough grain to maintain this floor level of consumption must import grain from other provinces. Grain-poor provinces (excluding China's three municipalities) collectively imported an average of 4.5 to 5.5 million tons of grain per annum in the 1950s, and about 8 million tons per annum in the late 1970s. For example, Gansu, Nei Monggol, Shanxi, Ningxia, Qinghai, Guizhou, Yunnan, Guangxi, and Guangdong together imported more than 4 million tons of grain in 1979, greatly alleviating the shortfall of grain production in those provinces (Walker 1984). Although rural grain transfers have certainly greatly increased the proportion of the population whose basic food needs are met, the system does not satisfy everyone's food needs. This was most notably the case during the food crisis of 1959–62, but undernutrition is still prevalent in many rural areas, particularly in western China.

Mix of Food Consumption

The government has also used its control of agriculture to manipulate effectively the mix of food production and consumption. Until quite recently, government policy has favored direct consumption of grain over consumption of such preferred foods as pulses, vegetable oils, and animal products. As a result, the average Chinese now receives more food energy through the direct consumption of grain than do the inhabitants of almost any other country; only Koreans and Egyptians come close. In contrast, China's per capita consumption of pulses, separated oils and fats, and animal products is quite low by international standards. Consumption of preferred foods has increased rapidly in recent years, and the government plans to continue this increase for the foreseeable future.

Since grains produce greater food energy and protein per hectare of cropland than preferred foods, China's agricultural planners have chosen to restrict preferred foods and to maximize gross nutrient availability from the limited arable land available. This strategy explains why China has been able to attain the level of the average middle-income country in per capita availability of food energy and protein (but not fat), while the mix of food consumption is still typical of the average low-income country.

Maximizing nutrient availability in this way may have reduced malnutrition in China in two ways. First, of course, increased nutrient availability means more food energy and protein for everyone. Second, restricting the consumption of preferred foods may have brought about a more equal distribution of nutrient consumption. As the income elasticity of demand for preferred foods is by definition greater than that of less preferred foods, the distribution of consumption of preferred foods is likely to be less equal across income groups, compared to the distribution for less preferred foods (FAO 1976a). In effect, restricting preferred foods should have increased the availability of affordable food for China's poor. However, restricting preferred foods may also have had nutritionally deleterious effects. Specifically, the chronic short supply of nutrient-dense weaning foods, typically derived from preferred foods, may have adversely affected infant health. In addition, the steady drop in per capita availability of soybeans and other pulses since the mid-1950s has reduced complementary proteins in the average diet. Although the trend was dramatically reversed beginning in 1979, per capita production of oilseeds also declined steadily after the mid-1950s and may have resulted in undesirably low fat intake during the 1960s and 1970s.

International Agricultural Trade

A primary objective of China's international agricultural trade has been to generate foreign exchange to pay for imports of capital goods. China has maintained a positive agricultural balance of trade since 1949 in all years except 1961–64 and 1980–81, and planners have never considered food imports to be a viable long-run solution to domestic shortfalls in food production. The relatively large annual grain imports of more than 10 million tons in recent years, which have been misunderstood as a sign of insufficient domestic grain production, are instead more convincingly explained by internal transport constraints and grain procurement shortfalls (Surls 1982; Kirby 1972).

Maintaining a positive agricultural trade balance, however, cannot explain the astounding fact that China increased net grain exports during the first two years of the food crisis of 1959–62. China's grain trade and its impact on domestic grain supplies are summarized in table 36-2. Annual net grain exports, which had averaged close to 2.0 million tons during 1950–57, doubled to 4.2 million tons in 1959. In 1960, at the height of the famine, the government approved net grain exports of 2.7 million tons. It was not until 1961 that China responded to the food crisis with massive grain imports. Grain exports were cut in half and imports increased from less than 100,000 tons to over 5.8 million tons; net imports approached 4.5 million tons. The effect was dramatic. The estimated average per capita energy availability in 1961 of 1,763 kilocalories was 11.5 percent greater than the 1,578 kilocalories available in 1960, with about two-thirds of the increase resulting from the switch to net grain imports.

The government's failure to respond to the food crisis with large grain imports in 1959–60 is largely attributable to the systematic falsification of agricultural production data at the end of the 1950s. Government leaders apparently were unaware of the extent of the collapse of agricultural production and the resulting loss of life (Ash-

Table 36-2. *International Grain Trade, China, Selected Years, 1950–65*

(millions of metric tons, except as specified)

Year	Total grain production[a]	Grain exports	Grain imports	Net grain imports	Domestic grain supply	Per capita grain supply (kilograms/ year)[a]
1950	129.6	1.2	0.1	−1.2	128.4	234
1955	180.2	2.2	0.2	−2.1	178.1	294
1959	165.2	4.2	0.0	−4.2	161.0	246
1960	139.4	2.7	0.1	−2.7	136.7	210
1961	143.1	1.4	5.8	4.5	147.6	229
1965	197.5	2.4	6.4	4.0	201.5	282

Note: Columns may not add to totals because of rounding.

a. The tuber component of total grain production has been included at one-fifth its wet weight for 1950–63.

Source: State Statistical Bureau (1983).

ton and others 1984). The two-year delay in responding to the food crisis entailed tremendous human cost.

Food Availability and Distribution

Since 1949, per capita food availability has increased greatly, and regional and local disparities in food consumption have been reduced. As a result, the average Chinese today consumes considerably more food than did the average Chinese 30 years ago, and the number of malnourished Chinese has declined significantly. However, food availability has not increased steadily over time, nor have all Chinese benefited equally from the increase. Thus, although the situation is now generally much better than it was in the early 1950s, extreme setbacks have occurred along the way and serious regional and localized food shortages continue to afflict part of rural China.

Food Availability

Trends in national average daily per capita nutrient availability in China for the years 1950–82 are illustrated in figure 36-1 and summarized in table 36-3. Despite wide fluctuations, per capita nutrient availability has increased markedly and now exceeds estimated nu-

Figure 36-1. *Average Daily Per Capita Nutrient Availability, China*

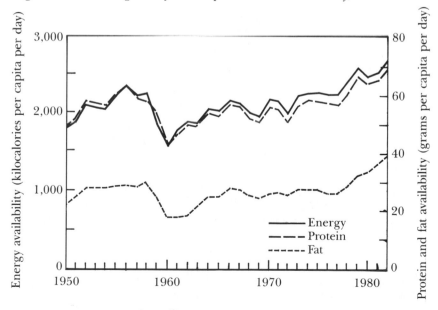

trient requirements by a large margin. From 1950–52 to 1980–82, per capita availability of food energy grew by more than one-third, increasing from about 90 percent to about 115 percent of estimated energy requirements. Per capita availability of protein grew by more than one-quarter, increasing to more than 150 percent of estimated safe levels of protein intake. Per capita availability of fat grew by more than one-half. (Estimates of food energy requirements and safe levels of protein intake in 1980–82 were about 9 and 10 percent greater, respectively, than in 1950–52. Consequently, the increase in food energy and protein reported in table 36-3 appears somewhat less when measured as a percentage of requirements than when measured in absolute terms.)

The increase in per capita nutrient availability since 1949 has been closely tied to long-term trends in China's agricultural production (Walker 1984; Lardy 1983b; Barker and Sinha 1982). Agricultural production increased sharply during the early and mid-1950s as China recovered from the devastation of World War II and the civil wars of the 1940s. Per capita nutrient availability increased rapidly and by the mid-1950s, daily per capita availability of food energy topped 2,200 kilocalories—slightly greater than energy requirements. During the food crisis of 1959–62, however, agricultural production declined disastrously because of the chaos created by the "Great Leap Forward" and the sudden implementation of the commune system (1958–59), policy-induced reductions in sown area (1959), and widespread bad weather (1960–61). Per capita nutrient availability fell below the 1950 level and by 1960 daily per capita availability of food energy had declined to less than 1,600 kilocalories—only 75 percent of energy requirements. Estimates put the number of deaths due to malnutrition and starvation during the food crisis at 16 to 30 million or more (Ashton and others 1984; Coale 1984).

Agricultural production recovered only slowly during the next 15 years, 1963–77, and it was not until the mid-1970s that per capita

Table 36-3. *Per Capita Food Energy and Protein Availability and Requirements, China, Selected Three–Year Averages*

Period	Energy availability		Protein availability		Fat availability, grams/day
	Kilocalories/ day	Percentage of requirement	Grams/ day	Percentage of requirement	
1950–52	1,894	91	53	133	25
1960–62	1,736	82	46	114	18
1970–72	2,040	97	53	132	25
1980–82	2,570	114	66	151	37

Source: Piazza (1986).

nutrient availability regained the level achieved in the mid-1950s. During 1978–84, agricultural production grew at a rapid pace and per capita nutrient availability increased commensurately. Daily per capita availability of food energy and protein now exceeds estimated nutrient requirements by a large margin and compares favorably with the average for middle-income countries. This positive situation is expected to continue for the rest of the century, both because of highly successful production incentives and because population growth has been reduced to less than 1.5 percent per annum.

Since food is unevenly produced and distributed, the nutritional status of the Chinese population may not be directly inferred from these estimates of per capita nutrient availability. Although per capita availability of energy and protein now greatly exceeds requirements, a large segment of the population may still suffer from malnutrition. The extent to which a given margin of nutrient availability over requirements will lead to insufficient food consumption among a portion of the population depends on both the income distribution and the income elasticity of demand for the nutrient. (Limited data from China confirm the standard finding that the income elasticity of demand for protein far exceeds that for energy. Hence the distribution of protein consumption is probably more unequal than that of energy, and it cannot be concluded from table 36-3 that there are likely to be more individuals suffering from energy deficiency than from protein deficiency.)

There appears to be a strong positive relationship between overall nutrient availability and health. Figure 36-2 illustrates the strong negative relationship between the infant mortality rate and per capita food energy availability in China during 1950–82. The 1959–62 food crisis caused great human suffering, reflected in a sharp increase in infant mortality and an actual decline in the total population in two of those years. The long-term decline in infant mortality resumed after the food crisis with the recovery of growth in per capita nutrient availability during the last two decades.

Distribution

Malnutrition is significantly curtailed only when an increase in per capita food availability benefits the entire population and not just those already enjoying an adequate diet. For China, the available provincial food production data and county and production team income distribution data show that the benefits of the increase in per capita food availability since 1949 have been widely distributed. The combination of increased per capita food availability and greater equality of food consumption have together brought about a major

Figure 36-2. *Infant Mortality and Per Capita Food Energy, China*

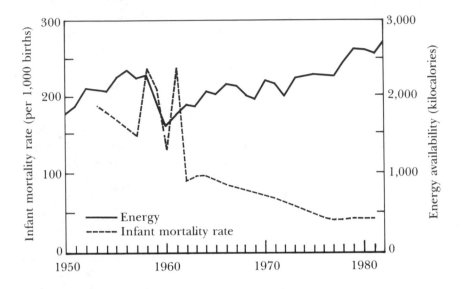

Table 36-4. *Grain-Poor Provinces, China 1953–57 and 1979–82*

Period and province	Per capita unprocessed grain production (kilograms/year)	Population (millions)
1953–57		
Shandong	220	52
Henan	240	46
Hebei	243	40
Qinghai	257	2
Liaoning	260	21
Shanxi	265	15
Jiangsu	274	43
Seven grain-poor provinces		220
National	291	610
1979–82		
Guizhou	229	28
Qinghai	230	4
Xizang	237	2
Gansu	242	19
Yunnan	272	32
Five grain-poor provinces		85
National	348	991

Note: Provinces that produced less than 275 kilograms of unprocessed grain per capita per year are considered to be grain poor. No data were available for Xizang for 1953–57. Columns may not add to totals because of rounding.

Source: Piazza (1986).

improvement in the nutritional status of the Chinese. In addition, China's advances in controlling infectious disease have undoubtedly contributed substantially to improved nutritional status, especially among children, since infectious diseases are important causes of malnutrition in children (see Leslie in part V).

The comparison of provincial per capita grain production in 1953–57 and 1979–82 in table 36-4 provides some of the most convincing evidence that food consumption is now more equally distributed in China. Specifically, the figures show that the number of Chinese residing in grain-poor provinces declined from about 220 million in the mid-1950s to about 85 million by the early 1980s. Since total population grew by about 60 percent during the period, the proportion of the population residing in grain-poor provinces declined by an even greater margin, from about 35 percent in 1953–57 to less than 10 percent in 1979–82. These figures are encouraging, but they also document the emergence of a serious and chronic shortfall in grain production in northwest and southwest China. Thus, although food supplies are adequate at the national level, and despite grain transfers from other provinces, provincial food balance sheets for 1979–81 show that per capita availability of energy in Gansu in the northwest and Guizhou, Guangdong, and Yunnan in the southwest was below requirements. The situation in Guizhou appears to have been particularly bleak.

It is also clear that national land reform and the adoption of the commune system greatly reduced rural inequality at the level of the village and the production team during the 1950s. Between 30 to 45 percent of China's arable land and somewhat less of other productive assets were redistributed during the national land reform of 1950–52, bringing about an immediate and substantial reduction in the disparity of wealth and income at the village level (Wong 1973; Schran 1969). With the formation of the commune system in the mid-1950s, moreover, the system of private ownership of land and other agricultural assets was virtually eliminated in the countryside. Land, tools, and farm animals were jointly owned by production team members, and consequently income disparity within the production team was greatly reduced.

However, income disparity between teams, communes, and counties was not affected by the national land reform or the formation of communes. Substantial differences in average household income between these larger administrative units have remained largely intact. Sharp curtailment of internal migration has helped to maintain geographic pockets of poverty, but the incidence of extreme rural poverty has diminished greatly in recent years. National surveys of household income have documented that, with the upsurge in agricultural production since 1978, the number of poor counties and production teams has declined tremendously. During 1977–81, the number of poor counties declined by 60 percent and the percentage of poor production teams declined from 39 percent to less than 20 percent of all teams (Lardy 1983b).

Improvements in Nutritional Status

Anthropometric surveys of children undertaken mostly in and around urban areas during the 1950s and in 1979 make possible an assessment of trends in the nutritional status of the Chinese. Rural data are scanty, and what data are available are principally for very well-off rural areas on the outskirts of Beijing and Shanghai. As the available anthropometric data suggest that nutritional status improvement in these rural areas has equaled the gain in urban areas, the urban data probably provide a reasonable proxy for trends in nutritional status of the general population. The data also show that nutritional status in rural areas lags far behind that in urban areas, so the urban data overstate the absolute level of the nutritional status of the general population. The data also overstate nutritional status in general because the surveys exclusively measured students, and students are, on average, taller than the general population (Tanner 1978). Another concern is whether the specific years for which data are available represent average years for agricultural production and general food availability, as short-term food shortages or surpluses in the survey year could be reflected in the weights of children. It is far less likely, however, that heights would be markedly affected by short-term food availability, so that height measurements provide a useful indication of longer-term growth trends. Despite these limitations, the anthropometric data are useful for assessing change in nutritional status over time.

Table 36-5 summarizes national average heights and weights for boys of several ages in 1915–25, 1951–58, and 1979. The national averages are calculated from anthropometric surveys of 3 provinces conducted in 1915–25, 15 provinces in 1951–58, and 16 provinces in 1979 (Piazza 1986; Research Group 1982; Stevenson 1925). These figures document tremendous improvement in urban nutritional status between 1951–58 and 1979. The height and weight of male and female children in 1979 exceed those of 1951–58 by a large margin for all ages. Males between the ages of 7 and 20 in 1979 were on average 7.6 centimeters taller and 4.3 kilograms heavier than males of the same ages in 1951–58. Females in 1979 were on average 6.6 centimeters taller and 3.0 kilograms heavier than were females of the same ages in 1951–58. These differences correspond to an average

Table 36-5. *Heights and Weights of Male Children, China, 1915–25, 1951–58, and 1979*

Indicator	1915–25	1951–58	1979	Improvement per decade, 1951–58 to 1979
Height (centimeters) at age				
7	114.6	114.5	120.7	2.6
12	136.3	135.7	144.7	3.8
18	163.1	163.6	168.9	2.2
Weight (kilograms) at age				
7	18.4	19.8	21.1	0.5
12	29.4	29.2	33.6	1.8
18	50.1	51.6	56.2	1.9

Source: Piazza (1986).

increase in height and weight of about 1.2 and 0.6 standard deviations, respectively. Similar improvements have also been reported at the provincial level (Piazza 1986; Jamison and Trowbridge 1984).

Data on change and anthropometric status are often reported as growth rate per decade. Tanner (1978) reports, for example, that European children of average economic circumstances aged 5 to 7 years have increased in height by 1 to 2 centimeters per decade since 1900, and that the height of Japanese 7-year-olds increased by about 3 centimeters per decade during 1950–70. By comparison, the national average increase in height for Chinese 7-year-olds for 1951–58 to 1979 was about 2.6 centimeters per decade. Thus, the decennial increase in height for age in China surpassed that of many European countries during the 20th century and almost equaled that of Japan during its most rapid period of anthropometric improvement. If the European experience is any guide, moreover, the increases can be expected to continue well into the next century. Tanner also observes that conditions that lead to increase in height have two effects: to increase the ultimately attained height and to increase the rate of maturation. The increased maturation rate results in higher rates of change in height in youths ages 10 to 14 than in young adults. This tendency is clearly evident in the last column of table 36-5.

The data for 1915–25 are not as useful for comparisons of change over time, since they are probably more positively biased than the data for the 1950s and 1979. Nevertheless, the contrast between the rapid improvement in nutritional status during 1951–58 to 1979 and the lack of any significant change in nutritional status during 1915–25 to 1951–58 is quite striking. The post-1949 improvement in nutritional status is largely explained by the increase in per capita food availability and its more equal distribution and by improvements in health. As per capita food energy and protein availability did not increase during 1958–77 (figure 36-1), the improvement in nutritional status during this period does not appear to be related to changes in nutrient availability. This suggests that improvements in health—principally the reduction of diarrheal infections—have played a key role. Another possibility is that the distribution of food has changed in favor of the relatively well-off areas from which most of the anthropometric data come. The national land reform carried out during 1950–52 may, in addition, have created preconditions for subsequent improvements in nutritional status by greatly reducing intraregional food production disparities. This, combined with protection of the very poorest against complete food deprivation, may have contributed substantially to the reduction in malnutrition-related child deaths since 1950.

Nutritional Status Today

The increasing implementation of a one-child-family policy in China has generated strong concern among parents that each child have full opportunity for optimal physical, mental, and psychological development. Prenatal nutrition counseling for expectant mothers is one important facet of policies to improve child development. The empirical evidence, although highly selective, does suggest that the prevalence of low birthweight (less than 2.5 kilograms) is low.

China's success with fertility limitation has also benefited the health of children actually born. Children seem well protected against vaccine-preventable diseases and, although problems of diarrheal, respiratory, and parasitic infections remain in much of China, substantial progress has been made to transform these from major sources of mortality to lingering problems of morbidity. Progress against malnutrition has been so substantial in urban areas that it can no longer be considered a problem of child development. Rural areas, in contrast, continue to suffer substantial amounts of moderate to serious child malnutrition with likely adverse functional consequences (Jamison 1986; Berg 1981).

Rural-Urban Differences

China's 1979 anthropometric survey of 16 provinces and municipalities provides valuable data for a careful assessment of urban-rural and interprovincial differences in child malnutrition (Research Group 1982). A second data set from 1975 provides information on a more limited sample of nine cities and the suburban areas immediately outside them: three cities in northern China, three in central China,

Table 36-6. *Malnourishment among Boys, Age 7, Selected Provinces of China, 1979*

	Percentage stunted[a]		Percentage with low weight for age[b]	
Province	*Urban*	*Rural*	*Urban*	*Rural*
Beijing	0.7	8.4	3.8	10.2
Tianjin	0.5	3.8	2.9	4.4
Shandong	2.1	11.9	6.2	11.3
Heilongjiang	1.3	19.5	5.9	15.4
Guangdong	1.3	19.2	6.4	23.0
Sichuan	7.5	37.1	11.1	26.4
National average	2.6	12.7	7.6	13.1

a. Stunting means that a child's height is less than 90 percent of the median height of children of the same age under the standards compiled by the U.S. National Center for Health Statistics (NCHS). The percentage stunted can be calculated from the mean and standard deviations of the distribution of height at a given age, assuming, as is reasonable, that the distribution is normal.

b. Calculated under the assumption of a normal distribution for weight (which is not a particularly good approximation). Low weight for age is defined as below 75 percent of the NCHS median. This corresponds to either Gomez II malnutrition (60–75 percent of the NCHS median) or Gomez III malnutrition (below 60 percent of the NCHS median).

Source: Jamison and Trowbridge (1984).

and three in southern China (Jamison and Trowbridge 1984). A clear pattern of rural malnutrition, but relatively little urban malnutrition, can be seen in these data. Table 36-6 reports both the proportion of 7-year-old boys stunted (that is, with unduly low height for age) and the percentage low in weight for age in the 1979 survey. The table illustrates, first, that rural-urban differences are marked, although somewhat less so in weight for age than in height for age. (Available data consistently show rural Chinese children to be as high—often higher—in weight for height as their urban counterparts. Greater stockiness of rural children may, then, partially compensate for lower stature in reducing rural-urban differences in weight for age.) Almost no stunting shows up in the most favored locations, urban Beijing and Tianjin. Second, both urban and rural malnutrition vary considerably from province to province. About 37 percent of rural boys in Sichuan are stunted, in contrast to only 12 percent in rural Shandong and less than 4 percent in rural Tianjin. Although the table does not show the corresponding data for females, the data indicate no major differences between males and females in percentage stunted.

Sources of Differences

One possible source of the differences in prevalence of malnutrition reported in table 36-6 is genetic variation between northern and southern Chinese. However, the relatively small differences between cities in northern and southern provinces (compare Beijing and Guangdong) suggest that genetic differences are relatively unimportant, and they certainly could not explain rural-urban differences in the same province. A second and well-established source of variation is disease prevalence, particularly diarrheal disease. Although the hard evidence is scant, diarrheal disease almost certainly remains an important problem in rural China. Hygienic improvements that reduce diarrheal incidence would likely have beneficial nutritional effects. Finally, differences in the quantity and quality of available food probably account for much of the rural-urban difference in prevalence of malnutrition. The State Statistical Bureau reports that in 1978, average urban residents consumed 22 percent more food energy, 14 percent more protein, and 90 percent more fat than their rural counterparts. Although the relative difference had decreased by 1982–83, it still amounted to about 400 kilocalories of energy and about 40 grams of protein and fat per capita per day (State Statistical Bureau 1981, 1984).

Efforts to reduce rural malnutrition will, therefore, need to address directly the problem of providing more food, and possibly food of higher protein content, to rural children and youths. Diarrheal disease control efforts may also be important, but probably relatively less so than in many countries. The increases in rural income that have ensued from economic reform in recent years will undoubtedly be important for many areas in providing the food required to reduce malnutrition. However, close surveillance of children's growth to allow targeting of food to the malnourished is a contribution the health care system can make to reducing rural malnutrition, and, where it is not now done, this effort should be a priority of the maternal and child health system.

Micronutrient Deficiency Diseases

Micronutrient deficiencies appear to be less of an issue in China than in many low-income countries. However, mild anemia is widespread, partly because of inadequate iron in the diet and partly because of iron losses due to hookworm infestation. In southern China, hookworm infection appears to be endemic, but the problem seems to receive little attention from health authorities.

Other deficiency diseases that remain important in China are rickets (vitamin D deficiency) and goiter (iodine deficiency). Vitamin A deficiency, which in a number of other countries is an important cause of impaired vision and perhaps of higher mortality rates (see Latham in part V), is relatively uncommon. Control of goiter has been the subject of extensive campaigns in recent years and, if these efforts continue at an adequate level, goiter could soon cease to be an important problem. Keshan disease, a result of selenium deficiency, is found only in about 15 provinces in China and is virtually unknown elsewhere in the world. It frequently leads to death through heart failure among children or women of childbearing age. Almost half of China's nutrition research is directed to understanding this disorder, which is now relatively unimportant as a public health problem. Selenium supplementation of food in affected areas has reduced the incidence of Keshan disease.

Issues for the Future

The Chinese government has been active in setting food policy, resulting in both major failures and major successes. The most notable failure was the policy-induced famine of 1959–61, which caused premature loss of perhaps 16 to 30 million lives (Ashton and others 1984; Coale 1984). The government allowed net exports of grain to double during the first two years of the famine, contributing to the tragedy. The government may also be faulted for having brought about reduced production of soybeans, other pulses, and oilseeds during the 1960s and 1970s. This action further diminished protein complementarity and fat availability in the average diet.

On the positive side, government policy has been instrumental in achieving a long-term increase in per capita food availability and reducing local disparities in food consumption. The rationing system helped virtually to eliminate malnutrition from major urban areas, and grain transfers have moderated regional shortfalls in food production. Until recently, the government had also constrained the growth of meat consumption, with the positive effect of making grain available to China's poor at affordable prices. In sum, although serious errors occurred along the way, food policy has played an important and generally positive role in reducing the incidence and severity of hunger and malnutrition in China since 1949.

As a result of the success of these policies, China's food problem is no longer one of insufficient national production. To the contrary, per capita nutrient availability in China now equals that of the average middle-income country (table 36-1). The remaining nutrition problems are to guarantee adequate levels of food intake among the poor and to avoid problems of overnutrition, with its concomitant enhanced risk of heart disease, stroke, and some cancers.

At least three issues arise concerning China's current food and nutrition policies. First, the centerpiece of recent agricultural reform in China, the "production responsibility system," and related reforms of the commune system (Khan and Lee 1983), may prove inimical to the welfare of indigent households and individuals. The reforms emphasize the link between income and individual work effort and have been central to the revitalization of agricultural incentives. However, since households with few or no able-bodied workers participate in agricultural production only to a limited extent, they have not directly benefited from the recent increases in production. Such indigent households depend on local relief programs for food, medical care, education, and other basic needs (Dixon 1981). Unfortunately, the ongoing reform of the commune system, including elimination of communes as political organizations, may reduce or disrupt such welfare activities, at least in the short run. These problems are, at least potentially, counterbalanced by the major production gains resulting from implementation of the responsibility system.

Second, the government has ambitious plans to double per capita consumption of red meat and other preferred foods by the year 2000 (Daxin 1982). Increased production of preferred foods need not necessarily reduce the grain available for direct consumption by China's poor, as national grain supplies more than meet current demand and grain production is expected to continue to increase more rapidly than population. However, if upward pressure on grain prices occurs, it will have a particularly adverse effect upon the poor. Furthermore, the task of increasing meat production for the majority of Chinese may distract the government from the task of increasing grain consumption for the malnourished. Unfortunately, guaranteeing adequate food intake among China's poor is both a less tractable and a less politically rewarding endeavor than increasing the consumption of preferred foods. It would, however, represent a far more important contribution to nutritional status in China.

A final issue about Chinese food and nutrition policy concerns the medical consequences of satisfying a much higher percentage of dietary requirements from animal sources. Reduction in mortality due to infectious disease and undernutrition have brought China health problems—stroke, cancer, and heart disease—remarkably similar to those of industralized countries. While definitive conclusions about the relationship between chronic disease and excess consumption of animal products cannot yet be drawn, the available epidemiological evidence strongly suggests that if the Chinese substantially increase their consumption of animal products, particularly animal fat, this will result in a significant increase in mortality from heart disease, stroke, and some cancers. Substantial taxes on animal consumption, and possibly production controls, could help China avoid the worst problems of overnutrition, improve state revenues and foreign trade, and maintain lower grain prices.

37

Dilemmas and Options in the Formulation of Agricultural Policies in Africa

Alain de Janvry

Sub-Saharan Africa is facing a severe economic, food, and social crisis. It is the only major region of the world where the rate of population growth is continuing to rise and where per capita food production has declined during the last 25 years. The current rate of population growth, 2.8 percent per year, will continue to rise in the next 15 years to 3.3 percent. The average annual increase in food production between 1970 and 1982 was only 1.7 percent, meaning a 1.1 percent drop per year in production per capita. This production shortfall leaves little margin for food security when agriculture is subject to climatic shocks and disruptions caused by civil war and misguided economic policies.

Agriculture and Food in Africa

Under the pressure of higher food demand associated with urbanization and higher incomes among certain segments of the population, African grain imports rose 640 percent between 1961–63 and 1980–82 and their cost increased 1,936 percent. This greatly heightened food dependency poses particular problems given that (a) the international terms of trade for Africa have worsened significantly (a decline of 15 percent between 1978 and 1981); (b) agricultural ex-

Translation of "Dilemmes et Options dans la Definition de Politiques Agricoles pour l'Afrique," a background paper prepared for the Economic Development Institute seminar on Agricultural Policy and Its Relationship to Food Policy in Sub-Saharan Africa, held in Berlin, March 18–22, 1985, in conjunction with the German Foundation for International Development.

ports are increasingly represented by certain products whose prices are now markedly unstable; (c) the prices of imported grains have been destabilized by monetary phenomena and protectionism in the developed countries; and (d) foreign exchange reserves are compromised by high interest rates, which push up the carrying charges on external debts, and by the drying up of sources of new loans.

Despite a grain surplus in the United States and Europe, the volume of international food aid has declined significantly since the mid-1960s, largely because of the United States' trade balance crisis. For sub-Saharan Africa, food aid rose by 75 percent between 1978 and 1982. However, the share of African agricultural imports represented by food aid is already 23 percent and a sustained increase in this source of supply is unlikely (see Huddleston in part III). Projections for the decade ahead suggest that food dependency will continue to intensify rapidly unless governments make major efforts to improve domestic production. For the short term, the consequences of this food shortage are critical. People in 36 African countries are going hungry, more than three-fifths of Africa's population is chronically malnourished, daily food energy intake is below 90 percent of needs in 15 of the 39 countries in sub-Saharan Africa, and average life expectancy is only 49 years.

Despite rapid population growth, the food problem is not basically a demographic one. Many countries are, in fact, sparsely populated, and food production is often limited by a shortage of labor. The labor shortage is exacerbated by rapid rural-urban migration due to (a) the very low productivity of labor in food-crop production owing to the poor quality of natural resources and the dearth of investments in infrastructure, irrigation, and technology; (b) the rapid growth of certain industrial sectors and urban services prompted by the influx of foreign capital, particularly under international aid; and (c) high urban wages and access in the cities to government subsidies, on food in particular, provided in response to urban pressure groups. In addition to urban unemployment, the rural exodus causes heavy consumption of imported goods (wheat, rice, and luxury industrial products), which shifts effective demand away from the production of domestic food crops (maize, millet, sorghum, and tubers) and from local industry.

Agricultural Price Policies in Africa

One of the major themes of the World Bank's first report on development in sub-Saharan Africa is that the stagnation of agriculture is rooted largely in the undervaluation of producer prices for both export crops and food grown for local consumption (World Bank 1981). In the case of export crops, the aims of undervaluing agricultural products are to raise funds for public investment in development and to ensure low-cost inputs for the local processing industries of those products and high revenues for the bureaucracy overseeing their marketing. These mechanisms are implemented by parastatal corporations, which have a monopoly on the purchase and export of agricultural products. Many were set up during the colonial period and later became the primary source of revenue and foreign exchange for the African countries. As shown in table 37-1, the producer price is generally below the world price, often by a 25 to 50 percent margin.

Food grown for domestic consumption was often also undervalued by a host of measures resulting from overvalued exchange rates (and hence competition from cheap imports) or below-market prices set by parastatal monopolies. These artificially low prices have frequently led to black markets and smuggling. Governments adopt such measures chiefly out of their need to maintain their legitimacy and to respond to the demands made by the urban population for protection of their real income against inflation. The less political autonomy and legitimacy a government has, the more it has to yield to those demands. Another objective is to keep nominal wages low by fixing low producer prices, hence subsidizing the cost of labor for processing in both the private and public sectors. These food subsidies for urban consumption are often provided through a system of monopolistic purchases from the producers at low prices and distribution to consumers through state warehouses. Consumer price distortions also result from industrialization policies which favor import substitution. An overvalued exchange rate—usually a component of such policies—actually subsidizes imported capital and intermediate goods for industry.

Low producer prices are frequently offset by subsidies of inputs, although this poses four types of problems. First, the subsidies are in general aimed primarily at export crops, leaving food production with unfavorable terms of trade (Christensen and Economic Research Service, USDA 1981). Second, the supply of subsidized inputs is often limited by the heavy burden that those subsidies represent to the government. Third, unlike price mechanisms, the distribution of public funds through institutional mechanisms is highly biased in favor of farmers with the greatest political and social clout. Last, input subsidies benefit modernized farmers more than traditional ones, who are thus not compensated for the low prices of their output.

Despite these general trends for agricultural price policies in sub-Saharan Africa, such policies can vary greatly from country to country. For example, Nigeria's domestic prices for export crops are above world market prices. Products such as rice in Ghana are favorably

Table 37-1. *Nominal Protection of Agricultural Exports*

Country	Per capita GNP, 1982 (1980 U.S. dollars)	Share of agriculture in GNP, 1980 (percent)	Export product	Nominal protection[a]
Mali	190	42	Sesame	0.50
			Cotton	0.50
Burkina Faso	210	40	Sesame	0.75
			Cotton	0.75
Malawi	230	43	Tobacco	0.40
			Cotton	0.75
			Groundnuts	0.75
			Maize	1.50
Tanzania	280	54	Coffee	0.40
Togo	410	26	Coffee	0.47
			Cocoa	0.47
			Cotton	0.94
Sudan	410	38	Cotton	0.50
			Sesame	0.50
			Groundnuts	0.50
			Sugar	0.84
Kenya	420	34	Tea	0.73
			Coffee	0.73
			Cotton	0.91
			Maize	0.91
Senegal	450	29	Groundnuts	0.50
			Cotton	0.50
Zambia	560	15	Tobacco	0.84
			Maize	0.62
			Groundnuts	0.62
Cameroon	670	32	Cocoa	0.30
			Coffee	0.41
			Cotton	0.62
Nigeria	1,010	20	Groundnuts	1.33
			Palm oil	1.41
Côte d'Ivoire	1,150	34	Coffee	0.40
			Cocoa	0.40
			Groundnuts	0.73
			Cotton	0.83
			Palm oil	0.83

a. Nominal protection is defined as P_a/eP_w where P_a is the domestic price, P_w is the world price, and e is the equilibrium exchange rate.

Sources: World Bank (1982, 1984a).

priced because they are grown by large farmers wielding substantial political power (Bates 1981).

Many countries also reacted to the food crisis of the 1970s and to balance of payments difficulties by raising the real prices of foodstuffs and/or export crops. Between 1969 and 1980, Côte d'Ivoire, Ghana, Kenya, Madagascar, Rwanda, Tanzania, Togo, Zaire, and Zambia increased real producer prices for foodstuffs because demand was growing faster than supply, because of devaluations due to the external debt and to austerity policies, or as a result of policies designed to achieve food self-sufficiency. During the same period, Côte d'Ivoire, The Gambia, Kenya, Malawi, Nigeria, Sierra Leone, Zaire, and Zimbabwe raised real producer prices for export crops. These increases resulted from devaluations, lower taxes for exporting sectors, and policies to stimulate agricultural exports (Ghai and Smith 1983). Interestingly, during this period no countries lowered the real prices of food or export crops, indicating the beginning of a turnaround, even if only slight, in the attitude of African governments toward their agriculture sectors.

Multiple Policy Objectives and Price Instruments

One of the big problems in using agricultural prices as a political tool is that prices fulfill many contradictory functions (see Streeten in part IV). They simultaneously affect economic growth and general welfare, but in opposite ways, as prices are a source of income for certain classes and a cost for others. Low agricultural prices can stimulate industrial growth but lead to stagnation of agriculture. They can bring up the real income of consumers but lower that of farmers and reduce job opportunities for farm workers.

There is also a conflict between short- and long-term objectives, as the short-term redistributional effects obtained through price manipulations for a given agricultural supply are often offset by the long-term consequences once the effects of the prices on economic growth are felt. Such is the case with consumer subsidies accorded to the detriment of public investment. Urban workers gain in real wages in the short term but lose in employment and nominal wages in the long run. Most governments are therefore reluctant to let market forces set agricultural prices and try to control their effects through a host of institutional measures. The objectives of agricultural price policies include, in particular, safeguarding consumer welfare, filling public coffers, generating farmer income, producing foreign exchange, increasing food security, stabilizing prices, improving nutrition, and distributing revenue between regions and individuals.

The dilemma surrounding price policies is thus that too few tools have to satisfy too many objectives. This leads to pronounced contradictions including, for example, the stagnation of food production and the rural poverty currently widespread in Africa. Two solutions exist. The first is to trim the number of objectives. This is essentially the neoliberal solution, which abandons concern for general welfare and lets prices—set adrift to respond to market forces—and private enterprise control the allocation of resources. The second solution is to increase the number of instruments so as to strip prices of certain functions that official measures have sought to assign them. For example, equity for rural groups can be achieved through agrarian reform and higher productivity of rural labor, public revenue can be generated by land taxes, the nutrition of the poor can be improved through the creation of jobs and income transfers, and so forth. This increase in the number of instruments allows the role of prices to be confined to what they do best: guiding resource allocation in an institutional context created by a set of structural measures.

Investment in Agriculture or Industry

Most developing countries have gone through a phase of import substitution–led industrialization followed, in the most successful growth cases in the last 15 years, by a phase of export-led growth. The success of these two models is now limited. The problem with the first is that protectionism created inefficiencies and industrialization oriented toward the production of luxury goods skewed income distribution. The difficulty with the second model is that the current international market severely limits the possibilities for sales of industrial goods in the developed countries.

In the current economic context, an investment strategy that favors food production within the rural economy, and that bases industrialization on agricultural growth, seems the best way to ensure both stable growth and general welfare. The experience of China, the Republic of Korea, and Taiwan, as well as the experience of the industrialized countries in the 18th and 19th centuries, shows the possibilities of sustained industrialization through stepped-up agricultural development. Small-farmer development was proposed as a strategy for India by Mellor (1976) and for the Republic of Korea by Adelman (1984). For Korea, Adelman shows how the reallocation of investment from the services and industrial consumer sectors toward rice production—provided that technological change allows for a steady increase in agricultural productivity—leads to a higher GNP and more uniform income distribution than the current strategy of growth based on industrial exports.

Agricultural Development: Prices and Other Instruments

The neoliberal school stresses the importance of raising agricultural prices to stimulate production and scale down the public sector, particularly to reduce the taxes levied on the agricultural sector. This is, for example, the philosophy of the World Bank's first report on development in sub-Saharan Africa (World Bank 1981). Although prices must indeed be set at the market breakeven point, policymakers must also realize that (a) price equilibrium is necessary but not sufficient to guarantee agricultural development, and (b) technological and structural alternatives exist that are conducive to more rapid increases in agricultural production with more progressive consequences for income distribution than those achieved by price supports.

Raising agricultural prices has a limited overall linkage effect on rural community development because farmers are unable to increase their output quickly in most African countries (Bond 1983). This is due chiefly to a lack of new technical options and to the constraints farmers face in acquiring modern inputs. Thus higher agricultural prices result in a transfer of income from consumers to those farmers who marketed the largest surpluses. The efficient use of price policies requires prior structural policies to make agricultural supply more elastic.

A recent study of a general equilibrium model in India shows how the poor (landless farm workers, small farmers who are net purchasers of food, and urban workers) benefit from a policy of technological change in agriculture with flexible prices, while they are adversely affected by a policy of agricultural price supports designed to stimulate supply when elasticity is low (de Janvry and Subbarao 1984).

The key to agricultural development lies in the implementation of policies aimed at structural change, even if they are more difficult to manage than price incentives. Such policies must attempt to stabilize access to land, stimulate technological change (in particular, change that reduces the need for manpower where the rural labor force is limited), promote research, encourage investments in infrastructure (transportation, communications, and irrigation), train managers, organize rural extension, and so forth.

The Costs of Uneven Sectoral Development:
Why Does Success in Some Sectors Cause Famine?

In the 1970s, many countries experienced rapid growth in certain export sectors, including extraction (petroleum and natural gas) and certain branches of agriculture (for example, tea, coffee, and fodder grains). Other sectors moved into recession precisely because of this growth and the resulting massive inflow of foreign exchange. The same effect can be caused by a rapid increase in the external debt or by an influx of capital from international aid. In all these cases, success in a sector that generates foreign exchange creates two types of perverse impacts on the food-growing sector, which competes with imported foods. The first is a shift of resources toward the sector undergoing rapid expansion—for example, by emigration—to the detriment of food production. The second is an adverse impact on domestic prices for food products because of the inflationary push created by the revenue in the expanding sector and by the resulting tendency to overvalue the currency. An abundance of foreign exchange makes it possible to avoid devaluation, which is always unpopular in the urban sectors, and hence to keep domestic food prices low.

If small farmers produce mainly foodstuffs and if the reallocation of resources is insufficiently smooth to enable them to produce for the sector undergoing rapid expansion, the rural sector is hit by recession and untenable prices. The result is emigration toward the sources of employment created by the sector that is expanding. If not enough jobs are created, the result is poverty and often famine.

There are five ways to protect small farmers from the deleterious consequences of this type of uneven sectoral development.

○ To help the rural sector produce for the sector undergoing rapid expansion, as with coffee and cocoa production in the Côte d'Ivoire (Hecht 1983.) As these export crops are often capital-intensive (planting of trees, irrigation for sorghum in Mexico), this assistance to small farmers requires large-scale credit and technical assistance programs together with stable prices for the product in international trade.

○ To increase the productivity of rural labor in food production so that domestic food can compete with low-cost agricultural imports. This is the goal of integrated rural development projects and research on improving traditional production systems.

○ To introduce protectionism against imported foodstuffs that compete with local production, keep producer prices above consumer prices, or subsidize inputs to compensate for the unfavorable prices of the products. This is what Mexico tried under Lopez

Portillo but had to drop because of the high cost of the program and the austerity policies made necessary by the external debt crisis.

○ To create enough jobs in the sector undergoing expansion, together with emigration opportunities, to absorb farmers driven from the land by untenable agricultural prices

○ To increase the food self-sufficiency of farmers by enabling them to end their reliance on the inputs and credit market. This entails in particular the promotion of organic farming methods.

Food Security Strategies: For Whom?

The two extreme solutions to a food strategy are unacceptable—food self-sufficiency because the cost is generally too high, and the application of the pure theory of comparative advantage because its risks are too great and it has negative effects on some groups that have very low income (see Reutlinger in part III). Most countries have therefore tried to formulate food security strategies that judiciously balance these two extremes. The main problem is, however, not to formulate an optimum national strategy but to formulate a strategy that ensures food security for all population groups.

Nationally, the formulation of a food security strategy can be based on the optimum allocation of resources among production for the domestic, export, and import markets. The objective function can be specified mathematically, for example, as the maximization of expected production and the simultaneous minimization of the variance in the net foreign exchange income of the agriculture sector once a given set of consumption needs has been satisfied (Sarris 1983). The sources of random variability are domestic yields and world prices. However, this national strategy is not necessarily satisfactory for specific social groups. For the poor, food security means the security of their real income—and hence of their source of employment or other means of earning their livelihood—as well as access to food subsidies (see Sen in part III). For farmers, a food security policy consists of protecting them against the adverse effects of rapid growth in certain sectors or against the vagaries of climate in production for self-consumption.

Agricultural Development or Rural Development?

In the face of the food crisis and the demand of urban populations for low-cost food, governments are tempted to solve the problem of production stagnation through an increase in production in the framework of large, modern enterprises, whether capitalistic, cooperative, or state, that are highly integrated with agroindustry. This is the easy solution, as these types of enterprises are the more readily controlled, are often more productive when there is a shortage of labor, and can directly adopt a good number of techniques, particularly farm mechanization, from the developed countries.

This easy short-term solution, however, has its medium- and long-term difficulties. First, large-scale cooperative or state farm projects are often highly inefficient. Second, concentrating investments on a small number of large producers tends to concentrate income distribution and induce development based on consumption of luxury goods. Last, this approach leaves the rural masses with minimal income and employment opportunities, possibly triggering famine even when efforts to expand food production are successful.

Although it is more difficult to implement and requires a sustained commitment over time—including international aid—rural development based on an increase in small-farmer productivity seems to offer better guarantees for egalitarian and stable growth over time (Johnston and Clark 1982).

Food Aid: Supplement or Substitute for Rural Development?

There is no doubt that international food aid to refugees and the starving is necessary. Long-term food aid is more controversial. It is often denounced because it (a) reduces pressure for the implementation of needed reforms to improve food production; (b) depresses prices paid to domestic food producers; (c) causes great price uncertainty because it is unreliable; and (d) encourages food habits (wheat consumption) that domestic production cannot meet (Eicher 1983; Hopkins in part III).

A detailed study of the impact of food aid in Latin America shows, however, that the same tool, food aid, can be used with very different results, depending on whether it is an explicit component of a food security strategy or a substitute for the implementation of such a strategy. In Colombia, for example, subsidized wheat imports (PL 480) depressed domestic prices and eliminated the wheat crop on commercial farms. In Brazil, in contrast, the government sold subsidized wheat to the mills at a price higher than that paid for PL 480 wheat and used the revenue from the transaction to offer domestic producers a price higher than the mill price. Unlike the case of Colombia, instead of competing with domestic production, food aid was a source of revenue for financing the transition toward greater food self-sufficiency (Hall 1980).

Changes in the Role of the Government?

Criticism of the inefficiency of parastatals and excessive taxation of the agricultural sector has led neoliberal critics to suggest reducing the role of the government and promoting market forces and private investment in its stead. It is doubtful, however, that the developing countries can grow rapidly without the government playing a strong role, as in Japan.

A recent reinterpretation of the fast growth in the Republic of Korea has shown, for example, that contrary to initial assessments, Korea's growth was an archetype of neoliberal development, with the government playing a very important role in formulating investment priorities and technical choices (Pack and Westphal 1984). In the case of Africa, the role of the government is vital in managing investments in public goods, such as research, education, and infrastructure; determining intersectoral investment priorities, particularly between agriculture and industry; subjecting foreign trade and international capital flows to a consistent development policy; managing a food security strategy; and structuring income distribution in conjunction with the investment policy. It is therefore clear that the government has to be made more efficient in managing structural mechanisms that complement market forces. This requires in particular the training of managers to take on these technocratic responsibilities.

Formulation of Agricultural Policy: Social Integration or Political Integration?

Rapid agricultural development has probably never occurred without a strong political representation of the economic interests of the agriculture sector. The safeguarding of those interests requires more than the social integration by which farmers have access to credit, information, markets, and so forth. It requires their political integration, enabling farmers to become full-fledged citizens in the political apparatus and to assert their rights through lobbying groups. The success of Japan's agriculture is based on the dominant role of farmers in the ruling party, and that of the green revolution in Colombian rice production is based on the power of farmer associations, which activated public research and rural extension from the bottom up. In Africa, Mellor (1984) observes that successes with cotton in southern Mali, tea in Kenya, maize in Zimbabwe, and cocoa in the Côte d'Ivoire have all had two central features: the existence of powerful producer associations and an active role by the government in research, rural extension, infrastructure, and market guarantees. If rural development is to be chosen over agricultural development and the farmers protected from the pernicious effects of uneven sectoral development, the vast majority of farmers must have a say in the formulation of agricultural policy alternatives.

38

Experience with Food Strategies in Four African Countries

Kees Tuinenburg

In 1981, the EC adopted the so-called "Pisani plan," an action plan to combat world hunger. Unhappy with conventional projects and standard food aid, the EC proposed a new kind of support for national governments.

In 1982, the EC Council of Ministers decided to assist four African countries, Kenya, Mali, Rwanda, and Zambia, to formulate and implement food strategies. The EC and its member states entered into a "mutual commitment" with the governments of these four countries. The governments committed themselves to implement policy reforms; the EC and its member states committed themselves to provide sustained resources and technical support and, where necessary, to arrange a safety net during critical and costly transition periods.

The food situation in the four countries selected for support by the EC is illustrative of the situation in most of sub-Saharan Africa. Per capita food production is decreasing and food imports, including food aid, have increased substantially. Malnutrition in the rural areas among small and marginal farmers and landless families, the latter a new phenomenon in sub-Saharan Africa, is on the increase. Urban employment opportunities do not keep pace with the growth of the urban population, which will cause increasing malnutrition among the urban poor.

In general, food systems have become more vulnerable than before. Even in countries with a reasonable degree of food security, the situation may change drastically in a few years if trends are allowed to

Excerpted from *Food Strategies in Four African Countries, A Study on Food Policy Formulation and Implementation in Kenya, Mali, Rwanda and Zambia,* prepared for the Commission of European Communities by the Royal Tropical Institute, Amsterdam, the Netherlands, January 1984.

run their course. Changing food habits and national food deficits have caused increasing dependence on imported food.

The deteriorating food situation in a number of sub-Saharan countries is undermining the survival of governments and people. Donors have become disillusioned with project aid that, in an unsuitable national policy context, has not produced the expected results. Thus governments and donors realized that the underlying cause of food insecurity is the lack of integrated national food policies covering all stages of the food system. This growing awareness that a fundamental rethinking of food and agricultural policies is essential led to the formulation of the food strategy concept at the World Food Council of Ministers in Ottawa in 1979. Since then, the food strategy approach has won wide acceptance, and a number of countries and development agencies have begun to support national food strategies as the method for coordinating policies and resources.

A national food strategy is a permanent instrument for policy planning and management that ideally ensures the coherence of diverse technical actions, investments, and social and economic policies related to a country's food sector. It does so in the following three ways:

○ By establishing a framework for food production and consumption objectives, thus helping to identify consistent policy priorities over time

○ By specifying within this framework short- and medium-term programs and projects

○ By providing a mechanism for more effective implementation of specific program and project proposals, both strengthening national institutional and management capabilities and exploiting development of the food sector in a more profitable way.

Thus, food strategies provide a framework for fundamental policy modifications that will put an end to short-term improvisation and stopgap measures. They further provide the framework for consistent donor assistance and for effective development partnerships in an ongoing policy dialogue.

In all four countries selected for support by the EC, debate on food policy issues has intensified since 1982. The governments have set up interministerial committees, and governments and donors have begun to discuss policy reform and donor assistance. It is too early yet to evaluate the practical results of these efforts, since it has become clear that policy dialogue by its nature—and given the need to implement radical policy changes—is a much longer-term affair than was first realized.

Experience so far has shown that there is no blueprint for policy design and policy dialogue, since both are country specific. Food policy dialogue and implementation have taken a different path in each of the countries. However, some common principles have emerged that are summarized below.

Food Security at the National and Individual Levels

Food security is the ability to acquire enough food to satisfy minimal nutritional requirements at both national and household levels. This concept is different from food self-sufficiency, which means that a country or household produces enough for its own consumption. A high degree of food self-sufficiency, therefore, is not necessarily a precondition of food security. Agricultural or nonagricultural exports, according to the country's comparative advantage in international trade, may provide enough foreign currency to bridge the gap between requirements and own production (see Reutlinger in part III).

However, in many African countries, national food deficits are growing, and the objective of food self-sufficiency seems a sensible one, particularly for the landlocked countries because of the costs of overland transport. The four food strategies under consideration all concentrate on national food self-sufficiency, particularly self-sufficiency in staple crops.

Currently, the governments are paying less attention to nutritional aspects, although the nutritional situation of the populations in the four countries has been analyzed. Severe nutritional problems affect at least 10 to 20 percent of the inhabitants in these countries. This percentage can be expected to rise, especially for the urban low-income populations whose growing numbers are not being matched by increased employment opportunities.

The strategies have not developed concrete ways to put an end to growing malnutrition, apart from the implicit belief that general economic development will take care of this problem. Possibilities for interim nutrition-oriented crash programs are still lacking, but in Zambia, for instance, the government did devote increased attention to urban gardening.

So far, the four strategies are in essence staple crop strategies rather than comprehensive food and nutrition strategies. Food policy planners, particularly development administrators with an agricultural background on the donor side, appear to have a blind spot for nutritional aspects. Within developing countries, nutritional aspects are recognized, but the most urgent priority remains how to deal with growing national food deficits.

Food Crops versus Cash Crops

Recent debate invariably includes the relative merits of food crops and cash crops. Two simplifications are frequently heard:

○ Export crops create hunger.
○ Governments must choose between food production and export crops.

Such arguments ignore the possibility that within farming systems both can exist. Cash crops may enhance the farmers' access to credit and inputs, which benefits food production as well. The area devoted to cash crops must not be allowed to expand excessively, and certainly not to the extent that it jeopardizes the small farmers' food security. Too often governments have stimulated the cultivation of export crops out of eagerness to secure the foreign exchange needed for their urban development. (See also Donovan in part II, who points out that food is often an important export crop.)

In southern Mali, increased attention to food crop production in the existing farming system does not seem to go against the objectives of cotton production for exports. In Kenya, the ideal balance of food and cash crops has not yet been thoroughly explored in food policy documents. In Zambia, agricultural exports are still very small and, in view of shortfalls in food production, top priority is currently given to self-sufficiency in staple crops. Objectives include simultaneous development of the food production and export crop sectors. Rwanda intends to increase resource allocation to boost food production without necessarily neglecting the need to improve productivity in the cash crop sector.

Food Marketing and Price Policy

Few people would argue about the need for an improved incentive structure for food and agricultural production. Low farmgate prices, overvalued exchange rates, and direct taxation of farmers have weakened the economic base of the rural sector in most African countries. Parastatal marketing boards have been subject to severe criticism, but within the margins set by governments, they seldom enjoyed much room for maneuvering. Parastatals have incurred huge deficits, caused both by high consumer subsidies and by operational inefficiencies in a situation where there was no incentive at all to apply the guidelines of economic management. Deficits were simply matched by government contributions. Although economists agree that higher producer prices enhance conditions for increased production, there are two reasons why government interference in marketing has usually resulted in keeping prices low:

○ Governments try to accumulate budget income through taxation of agricultural products, especially in the export crop sector.

○ Prices are maintained at artificially low levels in deference to the interests of urban consumers—the eternal conflict between producers and urban consumers—with the latter, who are close to the political center and better organized, generally on the winning side. At this moment, inappropriate marketing and pricing policies are the most significant obstacles to improving the production and distribution of food in most African countries.

Price Policy Design

The food strategies under review permit the distillation of certain basic principles for price policy formulation. Most economists accept that international market prices, that is, border prices, represent the actual opportunity costs of domestically produced and consumed food commodities, especially for small countries. Thus, long-term trends of international prices should provide a point of reference for domestic price policies (see de Janvry in part VI). As shown below, domestic prices for maize in the four countries were well below their import price level.

Country	Ratio of domestic to import price
Zambia, 1981	0.60
Mali, 1981–1982	0.64
Kenya, 1978–1980	0.77
Rwanda, 1982	0.88

These computations do not compensate for the overvaluation of domestic currency, estimated at 10 to 30 percent in many East African countries. These figures suggest that an increase in the price of food grains by roughly 20 to 60 percent is needed to approximate international long-term prices. (Since the original study was written, producer prices in a number of countries have indeed been increased to a level more commensurate with international prices.)

Options for Price and Market Policies

A challenge to food strategists is to design a policy mix that will simultaneously stimulate food production and increase the food consumption of the malnourished. Depending on social and economic conditions, the following three options, which are not mutually exclusive, can be distinguished:

o A policy of low consumer and producer prices, combined with subsidized inputs and services to farmers
o A dual price policy, with producer prices based on international prices, but with consumer price subsidies on basic foodstuffs targeted to vulnerable groups
o A policy of both producer and consumer prices at efficient levels, combined with income transfer schemes (cash or food) targeted to the poor and/or programs to generate employment and purchasing power for these disadvantaged groups, such as public works or food for work.

A problem with subsidized inputs is that small farmers rarely benefit from these incentives. The Rwanda food strategy envisages input subsidies for a transitional period to allow for institution building and for the adoption of new technologies. But in principle, these input subsidies should be phased out to avoid further income inequalities. Zambia is in the process of abolishing fertilizer subsidies and Kenya will no doubt consider this issue as well.

Dual price systems have been, to date, inefficiently implemented on both the producer and the consumer side. All four countries have heavy indirect consumer subsidies, either general in their effect or catering in reality to urban civil servants and the middle class. However, consumer subsidies are expensive, and in Zambia, for instance, large budget deficits have persuaded the government to put an end to untargeted consumer subsidies. None of the strategies under review have dealt with consumer price subsidies for nutritionally vulnerable groups.

An important problem with a policy that attempts to regulate producer and consumer prices at so-called efficient levels is that inefficient market structures absorb an excessive share of producer-consumer price differentials. In all four countries, the operation of food markets costs far more than it should. Inefficiency in marketing has immediate, substantive implications for producer and consumer response to incentives. If marketing fails and farmers are unable to sell their crops, they have little incentive to continue producing for the market.

There appears to be room to provide farmers with better incentives, without necessarily increasing consumer prices, through policy reforms that reduce the share of marketing costs taken by middlemen or state marketing boards with high operational costs. In Mali, a gradual liberalization of the cereal market (excluding rice) resulted in higher producer prices, while the impact of these higher prices on consumers is being cushioned by subsidies that will eventually be phased out. In Rwanda, the strategy includes the extension of local procurement and sales outlets in an effort to reduce excessive seasonal and interregional price margins.

Public Marketing Agencies

The role of public marketing agencies in domestic food grain markets has become a much-debated issue. Although many people are disillusioned with public food marketing boards, most accept the need for some state intervention.

Originally, marketing boards were set up for trade in export crops, but today, parastatal food marketing boards exist everywhere in Africa. While the original objectives were quite simple—to improve the economic position of the producers—a multitude of new goals were added. Advisory and regulatory boards gradually disappeared and political objectives were added, such as government control over important sectors of the economy, protection of urban consumers, and avoidance of exploitation by middlemen. Governments felt increasingly pressured to guarantee uniform prices to farmers, regardless of season or location, and these can only be enforced under a monopoly.

Analyses show that current state marketing operations largely fail to achieve their assorted objectives, while the costs are enormous. Governments are so intent on keeping urban prices low that margins between buying and selling are minimal, with the result that private traders are forced out of business and heavy government subsidies become necessary. The cost of state marketing agencies has become prohibitively expensive to governments. More public-private action therefore seems to be the solution, but governments regard private trading with suspicion, fearing that traders will exploit farmers. However, researchers studying private marketing systems in sub-Saharan Africa in the 1960s and 1970s have been consistently impressed with how well they operated (Jones 1984). Some found that indigenous private enterprise food marketing in developing countries in Africa is more efficient than statutory marketing of any agricultural product (Kriesel 1974).

The perception that the coexistence of public and private trading is not only possible but desirable has promoted serious efforts to restructure the cereal market in Kenya and Mali. In Mali, it has brought down consumer prices, while producer prices have increased. In Kenya, a step-by-step approach is being considered with careful monitoring. Liberalization of food marketing in Zambia does not yet seem to be politically feasible, but because of more economic pricing and the abolition of transport subsidies, signs indicate that private trade has been somewhat reactivated. Multiyear food aid commitments, such as Mali has achieved, can play an important role by enabling the governments to introduce these expensive structural reorganizations. At this moment, however, marketing and price policy measures are too often taken on an ad hoc basis, while careful monitoring of the effects on production and consumption is virtually absent.

Reserves

Two sorts of stocks should remain under the jurisdiction of public marketing agencies: a stabilization stock, financed by the marketing board, to stabilize cereal prices, and a food security stock as an insurance against emergency shortfalls, financed, at least in the short-term, with substantial donor assistance. The strategies under review have still given too little attention to the planning of these stocks. Food reserves and their various uses should indeed be a major theme during ongoing policy dialogue. Food aid and the procurement of local cereals with counterpart funds could play a more important role in maintaining the necessary stocks.

Research, Technology, and Input Supply

As stipulated earlier, higher producer prices are not enough to bring about a sustained growth of food production beyond initial increases. A long-term increase in production must ultimately come from more productive use of available resources, including a combination of modern inputs, such as fertilizers, improved seeds, and animal traction, together with improved use of indigenous resources, such as recycling of organic matter, intercropping, and agroforestry. The development and introduction of low-cost technological packages, especially for small farmers, is a prerequisite to increased food production. Action-oriented farming systems research should be rooted in traditional systems. Improved technology should be tested under on-farm conditions. In southern Mali, a start has been made in these directions, but in Zambia, farmers often have an unjustified preference for tractors. Attempts to make optimal use of existing farm resources certainly deserve full support, as does donor support for research strategies based on farming systems.

Extension services are an indispensable element in introducing improved technological packages. The same, of course, applies to a timely and uninterrupted supply of inputs, particularly of fertilizer, which is often impeded by serious foreign currency constraints. As mentioned before, it is advisable to phase out subsidies on inputs once the initial purpose of encouraging certain technologies has been achieved and producer prices have been sufficiently increased. Not only is much more emphasis on farming systems research advocated; applied research is also desirable to advance small-scale local agroprocessing, especially processing of traditional cereals such as couscous and of composite baking flour, preparation of weaning foods, and village-based oil pressing.

Credit

Food strategies are concerned not only with increasing total agricultural production but also with increasing the proportion of total food production by small-scale and subsistence farmers, who constitute the majority of the rural population. Although small farmers often produce high returns on small capital investments, their access to formal credit has remained anything but commensurate with these returns. Poor performance of credit programs in all four target countries has further damaged the prospects of farmers in search of loans. Formal credit still does not reach many farmers, with the result that dependence on private money lenders, who charge high short-term interest rates, has forced smallholders to sell a high proportion of their crop, with malnutrition as a possible consequence.

The issue of providing credit therefore deserves rethinking. Low-cost credit for small farmers might be realized through a group approach. For example, a number of farmers are organized into cooperatives or primary societies in Kenya and Rwanda and into village associations in Mali and bear mutual responsibility for repayment. Standardization of credit procedures for farmers in the same region with similar production patterns might also be a solution, although repayment might remain a problem.

The EC should support experimental programs to provide credit to farmers' groups for input supply as well as to improve village level storage capacity. Providing more credit to small farmers is pointless unless marketing systems are first improved, including prompt payment upon delivery. Many examples exist where, because of slow payment, farmers have been discouraged or have switched crops. This was reported in Zambia, where farmers substituted cotton for maize because prompt payment for cotton was more appreciated than the higher returns on maize, which could only be cashed after a long delay.

Direct Measures to Assist Vulnerable Groups

The four food strategies mainly focus on the supply side of the equation, although in Zambia, some attention has been given to the demand for food and to nutrition. Apparently, development administrators and food strategists feel ill at ease with nutritional considerations and do not know how to incorporate them into agricultural planning. Donors might well encourage governments to develop data collection in this area and assist governments with nutrition impact analysis of policies and projects.

Although vulnerable groups were identified in the four strategies, no specific direct measures to assist them have been defined as part of these strategies. Existing food subsidies in the countries were general, benefiting poor and better-off families alike. In Zambia, it was even found that the more expensive breakfast meal was more subsidized than the cheaper roller meal consumed by the lower-income groups.

Few examples of targeted food subsidies to nutritionally vulnerable groups in sub-Saharan Africa exist. For the moment, such rationing schemes appear too difficult to manage. Public works programs that provide food do exist, but they have not yet been an integral part of food strategies. A promising approach to assist vulnerable groups might be the targeting of food subsidies within the context of primary health care activities, as has been done in some countries in Latin America.

The four food strategies thus ultimately concentrated on increasing overall production of staple food crops and on marketing reform but neglected nutritional objectives and food security at the household level.

Food Aid and Food Strategies

Examples of indiscriminate food aid having a negative impact on consumption patterns and production abound in developing countries. It is therefore encouraging to note that donors and recipients have become aware that food aid should be integrated in food strategies. In 1983, the Commission of European Communities developed the following guidelines:

○ Adapt the system so that EC aid contracts with recipient countries will accord with the requirements of food strategies designed to boost productive activity in the present farming sector.

○ Allocate products in keeping with local dietary habits and with the intention of avoiding promotion of a high level of dependence on imported commodities.

There is a sound macroeconomic case for food aid. Disincentive effects on local agriculture are unnecessary and can be avoided by the appropriate use of food aid in the right policy environment. In the case of Mali, the proceeds from food aid sales on the urban market permitted the government to restructure the national grain market policy. However, there is still a lot of room for improved donor coordination and for collective donor food aid agreements in support of food strategy objectives. (See Hopkins in part III for an expanded discussion of this issue.)

Women and Food Strategies

Issues affecting women are conspicuously absent in the four strategies, although everyone is aware of their crucial role in African agriculture. It is too easy and certainly not fair to accuse policymakers of discrimination against women, but it is evident that they do not seem to know how to deal with the issue of women and agriculture. (See FAO in part II for an expanded discussion of this issue.)

Conclusion

It is too soon to evaluate the experience with policy dialogue since the introduction of the Pisani plan, but it is possible to single out some impressions.

○ Confusion has arisen about the formulation and implementation of food strategies. Ideally, first a strategy should be devised based on an analysis of the existing situation, followed by implementation of the necessary reforms, followed by project implementation. In practice, the three stages occur simultaneously, and this is likely to remain the case for some time to come. Radical policy changes cannot be devised and implemented in a short time.

○ At the beginning, partners were not always interested in the same things. Governments tended to continue to seek support for projects in the pipeline, while donors preferred to discuss policy reforms first.

○ People now realize that structural reforms are not easily implemented because of their sensitive political nature. Increased producer prices imply higher consumer prices. In some countries, governments did not survive higher food prices. Liberalization of marketing runs counter to many interests, while, rightly or wrongly, governments fear that traders may exploit farmers and consumers. Sometimes, private trading is simply contradictory to the established philosophy of the state.

○ Within recipient countries, the formulation of a food strategy involves a number of ministries, and coordination is difficult to achieve. Different ministries have different interpretations of food strategy objectives. Coordination must be vested in a lead ministry as close as possible to presidential or cabinet level (see Pines in part VI).

○ On the donor side, the situation is equally complicated. Each donor has particular concerns and procedures. Field officers generally have little flexibility in their mandate from headquarters, while frequent staff changes undermine the continuity required for policy dialogue. Donor coordination will not be easy. The best results occur when donors designate a leading partner with a thorough knowledge of the country.

○ The development of food strategies is thus inevitably a long-term process which requires the political will of the partners involved as well as the capacity of the recipient country to take the lead. Food strategy formulation and implementation is an ongoing process that requires patience, since by its nature, results cannot be expected overnight.

Bibliography

The word "processed" in this bibliography describes works that are reproduced from typescript by mimeograph, xerography, or similar means. Such works may not be cataloged or commonly available through libraries or may be subject to restricted circulation.

Academy for Educational Development, Inc. and Stanford University Institute for Communications Research. 1984. *Mass Media and Health Practices, Academy for Educational Development: Field Notes.* PN-AAR-252. Washington, D.C.: USAID.

Acharya, Meena, and Lynn Bennett. 1983. *Women and the Subsistence Sector: Economic Participation and Household Decision Making in Nepal.* World Bank Staff Working Paper No. 526. Washington, D.C.

Adams, J. M., and G. W. Harman. 1977. *The Evaluation of Losses in Maize Stored on a Selection of Small Farms in Zambia with Particular Reference to the Development of Methodology.* Report G-100. London: Tropical Products Institute.

Adams, Richard H., Jr. 1983. The Role of Research in Policy Development: The Creation of the IMF Cereal Import Facility. *World Development.* 11(7):549–63.

Adelman, Carol. 1975. Health/Nutrition Survey. Kinshasha, Zaire. June 19–July 20, 1974. Washington, D.C.: USAID. Processed.

Adelman, I. 1984. *Beyond Export-Led Growth.* Working Paper No. 309. Berkeley, California: University of California Department of Agricultural and Resource Economics.

Agarwal, Bina. 1983. Rural Women and the High Yielding Variety Rice Technology in India. Paper presented at the Conference on Women in Rice Farming Systems. September 26–30. Los Baños, Philippines: IRRI.

Aguilar, J., and Michael C. Latham. Forthcoming. Ascorbic Acid Supplementation and Vitamin A Fortification of Anemic Filipino Children and Its Effects on Nutriture. *American Journal of Clinical Nutrition.*

Ahmed, Raisuddin. 1979. *Foodgrain Supply, Distribution, and Consumption Policies Within a Dual Pricing Mechanism: A Case Study of Bangladesh.* Research Report No. 81. Washington, D.C.: IFPRI.

———. 1981. *Agricultural Price Policies Under Complex Socioeconomic and Natural Constraints: The Case of Bangladesh.* Research Report No. 27. Washington, D.C.: IFPRI.

Ahmed, Raisuddin, and N. Rustagi. 1985. *Agricultural Marketing and Price Incentives: A Comparative Study of African and Asian Countries.* Washington, D.C.: IFPRI for FAO.

Akino, Masakatsu, and Yujiro Hayami. 1975. Efficiency and Equity in Public Research: Rice Breeding in Japan's Economic Development. *American Journal of Agricultural Economics.* 57(1):1–10.

Alderman, Harold, and Joachim von Braun. 1984. *The Effects of the Egyptian Food Ration and Subsidy System on Income Distribution and Consumption.* Research Report No. 45. Washington, D.C.: IFPRI.

Alderman, Harold, Joachim von Braun, and Sakr A. Sakr. 1982. *Egypt's Food Subsidy and Rationing System: A Description.* Research Report No. 34. Washington, D.C.: IFPRI.

Alderman, Michael H., Paul H. Wise, Robert P. Ferguson, H. T. Laverde, and Anthony J. D'Souza. 1978. Reduction of Young Child Malnutrition and Mortality in Rural Jamaica. *Journal of Tropical Pediatrics.* 24(1):7–11.

Alfonso, Felipe B. 1983. Assisting Farmer Controlled Development and Communal Irrigation Systems. In David C. Korten and Felipe B. Alfonso, eds. *Bureaucracy and the Poor.* West Hartford, Connecticut: Kumarian Press.

Anderson, Kym, and Yujiro Hayami, with Aurelia George and others. 1986. *Political Economy of Agricultural Protection: East Asia in International Perspective.* Boston, Massachusetts: George Allen and Unwin, Inc.

Anderson, M. A. 1977. *CARE Preschool Nutrition Project.* New York: CARE.

Anderson, M. A., J. E. Austin, J. D. Wray, and M. Zeitlin. 1981. Study I: Supplementary Feeding. In James E. Austin, Marian F. Zeitlin, USAID Office of Nutrition, and Harvard Institute for International Development. *Nutrition Intervention in Developing Countries.* 5 vols. Cambridge, Massachusetts: Oelgeschlager, Gunn and Hain, Inc.

Arauz, J. R., and J. C. Martinez. 1983a. *Desarrollando Tecnología Apropiada para el Agricultor: Informe de Progreso del Programa de Caisan en Panamá.* Serie de Estudios Especiales No. 1. Panama: Instituto de Investigación Agropecuaria de Panamá.

————. 1983b. Institutional Innovations in National Agricultural Research: On Farm Research within the Agricultural Research Institute (IDIAP), Panama. In Cornelia Butler Flora, ed. *Proceedings of Kansas State University's 1982 Farming Systems Research Symposium: Farming Systems in the Field.* Farming Systems Research Paper No. 5. Manhattan, Kansas: Kansas State University.

Arroyave, G. 1983. Fortification of Sugar with Vitamin A: Bases,

Implementation and Evaluation. In Donald S. McLaren, ed. *Nutrition in the Community: A Critical Look at Nutrition Policy, Planning and Programmes.* Chichester, England: John Wiley Publishers.

Ascoli, Werner, Miguel A. Guzman, Nevin S. Scrimshaw, and John E. Gordon. 1967. Nutrition and Infection Field Study in Guatemalan Villages, 1959–1964. 4. Deaths of Infants and Preschool Children. *Archives of Environmental Health.* 15:439–49.

Ashton, Basil, Kenneth Hill, Alan Piazza, and Robin Zeitz. 1984. Famine in China, 1958–61. *Population and Development Review.* 10:613–45.

Asia Research Organization, Inc. 1976. *Evaluation of the Targeted Maternal and Child Health Program in the Philippines.* Manila.

Atwater, Wilbur O., and F. G. Benedict. 1899. Experiments on the Metabolism of Matter and Energy in the Human Body. *Office of Experiment Stations Bulletin No. 69.* U.S. Department of Agriculture. Washington, D.C.: Government Printing Office.

Atwater, Wilbur O., and E. B. Rosa. 1897. A Respiration Calorimeter and Experiments on the Conservation of Energy in the Human Body. *Annual Report, Storrs Agricultural Experimentation Station.* U. S. Department of Agriculture. Washington, D.C.: Government Printing Office.

Austin, James E. 1984. The Role of Parastatals in Food Policy Implementation. Boston, Massachusetts: Harvard Business School. Processed.

Austin, James E., Marian F. Zeitlin, USAID Office of Nutrition, and Harvard Institute for International Development. 1981. *Nutrition Intervention in Developing Countries.* 5 vols. Cambridge, Massachusetts: Oelgeschlager, Gunn and Hain, Inc.

Bachman, Kenneth L., and Leonardo Paulino. 1979. *Rapid Food Production Growth in Selected Developing Countries: A Comparative Analysis of Underlying Trends, 1961–76.* Research Report No. 11. Washington, D.C.: IFPRI.

Baertl, J. M., E. Morales, G. Verastegui, and G. G. Graham. 1970. Diet Supplementation for Entire Communities: Growth and Mortality of Infants and Children. *American Journal of Clinical Nutrition.* 23(6):707–15.

Baker, S. J., and E. M. DeMaeyer. 1979. Nutritional Anemia: Its Understanding and Control with Special Reference to the Work of the WHO. *American Journal of Clinical Nutrition.* 32(2):368–417.

Bale, Malcolm D., and Ronald C. Duncan. 1983. *Prospects for Food Production and Consumption in Developing Countries.* World Bank Staff Working Paper No. 596. Washington, D.C.

Bardach, John E., and E. R. Pariser. 1978. Aquatic Proteins. In Max

Milner, Nevin S. Scrimshaw, and Daniel I. C. Wang, eds. *Protein Resources and Technology: Status and Research Needs.* Westport, Connecticut: AVI Publishing Co.

Barker, Randolph, and Rahha Sinha, eds. 1982. *The Chinese Agricultural Economy.* Boulder, Colorado: Westview Press.

Barker, R., E. C. Gabler, and D. Winkelmann. 1981. Long-Term Consequences of Technological Change on Crop Yield Stability. In A. Valdés, ed. *Food Security for Developing Countries.* Boulder, Colorado: Westview Press.

Barr, Terry N. 1981. The World Food Situation and Global Grain Prospects. *Science.* 214(4525):1087–95.

Basta, S. S., Soekirman, D. Karyadi, and N. S. Scrimshaw. 1979. Iron Deficiency Anemia and the Productivity of Adult Males in Indonesia. *American Journal of Clinical Nutrition.* 32(4):916–25.

Bates, Robert. 1981. *Markets and States in Tropical Africa.* Berkeley, California: University of California Press.

Beaton, George H. 1983. Adaptation to an Accommodation of Long Term Low Energy Intake. In Ernesto Pollitt and Peggy Amante, eds. *Current Topics in Nutrition and Disease.* Vol. 11, *Energy Intake and Activity.* New York: Alan R. Liss, Inc. for UNU.

Beaudry-Darisme, M., and Michael C. Latham. 1973. Nutrition Rehabilitation Centers—An Evaluation of Their Performance. *Journal of Tropical Pediatrics.* 19(3):299–332.

Becroft, Thelma, and K. V. Bailey. 1965. Supplementary Feeding Trial in New Guinea Highland Infants. *Journal of Tropical Pediatrics.* 11(2):28–34.

Beghin, I. D., and Fernando E. Viteri. 1973. Nutritional Rehabilitation Centres: An Evaluation of Their Performance. *Journal of Tropical Pediatrics.* 19(4):404–16.

Behar, Moises, Nevin S. Scrimshaw, Miguel A. Guzman, and John E. Gordon. 1968. Nutrition and Infection Field Study in Guatemalan Villages, 1959-1964. 8. An Epidemiological Appraisal of Its Wisdom and Errors. *Archives of Environmental Health.* 17:814–27.

Behnke, R., and C. Kerven. 1983. Farming Systems Research (FSR) and the Attempt to Understand the Goals and Motivations of Farmers. *Culture and Agriculture.* 19:9–16.

Behrman, Jere R., and Anil B. Deolalikar. Forthcoming. Health and Nutrition. In Hollis B. Chenery and T. N. Srinivasan, eds. *Handbook of Development Economics.* Amsterdam: North Holland.

Behrman, Jere R., and Barbara L. Wolfe. 1984. More Evidence on Nutrition Demand: Income Seems Overrated and Women's Schooling Underemphasized. *Journal of Development Economics.* 14(1-2):105–28.

Bell, Clive, Peter Hazell, and Roger Slade. 1982. *Project Evaluation in*

Regional Perspective. Baltimore, Maryland: Johns Hopkins University Press.

Berg, Alan. 1981. *Malnourished People: A Policy View*. Washington D.C.: World Bank.

Bergsman, Joel. 1970. *Brazil: Industrialization and Trade Policies*. London: Oxford University Press.

Bergsman, Joel, and Pedro S. Malan. 1971. The Structure of Protection in Brazil. In Bela Balassa and associates. *The Structure of Protection in Developing Countries*. Baltimore, Maryland: Johns Hopkins University Press.

Berio, Ann-Jacqueline. 1984. The Analysis of Time Allocation and Activity Patterns in Nutrition and Rural Development Planning. *Food and Nutrition Bulletin*. 6(1):53–68.

Berry, R. Albert, and William R. Cline. 1979. *Agrarian Structure and Productivity in Developing Countries*. Baltimore, Maryland: Johns Hopkins University Press.

Betancourt, E. 1977. *Las Carencias Nutricionales en Colombia, Revisión 1977*. Bogotá: Instituto Colombiano de Bienestar Familiar.

Bhagwati, Jagdish N. 1978. *Trade Regimes and Economic Development: Anatomy and Consequences of Exchange Control Regimes*. Cambridge, Massachusetts: Ballinger Publishing Company.

Bhagwati, Jagdish N., and Sukhamoy Chakravarty. 1969. Contributions to Indian Economic Analysis: A Survey. *American Economic Review*. 59(4, Supplement):2–73.

Bhalla, Surjit S. 1980. *Measurement of Poverty: Issues and Methods*. Washington, D.C.: World Bank.

Binns, C. W. 1976. Food, Sickness and Death in Children of the Highlands of Papua New Guinea. *Journal of Tropical Pediatrics and Environmental Child Health*. 12(1)9–11.

Binswanger, Hans. 1978. *The Economics of Tractors in South Asia: An Analytical Review*. Agricultural Development Council and ICRISAT. New York.

Biswas, Margaret, and Per Pinstrup-Andersen, eds. 1985. *Nutrition and Development*. Oxford, England: Oxford University Press.

Bjorkman, James W. 1975. Public Law 480 and the Policies of Self Help and Short Tether: Indo-American Relations, 1965–68. In *Report of the Commission on the Organization of the Government for the Conduct of Foreign Policy*. Washington, D.C.: Government Printing Office.

Black, Robert E., Kenneth H. Brown, and Stan Becker. 1984. Malnutrition Is a Determining Factor in Diarrheal Duration, but Not Incidence, Among Young Children in the Longitudinal Study in Rural Bangladesh. *American Journal of Clinical Nutrition*. 39(1):87–94.

Blackie, Malcolm, Ron Schwass, and Richard Jones. 1979. Rural Development in Western Samoa Through Farming Systems Research. Part 1, The Problem and Perspective. *Fiji Agricultural Journal.* 41(2):87–94.

————. 1980. Rural Development in Western Samoa Through Farming Systems Research. Part 2, An Approach Through Multiple Cropping. *Fiji Agricultural Journal.* 42(1):1–10.

Blyn, George. 1983. The Green Revolution Revisited. *Economic Development and Cultural Change.* 31(4):705–25.

Bond, Marian E. 1983. Agricultural Responses to Prices in Sub-Saharan African Countries. *IMF Staff Papers.* 30(4):703–26. Washington, D.C.

Boserup, E. 1970. *Women's Role in Economic Development.* London: George Allen and Unwin, Ltd.

Bothwell, Thomas H., Robert W. Charlton, and INACG. 1981. *Iron Deficiency in Women.* New York: Nutrition Foundation.

Botswana, Government of. 1976. *Rural Income Distribution Survey.* Central Statistical Office. Gaborone.

Bouis, H. 1982. Rice Policy in the Philippines. Ph.D. thesis. Stanford, California: Stanford University.

Bourne, Malcolm C. 1977. *Post-Harvest Food Losses: The Neglected Dimension in Increasing the World Food Supply.* Cornell International Monograph No. 53. Ithaca, New York: Cornell University.

Boxall, R., and M. Greeley. 1978. Indian Storage Project. Paper presented to the Seminar on Post-Harvest Grain Losses, Tropical Products Institute. March 13–17. London.

Braverman, Avishay, Choong Yong Ahn, and Jeffrey S. Hammer. 1983. *Alternative Agricultural Pricing Policies in the Republic of Korea: Their Implications for Government Deficits, Income Distribution, and Balance of Payments.* World Bank Staff Working Paper No. 621. Washington, D.C.

Brewster, John M. 1950. The Machine Process in Agriculture and Industry. *Journal of Farm Economics.* 32(1):69–81.

Briscoe, John. 1984. Water Supply and Health in Developing Countries: Selective Primary Health Care Revisited. *American Journal of Public Health.* 74(9):1009–13.

Brooks, R. M., M. C. Latham, and D. W. T. Crompton. 1979. The Relationship of Nutrition and Health to Worker Productivity in Kenya. *East African Medical Journal.* 56(9):413–21.

Brown, Lester R. 1982. Global Food Prospects: Shadow of Malthus. *Challenge.* January–February.

Brown, Lester R., and Edward C. Wolf. 1984. *Soil Erosion: Quiet Crisis in the World Economy.* Washington, D.C.: Worldwatch Institute.

Burfisher, Mary E., and Nadine R. Horenstein. 1982. *Sex Roles in the*

Nigerian Tiv Farm Household and the Differential Impacts of Development Projects. Washington, D.C.: USDA Economic Research Service.

Butz, W. P., J. P. Habicht, and J. Da Vanzo. 1981. *Improving Infant Nutrition, Health and Survival: Policy and Program Implications from the Malaysian Family Life Survey.* Santa Monica, California: Rand Corporation.

Byerlee, Derek, and Larry Harrington. 1982. New Wheat Varieties and the Small Farmer. Paper presented at the Conference of the International Association of Agricultural Economists. August 24–September 4. Jakarta.

Byerlee, Derek, Larry Harrington, and Donald L. Winkelmann. 1982. Farming Systems Research: Issues in Research Strategy and Technology Design. *American Journal of Agricultural Economics.* 64(5):897–904.

Cain, M., S. R. Khana, and S. Nahar. 1979. *Class Patriarchy and the Structure of Women's Work in Rural Bangladesh.* Center for Population Studies Working Paper No. 43. New York: Population Council.

Caldwell, J. 1980. Mass Education as a Determinant of the Timing of Fertility Decline. *Population and Development Review.* 6(2):225–55.

Caldwell, J. S., and D. W. Newsom. 1984. *Vegetable Consumption and Production in Two Municipalities in Ilocos Norte, Philippines.* Technical Bulletin No. 14. Shanhua, Taiwan: Asian Vegetable Research and Development Center.

Canada, Science Council. 1976. *Population, Technology, and Resources.* Ottawa: Science Council of Canada.

Cantrelle, P., and H. Leridon. 1971. Breastfeeding, Mortality in Childhood and Fertility in a Rural Zone of Senegal. *Population Studies.* 25(3):505 33.

Caribbean Food and Nutrition Institute. 1975. *Evaluation of the Supplementary Feeding Program in Trinidad.* J-52-75. Kingston, Jamaica.

Carloni, A. 1981. Sex Disparities in the Distribution of Food Within Rural Households. *Food and Nutrition.* 7(1):3–12.

Cassen, Robert H. 1978. Current Trends in Population Change and Their Causes. *Population and Development Review.* 4(2):331–53.

Cathie, John. 1982. *The Political Economy of Food Aid.* New York: St. Martin's Press.

Cavallo, Domingo, and Yair Mundlak. 1982. *Agriculture and Economic Growth in an Open Economy: The Case of Argentina.* Research Report No. 36. Washington, D.C.: IFPRI.

Caves, Richard, and Thomas Pugel. 1982. New Evidence on Competition in the Grain Trade. *Food Research Institute Studies.* 18(3):261–74.

Centre for Monitoring Indian Economy, Economic Intelligence Service. 1984. *Basic Statistics Relating to the Indian Economy.* Vol. 1, *All India.* Bombay.

Chafkin, Saul H., James Pines, Gerald Keusch, Barbara Underwood, Robert Pratt, and James Brady. 1978. Technical Review of the Philippines Nutrition Program. Manila and Washington, D.C.: USAID. Processed.

Chakravarty, S. 1969. *Capital and Development Planning.* Cambridge, Massachusetts: Massachusetts Institute of Technology Press.

Chambers, Robert. 1983. Seasonality, Poverty and Nutrition: A Professional Frontier. Paper presented at the EFNAG National Workshop on Poverty and Malnutrition, Tamil Nadu Agricultural University. Coimmbatore, India.

Chambers, Robert, Richard Longhurst, and Arnold Pacey. 1981. *Seasonal Dimensions to Rural Poverty.* London: Frances Pinter Publishers, Ltd.

Chandra, R. K. 1982. Malnutrition and Infection. In Nevin S. Scrimshaw and Mitchel B. Wallerstein, eds. *Nutrition Policy Implementation: Issues and Experience.* New York: Plenum Press.

————. 1983. Nutrition, Immunity and Infection: Present Knowledge and Future Direction. *Lancet.* 1(8326 Pt. 1):688–91.

Chang, T. T. 1984. Conservation of Rice Genetic Resources: Luxury or Necessity? *Science.* 224(4646):251–56.

Chaudhry, M. Ghaffar. 1982. Green Revolution and Redistribution of Rural Incomes: Pakistan's Experience. *Pakistan Development Review.* 21(3):173–205.

Chaudhuri, P. 1982. Nutrition and Health Problems and Policies: Women and Children in India. British Society for Population Studies, Oxford Conference. Processed.

Chavangi, N. A., and A. Hanssen. 1983. *Women in Livestock Production with Particular Reference to Dairying.* Rome: FAO.

Chavez, Adolfo, and Celia Martinez. 1975. Nutrition and Development of Children from Poor Rural Areas. 5. Nutrition and Behavioral Development. *Nutrition Reports International.* 11(6):477–89.

————. 1983. Behavioral Measurements of Activity in Children and Their Relation to Food Intake in a Poor Community. In Ernesto Pollitt and Peggy Amante, eds. *Current Topics in Nutrition and Disease.* Vol. 11, *Energy Intake and Activity.* New York: Alan R. Liss, Inc. for UNU.

Chavez, Adolfo, Celia Martinez, and H. Bourges. 1972. Nutrition and Development of Infants from Poor Rural Areas. 2. Nutrition and Behavioral Development. *Nutrition Reports International.* 5(2):139–44.

Chen, Lincoln C. 1982. Malnutrition and Mortality. *Nutrition Foundation of India Bulletin.* October:1–5.

Chen, Lincoln C., and Nevin S. Scrimshaw. 1983. *Diarrhea and Malnutrition: Interactions, Mechanisms, and Intervention.* New York: Plenum Press.

Chen, Lincoln C., A. K. M. Alauddin Chowdhury, and Sandra L. Huffman. 1979. Seasonal Dimensions of Energy Protein Malnutrition in Rural Bangladesh: The Role of Agriculture, Dietary Practices and Infection. *Ecology of Food and Nutrition.* 8(3):175–87.

—————. 1980. Anthropometric Assessment of Energy-Protein Malnutrition and Subsequent Risk of Mortality Among Preschool Aged Children. *American Journal of Clinical Nutrition.* 33(8):1836–45.

—————. 1981. The Use of Anthropometry for Nutritional Surveillance in Mortality Control Programs. *American Journal of Clinical Nutrition.* 34(8):2596–99.

Chen, Lincoln C., Emdadul Huq, and Stan D'Souza. 1981. Sex Bias in the Family Allocation of Food and Health Care in Rural Bangladesh. *Population and Development Review.* 7(1):55–70.

Chen, Lincoln C., Emdadul Huq, and Sandra L. Huffman. 1981. A Prospective Study of the Risk of Diarrheal Diseases According to the Nutritional Status of Children. *American Journal of Epidemiology.* 114(2):284–92.

Chen, Lincoln C., Mizanur Rahman, and A. M. Sarder. 1980. Epidemiology and Causes of Death Among Children in a Rural Area of Bangladesh. *International Journal of Epidemiology.* 9(1):25–33.

Chen, M. 1983. The Working Women's Forum: Organizing for Credit and Change. *Seeds.* 6:120.

Chennareddy, V. 1967. Production Efficiency in South Indian Agriculture. *Journal of Farm Economics.* 49(4):816–20.

Christensen, Cheryl, and Economic Research Service, USDA. 1981. *Food Problems and Prospects in Sub-Saharan Africa: The Decade of the 1980's.* Foreign Agricultural Research Report No. 166. Economic Research Service. Washington, D.C.: USDA.

CIAT. 1981. *Report on the Fourth International Rice Testing Program Conference for Latin America.* Cali, Colombia.

CIMMYT. 1978. *CIMMYT Review.* Mexico City.

—————. 1981. *World Maize Facts and Trends: Analysis of Changes in Production, Consumption, Trade and Prices Over the Last Two Decades.* Mexico City.

Clark, C. 1981. The Use of the Household Production Model to Assess the Relation of Women's Market Work to Child Welfare. Paper prepared for the International Center for Research on Women's Policy Round Table, The Interface Between Poor Women's Nurturing Roles and Productive Responsibilities. December. Washington, D.C.

Coale, Ansley. 1984. *Rapid Population Change in China, 1952–82.* Washington, D.C.: National Academy Press.

Cochrane, Susan H., Joanne Leslie, and Donald J. O'Hara. 1982. Parental Education and Child Health: Intracountry Evidence. *Health Policy and Education.* 2(3/4):213–50.

Cohen, N., and D. Clayden. 1978. *Patterns of Growth of Children Receiving Food Supplements in Rural Lesotho.* Rome: FAO.

Cole, T. J., and J. M. Parkin. 1977. Infection and Its Effect on the Growth of Young Children: A Comparison of The Gambia and Uganda. *Transactions of the Royal Society of Tropical Medicine and Hygiene.* 71(3):196–98.

Condon-Paolini, D., J. Cravioto, F. E. Johnston, E. De Licardie, and T. O. Scholl. 1977. Morbidity and Growth of Infants and Young Children in a Rural Mexican Village. *American Journal of Public Health.* 67(7):651–56.

Cook, J. D., and E. R. Monsen. 1976. Food Iron Absorption in Human Subjects. *American Journal of Clinical Nutrition.* 29:859–67.

Cooke, T. M., and S. T. Romweber. 1977. *Radio Advertising Techniques and Nutrition Education: A Summary of a Field Experiment in the Philippines and Nicaragua.* New York: Manoff International, Inc.

Coursey, D. G. 1972. Biodeteriorative Losses in Tropical Horticultural Produce. In A. H. Walters and E. H. Hueck-Van Der Plas, eds. *Biodeterioration of Materials.* New York: John Wiley & Sons.

Cowan, Robert C. 1981. Gene Splicing Opens New World for Agriculture. *Christian Science Monitor.* July 7.

Cravioto, Joaquin, Herbert G. Birch, Elso R. De Licardie, and Lydia Rosales. 1967. The Ecology of Infant Weight Gain in a Pre-Industrial Society. *Acta Paediatrica Scandinavica.* 56(1):71–84.

Crompton, D. W. T., and M. C. Nesheim. 1984. Malnutrition's Insidious Partner. *World Health.* March:18–21.

Crook, N., and T. Dyson. 1981. Data on Seasonality of Births and Deaths. In Robert Chambers, Richard Longhurst, and A. Pacey, eds. *Seasonal Dimensions to Rural Poverty.* London: Frances Pinter Publishers, Ltd.

Dallman, Peter R., Martti A. Siimes, and INAGC. 1979. *Iron Deficiency in Infancy and Childhood.* Washington, D.C.: Nutrition Foundation.

Da Vanzo, J., and D. L. Poh Lee. 1983. The Compatibility of Child Care with Market and Non-Market Activities: Preliminary Evidence from Malaysia. In Mayra Buvinic, Margaret A. Lycette, and William Paul McGreevey, eds. *Women and Poverty in the Third World.* Baltimore, Maryland: Johns Hopkins University Press.

Daxin, Wu. 1982. Briefing on Agriculture of the People's Republic of China. In E. M. Reisch, ed. *Agricultura Sinica.* Berlin: Dunker and Humbolt.

Deaton, Angus. 1981. Inequality and Needs: Some Experimental Results for Sri Lanka. In *Three Essays on a Sri Lanka Household Survey.* Living Standards Measurement Study Working Paper No. 11. Washington, D.C.: World Bank.

Deere, C. D. 1983. The Allocation of Familial Labor and the Formation of Peasant Household Income in the Peruvian Sierra. In Mayra

Buvinic, Margaret A. Lycette, and William Paul McGreevey, eds. *Women and Poverty in the Third World*. Baltimore, Maryland: Johns Hopkins University Press.

de Janvry, Alain. 1981. *The Agrarian Question and Reformism in Latin America*. Baltimore, Maryland: Johns Hopkins University Press.

de Janvry, Alain, and K. Subbarao. 1984. Agricultural Price Policy and Income Distribution in India. *Economic and Political Weekly* (Bombay). 19:A166–78. December 22.

Delgado, Hernan, Elena Brineman, Aaron Lechtig, John Bongaarts, Reynaldo Martorell, and Robert E. Klein. 1979. Effect of Maternal Nutritional Status and Infant Supplementation During Lactation on Postpartum Amenorrhea. *American Journal of Obstetrics and Gynecology*. 135(3):303–07.

De Lima, D. P. E. 1973. *A Technical Report on 22 Grain Storage Projects at the Subsistence Farmer Level in Kenya*. Report Proj./Res./AG 21. Nairobi: Kenya Department of Agriculture.

De Sweemer, Cecile. 1973. Growth and Morbidity. D.P.H. thesis. Baltimore, Maryland: Johns Hopkins School of Hygiene and Public Health.

Devi, S. Y., and P. Pushpamma. 1978. *Rural Creche: A Longitudinal Study* Indo-Dutch Project for Child Welfare. Hyderabad, India: Agricultural University.

Dewey, Kathryn G. 1979. Commentary—Agricultural Development, Diet and Nutrition. *Ecology of Food and Nutrition*. 8(4):265–73.

———. 1981. Nutritional Consequences of the Transformation from Subsistence to Commercial Agriculture in Tabasco, Mexico. *Human Ecology*. 9(2):151.

Dey, P. 1981. Gambian Women: Unequal Partners in Rice Development Projects? *Journal of Development Studies*. 17:109–22.

Dinham, Barbara, and Colin Hines. 1983. *Agribusiness in Africa*. London: Earth Resources Research.

Dixon, John. 1981. *The Chinese Welfare System, 1949–1979*. New York: Praeger Publishers.

Dixon, R. 1978. *Rural Women at Work*. Baltimore, Maryland: Johns Hopkins University Press.

———. 1982. Women in Agriculture: Counting the Labor Force in Developing Countries. *Population and Development Review*. 8:539–66.

Domar, E. D. 1957. *Essays in the Theory of Economic Growth*. Oxford, England: Oxford University Press.

Dorner, Peter, ed. 1977. *Cooperative and Commune: Group Farming in the Economic Development of Agriculture*. Madison, Wisconsin: University of Wisconsin Press.

Dovring, Folke. 1959. The Share of Agriculture in a Growing Population. *Monthly Bulletin of Agricultural Economics and Statistics*. 7(8,9):1–11.

Drasor, B., A. M. Tomkins, and R. G. Feachem. 1981. Diarrhoeal Diseases. In Robert Chambers, Richard Longhurst, and Arnold Pacey, eds. *Seasonal Dimensions to Rural Poverty.* London: Frances Pinter Publishers, Ltd.

Drilon, J. D. 1977. *Agricultural Systems in Asia: Successes and Difficulties.* College, Laguna, Philippines: SEARCA.

Durnin, J. V. G. A., O. G. Edholm, D. S. Miller, and J. C. Waterlow. 1973. How Much Food Does Man Require? *Nature.* 242(5397):418.

Eckholm, Erik. 1976. *Losing Ground: Environmental Stress and World Food Problems.* New York: W. W. Norton Publishing.

Effendi, S., and J. L. McIntosh. 1983. Cropping and Farming Systems Research in Indonesia. In Cornelia Butler Flora, ed. *Proceedings of Kansas State University's 1982 Farming Systems Research Symposium: Farming Systems in the Field.* Farming Systems Research Paper No. 5. Manhattan, Kansas: Kansas State University.

Egeman, Ayten, and Munevver Bertran. 1980. A Study of Oral Re-hydration: Therapy by Midwives in a Rural Area Near Ankara. *Bulletin of the World Health Organization.* 58(2):333–38.

Eicher, Carl K. 1983. *Facing Up to Africa's Food Crisis.* Working Paper No. 8. East Lansing, Michigan: Michigan State University Department of Agricultural Economics.

Eicher, Carl K., and John M. Staatz, eds. 1984. *Agricultural Development in the Third World.* Baltimore, Maryland: Johns Hopkins University Press.

Engle, P., C. Yarbrough, and R. Klein. 1983. Sex Differences in the Effect of Nutrition and Social Environment on Mental Development in Rural Guatemala. In Mayra Buvinic, Margaret A. Lycette, and William Paul McGreevey, eds. *Women and Poverty in the Third World.* Baltimore, Maryland: Johns Hopkins University Press.

Evenson, R. E., and P. M. Flores. 1978. Social Returns to Rice Research. In *Economic Consequences of the New Rice Technology.* Los Baños, Philippines: IRRI.

Fagley, R. M. 1976. Easing the Burden of Rural Women, A 16-Hour Workday. *Assignment Children.* 36:9–28.

FAO. 1948. *First World Food Survey.* Rome.

———. 1974. FAO trade tapes. Rome.

———. 1976a. *Income Elasticities of Demand for Agricultural Products.* ESC/ACP/WD. 76/3. Rome.

———. 1976b. Production Yearbook tape, 1975. Rome.

———. 1976c. *The State of Food and Agriculture, 1975: World Review.* FAO Agriculture Series. Rome.

———. 1977a. *The Fourth World Food Survey.* FAO Statistical Series 11. FAO Food and Nutrition Series No. 10. Rome.

———. 1977b. *World Population Estimates and Projections, 1950–2000.* ESC/ACP/WD.76/1 Rev. Rome.

————. 1978. *FAO 1977 Fertilizer Yearbook.* Rome.

————. 1979. FAO trade tapes. Rome.

————. 1980a. Global Agricultural Programming System Supply Utilization Accounts tape. Rome.

————. 1980b. Production Yearbook tape, 1979. Rome.

————. 1981a. *Food Aid Bulletin.* Rome.

————. 1981b. Production Yearbook tape, 1981. Rome.

————. 1982a. *Integrating Nutrition into Agricultural and Rural Development Projects: A Manual.* Nutrition in Agriculture No. 1. Nutrition Planning, Assessment, and Evaluation Service, Food Policy and Nutrition Division. Rome.

————. 1982b. *The State of Food and Agriculture, 1981: World Review.* FAO Agriculture Series. Rome.

————. 1983. *Changing Patterns and Trends in Feed Utilization.* FAO Economic and Social Development Paper No. 37. Commodities and Trade Division. Rome.

————. 1984a. *Food Balance Sheets: 1979–81 Average.* Rome.

————. 1984b. *Integrating Nutrition into Agricultural and Rural Development Projects: Six Case Studies.* Nutrition in Agriculture No. 2. Nutrition Planning, Assessment, and Evaluation Service, Food Policy and Nutrition Division. Rome.

————. Various. *FAO Trade Yearbook.* Rome.

————. Various. *Production Yearbook.* Rome.

FAO, Government of Malaysia, and Food for the Hungry, Inc. 1977. *Report of the Action-Oriented Field Workshop for Prevention of Post-Harvest Rice Losses.* Kedah, Malaysia. March 12–30. Bangkok: FAO.

FAO and UNECA. 1977. Unpublished data.

FAO/WHO. 1973. *Report of a Joint FAO/WHO Ad Hoc Expert Committee on Energy and Protein Requirements.* FAO Nutrition Meetings Report Series No. 52. WHO Technical Report Series No. 522. Rome: FAO.

————. 1975. Energy and Protein Requirements: Recommendations by a Joint FAO-WHO Informal Gathering of Experts. *Food and Nutrition.* 1:11–19.

FAO/WHO/UNU. 1985. *Energy and Protein Requirements. Report of a Joint FAO/WHO/UNU Expert Consultation.* Technical Report Series No. 724. Geneva: WHO.

Federal University of Pernambuco and Secretary of Health for the State of Pernambuco. 1971. *Ciaconia Nutrition Project in Pernambuco.* Recife, Brazil.

Fertilizer Institute. 1982. *Fertilizer Reference Manual.* Washington, D.C.

Finch, C. A., and J. D. Cook. 1984. Iron Deficiency. *American Journal of Clinical Nutrition.* 39(3):471–77.

Finney, R. 1983. Food and Self-Sufficiency. Presentation given at the Plenary Session, Conference on Women in Development: A Decade of Experience. October 13–15. Washington, D.C.

Fleuret, Patrick, and Anne Fleuret. 1980. Nutrition, Consumption and Agricultural Change. *Human Organization.* 39(3):250–60.

Flora, Cornelia Butler. 1983. Farming Systems Research and the Land Grant System: Transferring Assumptions Overseas. In Cornelia Butler Flora, ed. *Proceedings of Kansas State University's 1982 Farming Systems Research Symposium: Farming Systems in the Field.* Farming Systems Research Paper No. 5. Manhattan, Kansas: Kansas State University.

Foote, Dennis. 1983. *The Mass Media and Health Practices Evaluation in Honduras: Findings from the First Year.* Institute for Communication Research. Stanford, California: Stanford University.

Fougere, W. 1972. *Mothercraft Centers in Haiti.* New York: Agricultural Mission, Inc.

Fox, E., and P. S. Gibson. 1979. *Evaluation of PL 480 Title II Program in Tunisia.* Rabat: USAID.

Fraenkel, F. R. 1976. *India's Green Revolution: Economic Gains and Political Costs.* Princeton, New Jersey: Princeton University Press.

Franklin, D. L., and I. Vial. 1981. *Food and Nutrition Policies: Does Women's Time Matter?* Chapel Hill, North Carolina: Sigma One Corporation.

Frazao, M. 1982. Home Day Care Centers. Clearinghouse on Mothers and Children. Washington, D.C.: American Public Health Association. Processed.

Freeman, Howard E., Robert E. Klein, Jerome Kagan, and Charles Yarbrough. 1977. Relations Between Nutrition and Cognition in Rural Guatemala. *American Journal of Public Health.* 67(3):233–39.

Freij, L., and S. Wall. 1977. Exploring Child Health and Its Ecology: The Kirkos Study in Addis Ababa, An Evaluation of Procedures in the Measurement of Acute Morbidity and a Search for Causal Structure. *Acta Paediatrica Scandinavica.* (Supplement) 267:1–180.

Fribourg, Michel. 1983. A Time for Decision. *Milling and Baking News.* (March 22)67–69.

Furtado, Celso. 1964. *Development and Underdevelopment.* Berkeley, California: University of California Press.

Galbraith, John K. 1979. *The Nature of Mass Poverty.* Cambridge, Massachusetts: Harvard University Press.

Gandra, Y. R. 1977. *Centres for Nutrition and Education of Preschoolers in Brazil (CEAPE).* Faculty of Public Health. São Paulo: University of São Paulo.

GAO. 1979. *Search for Options in the Troubled Food for Peace Program in Zaire.* Washington, D.C.

García García, Jorge. 1981. *The Effects of Exchange Rates and Commercial Policy on Agricultural Incentives in Colombia, 1953–1978.* Research Report No. 24. Washington, D.C.: IFPRI.

Garfield, E. 1979. *The Impact of Technical Change on the Rural Kenyan*

Household—Evidence from the Integrated Agricultural Development Program: A Research Proposal and Literature Review. Working Paper No. 358. Nairobi, Kenya: University of Nairobi Institute of Development Studies.

Gavan, James. 1977. *Recent and Prospective Developments in Food Consumption. Some Policy Issues.* Research Report No. 3. Washington, D.C.: IFPRI.

Gavan, James D., and Indrani Sri Chandrasekera. 1979. *The Impact of Public Foodgrain Distribution on Food Consumption and Welfare in Sri Lanka.* Research Report No. 13. Washington, D.C.: IFPRI.

Gbetibouo, Mathurin, and Christopher L. Delgado. 1984. Lessons and Constraints of Export Crop–Led Growth. In I. W. Zartman and Christopher L. Delgado, eds. *The Political Economy of the Ivory Coast.* New York: Praeger Publishers.

George, P. S. 1979. *Public Distribution of Foodgrain in Kerala—Income Distribution Implications and Effectiveness.* Research Report No. 7. Washington, D.C.: IFPRI.

Gershon, Jack. 1982. *Progress Report: Asian Vegetable Research and Development Center (AVRDC) Garden Program.* Shanhau, Taiwan: Asian Vegetable Research and Development Center.

————. 1983. Alleviating Vitamin A Problems with Home Gardens. Paper presented at the Fourth Asian Congress of Nutrition, November 14, 1983, Bangkok. Shanhau, Taiwan: Asian Vegetable Research and Development Center.

Ghai, D., and L. Smith. 1983. *Food Policy and Equity in Sub-Saharan Africa.* Working Paper No. 55. World Employment Program Research. Geneva: ILO.

Gibb, Arthur, Jr. 1974. *Agricultural Modernization, Non-Farm Employment and Low-Level Urbanization: A Case Study of a Central Luzon Sub-Region.* Ph.D. thesis. Ann Arbor, Michigan: University of Michigan.

Gibbons, Gayle, and Marcia Griffiths. 1984. *Program Activities for Improving Weaning Practices.* Information for Action Issues Paper. Washington, D.C.: American Public Health Association.

Gilbert, E. H., D. W. Norman, and F. E. Winch. 1980. *Farming Systems Research: A Critical Appraisal.* Michigan State University Rural Development Paper No. 6. East Lansing, Michigan.

Gilmore, Judith W., Carol C. Adelman, Anthony J. Meyer, and Melvyn C. Thorne. 1980. *Morocco: Aid and Nutrition Education.* USAID Project Impact Evaluation Report No. 8. Washington, D.C.

Gittinger, Mattiebelle. 1982. *Master Dyer to the World—Techniques and Trade in Early Indian Dyed Cotton.* Washington, D.C.: Textile Museum.

Goldman, R., and C. Overholt. 1981. Study 4: Agricultural Production, Technical Change and Nutritional Goals. In James E. Austin, Marian F. Zeitlin, USAID Office of Nutrition, and Harvard Institute for International Development. *Nutrition Intervention in Developing Countries.* 5 vols. Cambridge, Massachusetts: Oelgeschlager, Gunn and Hain, Inc.

Gomez, Federico, Rafael R. Galvan, Joaquin Cravioto, and Silvestre Frenk. 1955. Malnutrition in Infancy and Childhood with Special Reference to Kwashiorkor. *Advances in Pediatrics.* 7:131–64.

Gomez, Federico, Rafael R. Galvan, Silvestre Frenk, Joaquin C. Munoz, Raquel Chavez, and Judith Vazquez. 1956. Mortality in Second and Third Degree Malnutrition. *Journal of Tropical Pediatrics.* 2(2):77–83.

Goodell, G. 1980. *1979 Annual Report of Anthropological Observations from Villages in Central Luzon. Consequences of the New High-Yielding Varieties (HYV) Technology: Confusion at the Farm Level.* Los Baños, Philippines: IRRI.

Gopalan, C. 1983. *Small Is Healthy?* New Delhi, India: Nutrition Foundation of India.

Gopalan, C., M. C. Swaminathan, V. K. Krishna Kumari, D. Hanumantha Rao, and K. Vijayaraghavan. 1973. Effect of Calorie Supplementation on Growth of Undernourished Children. *American Journal of Clinical Nutrition.* 26(5):563–66.

Gopaldas, T., N. Srinivasan, I. Varadarajan, and CARE India. 1975. *Project Poshak: An Integrated Health-Nutrition Macro Pilot Study for Preschool Children in Rural and Tribal Madhya Pradesh.* 2 vols. New Delhi: CARE India, sponsored by Government of Madhya Pradesh, Government of India, USAID, and UNICEF.

Gordon, John E., Ishwari D. Chitkara, and John B. Wyon. 1963. Preventive Medicine and Epidemiology: Weanling Diarrhea. *American Journal of Medical Sciences.* 245(3):345–77.

Gordon, John E., Miguel A. Guzman, Werner Ascoli, and Nevin S. Scrimshaw. 1964. Acute Diarrhoeal Disease in Less Developed Countries: 2. Patterns of Epidemiological Behaviour in Rural Guatemalan Villages. *Bulletin of the World Health Organization.* 31(1):9–20.

Gordon, John E., Nevin S. Scrimshaw, Werner Ascoli, Leonardo J. Mata, and Miguel A. Guzman. 1968. Nutrition and Infection Field Study in Guatemalan Villages, 1959–1964. 6. Acute Diarrheal Disease and Nutritional Disorders in General Disease Incidence. *Archives of Environmental Health.* 16:424–37.

Grant, J. P. 1984. *The State of the World's Children, 1984.* New York: UNICEF.

Green, Arthur. 1977. *An Analysis of an FAO Survey of Post-Harvest Food Loss in Developing Countries.* AGPP:MISC/27. Rome: FAO.

Greenland, D. J. 1975. Bringing the Green Revolution to the Shifting Cultivator. *Science.* 190(4217):841–44.

Greer, J., and E. Thorbecke. 1983. *Pattern of Food Consumption and*

Poverty in Kenya and Effects of Food Prices. Ithaca, New York: Cornell University.

Griffin, Keith. 1972. *The Green Revolution: An Economic Analysis.* Geneva: UNRISD.

————. 1979. *The Political Economy of Agrarian Change.* London: Macmillan Press.

Griffiths, M. 1981. *Growth Monitoring of Preschool Children: Practical Considerations for Primary Health Care Projects.* Washington, D.C.: American Public Health Association.

Gross, Daniel R., and Barbara A. Underwood. 1971. Technological Change and Caloric Costs: Sisal Agriculture in Northeastern Brazil. *American Anthropologist.* 73(3):725–40.

Guerrant, R. I., L. V. Kirchhoff, D. S. Shields, M. K. Nations, J. Leslie, M. A. de Sousa, J. G. Araujo, L. L. Correia, K. T. Sauer, K. E. McClelland, F. L. Trowbridge, and J. M. Hughes. 1983. Prospective Study of Diarrheal Illness in Northeastern Brazil: Patterns of Disease, Nutritional Impact, Etiologies, and Risk Factors. *Journal of Infectious Diseases.* 148(6):986–97.

Gurley, John G. 1983. *Challeges to Communism.* San Francisco, California: W. H. Freeman and Co. Ltd.

Guyer, J. 1980. *Household Budgets and Women's Incomes.* African Studies Center Working Papers No. 28. Boston, Massachusetts: Boston University.

Guzman, Miguel A., Nevin S. Scrimshaw, Hans A. Bruch, and John E. Gordon. 1968. Nutrition and Infection Field Study in Guatemalan Villages, 1959–1964. 7. Physical Growth and Development of Preschool Children. *Archives of Environmental Health.* 17:107–18.

Gwatkin, Davidson R., Janet R. Wilcox, and Joe D. Wray. 1980. *Can Health and Nutrition Interventions Make a Difference?* Monograph 13. Washington, D.C.: ODC.

Habicht, Jean-Pierre, A. Lechtig, C. Yarbrough, and R. E. Klein. 1972. The Timing of the Effect of Supplementation Feeding on the Growth of Rural Preschool Children. In Pedro Arroyo, Samir Basta, Hector Bourges, Aldolfo Chavez, Marta Coronado, Miriam Munoz, and Sara E. Quiroz., eds. *Ninth International Congress of Nutrition, Abstracts of Short Communications.* Mexico City: Mexican Government and the International Union of Nutrition Sciences.

Habicht, Jean-Pierre, Reynaldo Martorell, C. Yarbrough, R. M. Malina, and R. E. Klein. 1974. Height and Weight Standards for Pre-School Children. How Relevant Are Ethnic Differences in Growth Potential? *Lancet.* 1(858):611–14.

Haggerty, P. A. 1981. Women's Work and Child Nutrition in Haiti. M.S. thesis. Cambridge, Massachusetts: Massachusetts Institute of Technology.

Hall, D. N. 1970. *Handling and Storage of Food Grains in Tropical and*

Sub-Tropical Areas. Agricultural Development Paper No. 90. Rome: FAO.

Hall, Lana. L. 1980. Evaluating the Effects of P.L. 480 Wheat Imports on Brazil's Grain Sector. *American Journal of Agricultural Economics.* 62(1):19–28.

Hamill, Peter V. V., Terrence A. Drizd, Clifford L. Johnson, Robert B. Reed, Alex F. Roche, and William M. Moore. 1979. Physical Growth: National Center for Health Statistics Percentiles. *American Journal of Clinical Nutrition.* 32(3):607–29.

Hanrahan, Charles E., and Joseph W. Willet. 1976. Technology and the World Food Problem: A U.S. View. *Food Policy.* 1(5):413–19.

Haq, Mahbub ul. 1971. Keynote Address to the 12th World Conference, Society for International Development. May. Ottawa, Canada.

Harberger, Arnold C. 1978. On the Use of Distributional Weights in Social Cost-Benefit Analysis. *Journal of Political Economy.* 86(2):S87–120.

Harbert, Lloyd, and Pasquale L. Scandizzo. 1982. *Food Distribution and Nutrition Intervention: The Case of Chile.* World Bank Staff Working Paper No. 512. Washington, D.C.

Hargrove, T. R. 1977. *Genetics and Sociological Aspects of Rice Breeding in India.* IRRI Research Paper Series No. 10. College, Laguna, Philippines.

Hargrove, T. R., W. R. Coffman, and V. L. Cabanilla. 1979. *Genetic Interrelationships of Improved Rice Varieties in Asia.* IRRI Research Paper Series No. 23. Manila, Philippines.

Harris, K. L., and C. Lindblad. 1978. *Post-Harvest Grain Loss Assessment Methods.* St. Paul, Minnesota: American Association of Cereal Chemists.

Harrison, Kelly, Donald Henley, Harold Riley, and James Shaffer. 1975. *Improving Food Marketing Systems in Developing Countries: Experiences from Latin America.* Research Report No. 6. East Lansing, Michigan: Michigan State University Latin American Studies Center.

Harriss, Barbara. 1979. Going Against the Grain. *Development and Change.* 10(3):363–84.

Harriss, John. 1977. The Limitations of High Yielding Varieties (HYV) Technology in North Arcot District: The View from a Village. In B. H. Farmer, ed. *Green Revolution.* Cambridge, England: Cambridge University Press.

Hart, R. D. 1983. An Ecological Systems Conceptual Framework for Agricultural Research and Extension. In *Readings for Farming Systems Research and Extension Methods.* Farming Systems Support Project. Gainesville, Florida: University of Florida.

Harvey, P., and P. Heywood. 1983. *Nutrition and Growth in Simbu.* Vol. 4. Papua New Guinea: Office of Environment and Conservation, Simbu Provincial Government.

Harwood, R. R. 1979. *Small Farm Development: Understanding and Improving Farming Systems in the Humid Tropics.* Boulder, Colorado: Westview Press.

Hayami, Yujiro, and Vernon W. Ruttan. 1971. *Agricultural Development: An International Perspective.* Baltimore, Maryland: Johns Hopkins University Press.

Hazell, Peter B. R. 1982. *Instability in Indian Foodgrain Production.* Washington, D.C.: IFPRI.

———. 1984. Sources of Increased Instability in Indian and U.S. Cereal Production. *American Journal of Agricultural Economics.* 66(3):602–11.

Hazell, Peter B. R., and Alisa Röell. 1983. *Rural Household Expenditure Patterns and Their Implications for Development Strategy: Studies in Malaysia and Nigeria.* Research Report No. 41. Washington, D.C.: IFPRI.

Hecht, R. 1983. The Ivory Coast Economic Miracle: What Benefits for Peasant Farmers? *Journal of Modern African Studies.* 21:25–53.

Heller, P. S., and W. D. Drake. 1976. *Malnutrition, Child Morbidity and the Family Decision Process.* Discussion Paper No. 58. Ann Arbor, Michigan: University of Michigan Center for Research on Economic Development.

Hendry, Peter. 1983. Land Use and Living Space. *Ceres.* 96:15–19.

Herdt, Robert. 1970. A Disaggregate Approach to Aggregate Supply. *American Journal of Agricultural Economics.* 52(4):512–20.

Herdt, R. W., and C. Capule. 1983. *Adoption, Spread, and Production Impact of Modern Rice Varieties in Asia.* Manila: IRRI.

Hernandez, Mercedes, Carlos P. Hidalgo, Juan R. Hernandez, H. Madrigal, and Adolfo Chavez. 1974. Effect of Economic Growth on Nutrition in a Tropical Community. *Ecology of Food and Nutrition.* 3(4):283–91.

Herrera, M. G., J. O. Mora, and N. Christiansen. 1980. Effects of Nutritional Supplementation and Early Education on Physical and Cognitive Development. In R. Turner and F. Reese, eds. *Life-Span Developmental Psychology.* New York: Academic Press.

Hewitt de Alcantara, Cynthia. 1976. *Modernizing Mexican Agriculture.* Geneva: UNRISD.

Hildebrand, P. E. 1982. Role, Potential, and Problems of Farming Systems Research and Extension: Developing Countries vs. United States. In W. J. Sheppard, ed. *Proceedings of Kansas State University's 1981 Farming Systems Research Symposium: Small Farms in a Changing World: Prospects for the Eighties.* Farming Systems Research Paper No. 2. Manhattan, Kansas: Kansas State University.

————. 1983a. *Designing Alternate Solutions: Case Study of Jutiapa, Guatemala.* An Audio-Visual Training Module Script. Farming Systems Support Project TSM 401. Gainesville, Florida: University of Florida.

————. 1983b. *Designing Alternate Solutions: Case Study of the North Florida FSR/E Project.* An Audio-Visual Training Module Script. Farming Systems Support Project TSM 403. Gainesville, Florida: University of Florida.

————. 1983c. Modified Stability Analysis of Farmer-Managed, On-Farm Trials. In *Readings for Farming Systems Research and Extension Methods.* Farming Systems Support Project. Gainesville, Florida: University of Florida.

Hildebrand, P. E., and E. G. Luna. 1983. Unforeseen Consequences of Introducing New Technologies in Traditional Agriculture. In *Readings for Farming Systems Research and Extension Methods.* Farming Systems Support Project. Gainesville, Florida: University of Florida.

Hildebrand, P. E., and R. K. Waugh. 1983. Farming Systems Research and Development. *Farming Systems Support Project Newsletter.* 1:4–5.

Hill, Kenneth. 1985. Demographic Trends in China, 1953–1982. Population, Health and Nutrition Department Technical Note PHN 85-4. Washington, D.C.: World Bank.

Hitchings, Jon. 1982. Agricultural Determinants of Nutritional Status Among Kenyan Children with Model of Anthropometric and Growth Indicators. Ph.D. dissertation. Stanford, California: Stanford University.

Ho, Teresa J. 1979. Women's Role in Domestic Food Acquisition and Food Use in India: A Case Study of Low-Income Households. *Food and Nutrition Bulletin.* 6:69–76.

Hoffman, A. 1977. The Effect of Processing and Storage upon the Nutritive Value of Smoked Fish from Africa. *Tropical Science.* 19(1):41–53.

Hofvander, Y., and R. Eksmyr. 1971. An Applied Nutrition Program in an Ethiopian Rural Community. *American Journal of Clinical Nutrition.* 24:578–91.

Hoge, Warren. 1983. Brazil's Poor Raiding Food Stores in the Rio Area. *New York Times.* September 11.

Holmes, A. Stewart. 1971. *Market Structure, Conduct, and Foodgrain Pricing Efficiency: An Indian Case Study.* New York: Educational Publishing Company, Inc.

Hopf, H. S., G. E. J. Morley, and J. R. P. Humphries. 1976. *Rodent Damage to Growing Crops and to Farm and Village Storage in Tropical and Subtropical Regions.* London: Centre for Overseas Pest Research and Tropical Products Institute.

Hopper, W. David. 1965. Allocation Efficiency in a Traditional Indian Agriculture. *Journal of Farm Economics.* 47(3):611–24.

Hornblower, Margot. 1984. Price Riots Imperil Dominican Government. *Washington Post.* April 30.

Hornik, Robert C. 1982. *Communications and Agriculture.* Stanford, California, and Philadelphia, Pennsylvania: Institute for Communications Research, Stanford University, and Annenberg School of Communications, University of Pennsylvania.

Hunter, Guy. 1978. Report on Administration and Institutions. In Asian Development Bank. *Rural Asia: Challenge and Opportunity.* Supplementary Papers. Vol. 1, *Administration and Institutions in Agricultural and Rural Development.* Manila.

IFPRI. 1977. *Food Needs of Developing Countries: Projections of Production and Consumption to 1990.* Washington, D.C.

————. 1981. Food Aid tape. Washington, D.C.

IMF. 1950–1984. *International Financial Statistics.* Washington, D.C.

INACG. 1977. Guidelines for the Eradication of Iron Deficiency Anemia: A Report. New York: Nutrition Foundation.

India, Government of. Planning Commission. 1961. *Third Five Year Plan.* New Delhi: Government of India Press.

Jackson, Tony. 1983. A Triumph of Hope Over Experience. *IDS Bulletin.* 14(2):53–55.

Jacob, F. 1975. *An Evaluation Study on the Preschool Health Program in Rwanda.* Field Bulletin No. 25. Nairobi, Kenya: Catholic Relief Services.

Jacob, F., and G. Gordon. 1975. *An Evaluation Study of the Preschool Health Program in Ghana.* Field Bulletin No. 24. Nairobi, Kenya: Catholic Relief Services.

James, Clive. 1983. Wheat and Maize: CIMMYT's Experience. *Courier.* 82:63–65.

James, D. 1977. Post-Harvest Losses of Marine Foods—Problems and Responses. Paper presented to the Institute of Food Technologists Annual Meeting. Philadelphia, Pennsylvania.

James, J. W. 1972. Longitudinal Study of the Morbidity of Diarrhea and Respiratory Infections in Malnourished Children. *American Journal of Clinical Nutrition.* 25(7):690–94.

Jamison, Dean. 1986. Child Malnutrition and School Performance in China. *Journal of Development Economics* 20(2):299–310.

Jamison, Dean T., and Frederick L. Trowbridge. 1984. The Nutritional Status of Children in China: A Review of the Anthropometric Evidence. Population, Health and Nutrition Department Technical Note GEN 17. Washington D.C.: World Bank.

Jamison, Dean T., John R. Evans, Timothy King, Ian Porter, Nicholas

Prescott, and Andre Prost. 1984. *China: The Health Sector.* A World Bank Country Study. Washington D.C.

Jenkins, Janet. 1983. Mass Media for Health Education. IEC Broadsheets on Distance Learning, No. 18. Nottingham, England: Russell Press, Ltd.

Jennings, Peter. 1976. The Amplification of Agricultural Production. *Scientific American.* 235:181–94.

Johnson, D. Gale. 1982. The World Food Situation: Developments During the 1970's and Prospects for the 1980's. In Emery N. Castle, Kenzo Hemmi, and Sally A. Skillings, eds. *U.S.-Japanese Agricultural Trade Relations.* Washington, D.C.: Resources for the Future.

Johnson, E. A. 1970. *The Organization of Space in Developing Countries.* Cambridge, Massachusetts: Harvard University Press.

Johnson, Harry G. 1969. Comparative Cost and Commercial Policy Theory in a Developing World Economy. *Pakistan Development Review.* 4(1, Supplement):1–33.

Johnston, Bruce F., and William C. Clark. 1982. *Redesigning Rural Development: A Strategic Perspective.* Baltimore, Maryland: Johns Hopkins University Press.

Johnston, Bruce F., and Peter Kilby. 1975. *Agriculture and Structural Transformation: Economic Strategies in Late-Developing Countries.* New York: Oxford University Press.

Johnston, Bruce F., and John W. Mellor. 1984. The World Food Equation: Interrelations Between Development, Employment and Food Consumption. *Journal of Economic Literature.* 22(2):531–74.

Jones, Christine W. 1982. Women's Labor Allocations and Irrigated Rice Production in Northern Cameroon. Paper presented to the 18th International Conference of Agricultural Economists. August–September. Jakarta, Indonesia.

————. 1983. *The Impact of the Société d'Expansion et de Modernisation de la Riziculture de Yagoua (SEMRY I) Irrigated Rice Production Project on the Organization of Production and Consumption at the Intra-Household Level.* Report to AID. Washington, D.C.: USAID.

Jones, J. C. 1983. The Farming Systems Approach to Research and Extension. Gainesville, Florida: University of Florida. Processed.

Jones, William O. 1972. *Marketing Staple Food Crops in Tropical Africa.* Ithaca, New York: Cornell University Press.

————. 1984. Economic Tasks for Food Marketing Boards in Tropical Africa. *Food Research Institute Studies.* 19(2):113–38.

Joy, Leonard. 1973. Food and Nutrition Planning. *Journal of Agricultural Economics.* 24(1):164–97.

————. 1978. Intersectoral Food and Nutrition Planning. In Leonard Joy, ed. *Nutrition Planning: The State of the Art.* Guildford, England: IPC Science and Technology Press for USAID.

Katona-Apte, Judit. 1986. A Commodity-Appropriateness Evaluation of Four WFP Projects. In Martin J. Forman, ed. *Nutritional Aspects of Project Food Aid*. Rome: Subcommittee on Nutrition, United Nations Administrative Committee on Coordination.

Kellogg, Charles E., and Arnold C. Orvedal. 1969. Potentially Arable Soils of the World and Critical Measures for Their Use. *Advances in Agronomy*. 21:109–70.

Kennedy, Eileen, and Bruce Cogill. 1985. Effects of the Commercialization of Agriculture on Women's Decision Making and Time Allocation. Paper presented at the Association of Women in Development Annual Meeting. April. Washington, D.C.

Kenya, Republic of. 1977. *Integrated Rural Survey, 1974–75*. Nairobi: Government Printer.

Ker, A. D. R., and IDRC. 1979. *Food or Famine: An Account of the Crop Science Program Supported by the IDRC*. Monograph No. 143e. Ottawa, Canada: IDRC.

Khaldi, Nabil. 1984. *Evolving Food Gaps in the Middle East/North Africa Region: Prospects and Policy Implications*. Research Report No. 47. Washington, D.C.: IFPRI.

Khan, Azizur R. 1983. Institutional-Organizational Framework of Egalitarian Agricultural Growth. In Allen Maunder and Kazushi Ohkawa, eds. *Growth and Equity in Agricultural Development*. Aldershot, England: Gower Publishing Company.

Khan, Azizur R., and Eddy Lee. 1983. *Agricultural Policies and Institutions After Mao*. Singapore: Richard Clay.

Khare, R. S. 1984. Women's Role in Domestic Food Acquisition and Food Use in India: A Case Study of Low-Income Urban Households. *Food and Nutrition Bulletin*. 6(1):69–76.

Khare, R. D., P. M. Shah, and A. R. Junnakkar. 1976. Management of Kwashiorkor in Its Milieu—A Follow-Up for 15 Months. *Indian Journal of Medical Research*. 64(8):1119–27.

Kielmann, Arnfried A., and C. McCord. 1978. Weight-for-Age as an Index of Risk of Death in Children. *Lancet*. 1(8076):1247–50.

Kielmann, Arnfried A., Carl E. Taylor, Cecile De Sweemer, Robert L. Parker, D. Chernichovsky, William A. Reinke, Inder S. Uberoi, D. N. Kakar, Norah Masih, and R. S. S. Sarma. 1983. *Child and Maternal Health Services in India: The Narangwal Experiment*. Vol. 1. *Integrated Nutrition and Health Care*. Baltimore, Maryland: Johns Hopkins University Press.

King, Robert P., and Derek Byerlee. 1978. Factor Intensities and Locational Linkages of Rural Consumption Patterns in Sierra Leone. *American Journal of Agricultural Economics*. 60(2):197–206.

Kirby, Riley H. 1972. *Agricultural Trade of the People's Republic of China*. Foreign Agricultural Economic Report No. 83. Washington, D.C.: USDA.

Kirchner, J., I. Singh, and Lyn Squire. 1984. Agricultural Pricing and

Marketing Policies in Malawi. Country Policy Discussion Paper. Washington, D.C.: World Bank.

Kirk, Dudley. 1971. A New Demographic Transition. In NAS. *Rapid Population Growth: Consequences and Policy Implications.* Baltimore, Maryland: Johns Hopkins University Press for the NAS.

————. 1978. World Population and Birth Rates: Agreements and Disagreements. *Population and Development Review.* 5(3):387–403.

Kneerim, J. 1980. Village Women Organize: The Mraru Bus Service. *Seeds.* 1:1–20.

Koester, Ulrich. 1982. *Policy Options for the Grain Economy of the European Community: Implications for Developing Countries.* Washington, D.C.: IFPRI.

Koppel, Bruce. 1978. *Technology Assessment and Research Management.* SEARCA Bulletin No. 4. College, Laguna, Philippines: SEARCA.

Korte, R. 1969. The Nutritional and Health Status of the Mwea-Tekere Irrigation Settlement. In H. Kraut and H. D. Cremer, eds. *Investigations into Health and Nutrition in East Africa.* Munich: Weltforum-Verlag.

————. 1981. Health and Nutrition. In Mwea Irrigation Scheme. Washington, D.C.: World Bank. Processed.

Korten, Frances F. 1983. Community Participation: A Management Perspective on Obstacles and Options. In David C. Korten and Felipe B. Alfonso, eds. *Bureaucracy and the Poor.* West Hartford, Connecticut: Kumarian Press.

Kothare, N. R. 1977. *Rainfall in India.* Reserve Bank Staff Occasional Papers. Vol. 2. Bombay: Reserve Bank of India.

Kozlowski, Z. 1975. Agriculture in the Economic Growth of East European Socialist Countries. In Lloyd G. Reynolds, ed. *Agriculture in Development Theory.* New Haven, Connecticut: Yale University Press.

Kraut, H., J. Kreysler, L. Kanti, K. Mndeme, H. Moshi, U. Oltersdorf, T. Plesser, E. Schach, and E. Boch. 1978. Rehabilitation of Undernourished Children in Tanzania Using Locally Available Food. *Ecology of Food and Nutrition.* 6(4):231–42.

Kreysler, J., and C. Schlage. 1969. The Nutrition Situation in the Pangani Basin. In H. Kraut and H. D. Cremer, eds. *Investigations into Health and Nutrition in East Africa.* Munich: Weltforum-Verlag.

Kriesel, Herbert. 1974. The Marketing Board System. In O. O. Onitiri and D. A. Olatunbosun, eds. *Proceedings of an Interministerial Conference.* Ibadan, Nigeria.

Krishnamurthy, K. A., and S. A. Kabir. 1977. *Report on Nutritional Rehabilitation Center and Its Activities.* Mandurai, India: Government Erskin Hospital.

Krueger, Anne O. 1974. The Political Economy of the Rent-Seeking Society. *American Economic Review.* 64(3):291–303.

————. 1978. *Foreign Trade Regimes and Economic Development: Liberalization Attempts and Consequences.* Cambridge, Massachusetts: Ballinger Publishing Company.

Kumar, Shubh K. 1978. *Role of the Household Economy in Determining Child Nutrition at Low Incomes—A Case Study in Kerala.* Department of Agricultural Economics Occasional Paper No. 95. Ithaca, New York: Cornell University.

————. 1979. *Impact of Subsidized Rice on Food Consumption and Nutrition in Kerala.* Research Report No. 5. Washington, D.C.: IFPRI.

————. 1986. Nutrition Problems in Sub-Saharan Africa. In John W. Mellor, Christopher L. Delgado, and Malcolm Blackie, eds. *Accelerating Agricultural Growth in Sub-Saharan Africa.* Washington, D.C., and Baltimore, Maryland: IFPRI and Johns Hopkins University Press.

Kutcher, Gary P., Alexander Meeraus, and Gerald T. O'Mara. 1986. Agricultural Modeling for Policy Analysis. Internal document. Washington, D.C.: Agricultural and Rural Development Department, World Bank.

Lambert, J. N. 1978. Does Cash Cropping Cause Malnutrition? Port Moresby, Papua New Guinea: National Planning Office. Processed.

Lancet. 1978. Editorial. Water with Sugar and Salt. 1:300–01.

————. 1984. Editorial. A Measure of Agreement on Growth Standards. 2:142–43.

Lardy, Nicholas R. 1983a. *Agricultural Prices in China.* World Bank Staff Working Paper No. 606. Washington D.C.

————. 1983b. *Agriculture in China's Modern Economic Development.* Cambridge, England: Cambridge University Press.

Lastigzon, Joseph. 1981. *World Fertilizer Progress Into the 1980s.* Muscle Shoals, Alabama: International Fertilizer Development Center.

Latham, M. C. 1984. *International Nutrition Problems and Policies in World Food Issues.* 2d ed. Ithaca, New York: Cornell University Program of International Agriculture, Center for the Analysis of World Food Issues.

Lee, Linda. 1978. *A Perspective on Cropland Availability.* Washington, D.C.: USDA.

Lee, T. H. 1971. *Intersectoral Capital Flows in the Economic Development of Taiwan, 1895–1960.* Ithaca, New York: Cornell University Press.

Lele, Uma. 1979. *The Design of Rural Development: Lessons From Africa.* 3rd ed. Baltimore, Maryland: Johns Hopkins University Press.

————. 1984. Tanzania: Phoenix or Icarus? In Arnold C. Harberger, ed. *World Economic Growth.* San Francisco, California: Institute for Contemporary Studies.

Lele, Uma, and John W. Mellor. 1981. Technological Change, Distributive Bias, and Labor Transfer in a Two Sector Economy. *Oxford*

Economic Papers. 33(3):426–41. Reprinted in World Bank Reprint Series, No. 205.

Leonard, David. 1984. What is Rational When Rationality Isn't? Comments on the Administrative Proposals of the Berg Report. *Rural Africana.* 19/20:99–113.

Leslie, Joanne. 1981. Evaluation of Mass Media for Health and Nutrition Education. In Manfred Meyer, ed. *Health Education by Television and Radio.* Munich: K. G. Saur.

————. 1982. Child Malnutrition and Diarrhea: A Longitudinal Study from Northeast Brazil. D.Sc. thesis. Baltimore, Maryland: Johns Hopkins School of Hygiene and Public Health.

Leslie, Joanne, Bal Gopal Baidya, and Kalpana Nandwani. 1981. Prevalence and Correlates of Childhood Malnutrition in the Terai Region of Nepal. Discussion Paper No. 81-35. Population and Human Resources Division. Washington, D.C.: World Bank.

Lev, Larry. 1981. *The Effect of Cash Cropping on Food Consumption Among the Meru of Northern Tanzania.* Working Paper No. 21. East Lansing, Michigan: Michigan State University.

Levinson, F. James. 1974. *Morinda: An Economic Analysis of Malnutrition Among Young Children in Rural India.* International Nutrition Policy Series. Ithaca, New York, and Cambridge, Massachusetts: Cornell University and the Massachusetts Institute of Technology.

————. 1982. Toward Success in Combatting Malnutrition: An Assessment of What Works. *Food and Nutrition Bulletin.* 4(3):23–44.

Lewis, Barbara C. 1981. *Invisible Farmers: Women and the Crisis in Agriculture.* Office of Women in Development. Washington, D.C.: USAID.

Lewis, W. Arthur. 1980. The Slowing Down of the Engine of Growth. *American Economic Review.* 70(4):555–65.

Liang, Kou-shu, and T. H. Lee. 1972. *Process and Pattern of Economic Development in Taiwan.* Taipei: Joint Commission on Rural Reconstruction.

Lipton, Michael. 1977. *Why Poor People Stay Poor: Urban Bias in World Development.* Cambridge, Massachusetts: Harvard University Press.

————. 1983. *Labor and Poverty.* World Bank Staff Working Paper No. 616. Washington, D.C.

Longhurst, Richard. 1981. Rapid Rural Appraisal—Social Structure and Rural Economy. *IDS Bulletin.* 12(4):1–2.

————. 1983. Agricultural Production and Food Consumption: Some Neglected Linkages. *Food and Nutrition.* 9(2):2–5.

Longhurst, Richard, and P. Payne. 1981. Seasonal Aspects of Nutrition. In Robert Chambers, Richard Longhurst, and A. Pacey, eds. *Seasonal Dimensions to Rural Poverty.* London: Frances Pinter Publishers, Ltd.

Lopez, Clara E. 1978. Nutrition and Government Policy in Colombia. In Beverly Winikoff, ed. *Nutrition and National Policy.* Cambridge, Massachusetts: Massachusetts Institute of Technology Press.

Lunven, P. 1983. The Value of Time-Use Data in Nutrition. *Food and Nutrition.* 9(2):33–38.

Lunven, P., and Z. I. Sabry. 1981. Nutrition and Rural Development. *Food and Nutrition.* 7(1):13–21.

Mackay, J., C. Capone, and F. Jacob. 1974. *An Evaluation of the Preschool Health Program in Lesotho.* Field Bulletin No. 20. Nairobi, Kenya: Catholic Relief Services.

Mahadevan, M. 1977. Les Creches Mobile en Inde. *Carnets de l'Enfance.* 40:68–87.

Mahai, B. A. P., and others. 1976. The Second Follow-Up Formative Evaluation Report of the Food Is Life Campaign. Paper for the Institute of Adult Education, Research and Planning. Dar es Salaam, Tanzania. Processed.

Mahalanobis, P. C. 1953. Some Observations on the Process of Growth and National Income. *Sankya.* 12:307–12.

Malthus, Thomas Robert. 1798. *Essay on the Principle of Population.* Reprinted London: Penguin Books, 1983.

Mann, Charles K., and Barbara Huddleston, eds. 1985. *Food Policy: Frameworks for Analysis and Action.* Bloomington, Indiana: Indiana University Press.

Manoff International, Inc. 1984. *Nutrition Communication and Behavior Change Component: Indonesian Nutrition Development Program.* Vol. 4, *Household Evaluation.* New York: Manoff International, Inc.

Martin, Michael V., and Ray F. Brokken. 1982. *Grain Prices in Historical Perspective.* St. Paul, Minnesota: University of Minnesota Department of Agricultural and Applied Economics.

——. 1983. Grain Price Historic Perspective Shows Real Weakness. *Feedstuffs.* December 5.

Martinez, J. C., and J. R. Arauz. 1983. *Institutional Innovations in National Agricultural Research: On-Farm Research within the Agricultural Research Institute (IDIAP), Panama.* CIMMYT Economics Program Working Paper 02/83. Mexico City.

Martorell, Reynaldo. 1980. Interrelationships between Diet, Infectious Disease, and Nutritional Status. In Lawrence S. Greene and Francis E. Johnston, eds. *Social and Biological Predictors of Nutritional Status, Physical Growth, and Neurological Development.* New York: Academic Press.

——. 1984. Genetics, Environment, and Growth: Issues in the Assessment of Nutritional Status. In A. Velazquez and H. Bourges, eds. *Genetic Factors in Nutrition.* New York: Academic Press.

Martorell, Reynaldo, and Teresa J. Ho. 1984. Malnutrition, Morbidity, and Mortality. In W. Henry Mosley and Lincoln C. Chen, eds. *Child Survival: Strategies for Research. Population and Development Review.* 10 Supplement:49–68. New York: Population Council.

Martorell, Reynaldo, Jean-Pierre Habicht, Charles Yarbrough, Aaron Lechtig, Robert E. Klein, and Karl A. Western. 1975. Acute Morbidity and Physical Growth in Rural Guatemalan Children. *American Journal of Diseases of Children.* 129(11):1296-1301.

Martorell, Reynaldo, Robert E. Klein, and Hernan Delgado. 1980. Improved Nutrition and Its Effects on Anthropometric Indicators of Nutritional Status. *Nutritional Reports International.* 21(2):219–30.

Martorell, Reynaldo, C. Yarbrough, S. Yarbrough, and R. E. Klein. 1980. The Impact of Ordinary Illnesses on the Dietary Intakes of Malnourished Children. *American Journal of Clinical Nutrition.* 33(2):345–50.

Mason, John B., Jean-Pierre Habicht, H. Tabatabai, and V. Valverde. 1984. *Nutritional Surveillance.* Geneva: WHO.

Mata, Leonardo J. 1978. *The Children of Santa Maria Cauque: A Prospective Field Study of Health and Growth.* Cambridge, Massachusetts: Massachusetts Institute of Technology Press.

Mata, Leonardo J., and E. Mohs. 1978. As Seen From National Levels: Developing World. In Sheldon Margen and R. A. Ogar, eds. *Progress in Human Nutrition.* Vol. 2. Westport, Connecticut: AVI Publishing Company.

Mauldin, W. P., and Bernard Berelson. 1978. Conditions of Fertility Decline in Developing Countries, 1965–75. *Studies in Family Planning.* 9(5):90–147.

Maxwell, Simon. 1983. From Understudy to Leading Star: The Future Role of Impact Assessment in Food Aid Programmes. *IDS Bulletin.* 14(2):32–39.

Mazingira. 1984. Chinese Reform Burial Customs. March.

McDermott, J. K. 1983. Farming Systems Research (FSR) Project Evaluation. In Cornelia Butler Flora, ed. *Proceedings of Kansas State University's 1982 Farming Systems Research Symposium: Farming Systems in the Field.* Farming Systems Research Paper No. 5. Manhattan, Kansas: Kansas State University.

McDowell, J., and V. Hazzard. 1976. Village Technology and Women's Work in Eastern Africa. *Assignment Children.* 36:53–65.

McDowell, R. E., and P. E. Hildebrand. 1980. *Integrated Crop and Animal Production: Making the Most of Resources Available to Small Farms in Developing Countries.* Rockefeller Foundation Working Papers. New York.

McLaren, Donald S. 1974. The Great Protein Fiasco. *Lancet.* 2(872):93–96.

McMillan, D. 1983. Land Use Within an Upper Volta Household.

Slides and tape recording. Farming Systems Support Project. Gainesville, Florida: University of Florida.

McNamara, Robert S. 1973. Address to the Board of Governors. Nairobi, Kenya. Washington, D.C.: World Bank.

McSweeney, Brenda G. 1979. Collection and Analysis of Data on Rural Women's Time Use. *Studies in Family Planning.* 10(11/12):379–83.

Medical Research Committee. 1917. Special Reports Series No. 10. United Kingdom.

Mehra, S. 1981. *Instability in Indian Agriculture in the Context of the New Technology.* Research Report 25. Washington, D.C.: IFPRI.

Meier, Gerald M., ed. 1983. *Pricing Policy for Development Management.* EDI Series in Economic Development. Baltimore, Maryland: Johns Hopkins University Press.

Mellor, John W. 1966. *The Economics of Agricultural Development.* Ithaca, New York: Cornell University Press.

———. 1973. Accelerated Growth in Agricultural Production and the Intersectoral Transfer of Resources. *Economic Development and Cultural Change.* 22(1):1–16.

———. 1975. *The Impact of New Agricultural Technology on Employment and Income Distribution—Concepts and Policy.* Occasional Paper No. 2. Washington, D.C.: USAID.

———. 1976. *The New Economics of Growth: A Strategy for India and the Developing World.* Ithaca, New York: Cornell University Press.

———. 1978. Food Price Policies and Income Distribution in Low-Income Countries. *Economic Development and Cultural Change.* 21(1):1–26.

———. 1983. Food Prospects for the Developing Countries. *American Economic Review.* 73(2):239–43.

———. 1984. *A Structural View of Policy Issues in African Agricultural Development.* Washington, D.C.: IFPRI.

Mellor, John W., and Gunvant M. Desai, eds. 1985. *Agricultural Change and Rural Poverty: Variations on a Theme by Dharm Narain.* Baltimore, Maryland: Johns Hopkins University Press for IFPRI.

Mellor, John W., and Uma Lele. 1973. Growth Linkages of the New Foodgrain Technologies. *Indian Journal of Agricultural Economics.* 23(1):35–55.

———. 1975. Interaction of Growth Strategy, Agriculture and Foreign Trade. In George S. Tolley and Peter A. Ladrozny, eds. *Trade, Agriculture, and Development.* Cambridge, Massachusetts: Ballinger Publishing Company.

Molla, A. M., Ayesha Molla, S. A. Sarker, and M. Mujibur Rahaman. 1983. Food Intake During and After Recovery from Diarrhea in Children. In Lincoln C. Chen and Nevin S. Scrimshaw, eds. *Diarrhea and Malnutrition: Interactions, Mechanisms, and Interventions.* New York: Plenum Press.

Mora, J. O., A. Amezquita, L. Castro, N. Christiansen, J. Clement-Murphy, L. F. Cobos, H. D. Cremer, S. Dragastin, M. F. Elias, D. Franklin, M. G. Herrera, N. Ortiz, F. Pardo, B. de Paredes, C. Ramos, R. Riley, H. Rodriguez, L. Vuori-Christiansen, M. Wagner, and F. J. Stare. 1974. Nutrition, Health and Social Factors Related to Intellectual Performance. *World Review of Nutrition and Dietetics.* 19:205–36.

Mora, J. O., J. Clement, N. Christiansen, J. Suescun, M. Wagner, and M. G. Herrera. 1978. Nutritional Supplementation and the Outcome of Pregnancy. 3. Perinatal and Neonatal Mortality. *Nutrition Reports International.* 18(2):167–75.

Mora, J. O., M. G. Herrera, J. Suescun, L. de Navarro, and M. Wagner. 1981. The Effects of Nutritional Supplementation on Physical Growth of Children at Risk of Malnutrition. *American Journal of Clinical Nutrition.* 34(9):1885–92.

Morgan, W. B. 1978. *Agriculture in the Third World: A Spatial Analysis.* Boulder, Colorado: Westview Press.

Moris, Jon. 1983. What Do We Know About African Agricultural Development? The Role of Extension Performance Reanalyzed. Draft No. 1. Washington, D.C.: USAID, Bureau of Science and Technology.

Moses, B. C., and M. S. Pandian. 1983. Tamil Nadu Drought Situation: View from a Village. *Economic and Political Weekly.* 18(23):996.

Murdoch, William W. 1980. *The Poverty of Nations: The Political Economy of Hunger and Population.* Baltimore, Maryland: Johns Hopkins University Press.

Murty, K. 1983. *Consumption and Nutrition Patterns of ICRISAT Mandate Crops in India.* Economics Program Progress Report No. 53. Hyderabad, India: ICRISAT.

Musgrove, Philip. 1978. *Consumer Behavior in Latin America.* Washington D.C.: Brookings Institution.

Mushi, A. M. 1978. Country Paper: Tanzania. Paper presented to the Seminar on Post-Harvest Grain Losses, Tropical Products Institute. March 13–17. London, England.

Nakajima, Chihiro. 1969. Subsistence and Commercial Family Farms: Some Theoretical Models of Subjective Equilibrium. In Clifton R. Wharton, Jr., ed. *Subsistence Agriculture and Economic Development.* Chicago, Illinois: Aldine Publishing Co.

NAS. 1975. *Underexploited Crops with Promising Economic Value.* Washington, D.C.

———. 1977. *World Food and Nutrition Study.* Washington, D.C.

———. 1979. *Tropical Legumes: Resources for the Future.* Washington, D.C.

National Institute of Nutrition. 1977. *Annual Report 1976*. Hyderabad, India: Indian Council of Medical Research.

———. 1981. Impact of Massive Dose Vitamin A Programme on Incidence of Nutritional Blindness. *Annual Report*. Hyderabad, India.

National Research Council. Commission on International Relations. Board on Science and Technology for International Development. 1978. *Postharvest Food Losses in Developing Countries*. Washington, D.C.: NAS.

———. 1982. *Nutritional Analysis of Public Law 480, Title II Commodities*. Washington, D.C.: National Academy Press.

Nelson, Gordon O. 1982. *Impact of Food Aid on Development in Africa*. New York: Agricultural Development Council.

Ness, Gayle D. 1979. Organizational Issues in International Population Assistance. In P. M. Hauser, ed. *World Population and Development: Challenges and Prospects*. Syracuse, New York: Syracuse University Press.

Newland, K. 1980. *Women, Men and Division of Labor*. Worldwatch Paper 37. Washington, D.C.: Worldwatch Institute.

New York Times. 1983. Poland Prepares for Unrest Over Food Prices. December 4.

Norman, D. W. 1983. The Farming System Approach to Research. In Cornelia Butler Flora, ed. *Proceedings of Kansas State University's 1982 Farming Systems Research Symposium: Farming Systems in the Field*. Farming Systems Research Paper No. 5. Manhattan, Kansas: Kansas State University.

O'Dea, J. 1982. An Examination of the Impact of Cash Crop Agriculture on Nutritional Status with Reference to Kenya. Report submitted in partial fulfillment of M.S. degree. London: University of London.

OECD. 1976. *Land Use Policies and Agriculture*. Paris.

OECD Observer. 1976. Should Agricultural Land be Protected? September–October. Paris.

Ogbu, J. 1973. Seasonal Hunger in Tropical Africa as a Cultural Phenomenon. *Africa*. 46:317.

Olayide, S. O., and Francis S. Idachaba. 1986. Input Supply and Food Marketing Systems for Agricultural Growth: A Nigerian Case Study. In John W. Mellor, Christopher L. Delgado, and Malcolm Blackie, eds. *Accelerating Agricultural Growth in Sub-Saharan Africa*. Washington, D.C., and Baltimore, Maryland: IFPRI and Johns Hopkins University Press.

Onchere, S., and R. Sloof. 1981. Nutrition and Disease in Machakos District, Kenya. In Robert Chambers, Richard Longhurst, and A. Pacey, eds. *Seasonal Dimensions to Rural Poverty*. London: Frances Pinter Publishers, Ltd.

Oram, Peter A., and Vishva Bindlish. Forthcoming. *Investment in Agricultural Research in Developing Countries: Progress, Problems, and the Determination of Priorities.* Washington, D.C.: IFPRI.

Orivel, François. 1983. The Impact of Agricultural Extension Services: A Review of the Literature. In Hilary Perraton, Dean T. Jamison, Janet Jenkins, François Orivel, and Lawrence Wolff. *Basic Education and Agricultural Extension: Costs, Effects, and Alternatives.* World Bank Staff Working Paper No. 564. Washington, D.C.

OTA. 1976. *Assessment of Alternatives for Supporting High-Priority Research in Such Areas as Photosynthesis, Nitrogen-Fixation and Plant Genetic Manipulation.* Washington, D.C.

Overholt, C., S. Sellers, J. O. Mora, B. de Paredes, and M. G. Herrera. 1982. The Effects of Nutritional Supplementation on the Diets of Low-Income Families at Risk of Malnutrition. *American Journal of Clinical Nutrition.* 36(12):1153–61.

Paarlberg, Don. 1982. The Scarcity Syndrome. *American Journal of Agricultural Economics.* 64(1):110–14.

Pachico, D. 1980. *Applying Efficiency Analysis to Small Farms in Low Income Countries: Some Theoretical and Empirical Considerations.* Cornell International Agriculture Monograph 84. Ithaca, New York: Cornell University.

Pack, H., and L. Westphal. 1984. Industrial Strategy and Technological Change: Theory Versus Reality. Paper presented at the Conference on New Directions in Development Theory. Massachusetts Institute of Technology, Cambridge, Massachusetts.

Palmer, I. 1977. Rural Women and the Basic Needs Approach to Development. *International Labor Review.* 115(1):97–107.

Paulino, Leonardo. 1984. *Food in the Third World: Past Trends and Projections to 2000.* Washington, D.C.: IFPRI.

Peck, Anne E. 1982. Futures Markets, Food Imports and Food Security. AGREP Working Paper No. 43. Washington, D.C.: World Bank.

Perkins, Dwight. 1966. *Market Control and Planning in Communist China.* Cambridge, Massachusetts: Harvard University Press.

Petersen, W. L. 1979. International Farm Prices and the Social Cost of Cheap Food Policies. *American Journal of Agricultural Economics.* 61(1):12–22.

Philippine Council for Agriculture and Resources Research. 1977. *Report on the International Conference on Potentials for Cooperation Among National Agricultural Research Systems.* October 17–21. Bellagio, Italy. College, Laguna, Philippines.

———. 1978. *Proceedings of the International Workshop on Mangrove and Estuarine Areas Development for the Indo-Pacific Region.* November 14–19, 1977. Los Baños, Philippines.

Piazza, Alan. 1986. *Food Consumption and Nutritional Status in the People's Republic of China*. Boulder, Colorado: Westview Press.

Pimentel, David, William Dritschilo, John Krummel, and John Kutzman. 1975. Energy and Land Constraints in Food Protein Production. *Science*. 190(4216):754–61.

Pinstrup-Andersen, Per. 1977. Decision-Making on Food and Agricultural Research Policy: The Distribution of Benefits from New Agricultural Technology Among Consumer Income Strata. *Agricultural Administration*. 4(1):13–28.

―――――. 1979. Modern Agricultural Technology and Income Distribution: The Market Price Effect. *European Review of Agricultural Economics*. 6(1):17–46.

―――――. 1981. *Nutritional Consequences of Agricultural Projects*. World Bank Staff Working Paper No. 456. Washington, D.C.

―――――. 1982a. *Agricultural Research and Technology in Economic Development*. London and New York: Longman Publishing Co.

―――――. 1982b. *Export Crop Production*. Chapel Hill, North Carolina: University of North Carolina Institute of Nutrition.

―――――. 1983. *Export Crop Production and Malnutrition*. Occasional Paper Series. Vol. 2, No. 10. Chapel Hill, North Carolina: University of North Carolina.

Pinstrup-Andersen, Per, and David Franklin. 1977. A Systems Approach to Agricultural Research Allocation in Developing Countries. In Thomas M. Arndt, Dana G. Dalrymple, and Vernon W. Ruttan, eds. *Resource Allocation and Productivity in National and International Agricultural Research*. Minneapolis, Minnesota: University of Minnesota Press.

Pinstrup-Andersen, Per, and Thongjit Uy. 1985. Seasonal Fluctuations in Food Consumption and Incomes in Northern Nigeria. Washington, D.C.: IFPRI. Processed.

Pinstrup-Andersen, Per, Norha Ruíz de Londono, and Edward Hoover. 1976. The Impact of Increasing Food Supply on Human Nutrition: Implications for Commodity Priorities in Agricultural Research and Policy. *American Journal of Agricultural Economics*. 58(2):131–42.

Plucknett, D. L. 1980. An Overview of Farming Systems Research. Paper presented at USAID-USDA-sponsored workshop on Farming Systems Research. December 8–10. Washington, D.C.

Popkin, B. M. 1980. Time Allocation of the Mother and Child Nutrition. *Ecology of Food and Nutrition*. 9(1):1–13.

―――――. 1981. Community-Level Considerations in Nutrition Planning in Low Income Nations. *Ecology of Food and Nutrition*. 10(4):227–36.

―――――. 1983. Rural Women, Work, and Child Welfare in the Philippines. In Mayra Buvinic, Margaret A. Lycette, and William Paul McGreevey, eds. *Women and Poverty in the Third World*. Baltimore, Maryland: Johns Hopkins University Press.

Popkin, B. M., and F. S. Solon. 1976. Income, Time and Working Mother and Child Nutriture. *Journal of Tropical Pediatrics and Environmental Child Health*. 22(4):156–66.

Poskitt, E. M. E. 1972. Seasonal Variation in Infection and Malnutrition at a Rural Paediatric Clinic in Uganda. *Transactions of the Royal Society of Tropical Medicine and Hygiene*. 66(6):931–36.

Prahladachar, M. 1983. Income Distribution Effects of the Green Revolution in India: A Review of the Empirical Evidence. *World Development*. 11(11):927–44.

Prebisch, Raul. 1971. *Change and Development—Latin America's Great Tasks*. Berkeley, California: University of California Press.

Prentice, A. M. 1983. Adaptation to Long-Term Low Energy Intake. In Ernesto Pollitt and Peggy Amante, eds. *Current Topics in Nutrition and Disease*. Vol. 11, *Energy Intake and Activity*. New York: Alan R. Liss, Inc. for UNU.

Prentice, A. M., R. G. Whitehead, S. B. Roberts, and A. A. Paul. 1981. Long-Term Energy Balance in Child-Bearing Gambian Women. *American Journal of Clinical Nutrition*. 34(12):2790–99.

Puffer, Ruth, and Carlos Serano. 1973. *Patterns of Mortality in Childhood*. Scientific Publication No. 262. Washington D.C.: Pan American Health Organization.

Quazi, Akef. 1978. Village Overspill. *Mazingira*. No. 6.

Rajagopalan S., B. Strassburger, R. B. Arumugam, and K. Roche. 1973. *The Tamil Nadu Nutrition Study*. Vol. 2, Section C. Haverford, Pennsylvania: Sidney M. Cantor Associates, Inc.

Ram, E. R., and V. M. Holkar. 1978. A Community Kitchen in the Kamanves Slum, India. *Assignment Children*. 43:47–56.

Randal, Jonathan C. 1984. Morocco's Unrest Has Its Roots in Economic Woes. *Washington Post*. January 27.

Rangarajan, C. 1982. *Agricultural Growth and Industrial Performance in India*. Research Report 33. Washington, D.C.: IFPRI.

Rao, D. H., and N. A. Nadamuni Naidu. 1977. Nutritional Supplementation—Whom Does It Benefit Most? *American Journal of Clinical Nutrition*. 30:1612–16.

Rao, D. H., K. Setyanarayana, K. Vijayaraghawau, J. G. Sastry, N. A. Nadamuni Naidu, and M. C. Swaminathan. 1975. Evaluation of the Special Nutrition Programme in the Tribal Areas of Andhra Pradesh. *Indian Journal of Medical Research*. 63(5):652–60.

Ravallion, Martin. 1983. *Method with Less Madness: Modeling Market Integration in Agriculture*. Oxford, England: Queen Elizabeth House, Oxford University.

Rawnsley, J. 1969. *Ghana Crop Storage*. PL:SG/GHA7. Rome: FAO.

Reddy, V., M. Mohanram, and N. Raghuramulu. 1979. Serum Retinol-Binding Protein and Vitamin A Levels in Malnourished Children. *Acta Paediatrica Scandinavica.* 68:65–69.

Reich, Michael R., Yasuo Endo, and C. Peter Timmer. 1986. *The Political Economy of Structural Change: Conflict Between Japanese and United States Agricultural Policy.* Boston, Massachusetts: Harvard Business School.

Research Group. 1982. *Research on the Physical Characteristics, Fitness and Vital Indicators of Chinese Children and Young Adults.* Beijing: Science and Technical Paper Publishing House.

Reutlinger, Shlomo, and Marcelo Selowsky. 1976. *Malnutrition and Poverty: Magnitude and Policy Options.* Baltimore, Maryland: Johns Hopkins University Press.

Riley, Harold M., and Michael T. Weber. 1979. *Marketing in Developing Countries.* Working Paper No. 6. Rural Development Series. East Lansing, Michigan: Michigan State University.

Riley, Harold M., Kelly Harrison, Nelson Suarez, James Shaffer, Donald Henley, Donald Larson, Colin Guthrie, and David Lloyd-Clare. 1970. *Market Coordination in the Development of the Cauca Valley Region, Colombia.* Research Report No. 5. East Lansing, Michigan: Michigan State University Latin American Studies Center.

Ritchie, Gary A., ed. 1979. *New Agricultural Crops.* Boulder, Colorado: Westview Press for the American Association for the Advancement of Science.

Robert Nathan Associates, Inc. 1978. *An Evaluation of the PL 480 Title II Program in Sri Lanka.* Washington, D.C.

———. 1979. *An Evaluation of PL 480 Title II in Morocco.* Washington, D.C.

Rody, Nancy. 1978. Things Go Better with Coconuts: Program Strategies in Micronesia. *Journal of Nutrition Education.* 10(1):19–22.

Rogers, Everett M. 1969. Motivations, Values, and Attitudes of Subsistence Farmers: Toward a Subculture of Peasantry. In Clifton R. Wharton, Jr., ed. *Subsistence Agriculture and Economic Development.* Chicago, Illinois: Aldine Publishing Co.

Rohde, Jon E. 1978. Preparing for the Next Round: Convalescent Care After Acute Infection. *American Journal of Clinical Nutrition.* 31(12):2258–68.

Rohde, Jon E., Richard A. Cash, Richard L. Guerrant, Dilip Mahalanabis, A. M. Molla, and Aree Valyasevi. 1983. Therapeutic Interventions in Diarrhea. In Lincoln C. Chen and Nevin S. Scrimshaw, eds. *Diarrhea and Malnutrition: Interactions, Mechanisms, and Interventions.* New York: Plenum Press.

Rosenberry, Paul, Russell Knutson, and Lacy Harmon. 1980. Predicting the Effects of Soil Depletion from Erosion. *Journal of Soil and Water Conservation.* 35(3):131–34.

Rosenzweig, M., and T. Schultz. 1980. *Market Opportunity, Genetic Endowments and the Intrafamily Distribution of Resources: Child Survival in Rural India.* Center Discussion Paper No. 347. New Haven, Connecticut: Yale University Economic Growth Center.

Ruddle, Kenneth, Dennis Johnson, Patricia K. Townsend, and John D. Rees. 1978. *Palm Sago: A Tropical Starch from Marginal Lands.* Honolulu, Hawaii: University of Hawaii Press for the East-West Center.

Rupert, James. 1984. Tunisians Riot Over Bread Price. *Washington Post.* January 4.

Rutishauser, Ingrid H. E., and R. G. Whitehead. 1972. Energy Intake and Expenditure in 1–3 Year Old Ugandan Children Living in a Rural Environment. *British Journal of Nutrition.* 28(1):145–52.

Ruttan, Vernon W. 1975. Integrated Rural Development Programs: A Skeptical Perspective. *International Development Review.* 17(4):9–16.

————. 1977. The Green Revolution: Seven Generalizations. *International Development Review.* 19(4):16–23.

Ryan, J. G. 1977. Human Nutritional Needs and Crop Breeding Objectives in the Indian Semi-Arid Tropics. *Indian Journal of Agricultural Economics.* 32(3):78–87.

Saarinen, U. M., and M. A. Siimes. 1977. Developmental Changes in Serum Iron, Total Iron Binding Capacity and Transferrin Saturation in Infancy. *Journal of Pediatrics.* 91(6):875–77.

Sahn, David. Forthcoming. The Effect of Price and Income Changes on Food Energy Intake in Sri Lanka. *Economic Development and Cultural Change.*

Sahni, S., and Ranjit K. Chandra. 1983. Malnutrition and Susceptibility to Diarrhea, with Special Reference to the Antiinfective Properties of Breast Milk. In Lincoln C. Chen and Nevin S. Scrimshaw, eds. *Diarrhea and Malnutrition: Interactions, Mechanisms, and Interventions.* New York: Plenum Press.

Sahota, Gian S. 1968. Efficiency of Resource Allocation in Indian Agriculture. *American Journal of Agricultural Economics.* 50(3):584–605.

Sanchez, P. A., and S. W. Buol. 1975. Soils of the Tropics and the World Food Crisis. *Science.* 188(4188):598–603.

Sanders, Thomas G. 1980. *PAN: A Description of the Colombian Nutrition Program.* Washington, D.C.: USAID.

Sarma, J. S. 1986. *Analysis of Cereals Feed in the Third World, Past Trends and Projections to 1990 and 2000.* Washington, D.C.: IFPRI.

Sarris, A. 1983. *Food Security and Agricultural Production Strategies Under Risk in Egypt.* Berkeley, California: University of California Department of Agricultural and Resource Economics.

Savane, Marie Angelique. 1981. Implications for Women and Their Work of Introducing Nutritional Considerations into Agricultural and Rural Development Projects. *Food and Nutrition Bulletin.* 3(3):1–5.

Scandizzo, Pasquale L., and Odin K. Knudsen. 1980. The Evaluation of the Benefits of Basic Need Policies. *American Journal of Agricultural Economics.* 62(1):46–57.

Schmidt, Guntur. 1979. *Maize and Beans in Kenya: The Interaction and Effectiveness of the Informal and Formal Systems.* Occasional Paper No. 31. Nairobi, Kenya: University of Nairobi Institute for Development Studies.

Schofield, Sue M. 1974. Seasonal Factors Affecting Nutrition in Different Age Groups and Especially Pre-School Children. *Journal of Development Studies.* 11(1):22–40.

————. 1979. *Development and the Problems of Village Nutrition.* London: Croom Helm.

Schran, Peter. 1969. *The Development of Chinese Agriculture, 1950–1959.* Ithaca, New York: Cornell University Press.

Schuh, G. Edward. 1981. Food Aid and Human Capital Formation. In Gordon O. Nelson, C. Peter Timmer, Matthew Guerreiro, G. Edward Schuh, and Patricia Alailima, eds. *Food Aid and Development.* New York: Agricultural Development Council.

Schulten, G. G. M. 1975. Losses in Stored Maize in Malawi and Work Undertaken to Prevent Them. *Bulletin of the European and Mediterranean Plant Protection Organization.* 5(2):113–20.

Schultz, Theodore W. 1960. Value of U.S. Farm Surpluses to Underdeveloped Countries. *Journal of Farm Economics.* 42(5):1019–30.

————. 1964. *Transforming Traditional Agriculture.* New Haven, Connecticut: Yale University Press.

Schultz, Theodore W., ed. 1978. *Distortions of Agricultural Incentives.* Bloomington, Indiana: Indiana University Press.

Schumpeter, Joseph. 1950. *Capitalism, Socialism and Democracy.* New York: Harper and Row.

Scobie, Grant M. 1979. *Investment in International Agricultural Research: Some Economic Dimensions.* World Bank Staff Working Paper No. 361. Washington, D.C.

Scobie, Grant M., and R. Posada. 1978. The Impact of Technical Change on Income Distribution: The Case of Rice in Colombia. *American Journal of Agricultural Economics.* 60(1):85–92.

Scott, Gloria L. 1979. *Recognizing the "Invisible" Woman in Development: The World Bank's Experience.* Washington, D.C.: World Bank.

Scrimshaw, Nevin S., John E. Gordon, John J. Kevany, Marina Flores, and Susana J. Iscaza. 1967. Nutrition and Infection Field Study in Guatemalan Villages, 1959–1964. 3. Field Procedure, Collection of Data and Methods of Measurement. *Archives of Environmental Health.* 15:6–15.

Scrimshaw, Nevin S., Miguel A. Guzman, and John E. Gordon. 1967.

Nutrition and Infection Field Study in Guatemalan Villages, 1959–1964. 1. Study Plan and Experimental Design. *Archives of Environmental Health.* 14:657–62.

Scrimshaw, Nevin S., Miguel A. Guzman, John J. Kevany, Werner Ascoli, Hans Bruch, and John E. Gordon. 1967. Nutrition and Infection Field Study in Guatemalan Villages, 1959–1964. 2. Field Reconnaissance, Administrative and Technical; Study Area; Population Characteristics; and Organization for Field Activities. *Archives of Environmental Health.* 14:787–801.

Scrimshaw, Nevin S., Miguel A. Guzman, Marina Flores, and John E. Gordon. 1968. Nutrition and Infection Field Study in Guatemalan Villages, 1959–1964. 5. Disease Incidence Among Preschool Children under Natural Village Conditions, with Improved Diet and with Medical and Public Health Services. *Archives of Environmental Health.* 16:223–34.

Scrimshaw, Nevin S., C. E. Taylor, and John E. Gordon. 1968. *Interactions of Nutrition and Infection.* Geneva: WHO.

Scrimshaw, Nevin S., Moises Behar, Miguel A. Guzman, and John E. Gordon. 1969. Nutrition and Infection Field Study in Guatemalan Villages, 1959–1964. 9. An Evaluation of Medical, Social, and Public Health Benefits, with Suggestions for Future Field Study. *Archives of Environmental Health.* 18:51–62.

Senghaas, Dieter. 1983. Abkoppelung als entwicklungspolitische Devise. *Ueberblick.* March:24–26.

Seoane, Nicole, and Michael C. Latham. 1971. Nutritional Anthropometry in the Identification of Malnutrition in Childhood. *Journal of Tropical Pediatrics and Environmental Child Health.* 17(3):98–104.

Seshamani, Lalitha. 1980. Food Consumption and Nutritional Adequacy in Iringa: A Case Study of Four Villages. Paper presented at the University of Dar es Salaam, Tanzania.

Shah, Mahendra M., and F. Willekens. 1978. *Rural-Urban Population Projections for Kenya and Implications for Development.* Laxenburg, Austria: International Institute for Applied Systems Analysis.

Shah, P. M. *The Kasa MCHN (Integrated Mother-Child-Health-Nutrition Model) Project.* Second Progress Report. 1976. Government of India, Government of Maharashtra, and CARE. Maharashtra, India: CARE.

————. *The Kasa MCHN (Integrated Mother-Child-Health-Nutrition Model) Project.* Third Progress Report. 1977. Government of India, Government of Maharashtra, and CARE. Maharashtra, India: CARE.

Shaner, W. W., P. F. Philipp, and W. R. Schemehl. 1982. *Readings in Farming Systems Research and Development.* Boulder, Colorado: Westview Press.

Shemilt, L. W., ed. 1983. *Chemistry and World Food Supplies: The New Frontiers. Chemrawn 2.* Willowdale, Ontario: Pergamon Press Canada.

Singh, Inderjit J. 1983. The Landless Poor in South Asia. In Allen Maunder and Kazushi Ohkawa, eds. *Growth and Equity in Agricultural Development.* Aldershot, England: Gower Publishing Company.

Smith, Carol. 1975. Examining Stratification Systems Through Peasant Marketing Arrangements: An Application of Some Models from Economic Geography. *Man.* 10:95–122.

Smith, Carol, ed. 1976. *Regional Analysis.* New York: Academic Press.

Smith, K. R. 1983. Presentation given in Concurrent Session, Frontiers of Food Fuel Policy and Programming, at the Conference on Women in Development: A Decade of Experience. October 13–15. Washington, D.C.

Smith, M. 1984. Nutrition and FSR/E (Farming Systems Research/Extension). In Cornelia Butler Flora, ed. *Proceedings of Kansas State University's 1983 Farming Systems Research Symposium: The Role of Animals in the Farming System.* Farming Systems Research Paper 6. Manhattan, Kansas: Kansas State University.

Smith, Thomas C. 1959. *The Agrarian Origins of Modern Japan.* Stanford, California: Stanford University Press.

Snaydon, R. W., and J. Elston. 1976. Flows, Cycles, and Yields in Agricultural Ecosystems. In A. N. Duckham, J. G. W. Jones, and E. H. Roberts, eds. *Food Production and Consumption: The Efficiency of Human Food Chains and Nutrient Cycles.* Amsterdam: North Holland.

Solon, Florentino S. 1978. Nutrition and Government Policy in the Philippines. In Beverly Winikoff, ed. *Nutrition and National Policy.* Cambridge, Massachusetts: Massachusetts Institute of Technology Press.

Solon, Florentino S., T. L. Fernandez, Michael C. Latham, and B. M. Popkin. 1979. An Evaluation of Strategies to Control Vitamin A Deficiency in the Philippines. *American Journal of Clinical Nutrition.* 32(7):1445–53.

Sommer, A. 1981. *Nutritional Blindness: Xerophthalmia and Keratomalacia.* Oxford, England: Oxford University Press.

Sommer, A., and M. S. Loewenstein. 1975. Nutritional Status and Mortality: A Prospective Validation of the QUAC Stick. *American Journal of Clinical Nutrition.* 28(3):287–92.

Spencer, D. 1976. *African Women in Agricultural Development: A Case Study in Sierra Leone.* East Lansing, Michigan: Michigan State University Department of Agricultural Economics.

Squire, Lyn, and Herman G. van der Tak. 1975. *Economic Analysis of Projects.* Baltimore, Maryland: Johns Hopkins University Press.

Stanbury, J. B., and A. Querido. 1983. Policy and Planning for Endemic Goitre Control. In Donald S. McLaren, ed. *Nutrition in the Community.* Chichester, England: John Wiley & Co., Ltd.

State Statistical Bureau. 1981. *Statistical Yearbook of China: 1981.* Hong Kong: Economic Information and Agency.

———. 1983. *Statistical Yearbook of China: 1983.* Hong Kong: Economic Information and Agency.

———. 1984. *Statistical Yearbook of China: 1984.* Hong Kong: Economic Information and Agency.

Stephenson, Lani S., D. W. T. Crompton, Michael C. Latham, T. W. J. Schulpen, M. C. Nesheim, and A. A. Jansen, 1980. Relationships Between *Ascaris* Infection and Growth of Preschool Children in Kenya. *American Journal of Clinical Nutrition.* 33(5):1165–72.

Stephenson, Lani S., Michael C. Latham, and A. Jansen. 1983. *A Comparison of Growth Standards: Similarities between the National Center for Health Statistics, Harvard, Denver and Privileged African Children and Differences with Kenyan Rural Children.* Cornell International Monograph Series No. 12. Ithaca, New York: Cornell University Program in International Nutrition.

Stephenson, Lani S., Michael C. Latham, Stephen N. Kinoti, and Martin L. Oduori. 1985. Regression of Splenomegaly and Hepatomegaly in Children Treated for *Schistosoma haematobium* Infection. *American Journal of Tropical Medicine and Hygiene.* 34(1):119–23.

Stetler, Harrison C., Frederick L. Trowbridge, and Alan Y. Huong. 1981. Anthropometric Nutrition Status and Diarrhea Prevalence in Children in El Salvador. *American Journal of Tropical Medicine and Hygiene.* 30(4):888–93.

Stevens, Christopher. 1979. *Food Aid and the Developing World.* New York: St. Martin's Press.

Stevenson, Paul. 1925. Collected Anthropometric Data on the Chinese. *Chinese Medical Journal.* 39:855–98.

Stoler, Ann. 1977. Class Structure and Female Autonomy. In Wellesley Editorial Committee, eds. *Women and National Development: The Complexities of Change.* Chicago, Illinois: University of Chicago Press.

Stone, Bruce. n.d. Unpublished data. IFPRI, Washington, D.C.

Strauss, J. 1983. Determinants of Food Consumption in Rural Sierra Leone. *Journal of Development Economics.* 11:327–54.

Sukhatme, P. V. 1972. Protein Strategy and Agricultural Development. *Indian Journal of Agricultural Economics.* 27(1):1–24.

Surls, Frederick. 1982. Foreign Trade and China's Agriculture. In Randolph Barker and Radha Sinha, eds. *The Chinese Agricultural Economy.* Boulder, Colorado: Westview Press.

Sverberg, Peter. 1979. The Price Disincentive of Food Aid Revisited: A Comment. *Economic Development and Cultural Change.* 27(3):549–52.

Swaminathan, M. C., D. H. Rao, R. V. Rao, M. V. V. L. Narasimhan, and N. S. Dumo. 1970. An Evaluation of the Supplementary Feeding Programme for Pre-School Children in the Rural Areas Around Hyderabad City. *Indian Journal of Nutrition and Dietetics.* 7(5):342–50.

Taiwan. Council for Agricultural Planning and Development. 1981. *Taiwan Food Balance Sheet, 1935–1980.* Taipei.

Tang, Anthony M., and Bruce Stone. 1980. *Food Production in the People's Republic of China.* Research Report No. 15. Washington, D.C.: IFPRI.

Tanner, J. M. 1978. *Focus into Man: Physical Growth from Conception to Maturity.* London: Open Books Publishing Ltd.

Taylor, Carl E., Arnfried A. Kielmann, and Cecile De Sweemer. 1979. Nutrition and Infection. In Miloslav Rechcigl, Jr., ed. *Nutrition and the World Food Problem.* New York: S. Karger.

Timmer, C. Peter. 1972. Employment Aspects of Investments in Rice Marketing in Indonesia. *Food Research Institute Studies.* 11(1):59–88.

————. 1983. *The Scope and Limits of Agricultural Price Policy.* Washington, D.C.: World Bank.

————. 1984. Corn Marketing and the Balance between Domestic Production and Consumption. In *Stanford-BULOG Corn Project. The Corn Economy in Indonesia.* Stanford, California: Stanford University.

Timmer, C. Peter, and Harold Alderman. 1979. Estimating Consumption Parameters for Food Policy Analysis. *American Journal of Agricultural Economics.* 61(5):982–87.

Timmer, Peter, and Matthew Guerreiro. 1981. Food Aid and Development Policy. In Gordon O. Nelson, C. Peter Timmer, Matthew Guerreiro, G. Edward Schuh, and Patricia Alailima, eds. *Food Aid and Development.* New York: Agricultural Development Council.

Timmer, C. Peter, Walter P. Falcon, and Scott R. Pearson. 1983. *Food Policy Analysis.* Baltimore, Maryland: Johns Hopkins University Press.

Tinker, Irene. 1976. Development and the Disintegration of the Family. *Assignment Children.* 6:29–37.

————. 1979a. *New Technologies for Food Chain Activities: The Imperative of Equity for Women.* Office of Women in Development. Washington, D.C.: USAID.

————. 1979b. *Women and Development.* Washington, D.C.: American Association for the Advancement of Science.

Tinker, Irene, and Michelle Bo-Bramsen, eds. 1976. *Women and World Development.* Washington, D.C.: ODC.

Tobisson, E. 1980. *Women, Work, Food, and Nutrition in Nyamwigura Village, Mara Region Tanzania.* Report No. 548. Dar es Salaam: Tanzania Food and Nutrition Centre.

Tolley, George, Vinod Thomas, and Chung Ming Wong. 1982. *Agricultural Price Policies and the Developing Countries.* Baltimore, Maryland: Johns Hopkins University Press.

Tollison, Robert D. 1982. Rent Seeking: A Survey. *Kyklos.* 35(4):575–602.

Tomkins, A. 1979. Folate Malnutrition in Tropical Diarrhoeas. *Transactions of the Royal Society of Tropical Medicine and Hygiene.* 73(5):498–502.

————. 1981. Nutritional Status and Severity of Diarrhoea Among Pre-School Children in Rural Nigeria. *Lancet.* 1(8225):860–62.

Toqero, Z. 1977. Assessing Quantitative Losses in Rice Post-Production Systems. In FAO, Government of Malaysia, and Food for the Hungry, Inc. *Report of the Action-Oriented Field Workshop for Prevention of Post-Harvest Rice Losses.* March 12–30. Kedah, Malaysia. Bangkok: FAO.

Torun, Benjamin. 1983. Environmental and Educational Interventions Against Diarrhea in Guatemala. In Lincoln C. Chen and Nevin S. Scrimshaw, eds. *Diarrhea and Malnutrition: Interactions, Mechanisms, and Intervention.* New York: Plenum Press.

Trairatvorakul, Prasarn. 1984. *The Effects on Income Distribution and Nutrition of Alternative Rice Price Policies in Thailand.* Research Report No. 46. Washington, D.C.: IFPRI.

Tripp, Robert. 1982. *Cash Cropping, Nutrition and Choice of Technology in Rural Development.* Mexico: CIMMYT.

Troll, C. 1966. *Seasonal Climates of the Earth: World Maps of Climatology.* Berlin: Springer-Verlag.

Tropical Products Institute. 1977. *The Reduction of Losses During Farmer Storage of Cereal and Legume Grains in Commonwealth Africa.* London.

Trowbridge, Frederick L., and Ladene H. Newton. 1979. Seasonal Changes in Malnutrition and Diarrheal Disease Among Preschool Children in El Salvador. *American Journal of Tropical Medicine and Hygiene.* 28(1)136–41.

Tsujii, Hikaru. 1982. Comparison of Rice Policies Between Thailand, Taiwan, and Japan: An Evolutionary Model and Current Policies. In *A Comparative Study of Food Policy in Rice Countries—Taiwan, Thailand, and Japan.* Kyoto: Kyoto University Press.

Tuan, Francis C., and Frederick W. Crook. 1983. *Planning and Statistical Systems in China's Agriculture.* USDA Economic Research Service Foreign Agriculture Economic Report No. 181. Washington, D.C.: Government Printing Office.

Tyagi, A. K., and G. K. Girish. 1975. Studies on the Assessment of Storage Losses of Food Grains by Insects. *Bulletin of Grain Technology.* 13(2):84–102.

UNDP. 1980. *Action Oriented Assessment of Rural Women's Participation in*

Development. Evaluation Study No. 3. New York.

UNDP and FAO. 1984. *National Agricultural Research: Report of an Evaluation Study in Selected Countries.* Rome: FAO.

UNECA Women's Programme. 1975. *Women of Africa: Today and Tomorrow.* Addis Ababa: United Nations.

United Nations. Various. *Monthly Statistical Bulletin.* New York.

United Nations, Department of Economic and Social Affairs. 1979. *World Population Trends and Prospects by Country, 1950–2000: Summary Report of the 1978 Assessment.* New York.

United Nations, ECLAC. 1976. *El Medio Ambiente en América Latina.* Santiago.

Unnevehr, J. L., and M. L. Standford. 1983. Technology and the Demand for Women's Labor and Management Skills in Asian Rice Farming. Paper presented at Conference on Women in Rice Farming Systems. September 26–30. Los Baños, Philippines: IRRI.

UNU. 1981. The Uses of Energy and Protein Requirement Estimates. Report of a Workshop. *Food and Nutrition Bulletin.* 3:45–53.

Urban, Francis, and Thomas Vollrath. 1984. *Patterns and Trends in World Agricultural Land Use.* Washington, D.C.: Government Printing Office.

USDA. 1980. *The World Agricultural Situation.* WAS–21. Economics, Statistics, and Cooperatives Services. Washington, D.C.

————. 1983a. *Agricultural Statistics 1983.* Washington, D.C.: Government Printing Office.

————. 1983b. *Latin America, World Agriculture Regional Supplement, Review of 1982 and Outlook for 1983.* Economic Research Service. Washington, D.C.

————. 1983c. *Foreign Agriculture Circular: Grains.* Foreign Agriculture Service. FG-23-83. August. Washington, D.C.

————. 1983d. *Foreign Agriculture Circular: Grains.* Foreign Agriculture Service. October. Washington, D.C.

————. 1984a. *Inputs Outlook and Situation Report.* Economic Research Service. Washington, D.C.

————. 1984b. *USSR Outlook and Situation Report.* Economic Research Service. Washington, D.C.: Government Printing Office.

————. 1984c. World Indices of Agricultural and Food Production, 1950–83. Economic Research Service. Unpublished printout. Washington D.C.

————. 1984d. *Foreign Agriculture Circular: Grains.* Foreign Agriculture Service. FG-8-84. May. Washington, D.C.

————. 1984e. *Foreign Agriculture Circular: Grains.* Foreign Agriculture Service. November. Washington, D.C.

U.S. Department of Commerce, Bureau of the Census. 1984. 1982 Census of Agriculture. Unpublished data. Washington, D.C.

Valdés, Alberto, ed. 1981. *Food Security for Developing Countries.* Boulder, Colorado: Westview Press.

Vandevenne, R. 1978. Note on Crop Loss after Harvesting in the Ivory Coast. Paper presented to the Seminar on Post-Harvest Grain Losses, Tropical Products Institute. March 13–17. London.

van Steenbergen, Wil M., Jane A. Kusin, and Maria M. van Rens. 1981. Lactation Performance of Akamba Mothers, Kenya: Breast Feeding Behaviour, Breast Milk Yield and Composition. *Journal of Tropical Pediatrics.* 27(3):155–61.

Vargas, G. W. 1976. Programas de Nutrición Aplicada en Zonas Rurales de Costa Rica. *Assignment Children.* 35:80–90.

Venkataswamy, G., and S. A. Kabir. 1975. *Report on Nutrition Rehabilitation Centres and Village Child Care Centers with Evaluations.* Mandurai, India: Government Erskin Hospital.

Vincent, W. 1982. Small Farm Characteristics, Problems, and Programs in the Third World. In W. J. Sheppard, ed. *Proceedings of Kansas State University's 1981 Farming Systems Research Symposium: Small Farms in a Changing World: Prospects for the Eighties.* Farming Systems Research Paper No. 2. Manhattan, Kansas: Kansas State University.

Visaria, P. 1980. *Poverty and Living Standards in Asia.* Living Standards Measurement Study. Working Paper No. 2. Washington, D.C.: World Bank.

Viteri, Fernando E., and Benjamin Torun. 1981. Nutrition, Physical Activity and Growth. In Martin Ritzén, Kirstin Hall, Anders Zetterberg, Anita Aperia, Agne Larsson, and Rolf Zetterstrom, eds. *The Biology of Normal Human Growth: Transactions of the First Karolinska Institute Nobel Conference.* New York: Raven Press.

von Braun, Joachim, and Hartwig de Haen. 1982. *Impact of Food Price and Subsidy Policies on the Agricultural Sector: Egypt.* Washington, D.C.: Ministry of Agriculture of Egypt, USDA, and USAID.

————. 1983. *The Effects of Food Price and Subsidy Policies on Egyptian Agriculture.* Research Report No. 42. Washington, D.C.: IFPRI.

Walker, Kenneth. 1984. *Food Grain Procurement and Consumption in China.* Cambridge, England: Cambridge University Press.

Wallerstein, Mitchel. 1980. *Food for War, Food for Peace: United States Food Aid in a Global Context.* Cambridge, Massachusetts: Massachusetts Institute of Technology Press.

Ware, Helen. 1984. Effects of Maternal Education, Women's Roles, and Child Care on Child Mortality. In W. Henry Mosley and Lincoln C. Chen, eds. *Child Survival: Strategies for Research. Population and Development Review.* 10 Supplement:191–214.

Warley, Thorald K. 1976. Agriculture in International Economic Relations. *American Journal of Agricultural Economics.* 58(5):820–30.

Waterlow, J. C. 1972. Classification and Definition of Protein-Energy Malnutrition. *British Medical Journal.* 3(5826):566–68.

Waterlow, J. C., and P. R. Payne. 1975. The Protein Gap. *Nature.* 258(5531):113–17.

Waterlow, J. C., and A. M. Thompson. 1979. Observations on the Adequacy of Breast-Feeding. *Lancet.* 2(8136):238–42.

Waugh, R. K. 1982. A Compendium of Notes on Farm Focused Research and Extension. Course Agg 4932. Gainesville, Florida: University of Florida Institute of Food and Agricultural Sciences International Programs.

Welsch, Delane E. 1965. Response to Economic Incentive by Abakaliki Rice Farmers in Eastern Nigeria. *Journal of Farm Economics.* 47(4):900–14.

WFP. 1972. *Evaluation of Nutrition Education and Supplementary Feeding of Vulnerable Groups.* Project Colombia 549. Rome.

WFP/CFA. 1979. *Guidelines and Criteria for Food Aid.* Rome: CFA.

————. 1983. *Review of Food Aid.* Rome: CFA.

Whelan, W. P. 1982. Incorporating Nutritional Considerations into Farming Systems Research. In Cornelia Butler Flora, ed. *Proceedings of Kansas State University's 1982 Farming Systems Research Symposium: Farming Systems in the Field.* Farming Systems Research Paper No. 5. Manhattan, Kansas: Kansas State University.

White, Benjamin. 1975. The Economic Importance of Children in a Javanese Village. In M. Nag, ed. *Population and Social Organization.* The Hague: Mouton Publishers.

————. 1983. Women and the Modernization of Rice Agriculture: Some General Issues and a Javanese Case Study. Paper presented at Conference on Women in Rice Farming Systems. September 23–30. Los Baños, Philippines: IRRI.

Whitehead, R. G. 1977. Protein and Energy Requirements of Young Children Living in the Developing Countries to Allow for Catch-Up Growth After Infections. *American Journal of Clinical Nutrition.* 30(9):1545–47.

Whitehead, R. G., ed. 1983. Maternal Diet, Breast Feeding Capacity and Lactational Infertility. *Food and Nutrition Bulletin.* Supplement No. 6. New York: UNU.

WHO. 1976. *Methodology of Nutritional Surveillance.* Technical Report Series No. 593. Report of a Joint FAO/UNICEF/WHO Expert Committee. Geneva: WHO.

————. 1979. *Collaborative Study on Breastfeeding: Methods and Main Results of the First Phase of the Study.* Preliminary Report. MCH/79.3. Geneva.

————. 1982. *Control of Vitamin A Deficiency and Xerophthalmia.* WHO Technical Report Series No. 672. Geneva.

Whyte, William F. 1975. *Organizing for Agricultural Development: Human Aspects in the Utilization of Science and Technology.* New Brunswick, New Jersey: Transaction Books.

Williams, Maurice J. 1982. *The African Food Problem and the Role of International Agencies. Report by the Executive Director.* Rome: WFC.

Williamson-Gray, Cheryl. 1982. *Food Consumption Parameters for Brazil and Their Application to Food Policy.* Research Report No. 32. Washington, D.C.: IFPRI.

Wittfogel, Karl. 1971. Communist and Non-Communist Agrarian Systems, with Special Reference to the U.S.S.R. and Communist China: A Comparative Approach. In W. A. Douglas Jackson, ed. *Agrarian Policies and Problems in Non-Communist Countries.* Seattle, Washington: University of Washington Press.

Wittman, W., A. D. Moodie, S. A. Fellingham, and J. D. Hansen. 1967. An Evaluation of the Relationship Between Nutritional Status and Infection by Means of a Field Study. *South African Medical Journal.* 41:664–82.

Wittwer, Sylvan H. 1979. Future Technological Advances in Agriculture and Their Impact on the Regulatory Environment. *BioScience.* 29(10):603–10.

Wong, John. 1973. *Land Reform in the People's Republic of China.* New York: Praeger Publishers.

Wong, John, ed. 1979. *Group Farming in Asia: Experiences and Potentials.* Singapore: Singapore University Press.

World Bank. 1978. *World Development Report 1978.* New York: Oxford University Press.

————. 1979. *World Bank Atlas.* Washington, D.C.

————. 1980. *World Development Report 1980.* New York: Oxford University Press.

————. 1981. *Accelerated Development in Sub-Saharan Africa. An Agenda for Action.* Washington, D.C.

————. 1982. *World Development Report 1982.* New York: Oxford University Press.

————. 1983a. *China: Socialist Economic Development.* Washington, D.C.

————. 1983b. *World Development Report 1983.* New York: Oxford University Press.

————. 1984a. *Toward Sustained Development in Sub-Saharan Africa: A Joint Program of Action.* Washington, D.C.

————. 1984b. *World Development Report 1984.* New York: Oxford University Press.

Wray, J. D. 1978. Direct Nutrition Intervention and the Control of Diarrheal Diseases in Preschool Children. *American Journal of Clinical Nutrition.* 31(11):2073–82.

Wray, J. D., and A. Aguirre. 1969. Protein-Calorie Malnutrition in Candelaria, Colombia. 1. Prevalence; Social and Demographic Causal Factors. *Journal of Tropical Pediatrics.* 15:76–98.

Youssef, Nadia, and Carol Hetler. 1983. *Rural Households Headed by Women.* Geneva: ILO.

Zandstra, H. G. 1980. Methods to Identify and Evaluate Improved Cropping Systems. In Hans Ruthenberg, ed. *Farming Systems in the Tropics.* 3rd ed. Oxford, England: Clarendon Press.

Zeitlin, Marian F., and Candelaria S. Formacion. 1981. Study 2: Nutrition Education. In James E. Austin, Marian F. Zeitlin, USAID Office of Nutrition, and Harvard Institute for International Development. *Nutrition Intervention in Developing Countries.* 5 vols. Cambridge, Massachusetts: Oelgeschlager, Gunn and Hain, Inc.

Index

Adelman, I., 490

Africa, 56, 57, 62, 100, 104, 167, 183, 190, 203, 206, 220, 228, 229, 248, 256, 280, 443; access to food in, 387; agricultural development in, 491–96; agricultural (food) policy in, 485–91, 497–507; aid and, 23, 486, 494, 498, 504, 506–07; buffer stocks and, 35, 504; cash crops versus food crops in, 500; credit in, 505; development strategy in, 490–91; employment in, 497, 502; exports of, 41, 45, 487, 489; food marketing system in, 65, 273, 500, 501–04, 507; food production in, 4, 9, 41, 46, 49, 74, 75, 89, 117, 168, 485, 504; food security in, 100–01, 493, 499; hunger in, 15, 17, 73, 486, 493; imports of, 485–86; input supplies and, 504–05; irrigation in, 29, 93; politics in, 495–96; population growth in, 485, 486; price policy and, 501–03, 507; prices and, 486–87, 489–90, 491; research in, 504–05; savings in, 55; sectoral development in, 492–93; subsidies in, 487, 506; vitamin A deficiency in, 337; women in food production in, 2, 7, 133, 137, 138, 139, 140, 176, 190, 191, 372, 507. *See also names of specific African countries*

Agricultural development: in Africa, 491–96; agricultural production structure and, 61–63; capital accumulation and, 58; dualistic (bimodal), 40; food policy and, 13; international financial system and, 78–81; international trade and, 24, 73, 81–87; nutritional surveillance and, 406–07; organizational requirements and, 63–66; rural development and, 60–61; self-sufficiency and, 74–78; social services and, 66–69

Agricultural production. *See* Production

Agricultural projects: food availability and prices and, 161–63; food price increases and, 159–60; income transfers and, 154–57; income variability and, 163–64; nutrition and, 153, 401; reduction in production for home consumption and, 157–59; trade and, 161–62, 163

Agricultural reform, 27; in China, 483–84. *See also* Land reform

Agriculture: in Africa, 485–96, 497–507; in China, 467–84; commercial, 132, 188–89, 191; farm family and, 122–24; international community and, 32–37; nutrition programs and, 449–51, 454; rainfed, 124–26. *See also* Green revolution; International food and agricultural system; *names of specific related subjects, such as* Farmers; Irrigation; Production

Ahmed, Raissuddin, 188–89, 288, 291

Aid, 71; African agricultural development and, 486, 494; cereal dependence and, 232; concessional food, 218–19, 224, 257–58; cost-effectiveness of, 237–39, 239–44, 244–45; decline in, 228–31; development and, 250–51, 251–52, 259; economic gains from, 254–55; effectiveness analysis and, 34–35; food security and, 213–14, 252, 258–59; forecasting need for, 232–33; human capital and, 257; imports and, 23, 249–50; income transfer potential and, 235; international community and, 33–34; legislation in U.S. and, 247; long-term contracts and, 255–57; prices and, 239–42; principles of, 246–48, 249–51; reasons for providing, 234; research and, 258; transportation and, 241, 254; trends in food production and, 49–50; ways of using, 235–37

Anemia, 330, 339–42, 482

556

Argentina, 90, 96, 217, 263, 287, 343
Asia, 4, 16, 57, 61, 63, 107, 108, 112,
    114, 142, 167, 176, 191, 206, 241,
    280; food consumption and
    production in, 45, 46, 75; food trade
    and, 23; hunger in, 17; livestock in,
    47; savings in, 55; water and, 29. *See
    also names of specific Asian countries*
Ateng, Benson, 262
Atwater, Wilbur O., 346
Austin, James E., 443
Australia, 221, 228, 229, 247
Autarky. *See* Self-sufficiency

Balance of payments, 220, 254
Bangladesh, 27, 75, 181, 228, 247, 254,
    279, 291, 382; access to food in, 385,
    387, 388; fuel gathering in, 382;
    illness in, 360, 365, 369; jute versus
    rice production in, 189
Bates, Robert, 64
Beaton, George H., 235, 328, 329
Behnke, R., 175, 176
Benedict, F. G., 346
Berelson, Bernard, 67
Berg, Alan, 327, 443
Binswanger, Hans, 112
Biotechnology, 49, 50, 84
Birthrate, 66–67
Biswas, Margaret, 6
Black, Robert E., 369
Bolivia, 100, 343, 462, 464
Botswana, 372
Bourne, Malcolm C., 311
Brazil, 75, 83, 90, 91, 250, 343, 379,
    458, 459, 494; childcare in, 440, 441,
    442; food aid and, 228; food subsidies
    in, 209; grain exports of, 217; income
    and food and, 304; price change in,
    285
Breastfeeding: childcare and, 379;
    decline in, 371; food distribution
    programs and, 425; nutrition
    education and, 440
Brown, Lester R., 7, 13, 74
Buffer stocks (food reserves), 35–36,
    213, 216–17, 257; in Africa, 35, 504
Burma, 124
Byerlee, Derek, 63

Caldwell, John S., 104
Cameroon, 375, 376
Canada, 91–92, 94, 221, 228, 229, 246,
    247, 250

Capital, development and, 53, 55–57, 70
Capital flows and trade, 86
Capital markets, 79, 82
Capule, C., 107
Cash crops, 132; in Africa, 500;
    agricultural projects and, 157–59;
    area devoted to, 181–83, 183–84;
    competition between staple crops and,
    184–86, 191–94; defining, 179–81;
    effects of income from, 189–90; food
    versus livestock feed and, 186–87; as
    men's crops, 137; nutrition and, 7,
    187–91
Cash payments to households, 291–92
Cavallo, Domingo, 286
Central America, 90, 107, 322, 337, 372
Cereal grain losses (post-harvest),
    313–16
Cereal Import Facility, 36, 37, 50
Chandra, Ranjit K., 349, 365
Chavez, Adolfo, 349
Chen, Lincoln C., 349, 356
Childcare, 379–80, 440, 441, 442
Children: access to food and, 191,
    385–88, 390; China's nutrition
    planning and, 478–79, 480–81;
    energy metabolism and malnutrition
    and, 349–50; influences on mortality
    of, 279, 349, 424; malnutrition and
    illnesses of, 356, 357, 364, 370;
    measles and, 335; protein gap and,
    53; supplementary feeding programs
    and, 413–28; undernourishment and,
    18, 19–20; value of time analysis and,
    87–88; women and seasonal
    agricultural labor and, 136, 137, 140;
    working women and nutritional status
    of, 377–78
Chile, 100, 221, 322, 462, 463; food aid
    and, 224, 248
China, 23, 85, 89, 142, 203, 219, 221,
    273, 443, 444, 457, 490; agricultural
    trade of, 469, 472, 483; agricultural
    reform in, 483–84; commune system
    in, 62, 474, 477; cropland loss in, 90;
    disease in, 480, 482–83; development
    in, 467–69; food availability in,
    473–75; health problems in, 484;
    income level and distribution in, 467,
    475–78; irrigation in, 93; nutritional
    status in, 478–80, 480–82; production
    controls in, 469–73, 474–75, 477;
    reduction of malnutrition in, 467, 471,
    481, 482, 483; urban sector and food

China *(continued)*
  subsidy in, 469, 470
Clark, C., 378
Climate: drought and, 397; food loss and, 314–15, 323; rainfed farming and, 124–26
Collaborative Research Support Program on Nutrition and Function (USAID), 353
Colombia, 56, 189, 221, 343, 365, 403, 459, 461, 462, 494; food aid and, 224
Committee on Food Aid Policies and Programs (of WFP), 249
Commodity agreements, 73, 80
Commodity markets, instability in, 79
Community development, 168
Community kitchens, 380
Congo, 381
Consultative Group on International Agricultural Research (CGIAR), 36, 73, 84
Consumers: food subsidies to, 26–27; price policy and, 268; technological change and poor, 112–13
Consumption, 70, 115; agricultural projects and home, 157–59; cash crops and, 188, 189; China and mix of, 470–71, 475, 477, 484; elasticities and substitutabilities and, 145–46; feed, 217; food policy and, 3–4; food security and, 21; FSR&D and home, 165, 166; inadequate levels of, 18; trends in, 45–46, 50, 70; women's food production and family, 138
Costa Rica, 69, 461; nutritional surveillance in, 404, 408, 410, 411
Côte d'Ivoire, 58, 489, 490, 495
Credit, 29, 30, 132; Africa and, 505; FSR&D and, 173; small farmers and, 27
Credit clubs, 383
Cretinism, 332, 343
Cropland, stagnation of expansion of, 89–94. *See also* Secondary regions
Crops, 125, 176; FSR&D and, 166–67; growth of yields of, 46; harvest forecasting and, 217–18; irrigation and multicropping of, 106–07; secondary, 143–44; technology and, 95–96; women and minor, 133–35. *See also* Cash crops; High-yielding crops; Subsistence crops
Cuba, 107
Currency: exchange rates and, 80–81; food policy and, 13; overvalued, 83

de Janvry, Alain, 444
Delgado, Hernan, 349
Demand: for consumer goods (rural sector), 57, 59; food security and, 16, 21, 24; price policy and, 266; rural markets and, 307; supply and, 40, 46–49, 51–52, 119
Desertification, 91
Developing countries: food imports and, 216, 217, 219–22, 223, 224–28, 229–31; food security analysis and, 205–14; international community and, 32–37; long-term food problems and, 28–32; special measures for poor and hungry in, 26–28; trade among, 49; trade deficits and, 82. *See also names of specific countries*
Development, 49, 195, 328; African strategy for, 490–91; capital-intensive, 55–57, 58; China and, 467–69; domestic food production and, 59–60; dualistic, 40, 53, 56–57, 70; farm labor and, 54; food aid and, 250–51, 251–52, 259; food and labor-intensive, 57–59; food security and, 207–08; nutrition planning and, 465; nutrition programs and, 453–56. *See also* Agricultural development
Dey, P., 375
Diarrhea: as cause of malnutrition, 360–61, 369; in China, 480, 482; malnutrition research and, 356–60; malnutrition as risk factor for, 361, 365, 369; nutrition education and, 440; oral rehydration therapy and, 335, 336, 437
Disease: deficiency (in China), 480, 482–83; interactions between malnutrition and diarrhea and other, 20, 328, 329, 355, 356–60, 360–61, 365, 369, 370; nutrition and infectious, 332, 339. *See also* Anemia; Diarrhea; Goiter; Measles; Protein-energy malnutrition; Rickets; Schistosomiasis; Smallpox; Vitamin A deficiency; Xerophthalmia
Distribution, 7–8, 24, 349; food policy and, 3, 4, 5; intrahousehold food, 385–91
Dixon, R., 376
Dominican Republic, 322
Donaldson, Graham, 196
Donovan, Graeme, 104
Durnin, J. V. G. A., 351

Economic growth. *See* Development

Economy. *See* Macroeconomic policies

Ecuador, 101, 167, 322, 343, 439

Education: farming system in secondary regions and, 151; rural, 66; women and, 384. *See also* Nutrition education

Egypt, 181, 229, 267, 291, 354, 452; food aid and, 241–42, 248; food prices in, 289

Eicher, Carl K., 6

El Salvador, 360, 461

Elston, J., 143

Employment, 40, 70, 287; access to food and, 389–90, 392; Africa and, 497, 502; capital-intensive development and, 55, 56; entitlements and, 202, 203; farm family and, 122, 123; food demand and growth in, 47; off-farm, 27, 30; rural, 54, 57, 110; technology and, 112; urban (Africa), 497; women and, 371–72, 372–73, 376. *See also* Labor force

Energy (fuel): fertilizer production and, 102; fuel collection and, 373, 382–83; secondary regions and, 142

Energy metabolism: energy balance equation components and, 348; energy intake and expenditure balance concept and, 351–54; food intake and, 347–48; law of conservation of energy and, 346–47; malnourished children and, 349–50; physical activity and, 350–51

Entitlements, 195; employment, 202, 203; food supply and, 203–04; modes of production and exchange, 201–02; ownership and exchange, 200–01; ownership relations and, 198–99; social security and exchange, 202–03; starvation and, 202, 203–04

Equilibrium (supply-demand and price) models, 265–71

Ethiopia, 212

Europe, 17, 23, 25, 49, 77, 94, 217, 223, 228, 250, 301, 344; food aid and, 247, 253–54. *See also names of specific European countries*

European Community (EC), 25, 49, 217, 223, 250

Exchange rates, 78–79, 80–81, 83, 263

Exports, 30, 59, 80, 85, 256; Africa and, 41, 45, 487, 489, 500; cash crops and, 179, 184, 192; China's agricultural, 469, 472, 483; food prices and, 48;

sugar, 344; trends in, 23, 41, 45, 50, 226–27

Export tax, 83, 163

Extension services, 128; nutritional education and, 432; training and visit, 130–31

Fagley, R. M., 384

Fair-price (target food rationing) shops, 208, 255, 280

Falcon, Walter P., 6, 11, 12

Famine, 201; in Africa, 15, 73, 486, 493; as transitory food insecurity, 211–12. *See also* Hunger

Farm classification, 165–66

Farmers: in Africa, 492, 493–94, 495–96; direct measures for small, 27–28, 30; green revolution and poor, 110–12, 116; incentives and, 2; institutional economic environment and, 30; price and production changes and, 121–22; technological change and family of, 122–24; technology and small, 63; technology and women, 139–40

Farming systems research and development (FSR&D): application of, 169–72; farm types and, 165–69; issues in, 175–78; in Panama, 175–78

Fertility (human), 66–67

Fertilizer, 94, 96, 102, 125, 131, 300

Finance: food issue analysis and, 25; international food and agricultural system and, 78–81

Flora, Cornelia Butler, 172

Food, access to: children and, 385–88, 390; discrimination against females in, 385, 387, 388–89, 390; employment and, 389–90, 392; intrahousehold distribution and, 385–91; nutritional risk and, 391–92

Food and Agriculture Organization (FAO), 5

Food Aid Convention, 219, 247, 253

Food availability: agricultural projects and, 161–63; in China, 473–75

Food delivery systems (supplementary feeding programs), 413–15

Food distribution, 3, 4, 5, 7–8, 24, 349; intrahousehold, 385–91

Food intake (energy metabolism analysis), 347–48

Food losses (post-harvest): causes of, 311–12, 317, 324; cereal grains and,

Food losses *(continued)*
313–16; data sources for, 312–13;
determining, 309–11; fish and,
322–24; perishable staples and,
316–22; storage and, 312, 314, 317,
324
Food marketing systems. *See* Marketing
systems
Food policy: in Africa, 485–96,
497–507; agricultural development
and, 13; cash crops versus subsistence
crops and, 191–94; consumption and
supply and, 3–4; currency and, 13;
discipline orientation and, 4–5; food
aid and, 252–54, 257, 258–59;
hunger and poverty and, 11–12;
income distribution and, 13; instability
of international trade and, 24–25;
international community and, 32–37;
international coordinated food stocks
and, 12–13; long-term aspects of,
28–32; nutrition planning and, 444;
nutrition programs and, 452–53;
price policy and, 2, 280–81; price
theory and, 262; production and,
13–14, 261; scope of (micro and
macro), 1–2; secondary (marginal)
regions and, 141–52; special measures
for poor and hungry and, 26–28
Food preferences: in China, 471; fish
catch and, 323; income change and,
19, 120
Food, preparation of, 312, 373, 381–82
Food production. *See* Production
Food purchasing, by households,
304–08, 312
Food reserves. *See* Buffer stocks
Food security: Africa and, 100–01, 493,
499; chronic food insecurity and,
206–07, 207–13; data on grain supply
and, 215–16; defined, 205; economic
growth and, 207–08; food aid and,
213–14, 218–19, 252, 258–59; food
imports and, 216, 217, 219–22, 223;
food issues *(1974–84)* and, 20–22;
food price subsidies and, 209–10;
foreign exchange and, 219; futures
markets and, 218; global grain market
integration and, 218; grain prices and,
215; harvesting forecast and,
217–218; income transfers and,
208–09; interest rates and, 219;
national food supply policies and,

210–11; stockholding and, 213,
216–17; supply and competition and,
217; temporary food insecurity and,
205, 211–13; trends in, 99–101
Foreign exchange, 219, 300; China and,
469, 471
France, 94
Fuel collection, 373, 382–83
Futures markets, 218

Galbraith, John K., 68
Gambia, The, 352–53, 364, 375, 380,
430, 431, 489
General Agreement on Tariffs and
Trade (GATT), 73, 251
Genetic engineering, 49, 50
Germany, Federal Republic of, 94, 219,
249
Gershon, Jack, 176
Ghana, 191, 322, 380–81, 461, 487, 489
Ghassemi, Hossein, 235, 329
Gibb, Arthur, Jr., 114
Goiter, 330–32, 342–43, 440, 482–83
Gopalan, C., 334
Government intervention, 128; in
Africa, 495; marketing and, 308; price
policy and, 264, 271–74, 275, 276
Green, Arthur, 313, 316
Green revolution, 168; economic gains
and, 109–10; food production and,
106–07; landless labor and, 112; land
tenure and farm size and, 110–11;
poor consumers and, 112–13; poor
farmers and, 110–12, 116
Guatemala, 169, 172, 337, 342, 343,
356, 379, 388
Guyer, J., 190
Gwatkin, Davidson R., 67

Haggerty, P. A., 378
Haiti, 372
Harberger, Arnold C., 155
Harris, K. L., 310
Hart, R. D., 176
Harvest forecasting, 217–18
Hayami, Yujiro, 61
Hazell, Peter B. R., 58, 104
Health sector: nutritional surveillance
and, 407; nutrition programs and,
449–51, 454
Herdt, Robert W., 107
High-yielding crops: farm family welfare
and, 123; FSR&D and, 168; green

revolution and, 107; investment in research and, 28, 29; landownership and, 57; secondary regions and, 144; technology and, 60
Hildebrand, P. E., 176
Hitchings, Jon, 190
Ho, Teresa J., 356
Holmes, A. Stewart, 307
Home gardens, 128
Home preparation: of food, 312, 373, 381–82; of weaning foods, 437
Honduras, 430, 431, 461
Hookworm, 335–36
Hopkins, Raymond F., 197
Hornik, Robert C., 329
Huddleston, Barbara, 6, 196
Huffman, Sandra, 329
Human capital, 85–86, 196; food aid and, 257
Hunger: causes and incidence of, 17–20; developing countries and, 26–28; entitlements and, 202, 203–04; evolving perception of food issues and, 16–17; food policy and, 11–12; food security concept and, 20–22, 100; international economic environment and, 22–26; national policies and, 38. *See also* Famine

Idachaba, Francis S., 65
Imports, 58, 256; Africa and, 485–86; agricultural projects and, 161; cash crops and, 184, 187; China's food, 472; Cereal Import Facility and, 37, 50; developing countries and, 224–28, 229–31; food aid as substitute for commercial, 249–50; food security and food, 216, 217, 219–22, 223; international trade and, 23; supplementary feeding programs and food, 425; supply and demand and, 47, 210; trends in, 41–45, 46, 48, 49
Import substitution, 56, 82–83, 254
Incentives: effective price, 278; farmers and, 2; food prices and supply, 282; output and input prices and, 300; production, 22, 261
Income, 132; access to food and, 392; agricultural projects and, 163–64; cash crops and, 187, 188–89, 189–90; in China, 467, 475–78; development strategies and, 57–58; food preferences and, 19; food price

increase and, 286; minor crops and, 135; nutrition and, 206, 327; productivity increases and, 77–78; spending of (by men), 137–38; spending patterns and, 119–20; spent on food, 304–05; tax on agricultural, 264; women and, 123, 372, 373–77
Income distribution, 8, 31, 160; adequate diets and, 206; in China, 475, 477–78; food policy and, 13; price policy and, 275
Income transfers, 117; agricultural projects and, 154–57; food aid and, 235; food security and, 208–09
India, 27, 60, 111, 142, 190, 337, 338, 490, 491; access to food in, 385, 386, 387, 388; childcare in, 379, 380; development in, 55–56; food aid and, 228, 249; food consumption in, 45; food prices in, 263; food production in, 46, 75, 108–09, 114; fuel gathering in, 382; illness in, 356, 365; imports of, 224; irrigation in, 93; nutritional intervention in, 451; nutritional risk in, 397, 400; savings in, 55; targeted food subsidies in, 290–91; tea consumption in, 120–21
Indonesia, 90, 172, 223, 254, 267, 285, 337, 338, 381, 431, 435, 437, 439; nutritional intervention in, 451–52
Industrial sector, 85, 490–91
Infrastructure, 73; farmer incentives and, 2
Input subsidies, 277
Input supply (Africa), 504–05
Insect pests: food loss and, 314, 323, 324; genetic resistance to, 109
Interest rates, 157–58, 219
International food and agricultural system: evolution of, 72–74; finance and, 78–81; self-sufficiency and, 74–78; trade and, 73, 81–87
International Fund for Agricultural Development (IFAD), 36
International Vitamin A Consultative Group (IVACG), 337, 342
International Wheat Agreement, 20
International Wheat Council, 35
Investment, 55; agricultural dynamism and, 271; developing countries and, 29; expanded food supply and, 77–78; farming system, 149–50; food aid as development, 250–51; human

Investment *(continued)*
  capital, 196; international, 36–37;
  marketing systems and, 273
Iodine deficiency, 332, 342–43
Iran, 221, 228
Irrigation, 29, 96, 111, 124; in Asia, 65;
  expansion of, 93–94; in Kenya (rice),
  381; multiple cropping and, 106–07;
  nutritional risk analysis and, 397–99;
  pumps (electric) and, 108

Jamaica, 372
James, D., 324
Jamison, Dean, 444
Japan, 23, 46, 54, 61, 62, 65, 67, 77, 90,
  94, 96, 219, 222, 223, 247, 302, 494
Java, 381
Johnston, Bruce F., 6, 13, 187
Jones, William O., 65
Joy, Leonard, 393

Katona-Apte, Judit, 196, 244
Kennedy, Eileen, 105
Kenya, 6, 54, 188, 190, 256, 262, 267,
  341, 354, 376, 381, 403, 404, 411,
  452, 489, 495; access to food in, 387;
  credit clubs in, 383; food purchases by
  households in, 305–06; food strategy
  in, 497, 500, 501, 502, 503, 505
Kerven, C., 175, 176
Klein, Robert E., 349
Knudsen, Odin K., 155
Koester, Ulrich, 49
Koppel, Bruce M., 104
Korea, Republic of, 61, 62, 65, 67, 229,
  490, 495
Kothare, N. R., 108
Kumar, Shubh K., 377
Kuwait, 223
Kwashiorkor, 332

Labor force: farm family, 123; farming
  system research and, 145, 167;
  landless, 112; rural, 40; rural African,
  492; structure and demographic
  characteristics of, 54; women in
  agricultural, 372–73. *See also*
  Employment
Land, agricultural: amount of, 89–94;
  cash crops and, 181–84; distribution
  of, 279; FSR&D and, 166; irrigated, 29;
  reclamation of, 90; use of unsuitable,
  101; women and, 138–39

Landownership, 30; high-yielding crops
  and, 57
Land reform, 30, 62, 111; in China, 477,
  480
Land tenure, 110–11, 176
Latham, Michael C., 327, 328, 336
Latin America, 4, 100, 107, 111, 183,
  273, 280, 343, 494; access to food in,
  387; desertification and erosion in, 91,
  101; food aid and, 228, 229; food
  production in, 41–42, 75; grain
  exports of, 217; land reform in, 62;
  price changes in, 283. *See also names of
  specific Latin American countries*
Leslie, Joanne, 329
Levinson, F. James, 397
Lev, Larry, 189
Lewis, W. Arthur, 49
Liberia, 461
Lindblad, C., 310
Lipton, Michael, 329
Livestock, 17, 120, 122; energy
  produced by, 125; FSR&D and, 175,
  176; grain feed consumption and,
  16–17, 24; growing demand for,
  47–48, 50; women and, 134, 135, 137
Livestock feed, 300; as buffer stock,
  216–17; competition between food
  and, 186–87; demand for, 16–17, 24
Lopez, Clara E., 459
Lopez Portillo, José, 459, 492–93

McDowell, R. E., 176
Macroeconomic policies, 29–30, 30–31
Malawi, 172, 190, 269, 489
Malaysia, 115
Mali, 253, 495; food strategy in, 497,
  500, 501, 502, 503, 504, 505, 507
Malnutrition, 5, 39, 89, 117, 205; Africa
  and, 497, 499; anemia and, 330,
  339–42; China and reduction in, 467,
  471, 481, 482, 483; interactions of
  diarrhea with, 356–61, 365, 369;
  disease and, 20, 328, 329, 330; energy
  metabolism and children with,
  349–50; food security and, 100; goiter
  and, 330–32, 342–43; identification
  and incidence of undernourishment
  and, 17–20, 327, 330; poverty and,
  327, 330; protein-energy (PEM) 330;
  supply and demand balance and,
  51–52; vitamin A deficiency and, 330,
  336–38. *See also* Hunger

Malthus, Thomas Robert, 39
Mann, Charles K., 6
Manoff, Richard K., 329
Marginal regions. *See* Secondary regions
Market exchange systems, 148–49
Marketing boards, 65, 500
Marketing systems, 29; in Africa, 65, 273, 500, 501–04, 507; efficiency of, 263; food policy and, 148–49; investments in, 273; low-income households and, 306–08; price formation and, 293–94; price policy and, 293–95, 298–302; processing and, 298; resource allocation and, 293; storage and, 295–97; transportation and, 297–98; welfare effects of, 299, 302–03
Markets: capital, 79, 82; commodity, 79; farming system research and, 146; grain (futures), 218; price formation and, 293; price policy and grain, 262; sugar, 25; U.S. in international grain and soybean, 80
Martorell, Reynaldo, 52, 349, 356
Mason, John B., 329
Mass media. *See* Media
Mauldin, W. P., 67
Measles, 335
Mechanization, 112, 125
Media: nutritional education and, 430, 431, 432, 434, 435, 438, 439, 440–41, 442; nutrition programs and, 448
Mehra, S., 108
Mellor, John W., 6, 13, 64, 115, 187, 287, 490, 495
Mexico, 83, 90, 93, 267, 343, 354, 376, 382, 492–93; nutritional risk in, 399–400
Micronesia, 430
Middle East, 23, 41, 47–48, 228, 372; irrigation in, 93
Migration, 112, 115, 137; Africa and, 486; China and, 477; research on, 145
Mitchell, Janice T., 329
Moris, Jon, 63
Morocco, 94, 229, 430, 439
Mortality, 279, 349, 424; social services and, 66, 67
Mozambique, 248
Mundlak, Yair, 286
Musgrove, Philip, 283

Nepal, 101, 375

Ness, Gayle D., 69
Nigeria, 91, 189, 322, 487, 489
Norman, D. W., 176
Nutrient availability. *See* Food, access to; Food availability
Nutrition: access to food and, 391–92; agricultural projects and, 153; cash crops and, 7; cost-effective food aid and, 237–45; estimating inadequacies in, 69; income and, 206; outcome indicators and, 408–09; problems of, 8; social welfare programs and, 408; supply and demand balance and, 51–53; technological change and, 113–14; women and, 136, 140
Nutritional risk: access to food and, 391–92; approaches to reduction in, 393–96; assessment of, 396–400; data collection and, 400–01; household background and, 393–94; identifying, 393; project planning and, 401
Nutritional status: cash cropping and, 187–91; China and, 478–80, 480–82; working women and child's, 377–78
Nutritional surveillance: agricultural and rural development planning and, 406–07; concept of, 402–03; data and surveys and, 409–12; design of system for, 405–12; health sector and, 407; nutrition outcome indicators and, 408–09; in Philippines, 404, 408, 410; purpose of, 403–05; social welfare programs and, 408; uses of, 406–08
Nutrition education: effectiveness of, 429–33; extension services and, 432; guidelines for, 436–45; implementation and, 433–35; mass media and, 430, 431, 432, 434, 435, 438, 439, 440–41, 442
Nutrition planning (national): integrated, 448–49; nutrition goals and, 465–66; organizational coordination and, 462–65; in Philippines, 461–62, 462–63, 464; political process and, 458–62; practical multisectoral, 457–58
Nutrition programs: development community and, 453–56; evolution of, 447–48; food policy and, 452–53; integrated planning and, 448–49; intervention analysis and, 451–52; sectoralization (health and agriculture) and, 449–51, 454; technology and, 448

Olayide, S. O., 65
Oral rehydration therapy, 335, 336, 437

Pakistan, 90, 93, 267; food aid and, 228, 241; fuel gathering in, 383; imports of, 224
Panama, 172–75, 378
Pan American Health Organization, 52, 450
Papua New Guinea, 440
Parasitic infections, 335–36
Pariser, E. R., 263
Pearson, Scott, 6
Peru, 101, 322, 343, 373, 461
Pests: food loss and, 314, 323, 324; genetic resistance to, 109
Philippines, 85, 114, 123, 167, 169, 337, 377, 379, 431, 452; access to food in, 387–88; national nutrition planning in, 461–62, 462–63, 464; nutritional surveillance in, 404, 408, 410
Physical activity: energy metabolism analysis and, 350–51; food distribution program analysis and, 424
Piazza, Alan, 444
Pines, James, M., 444
Pinstrup-Andersen, Per, 6, 104, 261, 262–63
Pisani plan, 497
Planning, 8–9; diarrhea and malnutrition interactions and, 369; food and nutrition, 443–45; nutritional risk and project, 401; nutritional surveillance and development, 406–07; nutrition (in China), 467–84; nutrition (national), 457–66; nutrition programs and integrated, 448–49
Policy. *See* Food policy; Price policy
Politics: African development and, 495–96; food issues and, 16; nutrition planners and, 444, 458–62; policy implementation and, 31–32, price policy and, 280–81
Popkin, B. M., 377
Population, 53, 70, 203; cropland area and growth of, 92, 102; food issues and increases in, 16–17; food security and, 100; growth of African, 485, 486; supply and demand and, 47
Post-Harvest Food Loss Group (FAO survey), 312, 316. *See also* Food losses (post-harvest)
Poultry, 84. *See also* Livestock

Poverty, 57, 69, 117; developing countries and, 26–28; entitlements and, 198–204; food policy and, 11–12, 279–80, 280–81; food price increases and, 279; food security and, 205–14; food supply and, 50; undernourishment and, 18, 19, 327, 330
Price policy: Africa and, 501–03, 507; complexity of, 261; equilibrium models and, 265–68, 268–71; food policy and, 2; food security concepts and, 21–22; government intervention and, 264, 271–74, 275, 276; market failure and, 271–74; marketing and, 293–95, 298–302; policy decisions and, 274–76; politics and food policies and, 280–81; price incentives and, 278; transition (rising food prices) measures and, 279–80
Prices: African agriculture and, 486–89, 491; agricultural development and, 65–66; agricultural projects and, 159–60, 161–63; border, 265, 275, 294, 299–300; buffer stock, 35; ceiling, 296, 297; compensation (for poor) and, 282, 285–86, 289–91, 291–92; cropland area analysis and, 102; domestic, 265, 294, 299–300, 301; entitlements and, 201; farmer reaction to, 121–22; floor, 296, 297; food, 48, 56, 69; food aid and, 239–42, 254; food policy and, 262; grain, 215, 221, 484; international, 32–33, 37; long-term decline in, 75–76; and poor, 283–85; producer and consumer, 261, 262–63, 277; rural development and, 64; rural market, 306–07; seasonal, 301; subsidized, 24, 209–10; supply and demand and, 47, 48–49; stability of, 50; transitory food insecurity and, 212, 213; of wage goods, 59
Processing: food loss and, 315–16; markets and price policy and, 298; women and, 373, 381–82
Production, 7, 101; advantages of domestic, 59–60; Africa and, 485, 504; agricultural projects and reduction in (for home consumption), 157–59; China and, 469–73, 474–75, 477; cropland area and, 89–94; dualistic development and, 56–57; entitlements and, 201–02; farm family

and technological change and, 122–24; food-deficit regions and, 16; food policy and, 13–14; green revolution and, 106–09; growth of, 58–59, 74–75, 119–22; income generation and, 77–78; inputs and, 103; levels of, 23, 37–38; price policy and, 266; research and development analysis and, 176–78; secondary regions and, 143–44; sugar beet, 344; technology and, 59, 121–22, 139–40; trends in, 41, 49–50, 104; variability in, 108–09; women in African, 133, 137, 138, 139, 140, 176, 190, 191, 372; women and food, 7, 137–139; women and minor crop, 133–35; women's time constraints and, 135–37

Projects. *See* Agricultural projects

Protectionism, 24; tariffs and, 86–87

Protein-energy malnutrition (PEM), 53, 344: assessment of, 330, 333–34

Rationing (target group), 208, 255, 280; China and, 469–70, 483

Reform. *See* Agricultural reform; Land reform

Refrigeration, 317

Research: Africa and, 504–05; agricultural, 99; biotechnological, 49, 50, 84; food aid and, 251; generation of new technologies and, 126–29; investment in, 28–29; neglect of, 63; nutritional planning and, 462–63; secondary regions and farming system, 145–47, 149, 151, 152

Research and development (farming systems). *See* Farming systems research and development

Resource allocation, 152; price policy and marketing and, 293; women and family, 373–77

Resource development, 28–29

Reutlinger, Shlomo, 51, 104, 195, 196

Rickets, 482

Rodents (food loss to), 315

Röell, A., 58

Rohde, John E., 364

Rosa, E. B., 346

Rosenzweig, M., 389

Rural development, 60–61; nutritional development and, 406–07, 465. *See also* Agricultural development

Rural sector, 115; consumer goods demand and, 57, 59; development

conflict in Africa and, 493–94, 495–96; disease in Chinese, 482; food prices and poor in, 263, 286–87; food purchases (household) in, 305, 306–07; nonfarm employment and, 30; price comparisons and, 301; social services in, 66; undernourishment and, 19

Rustagi, N., 288

Rutishauser, Ingrid H. E., 349

Ruttan, Vernon W., 61

Rwanda, 489; food strategy in, 497, 500, 501, 502, 505

Sahn, David, 287

Sahni, S., 365

Saudi Arabia, 249

Savings, 86; capital-intensive development and, 56; farm labor force analysis and, 55

Scandizzo, Pasquale L., 155

Schistosomiasis, 336, 341, 342

Schuh, G. Edward, 6–7, 11, 12, 13, 257

Schultz, Theodore W., 168, 272, 389

Schumpeter, Joseph, 272

Scrimshaw, Nevin S., 356

Secondary regions: administrative capacity and, 148–49, 151; defined, 140, 141; ecology and, 142–43, 146; energy import bills and, 142; farming system research and, 145–47, 149, 151, 152; high-yielding crops and, 144; secondary crops and, 143–44; soil erosion and, 143; technology support system and, 147–48, 149, 151

Self-sufficiency, 46–47; Africa and, 493, 499; cash crops and, 192; international food and agricultural system and, 74–78

Selowsky, Marcelo, 51

Sen, Amartya, 7, 61, 195

Senegal, 381, 458, 462

Shah, Mahendra M., 54

Sharecropping, 201

Sierra Leone, 191, 463, 489

Smallpox, 335

Snaydon, R. W., 143

Socialism, 62, 199, 272; in China, 469

Social security, 202–03

Social service programs, 66–69, 408

Soil erosion, 92, 101, 143

Solon, Florentino S., 377

Spoilage. *See* Food losses (post-harvest)

Squire, Lyn, 155

Sri Lanka, 248, 254, 263, 287, 290, 379, 452, 457
Staatz, John M., 6
Stephenson, L. S., 336
Storage, 369; food loss and, 312, 314, 317, 324; low-income families and, 305; marketing and price policy and, 295–97, 301
Streeten, Paul, 261
Subsidies: in Africa, 487, 506; consumer food, 26–27, 506; food aid and, 254, 255; food price changes and, 280, 282, 285–86, 289–91; food (targeted), 262, 263; input, 277, 487; pricing and, 24, 209–10; urban food (China), 469, 470
Subsistence crops, 184–86, 191–94, 500
Sugar beet production, 344
Sugar market, 25
Supplementary feeding programs: food delivery system effectiveness and, 414–15; analysis of, 413–14; benefits of, 415–24; costs of, 424–25; imported food and, 425; recommendations on, 425–28
Supply: data on grain, 215–16; demand and, 40, 46–49, 51–52; dependence on foreign food, 221–22; food policy and, 3, 4; food security and, 16, 21, 24, 215–16, 217; insecurity and national food, 210–11; price policy and, 266; prices and expanded food, 287–88; rural markets and, 307
Swaziland, 463–64
Sweden, 248
Syria, 228, 248

Taiwan, 48, 61, 62, 65, 67, 167; development and, 58–59
Tanco, Arturo, 449
Tanner, J. M., 479
Tanzania, 189, 254, 373, 375, 380, 430, 458, 462, 489
Target group food rationing, 208, 255, 280; in China, 469–70, 483
Tariffs, 86
Taxes, 277; agricultural income and, 264; export, 83, 163
Tea, consumption of (India), 120–21
Technology, 2; advances in, 95–98; 126–29; Africa and, 504–05; diffusion of new, 129–32; evaluating new, 171; farm family and changes created by, 122–24; food production,

59, 60, 104, 121–22; food supply increase and, 288; FSR&D and sharing and transfer of, 167–68; fuels and, 383; international trade and, 84–85; investment in, 29; mechanical, 112, 125; nutrition programs and, 448; price incentives and, 278; secondary regions and, 147–48, 149, 151; small farmers and, 63; time allocation of women and, 378–84; women and food production and, 139–40. *See also* Green revolution; Research
Thailand, 6, 48, 67, 181, 249, 267, 287, 379, 452, 458, 460, 461, 463
Time allocation of women: agricultural activities and, 373, 380–81; technological change and, 378–84; work activities and, 135–37, 373, 384. *See also* Women
Time, rising value of, 87–88
Timmer, Peter, 6, 261, 262, 295, 298
Tobisson, E., 375
Togo, 489
Tolley, George, 293
Torun, Benjamin, 350
Trade: Africa and international, 485; agricultural policies and instability of, 24–25; agricultural projects and, 161–62, 163; China and international, 471–73; food security and grain, 215–23; international food and agricultural system and, 73, 81–87; trends in, 23–24, 41–45, 49, 50, 69. *See also* Exports; Imports
Training and visit (T&V) extension system, 130–31
Trairatvorakul, Prasarn, 287
Transportation, 115, 369; food aid and, 241, 254; marketing and price policy and, 296, 297–98
Tripp, Robert, 191
Tuinenburg, Kees, 444
Tunisia, 6, 67, 228, 461
Turkey, 228

Uganda, 357, 360, 364, 381
Unemployment, 202–03, 382
United States, 23, 25, 45, 49, 50, 75, 77, 90, 172, 222, 223, 273, 301; cereal yield increase in, 95–96; cropland idling in, 99, 100; international monetary system and, 80–81; fertilizer and, 94; food aid and, 228, 229, 246, 247, 248, 250, 251; grain exports of,

217; international grain and soybean markets and, 80; irrigation in, 93; maize leaf blight in, 108; trade deficit of, 82

Urban sector: disease in Chinese, 482; food price policy and, 291; food purchases (household) in, 304–05, 307–08, 312; food subsidy for, (China) 469, 470; secondary regions and, 146; undernourishment and, 19

Uruguay, 231

U.S. Agency for International Development (USAID), 450

U.S.S.R., 17, 23, 25, 45, 55, 93, 94, 218, 223; crop shortfalls in, 99–100; food aid and, 228, 253–54; food imports of, 221

van der Tak, Herman G., 155

Venezuela, 322

Vitamin A deficiency, 330, 336–38

Vitamin C supplementation, 341

Viteri, Fernando E., 350

von Braun, Joachim, 105

Wages, and food price rise, 285, 286

Water, 29; rural collection and supply of, 123–24, 373, 382–83

Waterlow, J. C., 333

Weaning foods, 379, 437

Weaning practices, 415

Weather, 18; drought and, 397; rainfed farming and, 124–26

Welfare effects: marketing system and, 299, 302–03; price policy change and consumer, 268

Whitehead, R. G., 349, 353, 364

Willekens, F., 54

Women: access to food and, 385, 387, 388–89, 390; in African food production cycle, 133, 137, 138, 139, 140, 176, 190, 191, 372, 507; agricultural activities of, 7, 123, 137–39, 373, 380–81; in agricultural labor force, 372–73; anemia in pregnant, 339; childcare and, 379–80; education and, 384; employment and, 371–72, 376; energy metabolism analysis and, 352–53; female-headed households and, 372; food processing and preparation and, 373, 381–82; fuel and water collection and, 373, 382–83; income (family resources) allocation and, 273–77; livestock and, 134, 135, 137; minor crops and, 133–35; nutritional education and, 432; nutritional status of children and working, 377–78; research and development analysis and, 176; technological change and, 116, 139–40, 378–84; time allocation of, 135–37, 373, 378–84; under-nourishment and, 19

World Bank, 5, 36, 49, 57, 65, 450, 452

World Food Conference, 5, 6, 11, 12, 15, 16, 20, 22, 23, 35, 37, 73, 258, 327, 345, 402, 446, 447, 448, 450, 451, 455

World Food Council, 5, 12, 15, 16, 19, 20, 498

World Food Program (*1963*), 247

World Health Organization (WHO), 5, 330

Wray, J. D., 365

Xerophthalmia, 330, 336–38, 377

Yield growth: price and farmer reaction to, 121–22; research and, 131; sources of, 46; technology and, 95–96

Zaire, 223, 248, 383, 489

Zambia, 181, 489; food strategy in, 497, 500, 501, 502, 503, 504, 505, 506

Zandstra, H. G., 176

Zimbabwe, 249, 267, 489

The most recent World Bank publications are described in the catalog *New Publications*, which is issued in the spring and fall of each year. The complete backlist of publications is shown in the annual *Index of Publications*, which contains an alphabetical title list and indexes of subjects, authors, and countries and regions; it is of value principally to libraries and institutional purchasers. The continuing research program is described in *The World Bank Research Program: Abstracts of Current Studies*, which is issued annually. The latest edition of each is available free of charge from Publications Sales Unit, The World Bank, 1818 H Street, N.W., Washington, D.C. 20433, U.S.A., or from Publications, The World Bank, 66, avenue d'Iéna, 75116 Paris, France.